Rethinking Organisational Behaviour

Rethinking Organisational Behaviour

A Poststructuralist Framework

Second Edition

Norman Jackson and Pippa Carter

FT Prentice Hall
FINANCIAL TIMES

An imprint of **Pearson Education**
Harlow, England • London • New York • Boston • San Francisco • Toronto • Sydney • Singapore • Hong Kong
Tokyo • Seoul • Taipei • New Delhi • Cape Town • Madrid • Mexico City • Amsterdam • Munich • Paris • Milan

Pearson Education Limited
Edinburgh Gate
Harlow
Essex CM20 2JE
England

and Associated Companies throughout the world

Visit us on the World Wide Web at:
www.pearsoned.co.uk
_____

First published 2000
Second edition 2007

ISBN-13: 978-0-273-68359-9
ISBN-10: 0-273-68359-4

British Library Cataloguing-in-Publication Data
A catalogue record for this book is available from the British Library

Library of Congress Cataloging-in-Publication Data
A catalog record for this book is available from the Library of Congress

10 9 8 7 6 5 4 3 2 1
11 10 09 08 07 06

Typeset in Stone Serif 9.5/12pt by 30
Printed and bound by Ashford Colour Press, Gosport

The publisher's policy is to use paper manufactured from sustainable forests.

Brief contents

Contents

Acknowledgements

We would like to thank Penelope Woolf (then at Pitman Publishing) for starting us off on this project and for her support in the early stages, and Sadie McClelland for taking over this task at a later stage and being unfailingly supportive and helpful, and remaining cheerful at all times. We must also thank Linda Saddington and Moira Dearden, who inestimably facilitated the production of this book.

We should also thank our colleagues, who assisted in many ways, some of them closely associated with alcohol.

We have significant intellectual debts, but, in order to save those people embarrassment and ourselves from possible legal action, we will not name them – but you know who you are!

Last, but by no means least, we must thank our families and any friends we have left, who accepted being put firmly on the back burner for a long time with remarkable fortitude, or, perhaps, relief. (But be warned, the repressed are returning . . .)

In respect of this second edition, we must add also our thanks to Linda Dhondy – a person of remarkable persistence – for her support and her patience.

Publishers Acknowledgements

We are grateful to the following for permission to reproduce copyright material:

Figures and illustrations

Page 42: M.C. Escher, *Relativity*. © 2006 The M.C. Escher Company B.V. – Holland. All rights reserved. (www.mcescher.com). Reprinted with permission; 49: © Steve Bell 1992. Reprinted with permission; 106: © Bettmann / Corbis; 182: Copyright © Ashleigh Brilliant (www.ashleighbrilliant.com). Reprinted with permission; 185: Pablo Picasso, *Self Portrait*, 1972. Copyright © Succession Picasso / Design and Artists Copyright Society (DACS) 2006. Pearson Education Ltd has paid DACS' visual creators for the use of their artistic works ◨; 217: René Magritte, *La Trahison des Images*, 1952. © Photothéque R. Magritte – ADAGP, Paris 2006. Pearson Education Ltd has paid DACS' visual creators for the use of their artistic works ◨.

Text

29: From 'Mad dogs and Englishmen' from *The Guardian*, 23 January 1991. Copyright © Guardian Newspapers Limited 1991. Reprinted with permission; 76: From Paul Hoyland, 'Lighthouse keeper sacked for wanting a shower' *The Guardian*, 4 October 1985. Copyright © Guardian Newspapers Limited 1985. Reprinted with permission; 126: W.B Yeats, 'An Irishman foresees his death', 1919. Reprinted with permission of AP Watt on behalf of Michael B Yeats; 134: Tony Benn, (1992) *Hansard (House of Commons Daily Debates) Session 1992–93*, Volume 212, 21 October 1992, pp 502–3. Reproduced with permission; 180: Incentive Theory: The philosophy in 20 words. Designed by Christine Hankinson, Leeds Postcards. Reprinted with permission; 192: Excerpt adapted from Norman Jackson and Pippa Carter (1985) 'The ergonomics of desire' *Personnel Review*, 14, 3, pp. 20–28. Reprinted with permission from Emerald Insight; 213: Excerpt from D. Bohm (1983) *Wholeness and the Implicate Order*. London: Ark Paperbacks (Routledge). Reproduced with permission from the Taylor & Francis Group Ltd.; 284: Chartered Managed Institute, excerpt from Code of Professional Management Practice; 291: Larry Elliott and Charlotte Denny, 'O'Neill insists recovery is near', *The Guardian*, 25 July 2001. Copyright © Guardian Newspapers Limited 2001. Reprinted with permission.

In some instances we have been unable to trace the owners of copyright material, and we would appreciate any information that would enable us to do so.

CHAPTER 1

Introduction

It is not unusual for organisational behaviour problems to reach quite widespread public attention. A notorious case involved two government employees, he a chief executive and she a relatively lowly employee, who, at work, in 'company time' and on 'company property', engaged in behaviour which, ultimately, not only endangered the functioning and even survival of the immediate organisation, but also had potential repercussions on a global scale. As awareness of this behaviour began to leak out, the junior employee was moved from her job and the chief executive sought to evade both responsibility for, and consequences of, the behaviour by lying about it, both to colleagues and to interested 'competitors'. A third party was engaged to enquire into this behaviour, which led to the threat of dismissal for the chief executive, not just for the inappropriate organisational behaviour, but also for lying about it.

This is one way of describing the famous, or infamous, Bill Clinton/Monica Lewinsky affair. It has all the hallmarks of a typical organisational behaviour problem. Such behaviour, however 'private', because it occurs in an organisational context, can have serious ramifications for the organisation. Indeed, in this case, the focus of attention has been concerned, primarily, with the impact on the organisation of the behaviour of its employees. Yet it is also an example of extremely common dysfunctional organisational behaviour, an everyday occurrence in organisations. Even so, it is one about which the discipline of Organisational Behaviour has very little to say.

Organisational Behaviour ought to be about all behaviour in organisations. The implications of the behaviour may be great or small, but the task of Organisational Behaviour ought to be to provide means to understand and explain any behaviour that takes place in an organisational context. Bill Clinton is merely a very high-profile example of an organisational participant; his case is really no different, in essence, to any case of organisational behaviour.

A review of the events since the publication of the first edition of this book throws up any number of examples that are of interest and relevance to understanding organisational behaviour. Instances include the 2000 American presidential election, the ongoing Enron debacle and the behaviour of participants in organisations such as Abu Ghraib and Guantanamo Bay – the list of cases of corporate, political, social, environmental corruption, mismanagement, unethical behaviour, sheer incompetence and plain farce seems endless. These are, however, just the high-profile, public and negative end of the spectrum. Organisational life is also about myriad events that, quite properly, have no more than local interest, significance and impact, have no public profile, but that, nonetheless, constitute the very fabric of contemporary existence. And, at the other end of the spectrum from the big events can be found the interesting, and relatively new, phenomenon of organisational behaviour as prime-time entertainment. There seems to be an inexhaustible appetite for watching people behave in organisations, marvelling at their antics – classic examples are *The Office* and *The Apprentice*. Organisational behaviour seems to have moved into The Big Time!

The field of Organisational Behaviour is an important part of management education, yet the discipline is, generally, in a rather parlous state. It consists of theories which are not just old, but out of date; assumptions which are naive and which do not bear close examination; knowledge claims which are dubious and which consistently fail to live up to expectation. Students might be surprised to learn that many of those who teach them Organisational Behaviour have no faith in either the theoretical rigour or the practical relevance of what they teach, yet that is the case. Indeed, arguably, students are being short-changed by being taught a subject which is a crucial part of management in theory and in practice in a form which, although superficially attractive, has little utility: students are being taught things as fact which are, at best, unprovable and, at worst, just plain wrong. Why then yet another book on Organisational Behaviour? Well, this is not a book about Organisational Behaviour, it is a book about organisational behaviour. But, before we get into what might be meant by this apparently trivial distinction, it is worth considering why we bother with this subject at all.

Why study organisational behaviour?

A moment ago we said that organisational behaviour is a crucial part of management in theory and in practice, and this is generally and widely believed to be the case. Why is it so important? In the lives of most people there is, quite literally, no aspect of their existence that is not touched, in some way, by organisations. Everything we do – working, worshipping, being educated, belonging to a family, enjoying ourselves or suffering, waking or sleeping – implies organisation. This very ubiquity of organisation suggests that understanding how and why people behave as they do in organisations, and what impact organisations have on people's behaviour, would be a central concern, formally or informally, of absolutely anybody. But there is even more to it than this. There are large issues which revolve around these two sides of organisational behaviour – the ways people behave in organisations and the impact of organisations on people's behaviour – which are, ultimately, to do with the well-being of society in general and of the individual members of society.

Tremendous good flows from organisations – for example, food, health care, education, entertainment, as well as relative economic prosperity. But they can also do tremendous damage. Such damage can have many causes, such as the production of disaster, unwise practices with deleterious long-term consequences, the threatening of the well-being, health and sanity of individuals.

There has probably never been a time in human history when we have had so much organisation, been so organised. Yet we still know very little about what constitutes **good** organisation, what constitutes **good** organisational behaviour. Even after more than one hundred years of formal and extensive academic and practical study of organisational behaviour we really know very little about it and have solved very few of the problems associated with it – let alone produced identifiable betterment. For the study of organisational behaviour is not just about preventing disaster, or about damage-limitation, it is also about realising the benefits of organisation for the human condition: the study of organisational behaviour is not just about preventing bad, it is about producing good. Unless organisations produce benefits, and unless the good they produce outweighs the cost they entail, there is no point in having them.

This is a large burden to place on the shoulders of the study of organisational behaviour, but, given the overwhelming presence of organisations in our lives, it is inevitable that this should be expected from it. And, very necessary that this role should be fulfilled.

How is *Rethinking Organisational Behaviour* different?

If it is accepted that the study of organisational behaviour is so significant, then it is of no small import that it has so signally failed to deliver the goods. One way to address this deficiency is to reiterate, rediscover, reformulate and refurbish previously developed theories and practices which, though once seen as outmoded, inappropriate or ineffective, can be dusted off and re-presented, in the hope that they can now solve a problem that they failed to solve before. This approach has the advantage of familiarity and of not requiring any substantial modification of the status quo. It has the disadvantage of a demonstrably poor track record and of requiring a huge act of faith that it has a better chance the second – or third, or fourth, or fifth, or umpteenth – time around. Another way to address the deficiency is to develop a significantly different approach to the whole subject: to rethink organisational behaviour. The advantage of this approach is that it does not depend on reliving the past history of Organisational Behaviour today, but must depend on its explanatory power, its ability to explain experience. The disadvantage is that, being different, it is inevitably more demanding. On the other hand, the prize, better organisations, is worth the effort. It is this approach that we are seeking to develop in this book.

In *Rethinking Organisational Behaviour* we have, in effect, abandoned traditional approaches to the study of organisational behaviour, on the grounds that the failings and gaps of such traditional approaches are simply too numerous to rectify. Traditional Organisational Behaviour seems to be stuck in a kind of time warp. In other fields of study of human activity, thinking has moved on dramatically. While traditional Organisational Behaviour is really a product of North American creation, the principal stimulus to the new thinking about human life, individual and social, comes from European social theory, most especially the developments in that arena that began with the *second* half of the twentieth century. This thinking has been largely ignored by traditional Organisational Behaviour. Yet it offers a radically different way of understanding what people do in organisations.

Rethinking Organisational Behaviour presents a **framework** for thinking about organisational behaviour based on this theory. It explores the potential of contemporary social theory to offer a different, more appropriate, understanding of how and why people behave in organisations and of the impact that organisations have on people's behaviour, its potential to offer explanations of these phenomena which make sense of experience.

In *Rethinking Organisational Behaviour* the reader will not find a guide to managing organisational behaviour, will not find chapters on motivation, leadership, culture, and so on. The reasons for this absence are twofold. *Firstly, Rethinking Organisational Behaviour* takes a step back from that point, to examine the very assumptions on which management of organisational behaviour rests, and to present a different set of basic starting points for thinking about organisational behaviour, which themselves need to be developed before management of organisational behaviour could be possible. *Secondly*, as the reader will discover, these starting points emphasise that there are no universals, no absolute or transcendent rules, for managing organisational behaviour that can be invoked: *how organisational behaviour can be managed depends entirely upon factors such as what ends are to be achieved by its management, the capabilities of particular managers, whoever they may be and whatever their organisational role, and the understandings and inclinations of both manager and managed.*

Management of organisational behaviour, even understanding of organisational behaviour, is extremely complex and *Rethinking Organisational Behaviour* seeks to reflect that complexity in all its glory and inevitability. What *Rethinking Organisational Behaviour* offers is a way of thinking about, understanding and managing that complexity. In that process it, necessarily, addresses aspects of organisation which are rarely addressed by traditional approaches to understanding organisational behaviour and thus which may seem strange to the reader at first glance. For example, we start with an exploration of **semiotics** and **symbolism** as a fundamental starting point for thinking about and understanding the enormous variety of human behaviour, and the reasons for this variety. This is a subject and an approach that rarely figures in conventional texts on organisational behaviour, but is one that seeks to reflect the actual complexity of behaviour in organisations rather than reducing such behaviour to a simplistic model, based on what managers, and many theorists, would *like* it to be like.

Structure is another heading rare in traditional Organisational Behaviour textbooks, not because it is ignored but because it is regarded as part of some other aspect of organisation and management. However, given that structure could be seen as organisation itself and, thus, as having a huge impact on organisational behaviour, we include it as a necessary part of understanding that phenomenon. **Power** is an example of a topic that is sometimes to be found in traditional approaches to understanding and managing organisational behaviour. In such cases, however, it is usually treated predominantly in terms of issues of compliance, how and why managers may and should be obeyed. The approach here treats power as a ubiquitous ingredient of all human relationships, and, therefore, gives the concept of power much greater prominence. Similar points could be made about all the issues that figure in *Rethinking Organisational Behaviour*. It is, indeed, precisely our point that such topics should *not* be strange to anyone trying to understand organisational behaviour, and that they demand to be included if any adequate understanding is to be achieved.

Another difference in *Rethinking Organisational Behaviour* is that it focuses on **explanations** rather than on solutions. The reason for this is very simple: the principles on which behaviour can be understood are the same, whatever the behaviour and whatever its context, but the production of solutions is both situation-specific and person-specific. Traditionally, the discipline of Organisational Behaviour has been geared to the production of techniques for solving organisational problems but, inevitably, this process has reduced organisational problems to a level of generality which cannot reflect such problems as people actually experience them. They become abstract and purely theoretical and so the problem-solving power of the techniques is, also inevitably, diminished. The first, most important and most difficult, step towards effective problem-solving is always to provide a definition of the problem. Thus, for example, the French social theorist Michel Foucault has pointed out that the task of the theorist is to provide the means for developing adequate and appropriate definitions of problems. Solutions can only be developed on such a basis, but will always depend on the particular conditions and circumstances that exist in particular cases. The issue of adequate and appropriate definition of organisational behaviour, and its problems, is much less well developed than that of proposing techniques – a situation that Michael Cohen, James March and Johan Olsen (1982), in their 'garbage-can model' of organisation theory, described as solutions looking for problems. *Rethinking Organisational Behaviour* seeks to redress the balance.

Organisational Behaviour versus organisational behaviour

Let us return to the distinction we made earlier, between (upper case) Organisational Behaviour and what we have said is the subject of this book, (lower case) organisational behaviour. It has not been our intention to provide a detailed description of the body of knowledge known as Organisational Behaviour, nor to provide a comprehensive critique and evaluation of it. We use the term to typify a large and easily recognisable body of knowledge which is widely disseminated, principally through North American texts, many of which run to several editions. These texts reproduce a remarkably consistent content – there may be differences in detail, but the overall similarity between such texts is more noticeable than the relatively minor differences they may represent. The range of topics tends to be fairly consistent, and limited – topics such as motivation (rarely properly distinguished as motivation to work), leadership, group dynamics, culture, and so on. This narrowness is necessarily reflected in the use we make of the content of Organisational Behaviour. For example, when we refer to it the reader will notice the repeatedly limited lists of issues considered to be relevant by it. Our examples of Organisational Behaviour are repetitive because that is the way it is.

Traditional Organisational Behaviour texts are principally concerned, implicitly or explicitly, with providing techniques for manipulating organisational behaviour. There is an important implicit assumption in the majority of such texts that behaviour can always be manipulated so that it 'better' serves the purposes of 'the organisation' or of 'management' – to that extent, the *understanding* of organisational behaviour is something of a side issue. It might be expected that, in proposing techniques for manipulating behaviour, the *ethical* considerations attendant on such practice would be automatically addressed – as is the case with other areas of knowledge production which propose such manipulation, such as psychology, biology, genetic engineering, and so on. But such considerations are very rare indeed in Organisational Behaviour texts. This is despite well-known effects detrimental to the individual of such behaviour modification techniques.

Not only is there a virtual ethical void surrounding the techniques of the discipline of Organisational Behaviour, but there is also a remarkable silence about the *purposes* that such behaviour modification is meant to serve. 'The organisation' is treated as the same in kind across the globe, or, if not, as the nirvana towards which all those who have different forms of organisation must be seeking to progress. It is treated as a given, natural, inevitable and unquestionable. Because of this there is a failure to articulate and examine the particular political, social, economic and cultural conditions that inform the way organisations are. The purposes that organisations serve, and thus the purposes to be served by manipulation of organisational behaviour, are treated as obvious, and beyond question.

In our view, these characteristics of what we have variously called traditional, conventional or orthodox Organisational Behaviour are more salient than any differences that particular authors might propose. On that basis we justify grouping them all together within this general and broad term, Organisational Behaviour.

Our belief is that the proper purpose of the study of organisational behaviour is to provide an understanding of it, not to prescribe its uncontrolled manipulation. Such an understanding cannot be achieved independently of consideration of the purposes, practices and ethical issues surrounding behaviour in organisations and its management. Equally important is consideration of the social context in which behaviour in organisations occurs. These aspects of organisational behaviour are, indeed, *integral* to any effort to understand it. The organisational behaviour we are talking about is **generic behaviour in organisations**, not any particular configuration of it. Thus we have used (lower case) organisational behaviour to distinguish between that generic activity, the subject of this book, and the particular approaches known as (upper case) Organisational Behaviour, which deal primarily with its management and manipulation for specific and interested purposes, without reference to the basic principles that inform the subject.

It is important to note also the *scope* of what we mean by organisational behaviour. This can best be illustrated by looking at what we mean by the terms 'organisation' and 'behaviour'.

Organisation

What constitutes an organisation has long fascinated scholars. Even among those who study organisations specifically, there is no general agreement about what an organisation is. Organisations may have, for example, a formal legal identity, and/or occupy a finite physical space, and/or exist spatio-temporally. But none of these aspects could be considered to be comprehensive definitions of an organisation. Even though organisations may have non-human attributes, such as equipment, or bricks and mortar, *the essential component that makes an organisation an organisation is people*. Because of the uniqueness of people, if you change the people in an organisation you change the organisation, even though its legal or spatial identity may remain exactly the same. The concept of 'the organisation' is extremely difficult to define, and, additionally, depends on what use is to be made of the definition, in what context it is to be employed. It is, perhaps, not even very fruitful to expend effort on it.

For this reason, our focus is not on organisation as a thing but on **organisation as a process:** the activity of organising and of being organised. All particular organisations are examples of this process – this alone emphasises that this one common process can produce an infinite variety of examples. The process of organisation in this context is the configuration of people and things in ways that are not given in nature. The advantage of focusing on the process of organisation is that it is a focus on those characteristics that are common to all organisations, of whatever kind, and whatever their purpose. In this, it subsumes every particular characteristic of a particular organisation, and every particular characteristic of the people and things, both abstract and physical, that constitute a particular organisation.

What a person does in an organisation might be influenced by the quality of leadership, the physical building they inhabit, the *esprit de corps*, the reputation of the organisation, the goods or services they produce, and so on and on: **there is nothing about any organisation that can be ruled out, *a priori*, as insignificant to that organisation and the people in it**. Thus, when we talk about organisations we mean any organisation, whether big or small, multinational or local, formal or informal, for profit or not for profit, involuntary or voluntary.

Behaviour

Obviously, our interest is in people, in what people do or do not do. The conventional wisdom is that, in order to understand behaviour, what you must do is observe what is going on. Our approach is not limited to observable behaviour and certainly does not attempt to ascribe meaning on the basis of observed behaviour. Some behaviour is, quite literally, not observable – for example, it takes place in private, out of the sight of others – but, in any case, it is quite possible to observe behaviour without understanding what is influencing that behaviour and what it means. One may observe two people interacting without, for example, being able to observe the impact of power on that interaction. Treating observable behaviour as necessary and sufficient to its understanding also ignores the common-sense recognition that all behaviour is influenced by experience, itself creates experience and prefigures future experience: behaviour is influenced by previous interactions, itself takes place in interaction and gives rise to future interaction. Quite apart from all this, even descriptions of observed behaviour cannot be treated as anything more than descriptions produced by someone, an observer, of something they saw and then interpreted in the light of their own understanding, experience, prejudices, purposes, and so on.

Although, strictly speaking, behaviour, as a term, may refer to actions, demeanour and so on which are observable, people in everyday life do not consider that observing such things is sufficient for their understanding. We all know that behaviour is *influenced* by things like perception, emotion, preference, experience and understanding, which are not necessarily observable. Equally, we all know that such factors are central to *understanding* behaviour. However, it is more important to acknowledge that these factors do influence behaviour than it is, in general, to know what influence what factor is having in any particular case. Behaviour is extremely complex in every instance of its occurrence, not to mention unique to every person behaving.

This does not mean, however, that it is not possible to generate **a general understanding of behaviour, based on a proper appreciation of the basic principles of what makes each person's behaviour unique and what may influence that behaviour.** Thus, when we talk about behaviour we are referring to the complex and possibly observable outcome of all the influences to which each of us is subject. This also necessarily implies that what we refer to with the term 'behaviour' is everything that people do at any time. Behaviour is not just what happens while someone is standing at a machine, or sitting in front of a word processor, or sitting behind a desk. Behaviour is the totality of their activity.

Rigour versus clarity

The ideas that inform the perspective in *Rethinking Organisational Behaviour* are well established, but relatively uncommon in the particular area of the study of organisational behaviour. The study of organisational behaviour can be seen as part of a more general interest in the study of organisation, what might be called organisation theory, or organisation studies. Within this larger arena these particular ideas are very well represented and much used in the analysis of organisation(s). What *Rethinking Organisational Behaviour* seeks to do is to illustrate their applicability to understanding organisational behaviour. In this intention our focus has been on presenting the ideas and exploring their utility, rather than on describing them in detail, or tracing their evolution. This does not mean that their details and the history of their development are not both interesting and important, but that this is outside the scope of this particular book (but see Appendix 1, *History and ideas*, in this second edition). Much has been written on these aspects of contemporary social theory and the **bibliographies** to each chapter indicate some sources for further reading for those who wish to develop their understanding of the ideas themselves. *Rethinking Organisational Behaviour* seeks to present what are very complex ideas in a relatively accessible, and thus simplified, form. In so doing, we plead guilty to the sacrifice of rigour to clarity – for which we crave the indulgence of our fellow researchers. However, it has seemed more important to introduce the ideas to a non-specialist audience, in the context of their value for understanding organisational behaviour.

Another side of the problem of detailed specification is to be found in the use of generalisation – (upper case) Organisational Behaviour is one example of this in this book. Another example of it is our widespread use of the general distinction **manager/worker**. Its use does not mean that we do not recognise that there are obvious, and not so obvious, differences, gradations, variations within each of these terms. Nonetheless, the use of the general terms is quite deliberate. Its intention is to emphasise that **the significance of these groups is not the existence of infinite variety within them, but the existence of power relativities between them**. However myriad the subtleties of the distinctions between management roles, the significance of the management role in general is that it represents greater organisational power to influence both behaviour and events than is represented in the managed.

Some readers might think that the use of the term 'worker' in the dichotomy between manager and managed is itself outmoded. Indeed, sometimes we do use the more common (these days) term '**employee**'. But when we do this it is intended to refer to all those employed in organisations – that is, both managers and those they manage. The term 'employee' also allows us to get round the problem that most people in organisations very often embody aspects of both manager and managed. While to the 'integral' self this distinction may not be particularly significant, for some purposes of analysis it is useful to make the distinction between the two roles – though remembering always that *it is only an analytical device*.

It should also be noted that the generalised terms 'manager' and 'worker' are used broadly, to refer to all organisational contexts. While it is our intention, as noted above, to write about organisation and organisational behaviour *per se*, we do tend to illustrate our points most commonly with examples from work organisations. In such cases, the terms 'manager' and 'worker' are literal descriptions of the respective roles. However, the terms are also used figuratively, to refer to similar kinds of power relationships in other kinds of organisation, such as parent/child or teacher/student.

Rethinking Organisational Behaviour . . .

. . . is a book about understanding organisational behaviour. It presents an approach to that endeavour which is substantively different to that of conventional Organisational Behaviour texts. An important focus of contemporary social theory has been on what it means to talk about people as people, and their behaviour. Such ideas are well represented in many aspects of the study of organisation(s), but are, so far, much less common in the study of organisational behaviour. *Rethinking Organisational Behaviour* seeks to apply these ideas to the study of organisational behaviour and, in so doing, to examine their utility and potential in developing an understanding of this important arena of human activity. The aim is to develop a framework for thinking about organisational behaviour which reflects the actual complexity of human activity in organisational settings and to do that in the context of giving due attention to the embeddedness, not only of organisations but also of people, in their social, political, economic and cultural world.

The structure of *Rethinking Organisational Behaviour*

Because each chapter of the book deals with a particular topic, it is possible to read one in isolation from the others. However, **the intention of the structure is that each chapter builds on what has gone before**, and the reader should bear that in mind, whatever their approach to the text may be.

Each chapter concludes with an **annotated bibliography** of further reading related to the substantive issues raised in the chapter. Each bibliography generally follows the structure of its chapter. The bibliographies are not intended to be comprehensive or exhaustive, but simply to indicate some relevant sources. There is also a **glossary** of relevant terms.

The development of **semiotics** has been one of the most influential of recent times. Because it deals with the very nature of meaning, of communication and of understanding, it is a necessary starting point which is germane to everything that comes after it. Chapter 2 introduces the basic concepts of semiotics and examines their implications for understanding behaviour, particularly in organisational settings, as well as their more familiar associated concepts, symbolism and culture. Having examined the nature and significance of the signifier/signified relationship, we then turn to looking at the ways in which these relationships are organised into **structures**. Chapter 3 moves away from the prevalent understanding of structure as real, given and independent of people, and develops a poststructuralist approach which sees structure as a human construct, essential for making sense of the world but having no existence independent of that purpose. Not only that, but, since structures are unique to individuals and their purposes, different people create different structures from the same phenomena.

This approach is further developed in Chapter 4, which proposes that **knowledge** is to be seen as a construction of internal meanings, rather than as universal, objective and monolithic, with all 'bits' of knowledge produced contributing to some whole. Using the notion of knowledge paradigms, we introduce the concept of knowledge as discourse and explore the implications of such an approach in terms of the constitution of Organisational Behaviour and Management discourse(s). This is compared to the view that there are multiplicities of knowledges which cannot be evaluated or ranked in terms of each other. Knowledge cannot be viewed independently of **power** and Chapter 5 explores the concept of power and its relevance to organisational behaviour. We consider the preferred term in the discourse of Organisational Behaviour, **authority**, though it is a pale and insubstantial substitute which does scant justice to the nature of power relationships in organisations. We examine the role of power – particularly in its relation to knowledge discourses – in maintaining and prioritising certain normative understandings of organisational behaviour over others, especially significant to the whole issue of discipline at work, why some behaviours are labelled good and how other behaviours are constructed as deviant.

The inherent relativism of such understandings of power and its role, and of knowledge, requires a reconsideration of the concept of **rationality**, and this is the subject of Chapter 6. While power is often treated rather superficially in the context of organisational behaviour, rationality, on the other hand, is often considered as centrally significant. Rationality is traditionally viewed as having the potential to be objective and, therefore, transcendent. This leads to competing explanations being labelled either as deviant, or as obstructive, or as plain wrong. We explore the viability of concepts of transcendent rationality and examine the respective claims for the nature of rationality as objective or as subjective. If rationality is inherently subjective – as the semiotic approach would suggest – there are very important implications for authority and legitimacy in and of organisations, and particularly in the management of organisational behaviour, which are considered. People obviously do share understandings but, if rationality is not transcendent, then rationality cannot be the basis for such understandings, and some other basis for intersubjective agreement is necessary to explain it. Such a basis is provided by the concept of **ideology**. Chapter 7 develops an explanation of organisational behaviour as the outcome of understandings based in emotional preference for particular ideas and versions of reality. The concept of ideology is explored and its normally hidden, even ignored, nature is examined.

It might be imagined that, since organisational behaviour is about the behaviour of people in organisations, the notion of what people are like and the notion of **self** would be highly developed and central to this field of study. In practice, this is not the case in traditional approaches, where issues of the self are largely ignored, in favour of a focus on organisation as an objective process and relegation of people to the role of servants of this process – in other words, people are considered as selves only in so far as they serve the purposes of, and identify with, this objective process. Chapter 8 looks at the issue of self and its profound impacts on behaviour in organisations, particularly self as developed and perceived by the subject, rather than as something defined by theorists or by 'the organisation'. Tracing the development of the shift from the belief that people will find salvation through work to the contemporary idea that, cosmologically, human life is transient and irrelevant, we examine the impact of this shift on the organisation of work, especially in the contexts of motivation to work and the realisation of identity.

The idea of an uncertain self in an uncertain world indicates the need for some clearer understanding of how sense and order are created and sustained. Chapter 9 examines how people achieve this through the creation of **boundaries** to limit the inherent variety in the world, and explores the important and ubiquitous process of model-building, which facilitates living in the world. If, as poststructuralism argues, all structure is the outcome of cognitive processes, rather than a property of the external world, this has profound implications for understanding organisational behaviour and for understanding organisation itself. In this context, the concept of boundary, and its process, is considered in its relation to associated concepts of system and of complexity, and their impacts on organisational problem-solving. Organisational practice is also considered in light of contemporary ecosystemic notions of boundarylessness.

A dominating concept in the organisation and management of organisational behaviour in practice is that of **efficiency**, but efficiency rarely finds a place in texts about organisational behaviour. However, every aspect of organisational behaviour developed in this book has relevance for how efficiency is understood. Chapter 10 addresses these issues, exploring the 'semantics' of efficiency. Deconstructing prevalent notions of efficiency, and especially its apparent objective and common-sense qualities, we examine the assumption that money is a sufficient indicator of efficiency, and explore the distinction between money and wealth, in order to develop a different understanding of efficiency, based on the idea that it is a subjective concept, influenced by all the factors that influence the development of subjective preferences.

In a way, it could be said that the whole of organisational behaviour, and, most notably, of its management, is about **making decisions**, and this is the subject of Chapter 11. Although decision-making is well recognised as a constituent of organisational behaviour, it is conventionally portrayed as being a response to objective, or quasi-objective, organisational conditions. Rather than this view of decision-making as reactive, we develop a view of it as a process of constructing the subject within terms of the unfolding semiotic understanding of being in the world. This has profound implications for a number of associated issues, including perceptions of risk and of morality, which are also considered. The practice of decision-making is linked to every aspect of the approach developed in *Rethinking Organisational Behaviour*.

In conclusion, Chapter 12 draws together the approach developed in an overview, and locates it all in the context of contemporary social, cultural, political and economic conditions, focusing on Postmodernism. We also discuss the question of what, why and how organisational problems can and should be addressed, utilising the concept of the organisation as rhizome, and the potential for a revitalised study and understanding of organisational behaviour which is capable of effective problem-solving in the contemporary world.

Each chapter (except Chapter 12) also contains, towards its conclusion, two sections, one of which summarises the **existing applications** of the ideas developed in the chapter to the study of Organisational Behaviour, and to the study of organisation(s) more generally, and the other of which seeks to suggest ways that the ideas could be taken further, and what the implications of such **further potential** might be.

Although we have developed our arguments in a linear fashion, and suggested that each chapter builds on the material that precedes it, it is important to emphasise that linearity is only an inevitable device of the written medium. Thus, for example, although the line of development that we present here seems to us to be a reasonable progression in terms of our purposes, it could have been done differently. Such linearity does not actually reflect the relationship between the various elements, or indeed between the various theories, that we have explored. Rather, these relationships should be understood as **rhizomic**, as described in Chapter 12.

The second edition

What has changed since the first edition of *Rethinking Organisational Behaviour*?

The last few years have seen a pronounced intensification of management and its social and economic role. The claim that managers have a 'right to manage' has become more entrenched than ever, irrespective of the variations in how they do it, where they do it, and what they do. As an inevitable consequence of that, this has been accompanied by a corresponding extension of the issues, and even the characteristics, over which managers are claimed to have dominion. The roles of the professionals in, for example, education and health care are increasingly redefined as management. Almost daily there are new examples of managers issuing decrees about what organisational participants should wear, do, think. All this has been immeasurably enhanced and facilitated by the steady increase in the interpenetration of government and corporation. In the UK, for example, the government openly and explicitly portrays itself as fulfilling a managerial role in governing the state, and, in so doing, claims for itself a 'right to manage'. At the same time, government is increasingly tolerant and indulgent of what organisations do. Corporations increasingly supply personal data on their clients and customers to government for the purposes of managing the population.

Yet, the more that the exercise of managerial power is claimed as a right, and, therefore, not to be questioned, the more that it *is* questioned. The last few years have seen a significant increase in challenges, to managers and to the management process, in theory and in practice. And this has been reflected in developments in the (critical) study of organisational behaviour.

We have made some substantial changes to *Rethinking Organisational Behaviour* for this second edition. Most obviously, we have added a sub-title. There has been a general up-dating and broadening of the material. **Appendix 1**, *History and ideas*, charts, selectively, the development of some of the ideas that inform the book, and notes some of the more recent developments in the study of organisation.

Additionally, we have now included a number of case studies, which are intended as much as focuses for discussion as for exercises. Each chapter now has a case study that specifically addresses the ideas and issues developed in that chapter. **Appendix 2** contains a 'continuous' case study, on which there are questions, and some additional material, in each chapter. **Appendix 3** contains two extended case studies which are intended for reflection on the book as a whole, rather than on specific topics, although some indicative questions are raised. Some of the case studies are based on actual contemporary events, some are based on historical events, and some have been made up. Some others of the case studies represent recontextualisations of material from other, less conventional, sources – in this instance, literary texts. In particular, the two extended case studies in Appendix 3 are based, respectively, on the fable *The Pied Piper of Hamelin* and on Herman Melville's (c. 1889) short story *Billy Budd, Sailor*. This exercise is intended not only to supply a case study for discussion, but also to illustrate that such sources readily provide plenty of ideas and stories of relevance to the study of organisational behaviour. They also illustrate, at some level, the poststructuralist notion of organisation as text, and text as organisation.

Appendix 4, *The art of the case study*, offers some reflections on the case study method in light of the ideas developed in *Rethinking Organisational Behaviour*.

The developments of the last few years have only enhanced the appropriateness, and the urgency, of generating new ways of understanding organisational behaviour.

CHAPTER 2

Semiotics

This chapter introduces the basic concepts of semiotics and the nature of symbols. Starting with examples of simple symbols, issues of meaning and interpretation are explored. Particular emphasis is placed on the three crucial characteristics of symbols – absence, artibrariness and difference – together with the significant concept of metaphor. Extending these considerations to examples of the more complex webs of symbols which are experienced on a daily basis, the problems of communication are highlighted. The possibility of communication is retrieved through the concepts of text and intersubjectivity. The implications of semiotics and symbolism for understanding behaviour in organisations are drawn out. These foundational concepts are fundamental to the approach used throughout this book.

One of the most significant developments in understanding human behaviour has been the recognition of the symbolic nature of the social world. This development has, potentially, a profound impact on understanding behaviour in organisations. In the field of organisational behaviour it has been the conventional assumption that behaviour can be understood through observation, but, if everything in the social world is symbolic, then meaning is not necessarily obvious and trying to understand organisational behaviour simply in terms of observable behaviour is inadequate.

The science of symbols

One of the defining characteristics of human beings is that they are **users of symbols**. Symbols are the means by which we communicate and make sense of the world. Most people have an everyday awareness of the use of symbols, widely found in the realms of, for example, the state, the Church or the military, especially as indicators of authority and process. Thus the British state is frequently symbolised by the use of a crown, bread in a church service symbolises the body of Christ, stripes, pips and crowns symbolise hierarchical position in the British army. More recently, however, this ordinary understanding of symbols has given way to a more rigorous analysis of symbol usage, which has developed into a scientific discipline in its own right. The scientific study of the use of symbols is generally taken to have developed simultaneously, in Europe with the work of the Swiss linguist Ferdinand de Saussure, and in the United States with the work of the philosopher and mathematician Charles Sanders Peirce ('Purse'). In Europe the more influential work has been that of Saussure, although his book *Course in General Linguistics*, published posthumously in 1915, which draws his theories together in coherent form, was not literally written by him but was constructed from the notes of students who had attended his lectures! The most significant and far-reaching developments of Saussure's work have been made relatively recently, since it was taken up, particularly, by the French writer and critic Roland Barthes and by the French anthropologist Claude Lévi-Strauss. Latterly, it has been widely developed and used in virtually every discipline in the Social Sciences and the Arts, and has also penetrated into all aspects of management and organisation theory.

Somewhat confusingly, the scientific study of symbol systems is referred to both as **semiotics** and as **semiology**. Although technically there is a slight difference between the two terms, in practice they are used interchangeably. Thus, for example, the Italian professor Umberto Eco, more famous generally for what he calls the 'negligible accident' that he wrote the novel *The Name of the Rose*, calls himself a semiologist and what he writes about semiotics. The term 'semiotics' is the more generally used, and is the one that will be used here.

Characteristics of symbols

Inevitably, there is a technical language associated with semiotics. This language, like the terms 'semiotics' and 'semiology', is not always used consistently, different writers using the same words in different senses. Some writers, for example, distinguish between symbol and sign, but the basis for doing so is not always the same, and such nuances are not necessary for our purposes here – we shall use the term '**symbol**' generally. There are, however, two technical terms which are consistently used and which need to be understood: **signifier** and **signified**.

A symbol is something which signifies something else, i.e., it is a signifier. That which a signifier signifies is referred to as its signified.

There are various *types* of symbol, or signifier. For example, mathematical symbols express complex abstract numerical relationships; iconic symbols usually express some visual representation, for example, pictures of men and women, however stylised, to symbolise their respective public toilets; linguistic symbols – for present purposes, words, of which there are two types, written and spoken – express the normal form of human communication. Language is usually accepted to be the most prevalent symbol system, and a particularly significant one since language is the basis of the social: there would be no point in people gathering in groups if they could not communicate in some way; no other feature of social life is so essential to it.

The *purpose* of symbols of all types is to convey **meaning**. This meaning is not inherent in the symbol itself, but derives from what is represented, or signified.

At your convenience?

| Trousers | SIGNIFIER | Skirt |
| Male | SIGNIFIED | Female |

These are standard conventional symbols used to signify male and female public toilets. Most people can recognise them and distinguish between them, but they are conventionally rather than representationally accurate – and they contain a large number of implications which reflect complex cultural norms. The point it that, although on examination they are fraught with meaning, we can still recognise them.

- What assumptions are being made in the use of these symbols?
- Would they work in Scotland, where men wear kilts?
- Will they make sense for women who wear trousers?
- Should feminists object to such symbols?

Every symbol also has three main characteristics: **absence**, **arbitrariness** and **difference**.

In the sense that the fundamental characteristic of a symbol is that it represents something else, the something else is always **absent**. If the 'object' were present it would not be necessary to have a symbol for it. A common example is that of currency – a £5 note symbolises an equivalent amount of gold held by the Bank of England which is not needed, under normal circumstances, in any transaction in which the note is used. A red traffic light symbolises a prohibition but the enforcer of that prohibition is not usually present to ensure compliance. A word may symbolise an object but the object does not need to be physically present in order to be talked about.

All symbols are also **arbitrary**, in that there is no necessary form that they must take. There is nothing intrinsic to any symbol that dictates what form it can have. Symbols symbolise whatever they do by agreement among users. In so far as there may seem to be rules about how to symbolise a particular thing or about what a particular symbol means, this is only the effect of convention, habit or power. One example of this is the way different natural languages use different symbols to signify the same object. Thus, in English we use the word 'tree' to signify a certain kind of plant life, but in French the same thing is signified by the word 'arbre', and in German the word is 'Baum'. Similarly, in English we use the word 'management', but in French the appropriate symbol is 'gestion', and in German it is 'Geschäftsleitung'. That all people who speak English would use the same word to signify a concept is a matter of convention. That the relationship between the word tree and the object tree is arbitrary is demonstrated by the utter lack of any necessary connection between the letters t, r, e, e – the marks on the page – and the object which grows from the earth. This is equally the case with other types of symbol. For example, danger is most often symbolised by red in Western iconographies, but in Chinese iconographies red symbolises happiness – red is a colour to get married in, while white is reserved for mourning. There is nothing inherent to danger that is red. Even in Western iconographies, where red is used to symbolise danger and green to symbolise safety, such as in traffic lights, this is a relatively recent articulation which has occurred as the result of agreement to standardise. **The way we symbolise something does not correspond to the reality represented, symbols do not reflect reality**; signifier and signified are arbitrarily connected and the recognition of the connection is something we learn.

Symbols also function as symbols only because they are recognisably **different** from any other symbol. We always recognise what something **is** by differentiating it from everything it **is not**. Relatively minor changes in a symbol distinguish major differences in what it symbolises. A simple example is made by just changing a vowel in a series of letters: mate, mete, mite, mote, mute. On road signs the figure 30 on a blue background means minimum speed, but in a red circle means maximum speed.

In organisations it is often the case that distinctions in type of company car, office furniture, canteens, working hours, and so on, are used to signify relatively subtle difference. In a university we know, toilets for the use of staff are equipped with 'soft' toilet paper, while those for the use of students are equipped with 'hard' toilet paper. Where distinction is not recognised, meaning is not conveyed.

These characteristics of symbols – **that they represent something else, that what they represent is absent, that the relationship between the symbol and what it represents is arbitrary, and that it is based on perceptible difference** – mean that the term 'natural users of symbols' signifies an extraordinarily complex and sophisticated activity. When we consider the implications of these characteristics this becomes clearer.

Minimum speed limit   Maximum speed limit

Watch your speed!

Links between signifier and signified

So far we have suggested that symbols have specific and real meanings, but this has only been for illustrative purposes. They do not. Thus, for example, **the same symbol can have different meanings in different contexts, and have different meanings to different people.**

The English word 'cat' is a relatively simple word but its signification is not at all simple. Even according to our dictionary 'cat' has *fourteen* meanings. As a noun it can mean an animal, a woman, a piece of military equipment, a double tripod, a game, a whip, a man, a jazz fan, a sailing boat, and, as an abbreviation, a tractor and a double hulled boat. As a verb 'cat' can mean to secure anchor, to vomit and to beat with a whip. It is worth noting that while some of these significations are just different to each other, some are what we would normally think of as exact opposites, such as man/woman, yet denotable by the same word. Another such example is expressed by the well-known pair of sentences: 'A fast horse can run. A fast colour cannot run.' This complexity is just as evident whether we refer to spoken language or to written language. Consider the following variations, which all *sound* the same but have very different meanings: pain (as in ache), pane (as in piece of glass), pein (as in the end of a hammer). Also, consider the difference between 'the pain' and 'le pain'. Of course, it is also the case that **specific signifieds have more than one signifier.** Instead of pain one could say ache; instead of fast one could say quick, and so on.

What about dogs?

Lest you think that CAT is peculiar as a signifier in having multiple signifieds:

- DOG can signify a type of clutch, a lifting device, part of a gun, sulking, a woman, a man, God, to follow, etc.
- FROG can signify a problem with the throat, a fastening, a piece of railway equipment, part of a hoof, a feature in brickwork, part of a violin, a Frenchman, etc.
- HORSE can signify a punishment frame, an oppressive boss, playfulness, a clothes drier, a saw bench, etc.
- MOUSE can signify a cut of meat, a term of affection, a term of derision, a piece of computer equipment, a firing device, an anti-slip device, etc.

Of course, it is not just animal names that have multiple signifieds. Think of the following work-related signifiers: **office; table; file; type; desk; job; superior; boss.**

Do you know what, in organisations, is meant by: **a government job? Saint Monday? a Friday afternooner? a symposium? a flyer?**

If relatively concrete objects or concepts create problems in understanding, what about more abstract ones: **fairness? effort? excellence? success? performance?**

Generally speaking we do not have great difficulty in distinguishing between all these different significations, *providing* that they occur within a meaningful context. In other words, **all signification is context-dependent**.

Up to this point we have talked about symbols as simple and discrete items. However, it is not normal to use or to experience symbols in this way. Usually they occur in what are known as **chains of signification**. It is this that gives the context for meaning. In the case of iconic symbols, for example, the same symbol in different locations can mean different things, and we understand what is signified by reference to the other symbols in the context. Thus a road sign by the side of the road signifies something different from the same road sign in a museum. In the case of language, the chain of signification is often a sentence.

The construction of meaning within chains of signification occurs on two axes, the **syntagmatic** and the **paradigmatic**. In the case of language, the syntagmatic axis (sometimes also referred to as the horizontal axis) relates to words that precede and follow a given word, which constellation of words gives each specific symbol its meaning. The paradigmatic axis (sometimes called the vertical or associative axis) relates to the realm of other words that could be used but are not. In the former case, in a sentence such as 'Fly cat are green' the words surrounding 'cat' do not generate any guidance to its signification, whereas 'The cat is big' does convey a certain amount of meaning but still does not distinguish exactly which signified of 'cat' is intended. 'The cat is big and furry' is much more useful in identifying which signified of 'cat' is likely to be intended, though not totally specific. In the latter case, if, in the sentence 'The cat is big', the word 'whip' is substituted for 'cat' this also enhances the meaning context, though is less precise in other ways since 'cat' is a *particular* type of whip. Beyond definitional sentences substitution always involves changes, or shades, of meaning, and the same synonyms do not always signify similar meaning. While there may not be much difference between 'A fair day's work for a fair day's pay' and 'A fair day's labour for a fair day's pay', there *may* be a lot of difference between 'My wife has gone into work' and 'My wife has gone into labour'.

Meaning and ambiguity

As users of symbols we handle all this practical complexity with ease, and, given even very basic levels of skill, we are able to refine our use of symbols to signify precise concepts. But when we talk about multiple significations it is not just this complexity which is the issue. The creation of **meaning** is not just a matter of sending a message, communication is also crucially dependent on that message's reception. An individual's reception of a message passes through the filter of their own unique perception and experience. It may be quite clear that the signification of 'cat' intended is a whip, but what that means to different individuals is extremely variable.

Let us return to the issue of the arbitrary nature of the relationship between signifier and signified. It has already been suggested that there is no necessary connection between the thing which is to be signified and that which signifies it, its symbol. This arbitrariness works in the other direction too: **there is no necessary signified**

attached to any particular signifier. At one level this has been illustrated by the point that the signifier 'cat' can mean many different things. However, even though there are variable signifieds, it has been suggested that once the context is known, it is possible to agree on what 'cat' means in any particular circumstance – in other words, that once the context is specified there is a real relationship between signifier and signified. But this is not the case. For that to be so, meaning would have to be an attribute contained within the signifier, but **meaning is a characteristic of the understanding of the person/people who use the symbol.**

Take, for example, a well-known symbol, the flag known as the Union Jack (although, strictly speaking, it should be the Union Flag, and is only called the Union Jack when it is displayed on a boat). There may be general agreement that, in some way, the Union Jack symbolises the United Kingdom, but it also contains meaning beyond this simple fact. For some people the Union Jack may symbolise the cradle of democracy, equality of opportunity, but to others it may symbolise colonial oppression. For some people job enrichment may be seen as a benign way of increasing productivity, but to others it might be seen as an unwelcome increase in complexity in the demands made on them, or as labour intensification. Frederick Taylor's famous objective for Scientific Management, 'a fair day's work for a fair day's pay', can prompt wildly differing views on what constitutes fairness, even when there is general agreement about the desirability of fairness. Additionally, in this context, it is noteworthy that, since fairness is not a scientific concept, nor scientifically measurable, its inclusion as a primary objective by Taylor throws the signification of 'science' in the term, Scientific Management, into considerable doubt. **Whether any meanings have positive or negative significations is a further level of interpretation.**

These different levels of meaning are known as **second-, third-, etc. order significations** – meanings themselves have meanings. In other words, symbols do not have meanings which can, ultimately, be specified as *true* meanings. Meaning does not reside within particular signifiers, or even in the signified. **The meaning contained in a symbol is given to it by the people who use, or experience, it.**

Connotation/denotation

One of the difficulties attached to the claim that symbols do not have specific meanings is a common-sense feeling that they do. If we see a symbol such as £, we recognise that this symbol signifies a certain type of currency, and the ability to recognise this is an essential prerequisite of the ability to use currency. That £ signifies a unit of British currency is its **denotative signification** – it is what it is intended to mean, its 'authorised' meaning. However, while it is important to be able to understand the denotation of a symbol, there is also another realm of meaning attached to a symbol, its **connotative significations**, its affective meaning, meaning beyond what is intended – in effect, **surplus meaning.** Connotative significations are more extensive than denotative ones, and the two can even be at odds with each other.

For example, around the beginning of November every year it is common to see people wearing red imitation poppies. The denotative signification of the red poppy is intended, unambiguously, to be a symbol of remembrance –

▶

specifically, remembrance of the fallen of the First World War, the armistice of which was concluded at (some say, contrived to occur at) the eleventh hour of the eleventh day of the eleventh month of 1918. Acts of remembrance associated with subsequent conflicts have since been subsumed into this particular act of remembrance. Apart from this specific denotation, the red poppy has innumerable connotations for each individual, such as who they are remembering, why they do it in this particular way, their understanding of this 'Great War', and of wars in general, as well as symbolising an act of charity. However, in recent years a white imitation poppy has also made an appearance at this time of year.

The white poppy (which made its very first appearance in 1933) has been intended to be an alternative for people who see the red poppy as symbolising a celebration of militarism and who wish to associate themselves with a 'culture of peace'. The coexistence of these two kinds of poppy has stimulated considerable controversy about both the denotations and the connotations attached to them. Notwithstanding assertions to the contrary, the white poppy has been claimed by the 'reds' to symbolise disrespect to, and criticism of, those who died for their country. The emergence of the white poppy has called into question the apparently straightforward symbolism of the red one, but the red poppy has done the same thing for the white one. The existence of two kinds of poppy has generated a plethora of surplus meanings. Each has a clear denotative signification but these pale into insignificance in light of the conflict surrounding their connotative significations. Neither was intended to denote conflict – the red poppy symbolised remembrance, the white one peace – but the affective significations attached to each by their opponents have stimulated profound disagreements, even bitterness, both about what is to be symbolised, and about the correct way to do it.

Not only can denotations and connotations generate mutual ambiguity, they can also come to symbolise exact opposites. Take, for example, the word 'wicked'. For nearly a thousand years this word has denoted something bad, but, in recent years, especially among young people, it has come to connote something good. And, in some cases, connotative meanings can come to dominate denotative ones. For example, when the leader of a political party says of some troubled colleague that he/she has the leader's confidence and whole-hearted support, the connotations of this are usually taken to be the opposite, that the colleague's political survival is in doubt. While the connotations of the phrase are considered clear, the denotation is considered unclear – it is difficult to tell whether the statement is intended to mean what it says or not.

Although identification of denotations is very important in terms of understanding, and surviving in, the world around us, the intended meaning of a symbol is less significant than what the symbol connotes to those who experience it.

And, by the way, the symbol £ is also not as straightforward as it seems. £ is actually a stylised L and stands, not for pound, but for the Latin word *libra*, also the linguistic root of names for other coins, such as, in Italian, *lira*. Even used just as a price tag, its connotative significations can vary widely, depending, for example, on whether one has a lot of them or only a few.

There is, therefore, no way of ensuring that any two people who use/experience the same symbol attach the same meaning to it. Even if there may be some general agreement about the first-order signification, what *that* means to people will be infinitely variable. The examples we have used up to now have tended to be relatively concrete in that they relate to physical objects – a cat, a flag – but clearly not as simple as they might have seemed. How much more complex symbols must become when they refer to something abstract, as in the case of the word 'organisation'. To students of Organisational Behaviour it may seem strange, but there is no general agreement among those who write about organisational behaviour about what 'organisation' means (though this may explain some discrepancies or apparent inconsistencies they have already encountered!). It is possible, for the practical purposes of communication, to construct a definitional level of signification which allows those who use this word to appear to be talking about the same thing. But close examination of the degree of agreement about such signification reveals that it is really very small. This is the case with all language. All language is **ambiguous** and **the ambiguity resides in the communicators, and is irreducible**.

A further difficulty with abstract concepts is that there is no concrete object against which they can be tested, measured, verified. If we wish to explain to another person what a cat is, it would be possible to produce an object to show them. However, even in such cases it is not particularly efficient constantly to concretise words with their corresponding physical object – in other words, to replace the symbol with the object. In practice, all communication is characterised by abstraction (absence): we communicate through symbols, not through real objects. But when we deal with concepts which do not have a corresponding physical object, all we have is language. Management is an activity particularly replete with abstract concepts, including excellence, leadership, satisfaction, authority, and so on – concepts which cannot be concretised, even if they are used *as if* they can. We must rely on signifiers to convey meaning, even though this is imperfect.

When trying to convey abstract concepts we rely on **figurative** language. Typically, we do this by comparing what we want to convey to something else which is already familiar. For example, if trying to describe how an organisation functions we may compare it to a machine. Obviously, an organisation is not a machine, but it may possess certain similarities to a machine. To say an organisation is like a machine is a **simile**. Alternatively, we might refer to a department being the brain of the organisation, though animals have brains, not organisations. Such a description, which omits the comparator 'like', is a **metaphor**. Such comparisons, even though they describe things in terms which are literally inappropriate, can be very effective communicators by virtue of the connections they signify. But, because they are literally inappropriate, they always emphasise some particular aspects of what we want to describe, and downplay, or repress, other aspects, those aspects which do not fit the metaphor. This is why metaphors are sometimes referred to as 'ways of seeing'.

The technical term for such figures of language is **tropes**, though more usually, and perhaps somewhat confusingly, they are often referred to collectively as metaphors. A metaphor is defined as **the perception of similarity between things that are fundamentally dissimilar**. The effectiveness of a metaphor, the extent to which it conveys meaning, depends on such a perception being held by the receiver of the message – again emphasising that meaning is not held in the symbols themselves, but in the person who uses them.

Tropes generally represent the often unremarked point that in trying to convey meaning about something we usually begin by describing it in terms of something else which it is *not* like, and rely on the receiver to make a connection. **But since all language is metaphoric, because the connection between signifier and signified, word and meaning, is arbitrary, such 'imperfections' are an inevitable feature of communication.**

Tropicality

There are many other tropes besides metaphor, though these are generally seen as less important for students of behaviour in organisations. Tropes are complex and there is not much agreement about definitions and applications. Nonetheless, their use is surprisingly common in organisations.

- **Metonymy** is, linguistically, when an *attribute* of something is used to symbolise the whole thing. Thus, 'Human Resource Management' is a metonym, because people are more than just resources.

- **Synecdoche** is when a *part* of something is used to signify the whole, as in the term 'hand' to mean employee, from which we get 'charge-hand'.

- **Irony** is also very common in organisations, especially, for example, in meetings, in expressions like 'What genius thought this up?'!

The functions of symbols

Symbols have two fundamental roles, which highlight their significance in human affairs: **they contain information** and **they are the medium of all communication.**

Information

A recognisable symbol used/experienced in context will give us **information**. For example, road signs give information about regulations for traffic or the state of the road, price tags inform us about cost, certain forms of dress inform about the role a person occupies (such as, literally or figuratively, uniforms), a verbal expression can inform about how someone is feeling (such as, I feel happy, ill, sad). But **information should not be confused with truth**. A road sign may warn of road works where there are none, a price tag may indicate a previous price rather than a current one, a person in a policeman's uniform may be an actor, a person who informs you that they are feeling happy may be telling a lie. Information can be untrue for one of two reasons: *the untruth may be intentional or unintentional*. The road works sign whose removal has been overlooked when the work was completed can be seen in terms of unintentional untruth, while the person who tells you they are happy when they are not is lying intentionally.

As already noted, a symbol always denotes an absence, so the recognition of whether or not the information is true can only be achieved when what is absent is made present: **knowledge about whether information is correct or not is always deferred.** After driving past a road works sign, whether or not it is true will not be discovered until driving further. Of course, in some cases we may *never* know whether the information is correct, because there is no way of verifying it – to know whether or not a person is happy we are dependent on their description of their feelings and on our interpretation of that description; even apparently contradictory information, such as weeping, does not necessarily belie the statement that they are happy, and, furthermore, happiness is a very subjective description which may, and probably will, vary considerably from one person to another. Similar differences are attached to many Organisational Behaviour concepts, such as feelings of satisfaction, empowerment, equity, expectation.

Are you properly dressed?

The popularity of uniforms waxes and wanes according to the current socio-political climate – broadly speaking, a liberal climate will not favour uniforms, a more authoritarian one will favour uniforms. At the moment, uniforms are increasingly in vogue, both in schools, where there is a trend towards uniforms in primary schools where they are not traditional, though in secondary schools they have been traditional, and at work, where companies such as banks, retail outlets, pubs and fast food chains are adopting uniforms as common practice.

- If uniforms are 'necessary' and 'desirable' in schools and at work, should university students be required to wear a uniform too?
- Does office dress, such as a suit, shirt and tie, constitute a uniform? Do women have more discretion in office clothing than men?
- Some organisations require employees to 'dress down' on Friday afternoons. Why? What is the symbolism here?
- Do uniforms improve employee performance? If so, why and how? If not, are there any other functional reasons for insisting on the wearing of uniforms?
- Some schools require female teachers to wear skirts and not to wear trousers. Equally, male teachers, presumably, have to wear trousers and not to wear skirts. This implies that there is a functional link between the clothing of the teacher and the quality of their teaching.
- Recently, a wagon driver was sacked for not wearing a tie while driving his wagon. What significance should be attached to the wearing of uniform at work when transgression of the dress code can be a sacking offence?
- Is there a conflict between management beliefs that stress the uniqueness of employees and encourage use of initiative (e.g., empowerment) and those that require conformity to a strict dress code?

Neither information nor truth should be confused with meaning. Meaning is the understanding which is generated within us, whatever the originator of the symbol intends. Thus, seeing a road works sign informs of the putative presence of road works, but says nothing about what that implies to, or how it is interpreted by, individual road users. **Information is neutral, meaning is affective**, that is, involves emotion. Information stimulates an affective response, but that response is a function of the person who receives the information, not a part of the information itself. Seeing a road works sign may cause feelings of resentment about potential delays, seeing a price tag may make one feel happy if it is seems to be a bargain, seeing a policeman – even a fictitious one – may make one feel uncomfortable, someone declaring that they feel happy may cause one to feel glad on their behalf, and so on. *And*, of course, different, even opposite, reactions are just as possible. The responses we give to information are to do with the meaning we attribute to it, and are independent of the information itself. However, it is also the case that we *never* experience information in its neutral sense, because we always respond to it by giving it – by transforming it into – meaning, even if that meaning is that the information is not significant to us. In a primary sense, **information has only two states: it informs of what it is *and* of what it is not. Meaning, however, is infinitely polymorphous**.

It is also often the case that we do not have full information about anything and must therefore attribute meaning on the basis of the partial information available. As is well known in the context of perception, this can, and often does, lead to very risky attribution of 'meaning'; for example, halo effect, stereotyping. Sometimes it is risky merely because it is uncertain, but at other times it may be substantively wrong, as in the famous phrase 'Not waving, but drowning'.

Communication

The other major function of symbols is as the means of **communication**. What we communicate is information, with the intention of eliciting a response, and this response is what we have called meaning. We have already seen that symbols are an imperfect mechanism for conveying meaning. But communication itself is an imperfect process. Communication involves a number of coding and transmission processes, which are all potential sources of ambiguity and error.

Opposite is a typical model of a two-way communication process, known as a communication loop.

A wants to communicate with B. A must turn the concept/idea to be communicated into natural language, of which we already know three problems: arbitrariness, and the paradigmatic and syntagmatic aspects – in other words, the lack of a necessary connection between signifier and signified, the choice of one signifier from amongst all possibilities, and the location of that in a chain of signification. This has then to be **encoded** into the transmission medium, such as speech or writing. The **transmission** medium is susceptible to what is called **noise**, interference with the transmission of the message. For example, in the case of speech, this could be, literally, background noise, or an unfamiliar accent, or in the case of writing, it could be bad handwriting, or writing style, and so on. Then there is the **decoding** process at B, which contains the same kind of prob-

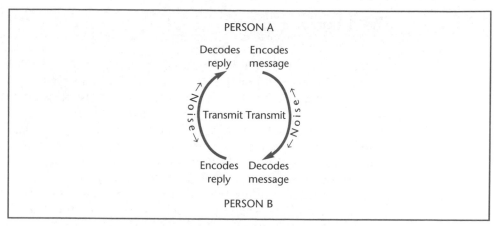

A two-person communication loop

lems as the encoding process. To close the loop the process is repeated, encoding, transmission and decoding all open to the same problems again, and compounding them.

One way to try to minimise errors is to build into the communication channel what is, rather confusingly, known as **redundancy**. Redundancy is a complex but useful concept in information and communication theory. For our purposes, it can be seen as the provision of an over-generous channel of communication in order to improve the chance of the message getting through. Examples might include repetition, alternative phrasings, tautology, and so on. A classic example of the problems of lack of redundancy is to be found in the children's game of chinese whispers. Another famous example is the transformation of the supposed message 'Send reinforcements, we're going to advance' into 'Send three and four pence, we're going to a dance'. Bureaucracy can be seen as a form of institutionalised redundancy, in that putting things in writing is supposed to make it less likely that they can be misinterpreted. However, written communication is no less subject to fallibility than spoken communication.

In this model of two-way communication, whatever B, the recipient of the message, understands by it is only an approximation, close or otherwise, of what A, the sender of the message, intends. But, by closing the loop – in other words, by responding – B can, potentially, improve his/her understanding of A's intention, by seeking clarification, for example. However, without the opportunity to close the loop any chance of gaining clarification is lost. This situation is characteristic of **one-way communication**. A lot of communication in organisations is one-way, the commonest example being the use of memos. Lectures of all kinds are predominantly one-way – as is this book. One-way communication inevitably eliminates many of the avenues for identifying the denotative signification of a message, and can have severe, even tragic, consequences, as in the controversial case of Derek Bentley, who was executed in 1953 as a consequence of shouting to his accomplice the ambiguous phrase 'Let him have it', which was alleged to mean that the accomplice should shoot the policeman who was trying to arrest him, rather than, as his supporters have claimed, an appeal to the accomplice to hand over the gun to the police.

Textuality

So far we have talked about short chains of signification, relatively discrete and simple. However, in practice we are immersed in a world of symbols, a world in which everything is symbolic, in which the symbols are interwoven, and in which symbols are so commonplace that we tend to overlook that they are symbols, treating this symbolic world as if it is uncomplicatedly material and real. This is to re-emphasise the point that **symbols are not just words, but that all aspects of the social have a symbolic dimension and can be understood semiotically as communication**. Consider the symbolic use of gestures, facial expression, and so on, which we commonly refer to as body language. Thus it is important to note that not just verbal language is symbolic, but also **all action is intentionally or unintentionally symbolic**. An example of intentionally symbolic action is any ceremony or ritual, such as the presentation of a gold watch for long service. Unintentionally symbolic action might be all other actions which, whatever the intention of the actor, are given a meaning by others. Action is symbolic in that it has meaning and it always, knowingly or unknowingly, reflects the meanings and interpretations given by the actor to the symbols he/she experiences. In that action is always a response to symbols, is itself symbolic and therefore elicits a response from others, it is more appropriate to talk about **interaction**. Action/interaction is a fundamental part of the chains of signification.

The infinity of chains of signification and their interconnectedness is nicely encapsulated in the concept of the **text**. The word 'text' derives from the Latin word for weaving. Its use in this context also reflects the pre-eminence of language, in whatever form, in society.

A text can have many forms and qualities. For example, it can be fictional or non-fictional, descriptive or analytical, it can be, intentionally or unintentionally, humorous, pathetic, ironic, serious, clear, obscure, allegorical, and so on. Such qualities of texts serve to underline the complexity of the process of interpretation, which is further complicated by the recognition that what constitutes any such quality is not universal, or agreed upon. Furthermore, the extent to which any quality may be understood to be present in a text is, fundamentally, a function of its relation to other texts. This is another example of the perception of difference, as discussed earlier.

This idea of the text can be applied, metaphorically, to any and all symbolic situations. This is already reflected in the idea of 'reading' a situation. In organisational life, for example, there are always key actors, bit-part players, stars, plots, sub-plots, comedies and tragedies, a narrative, descriptions of the action ranging from organisational stories to profit and loss reports. The use of tropes by organisational participants is common, especially metaphors, such as lean and hungry, family, jungle, brain, machine. All such tropes symbolise things about the organisation and are expressed in – and indeed refer to – symbols. Sometimes such symbolic expression is verbal, but by no means exclusively. Who someone is, what is going on, is also conveyed by such symbols as dress codes, modes of address, indicators of status, physical location, decor, artefacts, jargon, and many other things. To understand an organisation we need to **read** all these symbols and interpret them, in the same way that we would read a text.

War of words

This is an excerpt from a display, headlined 'Mad Dogs and Englishmen', that appeared in the *Guardian* newspaper on 23 January 1991, after only the first week of the First Gulf War. It describes use of language in reports in the national press about the war – all these expressions had been used in the national press in that week.

We have	**They have**
Army, Navy and Air Force	A war machine
Reporting guidelines	Censorship
Press briefings	Propaganda
We	**They**
Take out	Destroy
Suppress	Destroy
Eliminate	Kill
Neutralise or decapitate	Kill
Decapitate	Kill
Dig in	Cower in their foxholes
We launch	**They launch**
First strikes	Sneak missile attacks
Pre-emptively	Without provocation
Our men are . . .	**Their men are . . .**
Boys	Troops
Lads	Hordes
Our boys are . . .	**Theirs are . . .**
Professional	Brainwashed
Lionhearts	Paper tigers
Cautious	Cowardly
Confident	Desperate
Heroes	Cornered
Dare-devils	Cannon fodder
Young knights of the sky	Bastards of Baghdad
Loyal	Blindly obedient
Desert rats	Mad dogs
Resolute	Ruthless
Brave	Fanatical
Our boys are motivated by	**Their boys are motivated by**
An old fashioned sense of duty	Fear of Saddam
Our boys	**Their boys**
Fly into the jaws of hell . . .	Cower in concrete bunkers
Our missiles are . . .	**Their missiles are . . .**
Like Luke Skywalker zapping Darth Vader	Aging duds (*rhymes with Scuds*)
Our missiles cause . . .	**Their missiles cause . . .**
Collateral damage	Civilian casualties
We . . .	**They . . .**
Precision bomb ...	Fire wildly at anything in the sky
Our planes . . .	**Their planes . . .**
Suffer a high rate of attrition	Are shot out of the sky
Fail to return from missions	Are zapped

This is a relatively humorous instance of a phenomenon that is extremely common during conflicts of all kinds. It is a good example of the paradigmatic axis in operation. Just as significantly, it is a good example of the way symbols are used deliberately to manipulate the emotional response of the reader.

Source: 'Mad dogs and Englishmen' from *The Guardian*, 23 January 1991. Copyright © Guardian Newspapers Limited 1991. Reprinted with permission.

What is produced by such a reading is a **story** of what the organisation is like, it is not a definitive description. Other readings, and other readers, will generate other stories, which may be just as viable and just as relevant. Furthermore, in the way in which a more conventional sense of text has an **author**, someone who creates the text, there is a similar concept of **author-ity** in organisations, (see Chapter 5 on power). There is an **author-ised** model, or concept, of what the organisation is. A particular story may be intended by the disposition of symbols in an organisation, in the same way that an author intends a written text to be read in a particular way. But stories do not have only one meaning. Meanings, as already noted, are contained, not in the text, but in the interpretations given to it by the reader. **Whatever the intention of the author(s), it is only one possible interpretation among many**. Thus a text can have as many meanings as there are people reading the text. The more complex and varied the text, the more readings can be generated. **It is impossible to say that one is more correct than another, they are only different**. Such an approach provides a powerful insight into, for example, the occurrence of disputes and conflicts in organisations: they are the clashes of different readings of the organisational text.

Limitations of interpretation

A symbol is a representation. Throughout this introduction to symbolism and semiotics it has been strongly implied that there is a difference between symbols and that which they represent, the real. What might constitute the real, if anything, is a topic of much heated debate, both generally and in Organisation Theory. For present purposes we are using the term to describe what a symbol refers to. The **hyper-real** is the concept used to describe the condition when the recognition of difference, between a symbol and what it refers to, is lost and the symbol comes to be seen as 'more real' than its meaning. An example of this can be found in the well-documented phenomenon of viewers responding to events in television soap operas, such as weddings and funerals, by sending congratulations or condolences to the characters, as if they really existed. The history of organisations is replete with examples of people believing that an organisation, a process, or a product can confer on them some desired condition which is simply unachievable. Examples from the world of products would include the belief that alcohol makes one good at sport, that using a particular washing powder is synonymous with being a caring parent, that hair restorer will confer virility, that using a particular stock cube is conducive to a harmonious family life, and so on. It hardly needs to be said that **to believe that the symbol is the real is to live in a world of make-believe, to become detached from 'reality'**.

The problem we face, however, is an existential need to understand the world. This is not simply a desire, but a matter of survival, physically, socially, organisationally. The world is an inherently dangerous place to live in and in order to survive we need to be able to make sense from what is going on. But, because we have to do this through symbols, **we cannot gain unmediated access to the real**. Each of us interprets the symbols through our perception and, in that sense, every interpretation is unique, and there are infinite numbers of interpretations.

Since we cannot have direct access to the real, the best we can hope for is that our understanding is adequate to our survival needs. This is the same for everyone, *without exception*. To survive in an organisation, for example, it is imperative that we read, interpret, understand, the symbols. When we join an organisation it is imperative that we learn, as quickly as possible, to read the organisational text – for example, to understand what is appropriate behaviour, to recognise authority, to orientate ourselves. The importance of this is recognised in organisations, both formally and informally, in the induction process. The only difference between individuals in an organisation in this respect is that some people have a greater ability, or opportunity, to enforce their interpretation over other interpretations, because they occupy positions of power.

Intersubjectivity

That there are potentially infinite numbers of readings of a text might seem to imply that there is no possibility of **shared understandings**. Experience, obviously, tells us that this is not the case. People can agree about what things mean, **intersubjectively**. For example, workers in an organisation might agree that management's offer of a 2 per cent pay increase is derisory and symbolises management's lack of appreciation of the workforce; similarly, managers might see the workers' rejection of their generous offer of a 2 per cent pay increase as symbolising the economic naivety and inherent greed of the workforce. However, what such agreement in a group might consist in, the details on which agreement is constituted, is, often deliberately, nebulous, and itself is expressed symbolically. Even the use of such collective terms as 'managers' and 'workers' is only a convenient shorthand (symbol) which we use to communicate, and which masks the potentially profound differences and variety between individual managers and/or individual workers.

A more general example of intersubjectivity can be found in language itself. Even though we all understand meanings in a unique way, we do use language to communicate to each other and it is a relatively successful mode of communication. We tacitly and implicitly assume some agreement about what words mean. When we use the word 'organisation', under general circumstances we assume that others who speak the same natural language will understand what is meant. But this assumption of understanding bears very little scrutiny, and exploration of apparently common understanding usually reveals very quickly how little meaning is held in common. In effect, **intersubjectivity is about agreement to agree, rather than agreement about what is signified**. This is equally the case with any and all symbolic readings. The extent to which it is possible to establish intersubjectivity is dependent upon shared experience, shared culture, shared perceptions, and so on. This is reflected in the varied coalitions of organisational life.

Existing applictions in Organisational Behaviour

Semiotics has influenced two related but distinct approaches to Organisational Behaviour, though often implicitly rather than explicitly. The two approaches are **Organisational Culture** and **Organisational Symbolism**.

Organisational Culture

The relevance of Organisational Culture in the context of semiotics is the understanding of culture as aggregations of symbolic meanings, shared by groups and used by them to give and sustain group identity, and to delineate appropriate patterns of behaviour for group members. This is clearly relevant to, and has many attractions for, organisations.

The study of organisational cultures has encompassed two distinct approaches, one a rigorous attempt to analyse organisational cultures, akin to an anthropological approach, and the other, more common, an atheoretical attempt to manipulate organisational cultures. The first mentioned starts from the recognition that within particular groups there is a social dynamic based on tacit agreement about, for example, the nature of relationships, acceptable behaviour, duties, obligations, beliefs, custom and practice, tradition, and so on, which underlie and inform manifest behaviour. The approach seeks to uncover these hidden motivations for behaviour, in order to try to understand why things are the way they are.

The second approach, however, is less concerned with *de*scription than with *pre*scription. It views organisational cultures primarily in terms of being a major influence on organisational performance, and assumes that organisational cultures are 'perfectible' by what is often referred to as cultural engineering. The prescriptions of this approach are based on the claim that an organisation's current culture is suboptimal by definition, never as good as it can be, and that it can be improved, by strategic intervention, into a higher performing culture – the 'excellent' organisation. In this sense, this approach to organisational culture is simply not interested in the way things are, because it assumes, from the start, that the way things are is wrong, and both needs to be and can be improved. The approach owes a lot to the Organisation Development movement of the 1960s, and often uses Lewin's model of change to explain the process of engineering new cultures. This model proposes that first it is necessary to *unfreeze*, by destablising current understandings, then to *change*, by instilling the desired new understandings, then to *refreeze* behaviour patterns in line with the desired culture. It is well known about such approaches to change, however, that, while it is certainly not impossible to destroy current understandings, it is quite impossible to control how they '*refreeze*'. This problem has severely threatened the credibility of the manipulative approach to organisational culture.

The 'cultural engineering' approach to organisational culture is a top-down approach, which sees the preferred organisational culture as synonymous with management culture, which assumes that culture can be managed and that managers are the ones to do it. Such an approach to organisational culture ignores the basic lessons of semiotics and their implications for understanding how meaning is created, and the force of arbitrariness and difference in the nature of symbols. The other approach takes a much more cautious view, assuming that organisational culture is an accomplishment shared by all organisational participants and, though not impossible to change, difficult and dangerous to manipulate. Cultural change in this approach is seen as necessarily participative and long term, which conditions have made it less attractive as a proposition for practitioners, even though it may be more effective.

Organisational Symbolism

This interest is similar to the anthropological approach to organisational culture, in that it is, basically, an analytical approach which seeks to understand the meaning and use of symbols in organisations. Organisational Symbolism is informed, to a greater extent, by the underlying theory of semiotics. It has made three major contributions to the understanding of behaviour in organisations.

The *first* of these contributions has been the demonstration that symbols can have extraordinarily diverse, and often contrary, meanings within organisations, and that to ignore this is to leave out a major – perhaps *the* major – element of the jigsaw puzzle of problem-solving. The *second* contribution has been the provision of copious illustrations that behaviour in organisations is often widely at odds with ordinary conventional theories of Organisational Behaviour. Thus, while those understandings of organisation are often based on the premise that organisations exist solely for the efficient attainment of particular goals, such as optimising shareholder wealth, and that what contributes to the achievement of such goals is rational behaviour, Organisational Symbolism has shown that rational behaviour – that which is meaningful to the person behaving – can reflect an enormously diverse range of goals at all levels of the organisation, frequently at odds with achievement of organisational efficiency. The *third* contribution of Organisational Symbolism has been to establish a radical expansion of the range of factors in an organisation which must be considered relevant to understanding that organisation. The approach has highlighted that everything symbolises something, and that there is **nothing** about an organisation which should be excluded in attempting to understand it, for whatever purpose, whether to study it or to manage it.

Further potential

In spite of the work done in this area, there yet remain a number of implications of semiotics which have significance for understanding behaviour in organisations, and which have, so far, been insufficiently explored. Some of these are particularly relevant, not only to understanding organisational behaviour, but also to the issues of managing it.

Because the relationship between signifier and signified is arbitrary, and the interpretation of, and meaning attributed to, symbols are a function of individual experience, **it is impossible for managers to prescribe meanings for symbols.** For the same reasons, **people cannot be forced to understand a symbol, or the symbolic world, in a particular way.** In spite of this, traditional approaches to organisational behaviour tend to be highly prescriptive, and to offer such prescriptions as if they are transparent, rational and unproblematic – and, therefore, equally meaningful to all organisational participants. That those prescriptions often fail to deliver the benefits claimed for them is hardly surprising. Unless it is acknowledged that meaning and interpretation are individual, unique and highly variable, this will continue to be the case. Furthermore, although it has been conventional in the study of organisational behaviour to assume that it is possible to understand *why* people behave in particular ways simply by observing *how* they behave, a major implication of semiotics is that **observable behaviour, by itself, can tell us absolutely nothing about motivations**. That managers have accepted this fallacious idea, that behaviour itself demonstrates motivations, has left them operating in a hyper-real world.

Symbols often have diverse and contradictory meanings and so **there are NO incontravertible rights and wrongs, goods or bads, in organisational life**. This observation cuts across the grain of managerialist assumptions which permeate both organisational life generally and traditional approaches to understanding behaviour in organisations, and which imply that it is not only possible but also appropriate that managers should define what constitutes good or bad behaviour in the organsiational context. Some of the moral issues implied in this have been taken up by approaches which focus on the study of organisational ethics, and by more critical approaches to the study of organisational behaviour and of management, but there still remain some very salient issues to be addressed – the supposedly scientific nature of conventional Organisational Behaviour and its prescriptions, for example, have been insufficiently interrogated.

From what we know of information and communication, **it can never be assumed that the receiver of a message understands it in the same way that the sender does. Moreover, there is no way of ensuring that the two understandings can be made to coincide**. This situation afflicts everyone in organisations and all attempts to communicate. There is no possible basis for claiming that managers somehow have a better grasp of the process of communication than anyone else, nor for claiming that a manager's communication and interpretation are somehow more correct than that of others – managers are just as capable as anyone of imprecise communication and interpretation. Of course, a manager may *claim* that their view is the more significant, but this is nothing to do with the ability to communicate *per se*, and everything to do with power. Vast amounts of effort are devoted to attempts to perfect communication processes, usually by broadening channels of communication, but the awareness that meaning and interpretation cannot be controlled is widely parenthesised and remains undeveloped.

The conditions that might lead different members of an organisation to understand symbols differently, such as different perceptions of interest, different belief systems, and so on, emphasise that **there is no basis for unitary models of organisations** – the assumption that all organisational members have the same rationality and are pursuing the same goals, both of which can be prescribed by managers. Although this was widely recognised by the more liberal models of organisation and organisational behaviour of, for example, the 1960s, it has been largely forgotten in the conventional models of contemporary organisational analysis. In recent decades there has been a concerted attempt to restore both the unitary model itself and its moral and economic desirability, notwithstanding the increasingly divisive character of contemporary organisational practice. Decreeing that organisations are unitary ignores the plurality of meanings which are inevitable and irremediable. It encourages a version of organisational behaviour which cannot provide meaningful and useful solutions, because it starts out from an inappropriate and inaccurate definition of the problem.

Organisational behaviour and semiotics

The proper project for Organisational Behaviour should be to gain an understanding of behaviour in organisations. Traditionally, Organisational Behaviour has been preoccupied with developing insights and techniques intended to increase organisational performance, on behalf of management as symbolic of the organisation as a whole. Applied in organisations, however, such techniques – in so far as they are expressed in language and in practices – are irremediably symbolic. Yet managers cannot prescribe meaning. For example, in the case of techniques for increasing performance through increasing job satisfaction, it has been assumed that managers can, and should, define what is a satisfying job, yet satisfaction is something which can only be experienced or not, understood or not, by the person who performs the job. Nor can meanings be treated as if they are obvious, and uncontested. So, for example, actions taken to increase efficiency may be understood by workers as an emiseration of their conditions, and both understandings may be appropriate. It is not reasonable to deny contrary interpretations, or to expect them to be abandoned, but necessary, minimally, to accept their existence and therefore to include them in the 'equations' of problem-solving.

The principles of semiotics lead inexorably toward a radical reappraisal of the study of organisational behaviour. No interested parties can be seen as able to prescribe uncontested definitions or patterns for organisational practice. The role of manager has to be reconceptualised in terms of the symbolic significance of each and every managerial behaviour, however minute and whether intentional or not. And this is just as important with all organisational behaviour. Semiotics has the potential to offer enhanced explanatory power for the study of organisational behaviour, not least because it reaches the parts that other approaches cannot reach.

A TALE FROM THE VILLAGE PUMP (*SEMIOTICS*)

(See the Case Study in Appendix 2, pages 340–3)

There are a number of instances in the case of **signifiers** with multiple significations, and of those significations changing over time. One example is the signifier of the drinking water pump.

'Village' pumps were an inestimably important part of life. Not only did they provide the very stuff of life itself – drinking water – but, culturally, they signified a focal social point in the community: the whole notion of 'meeting at the village pump' signified an occasion for communication with one's neighbours, for chatter, for exchanging news and views, and for strengthening the fabric of

▶

social life. A very similar contemporary notion is to be found in the significations of the phrase 'meeting round the water cooler'. However, in the case, because of Snow's hypothesis about the causes of the 1854 outbreak of cholera, the signification of the public drinking water pump, for him, was dramatically changed – it started to acquire a more ominous signification, changing from being the source of life to something that spread deadly disease.

We have stated above that the characteristics of **symbols** are difference, absence and arbitrariness. What was important about the Broad Street drinking water pump was that there was a cluster of deaths from cholera in its vicinity, which was not the case with other drinking water pumps – this was the important *difference* that led Snow to his hypothesis about the causes of this outbreak. However, whatever it was that was actually causing the cholera *could not be made present*, since no one knew what it was – it was only an imputed relationship. Once the actual causes of cholera became identified scientifically (which did not happen until the 1870s), it became clear that it *was not really significant* that it was that particular pump that was involved in the outbreak, because it was the water that was the problem. On one hand, there is no connection between pumps and cholera and, on the other hand, the outcome would have been the same whatever mechanism was used to draw drinking water, if the water was contaminated. Nonetheless, this pump acquired significance for Snow that was way beyond its significance as a 'village pump'. It was the recognition of this that caused Snow to *act*. It is interesting to speculate whether the general signification of the 'village pump' changed as a result of Snow's action. For example, did people treasure their own local pump because it was not associated with cholera, or did they begin to doubt all drinking water pumps?

■ How could **semiotics** be used to analyse other aspects of the case?

Case   NO SMOKE WITHOUT FIRE?

Walter Ashton was a well-regarded manager parachuted in from another department to run the small Quality Audit Department (QAD) of a company, after the unexpected early retirement of the previous incumbent of the job. Ashton was well-connected within the company, although still relatively junior in the hierarchy. The QAD had always been regarded as functioning well, even though a rather relaxed and informal atmosphere prevailed in the department. Members of the QAD socialised together outside work and thought of each other as friends as well as colleagues. The work was quite technical and demanded extensive relations with the rest of the company. Members of the QAD had their own specialisms. They were professionals, such as engineers, accountants, personnel people. No one in the company outside the QAD had expressed any dissatisfaction with the department's performance, though its prevailing culture was well-known, somewhat unusual in the company and the subject of jocular comment at times. So Ashton was not being brought in as a fire-fighter, specifically to improve performance, but he was expected, at least, to maintain current levels of performance. He had little knowledge of the work, but was a very confident person, and perceived the move in terms of enhancing his career prospects within the company. Unfortunately, here ego exceeded talent. Ashton made little effort to understand the existing culture but preferred instead to try to bring the culture into line with what he thought it ought to be like. He instigated a number of new practices, of varying significance, such as random spot checks on people's whereabouts, and banning the traditional departmental provision of chocolate biscuits to be had with coffee, in favour of something, anything, cheaper.

Some time after Walter Ashton took over QAD, the company introduced a No Smoking Policy. This was not a total ban, and allowed individual departments some discretion in their implementation of it. Ashton, who was a non-smoker, did not consider it necessary to discuss the matter with other members of the QAD, several of whom were smokers, as he knew, and made a unilateral decision about implementation of the new policy. He sent the following memo:

INTERNAL MEMORANDUM
Date: 1 April 1994
From: Walter Ashton
To: All Members of QAD

No Smoking Policy
1. As you know, we are required to implement the Company's No Smoking Policy from today.
2. Smoking is no longer allowed in communal areas such as corridors and stairwells, although I am empowered to designate rooms as smoking rooms.
3. I have reviewed all the options and, as I feel that there is a lack of space, I will not be designating any rooms as smoking rooms.
4. Sadly, this means that employees may no longer smoke in their offices.
5. This is not an April Fool.

WA/jrk

- What are the denotations and the connotations of this memo?
- What does the memo imply about Walter Ashton's 'management style'?
- What can be deduced about the QAD's interpersonal relations from the memo?
- What is likely to be the effect of this communication on the members of the QAD?
- Were there any other ways of handling the situation that might have had a different effect?

(Other chapters that would be useful and relevant in analysing the case *include* Power (5), Rationality (6), Self (8), Efficiency (10) and Decision-making (11). See also the concept of Deconstruction, in the chapter on Boundary (9) and in the Glossary.)

Bibliography

The literature on semiotics and on its relevance to organisations is diverse and diffuse. Indeed, much of the literature, although relevant, was not intended as a contribution to the study of organisational behaviour. Going back to original sources, Saussure (1983) is less daunting and more accessible than it may seem at first glance. To go back to Peirce, however, is a more challenging prospect as his contribution is highly diffused throughout his work, though relevant to advanced studies. Several works by Barthes offer a useful overview of the principles of semiotics, notably Barthes (1967, 1972). The paper in Barthes (1972) called 'Myth Today' is especially useful, while the rest of the book consists of a number of brief vignettes which illustrate the process. The extensive anthropological work of Lévi-Strauss represents an important contribution to the development and application of the concepts of semiotics, notably Lévi-Strauss (1972), in which see, in particular, the concept of *bricolage*. Eco's novel *The Name of the Rose* (1984) is, in many ways, an exemplar of the principles of semiotics which is at once entertaining and informative. From his more 'serious' academic work, Eco (1976) offers a more technical exposition.

However, the most accessible routes to the concepts of semiotics – as to many other concepts – are often to be found in what are called secondary sources, in the work of authors who are drawing together the ideas of a number of theorists in order to focus on the central concepts and issues. A particularly clear exposition of semiotics is to be found in Hawkes (1983). Sturrock (1979), on the other hand, collects together studies of individual theorists which summarise their work and highlights links between them. Another useful, but less detailed, survey of key contributors is provided by Lechte (1994). Another way of gaining access to these complex ideas, though much undervalued, is through what might be called, generically, 'beginners' guides'. There are various series which do this, in varying detail and emphasis, but almost always in modest length, such as the Fontana Modern Masters series, Teach Yourself books (Hodder and Stoughton), the Key Sociologists series (Tavistock and Ellis Horwood) and the Key Ideas series (Routledge). A particularly entertaining, though quite rigorous, series is Icon's . . . *For Beginners*', which uses a cartoon format and some of which are also available on audio tapes. This series was relaunched in 1999 as '*Introducing* . . .'. (The '. . . *For Beginners*' series now continues with the publishers Writers and Readers.) There is one on semiotics (Cobley and Jansz 1997, now retitled, Cobley and Jansz 2004). There is also a good web-based book, by Chandler, *Semiotics For Beginners*, at **www.aber.ac.uk/media/Documents/S4B/semiotics.html**. See also Chandler (2002).

A well-known and persuasive example of using metaphors to understand organisations is Morgan (1997) and its companion volume, Morgan (1989). However, the role of metaphors is not uncontested and a good example of the issues is to be found in Morgan's debate with Bourgeois and Pinder (Pinder and Bourgeois 1982, Morgan 1983b, Bourgeois and Pinder 1983). It is interesting to note that, from a semiotic point of view, the protagonists in this debate employ different interpretations of the meaning of metaphor. Another metaphorical approach which has enjoyed some popularity in organisation studies is the dramaturgical or theatrical metaphor – Mangham (1986) is an example. An interesting, highly relevant and perhaps somewhat quirky approach is to be found in Skoldberg (2002).

There is a huge literature on information and communication, some of which is relevant to organisational behaviour, though the most accessible material seems to be in Media Studies – see, for example, Watson and Hill (1997), Ellis and McClintock (1994) and Fiske (1990). Hodge and Kress (1988) provide a good example of the use of semiotics to analyse communication and culture in their broad social context. Jamieson (1985) also focuses on communication from an explicitly semiotic perspective. Bateson (1973) contains much of interest about information. A very good example of the idea of the situation as a text to be read is provided by Barthes (1972). A variety of approaches which apply the concept of text(ure) in the context of organisation can be found in Fineman and Hosking (1990). A somewhat different aspect of the issue of text is to be found in approaches which argue that literary texts can be used fruitfully as metaphors for understanding organisational behaviour. An early example is Waldo (1968), a more recent one is Czarniawska-Joerges and Guillet de Monthoux (1994). For a specifically organisational take on storytelling, see Gabriel (2000). For a more visual approach to the idea of text, see Hassard and Holliday (1998). The most famous exponents of the concept of the hyper-real are Baudrillard (for example, 1988) and Eco (1987) – it is interesting to note that when first published in the UK this book had a different title, *Faith in Fakes*, and that that is the title of the current edition, with the other title, *Travels in Hyper-Reality*, as a subtitle.

The literature on organisational culture is extremely extensive – most textbooks on organisational behaviour have at least a chapter on organisational culture, though these may vary widely in perspective. The subject even supports at least one journal, *Culture and Organization*, previously *Studies in Cultures, Organisations and Societies*, which, incidentally, started life as *Dragon*, which was the journal of the Standing Conference on Organisational Symbolism, an international research group in the field. It is worth noting some texts in particular. Smircich (1983) develops a distinction between seeing organisational culture as a variable or as what she calls a root metaphor, a useful and quite influential distinction. Martin (1992) offers three different ways of conceptualising organisational culture, illustrated through one case study. See also Martin (2002). Allaire and Firsirotu (1984) provides an extensive overview of different definitions which have been used. An exploration of the value of understanding organisational culture from an anthropological perspective is included in Czarniawska-Joerges (1992). Frost *et al.* (1985, 1991) were early contributors to the then relatively new interest in organisational culture, and represent a wide variety of approaches and of perspectives. More generally, though still relevant, see Nuckolls (1998) and Ray and Sayer (1999).

There are also a number of critical assessments of organisational culture in theory and in practice. Linstead and Grafton-Small (1992) uses a deconstructive approach to analyse the literature, as does Smircich and Calas (1987). Meek (1988) critically connects organisational culture to its anthropological origins. Schwartz (1986a, 1986b) addresses the concept of cultural engineering in organisations. From a different angle, Mumby (1988) offers a critical perspective on organisational culture in the context of communication and power. See also Parker (2000) and Alvesson (2002).

An influential study by Hofstede (1991) links organisational culture and national cultural characteristics. For the more manipulative approach see Deal and Kennedy (1988) and Peters and Waterman (1982). Watson (1994) is an example of a long-term study of an actual attempt to change an organisational culture, but there are also many other cases documented from before the development of organisational culture as a subject in its own right, which chart similar experiences without using the language of culture or of semiotics – just one example is Flanders (1964). On the other hand, the approach known as Organisation Development was specifically concerned with cultural change. What is often seen as the definitive expression of Organisation Development can be found in French and Bell (1973). Another influential and relevant book from that period, still much used, is Schein (1988, 3rd edition), which also provides an accessible introduction to Lewin's model of change.

Work on organisational symbolism is very dispersed. There are, however, some useful books which collect material, notably B.A. Turner (1990). Alvesson and Berg (1992) charts the development of the approach and explores its links with other approaches. Another collection, this time mainly American, is Pondy *et al.* (1983). An interesting synoptic overview of various aspects of management which uses semiotics is Broms and Gahmberg (1987). Another which is not explicitly semiotic, and which focuses on researching symbolism in organisations, is Jones (1996). Rosen (1985, 1986) are examples of accessible studies of the symbolisation of structure. Linstead *et al.* (1996) links organisational symbolism and organisational culture, as does Gherardi (1995), with the additional specific focus on gender issues in organisations. There are also many books, particularly studies of individual organisations, from before the era of organisational symbolism as a specific subject, which recognise, if implicitly, the importance of organisational symbols. A notable example is Beynon (1973).

CHAPTER 3

Structure

This chapter examines the influence of structure on behaviour in organisations. To start with, structure is defined in terms of supporting and relational properties. Structure has the qualities of creating order, of being purposeful, of variety and of providing opportunities and constraints. We focus on three particular versions of the nature of structure: Structural Functionalism, which sees structure as real and as the inevitable consequence of systemic functions needing to be fulfilled; Structuralism, which sees structure as the 'deep' logic which explains interrelations and interactions, which are themselves the signifiers of this underlying structure, still understood as real; Poststructuralism, which sees structure as a product of the human mind, and as created by explanation, rather than discovered through explanation. The chapter focuses on Poststructuralist approaches, particularly on the implications of understanding structure as a human and subjective construct and on the question of why, if structure is unreal, it is experienced as if it is real. To address this latter issue concepts of power, intersubjectivity, alienation, ideology, order and disorder are introduced.

As noted in the previous chapter, the world is, intrinsically, a dangerous place. One of the ways we protect ourselves existentially from this danger is through development of structures. An understanding of structure is essential to understanding of behaviour in organisations. In recent years, the conventional view of structure as objective, given and obvious has been challenged, particularly by what has come to be known as Poststructuralism, an approach intimately linked with semiotics. It is this latter approach that will be explored in this chapter.

Physical structure

Structure has two basic functions, providing support and organising relations. An obvious way in which we use structure to protect ourselves can be found in the Latin root of the word, which is 'to build'. Thus, for example, we construct buildings to provide shelter from natural threats such as the weather, and from social threats such as undesired intrusion. Apart from providing shelter from what is

Structure in the eye of the beholder

outside, buildings also, inevitably, organise what is inside. Buildings contain organised space – different rooms, different functions for rooms – and, in so doing, they organise the relations between the people who inhabit the building, and differentiate both space and people from any other structures – your family from the family next door, for example.

Structure allows us to create a certain amount of **order** in our world. Imagine a secondary school of a thousand pupils, all contained in a single classroom. This would create severe problems for both teaching and learning. By the simple expedient of building internal walls pupils can be grouped, by, say, age and subject, into units which facilitate the educative process. Thus it can be seen that structure is also linked to **purpose** – we create structures to achieve certain outcomes. One type of structure facilitates the education of a thousand pupils, but a different kind of structure would be needed to facilitate the incarceration of a thousand prisoners, and another kind again to facilitate the employment of a thousand workers. Not only is there a potentially infinite **variety** of purposes that structures fulfil, but also each purpose can be fulfilled in a variety of ways: structures for housing can be apartments, villas, mud huts, palaces, cardboard boxes, and so on. However, there is an **opportunity cost** in selecting any particular structure, in that all other possible structures are forgone. As well as enabling certain purposes, structures also impose **limitations**. If, for example, we select, for housing purposes, detached houses, then more ground space is needed to house a particular number of people than would be needed if we selected, say, blocks of flats, and the use of that space for other purposes is lost.

Structure in the sense of building is a supplement to what occurs in nature. We reconfigure nature into a form that we deem more convenient to us than what occurs naturally. And, although we have, so far, talked about structure as the outcome of human purposes and action, it is also the case that some structures are naturally occurring – the cellular structure of organisms, for example. The question of the 'naturalness' of structure is something to which we shall return.

Abstract structure

It has been suggested that structure is order-creating, has purpose and variety, and imposes limitations, in the context of physical structures. In the context of organisation, however, the term 'structure' is most commonly used to refer, not to the physical building, but to the abstract ordering of social relations. Two points need to be noted. *Firstly*, this should not be taken to imply that the physical and material structure of organisations is not important – symbolically, for example, style of building, location, internal differentiation of space, and so on, all convey significant information and meaning about an organisation. *Secondly*, **abstract structures have the same characteristics as physical ones**.

At its most basic, organisational structure refers to the **form** of organisation, its skeleton. What gives flesh to this form are the rules, regulations, procedures, roles and systems that constitute the normal pattern of operation. What the structure does is to prescribe and regulate interactions, and so has a profound influence on behaviour in organisations. These structures do not have any physical properties, though they may be symbolised (for example, by status symbols, such as size of office, type of company car, or by an organisational chart), and the symbols may themselves be physical. However, the structures are abstract, conceptual, though we very often experience them *as if* they are physical.

These abstractions perform the same functions as physical structures. In the sense that they constitute the form of organisation, they give **order** to organisational activity. Without structure, people would not know why or how to act, why or how to choose between alternatives, why or how they related to each other – in short, **without structure there would be no organisation**. The kind of structure an organisation embodies depends on the **purpose** for which the organisation is created – the structure of an army will be different to the structure of a theatre company, for example. Not only are there different structural forms for different kinds of organisation, but organisations of the same kind may select different structures to each other – an organisation that manufactures cars might be organised on the basis of production lines or on the basis of autonomous work groups; organisations might directly employ all those who perform organisational functions or contract out some of those activities (indirect employment). There is potentially infinite **variety** in the forms organisations can adopt. No form is inevitable, even though some may be more popular – or, at least, more common – than others. Any structure has both advantages and disadvantages and, therefore, constitutes both **opportunities** and **constraints**. When a particular form is chosen the advantages and disadvantages of other forms are forgone. A bureaucratic structure may be difficult to change, a matrix structure may be difficult to control, an autocratic structure may be demotivating, a democratic structure may be inefficient, and so on. This is why it is always important to remember that there are benefits *and* costs attached to any particular structure.

The ontology of structure

All the above is a fairly uncontentious basic description of the nature of structure. Yet structure is the subject of much heated debate in Organisation Studies. What *is* considered to be contentious is what can be called the ontology of structure. In other words, how *real* are these forms? How this question is answered is a major influence on how we understand organisational behaviour.

The root of the word **ontology** comes from the Greek 'to be'. The term refers to the theory of what is real. It is the source of much debate in philosophy and may *seem* somewhat esoteric – yet we are constantly making decisions on the basis of what we consider, or believe, to be real, even if we are not conscious of doing so. Take, for example, astrology, the idea that the dispositions and movements of planets, stars, etc., have influence on behaviour and events. Some people believe that astrology is a description of real determinate factors, actual influences on our lives which are beyond our power to control or change. Other people believe astrology to be complete nonsense and that, while the dispositions and movements of planets and stars may be real, their influence on us is not. Some people believe that job enrichment strategies lead to increased job satisfaction and improved motivation to work. Others believe that job enrichment is just another cynical management technique to extort more effort from labour. Some people believe that repetitive strain injury is a real medical condition.

What is a university?

It is widely accepted that organisations are more than their physical assets and legal status – that organisations require people to make them organisations.

Imagine a university full of buildings, equipment, staff, students, etc. The Physics Department, while studying a neutron bomb, accidentally detonate it. Neutron bombs have the characteristics of killing people but not destroying buildings. Many people would accept that the sudden loss of all staff and students would terminate the identity of the organisation as a university, even though the physical assets remained.

However, rather than eliminating everyone with a neutron bomb, what happens to the identity of the university if all the people simply go home, after work for example? Does this mean that it is a university during the day but not at night? What about, for example, the Open University, where most of the members do not physically inhabit its buildings? What, in such a case, constitutes its identity as a university?

If an organisation needs people, can there ever be virtual organisations – a virtual university, for example?

Others believe that it is a figment of the imagination, at most psychosomatic. **Whether we believe something to be real or not shapes our entire understanding of the world and is a primary factor in all our actions and decisions.**

The debate in Organisation Studies about the ontology of structure is often expressed in terms of the debate over structure versus agency (conscious, intentional, free-willed action). Put very simply, this boils down to the question of whether action is determined by structure, or structure is determined by action. In other words, do we act as we do because we have no choice, as the structure dictates what can and cannot be done? Or, do we have free will, in which case we can choose how to act and it is our own action that creates structure? Adherents to the different positions in this debate have utterly different, and incommensurable, ontologies.

Realist approaches to structure

In Organisational Behaviour it has been conventional to view structure from a realist position: notwithstanding that structures are abstract, they are still real, they exist. An analogy might be the ordinary language understanding of gravity, which does not have physical properties but we have everyday experience of its existence. Earlier, we stated that structure has two characteristics, support and relational. Both of these elements are to be found in conventional approaches to understanding organisational behaviour, but different approaches place different emphasis on them.

Structural Functionalism understands organisations as purposeful components of a total social system, whose purpose is to contribute to the viability of the social system (society as a whole). Organisations are seen as themselves microcosms of that total system, which, likewise, have parts which contribute purposefully to the viability of the organisation as a whole. In other words, organisations have parts/subsystems that function in such a way as to ensure the stability (equilibrium) of the organisation as a whole and whose existence is, ultimately, for this purpose alone – to enable the organisation to fulfil the purpose within the social system for which it was created. From this point of view, structure fulfils a primary supportive role within the system: it supports the achievement of organisational goals. To return to the example of a building: a supporting wall in a building allows it to retain its integrity as a building – if the wall were not a supporting wall, the building would collapse. Thus, the supporting wall is linked dynamically to the other parts of the building. In this view, structure is both difficult to change and necessary *by definition*. But the fact that it may be a supporting wall is irrelevant to what takes place either side of the wall.

It is these relational aspects of structure that are associated with Structuralism. Structuralism shares many features with Structural Functionalism, but has three major differences. The *first* of these is that, while Structural Functionalism prioritises structure itself, Structuralism focuses on the relational dispositions which are the effect of structure. *Secondly*, while Structural Functionalism treats structure as a 'surface' phenomenon of which we can be directly aware, Structuralism argues that it is only relations of which we can be aware and that structure is the underlying 'deep' logic which gives coherence, meaning and explanation to these relations. *Thirdly*, Structuralism is strongly influenced by **semiotics**, especially by the concept of the signifier/signified relationship – hence, Structuralism assumes that the relations which can be observed are signifiers whose meaning is to be understood only by reference to the underlying structure – and by the idea that this underlying structure is, like a language, the system of rules, conventions, regulation, which defines what relations are possible. As with words, it is necessary to understand the language in order to understand the words, so with behaviour, it is necessary to understand the structure in order to be able to interpret behaviour. To use an organisational example: Structural Functionalists might interpret hierarchy as a support structure which facilitates the optimum use of resources, decision-making and the rational division of labour, without which the organisation could not discharge its function; Structuralism, on the other hand, might understand hierarchy as a deep structure symbolised by differential power relations, unequal distributions of freedom of action, and so on. Structural Functionalists would be concerned with how effective the hierarchy was in contributing to the viability of the system, while Structuralists would be seeking to explain how hierarchy organises relationships both within the organisational context and in the wider social context, one reflecting the other.

Description versus prescription in realist approaches to structure

Structural Functionalism and Structuralism emerged as opposing views of structure, particularly in anthropology, in the 1920s, but had rather different trajectories of development. In Organisation Studies, Structural Functionalism reached its most prominent development and influence with the work of Talcott Parsons in the 1950s, since when it has been much modified as a theory, but not really extended. Structuralism, on the other hand, took much longer to make its presence felt in Organisation Studies. It was following the work of Claude Lévi-Strauss in anthropology, also in the 1950s, that use of the insights of Structuralism was considerably developed, in Organisation Studies and in social theory more generally.

Structural Functionalism represents the last stages of a more *general* Functionalism, which exhibited concern for interpreting the significance of events and actions – that is, people's behaviour was best understood in terms of what they did and how they did it. This approach to explanation was dominant, certainly up to the development of Structuralism, and is, even now, still popular. Thus, for example, with Taylorism, organisational performance was understood in terms of job design, bonus payments and the superordinacy of management in planning and control. More recently, approaches such as Organisation Development, while paying a bit more attention to issues of process, still concerned themselves with the effects of events and actions such as team-building, the perfection of organisational culture and the release of latent energies and talents 'for the benefit of the organisation'. In contrast, Structuralism pays little attention to events and actions, preferring to understand the operations of organisations in terms of relationships as a **text** to be read in order to understand organisational structure, and whose meaning is underlying what can be observed. This approach represents organisation and organisational structure as far more complex than the basically unitary view of (Structural) Functionalism. From a Functionalist point of view, for example, low motivation might be seen as a consequence of poor job design and remediable by a job enrichment programme. A Structuralist understanding of low motivation, however, might see it as a negative reflection of differing expectations and rewards characteristic of different roles in the organisation – in essence, an effect of the structure itself. A strike, from a Functionalist point of view, might be a dispute about terms and conditions which, in principle, can be resolved, so ending the problem. But, from a Structuralist point of view, a strike might be simply a signifier of class antagonisms which is very unlikely to be resolved – the strike might be brought to an end but this would not resolve the underlying problem, which will inevitably recur though, perhaps, in a different form.

These examples also illustrate the point that, while Functionalism tends to see organisations as discrete entities, Structuralism tends to see organisations as embedded in their social context. In this latter view, problems in organisations are as likely as not to reflect conditions in that social context, rather than being just organisational events, and, therefore, to be beyond the capacity of management to resolve. Functionalism claims a highly **prescriptive** role, based on the assumption that structure determines action and therefore action is predictable. Structuralism is much more **descriptive**, and avoids prediction.

Making sense of making sense

We use the terms 'organisation' and 'management' frequently in this book, which is hardly surprising, given its subject matter. But what the terms mean, here or anywhere else, is far from clear. Any decent conventional text in Organisational Behaviour will acknowledge this problem, more or less explicitly, but will then tend to proceed as if such uncertainty and ambiguity is unproblematic and can be safely ignored. However, if our task is to *understand* organisational behaviour, then the uncertainty and ambiguity need to be investigated more thoroughly.

Organisation derives from the Greek word *ergon*, meaning work (thus making the phrase 'work organisation', technically, a tautology), and it refers both to the act of organising and to the state of being organised. The word **organise** refers to the forming of organic wholes. An **organ** is an instrument for doing something. This all fits quite well with the common type of definition of organisation as 'a structured arrangement of resources (human, material, financial, etc.) for achieving collective goals through controlled performance'.

However, as we suggest here (and also see Chapter 6), the existence of *collective* goals in an organisation is unlikely, and certainly not necessary for the organisation to function – think of a prison, or a school. If a society has a legal system which can decree that some people, because of behaviour that is defined by that legal system as criminal, should be segregated from the rest of

▶

society, then it is necessary to have prisons – but it would be unrealistic to expect every member of this organisation to have the same goals: staff are likely to want to keep prisoners in, but prisoners are likely to want to get out. And so it is, to a greater or lesser extent, with all organisations. Although organisations appear to be, and claim to be, purposeful, this cannot be taken to signify that all members of the organisation have the same goals. The purported goals of an organisation are not literally the 'organisation's goals', but are the goals of certain people – managers, shareholders, entrepreneurs, politicians, for example – and not even all of *these* people, but only of those who have sufficient power to determine what the goals will be, according to their wishes. Additionally, the goals of individual members or groups may be in conflict, so the 'organisational goals' may also be a trade-off between the conflicting desires of those with influence, not all of whom even belong to the organisation. So, just what is this 'organisation', and what are these 'collective goals'?

The term **management** is used to refer to the act of managing and to a body of managers. A 'body', in this sense, refers to 'a number of persons united by some common tie' – in this case, possibly, being employed by the same 'organisation', whatever that is, or, possibly, by a set of common organisational roles: planning, organising and controlling? But take the example of a bartender. A bartender obviously plans – for example, ensuring that necessary supplies of goods are available; a bartender organises – for example, using procedures to deal with customers, to handle money, to preserve ambiance (cleaning up and so on); he or she also controls – for example, exercises power over customers in a variety of ways. Such a person may even be called a 'bar manager'. But would they really be considered to be part of 'the management'? Probably not. Another way to think about management is to see managers as those who organise rather than those who do. Of course, this is no more use in defining management except in the most general sense. Clearly, many jobs include both organising and doing. And, what about a small organisation with just one person acting as accountant? This might be almost wholly a 'doing' job, but the person is likely to be regarded, organisationally, as a manager. It could be argued that this person manages financial resources, rather than, say, human ones, but this does not then give us a clear distinction between 'organising' and 'doing'.

Confused? You ought to be!

Poststructuralism and structure

Matters have not simply rested here, however, because another approach, quite distinct from either of the two discussed so far, has been developed out of Structuralism, known as **Poststructuralism**. Like Structuralism, Poststructuralism has its roots in semiotics, but is based on a much more rigorous application of semiotic thinking. It has become very influential, not least in its understanding of the ontology of structure, and it is to this approach that we now turn.

For Poststructuralists, the problem with Structuralism is that it assumes the presence of real deep structures, knowledge of which we gain by signifiers (social relations). Yet we know from semiotics that there can be no *necessary* connection between a signifier and what it signifies. This connection is supplied by the individual user who perceives a link between a signifier and its signified. The connection is unique to each individual and cannot be specified from an external source. The process of connecting signifier and signified derives from the attempt by individuals to make sense of the world as they experience it. From this, Poststructuralists conclude that there are no real structures that give order to human affairs, but that the construction of order – sense-making – by people is what gives rise to structure. **Structure is the explanation itself,** *that which makes sense, not that which gives sense*. It follows from this that **structure cannot be seen as determining action because it is not real and transcendent, but a product of the human mind**.

There has been considerable debate about when and/or who initiated the development from Structuralism to Poststructuralism, though it is generally agreed that the development is associated with the work of a number of European (especially French) theorists. It is not particularly useful for our purposes to chart this debate, partly because there are various continuities between Structuralism and Poststructuralism, and partly because many of the theorists concerned started out as Structuralists and, driven by the logic of their own arguments, went on to develop Poststructuralism. However, it is worth mentioning who some of the key figures are. We have already noted the significance of the anthropologist Claude Lévi-Strauss and, in the previous chapter, that of the writer and critic Roland Barthes. One can also cite the psychoanalyst Jacques Lacan, the historian of ideas Michel Foucault, the literary theorist Jacques Derrida, the philosopher Gilles Deleuze and the psychoanalyst Félix Guattari. Many would also include the philosopher Jean-François Lyotard.

Deconstruction comes out of the closet

In 1992 a proposal to give Jacques Derrida, by then a world famous philosopher, an Honorary degree from Cambridge University was contested in a vote by Cambridge dons. This was seen by those who supported Derrida as characteristically expressive of Anglo-Saxon closed-ness to new ideas, especially French new ideas. On the other hand, it gave great publicity to Derrida's work and, no doubt, hastened the adoption and application of his ideas in many other fields, including organisation studies. This cartoon by Steve Bell, which appeared in *The Guardian* newspaper at the time, reflects these events and illustrates the ideas.

Source: Copyright © Steve Bell 1992. Reprinted with permission.

Poststructuralism emerged partly from work in literary criticism, which, for many years, had been concerned with the issue of establishing what a text meant, by reference to the author's intentions. It had become clear to some theorists that a text could not have a *single* meaning. For example, is the classic book by George Orwell, *Animal Farm*, an amusing, if cautionary, tale about animals taking over the farm, the agricultural equivalent of lunatics taking over the asylum? Or, is it, as assumed when it was first published, a satire on Stalinism? Or, is it, as sometimes seen today, a more general allegory of the dangers of any kind of authoritarianism? From a semiotic point of view, it can be any, or all, of these, and, indeed, many other possibilities, depending on the interpretation of the reader. Many have claimed that the Beatles' song, *Lucy in the Sky with Diamonds*, is a reference to drug taking (Lucy in the Sky with Diamonds). The Beatles themselves said not, but this has not prevented people from persisting in their belief. We cannot know what the authors' intentions were, especially if they are dead, but even if they have declared their intentions, since this may not be consistent, and certainly cannot be verified. Nor could it be given primacy, given the nature of texts. Texts can also acquire significant meanings which they quite clearly could not have had at the time, as the effect of changing historical conditions. For example, Shakespeare's plays have been given many different interpretations, on stage and on film, which reflect contemporary events, or even recast them into a wholly different form, as in the case of *West Side Story*. Beethoven's *Symphony No. 5* acquired, in the twentieth century, a wholly new significance from the use of its opening four notes by the Allies during the Second World War as a call sign representing the Morse code letter V, for Victory.

In the previous chapter we said that **text refers to more than just literal texts, that it refers to any symbolic configurations, such as social situations.** Therefore, the same principles of interpretation apply to all cases. Thus, organisations can be read textually to produce potentially infinitely varied 'stories', none of which can have any transcendent meaning.

Textuality revisited

It was noted earlier that this idea of producing textual readings is also part of structuralist approaches, in which social relations, interactions, behaviours, and so on, are 'read' to reveal the underlying structure which gives order and meaning to, organises, activity. In the case of Structuralism, however, the deep structure which can be revealed is held to be real and, therefore, readings can be defined as more or less accurate, more or less appropriate, in terms of this structure. In effect, readings can be measured against a 'standard', which is the actual structure. In Structuralism the structure is immanent in what is being observed. Poststructuralism utilises the idea of producing readings of organisational texts with very different implications. **From the poststructuralist point of view, what readings reveal are potentially infinite, and potentially infinitely varied, orderings, sense-makings, of the experienced world of organisation.** Readings may be utterly different, may contradict each other, but none has a right to be considered more correct than any other and none may be considered, *a priori*, inappropriate – a manager, for example, does not have an intrinsically

The magic roundabout

'In the Paint Shop the car, after an early coat of paint, passes through the Wet Deck where a team of men armed with electric sanders – "whirlies" – sand the body while it is being heavily sprayed with water . . . The lads on the Deck played in a football team, went away on coach trips, drank together in the pub. They had their own nicknames for each other. A lad called John Dillon worked there. So they all took Magic Roundabout names. Dougal, Florence, Zebedee . . . The lads didn't like working [on the Wet Deck]. They looked forward to the weekends. The Friday shift was the worst. Particularly on nights, because it messed up your Saturday as well. So the Magic Roundabout lads decided to have a rota. Eight of them contributed to a pool. Every eighth week one of them took the Friday shift off and got paid a shift's money from the pool . . . [Eventually] management intervened with threats and the pool was abandoned.'

(Abstracted from Beynon, *Working for Ford*, 1973, pp. 140–8.)

Clearly, there are different interpretations of the meaning of work involved in this situation. Does it represent:

- a jolly band of workers trying to create a bit of space for themselves to escape the dreary reality of work, being thwarted by oppressive management?

- a band of feckless, irresponsible workers subverting the trust relationships of the work situation, thus requiring the necessary firm hand of management to restore order?

- a group of workers engaged in the class struggle, trying to sabotage the organisation, and, thereby, the perceived excesses of capitalism, being restrained by managers in their role as agents of capitalism?

- irrational acts of immature workers being protected from damaging their self-interest by benign, rational management?

What other interpretations are possible?

'better' view of the organisation than a worker. For Poststructuralists, it is the explanation itself that creates order, gives structure to experience. **Structure is the meaning given to experience. Structure is immanent in the subject not in the object, in the observer not in the observed.**

For example, two people at different levels of the same hierarchy, one a manager, the other managed, are likely to see the organisational structure differently. One may see it as decentralised, democratic and empowering, the other as highly centralised, dictatorial and limiting. In that each experiences the organisation in their own way, though they may disagree, neither can deny the experience of the other and there is no appeal to arbitration to decide whether one is a more accurate description than the other – all a third person can give is their own, equally individual, view. Or again, two people at the same level of the same hierarchy may experience, for example, appraisal in different ways: one may see it as an opportunity for personal growth, the other as increasing levels of managerial control. It is not that one is right, the other wrong; they are simply different meanings attributed to the same signifier, different understandings of the nature and purpose of organisational structures.

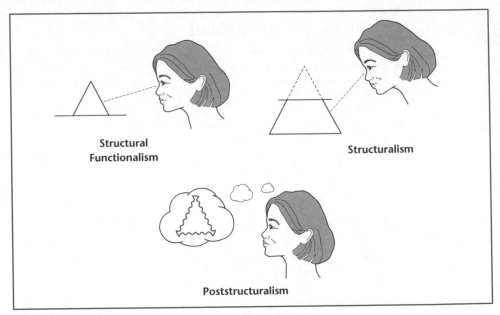

The structuralisms

Power

However, some explanations, or orderings, do seem to have more influence than others, are more difficult to refute even though they may be dissonant, bearing little resemblance to someone else's understanding of their experience. The reason for this is not that they are necessarily better explanations, but that the explanation is supported by more powerful interests. From a poststructuralist perspective, **power is the power to ordain significations**, to prescribe how signifiers should be understood, or to prioritise one set of meanings and, by implication, repress all others. If your boss tells you that down-sizing your department is beneficial to the organisation, and therefore to you, even though your understanding of its significance is different, you will find it difficult to substantiate your understanding in the face of your boss's power. (See also Chapter 5 on power.)

An important point to emphasise is that **meaning should not be confused with behaviour.** Because people in organisations have to act in accordance with certain requirements legitimated by certain rationalisations, it does not mean that the actors themselves share those understandings. If you are asked to work unpaid overtime at short notice because, you are told, it is essential to complete an order, that you may do the overtime does not signify that you share the view of its essential nature. You do it because you must, not because you share the belief that it is essential. **Behaviour does not necessarily signify shared understanding, it may only be the effect of power relationships.**

Intersubjectivity

If it can be argued that structure, rather than being real, is just individual attempts at sense-making, how is it that groups of people can apparently share a common understanding of a situation? Indeed, how is it possible to organise at all, if everyone sees the situation differently? The answer to this lies in the concept of intersubjectivity, which was introduced in the previous chapter. Organisation is driven by the desire to achieve certain outcomes, not by shared meanings. The purposes may, indeed, be very different, but still achievable by the same process. That there is common recognition of signifiers, and that these may lead to certain kinds of behaviour, says nothing about the individual meanings attached to those signifiers. **The cooperation necessary for organisation does not signify agreement about meanings or agreement about ends, but rests on the desire of individuals for particular outcomes.** In a theatrical performance, for example, the writer may have written the play to satisfy a creative urge, the producer may seek the opportunity to make an investment pay, the actors may seek fame and recognition, the ushers may seek financial survival, the audience may seek entertainment. All cooperate in the organisation, but for different reasons. And, while the play may represent a common set of signifiers, there is no reason to assume that they all understand it in the same way.

Alienation

Equally, if structure is a product of human sense-making, why do we experience it as if it is objectively real, beyond our power to influence? Two factors underlie this: *firstly*, there is our need to make sense of the world in which we live and, *secondly*, as human beings we experience real events, emotions, etc. We are all born into a world in which social relationships already exist. These are social relationships that are not of our choosing, into which we do not choose to be born and about which we are not consulted. This gives us a sense that there is an external logic to events into which we must fit, and which gives us a means of understanding things that we experience. So, for example, at an early age we are sent to an educational establishment in which we have real experiences, such as fear, pleasure, pain, enlightenment, understanding, and so on, and we experience social interactions with people like ourselves and with people who have more power than we do. We come to understand this experience in terms of these apparently pre-existing structures. We become socialised, that is, we are taught our role in society, and this reinforces our sense that society has structures which are external to us, and real. We feel powerless in the face of these apparent structures, and this sense of powerlessness can be so strong that we may feel oppressed, without freedom of action, estranged – in short, we feel **alienated**.

However, even here what we experience is not structure, but what Michel Foucault called **micro-power** (this concept is further developed in Chapter 5). Foucault argued that all interactions, however small or large, however intimate or public, are characterised by the exercise of power which resides in individual subjects who seek to gain control, to be able to prioritise *their* understanding of order, *their* view of the way the world is – in effect, to be able to achieve the power to signify. **It is not structure that is being experienced, but the force of other people's desires.**

Twenty ways to monitor a student

1 Closed circuit television cameras on campus.
2 Attendance registers.
3 Swipe cards to enter certain buildings, such as the library.
4 Course work.
5 Examinations.
6 Course work submission records.
7 Meetings with tutors.
8 Class appraisals.
9 Student records.
10 ....
11 ....
12 ....
13 ....
14 ....
15 ....
16 ....
17 ....
18 ....
19 ....
20 ....

Can you fill in the rest?

Ideology

There appears, however, to be some coherence and consistency in social relations, in the exercise of micro-power. But, again, it is not necessary to have a realist concept of structure to explain this. We can turn to the concept of **ideology** (which is also the subject of Chapter 7). This is an important concept in Poststructuralism, which, for the moment, can be described as a set of meta-beliefs that people can share at a general level while ignoring any inconsistencies between individuals. Thus large numbers of people subscribe to Christian beliefs, or to beliefs about the value of democracy, although they may disagree about what these mean in detail. (Differences in detail can be productive of extraordinary levels of **dis**unity, **in**consistency and **in**coherence.) Ideology provides a rationale for specific actions. It is a set of over-arching ideas about what the world is like, what is good and what is bad, what is right and what is wrong.

   The whole process of sense-making, order creation, that we have been discussing does not take place within a vacuum, or on a so-called *tabula rasa*, but is an attempt to fit experience into these sets of beliefs. Actions make sense, or have coherence, in so far as they conform to, or can be construed as conforming to, one's ideology. The unavoidable implication of this is that **organisation is never a value-neutral process, and no description of an organisation is value-neutral. Organisation, and theories of organisation, are always the product of ordering processes based on ideological preferences.**

Order/Disorder

We said earlier that structure is a way of creating order. It should be clear now that, from a poststructuralist point of view, there is no such thing as a natural social order of any kind and, therefore, there is no social order that is inevitable. **Such order as is perceived is a function of human agency – it is managed.**

The normal state of the world is disorder. Order is created, is temporary, and is always at the expense of some other order that could have been created. In this respect, Poststructuralism has strong affinities with some contemporary theories of **chaos**. We carve out areas of order from disorder. We gain the appearance of order through the use of attenuating devices – filters, templates, rubrics, sieves – which are ideas about what order should look like. In other words, which are ideology. (What derives from this is ontology, beliefs about the way the world *is*, about what is *real*.) Some aspects of what is possible are suppressed, other aspects are emphasised. Which are suppressed and which emphasised is not inherent or inevitable, not features of natural order, but a consequence of ideologies about what might be *desirable* order.

Order is the outcome of our (conceptual) structuring of disorder. It is obvious from this that, if an order is produced through the filter of a particular ideology, then a different ideological filter would produce a different order. Conversely, it needs to be recognised that *any particular form of organisation is not natural, not permanent and not inevitable*.

Making sense of making sense, continued

Perhaps the issue should not be one of providing clear and precise definitions of the terms 'organisation' and 'management', but one of acknowledging that there are problems in the way we think about what they mean, the way we *make sense* of them. Although we may not be able to provide clear and precise definitions, we think we recognise them when we 'see' them. So perhaps understanding them precisely is not important? In our day-to-day lives we find these concepts useful, and cope well with their ambiguity. This is because we make use of them as **tropes**. The problem arises when we forget that this is what they are, and accept as 'real' the illusions that such tropes evoke (see also **'the hyper-real'** in Chapter 2). This misapprehension is based on three closely related fallacies, all very common, but all founded on invalid arguments.

The *first* fallacy is **reification**. The root of this word is *res*, the Latin word for 'thing', and reification is the attribution of materiality to the non-material, the abstract. The classic example of this is to talk about 'the organisation' as if it (its entirety) has a real 'physical' existence, independent of our awareness of it. As noted earlier in this chapter, obviously most organisations have physical

▶

assets, but these assets are neither necessary nor sufficient as descriptions of them. To reify 'the organisation' is to deny most of its complexity. The *second* fallacy is **depersonification**. This fallacy involves thinking, or talking, about people as abstractions or things. The classic example here is 'the management', as in, say, 'the management's right to manage'. 'The management' masks the recognition that those who manage are people, and implies a transcendent and autonomous system, independent of human characteristics. The *third* fallacy is **anthropomorphism** – the attribution of human characteristics to the non-human. Classic examples here are descriptions of organisations as 'acting', or 'needing', talk of 'caring organisations', or 'healthy organisations', or 'lean and hungry organisations'. Organisations cannot have goals, people have goals. People act, or need, people care, or are healthy, or are lean and hungry, not organisations.

This is not to suggest that such expressions should never be used but that, if they are used, it should always be borne in mind that they are not literal descriptions, but metaphorical ones. All of these fallacies are used, wittingly or unwittingly, to evade the acknowledgement that 'organisation' and 'management' are processes that are outcomes of human agency, and implicitly, wittingly or unwittingly, to evade the responsibility that such agency entails. This is precisely the significance of recognising these fallacies in the context of understanding structure.

Existing applications in Organisational Behaviour

The argument that **structure is not real but is a function of human cognition and perception reflecting certain interests** has made considerable impact on Organisation Studies in general, and studies of organisational behaviour in particular. However, it is, inevitably, part of a critical literature, radically opposing conventional views of organisation and organisational behaviour, because it introduces into the field a different agenda, based on different questions to be addressed.

Traditionally, the field of Organisational Behaviour has been concerned with 'how' questions. It has identified certain 'problems', such as leadership, motivation to work, culture, and so on, and then sought to find prescriptions for solving those problems. However, the implications of a poststructuralist approach to structure include the point that **even what we see as a problem is a product of particular ways of perceiving disorder in the 'system' and thus also a product of ideology**. In recent years, for example, Organisational Behaviour specialists, and managers, have identified supposed problems with organisational culture. The solution has been to find ways of 'improving' organisational cultures which can be implemented by managers, together with measurements of improvement, such as increased output. But if organisational culture is not just something defined by management (which would cast doubt on its utility as a concept), but is a joint enterprise based on shared understandings of all organisational participants, say, then a unilateral declaration by managers that there is something wrong with the culture is not likely to be embraced by those who may be quite happy with it. Such solutions, externally imposed, are unlikely to resolve any supposed problems, and are as likely to make things worse as to make them 'better', emphasising conflicting understandings and highlighting unequal power to signify.

Poststructuralist approaches, in contrast, are concerned with 'why' questions. Given a poststructuralist understanding of structure, in phrasing a 'why' question – such as, why are things organised in the way they are? – the answer will always involve issues of power, interest, ideology, meaning and agency, concepts with which traditional Organisational Behaviour is generally uncomfortable. If such concepts are placed at issue, and, in particular, if structure is construed as the outcome of individual ordering processes, an attack is made on all the usual legitimations and justifications for organisational activity. **The poststructuralist approach removes the basic axioms or assumptions of traditional approaches to organisational behaviour, especially that the structure that orders and regulates activity is real, given and inevitable.** Instead of management being basically a technical process, the competent operation of a particular structure, it becomes, from a poststructuralist point of view, essentially an issue of power and control. Poststructuralist approaches have often argued, indeed, that all organisational behaviour should be seen in such terms.

Attempts to apply poststructuralist insights to understanding organisational behaviour have tended to reflect the work of particular poststructuralist theorists. Of these, Foucault has probably been the most prominent. Out of the broad range of Foucault's work, one of the most popular concepts for application in understanding organisational behaviour has been that of **surveillance**. This approach to understanding the form of organisation, and its impact on behaviour, rejects the idea that it is about the efficient production of goods and services (which becomes merely a rationalisation after the fact), in favour of the idea that organisations are designed to permit the maximum amount of surveillance of those who work in them, to afford the maximum opportunities for control. Such surveillance is exercised in myriad ways, ranging from direct visual supervision, through recording procedures, such as clocking on and off, output measurements, keystroke measurements, to more subtle and personal measuring techniques, such as appraisal. In such a view, hierarchy, for example, becomes a device for surveillance and control, rather than a functional pyramidic structure of authority. Labour itself ceases to be merely a value-adding process, and becomes a performance of conformity to be observed (see also Chapter 8). This has important implications for organisational behaviour. If one views employees as people who are trying to resist control, this leads to a very different view of organisational behaviour compared to an assumption that employees are simply producers of goods and services. None of this is to deny the obvious point that organisations *do* produce goods and services, but it is to argue that particular organisational forms are *not* chosen with that function as a primary consideration.

If particular organisational forms are seen as the realisation of certain interests, this generates a whole new set of questions for Organisation Studies, such as: Which interests are served by particular forms? Are these the interests most beneficial to organisational members, or society in general? Could other interests be served, by these or other forms? These questions, and many others, arise simply from changing our understanding of the nature and role of structure in organisation.

Further potential

Despite its impact so far, the application of poststructuralist thinking to organisation is still embryonic, and a much wider application of its analytic potential is needed. Given the supposed ubiquity of structure in organisations, there is no aspect of organisation that does not lend itself to poststructuralist analysis. In the context of behaviour, Poststructuralism implies that **we need a whole new set of models and 'tools', and a different agenda, for understanding organisational behaviour.** For example, there has long been an implicit assumption in conventional approaches that the function of the employee is to work, if not harder, at least more efficiently – a problematic concept itself, as will be developed later (Chapter 10). The obviousness of this understanding cannot be sustained within a poststructuralist perspective. It becomes just an idealisation, a fantasy of managers. Quite how an employee might be conceptualised has yet to be fully explored, however.

Such questions can only be addressed in the light of what ideologically driven ends organisations are to serve. Here, again, Poststructuralism has yet to make its full contribution. This is particularly pressing, given, for example, the growing recognition of the global implications of the ways we organise. One view suggests that we are organising ourselves into oblivion by mismanagement of world resources, whether human, material or symbolic. This recognition ought to lead to a new set of priorities for organising, never forgetting that each prioritised form has its own opportunity costs which also need to be understood.

These ideas are gaining ground as the problems become more urgent and as this urgency is increasingly more widely recognised and accepted. It is more common now for there to be challenges, to the dominant structural form of organisations, to their structural relations and to the structures of explanation that are used to justify particular actions. All such challenges must, in the end, propose new structures and new structural relations, however understood, and this needs further development.

Organisational behaviour and structure

Poststructuralist approaches to the issue of structure have enormous implications for understanding organisational behaviour. The attachment to a realist ontology of structure has allowed organisational members to be classified according to various measurements, which have been claimed to be absolute measurements in relation to this 'real' structure, and which have legitimised and facilitated attempts by managers to modify behaviour. Thus we have measures of motivation to work, leadership, commitment, satisfaction, competence, efficiency, potential, psychological types, and so on. Where organisational members failed to reach the required standards, Organisational Behaviour supplied techniques for remedial treatment, or displacement. People ceased to be seen as people as they entered an organisation, instead to be treated as behaving units. From a poststructuralist position, such categories have to be seen as meaningful *only* in terms of a particular ideology informing organisation, and Poststructuralism also provides a means of analysis whereby such ideological interests can be uncovered. These measures are just labels, signifiers of this ideology and, therefore, intrinsically meaningless, except to proponents of the ideology.

Realist views of structure reduce people to employees, attentuating out most of their variety, except those bits deemed 'useful to the organisation'. This process 'allows' them to be managed in particular simplistic and manipulative ways. Understanding human behaviour in a poststructuralist world demands a holistic concept of the person. Nonetheless, it is important to note that Poststructuralism is not a humanist approach – it does not prioritise the human being and require the rest of the world to be arranged for its benefit. It recognises the functional use of power in achieving desired ends. What it questions is what purposes are served by organisational forms, how they are sustained and whether the ends currently served are desirable, let alone sacrosanct.

It is necessary to understand structure to be able to understand organisational behaviour at all. People need the security and ordering benefits that structure provides. But, in the absence of real external structures, we have to create our own. It is this personal structuring that allows us to make sense of the world, creates meaning. Once we understand structure to be subjective rather than objective, we start to generate vastly different explanations of organisational behaviour, compared to those rooted in a realist concept of structure. We can start to understand our experience of organisation, *not as it should be, but as it is.*

A TALE FROM THE VILLAGE PUMP (*STRUCTURE*)

(See the Case Study in Appendix 2, pages 340–3)

There are some significant examples in the case of the **structuring** of information in order to make sense of it. One such example is the miasma theory. It was widely believed at the time that noxious smells carried disease. The ardent supporter of the miasma theory, Edwin Chadwick, claimed:

> All smell is, if it be intense, immediate acute disease; and eventually we may say that, by depressing the system and rendering it susceptible to the action of other causes, all smell is disease. (*Parliamentary Papers*, 1846, Volume 10, p. 651)

It is also relevant to note that Snow did not *discover* the cause of cholera, but *hypothesised* it, on the basis of his observations.

- How does the concept of **structure** help explain how the key actors in the case came to different understandings of the data on cholera outbreaks?

STRUCTURING THINKING ABOUT STRUCTURE

Sam is an A-level student who is planning to go to university. Sam is not really sure what career to pursue, but has a leaning towards becoming a manager. Encouraged by the Careers Officer at school, Sam makes a fairly thorough investigation into what programmes are available at which universities. There are, Sam realises, a great many factors to take into account, to weigh in the balance, such as type of degree, location of university, duration of programme and, of course, programme structure, amongst other things. Sam approaches this range of possibilities in a very systematic way, trying to organise the information in the most logical manner, anxious to make the right decision. Having made a selection, Sam applies for a place on a degree in Business Studies, this seeming the most obvious and most useful foundation for a career in management. However, surprisingly, Sam fails to get sufficiently good grades for a Business Studies programme, and ends up going into the Clearing system at the end of the summer, to get a place at any university on any programme – depending on what is on offer. Sam feels that the process undergone in Clearing is the very antithesis of the previous process, involving a very different range of factors for gaining admission to a university. Still, at this point all Sam wants is to get a place somewhere. To this end, Sam accepts a place on a Development Studies degree. This degree seems unlikely to lead to a career in management, but Sam thinks that maybe it will be possible to get a job with a charity, or possibly to go into teaching.

Sam decides that, to maximise employability after the degree, a good grade – 2.1 at least – is needed. To achieve this, and especially bearing in mind the recent fiasco at A-level, Sam determines to attend all lectures, to submit all required work on time, to study hard for exams and to make full use of additional facilities available, such as the usual wide range of 'how to . . .' courses, courses in computing, courses to improve presentation skills, and so on, and perhaps modules of relevance on other programmes, where possible. It is obvious, Sam thinks, that diligent application will lead to success in end of year exams, to progression to the next year and ultimately to a good final grade. Clearly, Sam concludes, all the programme requirements must be necessary ingredients of the degree. The subjects, the work, the reading lists, all fit together like a well-designed machine, to create an educated graduate in Development Studies. Successful progression through the system leads to a degree.

However, once actually at university these good intentions start to weaken. Sam likes sport and, at the Freshers' Societies Fair, joins the university's football club, to play 5-a-side. Being a useful player, Sam is soon selected to play for the university. There are training sessions to attend, which get in the way of study, and sometimes get in the way of attending lectures. There is also the Student Bar – people to see, things to talk about (other than work). Early morning lectures start to look less attractive, as do afternoon lectures, when there are so many other temptations, such as must-see afternoon television, shopping, relaxing, etc. Gradually, Sam discovers that it is quite possible to miss lectures, to catch up from the notes of fellow students, and still to pass the exams. Submission deadlines, although supposedly non-negotiable, can be got round. While some lecturers insist on deadlines, as per the rules, others are more flexible. Good excuses – computer problems, grandparents' funerals, dogs eating essays – may lead to extensions. One of Sam's lecturers is the coach for the 5-a-side football team and can be very understanding. Sam becomes proud to be rather adept at fooling gullible lecturers, until put straight one evening at a staff/student booze-up. It seems that lecturers are fully aware of the nature of the excuses offered by students, particularly as the same ones crop up year after year, thus stretching the boundaries of statistical credibility. Some lecturers just don't care, or cannot be bothered, or do not have time to check out claims, or do not believe in uniformly fixed deadlines, or for other reasons, in effect, collude with the students.

It also begins to dawn on Sam that, although the programme consists of a specified number of modules equally weighted, with the same number of lectures and tutorials, same size of assignments, same number of study hours, and so on, they do not all require the same amount of effort. Some require much more than the supposed amount of work necessary, for various reasons, and some less. Sometimes lots of work produces a low grade, and vice versa. By judicious selection of electives, it is possible to minimise the work required. Furthermore, though definitely a risky strategy, it is not impossible to use other people's work and to pass it off as one's own, with or without their permission. It is even possible to pay someone else to write one's essays. Sam discovers that even a genuine illness on the day of an exam can lead to a higher mark than that justified by the amount of work actually done.

What Sam works out is that there are key events in the completion of the degree programme that have to be negotiated, but that to succeed in this does not necessarily require following any particular – or even authorised – path. What matters is getting there. As long as submitted work is accepted as valid, exams at year end are passed, it is not particularly important, from Sam's point of view, how it is achieved. Over time, Sam comes to think that interactions and personal relationships with faculty members and, perhaps most significantly, with secretaries and administrative staff are just as important as studying, and can even be more important, in gaining the same end result.

Sam prospers as a student and is heading for a good final grade. During Sam's final year a Recruitment Fair is held at the university, and Sam goes along to have a look at what is on offer. One especially eye-catching stall, though at that moment empty of customers, is run by Charlie, on behalf of a consultancy company seeking to recruit trainee managers. Sam has long since abandoned the goal of management as a career but is gazing idly at the promotional material when Charlie starts chatting in a general way. It turns out that they both come from the same town, and even have some of the same interests. They take to each other. Charlie turns the discussion to a more purposeful direction. 'Have you ever thought of becoming a trainee manager?' Charlie enquires. 'Oh, I'm only doing Development Studies,' Sam replies. 'I haven't done anything relevant to management. I haven't studied the right things, or had any management experience, or anything.' 'That's not necessarily a problem,' says Charlie. 'We are just as interested in extra-curricular activities, and in personality and things like that. We put likely people

▶

through our own selection procedures, to check out their potential, not their history. We also have our own training programmes. We decide who would make a good recruit for us. We don't just go by degree programmes.'

In due course Sam undergoes some psychometric tests of the sort that ask 'Which do you prefer: snowboarding or pasta?' and 'Which makes you feel good: a bicycle or an empty bottle?' Sam cannot see the relevance of such choices, or how they can possibly aid selection. Perhaps they do not, Sam thinks. Perhaps they are just procedures, designed to make selection seem to be a rational process. Sam feels that that would not be too inconsistent with what experience at university had been like. Still, Sam is somewhat bemused to be offered a place on the company's training scheme. But, not wanting to look a gift horse in the mouth, Sam rapidly accepts.

Later, Sam reflects on this unexpected turn of events. Sam's career is not to be a function of knowledge gained on a particular degree programme. The company is not interested in what Sam has learned formally – they will teach the recruits what they want them to know. On the training course Sam discovers that fellow recruits have vastly differing backgrounds – a range of different degrees, or no degree at all, different experiences, and so on. Decisions about recruits seem, indeed, to be made on the basis of answers to questions that have no obvious relevance to the job, or to anything at all. It appears that any experience, or qualification, or whatever, could be seen by those recruiting as indicating future potential. Whatever criteria they are using to decide what is, in effect, the future of the company, they are not clear to Sam, even if they are clear to, say, Charlie (and Sam has not seen Charlie again since the Recruitment Fair). It's just not the way that Sam thought it would be. Nonetheless, Sam has ended up in just the kind of job hoped for at the start of this long process. So was it all just coincidence? Had the world changed? Or had Sam misunderstood the way the world worked?

This case illustrates three different versions of the nature of structure.

- Can Sam's experience at the Recruitment Fair and thereafter be explained adequately from a Structural Functionalist point of view?

- Can Sam's early, pre-university, approach be explained adequately from a Poststructuralist point of view?

- How might the changes in Sam's view of structure be explained?

- Given the conversation between Charlie and Sam, how might the structural relationship between education and career be understood?

(Other chapters that would be useful and relevant in analysing the case *include* Semiotics (2), Knowledge (4), Power (5), Rationality (6) and Decision-making (11).)

Bibliography

Architecture and the organisation of space have been particular sites for consideration of the role of structure, notably in respect of the ideas to be found in Poststructuralism and Postmodernism (see Chapter 12). Some relevant and interesting reflections are to be found in Harvey (1989) and also in, for example, Jencks (1985) and Rogers (1990). The semiotics of space also form part of Baudrillard's considerations in *The Ecstasy of Communication*, in Foster (1985) – Hodge and Kress (1988) is also relevant. An interesting study which relates the structure of a building to the problems of restructuring the organisation within is to be found in Schneider and Powley (1986). More recently, there has been some work exploring the relationships between organisation, in theory and in practice, and architecture. See, for example, Dale and Burrell (2003) and Burrell and Dale (2006).

Most books on organisation (as distinct from those on organisational behaviour) have something to say about structure. There are some studies that relate structure to process which are considered to be 'classics' – for example, Weber (1947), Burns and Stalker (1961), Woodward (1965). A synoptic approach which includes excerpts from these and other writers on organisational structure can be found in Pugh (1990) and Pugh and Hickson (1989) – there are various editions of these popular texts and contents do vary slightly from edition to edition.

For an introduction to the philosophical concept of ontology, good starting points are reference books such as the *Fontana Dictionary of Modern Thought, A Dictionary of Philosophy* (Pan) and the *Oxford Concise Dictionary of Sociology*. For its use in relation to organisation theory, see Burrell and Morgan (1979). A particularly influential book which considers the structure/agency issues, and introduces his concept of structuration, is Giddens (1979).

There is an awful lot on Structural Functionalism, and some books on Organisational Behaviour actually represent a Structural Functionalist approach without ever saying so. One of the most influential Structural Functionalists is Parsons (e.g., 1949). There have been many modifications to Structural Functionalist theory which have sought to fine-tune it *vis-à-vis* organisational practice. Notable examples include: Merton (1949), who introduced the notions of manifest and latent functions and of dysfunctions; Selznick (1949), who argued that legitimacy is not established once and for all but is a recurrent organisational issue; Gouldner (1967), who argued that any integration exhibited by organisations is not natural but managed. Critiques of Structural Functionalism are legion. Particularly extensive is Gouldner (1970), and, in the particular context of Organisation Studies, see also Burrell and Morgan (1979) and Silverman (1970). For those who wish to access a more traditional Functionalist literature on organisations, see, for example, Donaldson (1985, 1996). In this tradition the daddy of them all is, of course, Taylor (1911) – it really is worth going back to this original in order to understand the context and purposes which Taylor perceived to be relevant to Scientific Management since, although 'Taylorism' or 'Scientific Management' are widely paraphrased in organisational texts, these perceptions are rarely cited but do have an impact on Taylor's precepts.

Many books that chart the development of Structuralism do so in its relation to Poststructuralism – see, for example, Hawkes (1983), Harland (1987) and Sturrock (1979, 1993). For an example of renewed interest see Lounsbury and Ventresca (2003). A description of how Structuralism can be used to study organisations is to be found in Turner (1983). It is worth noting that all these approaches – indeed, all approaches – have implications for methods of producing knowledge about organisations. A broad sample of individual examples of this can be found in Morgan (1983a). See also Alvesson and Deetz (2000). An introduction to Poststructuralism can be gained from the relevant entries in Lechte (1994). For examples of the particular authors mentioned in this chapter, see Lévi-Strauss (1972), Barthes (1968), Lacan (1977, 1980), Foucault (1974), Derrida (1978), Deleuze and Guattari (1984), Lyotard (1984). A collection which seeks to draw out the implications of some of these authors for studying organisation(s) is Linstead (2004). Barthes (1968) particularly focuses on the argument that there cannot be a single, ultimate, interpretation of the signifier. Derrida (e.g., 1976, 1981) develops the concept of undecidability to capture the extensive ramifications of this argument. The Fontana Modern Masters book on Derrida (Norris, 1987) gives a useful synopsis, and there is an *Introducing Derrida* (Collins and Mayblin, 2005). On textuality, see the references to Chapter 2. Morgan (1997) might be seen as an example of this in the context of organisational analysis.

A bibliography on power follows Chapter 5, which focuses on that concept. However, Lyotard (1988), on the existence and effect of different languages in the same situation, where one language is dominant and others repressed, is relevant. Intersubjectivity was also considered in Chapter 2. The principle of the impacts of subjective preferences in managing organisational behaviour could be seen as having been articulated in Vroom (1964) – but see also Carter and Jackson (1993). Alienation is a concept widely used in studies of organisation and in organisation theory, but often in a dilute ordinary language sense which ignores the theoretical rigour of the concept. The most famous exponent of the concept of alienation was Marx (e.g., 1975). See also a development of Marx in Marcuse (1986), a psychoanalytic approach to alienation in Lacan (1977) and a poststructuralist analysis of alienation in contemporary capitalist society in Deleuze and Guattari (1984). Blauner (1964) is a post-Marxist analysis of alienation in organisations. Baxter (1982) also offers consideration of alienation in the context of the organisation of work.

The concept of micro-power is prevalent in Foucault's work generally. See, especially, Foucault (1979a) and Gordon (1980). There is really no substitute for reading Foucault's own work but there are some useful introductory commentaries, such as Smart (1985), McHoul and Grace (1993) and Danaher, Schirato and Webb (2000). There is also a *Foucault For Beginners* (Fillingham 1993). See also Horrocks and Jevtik (2004).

Chapter 7 focuses on the concept of ideology, and the bibliography to that chapter is relevant here. It is worth mentioning Mumby (1988) in particular. For examples of the influence of ideology on research into organisations see, for example, Carey (1967) and Baritz (1975). The relation between Poststructuralist approaches to issues of order/disorder and chaos theories is widely recognised. Prigogine and Stengers (1984) specifically noted the links, especially to the work of

Deleuze and Guattari, though, interestingly, this was omitted from the standard English translation, as noted by Massumi (1992). Cooper (1986) is an important contribution on the interconnectedness of order and disorder as relevant to processes of organisation. For just two examples of suggestions of other kinds of organisational 'order', see Vanek (1975) and Rothschild and Whitt (1986).

There is much dispersed throughout Foucault's work on issues of the role of theory in problem-solving and what sort of problems it ought to address – Foucault (1974) is one example, but various collections of Foucault's shorter writings and interviews are also fruitful on these questions, Gordon (1980) and Kritzman (1988) being examples. There are a number of texts that seek to relate particular poststructuralist ideas to organisation, either at a general or at a specific level of analysis. Cooper and Burrell (1988) is often regarded as a seminal paper in this respect. Burrell (1988) is directly relevant to the impact of Foucault's work in organisation theory. Burrell (1997) is an attempt to write a text on organisation according to poststructuralist ideas. McKinlay and Starkey (1998) collects a range of contributions focused specifically on the application of Foucault's work to thinking about organisations. Another example of a text which, by its analyses, implies different kinds of problem definition is Alvesson and Willmott (1992) – whilst overtly a contribution to Critical Theory, much of its content can be seen as relevant to Poststructuralism. Alvesson and Willmott (1996) attempts a closer and more direct rapprochement between Critical Theory and Poststructuralism. For a detailed and more general exploration of such issues, see Dews (1987).

Foucault (1979a) has much to say on matters of surveillance and on the concept of panopticism – though his work on these issues is not limited to this book. For the implications of surveillance in various aspects of organisation, all relevant to organisational behaviour, see, for example, Doray (1988), Kling (1991), Townley (1994), Jacques (1996), Bogard (1996).

CHAPTER 4

Knowledge

This chapter explores the implications of semiotics and Poststructuralism for epistemology, focusing on the nature of knowledge and knowledge production. It examines the vulnerability of the concept of the fact and of the unity of knowledge promised by post-Enlightenment science. The multiplicity of knowledges is highlighted through the concept of knowledge paradigms and three particular facets of knowledge paradigms are developed: diachronicity, synchronicity and incommensurability. The function of the public channel in the transformation of research into knowledge is described. The Foucauldian concept of discourse is then developed, with particular attention to its relevance to knowledge production in terms of who, what, where, how and why, and in terms of the rules of inclusion and exclusion which regulate discursive activity. The question of why we continue to accept the view that knowledge is unified, linear and objective, and thus neutral, when this is demonstrably not the case, is raised, and the role of rhetoric in legitimating knowledge claims is addressed.

In the previous chapters we have said that signifiers, the vehicles by which we communicate and make sense of the world, have no specific or specifiable meaning (signified), and that such order and structure as we perceive in the world derives, not from nature, but from individual sense-making processes. This has enormous implications for what it is possible to know about the world, because it suggests that knowledge is about constructing sense, not about discovering facts. Knowledge is the ordering of information. If order, coherence and regularity are conditions which we *perceive*, rather than ones which exist independently of our awareness, then this applies equally to what we might call facts, knowledge of the world. And, if the media for recording and communicating knowledge are signifiers which have no inherent meaning, then the possibility of unequivocal knowledge – uncontestable and, therefore, transcendent, because we all agree – evaporates. This argument is the basis of the claim that **there is no such thing as a social fact**, *no knowledge about human affairs which is incontravertible and universally accepted.* This suspicion has occasioned considerable debate about what knowledge is, and how it can be used, which has been particularly influential in the field of knowledge about organisations and organisational behaviour, because it throws doubt on to apparently common-sense understandings of organisations and organisational behaviour as observable and predictable, in favour of understandings which emphasise that both are contested and complex. It is to this question of what and how we can know about organisations that we now turn.

Knowledge as a problem

Broadly speaking, we can differentiate two types of science, one which claims knowledge about the natural world – natural science, and one which claims knowledge about human affairs – social science. The division between the two is not always clear: psychology and economics are examples of disciplines which some see as social science and some see as natural science. Social science has traditionally modelled itself on natural science, especially in terms of procedures and of how it is expressed. Our concern here is with social science, the validity of its claims to be a science and the relevance of scientific procedures in producing knowledge about the social world. Our argument is that the claim of social science to be scientific in the way natural science is scientific, is *not* valid, for the very reasons stated at the beginning of this chapter. If the claim to be scientific is not valid, however, then social science loses the particular cultural authority which being a science conveys. Some people question the validity of natural science in this sense, too, but this is not part of our concern here (but see '**A Periodic Table**', page 70).

Each of us reached postgraduate level in our education before being *taught* that there was a problem with the idea of a social fact. If, like us, you have encountered radically different interpretations of the same thing, then, under the regime of facts, all except one of those interpretations (at least) must be wrong. But if it is the concept of the fact which is inappropriate, then this has very different implications. The problem shifts from *the knower* to *the knowledge*. It can come as quite a surprise to be told that there are no such things as facts and that there are problems with the whole concept of knowledge, when it is likely that for the first two decades, at least, of our lives we have been taught that the world is full of facts, we have been inundated with facts, learnt them and been tested on them, and our success in learning facts has been the main instrument of our progress. Education itself is conceived as being about people learning facts. Facts are the medium of education. There are facts of history, such as that the Battle of Hastings was fought in 1066; facts of geometry, such as that the square on the hypotenuse is equal to the sum of the squares on the opposite sides in a right-angled triangle; facts of physics, such as that water boils at 100°C; facts of grammar, such as that a sentence contains a subject, an object and a verb; and so on. Whatever cannot be expressed as a fact is not worthy to be taught. Even in subjects where there is recognised scope for interpretation, such as art and literature, we are taught *rules* for interpretation, rules for re-expressing our feelings about a work in terms of objective criteria. When we start to study management and organisations we learn, for example, that there are three types of authority (theorised by Weber), that management styles are either Theory X or Theory Y

Epistemology

In the course of our normal daily lives we are constantly making decisions about what constitutes knowledge of something (the formal study of which is called **epistemology**).

Suppose that you wish to know the time. A public clock showing Ⓥ (analogue) or 12:55 (digital) would probably be acceptable, but what about one that showed 1100.110111? We know that some clocks tell the wrong time, sometimes because they have stopped. Would you rather believe a twelve-hour clock that had stopped or one that lost one minute per day? The stopped clock is correct twice a day but the losing clock is correct only once every two years!

It is a well-known maxim that 'if you want to know the time, ask a policeman'. But how do you know if your policeman is a real one and not, say, an actor dressed as one (a problem of ontology)? Would knowledge that the person is impersonating a policeman affect your trust that they know what the time is? If the sun is visible more or less overhead but the person you ask tells you that it is six o'clock, do you assume that they are lying to you, that they have a faulty watch, that they are using a different time zone?

Clearly, deciding what constitutes knowledge of the correct time is a complex process. Even the concept of correct time itself is problematic, since it depends on your beliefs about the nature of time. Additionally, supposing you have a fairly conventional view of time, most common devices for measuring time are acknowledged to be relatively inaccurate.

There is also the issue of why you want to know the time. If you are a scientist, you may need to be able to measure time to within millionths of a second, but if you are an historian you may only be able to measure the time of an event to within, say, a day, and if you are an archaeologist it might be a triumph to identify a time to within a few centuries. But if you are a scientist, an historian or an archaeologist wanting to catch a train, you will need to know what the time is to within, say, a minute.

(invented by MacGregor), that Taylor introduced science into management, and so on, all construed as facts. Knowledge, in this view, is a fairly straightforward activity of discovering events, processes, relationships, which eventually lead to the establishment of facts, differentiating what is correct from what is incorrect.

This idea that it is possible to distinguish true (objective) knowledge from other sorts of knowledge, such as opinion or prejudice (characterised as subjective knowledge) goes back to the **Enlightenment**. The Enlightenment is the name given to a historical period when science took over from other kinds of explanation, such as religion (though there is no agreement – no fact – about when this period began). Apart from developments in Science, it was also, and relatedly, characterised by the emergence of liberal, democratic forms of society and the decline of absolute monarchies, feudalism and the superordinate influence of the Church. Obviously, such changes took place over a long period of time but, for our purposes, the roots of the Enlightenment can be located in the seventeenth century. From this period on, there was a decline in knowledge based on superstition, the discovery of natural physical laws, the emergence of a formalised body of science and a wholesale conversion to the idea that knowledge could, and should, be objective, demonstrable and universal, and applied to all aspects of human existence. Science, it came to be believed, could, and should, be used to understand and control nature for the benefit of humanity, and to provide means of ordering the social world to the same ends. Following from this, there was a rapid expansion of understanding of, for example, agriculture, engineering, education, public health and housing, industry, management. Differentiating scientific knowledge from opinion, superstition, and so on, allowed vast improvements in the human condition, through the use of science to alleviate suffering from ignorance, pestilence and disease. A term associated with this epoch is **Modernism**, to which we shall return.

A place in the sun?

For many centuries in Europe the Catholic Church determined what was scientific knowledge. It was essential that scientific knowledge conformed to Church dogma. One of the assertions of approved science was the geo-centric universe – the Sun moves round the Earth.

However, the noted Italian scientist Galileo (1564–1642), with the advent of improved telescopes, could not make his observations fit with Church-approved theory. His observations led to the conclusion that the Earth moves round the Sun – that the 'universe' is helio-centric. This, of course, is now accepted as correct. But, as far as the Church was concerned, it was heresy. Galileo was forced to recant and was lucky to escape with his life, the remainder of which he spent under house arrest.

As recently as 1992 the Catholic Church, after careful consideration, decided that Galileo was indeed correct, forgave him and finally acknowledged that the Earth did move round the Sun.

Science was seen as a continuous process of accumulation of factual knowledge, with the implicit but logical implication that, ultimately, it would be possible to know everything about everything. There might be the occasional wrong turning, such as phrenology (the science of mental faculties investigated by the contours of the skull), which might lead to a cul-de-sac. There might also be areas developed, later to die out, only to reappear in the future with renewed interest, such as eugenics. In other words, progress towards total knowledge was not seen as *strictly* linear and inexorable, but as *principally* so. For these, among other, reasons, science, with its claims to objectivity, neutrality and generalisability, became almost universally viewed as a desirable form of knowledge, more true as knowledge than any other form. Science gained very high levels of *cultural* acceptability.

A Periodic Table

Let us suggest, for the sake of illustration, three stages in the development of the relationship between the Natural Sciences and the Social Sciences over the last hundred years or so.

Period 1

The Natural Sciences establish procedures and routines whereby, it is claimed, True Knowledge is produced, and these are, at the level of principle, universalised across all Natural Sciences. The primary goals of the Natural Sciences are seen to be the elimination of uncertainty and the control of Nature. The Natural Sciences claim to be value-free. The emphasis is on method, not content – application of the correct methods will produce the correct answer, independent of the preferences, values, etc., of the scientist. Proper procedure is the *sine qua non* of True Knowledge. The relatively young Social Sciences seek to emulate the procedures and routines of the Natural Sciences in order to be able to claim that *their* knowledge is True in the same sense that Natural Science knowledge claims to be True.

Period 2

Some social scientists think that it is neither possible nor appropriate for the Social Sciences to emulate the Natural Sciences. The argument is that the subject matter of the Social Sciences (people) is different in kind to that of the Natural Sciences and that, therefore, the methods of the Natural Sciences cannot be replicated in the Social Sciences. It is also argued that there are important ethical issues involved in experimentation in the social context and, therefore, there are limits to how knowledge can be acquired. These social scientists argue that the primary goals of Social Science should be to live with uncertainty as part of Nature. At the same time there is considerable turmoil in the Natural Sciences, especially in relation to the wide-ranging implications following from Einstein's theories of Relativity. The impact of factors extraneous to method on production of knowledge in the Natural Sciences – notably, how the research is funded and the personal preferences of knowledge producers – is increasingly acknowledged.

Period 3

The Natural Sciences become more like the Social Sciences, not through desire to emulate them, but through loss of faith in the precepts of Newtonian models of Science, through a shift of focus from method to content and through a recognition of the impacts of bias and values on how, and what, Science is done. Many natural scientists also come to believe that the goal of (all) Science is to live with uncertainty as part of Nature. Nonetheless, some social scientists, and some natural scientists, still cling to the Newtonian model.

Paradigms

The idea of a rational, linear, cumulative development of knowledge had its most potent challenge in the 1960s, with the development of the concept of knowledge paradigms. **Paradigm** is the name given to the conceptual framework(s) within which knowledge is produced. A paradigm is constituted, in part, by the **rules** which are generally accepted as necessary to follow in order to produce 'good' knowledge. More significantly, **a paradigm consists of the shared beliefs and assumptions of knowledge producers about what knowledge is**, which shared beliefs and assumptions are institutionalised through support structures, such as universities, and through training. A paradigm constitutes **a model for solving problems** – it is not a real structure.

In that the root of the word 'paradigm' is 'to show side by side', it is clear that there cannot be only one paradigm, but always must be more than one, which are compared to each other – usually on the basis of their ability to provide solutions to problems. Even in natural science there is not only one paradigm – a chemist will have one way of doing science, a physicist another, a biologist another, and so on. What is likely to be common to all these, however, is a general set of beliefs about what science is and about what good scientific practice is. It is increasingly accepted that **all disciplines have various paradigms within them**, groups of people who share beliefs and assumptions about what 'good' knowledge in their field should look like, and how to produce it, but who may not agree with other such groups, even in the same field of knowledge.

Diachronic paradigm models

The concept of a knowledge paradigm is particularly associated with the work of Thomas Kuhn, a philosopher and historian of natural science, who, in 1962, published a book called *The Structure of Scientific Revolutions*. Kuhn was looking at **dis**continuities in the historical development of natural science which, by their very existence, challenged the linear, cumulative view. Kuhn argued that scientific knowledge production was characterised by periods of calm, followed by periods of upheaval when ideas about science changed in fundamental ways, which then themselves developed into periods of calm before another revolution in thinking.

The dominant view of science in the quiet periods Kuhn called the **normal science paradigm**, which represents a general consensus among scientists about what knowledge is, and how to produce it. However, during this period some scientists, notably the younger ones, start to have doubts about the ability of the normal science paradigm to solve problems. These people start to do science in a different way and gradually develop what Kuhn called a **revolutionary science paradigm**. A conflict then develops between the two different ways of doing science – between the normal paradigm and the revolutionary paradigm. If the revolutionary science paradigm becomes sufficiently powerful, it overthrows the normal science paradigm and then becomes, itself, the *new* normal science paradigm. A significant requirement for success is that the revolutionary paradigm has to be able to solve *all* the problems that the normal paradigm can solve, *plus* some that it cannot. Eventually a new revolutionary science paradigm will start to emerge and the whole process is repeated. It is important to note two points: a revolutionary paradigm can only take over as the new normal science paradigm if it has better explanatory power (is better at solving problems) than the old normal science paradigm, and it must be sufficiently strong (enough people are part of it) to *eliminate* the old normal science paradigm – hence the idea of a scientific *revolution*.

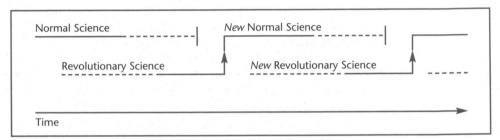

Kuhn's model of diachronic paradigms

The idea of a paradigm in this case refers to a particular way of doing science, a particular view of what constitutes knowledge. Kuhn has a fairly conventional, Enlightenment, view of what science is and how it is produced. Importantly, he holds the view that all scientists share the same goal of solving problems, and that the ultimate test of scientific knowledge is its ability to solve problems and contribute to progress. It is rather ironic that Kuhn's work is seen as representing this major challenge to the assumption that science is rational, cumulative and unified in nature, because this is precisely Kuhn's own view of science, as he was at pains to point out on many occasions. His own view of what he was examining was that it was to do with a concern for quality, with the development of better or worse ways of doing science. **For Kuhn, science is rational, but the way it is done is not.** This point is exemplified in the way in which Kuhn's model sees the production of science as changing and improving over time. It is a **diachronic** model – it has a time dimension, over which things change.

Incommensurability in diachronic paradigm models

One of the most controversial aspects of paradigm models is their incommensurability. **Different knowledge paradigms are incommensurable with each other.** So, what does this mean? The word commensurable means, literally, having common measures, being capable of being measured exactly by the same unit of measurement. Thus, **in**commensurable means *not* having common measures. If two things are incommensurable, they cannot be evaluated by the same means and, therefore, cannot be evaluated in terms of each other, or compared precisely to each other, or synthesised. For example, a length of road and a stick of rhubarb are commensurable in the sense that they can both be measured by the same unit of length, but incommensurable as items of food. In one sense they can be compared but, in another, they cannot. Of course, measures do not have to be physical and do not necessarily have reference to specific units. They can also be qualitative and conceptual. Shakespeare's *Macbeth* and Disney's *Snow White and the Seven Dwarfs* are commensurable in, for example, length of time occupied, and could be compared, if so desired, in terms of historical significance, or effectiveness as political allegory. They *might*, however, be incommensurable in terms of their value as children's entertainment, or as historical record.

In terms of diachronic knowledge paradigms, incommensurability suggests that there are no common grounds between the different paradigms. Different paradigms are different in nature and there are no *independent* measures against which the different paradigms can be compared. They are just different. They cannot be synthesised. They attempt to do the same thing in different ways. **The incommensurability arises because the proponents of each paradigm do *not* share beliefs and assumptions about what knowledge is and how it should be produced**. Kuhn argued that, over time, the revolutionary paradigm becomes the new normal paradigm, but this is *not* because they are synthesised, with everyone agreeing that the revolutionary paradigm is better at science than the old normal paradigm, even though this is, in practice, the case. The development of the revolutionary paradigm into the new normal paradigm occurs because it eliminates, in one way or another, the acceptability of the old normal paradigm. Kuhn says that the transformation is only complete when the proponents of the old normal paradigm are either converted to the revolutionary paradigm or, literally, they die out. He compares the incommensurability between the two paradigms to two groups who speak different languages. In other words, there is a 'normal' language and then the revolutionary group starts to use a new language. It is as if these two languages vie with each other for domination. When one becomes dominant you either learn that language or you cease to be able to communicate.

Kuhn's diachronic paradigm model has been extremely influential in thinking about how knowledge is gained but, when it comes to thinking about organisation(s) and organisational behaviour – and, indeed, any other social context – it has a major drawback. Kuhn's model is inherently concerned with the natural sciences, and could only be applicable to the social sciences in so far as the social sciences could be seen as unified and evolutionary in the same way as Kuhn sees the natural sciences. We have already suggested that the social sciences cannot be seen as commensurable with the natural sciences.

Synchronic paradigm models

In 1979 another model of knowledge paradigms was proposed, but this time one which specifically addressed the study of organisations: Gibson Burrell and Gareth Morgan's *Sociological Paradigms and Organisational Analysis*. This paradigm model seeks to provide a means of organising and structuring the enormous variety of theories about organisations. Unlike Kuhn's model, it is specifically about social scientific knowledge. Also unlike Kuhn's model, it is a **synchronic** model – that is, there is no time dimension, the model being like a snapshot of the state of organisational analysis. Again unlike Kuhn's model, Burrell and Morgan are not setting out to describe the historical development of a discipline, but are asking why there are so many, and so many contradictory, theories about organisations.

In Burrell and Morgan's model there are four knowledge paradigms, each representing a different set of beliefs and assumptions about science. These beliefs are of two types, one set being about the nature of the world and the other set being about the proper role of science. Each set of beliefs comprises an axis between two polar opposites, which allows the construction of a useful four-cell matrix to demonstrate how each paradigm stands in relation to all the others. The opposing beliefs about the nature of the world are, at one extreme, a realist view, believing in an external, objectively real world, existing independently of people and available to everyone's observation (akin to a natural science approach), and, at the other extreme, a view that the world is socially constructed, a product of individual meanings and, therefore, subjectively real, and that we gain knowledge of the world through our experience of it, so that, potentially, everyone's knowledge of it is different. As regards the role of science, one polar belief is that the proper role of science is to describe the world and, possibly, to suggest minor adjustments which might improve its functioning, but to claim no opinions as to whether the world is correctly ordered or not (sociology of regulation). The opposing view is that the role of science is to make judgements about the way the world ought to be and to offer suggestions as to how this could be achieved (sociology of radical change)

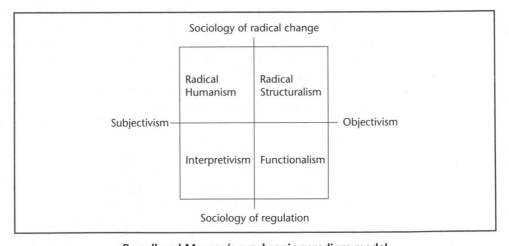

Burrell and Morgan's synchronic paradigm model

The cell at bottom right is the **Functionalist** paradigm, which is objectivist and regulatory. Most conventional theories of organisational analysis and organisational behaviour fall within this paradigm. Organisation theorists in the paradigm see organisations as, primarily, structures for economic activity, take a managerialist viewpoint (that is, see managerial interests as paramount), and, in general, address issues about maintenance of stability, equilibrium and control. The cell at bottom left is the **Interpretivist** paradigm. This paradigm is also concerned with regulation but understands the world as socially constructed.

Theorists in this paradigm are principally concerned with issues of interaction and how the construction of meaning and understanding occurs. For Interpretivist theorists, organisations are not independently existing structures, but the outcome of interactions manifested as shared meaning – they are to be seen as social constructs.

The cell at top right is the **Radical Structuralist** paradigm. Organisation theorists in this paradigm share the view of Functionalist theorists about what an organisation is, but see them as devices for maintaining class interests and power. To Radical Structuralists, organisations are microcosms of society, reflecting social inequalities, and it is not possible to understand organisations independently of the social context of which they are a part. In this view, organisations need to be understood as structures of domination designed to maintain existing unequal distributions of power, wealth and influence, but also represent vehicles for social change. The cell at top left is the **Radical Humanist** paradigm, which shares the Interpretivist view of organisations as social constructions but also shares the Radical Structuralist view of organisations as instruments of power and domination. However, whereas Radical Structuralists concentrate on the material aspects of domination, including the economic, Radical Humanists extend this to include psychological domination. This has been neatly described by Gareth Morgan in another of his books, *Images of Organization*, as 'the psychic prison', the idea that, although organisations are socially constructed, we tend to treat them as if they are real independently of our awareness and to experience them as oppressive, yet accept this repression as necessary and inevitable (see also the section on **Alienation** in Chapter 3).

Each of these paradigms represents theories of organisation, all of which co-exist simultaneously, symbolising fundamentally different and contradictory views about what an organisation is and what, and how, we can know about it. The important point that the model emphasises is that **gaining knowledge about organisations is not a matter of discovering facts but a reflection of the pre-existing beliefs and assumptions of the people who study them**. Each paradigm represents a radically different view of what is meant by organisation (its *signified*). Because this is not a matter of facts but of beliefs, this inevitably means that **there can be no unified understanding of organisation or organisational behaviour**. People seeking knowledge about organisations inevitably buy into one paradigm or another, a selection based, not on scientific explanatory power, but on ideological preference for a particular view of the world and the role of science in it.

Incommensurability in synchronic paradigm models

Like diachronic paradigms, synchronic paradigms are also incommensurable, but their incommensurability functions in a rather different way, precisely because of the lack of a time dimension. Incommensurability between paradigms is overcome in a diachronic model by the elimination of one paradigm by another. Because all scientists are seeking the same goal, the paradigm with the best explanatory power triumphs, even though it may have to overcome the rearguard emotional and ideological attachment to a dying paradigm of those whose

Shedding light – different paradigms, different explanations

Lighthouse keeper sacked for wanting a shower

An assistant lighthouse keeper who was sacked for refusing to work in 'primitive conditions' at the only Trinity House station without proper washing facilities was awarded £1,800 by an industrial tribunal yesterday.

Mr John Clarke, aged 33, told how he had campaigned for a year without success to get a shower installed at the 145-year-old Smalls Lighthouse, 20 miles off the Pembrokeshire coast.

He then refused to return to his 120ft high outpost clinging on to a rock in the Irish Sea until a shower was fitted. He was sacked, and the following day Trinity House sent an engineer to the station. He arranged for a shower to be put in at a cost of £5,289.

Mr Clarke won an appeal against dismissal, but was sacked again when he refused to accept penalties involving the loss of three years' seniority and increments.

After reviewing the case in Cardiff yesterday the tribunal chairman, Mr David Powell, concluded: 'It does seem unnecessarily primitive in the 1980s for a lighthouse keeper to have a strip-down wash in a plastic bowl in the kitchen; more reminiscent of the old days in coal mining villages.

We are unanimous that it was excessively severe to have dismissed Mr Clarke, for taking his admittedly reasonable complaint to the length that he did.'

Mr David Vennings, a Trinity House engineer, said he had been led to believe that there would be electrical difficulties in fitting a shower and, as the Smalls was to be automated next year, it was decided not to proceed. 'I was loath to do so, given the total cost', he declared.

The three kilowatt shower which was commissioned after Mr Clarke was sacked will have to be taken out when the lighthouse is gutted to prepare for automation. A new shower will then be installed for maintenance men.

The tribunal considered a letter from another keeper on the Smalls, Mr Peter Riches, who had complained last year: 'When are they going to realise that we are now living in the 20th century? This is the most isolated station, and has the unenviable reputation of being the worst.'

Mr Clarke, who had served in 15 of the 96 Trinity House lighthouses since 1974 and is now unemployed, said he was delighted.

Source: Paul Hoyland, 'Lighthouse keeper sacked for wanting a shower', *The Guardian* 4 October 1985. Copyright © Guardian Newspapers Limited 1985. Reprinted with permission.

A **Functionalist** in the **'scientific management'** mould might describe this situation in terms of control of expenditure and management's right to manage. As a Rational Economic Man, Clarke should have accepted the rationale of the organisation. A **Functionalist** in the **'human relations'** mould might suggest that this should have been more clearly explained to Clarke and, thus, his commitment to the acceptability of the situation elicited.

An **Interpretivist** might see it as a dramatic enactment of a clash of subjective realities, Clarke wanting an improvement in his working conditions and Trinity House wanting to optimise their efficiency, as they defined it. The drama was played out until one version of reality was declared more correct.

A **Radical Structuralist** might see the situation as an example of class conflict. Trinity House, an organisation traditionally run by, largely, senior ex-naval personnel (their current patron is the Duke of Edinburgh), was exercising economic and social domination over its employees, relatively powerless members of the working class, and replicating the deeply engrained structures of class interest. Yet the organisational situation also turned out to be a site of struggle for change.

- What do you think a **Radical Humanist** interpretation might be?

best interests are served by the survival of that paradigm, (for example, career, reputation, emotional investment). But, because there is, ultimately, an independent test of the paradigms – their ability to solve problems – then the one which is best at doing this will eventually become dominant. But **in synchronic paradigms the proponents of each paradigm are not trying to solve the same problems, do not have the same objectives, so there can be no ultimate agreement about which has the best explanatory power.** As with diachronic paradigms, each paradigm has its own language but, unlike diachronic paradigms, there are different goals being pursued, with different criteria for success.

Although we called the synchronic model a snapshot, this does not mean that the *individual* paradigms are static. Indeed, each one could be seen as containing within it the potential for a diachronic model such as that of Kuhn. However, the relations *between* the paradigms are static. They are mutually exclusive, contradictory to each other, and there is no way that time can resolve differences. There is no independent point from which one can be seen to have the best explanatory power. As previously noted, the proponents of each paradigm have fundamentally different views of what an organisation is, and of what its purpose is. This, combined with their incommensurable beliefs about the nature of the world and about the purpose of knowledge, means that there is no common, independent, transcendent standard against which explanatory power can be judged.

Take, for example, the 'problem' of low productivity – problem in quotation marks because not everyone would see it as a problem, or have the same view about what constitutes low productivity, there being no absolute measure. From a Functionalist point of view, it might be seen as a problem of low motivation, caused by structural weaknesses, in job design, say, which can be corrected by management action. From an Interpretivist point of view, it might be seen as a reflection of cultural values shared by workers, about the appropriate amount of work to do in a given period. From a Radical Structuralist point of view, it might be seen as a device used by the workforce to resist what they see as attempts to increase exploitation by management. From a Radical Humanist point of view, it might be seen as reflecting a sense of alienation caused by perceptions of negative worth and the requirements of a job which treats people as less than human beings and denies them positive identity. Each interpretation of the 'problem' stems from fundamentally different views of the nature and purpose of organisations. Just as importantly, each way of defining the 'problem' leads to fundamentally different proposed 'solutions'.

While the idea of knowledge paradigms has gained wide acceptance, what has seemed less acceptable to theorists has been this incommensurability. The reasons for the reluctance to accept incommensurability seem to stem from various causes. For example, incommensurability implies that communication between paradigms is, at least, difficult, because proponents use 'different languages' – they may use the same signifiers, such as organisation or management, but they do not agree about what those signifiers signify; it implies a threat to the status of knowledge producers, in that no theorist can claim transcendent authority for their knowledge, but can only seek to argue and persuade. Perhaps it can be said, therefore, that resistance to incommensurability is, just like the model itself, based on emotional and ideological preference. But incommensurability is, on one hand, simply a logical consequence of the model – it is, for example, not possible to synthesise beliefs in objectivism with beliefs in subjectivism, they are opposites and mutually exclusive. (You might convince an objectivist that subjectivism is a better approach, but that is merely to shift from one side of the argument to the other, not to synthesise them, or to *prove* that one is better than the other.) On the other hand, incommensurability can be seen simply to reflect our experience of organisation theories: there *are* radically different theories, they *are* mutually exclusive, and there *is* no way of proving, in the sense of scientific proof, that one is correct and the others are incorrect. If there were no incommensurability, there would be no need for the concept of paradigms – but then we would need some other way to structure the variety and contradiction in organisation theories.

While incommensurability is an important feature of paradigm models of knowledge, **the significance of such models which we have sought to highlight is their challenge to the claim for a rational, linear, cumulative, unified body of knowledge.** However, such models tell us little about why, and by what process, paradigms emerge, develop and prosper. It is to this that we now turn.

Knowledge and the public channel

In the opening sequence of Douglas Adams' *The Hitch Hiker's Guide to the Galaxy*, there is a girl sitting in a small café in Rickmansworth, on whom suddenly dawns the answer to the question of how to make the world 'a good and happy place'. But a moment later, before she can even express it, our sage is obliterated by the arrival of construction workers for the hyper-spatial express route, which requires the demolition of the planet Earth to make way for it. So this insight was denied to humankind, and necessitated the rest of the book. Suppose, however, that this revelation was not about the meaning of life, and so on, but was a total understanding of organisational behaviour, and our sage is not blasted into oblivion. In the current system of knowledge production, her insight would *still* have counted for nothing, because what counts as knowledge is not Truth, but what is communicated through the appropriate **public channel**.

Usually, knowledge is that which is written down, rather than just spoken, and written in the form of, for example, books or articles in learned journals. Different channels, such as different journals, are appropriate to different disciplines. So, you write an article and submit it to a journal in your field of knowledge, and the editor of the journal sends it to be reviewed by two or three of your peers, for acceptance or rejection. They comment on things like originality, appropriateness to the other knowledge in the field, style, and so on. You then respond, usually by modifying your original text. This is then accepted or not. If it is accepted, it may then take about two years to be published. It is only when it is published that it is given the status of knowledge. Thus, **knowledge is that which three or four people agree to be knowledge**.

Suppose our sage had had the opportunity to write down her revelation, the Truth about organisational behaviour, and submit it to a journal. Because she is not an appropriate person, such as an academic, and has no appropriate institutional affiliation, such as a university which employs her as an academic, her article may never get to be reviewed. Even if it does, it might or might not convince her reviewers, who, anyway, may have vested interests in rejecting it, if it seems to threaten their own careers or reputations, for example. In knowledge production it is not Truth that matters, so much as who you are, how you communicate and what your reviewers are prepared to tolerate.

This issue of the control of knowledge and knowledge production is one which has been addressed by many poststructuralist theorists. Of particular note is Jacques Derrida, who has written about what he calls **techno-mediatic power**. By this he refers to a *collusion* among various interests – political, media and academic – in various public channels. The public channels he refers to are much wider than those we have already described. Although in the academic world – the world where the job itself is to produce knowledge – the initial public channel is the publication of articles, etc., the general channels available for dissemination of knowledge are much more extensive. Thus popularised scientific knowledge and other forms of non-scientific knowledge are also disseminated through, for example, television, radio, video, the internet, advertising. This gives knowledge a much wider audience, of non-specialists. Derrida argues that the objective of the collusion is to reinforce the status quo, to damp down criticism represented in contradicting knowledge claims which might excite uncontrollable demands for change, to maintain stability and to reassure people in general that 'it's all for the best in the best of all possible worlds'. The effect of this is also to preserve the power and authority of those who have access to these public channels.

An example can be found in the ongoing problem of BSE in cattle in the UK. It was thought at first that this had arisen through the relaxation of cattle feed regulation by government, but this was later discounted, although problems with contaminated cattle feed did appear to be a significant cause of transmission of BSE. Its discovery led to veterinary restrictions, which alerted the public to its existence and led to widespread alarm in the population, who expressed this, especially, by ceasing to buy beef. This was promptly seen by government and other interested parties, such as farmers and butchers, as a political and economic crisis. Extensive use of techno-media was made to try to resolve the apparent crisis. Scientists declared authoritatively that there was no evidence that BSE could be passed to humans and politicians then declared that beef was safe to eat. Widespread coverage was given by the media. This was conveyed as the Truth. Nonetheless, evidence that contradicts this has become available. There were, of course, always scientists, politicians and journalists who disagreed with the official Truth, but they had little impact in the face of such authoritative and massive denial, and there is now also evidence that individual critics were denied access to public channels and research into the problem was restrained, especially by the withholding of funds. It is interesting to note that this contrary view did eventually achieve public dissemination, largely because of the extent of public concern. Subsequently it has been acknowledged that BSE can be passed to humans, in the form vCJD (variant Creutzfeldt-Jacobs Disease), and that beef was not safe to eat at that time.

Organisational issues are rarely accorded such attention, though this might be seen as surprising, since organisational issues affect as many people as BSE does, if not more. Indeed, the whole BSE scandal might usefully have been construed as an organisational problem, but was not. Nor was it construed as a problem of knowledge and its dissemination, but, in the main, as a problem of reassuring consumers – or not.

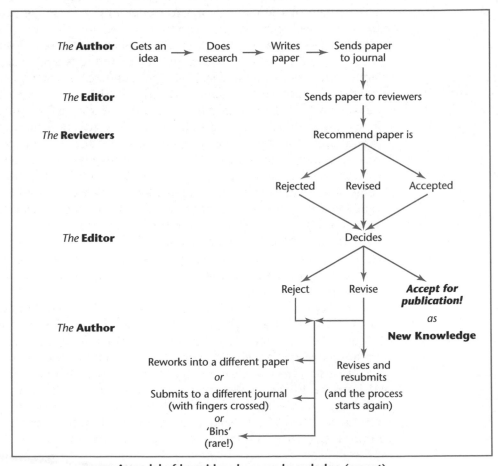

A model of how ideas become knowledge (or not)

Discourses of knowledge

A term which has, in the last twenty years or so, come to be widely used to refer to the processes and procedures of knowledge production is that of **discourse**. In this context, discourse is strongly associated with the work of Michel Foucault, and should not be confused with its usual, ordinary language, use. There are many discourses, each representing a field of knowledge. Discourses are relatively coherent and embody systems of rules considered to be appropriate to a particular field of knowledge, and reflect prevailing values, norms, beliefs and relations of power. Foucault's use of the term is part of a very complex formulation but, for our purposes, we will reduce this to the issue of **who can say what, where and how – and why**.

Who?

A discourse defines **who is allowed to speak authoritatively** on a particular topic. For example, to be recognised as a competent commentator on organisational behaviour it is necessary to be, usually, an academic in a relevant field or discipline, or, perhaps, a management consultant, or a manager – but rarely a worker, since workers are the **object** of the discourse. People outside this perceived eligible group will find great difficulty in getting their ideas into the public channel and even if they succeed are unlikely to be taken seriously by this 'community' of organisational behaviour specialists. It is possible to try to circumvent this by engaging in a competing discourse in which one *is* eligible, such as trades unionists writing on organisational behaviour in the discourse of Industrial Relations, but this will not necessarily be perceived as relevant in the Organisational Behaviour discourse.

It is an inevitable implication of such a view that those who are entitled to speak have **status**: they need status to be able to enter the discourse and entry enhances that status. They also have a function of **regulating who else can enter the discourse**. This also means that status is more significant than expertise. There is no guarantee that those who are entitled to speak have expertise. Furthermore, they will act as a brake on development of the discourse in directions that might not suit their own interests.

What?

Within a discourse there are **things that it is appropriate to say, and things that it is not**. Those that are not appropriate will be excluded from the discourse. There are two aspects to this. *Firstly*, there are rules about what can be considered to be **relevant** to the discourse. In the discourse of Organisational Behaviour, for example, it is acceptable to talk about motivation, leadership, culture, group dynamics, and so on, but to try to introduce issues of, say, music, art, diet, brain surgery, will be unlikely to be seen as appropriate, even though they may be so. *Secondly*, and more importantly, there are rules about what can be said about those issues that are considered appropriate: there are **rules about how problems can be defined and, therefore, about what kind of solutions can be proposed**. For example, while stress is widely recognised as relevant to organisational behaviour, acceptable solutions are those that teach people to manage their stress. Solutions that suggest that the causes of stress, such as overwork, low pay, lack of job security, should be addressed have been much less acceptable with the Organisational Behaviour discourse. The idea of 'a fair day's work for a fair day's pay' is one to which most people would subscribe, but the idea that workers might be appropriate people to contribute to defining what 'fair' means is rarely acceptable. One reason for this is that, as noted, workers are not part of the acceptable 'who' of the discourse, they are its object, what it studies.

Where?

Discourses also have rules about **where knowledge is located**, which affect its acceptability. This may be in terms of **actual classes of individuals** who can claim to be knowledgeable about, in this case, organisational behaviour – occupations that are OK, or not. Or it may be in terms of **physical locations for knowledge dissemination**: some journals are 'proper', others are not; some institutions are 'better' than others; some types of written knowledge, such as articles in learned journals, are more 'significant' than others, such as newspapers articles, or novels – many novels deal with organisational life but such locations are rarely seen as either appropriate or conforming to the rules of 'good' knowledge. There are also forums which are considered to be more appropriate than others – an academic conference is more 'important' than a conversation in a pub. Different discourses may have different rules about this. It has long been considered acceptable to use tele-media, especially video, to disseminate knowledge about organisational behaviour but other disciplines, such as philosophy or history, have been much slower to give legitimation to such channels.

How?

The discourse has **rules about what forms are appropriate for knowledge**. Knowledge claims in the discourse of Organisational Behaviour need to be expressed in ways commensurate with the causal logic of the natural sciences. Ideally, one should go out and collect data which can be converted into regularities through statistical procedures. Additionally, such data should point, unequivocally, to solutions that are acceptable under 'what' conditions – not just any old data will do. There are also **rules about appropriate style of presentation**, reference to other material in the discourse, linguistic form and, especially, technical language. For example, it is acceptable to speak about techniques to increase motivation, commitment, efficiency, productivity of workers, but it would not be acceptable to speak about this in terms of increasing exploitation of labour power, even if that is the same thing.

Why?

Implied in all the who, what, where and how rules are **rules about appropriate reasons for speaking**, about what interests should be served by knowledge. For example, in the discourse of Organisational Behaviour the only reason to discuss the behaviour of organisational members is to improve organisational functioning. You do not talk about why people behave the way they do in general terms, but only in terms of whether such behaviour is good or bad for organisational efficiency. You do not talk about modification of behaviour in terms of benefits to individual actors, but only in terms of benefits to 'organisational goals'.

Clearly, as all this shows, a fundamental quality of all discourses is the rules about what can be included and what must be excluded from any specific discourse. To that end, considerable effort is spent on managing discursive boundaries. While the overt purpose of this activity is to protect the quality of knowledge production within the discourse, it is also inevitable that it will, additionally, exclude potentially valid knowledge claims, just because they do not follow all the rules.

There are challenges to discourses and it is possible for a discourse to change from within, but debate about change has still to be acceptable within the rules of the discourse. A discourse might change its view of what is appropriate to its subject matter, for example, or it may even change other rules of acceptability, but what will not change is that there *are* rules. Equally, the discourse cannot control external challenges, such as material claiming to be relevant being part of other discourses – but it can ignore them. Thus, for example, knowledge claims in the discourse of Industrial Relations have often addressed organisational behaviour issues, in ways very different to those of the discourse of Organisational Behaviour itself, but these have made negligible impact in what is defined as the field of Organisational Behaviour.

Foucault argued that all knowledge belongs to some discourse or other. But he was not merely describing it to say 'this is the way it is'. His point was that, *given* that this is the way it is, **it is essential that any knowledge claim should be interrogated in terms of who is saying what, and why they are saying it at such a moment.** In other words, an essential part of the evaluation of knowledge claims is to understand what interests are served by a particular knowledge claim.

The discourse of efficiency – or of revenge?

In 1984–5 there was a major, and very bitter, strike in the coal industry in the UK. Both the union (National Union of Mineworkers, NUM) and the employers (National Coal Board, NCB) used a similar language in terms of their proposed intentions for the coal industry. For example, both sides stated that they wanted an efficient coal industry – they used the same signifier 'efficient'. They did not, however, intend the same signified – one version, for example, was based on maintaining the coal industry, the other version was not. In the end, only one signified of 'efficient' could triumph, become the 'reality'. However, it was not a matter of comparatively evaluating the two signifieds, but of the degree of power that could be brought to bear in the support of each particular signified.

It is widely held that the then Conservative Government wished to destroy the power of the NUM for historical reasons, the union, in a previous dispute, having won their demands and being seen to have humiliated the Conservative Government of the time. The Government was, therefore, willing to support the NCB in imposing their definition of 'efficient' and, ultimately, the miners lost. The eventual result of this was massive job losses, widespread pit closures, a vastly slimmed down and, ultimately, privatised coal industry and an increase in importation of coal from abroad to meet Britain's needs – the Government/NCB version of 'efficient'.

However, it is impossible to say whether or not this version is, in any sense, more efficient than that of the miners. It was not an issue of economics, but one of power – the power to dictate meaning. It was a clash of incommensurable discourses, in which one set of discursive rules would inevitably be declared inappropriate. It is not possible properly to understand this clash without asking who was saying what, and why they were saying it at that moment.

Regimes of truth

Foucault argued that, not only is all knowledge part of some discourse, but it always has been. But, obviously, what is thought of as acceptable knowledge has changed over time. He suggested that these changes are brought about by major shifts in social development and produce what he called regimes of truth – one such shift was effected by the Enlightenment, as discussed earlier in this chapter. The point here is that it is not just knowledge producers who define what the rules of a discourse might be, but that these rules are part of much wider social conditions. **It is not just knowledge producers who define what may be regarded as acceptable knowledge, but also other significant and powerful groups in society.** More than this, the rules about what is 'good' knowledge evolve through social, political, economic and cultural conditions as much as through intellectual ones. **The regime of truth defines what can be called truth in any epoch and whose interests can legitimately be served.** For example, once upon a time truth was a matter of understanding divine will, but this gave way to understandings of truth as based in science. Foucault himself defined three such regimes of truth throughout history, the current one being what he called the **capitalist regime of truth**. This concept has important implications for relations of knowledge and power, which will be developed in the next chapter.

Knowledge and rhetoric

We have argued against the idea that knowledge can be seen as objective, neutral, linear, cumulative and unified. Yet this is still how knowledge is, normally, presented to us and is still the dominant view of what knowledge is like. How is it possible for this view to persist if it is not the case? The answer lies in the concept of rhetoric. Like discourse, rhetoric has an ordinary language sense, where it is usually pejorative and signifies language empty of genuine meaning. However, rhetoric has a more rigorous and technical signification, as a form of logic. **Rhetoric is the logic of argument and persuasion**.

There are various types of logic but, for our purposes, we can focus on two in particular, formal logic and rhetorical logic. Formal logic is associated with science and, principally, refers to causal relations of the type 'if A, then B'. Management knowledge abounds with this kind of statement, such as if your job is enriched, then you will feel satisfied, or if supply exceeds demand, then prices will fall. Indeed, within the discourse of Management Knowledge, with its pretensions to the status of a science, it is often regarded as a requirement (rule) that knowledge claims should conform to this style. In contrast, rhetorical logic is the logic of argumentation: it is the logic employed to convince someone else that what you are saying is true. The most obvious use of rhetorical logic is in the legal system, where, for example, guilt or innocence is the function of an advocate's ability to persuade, for example, a jury that their interpretation of the evidence is the correct (most appropriate) one. When a person is pronounced guilty or innocent, what is being pronounced is the opinion of those sitting in judgement, not a fact – as evidenced by the well-known possibility that those who are actually guilty can be found innocent, and those innocent found guilty.

In formal logic truth resides in facts in nature, whereas in rhetorical logic truth resides in the ability of someone to persuade. In formal logic, no matter how badly a case is presented, it is axiomatic that truth will out, since truth is independent of its presentation. In rhetorical logic truth resides solely in the degree to which an argument convinces. The proposition that there is no such thing as a social fact implies that all knowledge claims about human affairs must be based in rhetorical logic, not in formal logic, notwithstanding claims to be based in the latter. Indeed, such claims are well-recognised **rhetorical devices** – techniques of argument. Such claims are merely **rhetorical logic pretending to be formal logic**. Thus, the claim that if your job is enriched then you will feel satisfied is a statement presented in formal logic style, but its truth depends crucially upon the ability of its proponent to convince that there is a relationship between enrichment and satisfaction, to convince that there are acceptable measurements of the relationship, to convince that what is measured is relevant to the relationship, and to convince that identifiable benefits will flow from it.

The process of persuasion is not just a matter of the quality of the argument itself, but is facilitated by the devices of rhetorical logic. These also include that **a speaker does not communicate with everyone in general but only with selected parts of the potential audience, and that those selected are those receptive to what is to be said.** Thus, Organisational Behaviour specialists do not communicate their ideas to the world at large, or even to all members of organisations, but, principally, to managers. Furthermore, the things that they communicate to managers about are things that managers want to hear, such as how to improve efficiency or control. If they try to communicate things that managers do not want to hear, they will not persuade. It will be clear by now that there are many resonances between the concept of rhetorical logic and that of discourse and, indeed, rhetorical logic has been influential in recent developments of theory about what knowledge is, how it can be produced and how its dissemination operates.

Existing applications in Organisational Behaviour

Burrell and Morgan's synchronic paradigms model has been hugely influential, especially in two particular ways. *Firstly*, it has stimulated considerable debate about the nature of knowledge in the field of organisations, and, especially, about influences on knowledge production in this area which are external to the knowledge itself, both the prior assumptions which are brought to knowledge production by its producer and the issue of whose interests are represented in that knowledge production, and how they are represented. For example, is organisational knowledge primarily to serve the interests of managers, or should it be legitimate to represent other interests, such as employees, and/or the wider community? *Secondly*, it has stimulated an expansion of what is considered to be appropriate knowledge about organisations and organisational behaviour. Within a Kuhnian-type diachronic model the revolutionary paradigm always has to justify itself in terms of the normal paradigm, because they are both pursuing the same objectives (and it is by no means inevitable that the revolutionary paradigm will triumph, even if it does have better explanatory power, unless it gains sufficient support). But within a synchronic model such justification is irrelevant – the various paradigms are not pursuing the same objectives, so it would be pointless to try to judge one paradigm in terms of another. It would be meaningless to criticise, for example, a Radical Humanist for not being a Functionalist, since that is not what they intend to be. This has allowed each paradigm to develop and flourish independently. Each paradigm has provided a 'home' for knowledge producers, a conceptual space in which like minds can congregate without having to justify why they are not working in some other paradigm. This has produced a flowering of approaches which are different, particularly to the conventional, orthodox, objectivist and managerialist approaches represented by the previously dominant Functionalist paradigm.

Many knowledge producers in the field of Organisation Studies have long believed that knowledge and ideas about organisations and organisational behaviour which do not fit into the assumptions of the Functionalist paradigm are, nonetheless, necessary for a fuller understanding of the subject – which is *not* to imply that they all agree about what kind of knowledge this might be. For example, knowledge producers in the Interpretivist paradigm have focused on micro-political aspects, such as culture, emotion, theatrical metaphors; those in the Radical Structuralist paradigm have focused on macro-political aspects, such as the impact of the interrelations between organisations and the state and the capitalist control of the labour process; those in the Radical Humanist paradigm have focused on the nature and role of organised life and how this might be made more suitable in terms of human needs – a direct inversion of Functionalist approaches, since Functionalism concerns itself, primarily, with how to get individuals to fit 'the needs of the organisation', while Radical Humanism concerns itself, primarily, with how to get organisations to fit the needs of people, both materially and psychologically.

The concept of discourse has also been very influential. While Burrell and Morgan's paradigm model can be seen as a system for classifying knowledge about organisations – they call it a map – which, therefore, says little about organisations themselves, Foucault's work can be seen to be about the process of organisation itself. It has been applied to a lot of specific areas of Organisation Studies, such as human resource management, business history, corporate governance, accounting, management control, organisational discipline. However, the full flavour of the concept of discourse, and, indeed, of its applications in Organisation Studies, cannot be properly appreciated without consideration of the concept of **power**, which is central to this work, especially in its relation to knowledge. This will be developed in the next chapter.

Further potential

In spite of the impact these concepts have had in Organisation Studies, the work which has been stimulated is still relatively disparate, and the assumption that it is managerial interests, rather than any other interests, which need to be served by knowledge production in the field is still a powerful influence. Thus, management knowledge is still often taught as being true and unproblematic, and relatively little attention is drawn to the fundamental issues concerning both the knowledge itself and the interests it serves. Even where knowledge is not part of this managerialist approach, there is a tendency to present it *as if* it were part of a unified body of knowledge about organisations and organisational behaviour. This is driven partly by the requirements of the dominant discourse, with its demands concerning who, what, where, how and why. Knowledge production that ignores these constraints finds difficulty in being legitimated as 'Organisational Behaviour knowledge'. It is also partly because many theorists, while recognising that there is not a unified body of theory, wish that there were.

However, **conformity to the requirements of a discourse which they are trying to oppose both stunts the impact of these different approaches and is confusing for those seeking to learn about organisations and organisational behaviour**, who are left with the impression that there is a unified body of relevant knowledge but are aware that a lot of this theory is contradictory. It is vital that problems of knowledge and knowledge production in this field are recognised and examined, not least because, without this, not only will the field remain confusing, but also the potential variety of ways of defining and solving organisational problems will not be realised. The dominant Functionalist approaches to understanding organisational behaviour have been addressing the same problems for the last two centuries without producing definitive solutions, but the tendency of managerialist approaches to go round in circles, reiterating approaches which have not worked in the past, will not be escaped unless their claim to be the *only* legitimate approaches is challenged. The problems remain. Other approaches are available – but they are part of different understandings of what knowledge is and how it can be produced. Functionalism has been legitimated by its scientific-ness. If that scientism can be shown to be spurious, it loses its claim to primacy and other approaches can make claims to produce legitimate knowledge. **The legitimating test of validity should not be conformity to a particular type of knowledge, but should *only* be the ability to solve problems.**

Organisational behaviour and knowledge

Suppose that all cookery books were written by deeply committed vegetarians – we might suspect, in that case, that our knowledge of possible foods would be somewhat limited. Yet this situation is precisely analogous to Organisational Behaviour: texts have tended to reflect a very partial view of what constitutes human behaviour. Generally speaking, organisational employees are seen as a sub-optimally performing resource that, with carrot or stick, can be improved. A certain amount of structural and environmental awareness may be needed to obviate problems such as group think, halo effects, 'poor' cultural values, but, with the application of the right techniques, all these things can be corrected. Abilities and capabilities are assumed to be distributed hierarchically – the higher up you are, the cleverer you must be – and, therefore, it is possible to furnish some people (managers) with techniques for optimising the contribution of the others (the managed). End of story.

In the light of what we have discussed in this chapter, this can be seen as a very particular view, sustainable only within one particular perspective. **If behaviour is understood as a signifier, then what it means cannot be specified and depends on who is doing the interpreting.** All interpretations are equally valid. To take account of only one – that of the manager – is to demean (de-mean) the understanding of the actors by treating them as merely passive reactors to managerial directives. It is also to prioritise managers' power to signify over consideration of the supposed problem, and to forego the insights that might be offered by other approaches or understandings. Of course, not to take this one-sided approach would inevitably result in seeing people as more than just employees and as having concerns beyond organisational productivity, effectiveness, and so on. This would necessarily make management a more complex activity.

On the other hand, management *is* a complex activity, and ignoring complexity does not make it go away, it only generates inadequate solutions to problems. Thus, for example, managerialist approaches, focused principally on issues of *organisational* benefit, frequently result in labour intensification, based on the assumption that people are never working as hard as they can. But it is recognised by other approaches that this leads, at the *individual* level, to stress, absenteeism, workaholism, work-related illness, and so on, which has important, and negative, repercussions at the organisational level. This would seem to imply that labour intensification is counterproductive. Or, take the example of group dynamics: from a managerialist point of view, the purpose of group dynamics should be to improve operational efficiency, but other approaches recognise that the dynamics of any social group are bound to be more extensive than those that managers believe to be suitable. Such dynamics cannot be simply ignored, they are part of what it means to be human – and they are not necessarily dysfunctional in management terms. It is this existing plurality of behavioural understandings and purposes that needs to be foregrounded in thinking about organisational behaviour. Its continued underestimation is not a problem of behaviour but a problem of the rules of appropriateness in knowledge production.

A TALE FROM THE VILLAGE PUMP (*KNOWLEDGE*)

(*See the Case Study in Appendix 2, pages 340–3*)

Knowledge is, undoubtedly, a key factor in this case. It could be suggested that Farr, as an important member of the 'Establishment' of the time, was part of a Kuhnian normal paradigm of the understanding, explanation and investigation of the causes of cholera. Snow, on the other hand, was a more minor figure in these terms – even, perhaps, more appropriately seen as a member of a different field: a doctor rather than, primarily, a statistician, for example. Snow was widely criticised by the scientific establishment, on the grounds that he did not do science 'in the right way', and it was claimed that this was why his hypothesis was not acceptable.

- How does Foucault's concept of discourse help explain the resistance to Snow's claims?

Case   EXPERT KNOWLEDGE

In France in 1863 there occurred what amounted to a revolution. It was an election year, and one that was taking place during a fairly prolonged period of social turmoil. There was a great deal of pressure on Emperor Napoléon III, both from the governing elites, who sought to maintain the status quo, and from others who demanded that the power of these elites should be curtailed, in the context of more general demands for liberalisation. Napoléon III wanted to satisfy both camps – the trick was to answer calls for liberalisation while, at the same time, not alarming the elites unduly. One of the many arenas in which conflict was to lead to a kind of liberalisation was that of the Fine Arts, and painting in particular. The revolution in question here was one of Art, but it was also, certainly, intimately connected with power and politics.

What constituted Good Art was, and still is, determined by experts. Good Art – in this case, painting – was allowed to be exhibited in the Salon of the French Académie des Beaux Arts. This was, and had been for almost two hundred years, in effect, the only public exhibition of such art, and therefore the only means by which artists could publicise, and so sell, their work. However, in the 1860s a new way of painting was emerging. This new style did not find favour with the guardians of Good Art and they successfully blocked the showing of the new approach. Such was the unrest among artists caused by this 'censorship' that Napoléon III decreed (or permitted, depending on which expert you believe) that there should be an exhibition space available for paintings rejected by the Salon – the Salon des Refusés. The establishment of the Salon des Refusés broke the stranglehold that the official Salon had had on exhibiting and fundamentally challenged the claimed right of the official experts to define what constituted Good Art.

In 1874 a group of painters, some of whom had experienced rejection of their work by the official Salon, mounted their own exhibition. This group

▶

called themselves the Société Anonyme des Artistes Peintres, Sculpteurs, Graveurs, and included Monet, Sisley, Renoir, Pissaro, Cézanne, Berthe Morisot, Guillaumin, Manet and Degas, though not all of these exhibited in 1874. One of the paintings in this first exhibition was of the harbour at Le Havre in early morning mist. It was called *Impression – Sunrise* and was painted by Claude Monet. One critic of the exhibition, Louis Leroy, adopted the title of this painting to label the group of artists 'The Impressionists'. This was intended to be uncomplimentary, indeed derogatory. Although this name was at first disliked by the artists, they quickly adopted it themselves. This approach to painting was what we now know, imprecisely, as Impressionism, and led to the equally imprecise notion of an 'Impressionist School' of artists. The growth in public appreciation of this 'School' took considerably longer.

The hostile reaction to the Impressionists was widespread among art 'experts'. They were described in such terms as 'so-called artists', 'madmen' and 'lunatics', and their work as 'supposed paintings', 'aberrations' and 'rubbish'. However, not everyone was opposed to this radical new art. In particular, one art dealer and expert, Paul Durand-Ruel, actively supported them and, by purchasing their work, enabled a number of them to continue working. Durand-Ruel came close to bankruptcy himself through his belief in Impressionism and it was a further 10 years before his faith in the Impressionists was proved to be well-founded, when he took a large number of paintings to New York and found many willing buyers. However, even in the early twentieth century the art establishment, and not just in France, was still exercising a negative controlling influence on the work of the Impressionists.

During the first half of the twentieth century Impressionism came, gradually, to be recognised as a valid approach to painting, and became a starting point for many further developments in painting. Its products became highly sought after by both public and private collections. Today, works by the Impressionists which were regarded as virtually worthless when they were painted, fetch prices in the tens of millions of pounds. Many are bought by corporations purely as investments and are kept in storage, rather than displayed.

Not surprisingly, as the approach of the Impressionists has become normalised, new ways of doing art have emerged, approaches seen as opposed to the 'naturalistic' art developed by the Impressionists, non-representational and non-naturalistic approaches, such as Abstract Art. The revolutionary insights of the Impressionists are now seen as ordinary, and incapable of capturing whatever it is that an artist seeks. But the Salon des Refusés can be seen as giving rise to what has become a 'tradition' of alternative showcases for revolutionary, or just experimental, art, such as the Edinburgh Fringe and off-Broadway. Now, rejection by the principal experts is no longer seen as fatal, to careers or to ideas, and artists simply go away and start up a new discourse, seek other experts or become their own experts. On the other hand, Impressionism remains very popular – some suggest that it is this very popularity that has, once again, 'devalued' it, as Art if not as investment. But then, it is sometimes said that, in our post-Modern times, the distinction between 'high art' and 'low art' is itself only the expression of expert opinion, expert power.

- To what extent can this history of the reaction to a new style of art be seen as a matter of politics, rather than of aesthetics?

- What does this history suggest about the nature of discourse?

- What does this history suggest about the nature of expert knowledge?

- Given Durand-Ruel's almost lone persistence in the face of other expert opinion that Impressionism was 'rubbish', does this indicate better or worse expert opinion in his case – or can his persistence be explained in other ways?

(Other chapters that would be useful and relevant in analysing the case *include* Semiotics (2), Structure (3), Power (5), Ideology (7) and Boundary (9).)

Bibliography

There is a big industry engaged in asking questions about knowledge, such as what is knowledge? what is science? what is the relationship between the social and the scientific? is social science the same as natural science? is natural science the same as social science? and so on. Not surprisingly, there is a massive literature. Just one or two relevant contributions are Polanyi (1962), Ravetz (1971), Feyerabend (1978). For an interesting more recent twist to the debate, see writers on what is known as 'New Physics', such as Bohm (1983), Capra (1983), Jones (1983), Zukav (1984). Another interesting slant can be found in personal accounts of the social process of scientific discovery, such as Watson (1968) on the discovery of DNA. A more general approach to issues of science is, for example, Lawson and Appignanesi (1989). It is also not surprising that these disputes are well represented in Organisation Studies. There are those who argue that the only true knowledge about organisations and management is knowledge produced by methods analogous to those of the natural sciences – Donaldson (1985, 1996), for example. There are those who argue that knowledge about organisations and management could be scientific but has not yet achieved that – Whitley (1984), for example. A notable attack on the claim of management knowledge to be scientific was made by the philosopher MacIntyre (1985) – a response to this can be found in Anthony (1986), another in Mangham (1995), which is also followed by a number of commentaries. There are lots of different angles on the issues in knowledge and its production in Organisation Studies, ranging from quality as science to the social, political and ideological process of knowledge production. See, for example, Carey (1977), Rose (1978), Thompson (1983), Reed (1985), Jackson and Carter (1995a), Clegg and Palmer (1996), Willmott (1997).

For a useful overview of the intellectual history of the Enlightenment, see Porter (2000).

An accessible and relevant introduction to the issues of what we can know is Baggott (2005). See also Borgmann (1992).

There is also a lot of material on paradigms, both outside and inside the field of knowledge about organisations, ranging from a strictly rigorous analytical approach to a generally ordinary language use of the term. Seminal works are Kuhn (1970) – but see also Lakatos and Musgrave (1972) – and Burrell and Morgan (1979). Other uses are represented by, for example, Lincoln (1985) and Guba (1990). Burrell and Morgan's approach has been very influential, and Morgan has extended this, particularly through his work on metaphors – see, for example, Morgan (1980, 1990, 1997) – and Morgan (1983a) also reflects the paradigm model. The aspect of the paradigm models which has been most con-troversial has been that of incommensurability – see, for example, Reed (1985), Hassard (1988), Jackson and Carter (1991, 1993), Willmott (1993). See also Hassard and Keleman (2002). Clegg *et al.* (2006) widely reflects the continuing debate about paradigms and, in 1998, the journal *Organization* devoted a special issue to the 'problem' of incommensurability (Scherer, 1998).

Derrida's concept of techno-mediatic power is particularly developed in Derrida (1994). The idea of, and the prevalence of, the management guru is espe-cially relevant to this issue – see, for example, Huczynski (1993), Clark and Salaman (1996), Jackson and Carter (1998b).

For the concept of discourse in Foucault's work see, for example, Foucault (1970, 1971, 1974). Commentaries on Foucault's work often provide a useful introductory overview of the concept – for example, Sheridan (1980), Dreyfus and Rabinow (1982), Cousins and Hussain (1984), Smart (1985), Fillingham (1993). This usage of the concept of discourse needs to be distinguished from other uses, such as the interpretive approach known as discourse analysis. The capitalist regime of truth figures especially in Foucault (1979b), and in Gordon (1980) and in Burchell *et al.* (1991). A similar idea given special prominence in a study of contemporary organisation can be found in Deleuze and Guattari (1984). The sigificance of capitalism as the context of organisation and organisa-tional behaviour is not widely addressed but there are exceptions, notably in Labour Process Theory – see, for example, Thompson (1983), Knights and Willmott (1990). See also Clegg and Dunkerley (1980) and Nichols (1980). Alvesson and Willmott (1996) is another example.

The concept of rhetoric is another one that is used in various ways – see, for example, Legge (1995). The particular use that we are referring to in this chapter is based on Perelman (1979, 1982) – a paper further developing this approach is Carter and Jackson (2004a). On relevant issues connected with law, see Bennett and Feldman (1981).

The application of Foucault's work to organisational issues is flourishing but dispersed. An accessible collection which covers many of the topics mentioned in this chapter is McKinlay and Starkey (1998). See also, for example, Burrell (1988, 1996, 1997), Donzelot (1991), Deetz (1992), Townley (1994), Jackson and Carter (1995b).

There are other perspectives which have challenged the conventional approach to knowledge and its production, in Organisation Studies and in other disciplines, without necessarily using a Foucauldian approach. Gender Studies is a particular example – see, for example, Spender (1981).

CHAPTER 5

Power

This chapter proposes an interactional view of power, rather than a purely structural view. Taking the relatively neglected concept of property rights as the basis of the legitimation of power, the concept of power is compared to that of authority, via consideration of why people work and of the significance of a wage labour economy in issues of compliance. Locating organisations as part of the contemporary system of governance, a poststructuralist approach to understanding power is explored, and concepts of normalisation, surveillance, micro-power and disciplinary power are elaborated. Building on the discussion of knowledge in the previous chapter, the mutuality of power and knowledge is emphasised, together with their role in the active formulation of what constitutes truth, which then provides the measure of good or bad (deviant) organisational behaviour.

It has been argued so far that signifiers – devices for communicating and understanding – have no intrinsic meaning, and, therefore, no correct meaning, and that such understandings as we do have arise from the ability of individuals to impose a perceived structure, a perceived order, on them. This has implications for what it is possible to know. But, even though it may be recognised that, in practice, knowledge is relative, it is still treated as if it is cumulative, objective, unified and available to all – it is treated *as if* there is *the* correct knowledge, *the* correct solution to problems, *the one best way*. How this apparent contradiction comes about can be explained in terms of the way in which knowledge, though always partial, is contained in a particular discourse which regulates legitimacy for certain *kinds* of knowledge. To understand why some discourses are more prominent than others it is necessary to have a concept of power.

Concepts of power are not well developed in the discourse of Organisational Behaviour. In this chapter we will explore ways of thinking about power, and the reasons for its negligent treatment in the discourse of Organisational Behaviour, together with the implications for understanding organisational behaviour without a concept of power. We will then turn to consider the different understanding of it that follows when the what and how of power are included.

The power of ownership

In an organisational context **power is the ability to get someone to do something that they do not particularly want to do.** This seems relatively uncontentious. Indeed, one could argue that such reluctance is precisely why organisations need managers. If people in organisations always wanted to do what they had to do, then much of the need for managers, whether parents, teachers or bureaucrats, would disappear. Children would always get up for school on time, and would demand to do the washing up after meals; in schools, registers would become redundant and homework would inevitably be submitted on time; at work, workers would never arrive late or work slower than their maximum pace. Clearly, this does not describe organisational life and so managers are required to ensure compliance – to ensure that people do what is required of them, obey, discharge their **proper duty**. But where does this idea of 'proper duty' come from? How do we know what people should do and how they should behave? In terms of modern work organisations, the idea can be traced back to the concept of **property rights**.

Property rights represent a deeply embedded value, certainly in the capitalist world. This value stems from the belief that if someone owns something, then, providing that they do not damage the rights of other people, they are free to do what they like with their property. Thus, if you own, say, an expensive watch, you may choose to wear it, sell it, give it away, smash it to pieces, or almost anything else you may wish. If you own land then, generally speaking, you can prevent other people from coming on to it, even if you are not using it. If you own a factory then you can decide to use it to produce widgets or, if you wish, you can shift your widget-making to another country. Even if you own something which you do not need but others need desperately, there is no obligation on you to share what you have. So fundamental and ubiquitous is the concept of the rights of ownership that it is very rarely discussed, especially in the context of organisational behaviour. Yet it is central to our understanding of organised work.

Suppose that, at the start of the Industrial Revolution, you decide to set up as a self-employed widget maker. You can decide how much time you want to devote to widget-making, and how hard you work during that time. After a while you decide that you need help in making your widgets, so you employ an assistant. Obviously, you do not want this person slacking and harming your ability to produce widgets, so you employ them on a piece rate carefully calculated so that, if they are industrious, they can help you to produce the necessary widgets and, at the end of the week, they will have earned enough to make it worthwhile continuing in your employ. If the piece rate is too low their earnings will not be sufficient to attract them to work. If it is too high they will be able to earn what they need from doing less work or from attending fewer hours. This is something in your control because you own the business – in other words, because of property rights. And it must be noted, this delicate calculation is the basis of all the principles of wage labour, whether piece rate, hourly rate, salary or whatever. After a while, and after taking on more assistants, you decide to retire from running your business, to enjoy the profits that you have made. You do not want to close down your business as it is a nice source of income for you, but you cannot trust your workers to keep up production in your absence, and, therefore, you employ a different kind of worker – an agent, or, as we call them nowadays, a manager. This person's job is

Property rights

In an incisive contribution to the ongoing debate on the philosophy of property rights, the eponymous Crocodile Dundee of the film (played by Paul Hogan) makes the point that arguing over who owns what land is like two fleas arguing over who owns the dog they are on! In the UK, for example, the idea that there should be land that nobody owns is anathema to the 'owning classes' – see the periodic and often successful attempts by landowners to enclose common land – but in Australian Aboriginal culture there was, apparently, no equivalent concept of property rights over land (see, for example, Bruce Chatwin's *The Songlines* (1987)). In any case, since ownership of land is not God-given, it is acquired, ultimately, through the exercise of power. One of the most obvious examples of this occurs after war, when the victorious side acquires for itself the land it has 'conquered' – in the UK a significant proportion of the pattern of current land ownership can be traced back to the last time the country was conquered by a foreign power, in 1066. In other parts of the world, however, land ownership is still an issue. Much land was acquired by force of power in, for example, Africa, Australia and the USA, during the eighteenth and nineteenth centuries through one kind of colonisation or another. Dispossessed native peoples are still in dispute with the successor governments over the appropriation of their land. Similarly, Jews are in dispute with various governments about the land, and other property, appropriated from them by the Nazis before and during the Second World War. More recently, property rights have changed hands in the former Yugoslavia as part of the process of 'ethnic cleansing'. Another example of a famous and long-running debate over ownership is that between the UK and Greece over the Elgin Marbles.

A current debate which affects us all is the question of who owns the fish in the sea. Countries are legally entitled to declare that they own a certain amount of sea around their coastline and this has been assumed to include the fish in it. One problem with this assumption is that the fish move around. Presumably, it is not necessary for the fish to be aware that they are owned, but the usual purpose of at least one of the parties to any dispute about ownership of fish is to claim the right to kill them. The whole issue has proved particularly problematic in the EU and recently the UK had to pay compensation to Spanish fishermen for having excluded them from UK waters.

Property rights can be an issue in some hitherto unexpected contexts. In recent years the question of who owns the semen that a man leaves in a woman after sexual intercourse has been the subject of various legal judgments. The problems revolve around the question of whether a woman has the (property) right to use the semen to have a child, irrespective of the wishes of the man who gave it to her – and, certainly in the USA, it has been judged in law to be a gift – when the man subsequently becomes financially responsible for the support of such a child. Similar problems have arisen in other related areas, such as fertility treatment. A more penetrating use of the concept of property rights in human affairs is hardly conceivable.

not to produce widgets themselves, but to ensure that the other employees do, at the required rate. In other words, this agent, or manager, is employed to look after your interest as owner, to safeguard your property rights.

This right of owners to determine, through their agents, what is the proper duty of employees has not changed significantly over the years and is still characteristic of contemporary work organisations. Certainly, there may be some legal restrictions on what an owner, or manager, can demand, such as health and safety regulations, and certainly, employees can try to modify these demands, to a greater or lesser extent. But, ultimately, the owner has rights in the workplace that the employee does not have: ownership of the jobs. In the context of work organisations this is referred to as **ownership of the means of production**. However, the full import of property rights cannot be understood without the dimension of **abstract property rights**.

Not everyone owns enough material goods to be able to ensure their own survival – they do not have control over those things necessary for their continued existence. What they do have, however, is **labour power** – briefly, the ability to do work. In order to survive, therefore, they can sell this labour power, that is, become employed by someone who can supply the opportunity to work in return for payment, and thus the means to survive. In effect, some people control the means of production and, in so doing, create the necessity for other people to sell their labour power. The significance of this transaction is that, even though labour power is not a physical thing, it is nonetheless implicitly assumed that, in buying labour power (employing people), the buyer/employer gains property rights over the labour power that they have bought. By analogy with the ownership of things, they can then dispose of this labour power as they wish.

It is this idea of gaining property rights over labour power that underlies the assumption in organisations, and in Organisational Behaviour, that owners and managers have the right to expect compliance. Indeed, it underlies the whole concept of the right to manage. There is a problem: what is bought is the labour power, not the person, but you cannot have one without the other. The problem has been 'resolved', however, simply by tending to ignore the person who is the repository of the labour power. Conventionally, the discourse of Organisational Behaviour has dealt with employees in organisations as if they are workers rather than people, and organisations themselves are notorious, in general, for ignoring the parts of the employee that are not seen as precisely useful for their purposes (the use of the labour power), and that may even be seen by employers as dysfunctional to that purpose – as defined by the purchaser of the labour power. It is implicit in this that **if a person sells their labour power it becomes their duty to make sure that that labour power is available to its purchaser, so that the purchaser can do with it as they wish**, irrespective of the consideration that it resides in a person, who is not bought.

Power versus authority

Property rights as such are rarely questioned or challenged. Since most people would recognise that workers could probably find other things to do with their time than to fulfil the desires of the owners of their labour power, it is, therefore, necessary to have managers who can **enforce compliance** – in other words, managers who have **power** over others. Yet the concept of power is almost totally absent from the discourse of Organisational Behaviour. The preferred concept is that of **authority**.

The distinction between power and authority was suggested by the German sociologist, Max Weber. Weber was interested in the attempt to create effective organisations and, as part of this, considered why people in organisations did as they were told. He decided that people accepted this duty because that was what they wanted to do. Hence, he argued, obedience was not a matter of power, but one of authority. The distinction between the two is that **power is about getting someone to do something irrespective of their desire to do it or the extent of their resistance to doing it, while authority rests on the assumption that the person is willing to obey, and accepts the right of the person doing the ordering to expect compliance.** Thus, authority figures – managers – were there to get people to do what they wanted to do anyway but were not sure how to do it. In this model the job of a manager is to be a facilitator: to create the conditions where employees can do those things that they want to do. The notion that management is simply directing people to do what they really want to do but do not have the ability to organise is a much more pleasant rationale for management than the notion that it is coercive, forcing people to obey. Thus, the concept of authority as an explanation for compliance has been seized upon, to the exclusion of the concept of power.

Power/authority

In his book *The Assembly Line* (1981), about his time working for Citroën, Robert Linhart relates the story of Demarcy and his work bench. Demarcy repaired minor manufacturing blemishes on car doors, prior to their use in assembling the car. This was a highly skilled task requiring some difficult manoeuvres. Over the years, Demarcy had constructed a work bench from odd bits and pieces he had found lying around which aided this work. It was not pretty but it served its purpose admirably and he was very efficient at his job. One day, and without consulting Demarcy, the Work Study people removed his old bench and gave him a new one. Much prettier maybe, but no use for the job Demarcy had to do, and disruptive of the manoeuvres necessary to do it. Demarcy's supervisor knew that the new bench was useless, but felt that he could not question a management decision. Demarcy's work rate suffered, despite his best efforts to manage the new bench, and this attracted the exasperated attention of the management. He lost the ability to perform at his previous level. After a suitable period the new work bench was discreetly removed, and the old work bench returned. But it was too late. Demarcy had lost confidence in his ability, was experiencing his work as stressful, and eventually went off sick.

- Given the above definitions of, and distinction between, power and authority, which best describes Demarcy's situation?
- What arguments might be used to justify describing it in terms of **authority**?
- What arguments might be used to justify describing it in terms of **power**?

The difficulty with the concept of power

The general assumption in the study of organisations is that organisational members act **rationally** in an effort to achieve the goals of the organisation as defined by managers. By 'rational' is meant that, even though people might not literally want to work or to be required to obey, they make a calculation that this is what is necessary to achieve the desired outcome. This assumption is what informs the belief that employees act willingly and that management is the facilitation of the outcomes, that managers know best how the outcomes can be achieved. Even in areas of Organisational Behaviour where it is sometimes recognised that employees do not always act rationally (such as Organisation Development), it is assumed that, by the application of appropriate techniques, this can be overcome: people can be guided so that they do act rationally. This might be achieved through a wide range of techniques, such as the payment of incentives, or the use of techniques of behaviour modification.

The basis of such techniques is the belief that organisation itself is a rational process, even if the employees themselves are not rational. This belief in the rationality of organisations is important as a means of legitimating what organisations 'do'. If, as a student of management, you are asked to write an essay on, say, leadership, this appears to contribute to your education as a manager. However, if you are asked to go and wash your professor's car, this appears to be outside the scope of education and so loses legitimacy. To a significant extent, what is rational in an organisation is evaluated by reference to what the organisation meant to achieve. (The issue of rationality is explored in more depth in Chapter 6.)

In terms of the example, it is assumed that students want to do those things that contribute to their education, so the professor has the authority to get you to do them as necessary. There is no assumption that you want to wash the professor's car, so the professor has no authority to make you do so. In the same way, it is assumed that organisational effort is directed only to those activities necessary for the successful achievement of organisational objectives, including employee objectives. Conversely, it is assumed that whatever an employee is required to do is necessary for the achievement of those objectives. The justification of authority, moreover, is based on the assumption that all organisational members agree on what the organisational goals are, that all agree that the activities required are necessary for their achievement, and that all wish to do whatever is necessary.

Authority is assumed to relate to the achievement of organisational objectives, but **power** implies that the person with power can get people without it to do whatever they wish, *irrespective* of whether it contributes to the organisational objectives. In other words, **power is arbitrary** – it can be used for any purpose whatsoever. Clearly, it is impossible to sustain an argument for the rationality of organisations if those in control of them, the managers, can do it in any fashion they choose and towards any end. It is this arbitrariness that has contributed to the perception of the *unattractiveness* of the concept of power, together with its implications for organisational legitimacy.

Authority versus Power

Why people work

Also underlying the preference for the concept of authority in the discourse of Organisational Behaviour is a set of assumptions about why people work, based on the notion that it is voluntary, and that people are willing to be told what to do and to do whatever is necessary to achieve organisational goals. However, we live in a wage labour economy, the principle of which is that people sell their labour power in return for a wage which allows them to purchase those things that they want, need or desire. It follows from this, therefore, that **the primary reason for working is to obtain money**. This is not a popular view, however, and great emphasis has been placed on the social and psychological satisfactions to be derived from work. But the crucial test of why people work is that, if the employer stops paying them a wage, they will stop coming to work. Thus, any non-material motivations there may be for working must be seen as secondary to that of obtaining money. Unfortunately, to get the money one has, usually, to do more than just turn up – it is necessary to perform tasks, as directed by a manager. Nonetheless, *the object of going to work is not to do the work, but to get the money*. Working is merely a requirement for that outcome.

Once at work, people will, of course, have a vested interest in what they are required to do, and how they are required to do it. They may, indeed, make demands for improvements in, for example, working conditions, or the design of their job, but this cannot be taken to mean that these factors have precedence over the desire for a wage. Perhaps such demands might indicate the development of perceptions about what might constitute reasonable conditions of work in return for their effort. These might be informed by observation of what other people get – but it cannot be suggested that there are any general standards about what is reasonable. None of this is to argue that people do not get other things from work, apart from money, but it is to argue that such things should be seen as secondary. A wage labourer – anyone who survives by selling their labour power – can survive without job satisfaction, but cannot survive without a wage.

If the assumption that people work voluntarily and willingly in pursuit of organisational goals, such as profit, is taken away, then the justification for the prevalence of the concept of authority *fails*, and it becomes necessary to resort to the concept of power to explain compliance. The concept of authority implies that, in return for a wage, workers will perceive that they have a duty to do what managers require of them. It implies that people work because they wish to do so, that what they do is seen by them as a legitimate requirement, and that there is consensus about all aspects of the employment relationship – in particular, about the organisational goals that are being pursued. The concept of power, on the other hand, makes no assumptions about why people work, nor about the legitimacy of what is required of them, nor about consensus. **The single focus of power is compliance:** in return for a wage, people must do whatever is required of them, whether they accept its legitimacy or not. Power always involves the threat of sanction: if compliance is not forthcoming, then neither is the wage, and, in general, the wage is more important to the individual worker than the individual worker is to the organisation.

The focus of Organisational Behaviour on so-called intrinsic satisfactions, on the internal dynamics of organisation and the second-level characteristics of work is itself part of the tendency to treat people as workers rather than as people. It has economic advantages from a management point of view, since strategies that address issues of non-material satisfactions are always cheaper than matching expectations of financial reward. Yet it also symbolises the contradiction between the role of the manager as the agent of owners and the claim that the role of managers is principally to facilitate – it is only to state the obvious to say that if, for example, job enrichment strategies did not yield increases in productivity, they would not be implemented simply because they increased job satisfaction. The focus on intrinsic rewards is part of a double standard, where workers are supposed not to prioritise economic gain, but managers are supposed to do so.

Importantly, such approaches also ignore the extent to which organisations are part of a larger social milieu which influences people. The 'culture' of this milieu is what forces people to work, rather than simple individual desire to do so. We sell our labour power, not because this is what we want to do, but because we are part of a socio-economic system where this is what it is necessary to do in order to survive and where existence outside that system is only feasible if we are self-employed, very rich or prepared to tolerate the disadvantages of being economically dependent on the state, or on charity. But being part of a system cannot be taken to signify that that system is legitimate, whether at the macro level of society as a whole or at the micro level of the organisation of work. Compliance within the system can only be taken to signify that the alternatives are perceived to be less attractive, or perhaps unachievable. Given this, **the concept of authority is not only not particularly useful, appropriate or adequate, its persistent use actually serves to *mask* other experiences, understandings.** The concept of authority portrays an organisational world in which the use of power is actively disguised. This portrayal, on one hand, benefits some interests at the expense of others and, on the other, fails to accommodate widespread contrary experience. Yet its ubiquity is such that we may almost be led to conclude that such experience is 'incorrect', that the organisational world is really the way such theory says it is, rather than the way we experience it.

Resistance

Certainly, we may choose voluntarily to give up some autonomy in some situations, such as accepting employment in an organisation. In such a case, however, we may find ourselves giving up more autonomy than expected or intended – for example, if we are discriminated against in some way. Power has been described as a 'zero sum game' – the more power one person has, the less someone else has. If a person acquires the ability to make you do something that you do not want to do, your own decision-making power does not remain constant, but decreases in proportion to the power gained by the other. That you may not want to play the 'game' does not matter, you still lose. Imagine a resource that no one owns; it may be considered desirable, by some, for no one to own it, so that it can be available for anyone to use. But if someone gains control of the resource, the right of others to use it is lost. This is classically the case with land ownership, whether in relation to colonisation, enclosures of common land or corporate acquisition. A variation on this is the case where someone acquires land with the sole purpose of stopping someone else from using it – an example of this is the recent referral of some supermarkets in the UK to the Competition Commission, one of the issues being the buying up of development land simply to prevent competitors acquiring the sites. It is also very much the issue currently surrounding the appropriation of common resources such as air and water. And, although you may not want to participate in a struggle for power, you can, in effect, be co-opted – you may have no choice. If, for example, you live near an organisation that is polluting your environment, although you may have no connection with the organisation other than proximity, you inevitably lose the freedom to, say, breathe clean air. Those proactive in the quest for power tend to win, and those who do not want to play tend to lose. The only choices available are to suffer or to resist.

It should be expected, and considered normal, that the exercise of power, in whatever arena, will give rise to resistance, overt or covert. **Resistance is always a challenge to the powerful.** It can take many forms, ranging from small personal acts of subversion to collective action, which might itself be anything from local to global. The rewards that people seek from acts of resistance are also very varied – they might range from a sense of personal satisfaction to changing the balance of power, in a particular situation or more generally, to 'changing the world'. In the discourse of Organisational Behaviour it is conventional to see resistance as something, minimally, to be managed, and, at best, to be neutralised. Resistance is regarded as misguided, ill-informed, recalcitrant or deviant. A particular case is to be found in the phrase 'resistance to change', ubiquitous in texts on management, and probably a ubiquitous phenomenon. The phrase signifies the lack of enthusiasm on the part of the managed for those attempts by managers to 'make things better'. It signifies that change is always good and desirable, and that resistance is always dysfunctional. (See also Chapter 6.)

Nonetheless, resistance to the desires of those with power has a very long history of bringing about improvement, both within work organisations and more generally. Examples include improvements in health and safety at work, reductions in working hours, regulations regarding pay, legislation to outlaw discrimination on grounds of gender, and other forms of discrimination – and the liberation of entire nations from oppressive occupation. The fundamental quality of all resistance, whether large or small, is that it always represents alternatives to the views, or desires, of the powerful. Resistance represents the opportunities that have been, or will be, forgone by a particular course of action.

Governance

Recent social theories, notably Critical Theory and Poststructuralism, have conceptualised organisations as part of a general system of what Michel Foucault calls **governance**. These approaches place very strong emphasis on the need to see organisations as embedded in their social context if we are to understand them. The concept of governance, in Foucault's terms, refers to the broad process of organisation of people and things. One of the functions of the nation state is to regulate the behaviour of people within it, to create order, to organise. In a way, this is what defines the existence of a nation state – without it there is anarchy. In the past most countries had coercive systems of regulation, such as feudalism or absolute monarchies, and some contemporary societies, usually called totalitarian regimes, still use such methods, whereby people can be compelled, by threat of sanction, to behave in specified ways. The development of liberal democracy was partly motivated by resistance to such compulsion and by desire to limit the arbitrary power of some individuals to organise all the rest. Nation states can still, and do still, use coercive power on some elements of their citizenry, such as the criminal, the mentally ill and the young, but, generally, adult populations tend to resist overtly coercive regulation, such that its use has a tendency to destabilise systems. **The opposite of coercive regulation, however, is not absolute freedom, it is non-coercive regulation.** In contemporary societies governance, in general, is based on attempts to get people to comply voluntarily, as a minimum, and, optimally, to accept positively the legitimacy of those with power to direct them.

Nation states are also economies. In any society it is necessary for people to produce as much wealth as they consume, in order to ensure social reproduction (social continuity). Civilised society requires that people produce more than they can consume, so that the benefits of civilisation, such as education, health, the arts, entertainment, and so on, can be paid for. There is, therefore, a need to get people to work and to produce more than they themselves need to survive. In a capitalist system this is achieved through wage labour organisations. Such organisations have a **dual** function: they not only produce goods and services, but also produce consumers for these goods and services, by paying people. As previously noted, by selling labour power to an organisation people acquire the means to buy the goods and services they desire and if they do not work they experience considerable difficulty in participating in such consumption, however much they may desire to do so. If one exists outside wage labour organisations – for example, being unemployed – it is very difficult to survive economically without resort to, for example, the black economy, or crime. To most people this is not as satisfactory as working for a living.

Work organisations contribute to governance in two specific ways: they provide the opportunity for the wealth creation necessary for the state to flourish, and they also produce the ordered behaviour which is required of the citizenry. They do this through what is known as **disciplinary power.**

Organisations can be conceptualised in terms of hierarchised power, where individuals have little bits of control over other people, such as manager over worker. However, this is a relatively uninformative, and idealised, description of structure. To address the actual operation of power in organisations it is more productive to see organisational relations in terms of disciplinary networks – **matrices of power** – where most people have some power over others, but everyone has someone who has power over them. A few examples will suffice to give a flavour of the point: the power of clergyman over parishioner, of gamekeeper over rambler, of school prefect over other school-children, of doctor over patient, of conductor over passenger, of bouncer over clubber, of shopkeeper over customer, of waiter over diner, of car mechanic over car driver, of secretary over boss, of referee over player, of councillor over rate-payer, of school crossing attendant over other road users. The power exercised in these relationships is formal in the sense that the person who exercises power has a **formal** role *vis-à-vis* those over whom they exercise it, but it is obviously not formal hierarchical power. There is, in all cases, potential for a *reversal* of formal hierarchical power, in the sense that the person over whom power is exercised may, in other circumstances, be much more powerful than the one who exercises power over them – the example of the power of secretary over boss is a pertinent one. **The concept of disciplinary power focuses on how power is used in particular situations**, rather than on structural power relations.

Equally important is the existence of what might be called **informal** power relations, where power is exercised but is not formally legitimated through any means, and often is formally illegitimate. Again, a few examples will illustrate: the power of men over women, of the old over the young and, in other circumstances, of the young over the old, of some ethnic groups over others, of the physically strong over the physically weak. The same kind of power is exercised by anyone who controls any jointly used resource, such as the person who distributes stationery, or the person who sits nearest to the window, or the radiator. Although these examples may seem to represent different orders of significance, there is a common factor in the ability of one person to impose their will on others, to impose their definition of reality on others. This is **micro-power** in operation. However small or transient the moment, **what each person does is to try to exact conformity to their view of the world from others and to use their control of resources of whatever kind – from DNA to pens – to threaten sanctions for non-compliance.** Much of the time the power relation is not even consciously recognised – until it is exercised against us: the waiter who refuses to find you a table because you are not wearing a tie, the referee who chooses to ignore the foul committed on you, the car mechanic who declines your MOT (vehicle roadworthiness certificate) until you have spent some unnecessary money, and so on.

There is always an attempt, however offhand, to legitimate the exercise of power, to provide a reason for it. But the powerless are rarely in a position to determine whether the reasons are genuine or spurious. If the secretary refuses to give you access to your boss, is it because the secretary does not want you to see the boss, or because the boss does not want to see you? The two reasons have widely differing implications, but you will be likely to remain in a state of uncertainty about which is appropriate. **In that the exercise of power represents the imposition of the world view of the powerful, the powerless are always kept in a state of uncertainty about the validity of their own world view, which is denied.**

Each exercise of power is, on the part of the powerful, an ordering, a structuring of what is permissible over what is not permissible, but not with reference to any absolute standards of correct behaviour, or even, very often, with reference to a relative standard: it is just what can be achieved at any particular moment. Nonetheless, there do occur **coalitions** of people who seek to maintain a particular version of right/wrong, good/bad, to represent certain interests. In work organisations, for example, it is the job of a manager, in general, to represent the interests of the owner and if they do not do this they will themselves be out of a job. This does not mean that everything a manager does will be directed to serving those interests, but a sufficient level of such service will be required, although what is signified by 'sufficient' will vary from situation to situation, depending, largely, on the requirements of the owners. Such coalitions can become widespread, so that there appears to be general conformity to particular standards (see also Chapter 7). An important element of the creation of this apparent conformity is what Jacques Derrida called **techno-mediatic power**, as noted in the previous chapter. Although particular events and instances of the exercise of power may seem random, in general they are not, and will conform to the needs of governance, as defined by the governors. It may not be obvious how managers, school crossing attendants and referees all contribute to an overall coherent system of governance, but we shall return to this later.

Disciplinary power at work

Disciplinary power is exercised in multitudinous ways, some overt and some covert, and in all aspects of organisational activity. Connected to every aspect of organisational activity there are rules, norms, values which extend beyond simple functional rules for operation: these rules, norms and values are not just about what is done. All tasks have certain functional requirements necessary to the production of outcomes – widgets, or whatever. But there are also rules which regulate beyond this, but with which it is necessary to comply in order to be judged a satisfactory employee. A fairly straightforward example relates to dress and general appearance. Some rules about clothing have obvious safety implications, such as not having loose long hair near machinery. Yet many dress codes in organisations, such as the wearing of ties for men or of skirts for women, do not have equally obvious implications for job performance. The recently reported banning of beards for train drivers by some rail companies in the UK is an example of a rule that does not seem to be a requirement for the efficient driving of trains, but a requirement for the sake of discipline itself. Other aspects of such discipline are much more subtle, including the regulation of attitudes and behaviours, such as the requirement to be motivated, to show commitment, to be loyal – in other words, to exhibit the characteristics of a 'model employee', as defined by those in the organisation with the power to signify.

The notion of a model employee concerns far more than a worker who is competent and works hard. It is also to do with **conformity and compliance**, with willingness to adopt specified behaviours and, in general, with the delineation of attitudes and behaviours that are labelled as good and worthy of reward. By the same token, attitudes and behaviours that do not seem to conform and, more importantly, are not approved, are labelled bad, and deviant. By definition, deviant behaviour is not the norm and deviants are marginalised and risk sanction. Such sanctions either bring the deviant back into line or deny them the benefits of conformity. However, the term 'deviant' does not signify, for example, villainy or delinquency, but simply 'deviation' from what is considered to be the norm, defined by those who have the power to signify what the norm should be. Equally, what is deviant in one situation may not be similarly regarded in others. For example, in one school wearing something other than the prescribed uniform may be regarded as deviant by teachers, but not by pupils, and in another school it may not be seen as deviant at all. However, where work organisations have uniforms it is usually seen as very clearly deviant not to conform.

Normalisation

Normalisation is the tendency of people to accept as normal the expectations of those who govern them and to comply with them, even though they may not agree with them or see them as useful. It is a process whereby these requirements are acted upon without prompting in the usual course of events. Where there are relations of power it is impossible to ensure compliance in every instance. It is, for example, impossible to ensure that motorists always comply with traffic regulations, yet the system of traffic management clearly works, more or less. Motorists generally observe traffic lights and speed limits, accept rules of priority, and so on, and so traffic flows are maintained. In other words, motorists accept the need to conform to traffic regulations, even though they may not agree that they are sensible and useful and even though there are opportunities to flout them. In the same way, when a person is employed and once they have received instruction on the requirements of their job, even though they may not agree that the requirements are sensible and useful it is assumed that they will conform to such instructions and, indeed, in general they do. The shop assistant will serve customers, the meter reader will read meters, the manager will manage, without further prompting.

However, although there may be a general tendency to conform, it does not mean to say that everyone can be trusted to do everything they should at every opportunity. This being so, it is necessary to have devices for encouraging and ensuring compliance and mechanisms for applying sanctions for non-compliance. Thus, there are speed traps to catch the motorist who exceeds the speed limit. Similarly, work organisations check what workers do to ensure compliance and to correct for non-compliance. Awareness that one *might* be being checked is a spur to doing the job properly, even though there may be opportunities for doing something different. Techniques of **surveillance** are widespread and have an enormous range of sophistication, from timing how long a worker takes to go to the toilet to keystroke monitoring of home-working word processor operators and checking whether electronic mail has been read, from direct supervision to indirect supervision. Increasingly we are watched by cameras, increasingly everything we do is checked. The problem for any individual is that they do not know exactly when or how they are being surveyed. Indeed, the most effective checking systems are precisely those where such ignorance is possible and encouraged, so that people have to assume that they could be being checked at any moment. Given sanctions for non-compliance, the only possible response is to assume that one is always being checked and so to conform accordingly.

This was the principle of the **panopticon**, originally designed by Jeremy Bentham in the nineteenth century as a cheap and efficient way of monitoring the behaviour of prisoners. The panopticon was a type of prison, with cells built in a circle around a central watch tower. Each cell faced the tower and had a window in its rear wall so that the person in the tower could see into any cell at any time but could not themselves be seen. The prisoners knew they could be being watched at any time, but not whether they actually were being watched. The effect of this was to ensure that the prisoners behaved as directed all the time, whether being watched or not. This tendency is known as **self-policing**, controlling one's own behaviour without prompting, so that one always behaves in the way desired by those in control, those with the power of sanction. It is a fundamental element of disciplinary power. The concept of the panopticon was taken up by Foucault as a metaphor for the prevalence of surveillance and compliance in contemporary society. Indeed, Foucault argued specifically that there were very strong parallels between the treatment of prisoners and the treatment of workers, both historically and in the present. The process of surveillance is important in creating normalisation. We even come to think that the surveillance itself is normal and useful, because it controls us – and, more importantly, others – and ensures conformity.

A picture of a panopticon design

Power and knowledge

We have talked so far about how compliance is produced but the question remains as to how those with power know what to require compliance with, know how and for what purpose to exercise their power. The justification for wanting one behaviour rather than another is knowledge. In organisations, and in the discourse of knowledge about organisations, there is a belief that there are better and worse forms of behaviour for achieving organisational goals and that we can distinguish between these in light of knowledge about how organisations operate. Knowledge is seen as providing certainty that we are acting correctly, using power correctly. We 'know' that it is better to have empowered workers than not, better to have enriched jobs than not, better to have one kind of culture rather than another – 'better' meaning more effective at achieving the objectives that the organisation is there to fulfil, the service of the interests of the owners. In other words, we do not guess what is best, or consult chicken entrails, we know what is best because we have knowledge about it.

However, in the previous chapter we argued that knowledge is not objective, that it is constituted within and through discourses, that discourses are the outcome of social, political and economic conditions and that they represent rules about who can say what, where, how and why. Thus, members of a discourse have the power to determine what is correct knowledge and what is incorrect – in effect, to determine what *is* knowledge. Discourses, therefore, represent the particular interests and beliefs of those who are their members. If the people in a discourse changed or if a different discourse emerged, then knowledge would be different. Thus, **knowledge can never be dissociated from power.**

It is not possible to understand knowledge about anything unless the power base to which it is linked is also understood. As was noted in the previous chapter, there is no reason to assume that people who are members of a discourse are there because they have a particular expertise. They are there primarily because of rules that allow them to speak rather than others, because they have satisfied the rules of entry into the discourse. But these rules are the effect of certain social processes, rather than issues of knowledge itself. A professor of Organisational Behaviour does not necessarily know any more about the ways people behave in organisations than the proverbial man on the Clapham omnibus does, it is just that the professor has gone through certain social processes which allow him or her to be recognised as a member of the discourse of Organisational Behaviour. And people who exercise power in a discourse are not doing so because the knowledge is absolutely correct, but because it conforms to the assumptions of that discourse. It may be that having a beard really does not make you a worse train driver, that having an enriched job does not make you more satisfied, that being empowered does not release your hidden potential. But this does not matter. The explanatory power of any piece of knowledge is, in itself, much less important than that the knowledge should conform to the requirements of the discourse.

Rocket power/knowledge

On 28 January 1986 the US space shuttle *Challenger* exploded 73 seconds after launch, killing all on board. Information from previous launches had indicated a potential generic problem with a rocket motor seal. The leading expert in the US on the type of seal in question had been asked to investigate the problem. His research showed that the seal was likely to fail if the shuttle was launched when the ambient temperature was too low. He had concluded that *Challenger* should not be launched when the ambient temperature was below 53 °F. The forecast overnight temperature prior to the day that *Challenger* was to be launched was 18 °F. At a pre-launch conference the seal expert produced, for the management team, overwhelming scientific evidence that the seal would fail if the launch went ahead as planned. But this was knowledge that the management team did not wish to hear. A delayed launch would embarrass the rocket motor suppliers as the seals were supposed to operate correctly at a much wider range of temperatures. In the end it was decided that the decision to launch should be a management decision, not an engineering decision. The launch took place, the seal failed, the shuttle exploded, the astronauts died needlessly.

What we have here is, in microcosm, the operation of a discourse. It was not a case of making a decision on the basis of the best possible knowledge available, but of making a decision that conformed to the desires of some key decision-makers. By defining the engineering information as not relevant it was possible to use a different knowledge base, which allowed the decision to launch to be construed as the correct and reasonable thing to do.

Note: For a fuller account of the background to the *Challenger* disaster, see R.P. Boisjoly and E.F. Curtis: 'Roger Boisjoly and the Challenger Disaster: A Case Study in Management Practice, Corporate Loyalty and Business Ethics', in Hoffman and Moore (1990).

Power and truth

It is clear that, historically, conditions of truth have been different. All epochs need some view of what can be seen as true, some reference point to which all knowledge can be referred in order to judge its truth value. Thus, in the period when governance in Europe was principally influenced by the Church, truth was revealed by reference to Christian dogma. For example, the Sun went round the Earth because this conformed to religious reasoning and it was heretical to deny this, even on the basis of empirical data, as Galileo discovered; witchcraft was real and an acceptable explanation for untoward events; human beings were descended from Adam and Eve and so could not have evolved from apes, a lesser life form; and so on. The requirement to understand the world along these prescribed lines permeated all aspects of social life. In education, universities were for educating the clergy, and the clergy were the educators; there was virtually no concept of secular art or literature; in medicine, ill health was strongly linked to the presence of demonic forces; etc. More recently, in the fascist regime in Germany in the 1930s and 1940s there was a science rooted in the notion of Aryan supremacy, state-approved arts glorifying supposed Germanic characteristics, a medicine informed by the principles of eugenics to enhance Aryan physical characteristics, social structures and values that actively reflected Nazi ideology – and German companies had no difficulties or qualms about employing slave labour or manufacturing equipment for the death camps as part of their normal commercial activities.

The all-embracing force of any particular way of determining truth is what is meant by a **regime of truth**. Regimes of truth generally last for long periods and do not change or disappear overnight. Thus, in the UK, where strict Christian observance is maintained only by a minority, there is still a residual notion of Christian truth, such as that Sunday is a special day. However, it should not be implied that there is no dissent to any particular regime of truth – such dissent *always* exists. But it is likely to be marginalised as deviant by those in control of the dominant discourse.

The current regime of truth has been labelled by Foucault, and others, as capitalist (as noted in the previous chapter). As a doctrine, capitalism furnishes us with a particular logic by which we can judge truth claims and which enables us to choose between alternatives when decisions have to be made. This logic can be understood as informed by the primacy of principles of efficiency (see also Chapter 10). Capitalism is based on the fundamentally simple idea that money can be made to make more money. In this sense, the engine of capitalism is a conversion process and, therefore, the more efficient this conversion can be made to be, the more money is produced. Thus, what is truth under capitalism is what relates to improved efficiency in these terms. This is a regime of truth rather than a lesser, more specific, truth because, as with the previous examples, it permeates the whole of society. For example, education, which, as part of the Enlightenment tradition of improvement of the human condition, was seen as a good in itself, is now openly promoted as education for a job, to fit people for work; health has become an issue of utility rather than a right; the arts are now judged in terms of economic value and potential benefit to commerce, through sponsorship; and so on. The arena of knowledge about organisations has been particularly strongly informed by this regime of truth, because of the especially intimate relationship between all kinds of organisations and capitalism. The discourse of Organisational Behaviour has been formulated in terms of managing people so that they maximise their contribution to organisational efficiency, defined in economic terms, and whatever kind of organisation is under scrutiny, rather than in terms of trying to understand, *per se*, people in organisations and the interactions, impacts and implications attendant upon living in what is often called an organisational society.

The regime of truth is the referrant principle for the application of power in organisations. Whether you are an arts administrator, an educationist, a corporate manager, a parent, the regime of truth provides a guide for your actions and an aid to decision-making, provides goals to work towards. It provides coherence between different arenas of social activity, a common principle to which all actions and decisions can be referred in order to determine what is the right thing to do. You are not necessarily aware of it – indeed, an important quality of an operant regime of truth is that it is internalised and normalised to the greatest possible extent, and when we all understand this principle of truth we will all know how to decide, how to act, our proper duty.

The regime of truth is the principle through which governance is exercised, and this is why it is possible to say, as we did earlier in this chapter, that all functionaries, in no matter what sphere, contribute to governance through the exercise of disciplinary power. When we come to exercise our little bit of power, it is the regime of truth that guides us, and that legitimates what we do.

Existing applications in Organisational Behaviour

It has been a major criticism of Functionalist approaches to organisational behaviour that they lack a concept of power. There are, outside that paradigm, many, and some widely differing, formulations of power as a concept and its significance in organisations, to be found especially, for example, in Critical Theory and Labour Process Theory. However, these are predominantly structural models of power. We have focused on one particular approach to power which emphasises not structural but **interactional** power. This view of power figures in a number of approaches to understanding organisation and organisational behaviour that have been developed, notably those that seek to use poststructuralist ideas although, as already noted, these tend to focus on the work of particular poststructuralist theorists rather than on the approach in general. Such studies typically pay relatively little attention to the role of organisations as producers of goods and services, preferring to focus on **the matrices of power and discipline which enable organisations to fulfil their superordinate function, in the system of governance**. A major contribution of studies using concepts of discourse and disciplinary power to analyse organisations and organisational behaviour has been precisely this emphasis on the primacy of power as an operating principle and their active questioning of the claim that organisational activity can be seen as functional, rational and, therefore, neutral. Studies applying the concept of disciplinary power to, for example, accounting and human resource management have illustrated very effectively how the gathering of information necessary to these functions is not itself simply to facilitate production of goods and services, but, principally, to sustain and enhance existing power relations. In particular, the connection between knowledge and power has been a strong focus.

Functionalist approaches to understanding organisations have always emphasised the *differences* between organisations based on, for example, what they produce, production systems, cultures, and so on. Poststructuralist approaches, however, have rejected these differences as trivial compared to the *similarities* between all kinds of organisation, when considered in light of the role they have to play in maintaining the system of governance and the capitalist regime of truth. These approaches emphasise that organisations of all kinds are the primary vehicles for the exercise of power in society.

Further potential

In the discourse of Organisational Behaviour it has been traditional to treat the nature of 'organisation' as a given, and the focus has been on 'behaviour' within a taken-for-granted context. Recent developments in the field have started to redress this imbalance by placing the concept of organisation itself in question and, in particular, by focusing on **organisation as a process** rather than on **organisations as entities** – that is, focusing on the activity, and purposes, of organising itself as a common principle in all organisations and of which any particular organisation is just one example. It is already clear that, once this shift is made, even what constitutes organisational behaviour is to be seen in radically different ways. Yet the penetration of such approaches into 'micro-level' organisational behaviour has, so far, been somewhat limited. Concepts like motivation to work, leadership, culture, group dynamics and the like cannot be merely dismissed because they are so prevalent, but still await the rethinking that is implied by emphasising the matrices of power in organisations.

Since the emergence of the concept of knowledge paradigms it has been recognised that there are no general or universal definitions of what an organisation is, or what its purpose may be. There are only competing definitions. Yet definition of what an organisation is, how it may be conceptualised, must necessarily precede any understanding of organisational behaviour. The tendency there has been to talk about organisational behaviour without an attendant definition of organisation has made such pronouncements problematic. What is still needed is for discussion of organisational behaviour to be couched in openly specified definitions of the nature of organisation. It is our own view that organisation cannot be defined adequately without recognition of the primacy and centrality of power. This argument has enormous implications for understanding organisational behaviour. It implies that, fundamentally, **organisational behaviour is about either using disciplinary power or being subject to it**. From this starting point ensuing interpretations will be radically different to those approaches that ignore or underplay the significance of power in organisational contexts.

Organisational behaviour and power

It has been suggested here that organisational behaviour cannot be understood without taking into account the operation of power, both in the organisational context itself and in the more general system of governance. But even to talk of 'the powerful' and 'the powerless' is still to use a relatively neutral language. What needs to be recognised is that **the exercise of power makes victims**.

Jean-François Lyotard has defined victims as those who are spoken about in a language which is not theirs, language in which the signifieds, and often even the signifiers, are not shared: victims are those who are the objects, those who are talked about but cannot themselves talk. This is precisely the case with conventional approaches to organisational behaviour. Terms such as job enrichment, job satisfaction, motivation to work, cultural engineering, and so on, are signifiers from the domain of management and management academics. They are not terms typically used by workers to describe their experience. Indeed, they are a technical jargon, signifiers which have very particular meanings appropriate to a particular context and a particular discourse. For example, 'motivation to work', as an approved topic within the discourse, is not about motivation in any generally understood sense but about observable measures of increased performance.

Workers experience being sacked but managers let them go or, as has been used latterly, *empower* them to get on with the rest of their lives. That the equivalent language of workers is not seen as relevant or acceptable is because managers and management academics are the ones with the power to signify. There is, as yet, no generally accepted language in the discourse of Organisational Behaviour to describe the experience of people at work in their own terms, no matter who they are and irrespective of their functional role. And there never will be, until the operation of power and its effects are taken into account.

This is not just a nicety. The discourse of Organisational Behaviour is not like that of, say, geology, in terms of its topics – in geology you can talk about a rock as an object because it *is* an object. But the objects of the discourse of Organisational Behaviour are people. This discourse is about the experience of people at work but does not include *their* interpretation of what that experience is. The discourse defines what that experience is for itself, and what it means. This is an act of supreme power.

From the perspective of a model of disciplinary power, therefore, organisational behaviour is understood only in terms of the language and interests of those with power, in its currently dominant discourse. It is not that the view of the powerless is ignored but that there is no recognition that there is such a thing – to ignore something implies that its existence is at least recognised. The failure to recognise the view of the powerless derives from the failure to consider that there are relations of power at work in organisational behaviour. Their existence too is, thus, not recognised. A view of organisational behaviour that emanates from recognition that such power relationships do exist starts to generate different understandings and explanations. The point is not to eliminate power relationships, however, since that is impossible. Given this inevitably, though, their existence demands to be taken into account in efforts to produce adequate understandings of organisational behaviour.

A TALE FROM THE VILLAGE PUMP (*POWER*)

(See the Case Study in Appendix 2, pages 340–3)

The roles of **power** and of **micro-power** are important elements of this case. For example, although Snow had some structural power as a member of an elite, he had no formal power in this situation. However, he was able to influence the Board of Guardians – who were not really convinced of his hypothesis, but were, perhaps, convinced by his status. The removal of the pump handle, while an exercise of formal power by the Board of Guardians, was also an exercise of micro-power by Snow, over the pump users. As it happened, the pump handle was replaced quite soon after its removal, on the authority of the Board of Guardians, but, apparently, without consulting Snow.

- What aspects of the case illustrate the importance of the **power** to determine significations?

THE POWER OF PRAYERS?

The Anglican Church is a global organisation with about 77 million members. It is organised into 38 (geographically based) provinces. Each province is autonomous and has wide-ranging powers of self-governance – especially relevant in this context is that provinces decide independently who is suitable for ordination as a priest. The leaders (bishops) of the provinces meet every ten years at the Lambeth Conference, where they seek to reach general agreement on matters of faith and of social policy. However, it seems that policy decisions made at the Lambeth Conference are not binding on the provinces, though the Conference may, and often does, exhort all provinces to be tolerant of each other's practices, even where practices are not universally adopted. Dissent from a general policy is not regarded as disloyalty.

There has been a long-running controversy in the Anglican Church regarding the ordination of women into the priesthood. The pressure for the ordination of women can be traced back at least to the mid-nineteenth century, but it reached a climax in the late twentieth century, at which point general acceptance of the idea was established, though this was not, in practice, universal. As long ago as 1935, a Church Commission had stated that there were no theological reasons why women should not be ordained. The first case of a woman ordained as a priest seems to have been a wartime emergency measure, in 1944, in Hong Kong. It was, perhaps, a special case of the practice, common in both world wars, of allowing women into occupations usually closed to them, to supplement a shortage of available men. Generally, such practice did not survive the outbreak of peace. Indeed, Florence Li Tim-Oi surrendered her licence as a priest in 1946 to avoid incipient controversy.

Subsequently a small number of official or unofficial ordinations took place in various provinces. In 1974 three bishops in the USA decided unilaterally to ordain women, but the practice was not officially sanctioned for the American province of the Anglican Church until a General Convention in 1976. In 1978 the Lambeth Conference, in effect, ratified this ruling by affirming the right of the provinces to decide who should be ordained. By 1998 a majority of provinces had ordained women as priests, but there remained a sizeable minority that did not. The debate has moved on, however, and there is now a similar dispute about the elevation of women priests to bishoprics. In recent times some women have been publicly vocal about their inability, in general, to rise in the hierarchy of the Anglican Church. It is also obviously the case that, despite the official acceptance of women as priests, since there is a ceiling on their advancement they do not have much voice in the strategic governance of the Church, and could be seen as still there on sufferance.

The resistance to the ordination of women has been based on theological argument. Those who oppose it rely on claims to possess expert knowledge, based in Scripture, of God's intention that women should not be priests – what has been called 'the apostasy of women's priesthood'. Equally, those who support such ordination – or at least do not oppose it – also rely on claims to expert knowledge of God's intentions, but come to a diametrically opposite conclusion. (It is easy to see why Florence Li Tim-Oi's ordination

▶

might be controversial, since it had the added dimension of demonstrating that theological argument could be set aside under some circumstances, for the sake of convenience, or that, sometimes, other considerations might be judged to take precedence over theological argument.) Nonetheless, here are two incommensurable knowledge claims, and no prospect of an independent test to discover which is correct. Each will remain the correct view to its proponents, and the other view will continue to be judged incorrect. At the moment, in terms of influence, the supporters of women's ordination are in the majority and it is recognised in the surrounding debates that the likeliest outcome is that this view will eventually become dominant, but only when those who oppose it retire, or die, and can no longer exert influence.

Another way to understand this dispute is to see it as an issue of patriarchal power. In the UK the Anglican Church, historically, has been part of the system of governance, and, although its role and influence in the wider society has diminished in more recent times, its bishops still sit in the House of Lords. It is still the established religion. The monarch is still the Supreme Governor (head) of the Church of England and is officially 'defender of the faith'. The Anglican Church's 'senior management team' has always been male. It would not be surprising, then, if recruits to the priesthood absorbed this traditional male domination as a truth rooted in historical precedence. At any rate, there would be a long-established and official male culture. The idea that some of the 'rights' of men exclusively to run the Church could be ceded to women would be very likely to meet resistance. Various explanations for this resistance have been put forward – innate resistance to change, fear of women, etc. Allowing women to participate in the higher echelons of the Church reduces the number of jobs available for men, reduces men's influence and leads, inevitably, to a change in culture. Basically, the dispute can be seen as centring on a group of powerful men protecting their perceived interests by use of expert knowledge. The men also have had the power of the defender – they own the jobs, have property rights over the profession of priest. Since neither theological argument nor the legally binding responsibility to ensure that women have 'equal opportunities' have been effective, for women to succeed in their claim they have to challenge the power of men.

In so far as women have won the argument that they should be able to be part of the priesthood of the Anglican Church, they have achieved this with support. Firstly, some powerful men in the Church supported them, though whether from a genuine desire to acknowledge the rights of women or from some perceived self-interest remains a matter of debate. There was also more general pressure to accept women as priests, because of the increasing strength of feminism and because of the perceived need for the Church to reflect the social culture in which it is embedded. Nonetheless, it might be expected that these debates will become increasingly bitter, considering the separate but pertinent dispute about the ordination of openly gay people as priests, which has brought the threat of schism to the Anglican Church. Traditionally, the governance of the Church has meant that no province has been compelled to accept either women or gay people as priests, but this is no longer enough for some. In claiming autonomy for themselves, they also seek to compel other provinces to accept and adopt their view. Although it is claimed that this is an issue of theological appropriateness, perhaps it would be more realistic to see it as a struggle for domination.

■ Would these issues be easier to resolve if the Anglican Church had a more centralised structure?

■ Even in provinces where women are ordained as priests, some parishes refuse to accept them. What does this illustrate about the nature of discourse?

■ Why might it be argued that power is a more appropriate concept in this context than the concept of authority?

■ Is expert knowledge a relevant concept in matters of faith?

(Other chapters that would be useful and relevant in analysing the case *include* Knowledge (4), Rationality (6), Ideology (7), Self (8) and Decision-making (11). The chapter on Semiotics (2) is particularly relevant to understanding how and why different interpretations arise.)

Bibliography

It is not impossible to find conventional texts on organisation and organisational behaviour that use the word 'power'. However, this use generally takes one of two very similar forms: either power is seen as a synonym for authority and issues of coercion and/or threat are, simply, ignored, or a distinction is made between legitimate power, defined as authority, and an aberrant illegitimate form of power which must be eliminated or legitimised. In general, such Functionalist approaches tend to mystify, rather than clarify and facilitate, the recognition and analysis of power in organisations and their practical contribution to such analysis is actually to mask the operation of power.

There are a number of different perspectives on work and power but these tend to be part of sociology rather than of Organisation Studies or Organisational Behaviour, which have been much criticised by sociologists for ignoring the organisational power/social power dynamic. Lukes (2005) is widely regarded as a prime source on the concept of power, but see also, for example, Urry and Wakeford (1973), Burns, Karlsson and Rus (1979), Giddens and Mackenzie (1982). The contemporary concept of property rights derives, primarily, from the seventeenth-century work of John Locke – a summary can be found in, for example, Russell (1961). The most obvious source of material critical of the impacts of this version of property rights is the work of Marx – see, for example, *Capital* (1976) and *Grundrisse* (McLellan 1980), or, more synoptically, Bottomore (1991) or Brewer (1984). There is a *Marx's Kapital For Beginners* (Smith and Evans 1983). A book considered by many to be a classic on the issues surrounding organisations and property rights is Berle and Means (1932). Much of this material also discusses labour power, its purchase and the rights of its disposal.

From its earliest beginnings, management theory has been a promotor of the view that organisational participants are most 'usefully' seen as workers rather than as people. The classic example is Taylor (1911). Latterly, the very concept of 'human resource management' carries the same implication: people as resources to be utilised. However, there has been a coextensive and widespread humanist critique of this approach. An example from conventional organisation theory is Schein (1988), with his concept of 'complex man'. This humanist critique is also widely reflected in the radical paradigm metaphors in Morgan (1997). An early recognition is encapsulated in the concept of 'partial inclusion', in Allport (1924). One of the classics of the approach is Gouldner (1969). This critique is not exclusive to any particular approach to understanding organisations and organisational behaviour. For example, feminist theory has focused on the particular issue of the failure to recognise women organisational participants as women and, therefore, having particular 'needs' – see, for example, Cockburn (1991), Gherardi (1995). Some contemporary conventional theory, notably the Human Resource Management literature, has recognised the problem of the attenuated view of people as workers, but has sought to 'resolve' it by incorporating more and more of the person into the sphere of organisational control.

The conventional interpretation of the work of Weber, dominant in management theory and in the discourse of Organisational Behaviour, emphasises his concept of rational-legal authority. An accessible exposition of this concept can be found in Pugh and Hickson (1989). As already noted, the word 'power' is not totally absent from conventional approaches and a popular example, influential in the Organisation Development literature, is French and Raven (1968). However, as also noted, such approaches usually use the term as a synonym for authority. There are two particular well-established critical approaches which represent preference for the term 'power' as distinct from that of authority. One of these is Marxist organisation theory, where the so-called Weberian concept of authority is hardly taken seriously – see, for example, Baran and Sweezy (1966), Braverman (1974), Marglin (1980). Marcuse (1986) is an example from outside organisation theory but very relevant to understanding organisation as a process. The other approach is known as Radical Weberianism, in which the conventional interpretation of Weber is severely contested through a different reading of Weber's work – see, for example, Eldridge and Crombie (1974), Mouzelis (1975), Clegg (1989). Indeed, Clegg (1989) provides a very useful overview of some of the 'frameworks of power' which have been, and are, prevalent in the field. The influential concept of the 'iron law of obligarchy' from the work of Michels (1968) – originally published in 1915 – is also relevant in this context. For more recent, and very relevant, studies of oligarchic tendencies, see, for example, Dye (2000), Domhoff (2005). See also Scott (1991). For more on the links that tie corporations and governments together, see Bakan (2005).

Since early in the twentieth century the focus of conventional approaches to organisational behaviour has been on non-material rewards and satisfactions. This focus characterises the very basis of the discourse of Organisational Behaviour and the vast bulk of its literature is all about it. A well-known example is Herzberg, Mausner and Snyderman (1959) – the Hygiene/Motivation Theory, more usually associated simply with Herzberg, in which money is seen as a hygiene factor, not a motivator. This type of literature generally and routinely takes the social, political and economic contexts of work and organisation as given, even irrelevant, and therefore, unremarkable, and, indeed, does not comment on it.

Not surprisingly, there is not much in the conventional discourse of Organisational Behaviour that takes a positive, or even a neutral, view of resistance. There is a wide range of materials outside that discourse. Cohen and Taylor (1992) is a well-known and influential book on 'resistance to everyday life', first published in 1976. For a sample of some specific issues see, for example, Parker (2002a), which offers some reflections on 'Anti-Corporate Protest'; Bryman (2004), which discusses resistance in the particular context of what he has called 'Disneyization'; Sennett (2006a), which argues that resistance, especially in the form of strikes, is likely to make a come-back. See also Sennett (2006b).

The core concept of governance is in Foucault (1979b), but see also Burchell, Gordon and Miller (1991), Jackson and Carter (1995b), Simons (1995), Moss (1998). Reed (1985) summarises the whole of organisation theory as taking either the view that organisations and organisational behaviour can be studied as discrete units, or the view that they must be seen as part of, embedded in, their social context. Most non-Functionalist approaches take the latter view, though to various extents, and with varying degrees of emphasis on its necessity. The issue of legitimacy in this context is one famously taken up by Habermas (1976), and is also one of the themes of Gouldner (1970).

It is ironic – or perhaps not – that a lot of the literature in the discourses of Organisation Studies and Organisational Behaviour that deals explicitly with compliance is to be found in the literature on authority mentioned earlier. The question of whether formal hierarchical structures represent an idealised rather than a realistic view of how power is exercised in organisations is widely reflected in the literature on structure, cited in the bibliography to Chapter 3. The long-standing recognition of the 'informal organisation' – see, for example, Mayo (1933), Roethlisberger and Dickson (1939) – can alone stand as an example of the acknowledgement that power does not always, or, perhaps, even often, operate in the ways in which models based on hierarchy suggest. The significance of rules in the Weberian notion of rational-legal authority is boundless, since they are the very source of rationality and of legitimacy. A very powerful exposition of the argument that rules are not always purely functional is to be found in Marcuse's (1987) concept of 'surplus repression'. Issues of conformity and deviance are the implicit or explicit subtext of much of the Organisational Culture literature (see the bibliography to Chapter 2), where the purpose of organisational culture is seen as the production of conformity. A Foucauldian approach to these issues is to be found in Jackson and Carter (1998a). The main source on the panopticon in Foucault's own work is Foucault (1979a). It is not unusual, these days, to find books that explain how surveillance works – see, for example, Gibb (2005) and also Davies (1996). A particularly pertinent context to the conformity or otherwise to organisational rules, and organisational responses to that, is that of whistle-blowing, a significant focus of the literature on organisational/managerial ethics – see, for example, Jackall (1988), Punch (1996), Maclagan (1998), Jones, Parker and ten Bos (2005).

The whole issue of the power/knowledge matrix and the related issues of surveillance and disciplinary power are widely reflected in poststructuralist, and, especially, Foucauldian, approaches to understanding and analysing organisation and organisational behaviour. See, for example, Daudi (1986), Burrell (1988, 1997), Townley (1994), Bogard (1996), McKinlay and Starkey (1998). Deleuze and Guattari (1984) is also highly relevant. On Foucault, see Gordon (1980) in particular, but, really, anything on Foucault's work is likely to consider these issues. From a rather different, more Critical Theory, perspective, see, also, Alvesson and Willmott (1992).

Compelling and readable evidence of management/organisational complicity in the Nazi regime of truth is to be found in Schirer (1960). The impact of religious beliefs on the organisation of work is part of the argument of Weber (1930). A more recent and very relevant book is Anthony (1977). The managerialist orientation of conventional approaches in organisation theory and in the discourse of Organisational Behaviour is widely criticised by writers outside the Functionalist paradigm – see Burrell and Morgan (1979). A seminal work in this context is Burnham (1942).

CHAPTER 6

Rationality

This chapter begins with a brief description of what it means to be rational, which provides a basis for a comparison between the concepts of objective rationality and subjective rationality. Some of the rhetorical devices through which claims to be objectively rational are sustained are considered, notably the economistic equation between rationality and return on investment, quantification and technological imperative. We then turn to implications of different versions of rationality and, especially, the implications of accepting that rationality is inherently subjective. This is approached, primarily, through consideration of the issue of organisational and managerial legitimacy, at both macro and micro levels of analysis, the former focusing on the claim of the right to manage and the latter on the social role of management. The apparent contradiction between serving ownership interest and serving social interest is explored. The particular consequences for the management of organisational behaviour are highlighted.

The themes we have explored so far can be seen in terms of two distinct and opposing sets of beliefs about what the world is like. On one hand is what is known as a realist view, which consists of beliefs that the world in general and organisations in particular are objectively real and exist independently of the people who inhabit them. On the other hand is the view which we are developing, based on beliefs that the world in general and organisations in particular are socially constructed, the product of the interactions, understandings and power relationships that characterise human existence and human affairs. The differences articulated in these views are underpinned by distinct views about the nature of rationality, about how people think.

Rationality is one of the most important, and contested, concepts in the study of behaviour in organisations and yet, at the same time, one of the least examined. 'Rational' is a very commonly used term – most people believe that they are rational, and believe that this is a desirable quality. The underlying cause of all disagreements, however, is competition between *different* rationalities. All management of organisational behaviour not only itself claims to be rational but is also, implicitly or explicitly, informed by the attempt to produce, and induce, behaviour that is rational in others. The claim to be rational is of inestimable importance in all areas of organisation and management, particularly because it is, ultimately, the basis of acceptability – of legitimacy. Yet the discourse of Organisational Behaviour is informed by a peculiarly narrow view of what it means to be rational. Given such significance, it is important to enquire into what is meant by rationality. To do this it is necessary also to explore the broad socio-economic context in which organisations are embedded and within which claims to be rational are rooted. The chapter examines different approaches to understanding rationality and their implications for understanding organisational behaviour.

Being rational

Rational has the same linguistic root as reason, and both derive from the Latin for 'to think'. There is a long tradition of attempts to understand (to *think* about) rationality, particularly in terms of its relationship to action, especially in philosophy and sociology. These literatures are replete with attempts to define rationality, and, in particular, to distinguish between different bases of rationality. Thus, we find formal rationality, instrumental rationality, purposive rationality, functional rationality, value rationality, substantive rationality – even organisational rationality – and so on. There are also debates about the extent to which rationality is possible – a notable example in the field of Organisation Studies is the idea of bounded rationality. This concept is based on the argument that perfectly rational behaviour is not achievable because of cognitive limits on the ability to gather and process information and to rank it in order of significance. Therefore, it is argued, people seek to act as rationally as possible, given their circumstances and constraints. Perfectly rational behaviour would imply that, when making a decision of any kind, the decision-maker is able to gather *all* the information relevant to that decision, rank it in significance and make a reasoned choice between alternatives.

The significance of rationality in behaviour is precisely that it becomes operative as a factor only when decisions have to be made. The whole point about rationality is **its role in choosing between alternatives**. It is an important feature of **rational** behaviour that it refers to choices made *before* the event: it signifies planned and intentional behaviour. On the other hand, the term **rationalisation** is used to signify explanations for behaviour that are constructed *after* the event. The essence of the concept of rationality is **the relationship between means and ends**. In all decision situations certain ends will be desirable. However, there will be more than one means to achieve those ends. Equally, the courses of action (means) between which choice has to be made will have different outcomes. We will want to choose the best, or the least worst, outcome in terms of our desired ends. So, what is rational is the course of action that achieves the least worst outcome. Thus, when confronted with a situation requiring choice between alternatives, we employ reason to arrive at a rational decision, by thinking about the possible consequences of each alternative and then choosing the optimum course of action. The optimum, or best, in this sense is the one that furnishes the most **utility** – in other words, that delivers the most satisfaction, often understood in terms of the most pleasure or the least pain. So, if you are offered the choice between being given £10 or being given a punch on the nose, one could assume the rational choice to be taking the £10. This is because with the money you can purchase items of desire or need which will give you satisfaction – pleasure – whereas the punch on the nose will cause pain. However, if you are masochist, perhaps you would prefer the punch on the nose.

Cognitive limits

In his book *The Brain of the Firm*, Stafford Beer points out just how much information is present in our normal daily lives. He notes that if we consider a small organisation, one that has only 300 inputs/outputs, each of which has only two states – for example, in the case of the answer to a question, that answer can only be yes or no, not maybe – the amount of information present in the situation is 300×2^{300}, or 3 × 100000000000000000000000000000000000 000000000000000000000000000000000000000000000000000000000 bits. That is, the amount of implicit uncertainty present in this organisation is about 3×10^{92} bits.

This is, of course, an extremely simple organisation, so simple as to be pretty unlikely – as Beer points out, 'many companies have more than 300 employees, for a start, with more than 300 machines, more than 300 products, more than 300 customers' (1981: 48). Indeed, it would even be a low estimate if we were only considering the sensory capacity of our own brains. But also, this amount of information considerably exceeds the capacity of the human brain to comprehend it. How, then, is it possible to manage, or control, organisations that are much larger and more complex than this? The answer is that we use variety (another word for information) attenuators. Not all information is useful to our purposes and so we filter out whatever is not necessary. If we can reduce the amount of information sufficiently, then we can control the organisation. If we cannot, the organisation will be out of control.

The problem is, how do we know which information is necessary? The answer to this may be crucial, because if we filter out information that we do need, then, again, the organisation will be out of control. But, for the purposes of managing, we have to apply some criteria to make the decision about what we need to know. These criteria, whatever they may be, are based on what we believe to be rational. (See also Chapter 9.)

One of the difficulties with approaches to understanding rationality, especially those in the province of organisational behaviour, is that they rarely include the possibility that decisions about what is rational also involve aspects of the personality such as sexuality, prejudice and the so-called seamier side of our lives, in favour of what might be called a *polite* view of rationality. There is little reference in the discourse of Organisational Behaviour to masochists or sadists, for example, notwithstanding that there will be many such people in organisations. Although there may *seem* to be a lot in this discourse about the emotional and the psychological aspects of people, there is very little depth to these considerations, since they are limited to their perceived relevance to work and efficiency. There is very little recognition that employees are anything more than organisms that work. It is this attitude that has allowed the discourse of Organisational Behaviour to adopt *an extremely limited view of rationality*.

Rationality is very highly valued, in general cultural terms. It has even been described as that which distinguishes humans from other life forms. Rationality, as in 'able to think', is defined as the quality of sanity. To be **ir**rational is to be insane, and society will take steps to control a person who is deemed to be irrational – commit them to a mental hospital, for example. But a much more insidious manifestation of the cultural value of rationality is the idea that irrationality equates with emotion, or being emotional. This has significant links to the maintenance and exercise of power, with the implication that what is emotional should be controlled by what is rational. A particular example of this is the justification for the dominance of male over female on the basis that rationality is seen as typically a male attribute, while being emotional is seen as typically a female attribute.

Meaning and information

The French author, film-maker, member of the Académie Française (and, some say, pornographer) Alain Robbe-Grillet, in his article 'Order and Disorder in Film and Fiction' (1977), draws on Information Theory to make an interesting distinction between meaning and information. Information, he suggests, is something that tells us something that we did not previously know. Information is linked to improbability – the more improbable, the more we learn, but the more difficult the information is to comprehend. Meaning, on the other hand, is linked to probability – it is what we (already) understand. Robbe-Grillet offers an example: if we are in a room in Chicago, in August, and someone enters to say that it is not freezing outside, this statement has a great deal of meaning but very little information, since no one would expect it to be freezing in Chicago in August. We learn nothing. However, if the message is that it *is* freezing outside, that Lake Michigan has frozen over, then it would contain a massive amount of information, but very little meaning. The notion of frost in Chicago in August is incomprehensible.

Imagine a continuum between pure meaning and pure information:

Meaning 100%_____Information 100%

This suggests that pure meaning contains no information – so we cannot learn anything from it, and pure information contains no meaning – so we cannot understand it. As we move along the continuum from meaning to information, reducing meaning and increasing information, so our potential to learn also increases. But, at some point, the amount of information will become too large relative to our ability to understand it, and confusion will grow.

The zone in which meaning and information cohere in an optimal relationship can be seen as the source of our rationality. It is at this point that we believe that we can understand enough of the data/information to which we are exposed to *create* adequate meaning – that is, **adequate in terms of *our purposes***. In other words, it is the point at which we can make sense of the world.

Clearly, rationality is a concept of great significance with major ramifications, especially in the context of organisational behaviour. However, it is our view that the sifting of the concept into various types, as listed earlier, on one hand unnecessarily complicates discussion of rationality and, on the other hand, ignores a prior distinction which is much more important: the distinction between objective rationality and subjective rationality. It is, therefore, our intention to focus on this difference.

Objective versus subjective rationality

At its most fundamental, the big issue about rationality is reflected in the debate between those who view it as an objective phenomenon and those who view it as a subjective one. The discourse of Organisational Behaviour, overwhelmingly, reflects the former view.

Objective rationality

Those who maintain that rationality is an objective phenomenon view it as impartial, impersonal, value-neutral. Objective rationality is a matter of formal logic which is not influenced by individual subjectivity. Thus, in a given situation one decision, or course of action, is rational, and all other possibilities are, therefore, irrational by definition. Furthermore, on every occasion of this situation arising, *all other things being equal*, the same decision will be the rational one. Thus, for example, if a group of workers are offered improvements in working conditions – a bonus payment, say, or enriched jobs, or a different and better culture – then, because the offer furnishes improvements, makes the job 'better', the rational decision is to accept the offer. And, this is the rational decision for everyone to whom the offer is made. If a like offer is made to a different group, then they too should accept the offer. **The rationality resides in the situation, so that in all like circumstances the correct answer is the same**. This view is also referred to as 'the one best way', because it holds to the belief that there is only *one* rational approach, only one good means to achieve a desired end. However, there are some difficulties with this scenario. *Firstly*, it contains a value judgement; *secondly*, it assumes that all things are equal; *thirdly*, it assumes that all participants in the situation share the same objectives.

A **value judgement** is a judgement where there is no objective measure for its basis. If you are given a quantity of beer and asked how much there is, you can refer to constant units of quantity, such as litres, and your answer can be checked for accuracy. But if you are asked whether it is good beer, your response will be a value judgement: there are no constant units of goodness in beer and so your judgement will refer to your own, subjective, concept of good – it will reflect your personal e-valu(e)-ation of what is good. In the example of changes in working conditions, what constitutes an improvement is a value judgement, and it cannot be assumed that all the individuals involved will view the changes as an improvement. What is defined as an improvement is usually decided by managers, not by those who experience the working conditions. In the same way that a barkeeper cannot *make* you think that the beer they have just served you is good, a manager cannot make you see the changes in your job that they have introduced as an improvement. Similarly, **the assumption that 'all things are equal' is not an appropriate one**. Although the changes in the job may be the same for everyone, this does not mean that everyone will view them as equally desirable. A young person, at an early stage in their career and ambitious, may see advantages from the change and therefore choose to see it as improvement. A colleague nearing retirement, however, may prefer to stick with the job conditions with which they are familiar and, therefore, see such change as disadvantageous and a deterioration in working conditions. Equally, **not everyone in the situation can be assumed to share the same goals** and, if the desired ends are different, the perception of appropriate means will also be different. The outcomes desired by managers may not be the same as those desired by workers. For example, the managerial objective of improving the job may be to increase productivity by increasing performance, but those doing the job may not wish to work harder, especially if, as is so often the case, increases in productivity result in decreases in demand for labour – fewer jobs.

The sad fate of Buridan's ass

This well-known cautionary tale from Philosophy illustrates the problem of assuming that decisions can, and should, be based on objective criteria.

A hungry ass is confronted with two bales of hay. The ass carefully examines the first one and decides that it looks to be the most delicious, most desirable, bale of hay possible. The ass is about to take a mouthful when it hesitates. What if the other bale is even better? Since the ass would definitely prefer the best hay, then, surely, that would be the one to eat. So the ass examines the other bale of hay and finds that this one looks just as delicious and desirable as the first one. Just as good, not better. Now, while the ass would certainly choose for its meal the better of two bales of hay, which should it choose if they are both the same? The ass ponders on this. It racks its brains, but can think of no reason to reject one bale in favour of the other. Why, it thinks, should it reject one bale when it is just as good as the other? Why choose one when an equally good one is also available? Unable to find any rational argument for choosing one of the bales of hay in preference to the other, the ass starves to death, still puzzling over how to make a rational decision when there appear to be no grounds for such a decision.

It may seem obvious from all this that what is rational depends upon individual preference. Yet this understanding is largely absent from the discourse of Organisational Behaviour and, indeed, from Management Theory in general. To accept such a view of rationality would have enormous implications for the process of management as a whole, and especially for the management of organisational behaviour, as will be discussed later.

Subjective rationality

Those who see rationality as a subjective phenomenon see it, not as a function of particular circumstances, but as **a characteristic of the individual**. Some of the problems of the approach that views rationality as objective have already been indicated, but the argument that rationality is subjective goes much deeper than this.

Proponents of objective rationality might protest against our criticisms of the logic of their position in the context of the example, on the basis that the point that different individuals have different circumstances does not, in itself, invalidate the principle of objective rationality – they might argue that in a hypothetical situation where circumstances *were* the same the decision would be objectively rational. As noted, rationality, for the objectivist, is contained in the circumstances, in the situation. But, for proponents of subjective rationality, this could *never* be more than a hypothesis and, even then, a pretty unlikely one. On the basis of the arguments in our previous chapters, all deriving from the first principle of the signifer/signified relationship and the profound individuality of understanding and meaning, superficially shared at best, it must be concluded that: the possibility that, in any situation, the view of it is held equally by all participants is extremely unlikely, to say the least; the possibility that any situation could be an exact replica of another situation is also, and equally, extremely unlikely; even were such a situation to arise, the possibility that the same decision is valid because of the nature of the situation is untenable, because it assumes that the situation itself precludes the exercise of free choice by actors – that people must decide the same thing because they have no alternative. **From a subjectivist point of view *none* of these assumptions is valid and, therefore, the conditions of objective rationality cannot be satisfied in *any* situation that involves people.** Thus, objective rationality is not applicable in any aspect of the social world.

Proponents of rationality as a subjective phenomenon would argue further than this. If rationality is subjective, decisions only have to *appear* rational to the individual subject. Indeed, strictly speaking, they do not even have to appear to be rational. From the perspective of subjective rationality, it can be quite rational to make a conscious decision to follow a course of action which is acknowledged to be *ir*rational: there is no absolute reason why satisfaction/pleasure cannot be gained from an apparently irrational decision. Consider, for example, workers who go on strike to protest at job losses and, by so doing, lose their own jobs, thus precipitating by their action exactly what they are opposing. Obviously, such workers do not want to lose their jobs and so would probably recognise the irrationality of their actions in terms of their own ends. But the transient satisfaction of making a gesture may seem worth it at the time, and, hence, rational.

All this strongly argues that **the concept of objective rationality is not appropriate in the context of organisational behaviour**. It is worth recapitulating some of the points made so far, to emphasise this. We have stated that observable behaviour is a signifier, as is the language itself which is associated with organisational behaviour. Given this, there can be no absolute meanings attachable to these signifiers – meanings cannot be prescribed. Thus,

What is rational, anyway?

An Irish airman foresees his death

I know that I shall meet my fate
Somewhere among the clouds above;
Those that I fight I do not hate,
Those that I guard I do not love;
My country is Kiltartan Cross,
My countrymen Kiltartan's poor,
No likely end could bring them loss
Or leave them happier than before.
Nor law, nor duty bade me fight,
Nor public men, nor cheering crowds,
A lonely impulse of delight
Drove to this tumult in the clouds;
I balanced all, brought all to mind,
The years to come seemed waste of breath,
A waste of breath the years behind
In balance with this life, this death.

Source: W.B. Yeats, 1919. Reprinted with permission
of AP Wyatt on behalf of Michael B. Yeats

This poem was written by Yeats in memory of Major Robert Gregory, a pilot in the First World War, in which the life expectancy of pilots was extremely low. The pilot, being Irish, did not have to fight – for political reasons, Irish nationals were not conscripted in the First World War. No sense of duty or conscience impelled him to fight. He felt no emotion towards those he fought or towards those he sought to defend. He did not even feel that his fellow countrymen would be affected by the outcome of the conflict, for good or ill. This would seem to exhaust 'rational' reasons for fighting: compulsion, guilt, hatred of the enemy, love of the oppressed, a hope of betterment. This pilot risks – and loses – his life just for the transient excitement of flying, and aerial combat.

This is hardly objectively rational behaviour as conventionally understood. Nonetheless, it undoubtedly does describe typical human behaviour. Is it any different to taking, say, Ecstasy, knowing that it can be fatal, or even to drinking excessively, knowing that it will lead to a hangover, or eating too much, driving too fast, playing dangerous sports, overworking, and so on?

- Given the Irish airman's situation, what would constitute objectively rational behaviour?

Some people claim that organisations generally contain many people who are indifferent to the aims of the organisation, who have low commitment and little sense of identity with what the organisation does, whose motivation is not linked to productivity, for example.

- If this is the case, how does it affect notions of generalisable objective criteria for rational behaviour?
- What are the implications for managing organisational behaviour?

the explanations of behaviour to be found in the discourse of Organisational Behaviour only reflect the views of those who are members of that discourse, but membership does not confer some privileged access to signification. Similarly, if structural relationships are the product of individual cognition then, again, attempts to link behaviour with particular criteria for the purposes of measurement, such as motivation, leadership, culture, and so on, reflect only the understandings of those in the discourse. Organisational Behaviour represents attempts by one interest group to manipulate the behaviour of another group, which constitutes the exercise of disciplinary power. **Thus, one person may wish another to be more motivated, a better leader, or to adopt particular cultural values, but whether this occurs or not, even what these terms mean, will be judged by those in the discourse in terms of their understanding of organisational behaviour – and such judgement will not reflect success or failure in itself, but success or failure in the context of discursive appropriateness within the terms of the capitalist regime of truth.**

If this description can be accepted as a coherent basis for understanding behaviour in organisations and the discourse of Organisational Behaviour, then it should be accepted that **there is no aspect of organisational behaviour, in practice or in theory, that is not based on subjective values, norms and preferences, no aspect of which is available to be characterised in terms appropriate to the concept of objective rationality.** Indeed, it might be suggested that the only reason why objective rationality is an issue at all in this context – though it is an important reason – is that those with the power to signify use this concept to prioritise their own subjective preferences and to present these as unchallangeable and legitimate.

The discourse of Organisational Behaviour and the concept of objective rationality

Despite the coherence of the arguments against the applicability of concepts of objective rationality in the context of organisations generally, and especially in the context of organisational behaviour, the discourse of Organisational Behaviour shows a tenacious attachment to this concept. It is, therefore, appropriate to consider why this might be. The underlying rationale goes back, once again, to the concept of **property rights**, as discussed in Chapter 5. There it was pointed out that there is a deeply ingrained and rarely questioned cultural value assigned to ownership. Individuals have extensive rights over what they own and its disposal. Ownership in itself confers power and status. This is valid whether what is owned is a physical object or something abstract. Thus, if one owns money, one can use it as one chooses.

It is worth stating the case made by, for example, classical economics here, since it is pertinent. Money can be made to work and has the special characteristic of being able to be used to make more of itself. For this to happen, especially in conditions of industrial capitalism, an organisation is required. In other words, money needs to be invested in a process that will cause the investment to grow. Such organisations have, therefore, a single objective, that they should provide for money to make more of itself. The particular process by which this happens – for example, the goods and services that are produced – is irrelevant, as long as the money invested grows. Thus, just one objective is given to organisations, that of increasing investors' money. Therefore, the argument goes, any decisions about what must be done in order to achieve this objective can be judged rational by reference to that objective – there is, in other words, an objective rationality. That the objective of investment is to make the investment grow, rather than to make the goods and services that are necessary to produce growth, is easily demonstrated. Many investors have little or no awareness of what is actually produced with their money. If you invest £100 in a unit trust, for example, you can know whether your £100 is growing and at what rate, but you cannot know with any accuracy where your £100 has gone to in order to make it more productive. The argument that organisations have a single objective and that decisions and actions can be judged rational, or otherwise, in terms of that objective, is taken further: if this is the case, it follows that those employed to achieve this objective – to manage its achievement – must themselves behave in an objectively rational way. If they do not, and succeed in causing money to be lost rather than to grow, they will not be able to sustain their position.

The argument does not imply that investors do not exercise choice over the kind of organisation in which they invest, but it does imply that, whatever they invest in, they expect it to make more money for them. This is the whole purpose of investment. And it is a process necessary for the continuation of the system itself – if, each time that money was invested, it lost value, then the system would be unsustainable. Nor should it be taken that what we are implying is that managers *are* objectively rational. The point is that **the intended function of management is to be objectively rational**. Of course, managers can make subjective decisions which will lead to better or worse rates of return but, over some necessary but indeterminate time period, they must be able to provide positive growth of investment. *This can be seen as the basis of the claim, implicit or explicit, that management is an objectively rational process and that, by implication, managers themselves are objectively rational.*

Management of organisational behaviour simply repeats this claim to be objectively rational, on the same basis, though the immediate conditions are different. Management of those employed by the organisation is governed by the same principles as management of any other organisational resource: to produce a positive return on money invested in the organisation. That the object of such management is people, or rather workers, rather than, say, machinery, may mean that a different process is needed but does not mean that the objective is any different. This claim to be objectively rational has *two major benefits* for management: if you can claim that your decisions are objectively rational, then you can stave off challenges to your decisions because they are, by definition, correct decisions, and, if you believe this to be the case, it saves you from having to think too much about what you are doing.

Organisational Behaviour and measurement

The problem with claiming to be objectively rational is that of being able to demonstrate that this is indeed the case, to demonstrate that your decisions are congruent with the conditions necessary if the term 'objective' is to be correctly applied. This is difficult to do but various (rhetorical) devices and techniques are used to sustain the impression. One favoured device is the emphasis on **measurement and quantification**. Through positing a relationship between organisational behaviour and efficiency at the meta-level, it is argued that the implicated aspects of such behaviour – for example, attitudes, motivation, and so on – can be measured. What is measured is, in effect, increased efficiency, or otherwise. This broadly defined link between organisational behaviour and efficiency is too broad and too remote to be used directly in the workplace, however. At that level there has been a preference for more immediate measures of effect, such as psychometrics. The idea that it is possible to measure mental phenomena has enjoyed huge popularity in the discourse of Organisational Behaviour and is widely used in all stages of the management of organisational behaviour, from recruitment to severance.

Measurement in the context of organisational behaviour can cover a spectrum of applications ranging from attempts to attribute absolute numerical values to concepts such as motivation, through ordinal measures where, say, attitudes are ranked hierarchically in terms of their desirability, to pseudo measures such as devising grid coordinates of management style. In the case of measures of physical objects, what is measured can be made visible – a metre of this, a litre of that – but measures of what is abstract must always be a matter of belief rather than of substance. **Since there are no tangible measures of such phenomena as motivation or management style, any claim to be able to measure them cannot be demonstrated in any objective sense and ought to be seen as exercises in discursive power.** The inability to make tangible such units of measurement tends to produce instead ersatz measurements, measurements of what *can* be measured, such as increases in units produced or measures of expressed satisfaction. These are then attributed to the mental phenomena under investigation, motivation, management style, or whatever. The logic of this depends entirely upon faith that there is a connection between what is measured and what it is purported to represent. But the connection is not itself measurable (see also Chapter 10).

The inevitable effect of this is that organisational behaviour becomes subordinated to those things that can be measured, such as units of production or, indeed, profit and loss. Thus, the discourse of Organisational Behaviour ceases to be about understanding organisational behaviour itself, in preference for a means of producing quasi-measures, even spurious measures, of behaviour. Rather than a means of enlightening those with an interest in organisations, it becomes a device for manipulating behaviour in ways desired by managers. All this inevitably flows from a commitment to the concept of objective rationality.

Organisational Behaviour and the imperatives of technology

Another device used to substantiate the claim that management is objectively rational is to justify decisions on the basis of **the imperatives of technology**. Technology can be used in this way because it conforms to the laws of nature, which are immutable. Thus, the argument goes, if managers use technology competently, then they are only facilitating the applied use of these natural laws. For example, electricity is a natural phenomenon which can be used to produce rotary power from motors. If motors are better, more efficient, for powering, say, looms, then this is just a fact of nature for which managers cannot be blamed. If managers use electric power competently to power looms, they merely facilitate the application of natural power to produce goods and services. Prioritising the requirements imposed by technology is simply to respond to the needs and requirements of nature as technology and so becomes an objectively rational activity, since it would be irrational to go against the laws of nature. For centuries, and particularly since the beginning of the Industrial Revolution, technology has been cited as the 'engine' of progress and development, and explicitly characterised as independent of subjective preference, inexorable, value-neutral. It is not uncommon today, as in the past, for managerial activity to be attributed to the necessities of technological imperatives, as if this were some natural phenomenon which controls us and cannot be controlled. If it cannot be controlled, then no one can be to blame for its effects.

There are two difficulties with this position. In the *first* place, managers do not always use technology competently, nor do they always organise and manage on the basis of principles that prioritise the imperative demands of technology. Nuclear power stations blow up, planes crash, ships sink, computer systems fail to fulfil their purpose, drugs damage people, machines kill. The history of *in*competent use of technology suggests that the claim to objective rationality based on competence must always be in doubt. That technological imperatives are not adhered to in practice discloses this as, at best, *a rhetorical device* to justify decisions, implying subservience to some greater, and prior, neutral force rather than any personal desire. In the *second* place, it ignores the role of value judgement in the *use* of technology. Whereas technology itself may be neutral, its use rarely is, and we rarely experience it as neutral. A guillotine, for example, is a piece of technology for cutting things, but the decision to use it to cut people's heads off was clearly a reflection of subjective preference for its use. **If particular applications of technology represent value judgements, and therefore subjective preferences, then the associated requirement to adapt behaviour to fit technological imperatives must also be influenced by subjective preference.** Indeed, the decision to use a technology is not made because there is no alternative, or even because of a desire to give that technology an opportunity to perform. It is used primarily to increase profit, whether or not it actually does so. But, if the decision to apply technology is a matter of value preference in support of a particular interest, then it is not possible to argue that any effects of its use are not the responsibility of those who facilitate its use. Once again, the conditions appropriate to the claim to be objectively rational cannot be demonstrated.

Rationality and legitimacy

Because managers make the claim, implicitly or explicitly, that their actions and decisions are objectively rational, it follows that anyone who opposes them or resists them is, by definition, irrational. Yet organisational life is characterised by various challenges to managers' wishes, especially from the managed. That such disagreements reflect conflicts of interest is widely recognised and, indeed, it is seen as an important function of management to resolve such conflicts of interest in favour of managerial priorities – in other words, to transform 'irrational' behaviour into 'rational' behaviour. The attempt to get the managed to share the manager's vision underlies much of the impetus of training and development. Managing the inherent plurality in organisations towards consensus is seen as a necessary managerial skill.

Recognition that there are conflicts of interest is not the same as recognition that interests other than those of management are legitimate. There is an implicit assumption in the management of organisational behaviour, and in the discourse, that the *real* interests of the managed are congruent with those of the ones who manage. This does not mean, however, that, if they are the same, managers should adjust their world view to concur with that of the managed, but means that the managed should adjust to concur with the manager. An approach to managing behaviour that represented compromise between what managers wanted and what workers wanted would inevitably be sub-optimal and represent deviation from what is rational. This helps to explain why there has been, over the past decade or so, a return to a preference for unitary models of organisation, emphasising harmony, consensus and unity of interests, and where, once again, we see it made explicit that rationality is embodied in management and that workers' best interests are served by sharing that view.

We discussed previously (Chapter 5) the preference, in theory and in practice, for the concept of authority, rather than the concept of power. It was noted then that the concept of authority assumes that the managed voluntarily obey managers because of a desire to do their 'proper duty'. An important aspect of this relationship is that the managed should feel that the managers are competent and credible as authority figures – in other words, that their authority has a **legitimate** basis. What the managed can be asked to do must conform to some notion of what is reasonable. The test of reasonableness is the extent to which the demands of managers accord with their claims to be acting in an objectively rational manner. That is to say, **it is the claim of managers to be objectively rational that gives legitimacy to their role as managers**.

This is enshrined in the Weberian idea of **rational-legal authority** which is held to characterise contemporary bureaucratic forms of organisation. By rational-legal authority is meant authority that conforms to the rules formulated to facilitate the rational achievement of 'the organisation's goals'. It can be seen, therefore, that the particular rules and structures that organisations represent, the behavioural requirements imposed on employees and the right to apply sanctions for non-compliance are, *from this point of view*, held to be objectively necessary for the rational achievement of organisational objectives – this is their justification. By reference to this rationality, managers can exact compliance because, by definition, they are the ones who know what is needed. This is why the claim, and the devices to support the claim, to be objectively rational are so very important: ultimately, *they are the basis of the right to manage.*

Legitimacy, organisations and society

Clearly, the issue of rationality is very important in sustaining the role of management. If, however, as we have already suggested, the concept of objective rationality is not tenable in the context of organisations and organisational behaviour and, in particular, if managers do not represent objectively rational authority, what would this imply? In order to explore this question it is useful to look at the wider context of management, its social role, as well as the implications within particular organisations.

We suggested earlier that, in a wage labour economy, for most people, access to necessary goods and services and the opportunity to play a full role in society derives from the ability to sell their labour to an organisation. This implies that **it is an important role of organisations in general to generate social good**. In practice, this is in the hands of managers (those who govern organisations), and, from society's point of view, this is a major aspect of the management function. Managers control how many jobs there are in the organisations they manage, and access to those jobs. But the legitimacy of management and the claim to rational-legal authority depend crucially on pursuit of the organisation's prime objective of providing a positive return on investment, of making money grow. In other words, **the legitimacy and authority of the management process depends crucially on commitment to the interests of owners**. This means that the number of jobs available in a population reflects the number of jobs held to best serve the interests of ownership. Thus, we have a rather strange situation where, culturally, work is seen as extremely important and central to the functioning of both society and economy, but the mechanisms that furnish jobs reflect not this, but the desire of those with money to be able to make more money. This would make sense if the interests of society at large in the provision of means of survival and the attributes of civilisation were exactly congruent with those of investors wanting maximum return on their investment. The provision of jobs necessary to social survival and continuity, however, is only a *consequence* of the *prior* imperative of money earning more money – in effect, of the priority of unearned income over earned income. The underlying logic of this position is that those without money can best acquire it by ensuring that those with money get more.

It is often argued that the economy functions on what is known as a 'trickle-down effect': those with money increase what they have and, through investing or just spending, create benefit for those further down the socio-economic ladder, through stimulating demand and thus creating the need for more goods and services, thus creating jobs, and so on. Even if this does work – and the evidence is extremely patchy – the argument itself represents the recognition that the interest of those who invest money is **not** congruent with the interests of society at large, because any benefit to society is cast as a kind of accidental by-product of committing our efforts to the increase of return on investment. By this argument, benefit to society is not the purpose of wealth creation, but is just an epiphenomenon to be hoped for.

The iron law of oligarchy

Organisational Sociology has often been more perceptive about organisational life than has conventional Organisational Behaviour. Weber noted the apparently irresistible trend of organisations to bureaucratise, such that others, such as Swingle (1976), have claimed that, in contemporary society, virtually all organisations are bureaucracies. Clearly, notwithstanding the much-vaunted death of bureaucracy, it still flourishes, as the factors noted by Weber are still very much present in society. Another important contribution to understanding organisations was made by the German sociologist Robert Michels, who, in 1915, established his concept of **the iron law of oligarchy**, an idea which has much influenced the theory of bureaucratic organisations.

Briefly, the iron law of oligarchy suggests that:

a) all organisations are inevitably oligarchic (even those that both advocate and seek to represent democratic structures);

b) all organisations end up being run by elites who have little in common with the rest of the organisation's members;

c) these elites identify with similar elites in other organisations, rather than with members of their own organisation.

Thus, although the managing elite of an organisation, or sector of organisations, obviously have to have some sense of making the organisation perform what it is there to do, and, certainly, at a professional level, elites from different organisations, or kinds of organisation, will sometimes clash, there is, nevertheless, a significant common 'identity' shared by such elites. For example:

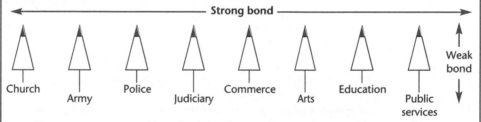

This sense of common identity is not really so surprising, given that, for example, many of the members of these elites have similar social and educational backgrounds, and will tend to socialise with each other. The contemporary idea of the professional manager who can manage any activity in any context supports and reinforces this oligarchical tendency, particularly with the increased use of 'business people' to run specialist services – education, health services, and so on. Yet it runs utterly counter to the idea that organisations and management are objectively rational processes.

■ If Michels is to be believed, what are the implications of the iron law of oligarchy for the concept of rational organisation?

One of the traditional aims of management is to reduce dependence on labour, and labour has always been seen as having interests at odds with those of capital. From a capitalist point of view, labour represents constraints on freedom of action, on one hand by being the repository of skills that capital needs to make money and, on the other hand, by making demands, such as claiming the right to a proportionate share of the benefits created by work. Traditionally, capital has moved, geographically, to areas where labour is seen as less problematic and demanding, and it has no allegiance to any particular socio-economic context, society or country. The preference for forms of technology that replace human work can also be seen as part of this trend. In a hypothetical capitalist utopia one might suppose that there would be no need for labour at all – but then capital would be making the money it wants but not providing the jobs society needs to be provided for its general good. **Thus, managers have a role of generating benefit for society *and* a role of regulating the supply of jobs, determining the amount of work that can be done, which is enacted on behalf of the interests that it is the manager's job to represent**. In practice, these two roles become incompatible, and it is the role as agents of ownership that – it might be said, inevitably – dominates.

The rationality of market forces

In the UK the coal industry, which was taken into State ownership after the Second World War because of its significance to industry and to the economy, has had a troubled history, less in terms of organisation than as a symbol of conflict between rationalities. On 19 October 1992 the then President of the Board of Trade, the Conservative minister Michael Heseltine, announced the intended closure of up to 31 coal mines due to a claimed excess of productive capacity. This provoked a considerable reaction from opponents, and from the general public, and, in particular, an unfavourable comparison with another industry which had similar problems, farming. The argument was succinctly encapsulated in a now famous contribution to the House of Commons debate on the proposal from the veteran Labour MP, Tony Benn:

'Entirely lacking from the Conservative Party has been any awareness of the sense of public outrage that people could be treated as the President of the Board of Trade did when he announced the closure of 31 pits . . . I say it was callous and brutal. That treatment came from a party that prides itself upon a citizens charter and a classless society . . . All my right hon. and hon. Friends know that these events are part of a sustained attack upon the mining industry. It is taking place because the previous Prime Minister [Margaret Thatcher] regarded the National Union of Mineworkers as the enemy within. That term was coined for that reason . . . The President of the Board of Trade said that he agonised over the decision that was before him. He is not the one who will suffer agony if pits are closed . . . Do not tell us that this is all about market forces. If those forces applied to the farming industry, half the farms in Britain would have closed years ago. We could get cheaper food from New Zealand and Australia . . . I am not in favour of applying market forces to farms. It is not possible to close a farm one year and open it the following year. We all know that the miners have not received set-aside grants. They have not been given money to stop producing coal . . . It has been said, "If there is surplus coal, why not give it to the pensioners?" That is a sensible argument. Coal could be supplied free of charge to the generators to pump it down the wire, as it were, in the form of cheap electricity . . . '

Source: Tony Benn, *Hansard (House of Commons Daily Debates) Session 1992–93*, Volume 212, 21 October 1992, pp. 502–3. Reprinted with permission.

The two industries, farming and coal mining, do make an interesting comparison:

Farming		Coal mining
Yes	Supply exceeds demand	Yes
Yes	Relevant products cheaper from abroad	Yes
Yes	Give surpluses free to pensioners, voluntary organisations, etc.	No
Yes	Subsidise producers from public funds	No

In the UK the Conservative Party has been associated, traditionally, with the owning class and the Labour Party, until recently, with the working class. Farmers have long been a significant constituency of the Conservative Party and Conservatives have supported, for many years, public subsidisation of the farming industry, including subsidies that encourage inefficient means of production, both for environmental reasons such as rural aesthetics and for artificial maintenance of the market. Amongst these subsidies has been 'set-aside', which pays farmers to take land out of production. In contrast, the Conservatives have shown virtually no interest at all in subsidising industries in order to protect jobs or to maintain the 'urban' aesthetics of, say, mining villages.

■ To what extent can it be seen as rational to treat two essential industries with similar problems in dissimilar ways?

Benn suggested that the actual cause of the decision to close pits was animosity to miners as an occupational group. This implies that punishing this group was more important than the social function of providing jobs.

■ In what sense could this be seen as rational?

Yet the social role remains. The effect is that managers, in general, exercise power on behalf *of* society and are supported *by* society but are not responsible *to* society. In theory at least, a country could be deprived of all its opportunities for jobs by managers acting in the interests of owners. Where would social benefit come from then? A potential brake on such a possibility is an extensive publicly owned sector, embodying different values regarding the provision of jobs, but with the fashion for privatisation such sectors as existed have been dismantled. Even what is left of a public sector is, in the UK at least, dominated by the principles, practices and values of private ownership, so that it is run *as if* for profit, and the idea that the provision of work is a social good in itself has all but disappeared.

The claim that managers are objectively rational in their actions and decisions is deeply implicated in all this. Their role in the process of production and distribution is pivotal and the effects would be serious enough if they *were* acting in an objectively rational manner. If, however, what managers do is to use the claim to be objectively rational to rational*ise* the enactment of their subjective preferences, albeit within the requirement of providing owners with some necessary but unspecified level of service, then the effects of such activity can no longer be seen as necessary, or inevitable, or inherently legitimate. The claim to be objectively rational can be seen as a means of moving the evaluation of what are essentially subjective preferences beyond question. But, because they *are* subjective, it is also obvious that they could be different. If managers are to fulfil their central social role, the assessment of what such preferences are, their legitimacy and how they are operationalised – their **rationale** – should be the province of more than just a partial interest.

Legitimacy and the management of organisational behaviour

From the particular perspective of organisational behaviour, a recognition of the subjectivity of preferences for managerial activity has enormous impacts. To put it at its baldest, it means that when a manager requires something to be done in a particular way, or requires particular behaviours from employees, this is not because there is some transcendent necessity for these demands to be satisfied, but because this is what seems to be required from their own subjectively rational point of view. If the claim to be objectively rational cannot be sustained, what remains is *subjective preference*, and that is influenced, as noted earlier, by all the aspects of a manager's personality, including areas like sexuality and prejudice, not just those aspects implicated directly in the work situation. A manager wants some behaviour, attitude or action because that is what they want, and that is all. Moreover, the requirement to comply is based not on what is rational, but on power.

When managers seek to influence behaviour, whether through payment of incentives, job appraisal, job redesign, employee development, cultural engineering or any other technique, in the absence of objective measures that demonstrate that this behaviour is better, or more productive, than that behaviour, the basis for choice can only be subjective. This explains why, as is now widely recognised, management is such a 'high fashion industry', attracted by the latest techniques in the same way as one might be attracted by the latest consumer product. If it is all a matter of subjective rationality, then the apparent legitimacy of demands for modification of behaviour in organisations disappears. All that is left is power. We do what is required of us in organisations, not because it is objectively rational to do it, but because someone has the power to ensure our compliance.

If managers cannot support the claim to be objectively rational, then they are no more rational, and no less rational, than employees. There has been a tendency in the discourse of Organisational Behaviour to dismiss the perspective of workers as self-interested, ill-informed, naive, and so on. **But if all are acting on the basis of subjective rationality, this must describe all, too.** So, if workers resist labour intensification because it causes them increased stress, if they resist pressures on them to identify more fully with 'the organisation' because it erodes their sense of autonomy, if they resist unsocial work patterns because of the impacts on their lives outside work, then these reactions must be seen as just as reasonable as the manager's desire for the contrary. Such differences cannot be resolved by one party claiming superior access to knowledge of what is correct, on the basis of their objectivity. Some other mechanism for judging priorities or for judging competing claims is necessary. This is not to suggest that all rationalities are equal, but the only differences are in the goals that are being pursued. Evaluation of those goals should be more extensive than that those of managers are superordinate because they are 'more' rational. Recognition of this would shift the entire basis of management of organisational behaviour. A discourse of Organisational Behaviour that reflects only a supposedly objectively rational managerialist interest cannot provide either an adequate explanation of the process of managing organisational behaviour or an adequate basis for defining and solving problems.

The meaning of rationality?

A particularly powerful view of the nature and purpose of rationality is offered by the American sociologist Alvin Gouldner in his book *The Dialectic of Ideology and Technology*:

'**Rationality is . . . the capacity to make problematic what had hitherto been treated as given**; to bring into reflection what before had only been used; to transform resource into topic; to examine critically the life we lead. This view of rationality situates it in the capacity to think *about* our thinking.' (1976: 49, first emphasis added)

In other words, Gouldner argues that rationality is not, and never should be, passive. We should never just accept what are presented to us as self-evident truths. It is, indeed, the very claim to self-evidence that should be interrogated. To be rational is to be active. We are only reasonable when we are questioning.

Existing applications in Organisational Behaviour

There is a strange situation in the field of knowledge about organisations and organisational behaviour, in which the conventional discourse, together with management practice, continues to adhere, implicitly or explicitly, to the claim to objective rationality in the face of widespread dissent and challenge to this claim. Virtually every critique of the orthodox position embodies a critique of the claim to objective rationality, emanating from an enormous variety of fields of knowledge with relevance to, and interest in, organisations and organisational behaviour.

Philosophical approaches have argued that managers do not and cannot represent the logical requirements of, the necessary and sufficient conditions for, objective rationality, especially that they are not and cannot be value-neutral. **Political** approaches, both those that examine the use of management techniques in politics and those that examine organisations from a macro or a micro political point of view, have argued that managers inevitably represent particular political interests which influence their preferences. Within these approaches there has also been a substantial focus on the intertwining of (especially macro) political and organisational processes, notably in the interventions of government on behalf of management to provide legal regulation of employee behaviour. Since politics is, by definition, the process of representing different and conflicting interests, involvement by managers in that process precludes objectivity. From the field of **economics** have come criticisms of managerial attachment to market mechanisms, such as the attachment to the concept of the market as a system operating, independently of human intervention, in obedience to some quasi-natural law, generating claims, for example, that employee behaviour must conform to the requirements of the market. From the field of **sociology** have come myriad studies of the management process which demonstrate that management practice does not conform to the prerequisites of objective behaviour or action – in particular, that it is reactive rather than characterised by forward planning – and that attachment to specific behaviour modification techniques owes much more to subcultural prejudices.

Within fields more specifically concerned with organisations there has been an even more focused critique. The burgeoning field of **managerial/organisational ethics** has developed the philosophical critiques, acknowledging and developing the specific recognition that moral values are – and should be – central to the management process, that concerns for, for example, efficiency have moral consequences, and that techniques for the modification and manipulation of behaviour require evaluation in the light of moral concerns. The widespread concern with the **knowledge base of management** generally, to which we referred in Chapter 4, has highlighted the prevalence of dehumanised, one-dimensional concepts of 'the worker'. This has stimulated exploration of aspects of the human condition that the discourse of Organisational Behaviour has consistently ignored. Recent examples include studies of **sexuality** in organisations and of the relevance and importance of **emotion** in the organisational context. One of the most obvious examples of this expansion has been the development of **gender studies**, which, until recently, was utterly absent from Organisational Behaviour. This has, in particular, addressed specific issues of management rationality, arguing that, far from being objective, it is predominantly a *masculine* rationality.

It has not been possible for the discourse of Organisational Behaviour utterly to ignore such a plethora of developments. Nonetheless, such acknowledgement as there is is usually superficial – the inclusion of a chapter, for example, on gender issues, or ethics, or emotion, in conventional organisational behaviour texts. It rarely includes acknowledgement that these developments constitute a profound challenge to the concept of objective rationality. That these challenges often come from outside the dominant discourse legitimates, from a discursive point of view, such casual treatment.

Further potential

The argument that all social situations can *only* be seen in terms of subjective rationality and the challenges to objective rationality have enormous implications, both within organisations and in society as a whole. In particular, two major and interlinked issues arise: **process** and **purpose**.

If the process of managing, and especially of managing behaviour, can only be a reflection of the subjective preferences of managers, this should necessitate a complete rethink of the basis of management. Whatever the purpose being served by managerial action, if that action can only be an expression of subjective preference, then **any unequivocal basis for judging managerial action is**

lost. This implies that managers are as likely to make bad decisions as to make good decisions in terms of the objectives being pursued, for reasons which are nothing to do with being objectively rational. There is a need for a body of theory that recognises that managers do actually *make* decisions, **that management is a process not of discovery but of invention**. If managers are objectively rational, then the correct/rational decision subsists within the situation and decisions are good or bad to the extent that this rational answer is *discovered*, and good or bad is merely a matter of management competence. If they are not objectively rational but are subjectively rational, then the good or bad decision is an effect of the manager's ability to interpret and to construct the situation – it is a matter of *inventing* the rationale for a particular decision, which is good or bad according to how persuasive it is at getting things done and achieving desired outcomes. It is worth emphasising that **there is no means of judging managerial decisions as good or bad in objectively rational terms because there is no way of assessing the opportunity cost of a particular course of action**. For example, when one person is selected for a job from a list of candidates, there is no way of knowing whether any of the other candidates would have performed better or worse than the one selected.

As regards purpose, it is not sufficiently recognised that **there is no such thing as management *per se*, there is only management for a specific purpose**. Under capitalism this purpose is to benefit the interest of owners, but, rather than make this explicit, there has been a tendency to claim that the purpose informing managerial action is that of serving an objective rationality. The explicit articulation of the purposes that management serves would, on one hand, give the lie to any notion of an over-arching objectivity and, on the other hand, require the development and assessment of a different basis of legitimacy. But a management process based on a spurious legitimacy is always vulnerable, as well as putting obstacles in the way of understanding what goes on in organisations. A legitimacy that was not spurious would provide management, as a profession, with firmer foundations, whatever that legitimacy was based on – and there are many possibilities, from the genuinely new (such as cooperation), to the genuinely old (power), each with its own far-reaching implications.

There has been a lot written about the problems of the claim to be objectively rational, many persuasive challenges. What is much less common is consideration of the full implications of this critique – there has been a reluctance to push it to its logical conclusions. Assuming that organisations and their management are an essential part of society, both now and in the future – could a society *without* organisation and management of *some* form or other be envisaged? – this step of addressing the full implications is the most important contribution to be made to the discussion. It is not enough to demonstrate, for example, that managerial decisions are subjectively rational, rather than objectively rational, because, **if the claim to be objectively rational fails, this has implications for *every* aspect of management and organisation**. If the claim to be objectively rational is not tenable, on what basis can legitimacy be claimed? What would an organisation look like that was based on some other kind of legitimacy? How could behaviour be managed, if the claim to be custodians of knowledge of what is correct behaviour fails? Could it be managed at all? These are questions that cannot be answered until the implications of a rationality that can only ever be subjective are explored.

Organisational behaviour and rationality

It has already been proposed that the proper function and purpose of the study of organisational behaviour is to try to gain an understanding of why people do the things that they do in the context of organisations. But, while the discourse of Organisational Behaviour retains its commitment to the idea of objective rationality, it is, largely, relegated to the role of identifying why workers tend to act 'irrationally' and, from this, to try to find and develop behaviour modification techniques that will bring them closer to 'rational' behaviour. Because Organisational Behaviour maintains an understanding of the proper role of workers as to give their maximum effort and commitment to 'the goals of the organisation', it has been obsessed with finding techniques to ensure that this potential is realised, be it through theories of motivation, cultural engineering, human resource management, training and development, or whatever else. Behaviour in organisations becomes understandable only in terms of performance.

An appreciation of the inescapably subjective nature of rationality, including the inevitable implication that, although managers and workers might have different goals, the status of their rationality is just the same, allows an expansion in the recognition of what is relevant to organisational behaviour. For example, conflict in organisations could no longer be viewed as a problem of, say, a recalcitrant workforce, but would need to be understood as the clash of equally valid rationalities. Though each may be equally rational they may not be equally desirable, but there could be no *a priori* judgement as to which was the more worthy. A profoundly different understanding of conflict in organisations would follow from the abandonment of objective rationality as a measure of behaviour and thus, too, would ensue profoundly different approaches to conflict management.

It has also been noted that there is a very simplified and attenuated concept of the person in the discourse of Organisational Behaviour and that many behavioural influences are barely recognised, such as sexuality, gender, ethnicity, religion, emotion, and so on. This has happened because such aspects of humanness are considered to be inimical to objectively rational behaviour. We all know that in our lives outside work these things are important and that they themselves constitute standards by which we measure our own behaviour as rational or otherwise. It is simply ridiculous to imagine that they are not equally important in our lives at work. If the issue of objective rationality is discarded, with it goes any theoretical barrier to including such aspects of behaviour in our understandings of behaviour in organisations. Then we will generate far richer and more appropriate understandings of why people behave as they do. An aspect of organisational behaviour that would be opened up, for example, is that of discrimination. Outside work organisations we know that discrimination of any kind is based on attitudes and prejudices, but these are the very aspects of personality excluded by basing the standards of behaviour on the concept of what is objectively rational. Thus, it is very common to find rationalisations of discrimination that seek to explain it in terms of objectively rational behaviour – it is not really discrimination but a necessary requirement in order to be objective. Take this prop away and the bases of discriminatory behaviour in organisations can be explored more productively and more appropriately. Unless we understand what the bases of discrimination are, we can never hope to deal with it adequately.

It is also long overdue for the discourse of Organisational Behaviour to admit that there are more organisations than just work organisations. Given the ubiquity of organisations in the contemporary world, it is not unreasonable to hope that Organisational Behaviour might have something to say about organisations of all kinds. Why is it that when people become members of organisations they accept it as perfectly rational to behave in ways that they would not do outside organisations? Why do members of paramilitary groups think it is rational to go out and murder, not only those they do not agree with, but also people who are not actively involved and may even sympathise with their views? Why, in families, can parents think it rational routinely to abuse their children? Why do members of a religion think it rational to persecute members of a different religion? Why does one ethnic group think it rational to eliminate another ethnic group through genocide? And why has the discourse of Organisational Behaviour nothing to say about *this* kind of organisational behaviour? All the people in cases such as the above believe themselves to be engaged in rational behaviour, but, obviously, it has difficulties in fitting such behaviour into its model of objective rationality. Surely, however, rather than simply ignore it, it would be better to abandon a model that simply does not fit experience?

A TALE FROM THE VILLAGE PUMP (*RATIONALITY*)

(See the Case Study in Appendix 2, pages 340–3)

The entirety of the events described in this case represents a narrative of competing **rationalities**. Both Farr and Snow were Men of Science, sons of the Enlightenment, and, at one important level, they shared the same purpose: the improvement of public health and welfare. But in other aspects they were profoundly different. Farr was looking for mathematical proof of the miasma theory, which would, purportedly, be the ultimate demonstration that the theory was objectively rational, True. He appeared to achieve this with his model, which demonstrated an inverse relationship between the incidence of cholera and height above the River Thames. The problem with this interpretation of the data was that it attributed causality to a relationship that was, in practice, coincidental.

Farr was relying on **formal** logic. Snow, on the other hand, had much more modest objectives – he merely wanted to demonstrate that a particular cluster of cholera victims was connected to a particular drinking water pump. To do this he relied on **rhetorical** logic (see also Chapter 4). Snow did not seek to furnish a proof, he only sought to furnish a plausible argument. In this, he was successful in so far as he got the pump handle removed, but he was unsuccessful in so far as he failed to convince other experts.

■ How does Gouldner's definition of **rationality** as 'the capacity to make problematic what had hitherto been treated as given' (see above) help to explain Snow's understanding of the problems?

THE STATE OF THE UNION

Makepiece Services was a medium-sized, family owned and non-unionised service company in an area where traditional industries had been in decline for many years, and unemployment was high. Inward investment to the region had been minimal and such jobs as had been created tended to be in organisations such as call centres and tele-sales.

Bill Thackery was the Chairman and Managing Director of Makepiece Services, and had had the same roles in Esmond Enterprises, another small company he had set up many years previously, having spotted an opening in supplying a large regional concern, Hoggarty Engineering. Esmond Enterprises had been a successful venture and had looked set for growth. New customers had been acquired, but Hoggarty Engineering had remained, overwhelmingly, the most important. But Hoggarty Engineering had become embroiled in a protracted union-led labour dispute, which became a lock-out. Esmond Enterprises could not cope with the loss of orders from Hoggarty Engineering that resulted from the lock-out and eventually the company folded. The dispute was finally settled in favour of the workers, but Esmond Enterprises could not be revived. Bill Thackery blamed the trades unions for the collapse of Esmond Enterprises and became very hostile to any attempt to introduce unionisation at Makepiece Services. He was also very vocal publicly in opposing government attempts to regulate working conditions. He opposed the introduction of the minimum wage, limits on working hours, and so on. He argued that self-regulation was the appropriate method for companies, and that government intervention was both unnecessary and unhelpful since any sensible company would treat its employees well, since they are an organisation's greatest asset.

Bill Thackery saw his management style as benign paternalism. The company was there for the benefit of his family and he should be allowed to 'know what was best' for what he owned. Working conditions at Makepiece Services were not very modern – indeed, were sometimes described by some as Victorian. Wages were low, there was little representation for the workforce, people were expected to work overtime as required and without regard to other commitments they might have, holiday entitlements were theoretical rather than real. On the other hand, Makepiece Services had a long history of providing employment opportunities for the family members of employees and it made uncommonly generous pension provision. Makepiece Services was not a high-tech company, it did not welcome innovation. Rather, what was wanted was a steady, reliable and undemanding workforce, loyal and long-serving. It seemed that this was just what the company had got. Although a change in the law gave workers the right to trade union representation if a majority of those working in any company wanted it, not having had a tradition of trade union membership and it being felt that, in spite of the relatively 'primitive' conditions, Makepiece Services was a reasonably fair employer, there had been no internal pressure to admit the unions to the company.

Some time after the change in the law a new, young and ambitious organiser had joined the local trade union organisation. Lori Byndon had been given, as her primary target, non-union employers in the area, to try to get union recognition and extra members in such companies. Makepiece Services was a prime candidate. She started by handing out leaflets at the main entrance to the company, holding meetings in the local Working Men's Club and getting featured in the local media.

Alarmed by these developments, Bill Thackery hired a consultant, Denis Penn, whose particular expertise was in blocking the attempts of unions to organise in non-union companies. Denis Penn started by sending out letters to the workforce of Makepiece Services. These letters suggested that there were dangers posed by unionisation, both to the company and to their jobs. Departmental meetings were called, at which Denis Penn developed these implied threats in terms of the particular difficulties that would face each department. If any employee was thought to be contemplating joining the trade union, they were interviewed on a one-to-one basis. Private detectives were hired to observe people who were thought to be speaking to the trade union representative and/or attending union-organised meetings.

Angela Titchmarsh was a departmental manager in her mid-50s who had worked for Makepiece Services since leaving school. She had never been particularly ambitious and her career had been strongly influenced by her desire to stay in the area, so she had been reasonably content at Makepiece Services, in spite of the conditions there. For her, work was, primarily, a means of survival and her main interests were outside work. The attempts of the union to gain admission to Makepiece Services and the response of the senior managers to this had increased tensions in the company. An especially worrying development for Angela Titchmarsh had been the company's threat to change the pension scheme, to something less favourable – Bill Thackery had claimed that a union presence would make the company less viable and so, to save money, it would be necessary to reduce the benefits of the pension scheme. As Angela Titchmarsh approached retirement age, she feared that her pension would be much smaller under the new scheme than she had anticipated under the existing scheme. The proposed new scheme sparked a great deal of discussion among the workforce, and many of the younger employees thought that the best response to the threat would be to have some help from the union in resisting the change. There were calls for a ballot to test support for joining a union.

Bill Thackery and Denis Penn redoubled their efforts to dissuade individuals from supporting the ballot. All staff were seen individually and the implications of voting to admit the union to the company, and of joining the union, were spelt out. In Angela Titchmarsh's case, the issue of the pension scheme was heavily emphasised. As the pressure from Bill Thackery increased, some employees felt that the only safe course of action was to back off, but others felt that it signified that the protection of union membership was increasingly necessary.

■ Each of the characters in the case acts rationally in their own terms. Is there any way that such a conflict of interest might be resolved rationally?

■ Even if the ballot is held but goes against unionisation, would it be the rational thing to do to introduce the new and cheaper pension scheme anyway?

■ Can the use of the various types of pressure applied at Makepiece Services be seen as a legitimate part of industrial relations?

■ What would be a rational decision for Angela Titchmarsh?

(Other chapters that would be useful and relevant in analysing the case *include* Power (5), Ideology (7), Self (8), Boundary (9) and Decision-making (11).)

Bibliography

For a general overview of the issues surrounding the concept of rationality see, for example, Wilson (1970) and Hollis and Lukes (1982). The concept of bounded rationality is in Simon (1976). For the general relevance of the concept of rationality to organisation and management, and their discourses, see, for example, Burrell and Morgan (1979), Bryman (1984), Thomas (2003). There is a huge literature on the concept of rationality *vis-à-vis* the social sciences and almost anything on the philosophy of the social sciences will have an argument one way or the other – see, for example, Ryan (1970), Pratt (1991). Those who argue for objective rationality are likely to be those who argue for the actual or potential scientific nature of social science – see the bibliography to Chapter 4. An influential contribution to the argument emphasising subjective rationality, in terms of the need for sociology to concern itself with the standpoint of the actor, is Winch (1958). Another very influential contribution is Berger and Luckman (1967). It may, of course, never be possible to resolve this argument conclusively, since the two positions are incommensurable – unless there were to be a Kuhnian-type revolution (Kuhn 1970). See also Baggott (2005).

Psychoanalysis made a big impact on understandings of the concept of rationality – see, for example, Lacan (1980) – and one of the major impacts of Poststructuralism has been to heighten awareness of these issues, not just among Poststructuralists. Rorty (1982) and Bernstein (1983), for example, both symbolise an attempt to move beyond the objective/subjective rationality issues in some ways, though perhaps not entirely successfully, as such a move seems to presuppose an argument for subjective rationality. Amongst Critical Theorists, who tend towards the objective rationality position, Habermas (1978) has made a notable contribution. His concerns are, perhaps, symbolised by the very title of Habermas (1987) – *Towards a Rational Society* – a commentary on the (especially student) protests of the 1960s. Such has been the impact of the critique of objective rationality that Postmodernism has been characterised by some writers as 'the flight from rationality' (that is, objective rationality) and the issue is one of the main focuses of the very active debate between Critical Theory and Postmodernism. Harvey (1989) gives a good introduction to the issues under debate. Holub (1991) presents some of the debates between Habermas and various Poststructuralist and Postmodernist writers. Compare, for example, Dews (1987) or Norris (1992, 1996) with Lyotard (1984) or Rosenau (1992). For a view of the implications of 'the flight from rationality' in management see, for example, Carter and Jackson (1990) or Jackson and Carter (1995a).

The economistic view of the role of organisation and management generally comes under the term 'the theory of the firm'. Savage and Small (1975) provide an accessible introduction. See also Cyert and March (1963). A closely related concept is that of Rational Economic Man, in the discourse of Organisational Behaviour extended to the idea that everyone is motivated by money and makes rationally calculated decisions to maximise economic self-interest. A useful synopsis of this, and of its implications, can be found in Schein (1988). See also Hollis (1975).

There is a really vast literature on measuring organisational behaviour elements such as attitudes and psychological states. For some interesting observations on the ontology of measurement, see Jones (1983). The argument against the impartiality of technology is also well represented in various literatures. For arguments related to the Industrial Revolution, see, for example, Clayre (1977) – an anthology of contemporary views – and also Marglin (1980), Berg (1994). Much of Labour Process Theory takes this view, following Braverman (1974). See, also, McKenzie and Wajcman (1985) and Scarborough and Corbett (1992). Again, Gender Studies has made a particular contribution in this area – see, for example, Cockburn (1983), Cockburn and Ormrod (1993), Bradley (1989). In the context of information technology, see, for example, Solomonides and Levidov (1985), Kling (1991). Latour (1987) is another influential contribution, from a different perspective. The rationality of the machine extended to organisational process is a particular concern of Marcuse (1986), in the concept of technocratic rationality – see also, for example, the machine metaphor in Morgan (1997). For a connection between technical rationality and ethics, see Adams and Balfour (2004). A more general, and perhaps more conventional, but relevant, disquisition on the management of decision-making is in Harrison (1999).

The literature on conflict and its management is particularly relevant to questions of rationality and legitimacy. Much of this literature is underpinned by implicit or explicit assumptions about whether organisations are typically unitary or pluralistic. A useful overview of the issues implied in such assumptions is to be found in Fox (1966), while Fox (1973) concludes that pluralism is really just a sophisticated version of unitarism, rather than substantively different – see also, amongst others who hold similar views, Playford (1971). An approach that opposes the pluralist one is represented in Conflict Theory. The classic examples of the general approach are Dahrendorf (1959), Rex (1961), and the relevance for theories of organisation, and, by implication, for theories of organisational behaviour, are explicitly explored in Burrell and Morgan (1979). Many Labour Process theorists take a Conflict Theory position – see, for example, Thompson (1983), Sturdy, Knights and Willmott (1992), Jermier, Knights and Nord (1994). Studies of actual conflict situations, such as those by Beynon (1973) and Hyman (1977), are similarly unpersuaded by the pluralist argument. For some relevant literature on authority, see the bibliography to Chapter 5. Ritzer (1993) provides an accessible study of the impacts of 'rationalisation' on contemporary organisations and society, from a Radical Weberian point of view. For an interesting overview of a range of relevant issues, see Ritzer (2004).

For the complex relations between capitalism, organisations and society, see, for example, Offe (1985), Urry and Lash (1987), Gorz (1989), Hutton (1995). Tugendhat (1971) offers a venerable but still relevant perspective, based on multinationals. There is a substantial literature from outside the conventional discourses of Organisation Studies and Organisational Behaviour on the social costs of organisational activity. See, generally, the radical paradigm metaphors in Morgan (1997) – also, from a variety of perspectives, Fromm (1979), Capra (1983), Bohm (1983), Hills (1987), Beck (1992), Punch (1996), amongst many others. A pertinent contribution is Foucault (2003). From a rather different angle, there is a burgeoning literature on issues of corruption that, while not necessarily focused directly on organisational activity, does make connections between states and corporations. See, for example, Green and Ward (2004), Harris (2003) and Rose-Ackerman (1999). Oligarchy is also obviously relevant here. The classic on this, as noted in this chapter, is Michels (1968), but see also Domhoff (2005), Dye (2000), Scott (1991).

That management is, and always has been, a 'high fashion industry' is not a contentious claim. This is reflected in a growing literature. See, for example, Jackson (2001), Collins (2000), ten Bos (2000).

Outside the discourses of Management and Organisational Behaviour no one really takes seriously the idea that management is the repository of objective rationality in organisations. MacIntyre (1985) puts the matter quite succinctly. See also, however, any study of management as process – such as Mintzberg (1980) or Stewart (1988) – for a picture of management activity as fragmented and reactive. A brief but representative sample of the literatures referred to in the section on 'Existing Applications in Organisational Behaviour' is, in order of appearance: MacIntyre (1985), Scott (1997), Hutton (1995), Polanyi (1971), Chia (1998), Parker (1998a), Hearn and Parkin (1987), Hearn, Sheppard, Tancred-Sheriff and Burrell (1989), Fineman (1993), Wilson (1995), Novarro (1980), Marshall (1984). See also Guillet de Monthoux (1993).

CHAPTER 7

Ideology

This chapter examines the nature of the concept of ideology. The extent to which an ideology is, can be, or ought to be, logical and systematic is considered, and the fundamental relations between ideology and action and practice are highlighted. The commonly pejorative implication of the term and its juxtaposition with 'reality' are both seen as inappropriate in light of the impossibility of being non-ideological. The functions of ideology as a rubric for making sense, enhancing survival and sense of security are described, and the concept is developed from micro to macro levels of analysis via the notion of coalitions, of people and of ideas. The role of ideology in forming perceptions of interest is highlighted, and its role In knowledge production and discourse is examined. Issues of the relationship of ideology to management and organisation as practices are explored, with particular emphasis on the significance of recognition of the ideological nature of capitalism as their rationale. As one particular example, it is shown how ideology is inextricably linked to the important arena of organisational ethics. The emphasis throughout is on the inadequacy of attempts to understand organisational behaviour that fail to recognise the ubiquity of ideology and its significance in informing behaviour and action.

We have been proposing an approach to understanding organisations and organisational behaviour that is considerably different to the orthodox approach. Rather than the approach that sees the study of organisations and organisational behaviour as part of the more general process of the scientific discovery of Nature's secrets, of the rational understanding of potentially rational behaviour, we have shown, through semiotics, that real meaning is absent, as are real structures; that knowledge of the (social) world is governed by discourses rooted in power; and that the claim to rationality is just that – a claim, not an actuality. Thus we have chipped away at the possibility of a rational, objective, scientific body of knowledge about organisations and organisational behaviour. Yet, even if there is no over-arching rationality informing organisational life, there is certainly some coherence to what occurs. Everything is not just random, accidental, chaotic. Things are achieved collectively, purposes are pursued. But this coherence is not a reflection of an external, given, rationality derived from nature. It derives from **ideology**.

The 'problem' with ideology

Ideology is not a popular concept in the context of organisations or of organisational behaviour, in theory or in practice, and thus its use as a concept is uncommon. Where it does occur it tends to signify something negative or undesirable – its use is almost always pejorative. There are two obvious reasons for this, relating, respectively, to issues of knowledge and to issues of practice. *Firstly*, natural science, in general, does not like the implications of the concept of ideology, because ideology implies subjective values and preferences, that science claims not only to eschew, but to render unnecessary. So a study of organisational behaviour that sought to base itself on the model of natural science would inevitably share this view. In representing itself as objective, rational and neutral the discourse of Organisational Behaviour has no truck with the trappings of ideology. *Secondly*, the 'people management' process likes to portray itself as universal and value-neutral, although, as we have shown, both theory and practice concern, specifically, behaviour in *capitalist* organisations. Capitalism is itself presented – where it is even considered – as a natural social phenomenon beyond the influence of subjective preference, or, indeed, of power, and, especially, of partial interests. If capitalism is natural, objective and rational, then any dissent from it must be, by definition, irrational. Or, as more commonly expressed, ideological.

If the discourse of Organisational Behaviour were to recognise the role and influence of ideology fully, it would put itself at odds with both science and capitalism. At a stroke, it would destroy the illusion of universality that scientific-ness confers and the utility for capitalism that universality and the denial of partial interests represent. Why? Because this would signify the potential legitimacy of other perspectives and other interests than those of capital, by placing them all on an equal basis – partial and subjective. Where the term 'ideology' *is* found is precisely in the labelling of views that do dissent from those of the powerful – of the kind of disparaging dismissal, 'I am rational; therefore, if you disagree with me, you must be ideological'. There is, however, no reason at all why the **concept** of ideology should be assumed to be value-laden. Although the **content** of an ideology is inevitably value-laden, the concept itself is merely a descriptive term for a more or less consistent system of ideas. This needs, however, to be explored in more depth.

Ideas and their logic

Imagine a person observing birds flying, noting that, while birds fly, humans do not, and noting that birds achieve flight by flapping their wings – devices having strong similarities with human arms. This person might then conclude that, if they were to fit appropriate wing-like attachments to their arms and flap them, they too could achieve flight. It would then be but a simple step to think that, if one jumped off something high, it might be possible, with these attachments, to achieve human flight. This is the concept of ideology at its most simple: **ideas systematically underpinned by logic**. The idea that humans could achieve flight by simulating what birds do has a logical flow – it seems reasonable. After all, we managed to swim by simulating what fish do, so why not flight by the same process? Jumping off high structures wearing and flapping bird-like wings is, of course, what a number of people attempted, usually with fatal results, because the logic underpinning their idea of human flight was flawed. As we now know, the logic of human flight generally implies more than human energy, an engine of some kind.

When ideology fails

In this simple example the accuracy of the logic of the idea of flight could be demonstrated. But imagine a much more complex scenario – ideas about how the economy works, ideas about ethnicity, or ideas about how to organise the production of goods and services. These are situations where the logic underlying the ideas cannot be tested. Such examples begin to indicate the significance of ideology in human affairs. For example, suppose you want to govern a nation state: you will have certain ideas, certain beliefs, about how this should be done, but it is not possible *scientifically* to test those ideas. When you come to power you can adopt certain policies to achieve the realisation of these ideas, but you will not know in advance whether they are achievable, or whether your policies are the best way to achieve them. If you are a Hitler, you may have ideas about eliminating a particular ethnic group and implement a Final Solution to do this; if you are a Kennedy, you may have ideas about halting the advance of global communism and start a war in South East Asia to do this; if you are a Thatcher, you may have ideas about the importance of the individual and the unimportance of society and start by reducing the influence of the state to do this; and so on. **The practices adopted follow the logic of the ideas** about what should be, about what government ought to achieve. You may, or may not, be correct – certainly, the originals in the examples above did not, in general, achieve their objectives.

Ideology is not only applicable at such a macro level, however. Suppose you are a manager in an organisation: you will have particular ideas about what people are like, about what structures should be in operation, about what constitutes a fair day's work, and so on, and all your practice will be influenced by the logic of your ideas. Suppose you are an owner who thinks that your employees should produce one thousand widgets per day: you would design a production system, a quality system, a payment system, which would seek to ensure this level of production. The logic of your ideas about how much should be produced and about the requirements for that production would inform how you organise and manage. Should your workers produce only nine hundred widgets a day you would need to investigate the causes of the under-production. You would need to decide whether it is because, for example, your workers are idle, or your production system is faulty, or your payment system provides insufficient incentive. The answer to the 'problem', however, is not a question of fact, but of what you believe to be the case – which, as with the flying example, may, or may not, be correct. The investigation you engage in would itself be driven by your ideas about what is an appropriate means to discover knowledge. **At its most basic level, this is what ideology is: a set of ideas and their underpinning logic, which inform action, decisions, preferences – everything.**

Ideology versus reality

Up to now ideology has been defined very simply, in terms of its linguistic relationship to 'ideas'. In some cases ideas can be tested and proved to be true, or not, and in other cases they cannot – they may be testable, but are not provable. For our purposes, ideas that can be proved can be consigned to the realm of science, and do not concern us here, since such proofs will be part of the natural world rather than the social world. Ideas that are not capable of scientific proof can be seen to lie in the realm of ideology. This statement points to the original sense of the term 'ideology'. It was coined to denote a systematic approach to the study of ideas – a science for analysing ideas – which would reveal any bias or prejudice in forming those ideas (as measured against reality). The term has subsequently acquired a number of connotations, some of which are descriptive and some of which are prescriptive. Thus, in some fields, such as sociology, ideology is a term used to refer to systems of beliefs, in a way similar to the use of the term 'culture', and there is, at the conceptual level, no value judgement necessarily implied.

On the other hand, in other fields, of which Management and Organisation Studies generally is one, the term 'ideology' is used to denote beliefs, whether systematic or not, which are not based on fact. In other words, ideology is counterposed to something called reality. The claim to be able to describe reality – the claim to represent the truth – is the correlative of the claim to be objective, rational and impartial. By implication, if you do not share the view of those who are objective, rational and impartial, you must be basing your view on something that is not true, either wilfully or through ignorance. However, as we argued in Chapter 6, to be objective, rational and impartial is not a condition available to human beings and, thus, the claim to be so *is* only a claim. It is, indeed, a claim most people would wish to make for themselves, but one that only those with the power to signify and with status in the discourse can seek to legitimate. Since it is only a claim, the use of the term 'ideology' to denote alternative views only signifies disagreement. **The term 'ideology', because it is counterposed to the claim to represent fact, is used to denigrate difference by classifying it as wrong.** But, given that there are no such things as social facts – and that, even if there were, there is no basis for any particular group to claim special knowledge of them – **any set of views, including the claim to be objective, rational and impartial, is ideological.** For example, managers are one such group who claim to be acting rationally, and, therefore, claim the ability to label any opposing group as ideological, whether they are recalcitrant workers, unwelcome pressure groups or interfering governments. And, as noted before, there is a strong *positive* cultural value attached to rationality, whose obverse is a strong *negative* cultural value attached to being ideological. This appellation, therefore, undermines the legitimacy of any opposing position. But denigrating an alternative position as ideological cannot be seen to represent a considered *evaluation* of it, since the position that denigrates is also ideological.

Given this situation, the use of the term 'ideology' in a pejorative way is effective in enhancing power, but does not convey any transcendent meaning. It is only a signifier and can thus mean what anyone wants it to mean, though those with the power to signify have the advantage in the contest to prescribe signification. This does not make them correct, however. Since the term 'ideology' is only a signifier, we wish to *rescue* it from this pejorative association. The implication of our position is that **there is no possibility for anyone to be non-ideological.** Being ideological is part of being human. It is like breathing, part of the human condition which cannot be escaped. All social organisation needs to accommodate the human characteristics of people and so, just as organisations have to provide toilets because people need toilets, even though toilets may not contribute directly to organisational objectives, it is necessary to recognise that all organisational members, be they owners, managers, workers, clients or anyone else, are ideological in their own way. The ideologies themselves may be different but the extent of being ideological is the same for everyone. They should do this, but they do not.

The functions of ideology

Everybody *needs* an ideology in order to be able to function in the world. Though people are rarely aware of its existence, **ideology is the coarse framework, or rubric, that we use for making sense of the world.** When we try to make sense, to understand significations and to render the world intelligible to ourselves, when we know what we know and decide what is real, we test our interpretations for adequacy against some set of ideas which we *already* have about how the world is. In this sense, **ideology prefigures any particular instance of making sense, and is the measure of what makes sense.**

We discussed in Chapter 2 the potentially infinite variety in the meanings ascribed to signifiers and in the interpretation of those meanings. The reason for this variety derives from the ways in which ideologies, in this sense, are developed. We acquire our ideology as we grow up and it continues to develop throughout adult life. It emerges as a consequence of the success, or failure, of processes of socialisation and is constantly monitored and modified in light of life experiences. This does not mean that we can be, inevitably, trained or indoctrinated into a *particular* ideology: we may be brought up as Christians and become atheists, we may come from a wealthy background and embrace poverty, we may be brought up as egalitarians and become elitists, and so on. On the other hand, we may, indeed, maintain the beliefs we are trained into at an early age. Our beliefs are not fixed, but they are not necessarily easy to change.

Changes in belief always come from within the individual even though the stimulus may be external. Our beliefs are the product of our experiences, but also of other influences, such as personality, emotion and cognition. Changes may be slow and gradual – for example, the *supposed* shift in political views from left of the spectrum to right of it as one gets older – or sudden road-to-Damascus conversions, often an effect of trauma. Nonetheless, that we have ideas which inform our attempts to make sense of the world is inescapable, inevitable, eternal. *The existence of ideology is not good or bad, it just is*. We may find the content of some ideologies more or less repugnant or attractive, but that is only in light of our own ideological positions.

The function of ideology is **not** to give us a correct or incorrect interpretation of the world – correct-ness is irrelevant, since ideology is not measurable against any absolute standard of truth. Its function is to give us the impression that we *are* able to make sense, to make us feel comfortable in the world – a psychological and emotional safety-net. In this sense, **ideology is a means of reducing our sense of uncertainty**. When we seek to give meaning to new, or different, information, this information triggers our ideology – we test it against other ideas and beliefs that we have, in order to discern a meaning. This is what underlies the capacity of different individuals to understand the same information in profoundly different ways. In testing interpretations against what we already believe to be the case, we generally accept interpretations, ideas, information that conform to our pre-existing beliefs and reject interpretations, ideas, information that do not conform – but not always. **The attempt to make sense of the world is not an attempt to discover reality, or truth, but an attempt to maintain stability, at a very individual level, so that we can continue to function, continue to believe that we do understand**. The maintenance of that belief is, to some extent, enhanced by the confirmation of others of our interpretation of the world. This, then, is the particular significance of the exercise of **micro-power**, *the opportunity to impose our own world view on others*.

Consistency and coherence

A common language sense of ideology always implies a degree of **consistency** and **coherence** in sets of ideas, implies a **system** of beliefs. However, in the sense in which ideology is being used here, the degree of consistency and coherence is a purely internal measure of the adequacy of our beliefs in serving their functional purpose of maintaining our ability to operate relatively effectively – in our own terms – in the world. What is necessary is that we should not *perceive* any direct inconsistency or contradiction in our ideas. This does not mean that individual ideologies are necessarily consistent and coherent by any objective measure – to anyone else. It is not necessarily dysfunctional to any individual to hold beliefs that seem inconsistent to other people – to be, for example, a Christian Darwinist, a capitalist socialist, an egalitarian racist – as long as that individual can convince themselves that they are not inconsistent. On the other hand, it is quite common for behaviour and actions to be inconsistent with beliefs – ideology in this sense is rarely so all-powerful as to-die-for, though, of course, it can be. Thus, a committed communist can work in, perhaps even manage, a capitalist organisation, an atheist can go to church, a pacifist can work in an arms factory, a vegetarian in an abattoir, and a person committed to honesty can be dishonest, without necessarily violating their ideology, or feeling forced to modify it. A well-known British executioner, who had a long career hanging people on behalf of the state, did not believe in capital punishment.

The ancient art of spinning

We tend to associate what is known as 'spin-doctoring' with contemporary corporate and political life, but it is by no means only a modern phenomenon.

A report from a Parliamentary Commission, *The Children's Employment Commission: First Report of the Commissioners – Mines*, was published in 1842. This Commission's task was to enquire into the employment of children and – despite the title – women underground in coal mining. Their report on the practices and conditions of work was so damning that, eventually, it led to a change in the law, banning women and girls, and boys under the age of ten years, from working underground. Prior to the change in the law women and children were employed for tasks such as moving coal and operating the heavy ventilation doors found in coal mines. They were preferred to men wherever possible because they were cheaper to employ. It was widely recognised that the publication of so critical a report made the prohibition of employment of women and children underground likely, and this had clear cost implications for the Coal Owners.

The immediate response of the Northern Coal Owners was '. . . the presentation of a short petition to both Houses of Parliament, denying the allegation of cruel practices . . . [which] would be the best mode of removing any impression disadvantageous to the coal owners'. This comprised a 27-point rebuttal of the Commission's findings and included the assertion – which the Coal Owners clearly thought reasonable and likely to influence public opinion in their favour – that no child younger than eight years was (officially) employed underground, and that children of that age 'seldom' worked more than 12 hours per day. (This is, however, somewhat at odds with the claim elsewhere in the rebuttal that 'boys of six years of age are never employed as putters; they must first go through the intermediate stage of trapper and driver'.) The general tenor of the spin is that, contrary to the evidence gathered by the Commission, miners, including women and children, were all healthy, happy and enjoying a fairly easy life. The spin doctors even got one 'Wm. Hardcastle, Member of Royal College of Surgeons, &c.' to write in support of this, and to claim that miners were not unduly affected by 'the perpetual inhaling of coal dust' – a somewhat unusual view, even for those times.

▶

The subsequent banning of such employment indicates that public opinion did not share the Coal Owners' view of what was reasonable.

- On what ideological basis might the Coal Owners and friendly doctors seek to deny evidence collected from miners and by observation?
- On what ideological basis might public opinion and, subsequently, Parliament reject the Coal Owners' rebuttal?
- What impact might the cultural perceptions of gender roles have had in this debate?

Source: The Rebuttal cited was produced by The Coal Office, Newcastle-upon-Tyne, 25 May 1842, and was later bound into a copy of the Official Commission Report, now held in the Library of the University of Newcastle-upon-Tyne.

Whilst in principle everyone has their own ideology, we do not, in practice, operate as isolated individuals: we share beliefs with other people. **People form coalitions** under particular ideological umbrellas, such as liberalism, nationalism, vegetarianism, Marxism, and so on – these coalitions symbolise relatively formalised, collective, ideologies. But because two people subscribe to the same ideology at the level of the signifier, it does not mean that they necessarily share the same view, the same interpretation, of that signifier in any detail. Thus, for example, in the Anglican church, there are people who believe in the propriety of the ordination of women as priests, and people who do not, yet both groups are Christian. There are also **coalitions of ideas**: some ideologies are more or less compatible with other ideologies. For example, in the UK, Conservatism, Capitalism and Anglicanism fit together, and members of one group are likely to be members of one or both of the others. The same was once the case with Socialism, Trades Unionism and Methodism. Equally, some '-isms' obviously do not fit together, such as Socialism and Individualism, or Conservatism and Egalitarianism. But ideologies are also malleable and -isms that might once have seemed inimical can become linked together – for example, Socialism and Capitalism, or Roman Catholicism and Marxism.

These collective ideologies, the -isms, generally derive from sources external to any individual believer. However, whatever their original articulation or form, they cannot be understood as homogeneous bodies of belief. Each individual adherent will have their own interpretation of what the tenets of the belief mean and what they imply for behaviour and action. No individual's ideology will be precisely the same as another individual's ideology. Where there is sufficient **intersubjective** agreement between people there will be the potential for a collective ideology, but this is unlikely to be total intersubjective agreement, not least because people adhere to more than one collective (as opposed to personal) ideology. To give a very simple example: if we consider Conservatives and Socialists in terms of attitudes to blood sports, the synthesis of formal political beliefs and sporting beliefs will not directly overlap, but may indicate a stronger or weaker combination. These are different orders of belief and belief in one does not entail belief in the other, but it may predispose particular individuals.

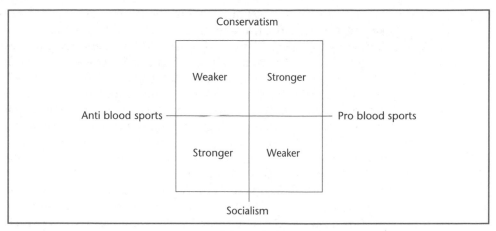

Coalitions of ideas

This is a very simple two-dimensional example. Individual, personal, ideologies are always much more complex than this, influenced by everything that it is possible to have ideas about – and people do, literally, have ideas about everything. Thus, in the case of the debate about blood sports, political belief is only one dimension and others might include, for example, attitudes to the countryside, attitudes to animal welfare, attitudes to tradition, attitudes to social hierarchy, attitudes to sport, attitudes to the role of the state, as well as much less formalised, more personal, attitudes, and all based on belief. While certain groups of attitudes might predispose individuals to one side of the argument or the other, there is no absolutely predictable pattern, because such beliefs derive from individual experience, cognition and interpretation. People may find emotional and ideological security in belonging to coalitions that reinforce their view of the world, and thereby suggest that this view is held by others as well as by themselves, but, in practice, neither the degree of intersubjective agreement nor the coherence of the ideology is likely to be very great.

Ideology and interests

It may sound as though ideology is always consciously and purposively developed, that choice of adherence to collective ideologies is deliberate and intentional, but this is *not* the case. In the course of normal, everyday, life it is rare that we have to consider our ideology – it is just there, functioning more or less adequately. Indeed, we are rarely even aware that we have an ideology. We take our beliefs for granted. We believe that what we believe is the way things really are, or should be; we believe that what we believe is correct, true – obviously, since, if we believed that what we believed was wrong, we would usually not believe it any more. We may be aware that other people have different views to our own, and will believe that they are wrong. But this is rarely significant, so long as those beliefs do not interfere with our own, in some way constrain our action.

Nonetheless, some ideologies are consciously adhered to which are inconsistent with other beliefs and ideas that we may hold. A further twist to the complex nature of ideology is that there may be what is often called **false consciousness** in one's beliefs. The usual implication of this term is that people have beliefs and subscribe to collective ideologies which do not serve their interests, although they may believe that they do. This itself is usually taken to imply that people's interests can be identified objectively, irrespective of what they may believe their interests to be. We are using the term rather differently, to illustrate the point that **people can even act against what they *believe* their interests to be**. We have already proposed that ideology prefigures efforts to make sense of the world and that the function of ideology is to provide us with a measure of what does make sense, to enhance our sense of security and certainty of being able, literally, to survive. At its most basic, this is our interest: to survive. Ideas about the way the world is and should be will also represent beliefs about what our proper place in the world is and should be – about what constitutes survival, about how 'the world' should treat us. In other words, **ideology defines perceived interests**. Yet it is quite possible – indeed, very common – for people to believe ideologies which are, in practice and even in theory, contrary to these personal interests.

For example, there were Jews in the 1930s and even in the 1940s, throughout the world but especially in Germany, who adhered to Hitler's Nazism; there are people who have to survive, socially and economically, by selling their labour who believe in the right of the rich to get richer; there are poor people who believe in elitism; and so on. The logic of such beliefs in serving individual interests may never be challenged. People may subscribe to particular ideologies and yet not share, or agree with the implications of, the specific beliefs of such an ideology. People vote for political parties that represent a particular view of what the state should be like, for example, yet do not agree with the policies that follow from that ideology. In the UK in the 1980s many people consistently voted for the Conservative Party but did not agree with many – or indeed, sometimes, any – of their policies, such as privatisation of publicly owned assets, attitudes to Europe, the emphasis on the individual, withdrawal of the state from its regulatory role. By the same token, the landslide election victory of the Labour Party in 1997 obviously included the votes of many people who would not welcome the introduction of policies designed to realise its vision. In the organisational context there are many managers, and would-be managers, who subscribe to the ideology surrounding the rights of ownership and the right of managers to manage on behalf of those interests, but who may not subscribe to the policies such representation entails, such as increasing insecurity for employees, down-sizing and casualisation. Thus many managers find themselves implementing policies which they believe to be morally distasteful, at least, but which are perfectly consistent with the over-arching role of the manager, as the representative of special interests, which is implied by the ideology.

Thus it can be said that, **while people may adhere to a particular ideology, or align themselves with one, this may not indicate the content of their beliefs**. Under normal circumstances, this ideology may function as if it does represent their beliefs, but, if brought into focus, such contradictions may become highly problematic.

Ideology . . .

Ideologies are complex and very nebulous, but they constitute the framework of ideas which informs all our thinking and actions. They have an all-pervasive and active presence, even though we may not be aware of it. **Ideology cannot be understood as the binary opposite of rationality** – indeed, rationality is itself but an ideology. Ideology is not opposed to anything – everyone has one, it is always there and always profoundly influential in action and behaviour. Yet the recognition of this influence is sadly lacking in the discourse of Organisational Behaviour.

Knowledge, discourse and ideology

We have already discussed the relationship between knowledge, discourse and power, but have not yet examined the basis of the predilections for certain types of knowledge and for certain types of knowledge production. The concept of ideology provides the key to understanding these issues. They can best be addressed in terms of form and content.

As regards **form**, there is, in the social sciences, a preference for producing knowledge in accordance with the rules and practices of knowledge production in the natural sciences. Given that, in the social sciences, it is impossible to replicate the conditions necessary for producing knowledge in ways commensurate with the natural sciences, the attachment to such approaches must be ideological. It is quite clear why such an attachment exists: if one can claim that one's knowledge claims are scientific, this lends, as we have already noted, an authority to that knowledge which would not attach to any other means of producing it. Yet such authority, based on the claim that science is the only way to produce truth, must be spurious, and could not be other than spurious if science is not applicable in the social arena – unless it is accepted that, by the standards of producing truth, social science will always fail. **The attachment to *any* form of knowledge production is ideological in the sense that it represents ideas and beliefs about what the social world is like and, therefore, how knowledge about it can be gained, because there are no transcendent measures against which truth content can be assessed** (see also Chapter 4).

The influence of ideology in the context of **content** is even more obvious. **Within a discourse the only things that can be said acceptably are those that conform to the prevailing ideology.** In other words, knowledge claims are *not* produced from abstract study of, for example, a problem, with the intention of discovering the causes of that problem, whatever they may be. Claims are based on sets of ideas and beliefs which are relevant to that problem *and* defined as acceptable, while sets of ideas and beliefs which *may* be relevant but are not ideologically acceptable are excluded as a basis for providing solutions. Thus, if there were a scientific study of motivation to work which demonstrated that the best way to motivate workers was to double their wages and halve those of managers, this would be unlikely to become even a subject of debate since it contravenes issues of ideological acceptability in the relevant discourse. Indeed, this situation is not uncommon in practice – scientific or quasi-scientific studies have produced techniques such as task-and-finish systems, have demonstrated the case for worker participation, have demonstrated that stress at work is directly attributable to overwork, but these findings have not met with general approval because they do not accord with a wide range of ideas informing the discourse of Management about, for example, the proper role of workers, how the amount of work a worker should do is to be measured, the nature and significance of intrinsic satisfactions from work, and so on.

By the same token, the recognition of the ideological nature of capitalism is rarely acceptable within the dominant discourses of Management and Organisation Studies in general. Such recognition would have serious implications for the legitimacy of capitalism as the over-arching principle of organisation and management, because, if capitalism is an ideology, then it is, in that respect, no different from any other possible system of ideas that might claim legitimacy as principles of organisation and management. Even the concept of ideology itself is hardly acceptable, except in so far as it can be used to denote dissent from puta-tively rational scientific principles and practices. However, as previously noted, **ideological acceptability** *cannot* **be seen as an absolute measure of relevance**.

The difficulty is that such findings and such ideas do not fit into the prevailing **regime of truth**. But any regime of truth is fundamentally an ideology – that is pre-cisely the force of the term in identifying the ways in which ideas about truth change over time and circumstance. It is, however, an extremely powerful ideology, and one that is none the less powerful because of its taken-for-granted nature.

The ideology of management

Managers are, just like everyone else, influenced in their work by their ideologies. Far from being technicians who merely competently facilitate the enactment of the laws of management, the performance of the management task is based on *beliefs* about what is good or bad for workers, good or bad for customers, good or bad for the organisation, and so on. In the specific case of organisational behaviour, management views about things like acceptable working conditions, what motivates workers, what can be asked of workers, how it can be asked, and any other aspect of the management of behaviour, are not based on science, but derive from ideology. An interesting example of the tacit recognition of this is to be found in Douglas McGregor's very influential characterisations, Theory X and Theory Y, which argue that management styles will be strongly influenced by beliefs and attitudes about the nature of workers *en masse*. It is not difficult to see that McGregor is referring to the ideological basis of management styles, but it is not normally referred to in terms of ideology, because this is a disapproved term.

Another example can be found in prevailing ideas about differentiation between managers and workers. It has long been an important part of manage-ment beliefs that managers should be demonstrably different from workers and an elaborate system of symbols has been created to highlight such difference, and justified as being necessary to the efficient functioning of the organisation. Such symbols range from matters of dress, working hours, working conditions to holidays and systems of payment. However, as an effect of the fascination with the success of Japanese companies and their advent in the West, much of this distinction has been, albeit reluctantly, eroded, in favour of the Japanese model of de-emphasising differences between managers and workers through the use of uniforms, common facilities, and so on. Such distinctions cannot have been purely functional in the first place, since, if they were functionally necessary, they would not change. **Changes in management practice follow changes in management beliefs – and what is believed to be functionally necessary is also only a matter of prevailing ideology.**

Work is wonderful

Certainly since the emergence of capitalism – and, no doubt, previous to that, too – those who do not have to work for a living have apparently believed that, for those who do have to work to survive, work is A Good Thing, and that they should do as much of it as possible (see the argument in, for example, Russell 1976). And certainly the conventional discourse of Organisational Behaviour has supported this view that people who work should work hard and should be encouraged to be as productive as possible – and, more than this, that this is what workers actually desire. Perhaps the most succinct expression of this view comes from McGregor, in his Theory Y assumption that '. . . work is as natural as play or rest' (McGregor 1960: 47). However, those who have to do the work are not as convinced by this argument, and neither are many commentators from outside the Organisational Behaviour discourse. Here are a few other views on work:

'Work is the curse of the drinking classes.'

(Oscar Wilde)

'Here, then, is the "curse" of our factory-system: as improvements in machinery have gone on, the "avarice of masters" has prompted many to exact more labour from their hands than they were fitted by nature to perform . . . A Dr. Ure . . . is trying, not to get the manufacturers down to *ten* hours' labour a day, but to lengthen the period to *fifteen* or *sixteen* hours a day . . . '

(John Fielden: *The Curse of the Factory System*, 1836, emphasis in original, quoted in Clayre 1977: 74)

'There is a very strong element of "ought" about work. Not only do we think that work ought to be undertaken but that, for the most part, it should be done well, with enthusiasm, even with devotion.'

(Anthony 1977: 6)

'The unwillingness of the workers to do a full day's labour, day after day, was the principal reason why the first factories went bankrupt. The bourgeoisie put this reluctance down to "laziness" and "indolence". They saw no other means of overcoming this problem than to pay the workers such meagre wages that it was necessary for the latter to do a good ten hours' toil every day of the week in order to earn enough to survive . . . In order to cover its need for a stable workforce, nascent industry in the end resorted to child labour as being the most practical solution.'

(Gorz 1989: 21)

▶

'The perception of a need to direct ideological appeals at workers is clearest with the capitalist organization of manufacturing process and the requirements associated with it for orderly, disciplined and committed workers. But capitalism breeds dissent, at least it is by definition based on competition, and it engenders conflict. The greatest need for committed workers is produced in conditions that make their commitment impossible.'
(Anthony 1977: 10)

'Wherever modern capitalism has begun its work of increasing the productivity of human labour by increasing its intensity, it has encountered immensely stubborn resistance . . .'
(Weber 1930 [2nd edition, 1976: 60])

'If you ask [the actual worker] what he thinks the best part of his life, he is not likely to say: "I enjoy manual work because it makes me feel that I am fulfilling man's noblest task, and because I like to think how much man can transform his planet. It is true that my body demands periods of rest, which I have to fill in as best I may, but I am never so happy as when the morning comes and I can return to the toil from which my contentment springs." I have never heard working men say this kind of thing. They consider work, as it should be considered, a necessary means to a livelihood . . .'
(Russell 1976: 21)

'Aversion – not desire – is the emotion – the only emotion – which labour, taken by itself, is qualified to produce . . . In so far as labour is taken in its proper sense, love of labour is a contradiction in terms.'
(Jeremy Bentham: *A Table of the Springs to Action*, 1817–43, quoted in Clayre 1977: 201)

'This book, being about work, is, by its very nature, about violence – to the spirit as well as to the body.'
(Terkel 1975: 1)

'Work's a bastard'
(Fax from recently graduated student of management)

If the discourse of Organisational Behaviour is correct and people really do (potentially) love work, want to work as hard as possible on behalf of their employer and willingly accept the direction and organisation of their work, then it could be argued that it is rational to proceed on this assumption, and those who dispute it are, at least, wrong and, possibly, mad. But if we accept that the conventional discursive view may not reflect actual attitudes to work but, instead, reflect an ideology, then the whole question of the organisation of work becomes an issue of whose ideology should prevail – an issue of discursive appropriateness.

- What is your view on this issue?
- What is your own attitude to work?
- Is your view the same for yourself as it is for others?

Of course, we are not suggesting that managers should be, or even could be, non-ideological. But if we are to understand the management process, the influence of ideology must be taken into account. As regards contemporary organisations, this influence can be seen as having two major focuses. *Firstly*, we do not just have organisations, we have capitalist organisations. Capitalism furnishes the principal over-arching ideology which defines how these organisations are to be managed – that is, for the benefit of the owners. This provides the overall logic that must inform managerial practice – for example, the need for cost minimisation, for maximisation of efficiency in economic terms, for prioritising generation of profit. *Secondly*, within this there is space for the functioning of the individual manager's ideology, in areas where they have discretion. Thus, a Christian manager might manage differently to an atheist manager, though both still within the capitalist system. Trying to understand the management process, and the behaviour of people in organisations more generally, without taking into account this profound influence on practice is simply inadequate. At best, it will lead only to partial explanations and, at worst, it will lead in wholly inappropriate directions.

There *are* alternatives . . .

As long as there have been capitalist bureaucratic organisational forms, there have also been alternative organisational forms. A particular example is that of **cooperatives**. Many cooperatives, though by no means all, eschew the ideology of capitalism, but **their principle focus can be seen as the ideology that informs the process of organisation.** The foundational ideas of cooperatives are that, *firstly*, organisation *is* ideological and *secondly*, therefore, it could be different – the ideology, values and principles of cooperatives are indeed profoundly different to those of conventional organisations, not least in respect of being explicit.

The International Cooperative Alliance (ICA), which has existed for more than a hundred years, offers the following definition of a cooperative: '*a cooperative is an autonomous association of persons united voluntarily to meet their common economic, social, and cultural needs and aspirations through a jointly-owned and democratically-controlled enterprise*'. It particularly emphasises that cooperatives are organisations that 'put people at the centre of their business, not capital'. Cooperatives embody specific and explicit values: '*cooperatives are based on the values of self-help, self-responsibility, democracy, equality, equity, and solidarity. In the tradition of their founders, cooperative members believe in the ethical values of honesty, openness, social responsibility and caring for others.*' These values are supplemented by principles that emphasise voluntary and open membership, democratic control by the members, equal contribution and democratic control of the capital of cooperation by the members, the autonomy and independence of cooperative organisations, the education and training of members within the cooperative, dissemination of information about cooperatives to the public, cooperation with other cooperatives and concern for the wider community. There is also a specific focus on a range of other issues, such as ensuring equality of opportunity for men and women, encouraging the involvement of young people, sustainability and

▶

fair trade. There is a huge range of types of cooperative and there is probably no sector of the economy where cooperatives do not exist. Cooperatives are a global phenomenon.

Perhaps because of the prevalence of the capitalist regime of truth, it is not uncommon for cooperatives to be seen as an insignificant sector of the economy, run by cranks in open-toed sandals. However, the ICA points out that, world-wide, cooperatives have 800 million individual members and provide 100 million jobs, which is 20 per cent more than are employed by multi-national organisations. To illustrate the point that cooperatives are not just for less developed countries: in the USA, about 25 per cent of people are members of cooperatives of some kind, 30 of which have an annual revenue of more than $1 billion, and the 'top' 100 of which have combined annual revenues of $117 billion; in Japan, one in three families, and 91 per cent of farmers, are members of cooperatives; in Canada, one in three individuals are members of cooperatives, and the Desjardins Savings and Credit Cooperative is the largest employer in the province of Quebec. In the USA Credit Union movement, 59 per cent of presidential, CEO and managerial positions are held by women.

Sources: Definitions and statistics, which refer to 2005, come from **www.ica.coop** and Davis and Donaldson (1998) is also relevant.

Organisation as ideology

In Organisation Studies it is relatively uncommon to see capitalism itself characterised as an ideology. Yet, plainly, it constitutes a system of ideas about how money can make money, about the social, political, economic and moral conditions necessary for this to happen, and about the social, political, economic and moral benefits to be derived from its occurrence. It embodies highly refined evaluations of the goodness and badness of the various conditions that might pertain, in terms of their capacity to deliver the best capitalist outcomes. It embodies, for example, beliefs about the optimum conditions for the operation of markets; beliefs about the rights of ownership; beliefs about the proper role for other agencies, such as governments and labour; and so on. If capitalism were to be recognised more fully as an ideology, rather than a rational system or a natural law, this would have major impacts on the significance, and legitimacy, of capitalism and its role in forming the world we live in. This extends to every aspect of the social world and has a particularly distilled form in the world of work organisations.

As we have noted, ideologies rarely stand alone but have sympathetic ideologies associated with them. As regards capitalism, the most obvious of these are Individualism, Conservatism and, in the Protestant tradition, Anglicanism. Certainly, contemporary organisations can be seen to reflect the beliefs embodied in these ideologies. Capitalism itself furnishes the prime principle of organisation, that of profit, which constitutes a meta-objective to which all other possible objectives must conform. Individualism, of particular relevance to organisational behaviour, furnishes the belief that the individual is more important than the collective. This extends into an active disparagement of all forms of Collectivism, except those prescribed by management, such as work groups. Conservatism furnishes beliefs in tradition, continuity, *esprit de corps*, paternalism, the master–servant relationship. Contemporary Conservatism has also furnished the belief that state ownership or regulation of organisational activity is, at least, unnecessary, and probably pernicious. It has also encouraged belief in the essentially unitary nature of organisations, where everyone's interest is served by the pursuit of profit in a harmonious, family-like culture. Anglicanism has furnished the belief that those in authority deserve respect and obedience. Indeed, Protestantism itself was described by Max Weber as fundamentally important and necessary to the development of capitalism and industrialised society, especially in terms of its own faith in the value of work. The **Protestant Work Ethic** is also very present in organisations, providing the belief that hard work is good and worthy in itself, which has obvious utility in supporting the creation of profit and a compliant workforce.

From these ideological influences we get the form of organisation that predominates in the contemporary world. The modern organisation, far from being merely an efficient mechanism for the production of goods and services, thus becomes a reflection of a highly complex set of ideological preferences about, for example, structure, work, organisational behaviour, and so on, which prefigure what, how and why we organise. And, perhaps inevitably under such circumstances, the relevant discourses tend to focus on the issues given by the ideology, rather than on processes of organisation and management in any independent sense.

Competition versus cooperation

Market capitalism engenders highly inconsistent attitudes with regard to competition and cooperation. At one level, for example, it is held that, in the market place that constitutes the modern economy, competition between a number of (non-oligopolistic) suppliers is good, the ideal being perfect competition. However, it is also claimed that beneficial economies of scale derive from having larger, fewer, organisations, and the tendency is to strive towards a monopolistic situation.

Within organisations, on the other hand, functional cooperation is preferred – marketing should cooperate with production, for example. Where there are sub-groups within a function, competition is often preferred – between sales teams, say. But within teams cooperation is preferred – though not in all circumstances. If it is, say, an issue of production, then cooperation is good, but if it is, say, an issue of promotion, then competition is good.

At the level of industries, owner cooperation through employers' associations is good, as is managerial cooperation through professional associations. However, the cooperation of workers through trades unions is bad – and, in some instances, such as secondary action to support fellow union members, is illegal. Cooperation between producers to fix prices is good, but cooperation between workers to fix wages is bad. Between suppliers and their customers as part of the supply chain, cooperation is good (at the moment), but between workers in negotiation over local pay agreements, competition is good.

- Why is cooperation seen as good when it favours ownership/managerial interests, but as bad when it favours worker interests?

This implies that, if the ideology were to change, so too would the way we organise, and the way organisations are studied. Should ideological changes occur, while now we study motivation, leadership, culture, and so on, then we might study, for example, cooperativism, environmentalism, sexuality – even motivation, leadership and culture, but with very different criteria of knowledge. However, unless such an ideological change occurs, such issues will remain, at best, at the margins, because the practices of organisations and the discourses of knowledge about them are based on ideology. **They are not based on questions of function or of efficiency *per se*, but on those issues as they are defined within the dominant ideology.** Organisation itself is a profoundly ideological process but this is very rarely explicit. Yet its lack of articulation is a serious impediment to understanding organisation.

Ideology and organisational ethics

There are many implications of this denial of the ideological basis of organisation. In particular, and as an example, the case of organisational ethics can be cited. Organisational ethics, as a subject of study and as criteria for managing, has enjoyed renewed popularity in recent years. However, in the absence of an explicit ideology of organisation, it might be argued that ethics is a relatively meaningless concept in the context of organisation. Ethics express concern for values but the injunction to be ethical can have no practical meaning in the absence of a specific set of criteria by which actions can be judged as ethical or not. Thus, a situation arises where particular decisions can be judged ethical in terms of some criteria, but unethical in terms of other criteria.

Take, for example, recent attempts to dispose of an oil platform by dumping it in deep sea water. The company owning the platform could be seen to be acting ethically, because they were adopting a least cost solution, to the benefit of shareholders, had the support of government and the approval of the scientific community. However, they could also be seen as acting unethically, because they were disposing of their rubbish in a communal asset which might be at risk from such activities, and were wasting re-usable material in finite supply. Similarly, a multinational company, one of whose overseas subsidiaries, in a Third World country, had malfunctioned causing pollution to the environment and poisoning the local population, successfully sought for its subsequent trial to be held in the Third World location, where damages awarded would be significantly less than if the trial were to be held in its home country. This company might be seen as acting ethically *vis-à-vis* its shareholders by minimising their liability, but unethically *vis-à-vis* its victims, for precisely the same reason.

Until specific ideological criteria by which organisations should be managed are made public, at least, there is no way of deciding what is ethical, because there are no explicit standards against which practice can be judged. Indeed, there is the rather ridiculous situation whereby most things that are done in organisations can be seen as both ethical and unethical at the same time, depending on which ideology is used to judge them. This is not an easy situation to resolve because there are many difficult and contested issues to be considered, such as how such an ideology could, or should, be generated, what weight should be given to various factors, who should be involved and how conflicts of ideology should be dealt with. Nonetheless, unless it is at least attempted, an ethical vacuum will persist or the whole issue of organisational ethics will come to be seen, as it has been in the past, as an irrelevance.

Existing applications in Organisational Behaviour

One unintentional and largely unrecognised use of ideology in recent years is to be found in the study of **organisational cultures** (see also Chapter 2). This approach is based on the idea that all members of organisations (but especially workers) have deeply ingrained ideas, attitudes, beliefs and values which influence their performance either positively or negatively. However, these phenomena are rarely called ideology in this context and that such ideas, attitudes, beliefs and values are relatively systematic is glossed over, in favour of presenting them as fairly atomised and malleable. The advantage of such presentation is that it implies that these ideas, attitudes, beliefs and values are available to be changed so that they form a mental set – a culture – which is unequivocally positive in terms of benefiting the organisation and conforming to managers' desires. For Organisational Culture, as an approach, to be of any use to capitalism it must be able to deliver improved performance and enhanced efficiency, and thus the possibility that such ideas, attitudes, beliefs and values constitute anything as cohesive as an ideology needs to be underplayed. Unfortunately, the approach is, therefore, based on an inadequate description of the phenomena and this is an important reason why Organisational Culture has failed to deliver the gains promised.

There have been some studies of ideology in the organisational context, particularly in relation to the nature of work, from a sociological perspective. However, its most notable presence is in the context of **Marxist** approaches to the study of organisations and organisational behaviour, such as Labour Process Theory. These approaches tend to utilise a particular interpretation of the concept of ideology, emphasising formal collective forms, to describe the basis of an intrinsic conflict between Capital and Labour. Ideology in these approaches tends to be used in the sense which counterposes ideology to, say, truth and reality, in that it is seen as forming a barrier, for all individuals in organisations, between them and a full consciousness of their real interests.

There have always been critiques of capitalism, both secular and religious, which are themselves ideological. Currently the most forceful of such critiques are those associated with Environmentalism and the Anti-Globalisation movement.

Poststructuralist approaches, on the other hand, shun binary oppositions, in favour of the guiding principle that 'the real' is constructed through language. Because language is never neutral and because it lacks any intrinsic or specifiable meaning, language acts to reflect the preferences of the user and their attempts to impose particular significations. From a poststructuralist point of view **there is no zero degree of meaning** – no possibility of a transparent language, of impartial non-ideological language and, therefore, given the role of language in constructing reality, **no non-ideological life**. Those approaches to understanding organisational behaviour that reflect Poststructuralism carry forward this underpinning principle and thus construe organisations and organisational behaviour to be profoundly ideological, in a descriptive sense – that is, to say that they are ideological is not, in itself, to criticise or even evaluate the contents of such ideologies, though that also happens. The emphasis, however, is on uncovering the role of ideology in the organisational process, and unmasking its operation.

This trend is developed by **Postmodern** approaches to understanding organisations and organisational behaviour, where, for example, the only reality is seen as being the **hyper-real** – the signifier is taken to be more 'real', more significant, than what it signifies. Through such approaches organisations and the behaviour within them are characterisable in terms of fantasy, though not recognised as such – a simulation of the real. Management becomes management of the signifier and organisational behaviour becomes the acting out of a desired image, irrespective of its substance. Thus, for example, when retailers instruct their salespeople to require customers to 'have a nice day', that this is meaningless and vacuous is not as important as that it should be said and taken to symbolise concern on the part of the organisation for the quality of its customers' lives. Or, when Human Resource managers talk of people as 'the most important asset', that this is said is far more important than that it should have any substantive meaning. Image is all.

Further potential

Approaches to understanding ideology in the discourse of Organisational Behaviour, such as they are present, tend to be sociological. As such, these approaches generally fail to give due recognition to **the deep psychological significance of ideology**. Unfortunately, the kind of psychological approaches to understanding organisational behaviour which are favoured in the discourse, such as Behaviourism, have little to offer in understanding the concept of ideology or its function in behaviour, focusing as they do on control of behaviour, the passivity implied by theories of conditioning and stimulus-response, and the emphasis on observable and measurable behaviour. Psychoanalytic approaches, especially those associated with Poststructuralism, offer to provide a much richer understanding of the individual (see also Chapter 8). These, for example, stress the myriad interconnections, at the psychological level, of the individual and the social, the impossibility of understanding human behaviour without understanding the society within which it is embedded, and how the manipulation of the psyche by capitalism promotes certain types of behaviour. In other words, they stress that **behaviour needs to be seen as a product of ideological influences**. Such an approach, applied more widely and generally to the study of organisational behaviour, would generate not only richer pictures of people in organisations, but also more appropriate ones. At present, the conventional view is highly over-attenuated, with a focus on only those attributes of people that seem obviously to be implicated in their potential as workers. What is needed is an approach that reveals the full complexity of human behaviour, particularly as a basis for understanding the impacts on and of organisation.

This kind of understanding of the role of ideology in human behaviour would have other major implications at all levels of organisational activity. For example, on the basis of the foregoing discussion it can be concluded that the obstacle to organisations operating in, say, a more environmentally responsible manner is not economics but ideology. While there is increasing recognition that organisations can be both environmentally and socially damaging, calls for improved ethical and environmental performance are largely ineffectual, and attempts by organisations to present themselves as responding to such calls are, necessarily, cosmetic since genuine improvement is ideologically sanctioned. The aspirations that people have for improvement in this respect will not be realised until the role of ideology is recognised. As regards Organisation Studies itself, this requires **the explicit recognition that contemporary organisations are informed by a specifically capitalist ideology which dictates the way they are managed**.

The commitment to the idea of an abstract organisation and a value-neutral process of management needs to be challenged and assessed. (This is not to ignore other ideologies at work in organisations, which also require recognition and assessment, but it is to acknowledge that that of management is the most significant, because managers are the more generally powerful group.) Once the principles which inform the management of organisational activity are explicitly recognised as deriving from a system of ideas – an ideology – the way would be opened to a fuller and more appropriate evaluation. This is not to imply that such an evaluation would be necessarily positive or negative, since the point is, simply, that all such management of organisational activity *is* informed by some ideology or other. It may be that capitalist ideology is indeed the best one for managing organisations – if so, making this explicit can do no harm. If, on the other hand, there are better ways of managing, according to some agreed criteria of judgement, then exposing the current ideological bias must be the first step, before such improvement could occur.

Organisational behaviour and ideology

The concept of ideology is of enormous significance in the context of organisational behaviour and needs to be rescued from the obscure and/or pejorative sense in which it is normally used. Within the conventional discourse of Organisational Behaviour it is a virtually unacknowledged influence on behaviour. This discourse has tended to seek after some 'organism' which is really only a compliant, obedient component of production whose only desire is to be a worker and to serve the greater purpose of the organisation as defined by managers. However, and perhaps unfortunately for the management process, this describes a wholly mythical creature. This explains why the management of people is such a high fashion industry in which what is defined as good and necessary practice is constantly changing.

Ideology, both in formal collective forms and in personal forms, is a major influence on behaviour of all organisational members, but the form of its influence is complex and idiosyncratic. It explains, however, why managers desire certain things from workers and why workers may not necessarily share these desires. Ideology forms the basis of all attitudes, interpretations, predispositions.

It is hardly amenable to being managed – it might be said that individuals hardly manage even their own ideology, because of its often taken-for-granted character. The discourse of Organisational Behaviour has a tradition of excluding those human attributes that are complex and difficult to understand, of reducing individuals to their simplest elements, but those elements that may be seen as the simplest and easiest to understand are not thereby to be assumed to be the most significant. To exclude ideology because it is complex is not the answer. Given the fundamental role that ideology performs in human understanding itself, as well as in predisposing attitudes, understandings, interpretations, behaviour, actions, its inclusion would seem to be a prerequisite to understanding organisational behaviour. It seems that, if our intention is really to understand organisational behaviour, it is utterly necessary to start with a comprehensive and appropriate understanding of people, as people. Perhaps the exclusion of the concept of ideology hitherto is part of the reason why the discourse of Organisational Behaviour has been relatively unsuccessful in explaining those aspects of human behaviour that it has sought to explain, such as motivation, culture, attitudes, and so on.

However, the introduction of the concept of ideology does more than just illuminate the complexity of human understanding and behaviour at the individual level. It also highlights the complex and multitudinous interconnections between individuals and the social world, the organisation and the wider social milieu. A person's interpretation of the world in general and organisations in particular derives from ideas which are formed from, and informed by, experience in an infinite variety of arenas. **For the individual there are no natural boundaries that contain experience or separate one kind of idea from another.** Thus, to try to treat organisations as in any way discrete units somehow distinguishable from other social milieux becomes a meaningless and fruitless exercise which does not reflect organisation as people experience it (see also Chapter 9). The boundary-lessness of people's experience is also represented in the interpenetration of personal and collective ideologies.

It is important to recognise, not just personal ideologies, but also more formal collective ideologies, partly because people adhere to them, but, more significantly, because they inform the very way we organise. The informing ideology of contemporary organisations is capitalism. It is the ideology of capitalism that prescribes how managers manage, for example. However, as an ideology capitalism must be recognised as historically specific. It is acknowledged that, in the past, organisations developed, in form, content and purpose, not because of scientific study but because of the specific interests that required to be represented. So, for example, the Catholic Church is not organised the way it is because of scientifically established principles of good organisation, but because of the requirements of Catholicism and of the Church hierarchy. The organisation of feudal society was not the product of social science, but of the power of feudal lords to ensure that it was their interests that were represented. But nowadays we do have a science of organisations and of organisational behaviour, and so, therefore, we tend to assume that our contemporary organisations reflect the distillation of scientific principles of organisation, and not sectional interest. But this is not so. What science has done is to provide a spurious legitimacy to the needs implied by the ideology of capitalism, especially by masking its ideological nature. The inclusion of the concept of ideology in the study of organisations and organisational behaviour would, itself, highlight this influence.

A TALE FROM THE VILLAGE PUMP (*IDEOLOGY*)

(See the Case Study in Appendix 2, pages 340–3)

Ideology played a significant role in the whole problem of identifying the causes of cholera. One example can be found in the person of Edwin Chadwick, professional civil servant and devoted supporter of the miasma theory. Chadwick was an ardent (some said, over-ardent) reformer who was engaged in a number of aspects of both social welfare and stricter control of the poor. In terms of his formal ideological commitments, Chadwick was a Utilitarian, a friend and disciple of Jeremy Bentham, and these beliefs deeply influenced all his efforts. He was also profoundly convinced by the idea – not uncommon in Victorian England – that there was a strong correlation between poverty and immorality. (Some people thought that cholera was divine retribution for sins and, after one outbreak, it was decided that the appropriate course of action would be a communal Day of Atonement.) Chadwick's commitment to the miasma theory led him to advocate flushing out London's sewers into the River Thames which, when done, actually made the problem worse, since the river was a main source of the capital's drinking water. Chadwick was so strongly committed to the miasma theory that he still adhered to it in the late nineteenth century, long after the actual causes of cholera had been established scientifically.

Another example of the impact of **ideas** is to be found in the way that the reputations of the key actors in the case have changed over time. For instance, Farr, although his theory about the transmission of cholera turned out (in his lifetime) to be incorrect, was highly regarded throughout his professional career, but suffered eclipse after his death, and a long period when he was sometimes portrayed as the proponent of a 'silly theory', yet is now being rehabilitated. Snow, whose theory about the transmission of cholera was shown to be correct, seems to have been highly regarded professionally until he published his theory that cholera was a water-borne disease, following which he was almost vilified by some people. Today, Snow's reputation could hardly be higher. It can be strongly suggested that the changes in the perception of the reputations of these men can be related to changes in the ideas and values of the wider social culture.

■ What was the role of **ideology** in the delay of more than a decade in Farr's acceptance of Snow's hypothesis?

Case

BY THE SWEAT OF ONE'S BROW?

There are many different approaches to understanding, and defining, what might constitute being ethical, or ethical behaviour. Two common and basic ones are consequentialism and deontology.

Consequentialism argues that what is good/right depends on outcomes – the 'better' the outcome, the more ethical the behaviour that achieves it. This, of course, leaves open the question of the criteria used to define good outcomes. A variation on consequentialism is **utilitarianism**, in which the consequence sought is 'the greatest good to the greatest number'. These are both calculative approaches, and there are obvious difficulties surrounding them, such as knowing the consequences of an action and being able to quantify them. There is also the problem of who defines 'good'.

Deontology (from the Greek *deon*, part of the verb 'to be necessary', 'to behave', and related to the word for 'duty') views being ethical as a function of duty – one must do one's duty, regardless of consequences. However, what is one's duty can be a problematic issue. For example, you may believe that it is wrong to kill another person – that there is a duty to respect life. But if someone were about to kill your child, whom you have a duty to protect, and you could only fulfil your duty of protection by killing the assailant, what would you do? One approach to resolving this sort of dilemma is to prioritise some duties over others, and to act in accordance with the highest duty. Of course, this too is not without difficulties. How do you know which are the higher duties? One solution is to calculate which duty will bring about the best likely outcomes – but then this begins to look like consequentialism. Although some duties may be easily recognisable as more important than others, it is by no means always so clear. If you feel that you have a duty to conserve the environment, should you put your empty wine bottles in your dustbin, or should you drive to the bottle bank, thereby using up other scarce resources such as fossil fuels and contributing to pollution of the environment with your car, or should you stop drinking wine?

As the above examples suggest, the question of what is ethical behaviour specifically relates to the behaviour of individuals. Given the difficulties and confusions at this level of analysis, it is hardly surprising that these difficulties and confusions become multitudinous when applied to a concept such as 'an/the ethical organisation'. It is worth considering some of the issues. For example, if everyone in an organisation acts ethically, does this make it 'an ethical organisation'? Does it matter if different people use different principles to define what is ethical for them? Everyone could be acting according to their own ethical principles, but the various positions might cancel each other out. Does it make a difference to the possibility of 'an ethical organisation' if some people have more power than others? Does it matter that some people adhere to different ideological beliefs to others? If senior managers devise a code of ethics for practice within the organisation, and everyone voluntarily adheres to this code, does this make it 'an ethical organisation'? Does it matter if some people do not share the ethics embodied in such a code? Is it meaningful to talk about 'an ethical organisation'?

As an example of the issues in the organisational context, let us take the case of **sweatshops**. There is considerable, and growing, ethical concern about the 're-emergence' of sweatshops, once thought to be a disgraceful relic of the Victorian age. A number of general factors are thought to be responsible for their popularity, such as globalisation, the easing of restrictions on business and the demand for cheap goods – consumerism. (Globalisation and information technology are also obvious factors in the increasing availability of information about the existence of sweatshops.) Sweatshops are characterised by some or all of the following: poor working conditions, often below legal requirements; low pay, often below legal minimums; long hours of work, often above legal maximums; employment of underage workers. It is frequently assumed that sweatshops are a Third World phenomenon, but they are also prevalent in developed countries, such as the USA. It has been estimated that as much as 50 per cent of the US garment industry comprises sweatshops.

At the general level, one of the justifications *for* sweatshops is the provision of jobs: conditions in sweatshops might be poor, it is argued, but they do provide work and, therefore, income that otherwise would not exist, and so people would be worse off without them. To improve conditions would be too costly, it is suggested, making the products uncompetitive. (However, wage costs for many goods amount to as little as 1 per cent, or less, of the selling price, so even a doubling of wages could be argued to be likely to have a negligible effect.) The arguments *against* this 'philanthropic' justification include the view that paying very low wages to people who are already poor condemns them to remaining poor, since they cannot acquire a surplus of income over essential expenditure, which would allow them to improve their situation. Such work may even worsen their position. For example, sweatshops, being unhealthy places to work, can increase health costs for workers, through industrial disease, injury, and so on.

The justificatory position seems to apply generally to the conditions in poorer countries – low incomes, shortages of jobs, low standards of living, low expectations, low levels of education and weak regulation of conditions of labour. However, this could hardly be said to be the case in the rich countries, such as the USA and the UK, where there are also sweatshop conditions to be found. This seems to reflect at least two other pertinent factors: lack of enforcement of labour law and the evidence that sweatshops are often peopled by illegal immigrants who are, therefore, in a very weak position for demanding their labour rights.

Nonetheless, it could also be suggested that sweatshops are a logical consequence of the ideology of capitalism, which holds that labour costs and production costs should be minimised and that profitability should be maximised. This, after all, is why enterprises based in rich countries seek presence in poorer countries in the first place.

■ Can consumer desires for cheap products be used legitimately as a justification for sweatshops?

■ If something is illegal, can it still be ethical, and vice versa?

- Is it ethically acceptable to have different ethical standards for different categories of people – for example, illegal immigrants, managers, etc.?

- Given that most people believe that they are acting ethically in the organisational context, is the idea of 'an ethical organisation' redundant?

(Other chapters that would be useful and relevant in analysing the case *include* Structure (3), Rationality (6), Self (8), Boundary (9) and Efficiency (10).)

Bibliography

There is a huge literature on ideology emanating from a variety of academic disciplines, ranging from conceptual overviews, often on a historical basis reviewing the contribution of major theorists, to detailed applications of the concept in specific arenas, and varying from using ideology in a pejorative sense to rigorous analytical treatments. The overviews vary in accessibility – some of the more accessible ones are Harris (1968), Hall (1977), Giddens (1979), Larrain (1979), Thompson (1986) – this last is a 'Key Ideas' text. Most writers on ideology emphasise, at some level or other, its systematic qualities – for example, Giddens (1979), Walton (1988). In general, discussions of the concept of ideology can tend to be rather abstract, and one of the reasons for this is an analytical connection between ideology and consciousness.

An important contribution, known as 'the end of ideology thesis', was made by Bell (1960). This thesis proved to be very controversial – see, for example, Rejai (1971) – and may have contributed to a strong revival of interest in the subject. On one hand, there was a flowering of positions tending to refute the end of ideology thesis by proclaiming their own previously unrecognised systems of beliefs, notably, for example, black power, flower power, feminism, environmentalism, religious fundamentalism. Relevant to this is some discussion about whether or not there is such a thing as a dominant ideology – see Abercrombie, Hill and Turner (1980) and Clegg (1989), for example.

Coextensively, there was a reinvigoration of philosophical approaches to ideology – a notable example here is Marcuse (1986). To some extent, this reinvigoration seems to have relocated study and analysis of ideology to Culture Theory. There are various overviews which reflect this trend. Eagleton (1994) is a useful collection which includes many of the (historically) foremost commentators on ideology and some of the most recent as well. Zizek (1994) focuses more on contemporary debates and encompasses both Critical Theory and Poststructuralism. Simons and Billig (1994) focus on the issues connected with ideology in light of Postmodernism. Various writers stress the relationship between language and ideology – for example, Simpson (1993). A more extensive analysis which also makes this connection is Bernstein (1979).

Almost all writers on ideology will, at some level of analysis, compare it to some view of rationality – see, for example, for varying points of view, Ryan (1970), Elster (1983) and, for particularly interesting and useful definitions,

Gouldner (1976). On the relationship of ideology to science, in addition to several of those already mentioned, see Meszaros (1986), Woolgar (1989), Ravetz (1990). Blackburn (1972) is an edited collection on the relation of ideology to social science, the topic also of Edel (1979).

For Poststructuralists, because of their view that it is not possible to be non-ideological, the concept tends to be under-articulated, since ideology is assumed to have a totalising presence. Thus, there is not a lot in poststructuralist work on the concept itself but a great deal on how it influences the construction of reality. Concepts such as discourse, episteme and regime of truth (Foucault 1970, 1971, 1974, 1979a, for example) and techno-mediatic power (Derrida 1994) subsume the concept of ideology and do not make sense without it. See Simons (1995) for an example of the significance of Foucault's work for political philosophy. There are also some poststructuralist studies of the contents of particular ideologies, such as Derrida (1994) on the influence of Marxism. Barthes (1968) can be seen as encapsulating the arguments about the impossibility of being non-ideological. Ideology is much more widely discussed in Critical Theory and tends to reflect the standard Marxist view that ideology is a distortion of reality and/or awareness of it and, thus, an impediment to emancipation. See, for example, Marcuse (1968), Habermas (1987, 1994). Jay (1973) is a highly regarded overview of the work of the Frankfurt School, to which both Marcuse and Habermas belonged, and a good source on Critical Theory's approach to ideology.

False consciousness is an important and controversial issue which is addressed in most studies of the concept – for a range of views see Lichtheim (1967), Bernstein (1979), Eagleton (1994). Also relevant are studies of particular ideological contents, especially Marxist ideology, since ideology is a term historically most closely associated with the work of Marx.

For the impact of ideology on the form of knowledge, and especially in the context of knowledge production, see, for example, Ryan (1970), Blackburn (1972), Burrell and Morgan (1979), Cashmore and Mullen (1983). For an example of the range of possibilities see Morgan (1983a). See also the bibliography to Chapter 4. It is in the very nature of orthodox and conventional approaches to the contents of a discourse that the impact of ideology on, for example, issues of appropriateness would not be acknowledged. One of the best illustrations of how ideology does impact on these aspects is to be found in Foucault's work on discourse, in commentaries on it (again, see the bibliography to Chapter 4) and, in the context of organisation and organisational behaviour, in Foucault-inspired studies thereof – for example, Donzelot (1991), Townley (1994), Jackson and Carter (1995b, 1998a), Burrell (1997), McKinlay and Starkey (1998).

The idea that there is an ideology of management and, though sometimes more implicitly, an ideology of organisation, is fairly well-established outside the discourse of Organisational Behaviour. There is a wide range of approaches, and a range between general and specific. The following, arranged by date, are a sample: Bendix (1966, 1970), Nichols (1969), Anthony (1977), Salaman (1979), Salaman and Thompson (1980), Clegg and Dunkerley (1980), Thompson (1983), Alvesson (1987a), Mumby (1988), Deetz (1992, 1994), Hutton (1995, 1997), Clarke and Newman (1997). For an interesting earlier study of ideology and organisation, see Brady (1943). A relevant and more recent development has been an interest in the concept of utopia in the context of its connections to the theory and practice of organisation(s). See, for example, Jones, Parker and ten Bos (2005), Parker (2002b), ten Bos (2000). There is, of course, a wide-ranging critique of managerialism. For three very different examples see Thrift (1999), Parker (2002a) and Jones and O'Doherty (2005).

The problems with the concept and the practice of organisational ethics are a matter of considerable debate in the contemporary literature, with different sides to the argument representing different degrees of optimism or pessimism. See, for example, Maclagan (1998), Parker (1998a, 1998b, 1998c). Walton (1988) specifically relates the issues to ideology. On the cyclical nature of interest in organisational/managerial ethics, see Jackson and Carter (1994). It could be argued that the rather optimistic flavour of earlier contributions is giving way to a more critical view. See, for example, Jones, Parker and ten Bos (2005) and a special issue of the journal *Organization* (2003a).

For the problems and issues associated with the concept and practice of organisational culture, see the bibliography to Chapter 2, especially those sources which are critical of conventional approaches to 'the management' of organisational culture. One example of a specific connection between culture and ideology is Alvesson (1987b). Previously noted references in this bibliography which locate interest in ideology in the realm of Culture Theory are also relevant.

One area of organisational analysis which has consistently given attention to ideology, and/or closely related concepts like managerialism, is Labour Process Theory – see, for example, Thompson (1983). The Labour Process Theory approach generally tends to reflect the Marxist view that ideology is a barrier, distortion or impediment, to be overcome. For an internal critique of some aspects of Labour Process Theory, see Beynon and Glavanis (1999). However, some more recent Labour Process Theory incorporates ideas from Poststructuralism, prominent among these being Alvesson and Willmott (1996) – Alvesson and Willmott (1992) is also relevant. A variety of poststructuralist approaches were cited earlier, in this and previous bibliographies. Of particular note because of its attention to capitalism is Deleuze and Guattari (1984). For a sample of approaches relevant to Postmodernism and its potential impact on the study of organisation and organisational behaviour, see, for example, Cooper and Burrell (1988), Power (1990), Gergen (1992), Hassard and Parker (1993), Chia (1996), Boje, Gephart and Thatchenkery (1996), Linstead (2004). Clegg, Hardy and Nord (2006) is also a useful source on this.

CHAPTER 8

Self

This chapter begins by describing the centrality of work to our sense of self and the way this has been impacted on by changing understandings of the cosmological significance of human life. Some early examples of dissent from the conventional notion of the integrated self, and of the appropriateness of contemporary organisational forms to that self, are noted, before going on to examine the view of self implied by contemporary social theory, rooted in psychoanalysis. An impression of the self as dispersed, differentiated and fragmentary is developed and the significance of interaction, communication and interrelationships with others in the development of our understanding of who we are, and of our intrinsic worth, is emphasised. To explore the implications of such a view of self for the organisation and management of organisational behaviour, the particular case of motivation to work is taken as an example. This is then developed at a more general level by the concept of employment of the self, to look at what people may gain or lose by their experience of employed work.

One of the implications of the issues that we have explored up to now is that the discourse of Organisational Behaviour has a remarkably limited view of what people are like. The concepts we have looked at imply that people are, for example, subjectively rational, make extensive use of power relationships, construct their own personal sense of meaning which is not easily accessible to others, or very responsive to external stimuli to change. People are very complex and creative, adept at organising and managing their own view of the world; they are adaptable and devious – there is a hidden genius in the ability of people to survive in an extraordinarily complex and existentially dangerous world. Recognition of such complexity is, however, sadly lacking in the conventional discourse. There the individual is, largely, passive and manipulable, and the self is simple, conscious, discrete and easily knowable to others. Interestingly, although Organisational Behaviour is always proclaiming the hidden potential in people, especially in terms of releasing it 'for the benefit of the organisation', it does not have much sense of what this potential might be, other than to work harder, longer, more loyally and more efficiently. In ignorance, whether wilful or otherwise, of the full complexity of people, the discourse of Organisational

Behaviour describes, and prescribes for, an organisational world much diminished from its actual state, for a world *as it wishes it to be* rather than *as it is*. Small surprise, then, if the discourse fails adequately to offer solutions to problems in organisations.

However, what constitutes this multifaceted self is far from clear. Self is a difficult and contested concept in modern social theory and has proved to be particularly elusive in attempts to define it – even though there is wide agreement about what it is *not*. But there is also wide agreement that a sense of 'who we are' is important psychologically. Understanding of the self has undergone a major shift in recent years, although this has hardly penetrated into the conventional discourse of Organisational Behaviour. We do not seek here to give any particular model for thinking about the self, but to highlight a range of issues relevant to its consideration. Given that the whole project of understanding organisational behaviour focuses on people, it is obviously important that some appropriate sense of what people are like is developed.

The meaning of life?

It has already been noted that, in Western capitalist societies, **theology** has had an important part to play in shaping the principles by which we organise in contemporary society (see Chapter 7). As part of this it has also had a key influence on understandings of the self, and what it means to be human. Traditionally, human beings have been seen as God's greatest creation, made in His own image and, because of this, occupying a very special position in the Great Chain of Being – less than the angels but greater than anything else on Earth. This casting of human beings in God's own image located us at the centre of the Universe, the most important of all, those whose purposes should be served by everything else, animate or inanimate, albeit in the greater service of God. Thus, life had a purpose, as a time of preparation for entry into Heaven – itself a special privilege accorded only to human beings. Entry into Heaven required that individuals lead a good life, or at least die repentant and forgiven. Although the details of what might constitute a good life varied between different Christian sects, the target of entry into Heaven itself gave a purpose to life. The Protestant Work Ethic was important in linking the good life to work. Being industrious became a virtue in itself.

It would be difficult to overestimate the significance of all this in forming attitudes to work, in whatever context, and its corollarative, that work constitutes identity and our role in society. Nowadays, for example, work is a primary descriptor of the self: people use what they do for a living as the second most important identification, after their name. This significance of work to our sense of self has not changed, even though organised religion can be said to have declined.

The significance of work went far deeper than earning a living. So important was work to human affairs that it was also a vehicle – perhaps *the* vehicle – for self-improvement. It was a widely held idea that people could grow and become better individuals through work. There were, and are, myriad social and cultural examples of the belief in improvement through work, from formalised learning processes, such as Mechanics' Institutes and the Workers' Educational

Association, through apprenticeships, to organisational practices such as incremental scales of pay, career paths and personal development strategies. In general, the idea that work improves people is deeply embedded in the discourse of Organisational Behaviour, in, for example, theories of motivation to work where it is assumed that, if people are going to 'self-actualise', it will be at work that they do it.

Another facet of this cosmology was that advancing age would bring its own rewards. Experience was thought to be cumulative and, therefore, worthy of reward. Also, as people grew older and approached death, they were seen as getting nearer to God, and this proximity merited respect in itself. These beliefs were formalised linguistically in terms such as *Elders* of the Church, and *Aldermen* in local government, but also in the common use of the term *Senior* to signify increasing achievement over time – in local government, for example, the hierarchical positions beyond this were Principal and Chief.

In general, therefore, this cosmology generated a view of life as purposeful, but fulfilment of that purpose requiring industry. This generated a cultural understanding of work as not just about the production of goods and services. Its, perhaps more significant, surplus meaning was that it was the passport to eternal bliss.

Or . . .?

Not only has religious observance declined but there also emerged, over the past century or so, a direct challenge to the whole ideology of religion in the development of what has been called **the post-Darwinian cosmology**. Far from being descended from God, it seems that humankind descended from apes, who in turn evolved from some more primitive life form. Life itself, rather than being a significant expression of God's creative intention, should, according to this view, be seen as an accident. Indeed, human life may well be only one of a number of such examples of organic evolution – other planets may host other life forms, for example. So humans, and their Earth, far from being the centre of the Universe, should be seen to be inconsequential, and irrelevant to Nature as created by, perhaps, the Big Bang. Not only is life to be seen as accidental, but so too is evolution. Therefore, human existence is not inevitable or necessary, possibly not even desirable, as some proponents of the Gaia Hypothesis have argued (see Chapter 9). The development of consciousness should be seen as just as accidental as the evolution of biological organisms. The apparently unique ability of humans to be able to think and reason, to be aware of ourselves and our surroundings, to reflect on our own existence, could not be used to justify our position in the Great Chain of Being because it is no more than an evolutionary coping strategy. In other words, human beings are to be seen as no more important in the cosmic scheme of things than bacteria or amoebas.

Life, therefore, has no intrinsic purpose, except perhaps, as some have argued, to perpetuate our genes. There is no Heaven to which we can progress. This means that there is no future, no life after death. Indeed, proponents of the Gaia Hypothesis argue that there may not even be a life *before* death for much longer, as humankind is becoming such an irritant to the planet Earth as a system that it may seek to self-regulate by eliminating human life. Failing this, global warming,

---

Who am I?

From the following list of characteristics, pick the five that best describe you.

Good sense of humour	Hardworking	Tidy	Trustworthy
Polite	Patient	Arrogant	Self-centred
Generous	Unreliable	Easy going	Boring
Good listener	Cultured	Careless	Clever
Clumsy	Short-tempered	Sarcastic	Lazy

Now ask some people from various spheres of your life – such as a parent, a sibling, a friend, a colleague at work, a boss – to pick the five characteristics that they think best describe you.

■ How might you explain any differences in how you see yourself and how others see you?

---

holes in the ozone layer, pollution, thermo-nuclear devices, and so on, may jeopardise human survival. The very existence of human life is not important in the context of the Universe.

The meaning of work?

Given the interrelationship between religious cosmology and the meaning of work, it is not surprising that the post-Darwinian cosmology should have brought about parallel changes in understandings of its significance, or, even if not causally related, understandings of the meaning of work which reflect these different understandings of the role of human life. If there is no future, then all we have is the here and now. Because human beings *per se* are no longer seen as important in the grand scheme of things and the whole idea of a Great Chain of Being is now discredited, there appears to be no virtue in treating human beings as special because made in God's image. People are just another resource to be exploited, a commodity to be bought and sold. Work has become merely the arena of a power struggle, where people use any competitive advantage they can to establish and protect their own significance, at the expense of others.

Thus, the role of jobs in forming identity is much changed. For example, it is no longer appropriate to assume that particular training or a specific profession can be sustained for a whole working life, whether or not such training or profession is an important part of one's identity. People may have to change what they do several times. This does not imply incremental change but wholesale shifts from one occupational sphere to another. Contemporary organisational practices such as down-sizing mean that, even if you have a job, there is real uncertainty about its continuation, and continuation is not governed by any considerations of human need in general. The meaning of tenure has changed to imply simply having a job, rather than implying some mutual contractual benefit to be derived from long-term employment, for both individual and organisation.

Technology is frequently used to eliminate jobs completely, and information technology is capable of changing the nature of jobs so much that they can be moved to locations inconceivable in the context of previous technology – for example, from a factory to a home, from an office in London to an office in Karachi. More than this, there is no implication that, even by job-hopping, individuals can complete a full working life. Age has become a liability. The contemporary cultural attachment to youth signifies that, in some spheres, a person over the age of forty is considered to be old, over the hill. Experience is not valued but considered to be stultifying. It is routine to ask people over the age of fifty to take early retirement. It is no longer believed that people will improve, or grow, with age – now, as we get older, we are seen as becoming less useful and a burden on society. It is ironic, in light of this, that, in the UK, for example, it is proposed to raise the state retirement age at least to 70 years of age. This is not a response to the desire of people to work longer (though some people do want to do this), but is a response to an ageing population, the degradation of pension provision through deregulation, the desire of corporations to reduce their pensions liabilities, mismanagement and, in some cases, corruption. It is interesting to speculate what jobs might be available to people in their late sixties.

The changes in the view of the place of people in the scheme of things have more general and more subtle implications as well. Thus, for example, when the purpose of life was to get into Heaven, if people felt alienated this was, to some extent, simply the price they had to pay – pain on Earth was there to be suffered until one got one's just reward in Heaven. Now that the prospect of salvation and eternal bliss seems, to most people, to be unlikely, suffering is no longer an investment, it is simply suffering. Since we no longer believe in suffering for its own sake, we become governed by the desire to minimise, not suffering in general, but just our own suffering – *there is a belief that nothing is, or could be, greater than the self.* This trend towards not believing in anything greater than the self has, as a logical consequence, a trend towards justification of prioritising self-gratification, especially the prioritisation of satisfaction of one's immediate desires. But, although this is an important and powerful motivation, the ability to gratify one's own desires is not equally distributed in any population – some people have a better chance of success in this than others.

The extent to which people can achieve success in gratifying their own desires is, probably entirely, a function of power. The exercise of **micro-power** – imposing your view of the world on others, getting them to see their role in the world as you see it, not as they do – is a primary vehicle for self-gratification, and emphasises that self-gratification, the relief of one's own suffering, usually implies the imposition of suffering on others. It is interesting to note, so central to our understanding of the self has self-gratification become, that what used to be called altruism – the giving of the self to the service of others without regard to one's own self-interest – is now usually seen as, itself, a form of self-gratification and satisfaction of self-interest. Our view of what it means to be human is now focused on defining and satisfying self-interest.

The meaning of the organisation of work?

All this is firmly entrenched in the ways in which work is organised. Human beings are regarded, principally, as resources to be used, as efficiently as possible. This guiding principle inevitably means that whatever about a person is not strictly implicated in their efficient use – as defined by those with the power to signify what efficient use means – is not just ignored, but actively denied. **What is denied is what makes people human**, and this ranges through biological characteristics, emotional characteristics, psychological characteristics. For example, it has already been noted that we live in a wage labour economy, where most people survive by selling their labour to an organisation, yet there is no obligation on employing organisations to pay a living wage. Organisations mark no contradiction between using up the hours people have available to work and not paying them enough to ensure that they can afford to continue working at that job. The deep commitment to paying less than a living wage is symbolised in the strong resistance to the idea of a minimum wage – though, at the same time, huge salaries are paid to *some* people, at the opposite end of the hierarchy.

Incentive Theory: The philosophy in 20 words

To Make The Rich Work Harder
You Pay Them More
To Make The Poor Work Harder
You Pay Them Less

Source: Christine Hankinson, Leeds Postcards. Reprinted with permission.

Another example is to be found in the routine and deliberate over-stressing of employees, with all its well-recognised physical, emotional and psychological dysfunctions. Yet the idea of relieving stress by making fewer demands is anathema and, instead, employees are, optimally, taught how to 'manage' their stress, even taught that stress is good for them.

Human beings have become an encumbrance in organisations, even though they are needed for organisations to function. If there is a human purpose to work, whatever it might be, it has become marginalised. The justification for all organisational practices has to be economic, whether it is paying less than a living wage, overworking people, or anything else, because, in the contemporary world, economic gain is the basis for ensuring the ability to gratify one's own desires, to serve one's self-interest. One might expect that such instrumental attitudes on the part of those who represent the owners' interest in organisations would be replicated throughout the organisation – after all, the same opportunities for gratification are at stake for everyone. Yet there is, within the theory and the practice of managing organisational behaviour, an extraordinarily strong emphasis on the requirement for employees *not* to have instrumental attitudes but, on one hand, to be loyal and committed to the organisation for itself and, on the other hand, to find gratification in this loyalty and commitment – to be, for example, satisfied by intrinsic, rather than extrinsic, rewards. Not surprisingly, such identification with organisations on the part of employees is rare, and needs to be enforced. This is done, most notably, through insecurity and through techniques of surveillance.

Work relationships have become increasingly characterised by low levels of autonomy and low trust relationships, notwithstanding a prominent rhetoric which claims exactly the opposite. For example, the concept of empowerment central to the rhetoric of Human Resource Management implies high levels of autonomy and high trust relationships (so that the benefit can accrue to 'the organisation'), but, in general, experience has shown a marked reluctance either to actualise such characteristics, or to recognise what might be necessary to actualise them. Some would argue, however, that the intention itself has never been more than to form a rhetorical device, rather than to make it an actuality.

Rules is rules

One of the problems faced by early factory owners was that of inculcating appropriately machine-like habits in their employees, a problem exacerbated by the situation that many such employees had been, originally, agricultural workers, geared to the rationality of nature and the rhythm of the seasons. Typical prohibitions enforced included:

- not leaving the work station without permission;
- not talking to other employees while working;
- not singing or whistling;
- not taking unauthorised breaks, including toilet breaks.

Such prohibitions are still commonplace in today's factories, particularly in the 'office-factory', and, nowadays, increasingly backed up by electronic surveillance media such as closed circuit cameras and rooms that require a swipe card to enter them, so that the length of time you spend in them can be checked.

- Can such prohibitions be seen as commensurate with the idea of the autonomous, mature and empowered self?

Towards an understanding of the self

There has been a big shift in the understanding of human existence, widely and strongly represented in shifts in the understanding of the whole concept of the role of work. The discourse of Organisational Behaviour, however, has retained a strong commitment to the model of workers as individuals who are integrated, job-oriented, (economically) rational and perfectible. This commitment is underpinned by a strong belief in the idea of an essential human nature, exemplified in concepts like Rational Economic Man, or Self-Actualisation. This notion of a human nature implies that there are certain essential characteristics which are present in all individuals, common to everyone irrespective of any other differences. This underlying assumption is extremely important in the discourse of Organisational Behaviour because it allows the guiding principle of techniques of managing organisational behaviour that treat everyone as the same – often known as 'blanket approaches'. Such approaches are rife in both the theory and the practice of the management of organisational behaviour, and are part of the general principle of trying to simplify such management. Thus, if you want to motivate people, the same approach or technique can be applied to everyone, because of this assumption of human nature. If the concept of human nature is abandoned, such approaches make no sense at all. Yet abandoning it is precisely what much contemporary social theory makes necessary.

Contemporary social theory, much influenced by the development of psychoanalysis, as noted in Chapter 3, has a view of the self which is, in many ways, the precise opposite of that which informs the discourse of Organisational Behaviour. Every self is seen as being **unique**, different to all other selves. It is also viewed as being **fragmented**, **inconsistent**, **incoherent** and **distributed** – the self is not the essential integrated core of a person, but **unfixed**, **in a state of flux**, **unstable**, **changing over time**, **unpredictable**, **differentiated** in the light of different perceived roles, so that, for example, someone might have one view of the world as a parent, another as an employee, another as a member of a community. In this approach, the self is **driven by the unconscious**, rather than the conscious; **subjectively rational and incapable of objectivity**; **wilful and power-seeking**; **self-gratifying and self-delusory**. From such a perspective the mere idea of an essential human nature is simply untenable.

Self-interest?

Source: Copyright © Ashleigh Brilliant (www.ashleighbrilliant.com) Reprinted with permission.

Some early contributions

Of course, it has long been recognised that all people were not really the same, that there were, and are, intrinsic differences between people, or, at least, between different classes of people. For example, the aphorism noted earlier, 'to make the rich work harder you pay them more, to make the poor work harder you pay them less', clearly represents the view that there are fundamental differences between rich people and poor people. This was given a rather different slant by Thorstein Veblen (1924) in his concept of **conspicuous consumption**, used to describe the evidence that rich people apparently feel that there is no point in being rich unless it can be flaunted, to other rich people but, especially, to those who are not rich.

Erich Fromm (1979) identified two broad philosophies of life which he differentiated in terms of **the having mode** and **the being mode**. Generally speaking, in the having mode the self is defined by possessions, by artefacts, while in the being mode the self, independently of possessions, is characterised by reflection, by focus on interpersonal relationships, and by the dynamic of personal growth, known as 'becoming'. In the being mode the self is, almost by definition, never complete or fixed. Fromm pointed out that the being mode is increasingly culturally devalued, overwhelmed by the having mode. It could be suggested that the ultimate symbolism of this is the marketing of goods in such a way as to imply that the possession of a particular good will itself realise a desired self, confer characteristics that will be identified and envied by others – for example, executive briefcases, business class travel, and so on. Fromm also noted that the having mode is based on the development of acquisitiveness, which breeds competition, which breeds conflict, while the being mode is based on cooperation.

The narcissism of minor difference

The concept of narcissism refers to 'excessive self-love'. **The narcissism of minor difference** links this sense of self to the delineation of small, and apparently insignificant, differentiations from others (see also Wilden 1980). These 'minor' differences acquire a disproportionately major importance to those who select them as the criteria of identification of positive value, in themselves and in others. The narcissism of minor difference *may* involve identification with a group who think such differences are important and *always* involves differentiation from others who do not. It can generate intense competition, but, more importantly, it can be the source of antipathy towards those who do not possess the difference, or towards those who do not think the difference is significant. The range of possible 'minor differences' is huge, and can stretch from the abstract to the actual, from the psychological to the material, from the imagined to the demonstrable, but in today's consumerist society, the possession, or otherwise, of **artefacts** is a very common focus.

Such obsession with minor difference is rife in organisations too: the proliferation of job titles, the minutiae of the allocation of office space, and office equipment, the provision of, and differentiation between, facilities, the provision of perks, and so on. Such differences easily become status symbols and differentiate the 'haves' from the 'have nots', the 'favoured' from the 'unfavoured'. But this belief in, and emphasis on, the significance of minor differences also generates its own filtering of information, on the basis of whether information confirms or counters the dominant interpretation of what matters.

▶

The narcissism of minor difference signifies differentiation that ignores important differences and pluralities among individuals in favour of differentiation on the basis of trivialities, slight differences being perceived as a greater threat to the sense of self of the narcissistic personality than more pronounced differences. Such differentiation stimulates action and behaviours based on the identification of tiny differences, magnified into significance that could not otherwise be justified. It generates valuations of the self and of others that neglect genuine difference and that emphasise signifiers rather than signifieds (see also **the hyper-real**, in Chapter 2). The characteristics that are considered to matter are, by definition, trivial, but the consequences of these valuations can be enormous, for the self that evaluates, for the selves that are evaluated and for the appropriateness of the assumptions on which the management of organisational behaviour is based.

The having mode is, of course, good for capitalism, because it promotes consumption. But the encouragement to consume has its own dysfunctions at the level of the self. Since the acquisition of material goods cannot create the self, the self remains dissatisfied and unfulfilled. Nonetheless the desire for material possessions is passionate, in the contemporary world – famously described by the postmodern, 'Baudrillardian', adaption of Descartes' aphorism, 'I think, therefore I am' into a motto for contemporary advanced capitalism, 'I shop, therefore I am'. This is also now signified in the very common idea of 'retail therapy'.

Another example of an early contribution particularly relevant to organisation is Ferdinand Tönnies' (1974 [1887]) comparative concepts of the *gemeinschaft* and the *gesellschaft*, usually translated as community and association, respectively, which characterise the basic principles of interrelationships. The *gemeinschaft* is characterised by community, interrelationships based on human fellowship, mutual exchange and the development of craft skills which serve the community. The *gesellschaft* is characterised by large-scale organisations, contractual and impersonal relationships, instrumentality and exchange mediated by money. The *gesellschaft* is obviously typical of most contemporary organisations, but this does not mean that it is the most appropriate form in terms of desired expressions of the self. The desire for the *gemeinschaft* is undiminished, represented, for example, by the consummate attractions of small, cooperative-style, organisations for many people, by membership of trades unions, and so on. It is also represented in the tendency of people perceptually to divide and fragment large organisations into smaller units such as departments or sections, to see cities in terms of collections of villages. Where the perception of being part of a small unit is simply impossible to sustain, this becomes part of experienced alienation. People rarely want to be units in a large mass, amorphous because beyond their ability to conceptualise (like the difficulty people have in conceptualising very large numbers).

Such approaches represent broad dissent from the idea of an essential human nature, and from the idea that people are primarily motivated by fundamentally economistic, rationalistic and materialistic drives or needs. But to gain greater depth in understanding the self it is necessary to turn to psychoanalysis.

Self-image?

Source: Pablo Picasso *Self Portrait, 1972*. Copyright © Succession Picasso/Design
and Artists Copyright Society (DACS) 2006.

Self and Other

Psychoanalytic theory associated with the work of Jacques Lacan has been
extremely influential in the development of contemporary understandings of the
self. The emphasis of this work is on seeing the self in **processual and develop-
mental** terms. Rather than the idea that the self is given, innate, organic, these
approaches start with the argument that the self begins to emerge in the developing infant, through social interaction. As we become aware of other people, our
idea of self forms as a reflection of interactions with others. As others respond to
us with, for example, approbation or disapproval, we come to see ourselves as a
reflection of such reactions.

We are born into the pre-existing world of the **Other** – the Other being all
people and things which are not us, or, rather, which are not I. We do not have
any choice about the Other, since it pre-exists us, we have to interact with it
because that is all there is. We become part of these social relations through the

acquisition of language but, because of the nature and structure of language, because of the arbitrary relationship between the signifier and the signified, our access to Otherness is always ambiguous, uncertain and necessarily open to inter-pretation. We are motivated by desires which are part of the unconscious; but our primary motivating desire is to become part of the Other, to be accepted by it – indeed, to *become* the Other. The basis of this desire is that if we were not accepted by the Other we would become isolated, meaningless, nothing – in other words, profoundly alienated. The *first* point to be drawn from this view, then, is that **the self is a product of social relations, never just an autonomous part of 'an individual'.**

Seeing ourselves as others see us?

In the famous story, *The Wind In The Willows*, by Kenneth Grahame, Mr Toad composes a song about himself.

> *The world has held great Heroes,*
> *As history-books have showed;*
> *But never a name to go down to fame*
> *Compared with that of Toad!*
>
> *The clever men at Oxford*
> *Know all that there is to be knowed.*
> *But they none of them know one half as much*
> *As intelligent Mr. Toad!*
>
> *The animals sat in the Ark and cried,*
> *Their tears in torrents flowed.*
> *Who was it said, 'There's land ahead'?*
> *Encouraging Mr. Toad!*
>
> *The Army all saluted*
> *As they marched along the road.*
> *Was it the King? Or Kitchener?*
> *No. It was Mr. Toad.*
>
> *The Queen and her Ladies-in-waiting*
> *Sat at the window and sewed.*
> *She cried, 'Look! who's that* handsome *man?'*
> *They answered, 'Mr. Toad.'*

Source: From Grahame [1906] (1951).

However, his friends, while recognising that Toad has some good points, do not share his view of himself. Ratty thought him an ass, trying, and undeserv-ing of true and loyal friends. Badger said he was a bad troublesome little animal. Mole thought him not sensible and asked, what are we to do with him? Even his own father said that, although he was a good boy, he was also very light and volatile in character, and simply could not hold his tongue.

The desire to be accepted, to become, the Other is, however, unachievable, because, if we were ever to become part of the Other we would become undifferentiated, indistinguishable – we would lose identity in being the same as the Other. The *second* point, therefore, is that **the self is based on perceptions of difference, of being in some way different to all other selves, of being unique**. According to this argument, our inability to become the Other leaves us with a 'lack' at the centre of being which we constantly strive to fill. The *third* point, then, is that **it is attempts to fill the lack that constitute motivation**.

Thus, **any particular self is a product of semiotic interpretations of Otherness**. To illustrate this, take, for example, a group of children having a lesson in a classroom: while all are participating in the same event, each child's understanding, experienced semiotically, of this particular expression of Otherness will be unique and, thus, the event, in terms of its impact on self, will impact differentially. All our experiences throughout our lives, and our interpretations of those experiences, form part of the self – and all this happens at the level of the unconscious.

Significant others

Obviously, a major part of the Other is other people, but, clearly, not all people have an equal impact on us in terms of forming the self. An idea originating with George Herbert Mead but which has become part of popular usage is that of the **significant other**. For various reasons some people have greater significance for us than others – significance, not necessarily in terms of the extent of their impact on our lives, but in terms of **the symbolic importance we give to them**. Such significance may be positive or negative. It simply signifies the relative potential to influence our behaviour, attitudes, ideas, and so on. A parent, or a boss, might be important in terms of the impact they can have on our lives, but may not be significant others – we may not attach much importance to them as others. Significant others are those whose ideas, attitudes and behaviours have particular importance for us. For some people, a pop star may be a significant other, but a politician may not, and, for others, it may be the other way round. A partner may not be a significant other, but the person who lives next door may be. It is just as possible that the impact of a significant other may be defined in terms of desire to be differentiated from them as it is possible that the impact may be defined in terms of admiration, say, or of a role model.

In the context of organisational behaviour the implications of this are to emphasise **the impossibility of *prescribing* significance to particular organisational participants**. It is often implied in, for example, leadership theories that managers should be assumed to be significant others, just because they are managers. On the basis of the above it can be said that there is no way in which significant otherness can be *ensured*. **Whether a person is a significant other to someone else is a matter of the latter person's own self, their perceptions, inclinations, attitudes and experiences**. Indeed, there is a well-known phenomenon in organisations where people's peer groups, their fellow workers, are far more significant to them than any manager could ever be.

Infantilisation at work

A potential problem for the sense of self developed and experienced in the organisational context is the ongoing tendency to **infantilise** employees. This has been a feature of capitalism, at least since the advent of factoryisation. It is prominent in the techniques of Scientific Management – Taylor, for example, maintained that it was not the job of workers to think, that managers should do the thinking and that the workers' job was to obey. It is also a feature of the **deskilling thesis** and the **degradation of work** associated with the analyses of Braverman (1974), was warned about in the work of Argyris (1957), and also identified as a problem in the work of Maslow, Herzberg and McGregor, amongst others. These writers of the 1950s and 1960s became influential in the advocacy of the more liberal and democratic styles of management typical of that era, based on the perception of employees as *adults*.

Other critiques have more recent pedigrees. They include Ritzer's (1993, 1998, and see also 2006) influential concept of **McDonaldization**, which involves high levels of standardisation and control, together with low levels of employee discretion (and 'McJobs'), and Bryman's (2004, especially Chapter 6) concept of **Disneyization**, amongst the features of which is the practice of presenting things in highly simplified versions that are easy to grasp, and in which only pleasant aspects are emphasised, and less pleasant ones are ignored or removed. The concept of **micromanagement** has emerged to describe the ascendant practice of 'over-management' of people, characterised by, for example, increased levels of surveillance and drastically reduced autonomy. In the contemporary organisation of work, it does not matter what the occupation is, these are the typical conditions that are experienced.

The infantilisation of people at work raises, in particular, two interesting questions. *Firstly*, why do managers have such low regard for the maturity of employees, notwithstanding the rhetoric of empowerment? *Secondly*, we live in a world that is generally regarded as increasingly complex, and are required to make intelligent decisions about politics, finance, the environment and all the other big existential issues that affect us. At the same time, we are treated like children in the very arena where the essential ingredients of survival are obtained, an arena where our capacity to make responsible decisions is increasingly regarded as minimal. How is it possible to rationalise these two conditions?

Desire and motivation

The impact of such views of the self has enormous implications in organisational behaviour, and its study. The issue of **motivation** will serve as a particularly pertinent example. Since the work of Sigmund Freud it has been recognised that **motivation stems from desire, and that desire lies in the realm of the unconscious**. Furthermore, we know from semiotics that behaviour, as an indicator of desire, is a signifier, but that its relation to the desire it signifies is arbitrary and unspecifiable. In other words, it is not possible to infer from observed behaviour what desire is motivating that behaviour. Even the self that is behaving may not – indeed, is unlikely to – be consciously aware of the desire that motivates them. Desire is a particularly important concept in poststructuralist thinking, because it is the basis for understanding, for example, meaning, structure, knowledge, power, ideology, and so on. **Desire is the primary motivating force**. It is the basis of the self. Lacan's model of desire emphasises desire for the Other as the means of creation of the self. **Motivation, here, could be seen as, not about the acquisition of satisfactions, material or otherwise, but about the search for identity, for a positive valuation from the Other.**

In a somewhat different, but also very influential, formulation, Gilles Deleuze and Félix Guattari have suggested that, rather than being focused on some unachievable, 'lost', object, **desire just *is***, a primary force that requires no focus. However, it is not entirely independent and can be channelled, and, under the contemporary regime of truth of capitalism, **desire is encouraged to desire those things that capitalism can provide**. Since the self is a reflection of desire, the channelling of desire in particular directions actively moulds the self: we are encouraged to become the people that the system needs for *its* survival and prosperity, *irrespective* of whether this serves our own interests, as we perceive them. Whereas, left to its own devices, desire might flow in any direction at all, but always in accordance with some perception of our own interests, under the capitalist regime of truth we are encouraged to, or made to, desire things that serve interests other than our own. For example, food is a well-recognised object of desire. Over-eating is also well recognised as personally and socially dysfunctional, and many organisations place increasing emphasis on the requirement for employees to be healthy. But there is an entire industry which actively encourages us to eat more, not because we are hungry but because, by so doing, our consumption will generate increased profits.

Another example might be found in the world of sport. Once upon a time sport was an activity valued in itself by participants and spectators alike. In a remarkably short space of time sport has been redefined in terms of its ability to generate profits. The recreational importance of sport is now much secondary to its importance as a business. Successful sport is about merchandising, sponsorship, media exposure, large salaries and profits for the few. Sporting events have to conform to the requirements of advertisers, media coverage, investors, and so on – and must offer endless opportunities for associated merchandise to be sold at a premium: endless opportunities for making money out of people's desire to participate in or spectate sport. Sport for its own sake has become, at best, a minority activity and, even then, successful participation is defined by the ability to use this as a stepping stone. The power of this version of sport is the increasing inability of people to imagine any other way for sport to be – in other words, this version has **become normalised as part of the capitalist regime of truth**. Yet, looked at with a detached eye, the interests of very few people are served by this reconstruction of sport. Football teams change their strip with increasing frequency without reference to the requirements of the game, and can make huge profits because of the desire of fans to wear this uniform. The desire for 'proper' – that is, commercial – clothing is just as significant at the non-professional end of the scale. Tales are commonplace of families who impoverish themselves to satisfy a child's desire for a particular strip, or a particular pair of trainers. The desire for capitalism's productions is increasingly portrayed as irresistible, and a desire for anything else as, at least, illegitimate.

This apparent irresistibility has widespread ramifications throughout society, since those who do not have the wherewithal to buy their desires are marginalised, which has further significant impacts on their sense of self. The same pattern is easily discernible in every sphere of social activity, including work organisations, the arts, education, health care, politics, and so on.

Implications

What does all this imply about motivation to work? *Firstly*, **it implies that motivation to work is not about the desire to work, but about the desire to gain whatever incentives to work are available.** Indeed, most theories of motivation to work are not about motivation itself at all, but about the provision of incentives, whether material or psychological. If motivation is the acting out of desires, then, given that it is felt necessary to provide incentives, it can be assumed that the motivation is to get the incentive, not to do the work – as is widely recognised in some spheres. Further, however, if motivated behaviour is a signifier, there is no way of inferring from that what the desire is that is generating the motivation. Thus, for example, observable activity at work is as likely to be a result of fear or insecurity, the desire to keep one's job or not to incur the displeasure of a manager, as it is to be the result of, say, job satisfaction. These are just simple and singular understandings of why people do what they do. **Given the description of the self as fragmented, distributed, contrary, there are, in practice, manifold desires which may be being acted out.** Such desires might also be complementary or contradictory – for example, peer group approbation, boredom, self-image, amusement, micro-power, and, of course, the desire to gain the means to satisfy other desires, for the productions of capitalism.

Secondly, **it implies that talk about motivation to work being based on the satisfaction of innate needs is seriously misplaced.** Some of the most influential theories of motivation to work are founded on the notion that people have innate needs which they seek to satisfy through work, such as physiological, social and psychological needs, in an ascending order of importance and sophistication, and of difficulty in satisfying. However, in light of contemporary understandings of the relationship of motivation and desire, and their nature, it must be concluded that **any sense of such need that people experience is only a social construction, and cannot be generalised.** Many logical problems concerning need theories have been pointed out, such as questions of whether physiological needs can ever be satisfied, whether needs are incremental, whether there is a 'natural' order of needs, and so on. But, on the basis of the sort of approach described here, it must be added that such theories are really circular and self-fulfilling: the idea of a need is constructed and then is sought to be satisfied. It cannot be inferred that such posited needs refer to any general or specific needs of those who are the subject of such theories.

Thirdly, **such an approach places the whole issue of motivation to work in serious question.** Given that motivation is an expression of desire and that both lie in the unconscious, they must also be inaccessible – they are inaccessible to the self who desires and is motivated, let alone to a manager, or any other self who may be interested. **Motivation to work is inescapably the province of the self. This means that it is not possible for one person to motivate another.** As noted, what theories of motivation to work do is to provide incentives, which may or may not be desirable, but this desirability cannot be prescribed, and no incentive can produce the desire to work *per se*, but only the desire or otherwise for the incentive.

Ironically, one thing that managers *can* do is to **de-motivate**, in other words, produce a desire *not* to comply or *not* to work harder. This might be because access to desired incentives is restricted, or because there is a failure, or a refusal, to provide incentives that are desirable. It might also be the effect of a management style, or the way people feel they are treated, for example, which may imply a negative valuation of worth. People in organisations may do what is required of them, but the reasons for such compliance are multitudinous and may very well not include the desire to do what is required, in itself. If such a desire were to exist, it would be nothing to do with incentives and everything to do with the self.

So . . .

If, as some theorists argue, people are motivated by the desire to gain acceptance from the Other, then the only thing that a manager can do to affect this is to give at least the impression of a genuinely positive valuation of each person – in the hope that a valuation from this person will be significant. The signification of such positive valuation would be found in every interaction, every communication, every single behaviour and attitude. It would not be enough to tell people that they are positively valued, since this could only be a signifier to be interpreted in light of the entire network of interactions, communications and meanings that constitute organisational life. Thus, everything a manager might do, whether deliberate or not, would contribute to the understanding and interpretation developed by each self of what valuation was placed on that self. Equally, it would not be possible to prescribe how such actions, behaviour, attitudes were understood, because they themselves would be signifiers. Thus, the most that any manager could do would be to provide the conditions in which people feel that, whatever their desire, there is some possibility that it can be achieved – this includes, of course, the most obvious reason why people work, for the money. If the argument about desire and motivation is taken further, to include the view of Deleuze and Guattari, this is even more so the case. But, whichever the particular view taken of how desire works, **motivation has to be seen as coming from within, and as inaccessible to being managed.** Most especially, *desire and motivation cannot be managed when the principal objective of those who seek to manage it is to satisfy their own desires, and to represent the desires and interests of those who benefit most from the way work is organised* – the owners.

From the perspective of a view of the self as represented by contemporary social theory, it must be concluded that the whole question of motivation to work is a non-issue. The discourse of Organisational Behaviour has constructed a set of theories and practices which, from the point of view of the discourse,

Mix me a ~~person~~ . . . *employee*

It is often assumed, implicitly or explicitly, that organisations somehow reflect the needs of the people who constitute them. People need encouragement to work, so we have incentives; people need guidance, so we have leadership; people need looking after, so we have Human Resource Management functions; and so on. However, some people have argued that, on the contrary, organisations are not suited to the psychology of those who work in them. Various writers have argued, for example, that organisational practice actually stunts the personal/psychological development of those who work in them.

If we look at the typical requirements that are demanded of people when they join an organisation as employees, it is possible to infer from those requirements a 'model of man' (sic) which is suggested. For example:

Employees are expected to	*Which suggests*
■ allow their time to be organised for them;	■ this is what parents do for their CHILDREN;
■ do what they are told to do, in the way they are told to do it;	■ a person who decides for him/herself is autonomous, one deemed unable to do this is treated as an AUTOMATON;
■ sell control of their bodies to their employer, along with control of their labour;	■ people who sell their bodies are known as PROSTITUTES;
■ allow themselves to be disciplined;	■ willingness to accept being disciplined might be a sign of MASOCHISM;
■ punish others who are naughty;	■ willingness to accept this role might be a sign of SADISM;
■ surrender moral responsibility for what they do, or produce, for the organisation;	■ the archetype who gave up his moral responsibility for gain was FAUST;
■ place the interests of the organisation before their own interests;	■ such self-sacrifice on behalf of others is ALTRUISM;
■ accept that those who manage them deserve more money, better conditions, etc., than themselves.	■ accepting that those with higher formal status than oneself are intrinsically better than oneself suggests feelings of INFERIORITY.

Put all this together, give a good stir, and what do you get as the typical employee? *A sado-masochistic Faustian altruistic child-like automaton prostitute with feelings of inferiority!*

Does this describe you? If not, you may not be suited to modern organisational life.

■ Should people fit organisations? Or should organisations fit people?

■ If the latter, what would such an organisation look like?

Source: Adapted from N. Jackson and P. Carter (1985) 'The ergonomics of desire', *Personnel Review*, 14, 3, pp. 20–8. Reproduced with permission from Emerald Insight.

might be nice if they were the case, but which form a house of cards. Of course, it is not impossible that work might be organised on the basis of satisfying the desires of all organisational participants, but, in that case, it would look very different to the normal work design of contemporary organisations. If, on the other hand, there is no intention to satisfy such desires, then the discourse of Organisational Behaviour would be a much more relevant one if it were to come clean about this. Then, at least, we might debate and consider what the intentions are, and what incentives might make compliance with them acceptable.

Although we have focused on motivation to work this is no more than an example. The same principles can be applied to any aspect of organisational behaviour and its management, such as group dynamics, cultural engineering, leadership, management style, and so on. It is no more than a cliché to say that the self is deeply implicated in all areas of organisational activity and for all organisational members – it is so obvious that we hardly understand what it really means any more. **Because behaviour is a manifestation of desire, anything that anyone does in an organisation needs to be understood as a manifestation of the self.** There is, moreover, no boundary between work and non-work activity as regards the self so, contrary to the common assumption of the discourse of Organisational Behaviour, *it is not possible to separate out a worker from a person* – people come as total packages and can only be understood as such. This also means that whatever is done to someone at work is done to them as a person. It is not, for example, a worker who is made redundant, but a person who becomes value-less.

Employment of the self

What qualities characterise employment in contemporary capitalist organisations? Labour is treated as a commodity to be bought and sold, and disposed of as thought fit; employees should be paid as little as possible and the maximum amount of work extracted from them – and it is assumed routinely that they can always work harder; employees are expected to subordinate their own interests to those of the employer, including how they organise their life outside work, holidays, other commitments, giving prime time to the organisation; because of low levels of autonomy and low trust relationships, employees are subject to high levels of surveillance; employees are subject to high levels of discipline, which include things like being told what to wear and how they should look in general; even though employment is a contractual arrangement, employers want, as well as work, loyalty, commitment, compliance; employees have relatively few rights, and, sometimes, even their rights as citizens, such as freedom of speech, are constrained and do not apply at work; they are also constrained in attempts to improve their situation; it is assumed that the survival of the organisation is more important than the survival of the people who constitute it. None of this is contentious, though different people might see these characteristics in different lights, as good or bad, positive or negative, necessary or unnecessary, enabling or repressive. But let us consider what this might mean for the self.

Given the fragmented nature of the self, it is not possible to speak definitively on this, but it is possible to suggest some implications. Despite the rhetoric to the contrary, organisations exhibit signifiers which suggest that employees are held in low esteem, that they are expendable, perceived as problematic, not viewed as human beings, that their interests should be subordinated, that they are only a resource, to be used like any other resource. It must be said that it is unlikely that, from this, people will be able to gain a positive self-image as members of organisations. The ideal-type image of the worker, beloved in the discourse of Organisational Behaviour, is someone whose interests are aligned with those of 'the organisation', obedient, compliant, undemanding, with a strong urge to work hard. This implies a person whose self-image might not be adversely affected by the experienced conditions, because they would agree that such conditions were necessary. This does not seem to be very realistic.

Of course, people do not experience work as unremittingly oppressive. Clearly, people do find positive things about work, do find opportunities for positive development of the self. It is not at all uncommon for people to like the job they do. **What they often do not like is the social organisation of how that job is done**. People may well get a positive sense of self from their occupation, whatever it may be, but this does not mean that they will find the conditions under which they have to do that job positive. Someone may like to be a secretary, or an electrician, or a refuse collector, a clerk or a shopkeeper, but may not like to do it in a particular organisation.

There are other aspects of work which are important to people but which are not generally under the control of managers, such as the informal social aspects. Work provides opportunities for meeting people, for establishing relationships, activity outside the home, and may provide opportunities to act out desires not otherwise satisfiable, such as the desire to exercise power. It can also provide opportunities for social advancement and even facilitate desires for activities outside work. For some people employed work may provide genuine opportunities for creativity not available outside employed work. However, **most of these opportunities are not things that are under the control of managers – and they are not, in general, things that are directly related to the achievement of organisational goals**. They are epiphenomena, or unintended consequences, of the way in which labour is organised.

There is a more general point to be made, too. Because people are creative, complex, talented, devious, and because work is only a part of the general network of life, employees, even if they are treated as just hired labour to satisfy the requirements of ownership, use the experience of work to create as meaningful and as beneficial a personal space as they can. Managers' desires can always be resisted, circumvented, subverted, bent to the benefit of the managed. Expending energy to thwart the attempts at control by managers can itself be a source of amusement, satisfaction and positive self-image. The opportunity to refute the dehumanised role given to workers by managers, and to re-establish, in one's own mind at least, an equitable sense of self can be of immense benefit and utility. For most people, **the self is not passive or controllable, but reasserts itself at every opportunity and in unpredictable ways**. Of course, some people can be psychologically destroyed or severely damaged by organisational life, but most people are not. This is not because of the way they are managed or organised, but because they find ways of building and sustaining a sense of self which is relatively immune to the depradations on it which characterise the ordinary experience of organised work. This does not mean, however, that this is a sensible way to organise work.

Sabotage

One effective way of combating the tendency of organisations to de-humanise – to deny the possibility of a positive sense of self – is sabotage. This can range from minor and harmless disruptive acts to criminal damage.

A True Story

I am the manager of a department, and my telephone develops a fault which is both irritating and disruptive of my work – after being in use for a few minutes it develops a crackle which soon blots out conversation. Swapping the handset with that of a colleague, which is known to be working properly, shows that the fault is in the telephone, not in the line. A technician checks the phone, but only for a few seconds, and declares it to be functioning correctly. Further reporting of the fault brings the same response. What to do? Reason has not prevailed. Apparently I am not believed. I cannot do my job properly. *Solution*: choose a quiet time, take the telephone from the desk, raise it to a suitable height, drop it on the (usefully) concrete floor. *Result*: a new telephone, no questions asked. I can now get on with my job. Common sense prevails. I win. They don't know. *Outcome*: smug satisfaction.

Studies of sabotage furnish some of the most entertaining literature in the field of Organisation Studies. One of the most renowned is the case of the disgruntled maker of sticks of rock, who replaced the usual message running through the rock with the message 'Fuck Off', thus ruining an entire batch of rock which had to be thrown away – though this solution does suggest a lack of imagination on the part of the Marketing Department. Another well-known example involves the insertion of fruit into car body spaces during their manufacture. The fruit obligingly rots and gives off a suitable stench – but not until the car is complete and perhaps not until it is with its proud new owner. Workers involved in the production of food have been known to add interesting body fluids to their products – apparently, milk puddings particularly lend themselves to this treatment!

- What satisfactions and sense of self might such activities give to their perpetrators?

Existing applications in Organisational Behaviour

There is a huge literature on what is often called 'the nature of work' and its impacts on the self. A lot of this literature is critical of standard contemporary theory and practice. Ironically, the view of the individual most commonly held within the discourses of Organisational Behaviour and Management Theory is almost unique to those discourses. Most people outside those discourses view such an approach as anti-humanistic and, just as importantly, unrealistic. It should not be overlooked, however, that even within these discourses there are approaches that take a more sophisticated view of what people are like. Thus, for example, expectancy theories of motivation to work identified, but left undeveloped, that desire and assessment of the likely pay-offs from particular actions were irremediably subjective judgements, and thus unique to each individual. Because this insight was at odds with the ideological conventions of the discourse of Organisational Behaviour, its utility, especially in blanket approaches to managing people, was limited.

Outside these discourses two broad approaches to questions of the self at work can be identified. On one hand, there have been numerous empirical studies, especially participant observations, which have painted a very different picture of what people at work are like, their motivations and actions, to that portrayed from a managerialist perspective. So fascinating have such studies been found that they have developed into a major strand of documentary film-making, shown on prime-time television. The portrayal of 'real life people' in such studies bears almost no relation to the received wisdom from the managerialist discourses. On the other hand are theoretical approaches that examine the impacts of the way that work is organised on people as individuals, and focus on the dysfunctions for individuals of various forms of work design. One of the most common subjects in such studies, for example, has been the inhumanities of the production line, which isolates people and reduces them to machine-like objects.

There is also some research, both theoretical and empirical, which takes as its central theme the idea of the self as represented in, for example, other contemporary theory, and examines organisation in general and work in particular in this context. Some take an explicitly psychoanalytic approach to consider the engagement of the psyche in work and in organisation. Freud himself noted that the potential benefits to the self of work were, in his view, indispensable, yet unrealised. More recent studies have focused on the role of the psyche in contemporary organisational life – its part in organisational culture, for example – or used psychoanalysis to try to understand what it is that people want or expect from organisations, what desires they may seek to satisfy by committing their energies to organisational life. Yet other studies have focused on the concept of the self developed from psychoanalysis in, especially, Poststructuralism. Typically, such studies do not focus exclusively on the self but combine it with, for example, issues of power, discipline, production/consumption, in which the self is immersed. In such cases, the concept of the self is the underlying conceptual framework within which such other issues are examined.

Further potential

As indicated above, there is a lot of material available which examines the impacts of organisation, of management and of work on the self. The most important development now needed is for this work to become acceptable, and represented, in the dominant discourse of Organisational Behaviour. Even in the discourse it has been recognised that people are complex, as in, for example, Edgar

Schein's concept of complex man (sic), but this is still only a pale reflection of their actual complexity. **Organisational participants, whoever they may be, are not people who are conveniently integrated, conscious and rational, but are people who exhibit a fragmented and dispersed self emanating from the unconscious, inaccessible and manifested semiotically.** This understanding needs to be taken seriously and integrated into the discourse. For this to happen, however, it will be necessary for the discourse to abandon many of its cherished precepts, such as the reductionist approach which sees people as workers and seeks to ignore or downgrade in significance any aspect of this worker which is perceived to be not directly relevant to organisational 'needs', and the attendant behaviourism which assumes that individuals can be understood simply by observing their behaviour and that modification of such behaviour for 'the benefit of the organisation', irrespective of benefit to the individual, is not just legitimate but a managerial prerogative. But if this other understanding of people is *not* developed, the discourse of Organisational Behaviour will be left pontificating about an organisational world that exists only in its own annals. Current models of man (sic) may be *discursively* appropriate and *ideologically* acceptable but, if that is not the way people are, their value is strictly limited.

Part of this development would, inevitably, have to be the abandonment of the discourse's attachment to the idea of the value-neutral organisation. It would require the recognition that **organisations represent particular ideologies and regimes of truth.** Currently, the regime of truth in sway is capitalism, and it is necessary to explore the very particular links between capitalism, work and the self.

Such recognitions would, obviously, imply major changes in the discourse of Organisational Behaviour, and would necessitate clearer articulation of the purposes of the discourse itself. For example, is the purpose perceived to be to provide genuine understanding of, and knowledge about, people in organisations, or is it perceived to be about providing techniques for manipulating people with the aim of intensifying labour in the hopes of increasing organisational efficiency? We have stated before our own conviction that it should be the former but, even if it is the latter, inadequate and inappropriate models of what people are like will hardly be likely to contribute to effectiveness in fulfilling such a purpose.

Organisational behaviour and the self

We live in a society economically reliant on wage labour organisations, yet there is a curious mismatch between the requirements organisations have of people and the requirements that people as selves have from organisations. One might imagine that, rather than people being bent to fit organisations, organisations ought to be designed to be more suitable for people, on the basis that, ultimately, organisations only exist to serve human purposes. The discourse of Organisational Behaviour does not even recognise this as an issue, generally taking the organisational context as given and assuming that people must be moulded to fit this given. It is rare to find considerations of what an organisation moulded to fit people might look like. Yet, arguably, this should be a primary focus for anyone interested in understanding organisational behaviour.

As we have noted, work tends to be seen as isolable from life in a more general sense, as epitomised in the common duality 'work/life balance', which seems very clearly to imply that work is not part of life! But, on one hand, work occupies a major proportion of our waking hours – that is, of our lives as a whole – and, on the other, the reductionist approach which seeks to establish and achieve this separation does so by dichotomising the self in unnatural and potentially destructive ways. As well, it bears no resemblance to anyone's *own* sense of self and its significance. It seems that such an approach is almost schizophrenic in wanting work to be the most important part of anyone's life, while not wanting to acknowledge that work, and experience in organisations more generally, has tremendous impacts on the formation and development of the sense of self.

The denial of selfhood manifested in theory and in practice in organisations can have damaging consequences for people. Indeed, psychological problems associated with work are increasing as an effect of the way people are treated at work and, undoubtedly, in some cases, these surround issues of selfhood. This also has notable impacts on the wider society. Equally, this denial contributes to the dominance of instrumental and materialistic attitudes, since people come to acknowledge that those kinds of rewards are the only recognition of selfhood that is available to them from work. The denial of selfhood also constitutes an active barrier to the process of understanding behaviour in organisations, since attempts to do this are based on inappropriate and inadequate models of what people are like. It is not even functional in organisational terms, since, although it may be *possible* to manage people as if they are machines, this will never help to solve organisational problems and will, indeed, itself cause problems.

We have suggested that the self is fragmented, rooted in the unconscious and active, rather than the integrated, conscious, passive, potentially rational individual of the model held in the discourse of Organisational Behaviour. Given that the self is as we have described it, it is necessary for the discourse to have models that incorporate this understanding – necessary for its own survival (see Chapter 9). It does imply that understanding, and even managing, is a much more complex and difficult process than that implied by the orthodox model. But, if the orthodox model is inappropriate, then that its implications make understanding simpler can hardly be relevant. People are very complex, the self is very complex, and the understanding of organisational behaviour needs to recognise this, even if it, itself, also has to become complex.

A TALE FROM THE VILLAGE PUMP (*SELF*)

(See the Case Study in Appendix 2, pages 340–3)

A friend of John Snow, Sir Benjamin Richardson, wrote 'A Biographical Memory of John Snow' in 1887, after Snow's death, published in the London-based journal, *The Asclepiad* (Volume 6, 274–300), which is informative about the sort of person that Snow was. For example, in his early adult life Snow was a vegetarian and a total abstainer (from alcohol). He somewhat relaxed these precepts later in his life, but remained certain that abstaining 'must' become universal in time, since it was obviously the most healthy way to live. He was quite athletic, and a strong swimmer. Nonetheless, he suffered from ill-health and died quite young. Snow was, apparently, rather timid and was reserved with strangers, though amiable, open and sincere with his friends, to whom he was always available. He did not go out into society and his social life consisted of these friends. He liked things to be orderly, and was also something of an inventor. He was bookish, though only late in life discovered the pleasures of novels, especially those of Dickens. He had a good sense of humour. He was a poor public speaker, but wrote well. In his role as a doctor, Snow attended the poor for free, but he also attended Queen Victoria for the birth of several of her children, to administer anaesthetic to her. He was never well-off. He never married.

- From this picture, we can imagine how Snow might have seen himself. How might Snow's **sense of self** explain his persistence with his hypothesis on the causes of cholera, in the face of strong opposition?

Case

NOBODY'S PERFECT!?

Knut Oil is a company in the oil extraction industry. In the late 1990s, Knut Oil attracted a lot of negative attention from pressure groups in respect of unwelcome, and international, publicity about a number of incidents which raised doubts about the ethical status of the company – these included paying bribes to obtain contracts, price fixing and environmentally damaging practices. Alarmed at this bad publicity, Knut Oil decided to set up a Department of Corporate Social Responsibility (CSR), whose role would be to give advice on good practice and to audit the company in terms of CSR. Over the next few years, great improvements in practice were effected.

The Department of CSR had to be established from scratch and a number of young graduates were engaged, one of whom was Cherry Burton. She joined Knut Oil fresh from university, having read for a degree in Comparative Religion, with a specialism in the relationship between religion and business. Cherry Burton was a rather serious and intense person who felt that working in a Department of CSR was the ideal place to be able to have a positive impact on the world. Her interests outside work involved her in a range of charitable activities and she was also a lay preacher.

Cherry was very keen indeed about her job. She was both highly motivated and well regarded. Eventually, she was given the task of introducing to the company its first explicit Code of Ethics, which had been designed and written by a senior management team. This was a very demanding task that not only required making the Code visible within the company, but also making it visible to the public at large – and especially to the pressure groups that were keeping a close watch on Knut Oil's activities. So devoted was Cherry to this task that she worked very long hours on it, and even forewent most of her annual leave. Her considerable success in realising the aims of the project was

▶

rewarded by a substantial merit increase in her salary, and, when the time came, she was voted 'Employee of the Year'.

For a long time Knut Oil had run a rather ad hoc and informal staff appraisal scheme which each department operated in different ways, and which no one took very seriously. However, a recent tightening of Human Resource Management policy had resulted in a much more formal and rigorous appraisal scheme being introduced, which was to be applied uniformly across the company. It was a fairly conventional scheme and was generally based on self-assessment of the previous year's work. As the date for appraisal approached, the person being appraised was sent a standard form which they had to complete and to take with them to the appraisal interview. The topics on the form then supplied the basis of the discussion in the interview. The appraiser, who was normally the appraisee's immediate superior, had the job of writing a report of the discussion. Both appraiser and appraisee were expected to reach agreement on the report before it was forwarded to the relevant Group Manager and then on to the Human Resource Management Department.

One of the sections on the form that Cherry had to complete for her appraisal was headed 'Weaknesses'. It contained the questions:

> How could you have performed your job better?
> What mistakes did you make?
> What do you think are your principal shortcomings?

When Cherry got to this section she left it blank. On reflection, she did not think that she could have done a better job, had not made any mistakes that she was aware of and did not recognise any serious shortcomings in herself. Given the praise and recognition she had received for her work, she felt quite satisfied with her performance.

However, when they got to this part of Cherry's submission in the appraisal interview, her appraiser, Earl Green, was surprised to see that she had not filled it in and told her that *all* sections must be completed – it was a rule of the new system. If the form was forwarded incomplete, it would just be returned with a tetchy reminder to do the job properly. Cherry protested that she did not have anything to put in that section of the form – after all, her recognition by the company showed that everyone thought that she had done a good job, much of it, as she reminded him, on her own time. Earl Green was very sympathetic but insisted that the questions had to be answered. Cherry countered this by asking him what he thought were her shortcomings, and he had to admit that, at that instant, he could not think of any. Earl then suggested that they could invent something relatively minor to put in, just so that the procedure could go ahead. He assured her that no one would take it seriously. But Cherry replied that it would be dishonest to do so, and that would run counter to her religious beliefs. At this point, Earl Green suggested that they should take a day out to reflect on these issues, but, having done so, they were still unable to resolve the impasse. Finally, Earl agreed to allow Cherry to leave the section blank but, as he had intended, once she had signed the form, in her absence and without her knowledge or consent, he added to the section on 'weaknesses' on Cherry's form that she could be a bit obstinate. He was fairly sure that she would never find out about it, but, if she did, he would say that it was for her own good. By that time, it would all be history anyway.

- In light of the introduction of the new Code of Ethics, should Cherry have been encouraged to lie?

- Built into all appraisal systems is the assumption that everyone can improve their performance. If this is the case, what does Cherry's refusal to fill in the appropriate section say about her sense of self?

- Given that Earl agrees with Cherry about the quality of her performance, what does it say about his sense of self that he was not prepared to support her?

- Is it a good idea to require people to confess to their weaknesses, inadequacies and faults when they are being appraised?

(Other chapters that would be useful and relevant in analysing the case *include* Semiotics (2), Power (5), Rationality (6), Boundary (9) and Decision-making (11).)

Bibliography

Perhaps *the* classic, and a very influential, argument about the role of religion in the development of attitudes to work is Weber (1930). A more recent, and useful, reflection on these issues is Anthony (1977). A number of early observers of the development of organisations into forms we might recognise today were unequivocal in their positive assessment of the spiritual benefits of work for the working classes – see, for example, Ure ([1835] 1967), Smiles ([1859] 1897). Thompson's (1968) historical study of *The Making of the English Working Class* has much to say about the complex involvement of organised religion in this 'making'.

A prominent example of the vaunted changes in the role of work in people's lives is to be found in the so-called flexibilisation literature. A useful way to gain access to these shifts is to look at the contemporary 'visionaries' of the future of work, because they offer an overview rather than technical prescription – some of the best known examples are Handy (1984, 1994) and Drucker (1980, 1981, 1993). On the relatively recent issue of age as a general basis for discrimination at work, see, for example, McEwen (1990), Blytheway (1995). A more general and more philosophical approach to understanding these changes can be found in the literature on Nihilism and on the rise of Individualism. Nihilism is particularly associated with the work of Nietzsche, an introductory overview of whose thinking can be found in *Nietzsche For Beginners* (Sautet and Boussignac 1990). On Individualism, see Lukes (1973). An interesting short history of the concept of the individual can be found in Williams (1976).

There has always been a substantial literature advocating other possibilities. Freud (1963), for example, reflected on the unrealised potential benefits to be derived for the self from work, and on its evident dysfunctions and lack of perceived attractiveness. As just one other example, Habermas (1978) also reflects critically on the role of (instrumental) work in reproducing society. Many writers have recognised that work is a site of what Freud called 'unnecessary suffering', which, Habermas notes, also after Freud, it should be the role of society to eradicate. On this, see also Moore (1965). A different strand of literature concerned with the depredations of organised work at the level of the individual can be represented by Gouldner's (1969) concept of 'the unemployed self' – see also Allport's (1924) notion of 'partial inclusion'. An emergent challenge to individualism can be seen in the concept of communitarianism – see, for example, Etzioni (1988), Avineri and de-Shalit (1992), Kingdom (1992). The idea that there are alternatives to Individualism in the organisational context is addressed by, for example, Hosking, Dachler and Gergen (1995).

There is a burgeoning literature on stress and its 'management' – the popularity of the subject has led to it being referred to as 'the stress industry'. Contrasting approaches to the issue of stress are represented by, for example, Cooper, Cooper and Eaker (1988) and Newton, Handy and Fineman (1995). An early and very influential examination of trust relationships at work is in Fox (1974) – this is an issue now often also addressed in the literature on organisational ethics. Also early and very influential was the contribution of Argyris (1957) to the debate on autonomy and maturity in organisational settings. Watson (1994) provides an interesting study of the problems of both formulation and implementation of policies directed at empowerment, in the context of a longitudinal case study. Both concepts and practices of empowerment are increasingly questioned – see, for example, Sewell and Wilkinson, in the generally useful Blyton and Turnbull (1992). See also Collins (2000). The question of Human Resource Management theories and practices is addressed by, for example, Legge (1995). The idea that all management theory and practice is based on a set of beliefs about what people are like is represented in the widely accepted concept of models of man (sic). A well-known example is Schein (1988), but see also Leach (1972). Similar issues which particularly address man/machine conceptual models can be found in, for example, Simons (1986).

The notion of an autonomous, integrated, individual simply does not figure in the poststructuralist literature. Instead, there is a fairly ubiquitous notion of 'the de-centred subject'. Outside this literature there have been some attempts to chart the shift in understandings of the self and its repercussions – Giddens (1991) may stand as one example. The notion of becoming is, however, a very significant one in contemporary social theory – Sturrock (1993), for example, actually defines Poststructuralism as a 'philosophy of becoming', in contrast to Structuralism which he sees as a 'philosophy of being'. The concept of desire is also a major element in Poststructuralism, including consideration of the significance of the desire for artefacts and the spurious supposition that artefacts can define identity. Deleuze and Guattari (1984) is a good source on this. See also Goodchild (1996).

Major examples of Lacan's work are Lacan (1977, 1980). However, his work is often intentionally difficult and it is useful to approach it through commentaries, though these also vary in accessibility. There is a *Introducing Lacan* (Leader and Groves (2005), and Bowie (1991) is a Modern Masters text. Slightly more demanding are Benvenuto and Kennedy (1986) and MacCannell (1986) – and Lemaire (1977).

There are a number of other approaches which draw on these ideas in the context of organisation. Notable is the work of Cooper (for example, 1983a, 1983b, 1987, 1993). See also, for a variety of approaches, for example, Baxter (1982), Leather (1983), Chia (1996), Tsoukas (1998) and Willmott (1998). There are also other interesting, and contrasting, approaches to these issues, including, for example, Jacques (1996), who provides a useful and informative overview of the development of the concept of the employee; Du Gay (1996), who focuses on the interplay of production and consumption as impacts on the realisation of identity at work; Meakin (1976), who charts these changes as they are reflected in contemporary literature. For a study that specifically links work, consumption and poverty in a discussion of work in 'postmodern' society, see Bauman (2005). For an extensive reflection on the implications of Postmodernism in the context of work and organisation, see Hancock and Tyler (2001).

There are a rather limited number of sources on sabotage at work, though what there is is generally well known. See, for example, Taylor and Walton (1971), Brown (1977) and Dubois (1979). A somewhat different attitude is represented by Analoui and Kakabadse (1991). There is a larger literature on the satisfactions to be gained by various levels of disruption to normal work patterns. Well-known examples are Roy (1960), Beynon (1973) and Linhart (1981). If you move outside the literature on management and organisation, to look at personal accounts of experiences at work, the issues of the pleasures to be derived from work itself versus the dissatisfactions of the way work is organised are often very clear. See, for example, almost any book – and there are many – written by people who have worked in the railway industry.

As noted, there is a substantial literature on what is sometimes generically called 'the meaning of work', from a variety of perspectives. Some of this literature addresses the issue directly – for example, Fox (1980) – and some more indirectly – for example, Thompson (1983). Another kind of contribution is based on consideration of the general benefits to be derived by people from work. An example is Jahoda, Lazarsfeld and Zeisel (1972), a landmark investigation of *un*employment in Austria during the Great Depression. See also Jahoda (1982). For something profoundly different, see Kane (2004).

On Expectancy Theory, see Vroom (1964) and, for an analysis of its unrealised potential, see Carter and Jackson (1993).

Amongst participant observation, or similar, studies of people at work, Beynon (1973) and Linhart (1981) are, as noted previously, two of the best known, and more graphic. Another well-known example is Nichols and Armstrong (1976). Also worthy of note is Tunstall's (1962) study of the fishing industry, and Aktouf's (for example, 1996) comparative study of the brewing industry in Canada and Algeria. An earlier, and also well-known, study is Hughes (1958).

Tressell's *The Ragged Trousered Philanthropists* (1965) is also well worth a read. Traditionally, organisations have been reluctant to allow access for academic studies of their work processes, particularly where there is potential for the outcome to be critical, which is seen as more likely where the subject is people's experience at work, than where the subject is, for example, more technical. Some organisations have operated a simple blanket ban on providing access for purposes of academic research. However, as noted, recently there has been a remarkable upsurge of provision of access for non-academic purposes such as the making of television documentaries. Such documentaries frequently display their subject organisations in an unfavourable light but, apparently, the distinction between academic research and entertainment removes doubt on the part of those providing access.

An early specific use of psychoanalysis for the study of organisations and organisational behaviour was De Board (1978). Its use is now becoming both more popular and more rigorous. The psychoanalytic approach offers some very different, and challenging, understandings, particularly of the impact of organisations on people. Notable examples are Schwartz (1990), which includes some unusual case material, and Sievers (1994). See also Diamond (1993) and, especially, Gabriel (1999).

CHAPTER 9

Boundary

This chapter looks at some of the basic characteristics of boundary, focusing, in particular, on its function as a limit, and as a differentiating device. Against the idea that boundaries are fixed, obvious and natural, the emphasis is on boundary as cognitive rather than actual, and as functioning semiotically to signify inclusion and exclusion. Boundaries are viewed as being purposeful human constructs, necessary but arbitrary, which function as control mechanisms and which structure acceptable extents of responsibility. The 'permeability' of boundaries is explored through the concept of system, stressing interconnection, interaction and communication, rather than discreteness, and the concept of the ecosystem is used to explore the idea of boundarylessness. We then turn to an examination of the process of model-building as a bounding activity, emphasising its informational characteristics. The idea that we manage through models, which are always and inevitably both partial and purposeful, is developed. This necessarily follows from the view that unmediated access to 'the real' is not possible and that, therefore, models are all we have. The issue of the adequacy of models is explored, in the context of their intended use. The relevance of processes of bounding and model-building to problem definition and solution is addressed. The use of bounding and model-building processes in both theory and practice of understanding and managing organisational behaviour, ubiquitous but rarely explicit, is highlighted.

Every concept that has been introduced so far implies a notion of boundary. In the process of semiotic understanding, for example, what a signifier signifies is separated from what it does not signify – what it means is bounded from what it does not mean. In the context of knowledge, the concept of discourse is defined, in itself, by issues of boundary between the allowable and the excluded, at all levels of consideration. Power is a relational concept defined in terms of boundaries between, for example, who has it and who does not. Rationality includes a process of bounding the rational from the non-rational. Ideology produces, at the cognitive level, boundaries between what is good and what is not, what is moral and what is not, and so on, depending on the logic of the ideas that constitute any particular ideology. The very concept of self presupposes some bounding mechanism which distinguishes self from not-self, or others. Perhaps the prime example is that of structure which, in itself, constitutes a bounding process between, for example, order and disorder, organisation and disorganisation.

Clearly, what we are describing here is the general process of distinguishing between different states, conditions, things, concepts, and so on. Indeed, all sense-making depends on such distinctions and should, therefore, be seen as a bounding process. Some kind of bounding process is necessary for survival in the world: it would not be possible to survive without engaging in the construction of boundaries, from the most literal, such as being able to distinguish what is dangerous from what is not, to the most abstract, such as being able to decide what something means and what it does not mean.

A major implication of the discussion up to now has been that the conventional, so-called common-sense, boundaries which are perceived to exist in the discourses of Organisation Studies and of Management are not as natural or as obvious as is assumed or claimed, and that they need to be interrogated and examined, in terms of their appropriateness to the task in hand. In now focusing on the concept of boundary itself the starting point is that there are no *natural* boundaries in human affairs that are obvious, inevitable or necessary. The bounding process is an utterly inescapable one, but it is not a matter of simply recognising boundaries that pre-exist our awareness of them, it is a sense-making process – **the bounding process is not to do with *recognition*, but to do with *cognition*.** Not only is this process fundamental, but it is also obvious that important and myriad consequences flow from the perception of a boundary of any kind, not only for the self but also for others, at all levels of the social. These are the issues that will be explored in this chapter.

Boundary as limit

In the American Civil War the military commandant of a particular post had acquired a large number of prisoners but had insufficient troops to guard them. To resolve this problem he inscribed a line in the sand, the original **deadline**: if the prisoners kept to 'their' side of the line they were safe and relatively free, but if they crossed the deadline they would be summarily shot. The situation represented a classic management problem. The commandant-manager's difficulty was that the demand on his resources was too great and he needed to control the behaviour of his 'organisational participants' in such a way as to reduce that demand. He did this by placing the responsibility for their behaviour on the 'participants', in the context of a penalty for non-compliance – a sort of exception reporting. The encouragement to self-policing in this case has many echoes in the modern parlance of management techniques aimed at the same outcome, such as incentives, empowerment, self-appraisal, self-surveillance, management by objectives. The contemporary sense of deadline, although now temporal rather than spatial, still retains this notion of relative freedom to self-manage before the deadline, but withdrawal of such freedom and exposure to sanctions once the deadline is crossed.

The boundary formed by the original deadline very clearly represented a **limit**. From the point of view of the prisoners the deadline differentiated between safety and danger, between relative freedom of movement and no movement at all, between a degree of self-management and subjection to total control. From the point of view of the commandant-manager, the deadline represented the limit of what would be tolerated, backed up by the power of sanction. However, let us examine the constitution of this boundary. The line in the sand is not a physical barrier but exists only **semiotically**. The literal boundary is **absent** and the line is only effective if people recognise what it signifies (though that, of course, does not mean that no one will try to cross it, challenge the signification). The line in the sand is also **arbitrary** – on one hand, it could very easily have been placed somewhere else and, on the other, it could have taken another form, both with the same effect. The deadline also represents **difference**. Crossing the deadline symbolises transition from one state to another, from inside to outside, from – in this case – life to death, or, if crossed successfully from the point of view of the prisoners, from captivity to freedom. All this is represented by the line in the sand.

This example is an illustration of the conventional approach to understanding boundary in the discourse of Organisational Behaviour, and in the discourse of Organisation Studies more generally. There the prevalent interpretation of what a boundary signifies focuses on its function as a limit, a cut-off point, the demarcation between *inside* (relevant, important, meaningful) and *outside* (irrelevant, unimportant, meaningless). The discourse of Organisational Behaviour concerns itself specifically with what goes on *inside* the organisation – in other words, construes a notional boundary between the organisation and the rest of the world which is quite clearly intended to represent a limit to the concerns of Organisational Behaviour specialists and of management. The basis of this is the strongly embedded idea that what goes on inside the organisation is separable from what goes on outside it. People may exist inside *and* outside the organisation, but the discourse of Organisational Behaviour treats them as if they are divisible. Thus, for example, within the notional boundary it is deemed legitimate – or, even more, a right – for managers to exercise highly detailed levels of control over people's behaviour which are not supposed to be appropriate outside the organisation. Even if such control has impacts outside the organisation, this is not a matter that should concern managers.

However, what constitutes this limit, and where it is, is far from clear, and raises questions about how the establishment of a limit takes place, what criteria are used to decide where it should be. In terms of physical criteria it is often assumed that the boundary of an organisation is represented by the metaphorical 'factory gates' – the literal entry/exit of the premises. From the organisational behaviour point of view the boundary is much more diffuse, as witnessed by the extent to which managers claim legitimacy in having an impact on behaviour outside the 'factory gates'. It is quite usual, for example, for managers to expect people to behave outside work in ways that are defined as not detrimental to good performance inside work, such as getting a 'sensible' amount of sleep, not inducing a hangover, not allowing social life to impinge on working life, and so on. Equally, if you are not allowed to wear a beard at work, then it will be very difficult to wear one outside work, should you wish to do so – the boundary is meaningless.

Such conventional approaches to understanding the nature of boundary do not imply that what is outside the limit does not exist, or even that it is not significant, but they do imply that it is much less significant than what is inside the limit. The limit itself is seen to represent areas of transaction between what is inside and what is outside the organisation, but the nature of those transactions is defined by what is 'good for the organisation'. What is outside is commonly called, in such approaches, the **environment**: it is the *background* to whatever the organisation does. The language with which managers assess the relevance of the environment to their activities is the language of **opportunity** and **threat**: the significance of the environment is seen principally in terms of what good or ill it can do for the organisation. In so far as it is recognised, the environment is defined in highly attenuated, very selective, terms – not even as 'the rest of the world', but, for example, as a market, as a repository of resources, as competition, as something over which control might be desirable, if difficult to achieve, 'for the benefit of the organisation'.

Difficulties

The examination of the nature of the boundary in the case of the original deadline also illustrates why the above kind of approach to understanding the nature of organisational boundaries is deeply problematic, simplistic and reductionist, and does not bear much close scrutiny. There is **no actual difference** between what is inside the limit and what is outside it. The organisation and its physical and social 'environment' are continuous. **A boundary, wherever it may be, is simply a cognitive device developed to aid differentiation** – it is not real, does not have physical presence, does not *actually* distinguish between an 'in' and an 'out'.

Importantly, however, **a boundary is always purposeful, and perception of a boundary is always related to the purpose the boundary is intended to serve**. Different purposes will entail different bounding processes. Take, for example, the case of domestic property. It is common to use a boundary to distinguish between what is one's own and what belongs to someone else. This is a semiotic boundary, similar to the deadline example. But a semiotic boundary may not keep out unwelcome intrusions so, for that purpose, we might choose to erect a physical manifestation of the change of ownership as a more powerful symbol of it – build a wall, grow a hedge. There is also a legal concept of the boundary, which may or may not be coextensive with the symbolic and/or the physical boundary. But none of these boundaries signifies actual separation: the ground that you own is continuous with the ground owned by the person next door; the legal boundary does not separate you from lawlessness, since those outside your boundary are bound by the same laws. Such a boundary merely distinguishes between what you own and what someone else owns, what you are responsible for and what someone else is responsible for – that is their purpose. But **they are just human constructs and they can be changed**. You may, for example, buy another piece of land and your boundary will change, but the land itself has not changed.

We can construct many different boundaries for many different purposes but the common factor is that the basic purpose is always to differentiate at some level. Differentiation is a process that has enormous impacts on behaviour, attitudes, ideas and action. But **differentiation is also only a cognitive process, necessary for survival but profoundly arbitrary**.

It is also important to recognise that differentiation not only distinguishes between things, but also links these very same things together, by defining one in terms of the other: **what separates also joins**. The boundary hedge that separates your property from that next door also joins your property to that next door. This important point is best illustrated at the level of meaning itself, which depends on distinction between what is and what is not (see the discussion of language, meaning and sense-making in Chapter 2). If something is defined by what it is not, then to exclude, marginalise, devalue what it is not – what defines it as something – is to threaten meaning itself. What, for example, could 'organisation' mean if it were not distinguishable from something else, 'not-organisation'? Certainly it is useful to make such distinctions, necessary to existential survival at the most basic level, but it is equally important to understand them in terms of their **ontology: they are not real, but purposeful devices of sense-making**. Though we may treat a boundary *as if* it is real, it is no more than a conceptual tool, a way of thinking about something, anything. This implies, inevitably, that it is possible to think about something in different ways, to have different purposes, different boundaries, different outcomes. That is the full implication of the proposition that **boundaries are not fixed, natural or obvious**.

DIY bounding

Choose an organisation of which you are a member – for example, family, work, college, church, club.

- Where do you think the boundaries of this organisation are?
- Are the boundaries physical? geographic? legal? social? psychological? cultural? temporal? symbolic? Are they all of these? Are they some, but not all of them? Are some more important than others? Can you think of any other kinds of boundary to your chosen organisation?

Consequences

The significance of this implication derives from the observation that **every instance of boundary location has consequences**. There could, indeed, be no point to boundary location, and purpose would be irrelevant, were that not the case. The issue that attaches to the acknowledgement of consequences, however, is that of **responsibility**. The idea that boundaries, of whatever kind, are given and real is very comforting psychologically. It suggests that all that is necessary for anyone to do is to recognise them. It suggests that there is no need to think about them, or to judge them, because they just *are*. Most importantly, it suggests that no individual is responsible for them. All someone can do is to mind what goes on, on 'their' side of the fence. If a boundary is given in nature, how can we be responsible for what goes on outside that boundary? At worst, it might be necessary to think about how to conduct transactions across the boundary, but we can bear no responsibility for the boundary itself, or for its consequences.

An obvious example at the broad social level is the acceptance of a meaningful boundary between different ethnic or racial groups, signifying natural superiority and inferiority, which allows things to be done to those on the wrong side of the boundary that those on the right side of it do not have to suffer. This was a particularly salient problem in the twentieth century (and shows no sign of going away in the twenty-first century), with the Final Solution for the Jews in Germany, apartheid in South Africa, ethnic cleansing in the Balkans, amongst other examples. Segregation was still common in parts of the United States of America until relatively recently, whereby blacks were legally denied civil liberties available to whites. Such ethnic boundaries meant that people in organisations could discriminate at will on grounds of race without any legal or moral responsibility for the consequences of their actions. At a slightly more localised level, in the case of the multinational chemicals company cited in Chapter 7, which polluted the environment and poisoned the local population of a Third World country, it was the invocation of legal boundaries that enabled the company to escape the financial obligations and moral responsibility for its negligence. At an even more localised level, subscription to management theories such as the idea of 'right-sizing' has had the same effect of absolving individuals of any responsibility for their actions relevant to such practice. The implication of the term 'right-sizing' is that there is a proper and natural boundary to the size of any particular organisation, which is sometimes transgressed. This perception legitimised decisions to rectify such a problem by getting rid of those people who made the organisation the wrong size. The whole process has been justified by the claim that there is a natural and inevitable boundary for an organisation and all managers have to do is observe this 'natural law'.

A few specific examples such as those above can give only an indication of the significance of boundaries in organisational practice. Awareness of 'the' organisational boundary has profound impacts on all aspects of organisation, and of organisational behaviour in particular. To be able to claim that this boundary is natural, given and obvious is undoubtedly extremely useful to managers because, while placing this as a 'fact' beyond discussion, it also absolves them of responsibility for their actions: things are done because they are inevitable, not because they are chosen. A successful challenge to the acceptance of the naturalness and given-ness of boundaries would place managers in a very exposed position and would constitute a challenge to the right to manage. In this sense, and in *whatever* sense it is used, **a boundary represents a control mechanism**, restraining freedom of action both inside and outside the boundary. **The ability to specify where the boundaries are, therefore, is the exercise of power.**

Boundary and systems

In examining the nature of boundary it is useful to take what is, basically, a **systemic** approach. By this we mean that the focus is on **interaction** rather than action, **interrelationships** rather than relationships, **process** rather than discrete events – in other words, on the **interlinking, interconnectedness and mutuality** of phenomena, events, concepts, and so on. Everything is linked together, and everything influences everything else.

It is common in Systems Theory to speak of closed systems and open systems. **Closed systems are self-contained and have no transactions across their boundaries.** On the other hand, **open systems are not self-contained, do have transactions across their boundaries and have environments.** It is also commonly accepted that social systems – any system in which there are people, which, obviously, includes organisations – are *always* open systems. However, although closed and open systems are significantly different in terms of Systems Theory, it is arguable that, in effect, **once an open system is defined – given a boundary – it becomes a *quasi-closed* system as regards its internal functioning.** This is because, when conceptualising an open system, the boundary should be located at a point where transactions across the boundary are not significant – in other words, where the system includes everything that is relevant to it and where it achieves what is known as dynamic equilibrium.

The identification of an open system boundary, of the point at which transactions across the boundary are not significant, is a question of human judgement. **Boundaries are defined in terms of the purposes of those who do the defining.** As such, boundaries do *not* reflect natural phenomena, but reflect human interests. An illustration will reinforce this point. Bearing in mind that all organisations of whatever kind involve people and are, therefore, social systems and, therefore, open systems, let us cite the continuing debate about the health implications of nuclear power. It has long been recognised that those employed in nuclear installations are at risk from radiation and they are routinely monitored, effectively or otherwise, to try to ensure that they do not receive, or have not received, excessive doses of radiation. The debate surrounds those living in the vicinity of such installations and for a long time it was asserted that these people were not at risk and, therefore, did not require the same level of monitoring and protection. The boundary between those at risk and those not at risk was coextensive with the physical boundaries of the organisation. Subsequent experience has shown that those 'external' to the organisation – sometimes a great deal further afield than the 'vicinity' – have also been exposed to excessive radiation (and not only people but also animals and, indeed, land, water and air), with widespread and serious implications. That is to say, there were significant transactions of unwonted radiation across the supposed boundary of the system, thus demonstrating that the initial bounding was premature and inappropriate.

Typically, challenges to, and redefinitions of, the boundaries of organisations tend to come, not from *within* the claimed boundary, but from *outside* it, from, for example, pressure groups. In the first instance, it was managers who decided where to locate the boundary of unwonted radiation, and they chose this boundary for managerial reasons. Prominent among those reasons was to locate the boundary at the furthest extent of their direct control and, equally, at the limit at which they were prepared to accept responsibility. The interest of those who have challenged this decision was to compel managers to accept responsibility for impacts of their decisions and actions over which the challengers had no control but from which they were suffering. This is, almost always, the pattern of the location of, and challenges to the location of, boundaries. In this case, it now seems rather obvious that the extent of unwonted radiation could not be controlled by management fiat, yet this is precisely what was attempted.

Collateral damage

'Collateral damage' is a euphemistic term that seems to have originated in the Vietnam war, to denote unintended damage (consequences) following from military action against the enemy – often, killing or maiming people outwith the *intended* boundary of effect.

A euphemism is a rhetorical device. Its function is to rephrase something that is regarded as unpleasant in terms that sound less offensive, to try to mask the unpleasantness. Managers are great users of euphemism – for example, they talk of 'letting someone go', when they mean sacking them; they talk of 'negative profit', when they mean losses; they talk of 'rationalisation', when they mean closing a facility. The purpose of a euphemism is to deceive either the intended audience or the user, or, more likely, both. It is, then, interesting to note that the term 'collateral damage' has metamorphosed into an accepted technical term within the military lexicon, where it is intended as a precise definition of one of the unfortunate, but unavoidable, inevitabilities of normally accurate, modern and virtuous warfare – in other words, killing a few innocent bystanders (often those that the action in question is intended to protect or benefit) for the greater good! The companion concept of 'friendly fire' is another example.

This term, 'collateral damage', is now to be found outside military circles, though often used more ironically. It also seems to be emerging, non-ironically, as part of what is called 'management-speak'. Non-military organisational activity is also well-known for its ability to generate collateral damage (unintended consequences). Such damage always, and by definition, results from premature bounding of the perceived area of effect of organisational action. Examples abound: some industrial processes are associated with life-threatening industrial diseases; keyboard operators can get repetitive strain injury; appraisal systems are recognised to produce high levels of anxiety; employing women as cheap labour has resulted in some very large payouts for being discriminatory; increasing surveillance can increase resistance; call centres can alienate customers. At all levels from the macro to the micro, things said can sometimes have devastating unintended consequences – a particularly well-known example is the case of Gerald Ratner, son of the founder of, and Chief Executive of, a large chain of jewellers, who said, in 1991, in a speech to the Institute of Directors, that some of his company's merchandise was 'total crap', which resulted in £500 million being wiped off the value of the company and his own departure from it in the following year – though the loss of confidence in the company was irretrievable and it only survived by changing its name.

Different people have different perceptions of where the boundary of a system is, depending on their own particular interest in it. In other words, when addressing the *same* phenomena, people will bound them differently, in terms of their interest. Challenges to the power to locate boundary occur when people are in dispute over the nature and extent of impacts of, say, organisational activity, and who should be responsible for those impacts. It is this notion of interest in the activities of organisations that underlies the concept of **stakeholder**. Thus, a stakeholder is someone who has an interest of some kind in an organisation but there is a huge chasm between those who perceive themselves as having an interest, and those who are recognised by, for example, managers as having an interest. When a stakeholder interest is recognised it may be the first step towards relocating – changing perception of – organisational boundaries. For example, when, as recently occurred, an oil company starts to include members of environmental pressure groups as advisors to its management, this may signify recognition of the legitimate interests of environmentalists in its activities – but it may not, and may only be a way of incorporating the opposition.

These examples represent boundary issues arising from physical impacts of organisational activity, but the same holds for perhaps more nebulous issues of social and/or psychological impacts. At an even more localised level than previous examples, recent research has shown that the work demands made by organisations are contributing to the breakdown of familial relations. By conventional wisdom, the quality of employees' family relations are not the concern of managers, yet, clearly, work and family are systemically linked. The current boundary between work and family determined by managers may be successfully challenged, should families gain recognition as having a stakeholder interest through the demands made upon family members by their employing organisations. The feminist movement has been relatively more successful in redefining organisational boundaries, in some respects, through, for example, forcing recognition of managerial responsibility for harassment and discrimination, of whatever kind.

The consequences of bounding

Most social ills, as well as most social benefits, derive from, or are a consequence of, people acting (or behaving) in organisations. Such actions tend to be conceptualised as local and in pursuit of particular interests – that is, they are conceived of as occurring within fairly narrow boundaries; we do not usually think of what we do as having large-scale consequences, but are more aware of the consequences for ourselves. Such actions rarely, if ever, reflect a holistic view.

David Bohm has argued that:

'. . . art, science, technology, and human work in general, are divided up into specialities, each considered to be separate in essence from the others . . . society as a whole has developed in such a way that it is broken up into separate nations and different religious, political, economic, racial groups, etc. Man's natural environment has correspondingly been seen as an aggregate of separately existent parts, to be exploited by different groups of people. Similarly, each individual human being has been fragmented into a large number of separate and conflicting compartments, according to his different desires, aims, ambitions, loyalties, psychological characteristics, etc . . . The notion that all these fragments are separately existent is evidently an illusion, and this illusion cannot do other than lead to endless conflict and confusion. Indeed, the attempt to live according to the notion that the fragments are really separate is, in essence, what has led to the growing series of extremely urgent crises that is confronting us today. Thus, as is now well-known, this way of life has brought about pollution, destruction of the balance of nature, over-population, world-wide economic and political disorder, and *the creation of an overall environment that is neither physically nor mentally healthy for most of the people who have to live in it.'*

Source: From D. Bohm (1983) *Wholeness and the Implicate Order*. London: Ark Paperbacks (Routledge), pp. 1–2 (emphasis added). Reproduced with permission from the Tayor & Francis Group Ltd.

▶

In other words, because we construct boundaries where there are none and then run our organisations as if these boundaries we have constructed are real, we are creating an unhealthy environment for ourselves to live in.

- Given the significance of the consequences of boundary location, what criteria should we use to establish boundaries?

- In the knowledge of the problems of the fragmentary approach described by Bohm, why do we continue to bound in this way? Indifference? Laziness? Stupidity? Sense of powerlessness? Some people's interests are served by it, even if other people's are not?

- Are there any consequences of the situation Bohm describes that make it worth enduring?

Boundarylessness

Once it is recognised that the boundaries of social systems are mutable and malleable, arbitrary and interested, that they depend entirely on who is defining them, it is but a short step to argue that **social systems have no boundaries**. Within Systems Theory this is recognised by writers such as Kenneth Boulding, who argues that systems do not have environments, that there is no natural boundary at all to an open system. If it is assumed that the system boundary should include everything that has an impact on, and everything that is impacted by, the system, then it is not difficult to sustain the argument that there are no obvious, or known, limits. This is recognised further in the concept of the **ecosystem**, *the system formed by the interaction of all physical, organic and abstract components*. The ecosystem is, in effect, a very large **closed** system. It appears that the smallest conceivable unit that could constitute an ecosystem is the planet Earth as a whole, although, arguably, this ought to be extended, minimally, to include the Solar System, since the Earth depends on the Sun's heat to function, and, probably, the entire Universe, because of, for example, the potential for regular, if at long intervals, large meteor impacts which can eliminate life altogether, as apparently happened to the dinosaurs. Such an event would, clearly, have a major impact on the social system, at any level one chooses to consider it!

The idea of the planet Earth as a system, or, rather, *the* system, has gained widespread recognition through the popular, if controversial, **Gaia Hypothesis**. In this approach, the Earth is seen as maintained homeostatically through the action of living organisms. As with all concepts of dynamic systems, the Earth has limits within which it can function homeostatically – in dynamic equilibrium. Within the range of its stability criteria the system will self-correct to negate tendencies pushing it towards disequilibrium. The Gaia Hypothesis maintains that this is not something that people can determine, but only something that they can influence, by reducing threats to system stability. If the limits are violated, it will lead to the terminal collapse of the system – in the case of system Earth this would mean the extinction of life as we know it. It seems possible that, in the terms of the Gaia Hypothesis, the activities of humankind could lead to the extinction of life itself, through, for example, runaway pollution, the so-called nuclear winter that would follow the use of nuclear weapons, the greenhouse effect, holes in the ozone layer, desertification, spiralling population, misuse of pesticides and antibiotics, and, perhaps, genetic engineering. The point about all these threats is that they derive from *organisational* activity, whether commercial, social, familial or anything else.

The argument of the Gaia Hypothesis would totally destroy the managerialist assumption that we can have no responsibility for those things over which we do not have direct control. In the case of the previous example of unwonted radiation from nuclear installations, managers cannot control radiation that escapes, so they claimed not to be responsible for it – or, rather, claimed that it did not exist. The counterargument was that, not only did it exist, but it had consequences for which managers *were* responsible, because it was an effect of their actions. The Gaia Hypothesis also places major emphasis on the argument that everything that anyone does, good or bad, has an effect on the system as a whole. Obviously, organisational behaviour is thoroughly implicated, at all levels. Decisions made by organisational members, however trivial they may seem and however putatively obvious and rational, may – indeed, are likely to – have consequences for the system far beyond the immediate objectives of the decision-makers.

Unintended consequences

The law of unintended consequences suggests that any human action will lead to at least one unforeseen outcome. In other words, no matter how carefully we define a problem, how elaborately we construct our model of 'the world', how well we understand what we are doing, something will always occur that we did not allow for. To put it another way, no matter how precisely we construct our **boundaries**, there will always be something outwith those boundaries that will catch us unawares. A metaphor that illuminates this phenomenon evokes the tornado-causing beat of a butterfly's wings, and is known as the **butterfly effect**. This hypothesis comes from Chaos Theory, and is more correctly known as *sensitive dependence on initial conditions*. It states that, in non-linear dynamic systems – of which an organisation is an example – minute differences in initial conditions can lead to vastly differing consequences (see also the concept of the **rhizome**, in Chapter 12). So, if things are not exactly the way that you think they are – in any case, an unachievable condition – they will not turn out the way that you expect!

In the conventional discourse of Organisational Behaviour, where it is assumed that it is possible to know what is relevant, that it is possible to know all the relevant variables, and that it is possible to control them, it is not very surprising that this insight is relatively absent. On the other hand, it has been a part of 'folk wisdom' for centuries. It may be more familiar in another form. For example, this nursery rhyme has been around since the fourteenth century:

For want of a nail the shoe was lost;
For want of a shoe the horse was lost;
For want of a horse the rider was lost;
For want of a rider the battle was lost;
For want of a battle the kingdom was lost,
And all for the want of a horse-shoe nail.

          . . . And, of course, that's not the end of it!

For those who prefer a more humorous approach to the important issue of boundaries, there is always the well-known folk anthem, '*I know an old lady who swallowed a fly . . .*'.

This is not to suggest that people in organisations *deliberately* take decisions, perform activities, behave, in ways that threaten system viability. One can hardly suppose, for example, that the desire of deep sea fishermen, in employing industrial fishing methods to fish efficiently and so to optimise profit from the activity, *intended* to eliminate fish stocks, since fish stocks were the basis of their livelihood. Yet, in some areas this is precisely what has happened. And the point is that **whether or not this was an intention is quite irrelevant in the face of the actual consequence**. This is a prime example of the problem of constructing boundaries which are arbitrary but which are then treated *as if* real and given – in this case, the boundary between sustainable and non-sustainable fishing. From the point of view of the Gaia Hypothesis it does not matter where we construe the boundary to be, or why we might want it to be there – human intentions as regards boundaries have simply no relevance.

Boundary . . .

We have used Systems Theory to illustrate the point that, in human affairs, boundaries are human constructs, not natural phenomena. **Whenever human beings construct a boundary, differentiate between two situations, physical or conceptual, this reflects a choice made in the context of particular interests, not a recognition of a given, natural boundary.** However, the intention *here* is not to pursue Systems Theory, but to address the issue of boundary. To say that boundaries are human constructs is not to say that they are a non-issue, or insignificant. We previously suggested that the bounding process was an inescapable and necessary part of human understanding. It is an interesting paradox about boundaries that, although they do not exist, they are essential to us. It is this imperative to bound to which we now turn.

Boundary and model-building

Human beings are great model-builders. They do it all the time. It is no exaggeration to say that we spend all our waking hours – and probably all our non-waking hours too – building models. It cannot be avoided, it is a necessary part of functioning in the world.

When we talk about models we may think immediately of, for example, little plastic or balsawood aeroplanes, clay models, or even mathematical models, but, while this is undoubtedly a kind of modelling, it is only one small and relatively insignificant part of the modelling process in general. So, what is a model? The defining characteristics of models are that **all models are made of information and all models contain less information than that which they model**. If the model contained the same amount of information as that which it modelled, it would not be a model at all, but a clone of the original. Some models are obviously made out of physical material, but that material is itself information. Whether a model is a three-dimensional object, a two-dimensional icon, a set of

The Betrayal of Images

Source: René Magritte, *La trahison des images,* 1952.
© Photothéque R. Magritte – ADAGP, Paris 2006.

mathematical symbols, words, or whatever, it has these characteristics of comprising information, and less information than the original which is being modelled. Clearly, **all models are signifiers**. Equally, **all signifiers are models**.

At the moment of writing this there is, in front of us, a wooden jigsaw pig. It is clearly a pig because of its shape – that is, it contains information which says that this is meant to be a pig. But it is clearly not a pig because it is made of wood and only a few inches long – again, this is information: size, colour, material. A real pig contains a lot more information than this, it can breathe, eat, move, has internal organs which our model does not have. If somehow we could expand the information in our model by making it a living, breathing, full-sized pig, it would then not be a model but would be a real pig. It is a model *because* it has less information than the real thing. It has enough information to tell us what it represents, but not enough to be a real pig. By the same token, the word 'pig' is also a model. It represents, in English, a particular sort of animal, contains information that tells us that it denotes this particular animal, but also that it is not itself a pig, cannot grow, does not have a curly tail, cannot be mated with another pig. Our model of a pig is, of course, not the only possible model of a pig. A common example is the piggy bank, the use of the form of a pig into which money can be placed. Again, there is information that identifies it as a model of a pig, but also information that denotes that it is not a pig – a slot in its back and a plug in its underparts, for example. Real pigs are full of complex internal organs, piggy banks are 'full' of a void. One might have a photograph of a pig – the information might be relatively detailed about appearance, but a photograph is only two-dimensional, much smaller than a pig and is constituted by non-pig-like chemicals. And there are many other possibilities.

All these models contain less information than the original. They also contain different information from each other. In other words, **some information is always deleted from the original, but it is not the same information in each instance of a model**. Whereas a piggy bank requires the retention of information about the three-dimensionality of a pig, this is not necessary for the word 'pig' as a model. This raises another important point about models: **the choice of**

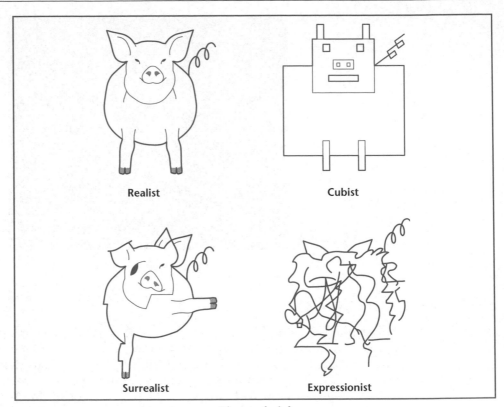

Realist　　　　　Cubist

Surrealist　　　　Expressionist

It's a real pig!

information to be retained or omitted depends on the purpose for which one is modelling. For example, if you wanted to explain, to someone who had never seen a pig, what a pig looked like, it would not be useful to show them the word 'pig', and some visual representation would be appropriate. On the other hand, if you wanted to ask a farmer how much it would cost to buy one of his pigs, the word 'pig' would be a sufficient model of what you wanted to buy, and a picture of the animal would not, usually, be necessary. This raises yet another important point: **models can be judged good or bad in terms of how effectively they fulfil their intended purpose – but not on any other basis**. If you want to inform what a pig is, a drawing that does not convey pig-ness would be a bad model. If, when trying to buy a pig, you mispronounce or misspell the word as pog, this would be a bad model. With redundancy (see Chapter 2) it might still communicate, but only sub-optimally.

There are two major reasons why we have models. The *first* is **for convenience and efficiency**. If, every time we needed to convey pig-ness, we had to have a real-life example to do so, this would make communication extremely difficult and unwieldy, if not an insurmountable problem. So we use models. The *second* reason is to do with **limits on our ability to handle information** (see, for example, Chapter 6). It would be extremely difficult, if not impossible, to understand the total amount of information in a pig, most of which would be unnecessary to any particular purpose, whatever it might be. So, if you want to buy a pound of pork sausages, the kind of pig, where it lived, its breed and diet, what it thought, are not likely to be *necessary* information for the achievement of your purpose (though might be thought *desirable* by some people). Of course, in the context of the BSE scare in the UK, if you wanted to buy *beef* sausages this information might be more relevant, given an additional purpose of remaining healthy. **It is possible to have more than one purpose at a time, and the same model can be used to serve all purposes relevant to it.** This may involve information that relates to the model in terms of another definition of what the model represents. If you want to buy a piggy bank for a child, any information about a real pig, apart from its shape, may not be useful to you, but you may want information about, for example, the quality of the materials, or safety – nothing to do with pig-ness.

Conceptual models

So far, we have discussed models in terms of physical representations of three-dimensional things, in order to convey the basic principles of models. However, the especial concern here is with organisations, and with organisational behaviour in particular, which are rather more abstract than pigs. **Precisely the same points can be extended to conceptual models.** An organisation does not have the materiality of a pig, and, indeed, it is not at all clear what an organisation *is*. It does have some materiality, but that is not enough to define it. Organisations have aspects, such as motivation, leadership, decision-making processes, and so on, which do not have literal substance but which are certainly part of them. Not only are organisations abstract to a significant extent, but they are also very complex and contain vast amounts of information. If it is difficult to encompass the complexity of pig-ness, of one pig, how much more so must it be to encompass the total information present in an organisation and which would be necessary to define it, let alone to understand it. This inability to process sufficient information in order to understand an organisation does not, however, prevent us from trying to do so. Instead of dealing with the totality, we make models – not necessarily physical models, but, more usually, models comprising, for example, ideas and concepts, mental models. **These models are multi-dimensional. They are also partial, selective, purposeful – and necessary – models.**

What kind of model we make depends on what our purposes are. If the desire is to understand the behaviour of employees, we might use, for example, a model such as Expectancy Theory, to produce a signifier of their behaviour. On the other hand, if it is financial performance which is to be understood, a balance sheet might be more useful. Although they are both models of the organisation, using Expectancy Theory to understand financial performance, or a balance sheet to understand motivation, will not be very helpful. The British Broadcasting Corporation, for example, is a very large, very complex, information-laden organisation. In spite of this, it can be represented with a very simple model, the letters BBC. If you want to know which channel a particular television programme is on, then this simple model will serve admirably. But if you want to understand, for example, the leadership structure and culture in that organisation, then you will need a much more complex model.

Given that model-building is purposeful, **it is necessary to decide what information is relevant to that purpose, and what is not.** Since we have cognitive limits, such decisions are *not* made by selecting some information as important from a position of knowing all the information there is to know. They are made

Models of models

Imagine a lecture in a course on Organisational Behaviour, on, say, group dynamics. There is a massive body of 'knowledge' on group dynamics, far too much to be comprehended, which we can call the '**real world**'. The lecturer, therefore, prepares a set of **notes** from which to deliver the lecture, which is a synopsis of the totality of knowledge about group dynamics. The lecturer then **presents** the lecture, which is based on, and abstracted from, the notes. The student hears what they think is being said – **reception** is only an approximation of what is actually said. The student then **records** notes, which are a précis of what they thought was said. Thus we have:

The 'real world' of
knowledge about
group dynamics
    ↓
Lecturer's notes   –   Model 1
    ↓
Presentation   –   Model 2
    ↓
Reception   –   Model 3
    ↓
Recording   –   Model 4

thus

Model 4
is a model of
Model 3
which is a model of
Model 2
which is a model of
Model 1
which is a model of the 'real world'.

So, no matter how good *your* lecture notes are, they are still a long way from the 'reality' of group dynamics.

by deciding that it is not necessary at all to know some information. Indeed, some information may not even be available, though, of course, this does not mean that it is not relevant. **This process of deciding what is relevant is, to some extent, conscious, but also, to an important extent, unconscious** – that is, it is affected by the influence of, *for example*, past experience, upbringing, socialisation, personality, on our judgement of what it is necessary to know. Relevant psychological processes, such as stereotyping and the halo effect, are well-known constraints on knowing, but there are myriad others, less easily defined though just as influential. Even at the conscious level, while we may *think* we are being wholly rational and functional in deciding what is relevant to our purpose, we are not, because of the multitudinous factors that influence our understanding, not just of the information, but also even of our purpose. If you want to know about an organisation's performance, you may decide that the balance sheet will give you all the relevant information you need to judge it. But it is not unknown for balance sheets not to represent a 'true' picture of organisational performance – one reason for this may be that people are dishonest, but another, more important, one is that it is not even possible for balance sheets to perform this function, since they are compiled by people who have themselves made judgements and decisions about what information they need, and what is relevant, and how it should be expressed – or modelled.

Tailoring Taylorism

It is not unusual to hear that, these days, Taylorism (Scientific Management) is irrelevant to understanding organisational behaviour. This could not be further from the case. Taylorism has an enduring popularity, albeit lacking the rigour that Taylor himself would have insisted on. It often masquerades under more modern titles, such as Just In Time, Business Process Re-Engineering, etc. The concepts of work measurement and payment-by-results schemes are to be found everywhere, even in areas which Taylor himself would never have envisaged.

Taylor was a fascinating character who often anticipated what later became theorisations of the discourse of Organisational Behaviour. However, as is often the case with management gurus, Taylor and his work are surrounded by much mythologising and inaccurate reporting – not helped by Taylor's own proselytising of his own work.

All the following points have been said by or about Taylor and Taylorism.

1. Scientific Management may well be the most powerful as well as the most lasting contribution to Western thought since the Federalist Papers.
2. It is difficult to discuss the 'contribution' of F.W. Taylor to the systematic study of industrial behaviour in an even-tempered way. The sheer silliness from a modern perspective of many of his ideas, and the barbarities they led to when applied in industry, encourages ridicule and denunciation.
3. Taylor believed that workmen should not be paid excessive wages. His experiments at Bethlehem Steel raised wages to $1.85 per day.
4. While working at Bethlehem Steel Taylor was charging $40 per day for his own services.
5. At Midvale Steel Taylor fined workers for being late.
6. Throughout his life Taylor was renowned for always being late for appointments.
7. Taylor believed that workmen should do exactly as they were told and should not think for themselves.
8. For people like himself, Taylor advocated that they should do more than just what they were told to do, always think what extra things they could do.

▶

9. Taylor thought of management as a science – and spoke of labour as an art.
10. Taylor's aim was for workers to do a fair day's work for a fair day's pay.
11. Fairness [*obviously not a scientifically measurable concept*] was to mean what Taylor thought was fair.
12. Taylor thought that workers should fear managers.
13. Taylor thought that work should be interesting and pleasurable.
14. Taylor believed that workers conspired together to control output.
15. Taylor was widely held to be a poor manager – he even said this about himself.
16. Taylor's life provides a splendid illustration of how unconscious concerns and preoccupations can have an effect on organisation, for it is clear that his whole theory of Scientific Management was the product of the inner struggles of a disturbed and neurotic personality.
17. Taylor's case presents a classic illustration of the anal-compulsive type of personality.
18. Taylor's own crippled and obsessive psyche is not irrelevant to a full explanation of the content of his system.
19. Taylor did not think that work measurement was particularly exact – that is, scientific.
20. Taylor found the spectacle of a man doing less than his best morally shocking.

Suppose that you are asked to write an essay on Taylorism (that is, construct a model of significant elements concerning Taylorism). Which of the above information would you consider to be relevant (worthy of inclusion)? Which would you consider to be not relevant (worthy of exclusion)? Describe why you have made these judgements.

Sources: Point 1 is from Drucker (1968: 337). Point 2 is from Rose (1978: 31). Point 18 is also from Rose (1978: 54). Points 16 and 17 are from Morgan (1997: 222). All the other points are taken from Copley's fascinating two-volume biography of Taylor (Copley 1923).

The process of judging between relevant and non-relevant information, the process of judging the limit of effect, the process of model-building itself, *is the process of boundary formation*. This is why it is possible to say that boundaries are not given in nature, but are human constructs, constructed according to human desires. For the purposes of illustration it is always easier to discuss discrete events. However, this is dramatically to understate the significance of models and boundaries in our understanding. **There are no discrete events. And there is nothing that is not modelled.** Everything that we think, and do, is based on a model, and this cannot be otherwise since we cannot comprehend the full complexity, the total information, all the variety, of our experienced world. Whether it is motivation, leadership, culture, the world economy, the natural environment, history, the next-door neighbour, last night's television programme, *Hamlet*, the people to whom we are closest or our perceived enemy, absolutely anything at all, our understanding, no matter how sophisticated, is based on models we construct, decisions we make about relevance, boundaries we impose. It is not a series of discrete models, either – they interact, they contradict, they confirm, they merge, so that it can be said that **such understanding of the world that we may have is no more, and no less, than the aggregation of all our model-building**.

As we noted before, however, there are good and bad models, according to their suitability in fulfilling their purpose. This is, first and foremost, an issue of **appropriateness**. By this is meant that the ultimate quality of a model depends on the extent to which it includes the information which, *in practice*, is necessary for the model to fulfil its purpose. That is to say, we may make the decisions about what information should be included or excluded, but it is possible for such decisions to be incorrect. The test of whether or not it is a good decision is whether the model provides an adequate basis on which to act effectively. For example, can we, on the basis of our model, produce an adequate solution to a problem, or not? The interesting aspect to this is that the quality of the outcome cannot be known until afterwards, and it is only by experience that we can tell whether the boundary was appropriate or not. In this sense, everything depends on our ability to assess, and to learn from, experience.

Generally, it is not very contentious to say that we cannot possibly know everything, and even that, therefore, we work on the basis of approximate understandings. Surprisingly, it is much more contentious to argue, from that, that we cannot fully understand anything (see, for example, the discussion of rationality in Chapter 6). But it is not only that we cannot comprehend all the information that there is (even about a single pig), but also that whatever information we do comprehend we gain through the filter of our own fragile perceptions. **There cannot be unmediated access to the 'real world'.** We *only* understand the world through our models of it. But, to us, that is our reality: we treat our models *as if* they are the real world. When we manage, what we manage is our models, not the real world – but we *think* we are managing the real world. Thus, the poorer or better the quality of the models in operation, the poorer or better the quality of management that ensues. In the context of organisational behaviour, for example, the quality of the models we have about what people are like profoundly influences our ability to understand their behaviour. **The issue of the**

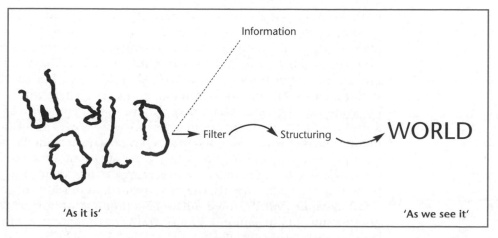

Seeing the world

quality of models rests fully on the boundaries that are established. Thus it might be said that the conventional discourse of Organisational Behaviour, in emphasising very narrow boundaries of what is relevant to understanding organisational behaviour, has produced poor models of what people are like and why they behave as they do, with profound impacts on their management.

Boundary and problem-solving

In Chapter 4 we described how the way a problem is defined has implications for how it is solved, presupposing some kinds of solution and precluding others. Now we are saying that this process of problem definition is a function of model-building and boundary location, which are arbitrary, interested and mutable. Management is often thought of as a problem-solving activity – arguably, if there were no problems of organisation, there would be no need for managers. If problem definition is a matter of model-building and boundary location, then it follows that this is the basis of the professional activity of management. This means that, rather than managing the real world objectively, rationally and dispassionately, managers manage through their own models, their own ideas about boundary location, their own perceptions about appropriate purposes, which are constructed from their own understandings and desires – just the same as everyone else. The only difference is that managers, generally, have more power than those who are managed (whoever they are, 'inside' or 'outside' the organisation) to define and defend their models. This does not mean, however, that they have generally better, or more effective, models in terms of a problem. They are just different models, built on different assumptions and different interests, for good or ill.

'Good or ill', however, depends on the capacity of a model to forward those interests – it is not an absolute measure of value. Suppose that managers decide that a workforce needs some incentive to improve performance: if they want to avoid increasing the wage bill, they may be attracted to solutions offering psychological incentives, such as job enrichment; if they decide that lack of motivation is caused by low wages, they may opt for a payment-by-results system. In other words, depending on how the problem is viewed, and what the pre-existing parameters of the decision may be, different solutions are generated. The parameters will include, for example, beliefs about what constitutes low motivation, about how it is measured, about the significance of performance in such measures, faith in measurement, and so on. There will be other models of the same situation, too, which may not even include the perception that there is a problem. Equally, there are many cases where, with hindsight, the management models of what the problem was have been shown to be inappropriate. For example, in the case of the previously cited situation of the proposal to dump an oil platform in deep sea water, managers appeared to define the problem in terms of how to transport and dispose of several thousand tons of scrap metal in the North Atlantic, but it turned out to be a problem of how to convince pressure groups, and public opinion more generally, of the rightness of this plan – something that they signally failed to address, let alone achieve.

We have concentrated on the cognitive aspects of boundary location – **boundary as a cognitive limit** – but it is also important to recognise that these cognitive limits also represent a moral aspect – **boundary as a moral limit**. When we decide what is appropriate and relevant information to include, we also, inevitably, prioritise that information and devalue what we exclude. Such decisions are not based on disinterested assessment but on personal experience and understandings, ideology, values and beliefs. Thus, what is prioritised is also given a moral status: once a prioritisation is decided on, it is not just a question of 'fact' but also one of moral worthiness. This is part of the reason why, as noted in Chapter 7, events can be simultaneously seen as moral, immoral and/or amoral. What is included in the model's boundaries becomes, by definition, morally good, what is excluded is, by the same token, morally suspect.

In consideration of the nature of boundary location and the processes that inform it, it is not just a matter of increasing understanding of how we understand. Boundary location is not simply an inner-directed activity concerning existential survival in the experienced world, though that *is* an important factor. The point is that **these decisions always have consequences**, for the self but also for others. In that **we act on our understandings** of the world in general, or of organisations in particular, and these understandings are founded on our models and our imposition of cognitive and moral limits on what is significant, these bases of action will inevitably affect others. So, for example, once managers decide that workers are different kinds of people to themselves, the consequence of that decision is that workers can be treated in ways that are different to the ways in which managers believe they themselves should be treated.

None of this has been intended to suggest that we should dispense with, or abandon, boundary location, since it has already been noted that this is an inevitable and necessary process. The first step is to recognise that, **although we treat them as obvious, natural, given, real, *they are not*.** Just as important is to recognise how we construct boundaries and what influences the decisions – and to accept that **consequences flow from how we understand which are not inevitable but, simply, a function of our particular understandings**. It is also important to acknowledge that, **although boundaries may represent cognitive and moral limits, these are not absolute limits**: it is possible to know more, or to know differently, to change our models and their boundaries. Equally, **the boundaries we construct are not literal limits, they are permeable**, whether we like it or not – what is outside our boundaries does not cease to exist just because we exclude it, is not somehow wrong while we are right, can intrude on our 'reality'. Indeed, it is precisely this that offers the potential to open up the possibility for reflection on how and why we understand and the impacts and consequences of that understanding.

Existing applications in Organisational Behaviour

The concept of boundary is widespread in the discourse of Organisational Behaviour, both explicitly and implicitly. Explicitly, it is found in concepts such as **bounded rationality** and **bounded discretion**, the former concerning cognitive limits, the latter limits to power, but both acknowledging that there are constraints on our ability to act. Implicitly, it is found in concepts like the **hierarchy of needs** and **motivation/hygiene theory**, where the idea of boundary plays an important, but generally unarticulated, role in delineating states or conditions, for example. In general, the concept of boundary tends to be treated as if it is either unproblematic, or self-explanatory.

There is also a fairly widespread ordinary language of models in the discourse. One of the most common cases is the idea of **models of man** (sic), which are seen to underlie and influence attitudes to people and their behaviour. Approaches to experiential learning in Organisation Development often make use of models, through, for example, **role playing** as a process of modelling supposedly real-life situations. **Quantitative models** are also used in the discourse, quasi-mathematical models such as those that have been applied to Expectancy Theory, to try to quantify motivation. These uses of models are often characterised by lack of recognition of the nature of the process of model-building and, indeed, in some cases, such as the quantification of motivation, that it *is* a modelling process is often overlooked in favour of treating the model as if it is the real. The idea that the same situation can be modelled from different perspectives is well represented in **Conflict Theory** in particular, but also in the discourse of Industrial Relations more generally. Much of the recognition of the philosophy of modelling is to be found in **Systems Theory**, where modelling is a process central to understanding control mechanisms and criteria of stability, as is the function of boundaries in defining what a particular system consists of. It is Systems Theory of various kinds that has, perhaps, come closest to explicit recognition of the process of model-building as a process of defining boundaries, and of the significance of boundary location as the criterion of effective functioning of a system.

However, the more extended use of the nature of boundaries and the process of boundary location comes from **Poststructuralism**, particularly the work associated with the general approach known as **Deconstruction**. This has highlighted the impossibility of transcendent meanings, notably in the concept of undecidability, and the impossibility of being able to specify meaning at all – and, thus, the artificiality of boundaries, whilst also recognising that boundaries, as the locus of differentiation, have a dynamic quality. (This is also a particular concern of Chaos Theory.) The creation of boundary conditions constitutes the basis for action and, in so doing, these boundaries represent a context of contestation, between different interpretations and between the included and the excluded. The specific relevance of such understandings for organisational behaviour remains to be more fully developed.

Although we have not explored Information Theory in any depth here, it, together with Communication Theory, has made relevant contributions. The problem of communication has, increasingly, become a matter of specific focus – treated for a long time as virtually unproblematic, it is more and more recognised as uncertain. The issue of boundary is particularly prominent in the context of the encoding–decoding of information, especially where that is linked to a semiotic approach (see Chapter 2).

Further potential

One of the difficulties with conventional approaches to understanding organisational behaviour is that there is a tendency to assume that there are, on one hand, modelling situations and, on the other, non-modelling situations, which are seen as 'the real world' and the proper domain of the management of organisational behaviour. Models are often seen as no more than educational tools which can be used, or not. In other words, there is assumed to be a boundary between the world of modelling and 'the real world'. In particular, this is both caused by, and results in, lack of recognition of the interconnections between model-building and boundary location, which itself relates to lack of recognition of the nature of these two processes and what informs them. If the process of boundary location is part of largely unconscious processes, such as ideology, desire, the need to manage information and the need to make sense, this must be recognised as constitutive of behaviour, so that more adequate and appropriate models can be used, rather than the model of the idealised worker which the discourse of Organisational Behaviour traditionally pursues. What is really needed is a **psychology of bounding and boundary**, as a basis for understanding organisational behaviour.

It has been suggested on a number of occasions in this book that an understanding of organisational behaviour needs, minimally, an appropriate model of what people are like, together with the recognition that different understandings inform different models. Given the purposefulness of models and their boundaries, to this should be added the recognition that **any model of what people are like represents particular interests and intentions**. From this it follows that it is of paramount importance that **all such models should be interrogated in terms of what interests they represent and why**. Without such awareness of interest it is hardly possible to judge whether a model is adequate to its purpose, or, indeed, whether the purpose itself is adequate and/or appropriate. Conventionally, the problems of information are treated lightly – they are, for example, noted and then ignored. A fuller awareness of how and why information is selected, divided, judged, prioritised, included or rejected – in other words, of the role of boundary location in dealing with information – would provide the basis for a much richer, and more rigorous, approach to understanding organisational behaviour.

There is a need for the discourse of Organisational Behaviour to be less blasé about boundary in the context of organisational boundaries in general, and, in particular, in the context of how the boundary of the *concept* of organisation *is* viewed. The current dominant approach to understanding what an organisation is is relatively undifferentiated, in favour of treating all organisations as if they are just examples of some universal organisation. What needs further recognition is that all organisations serve particular interests, that there is no such thing as the universal organisation – there are only particular kinds of organisation, ideologically, socially and historically specific. Such recognition would, of course, impose major constraints on the ability of the discourse to produce generalised, dogmatic and putatively objective statements. But it would make it possible for the discourse to become more relevant and more useful.

Organisational behaviour and boundary

The discourse of Organisational Behaviour contributes a major part of management knowledge but it is, increasingly, recognised that contemporary organisations are in crisis. The experience of work is making people ill, it is creating social problems, it is straining national resources – ironically, since its socio-economic purpose is to increase rather than to deplete them. Organisations themselves seem to be producing more disorder than order – the organisation of the family seems to be falling apart, sporting organisation seems to imply violence, caring organisation seems to imply abuse, and so on. Arguably, the discourse has, at best, failed to contribute to the solution of these problems, but, at worst, it has actively contributed to their occurrence, by its concentration on reductionist approaches to understanding people, and a strict demarcation between the 'inside' and the 'outside' of an organisation. It is surprising that such conceptual separation can be sustained in the face of the recognised extent to which problems in one are rooted in, and reflect, problems in the other. This mutuality, however, is not at all surprising, since people cannot be divided in such ways in practice, but come as total packages whose totality comprises more than just being a member of an organisation.

The relative failure of the discourse of Organisational Behaviour to contribute positively to these problem solutions can be laid at the door of its adherence to models and boundaries that do not recognise such variety and that deselect appropriate information. The boundaries and models established by the discourse, and within it, are treated *as if* they are 'the real world', rather than, inevitably, human constructs. Thus, awareness of the cognitive and moral processes involved, of the issues of purpose and interest, and the questions of adequacy and appropriateness to which such processes need to be submitted, are also, necessarily, ignored. Bounding and model-building are processes utterly necessary to organisational behaviour and to understanding of it, yet in the discourse of Organisational Behaviour they are virtually unrecognised in their proper complexity. That understanding, recognition and practice of such processes are inadequate is, therefore, hardly surprising.

There is a need to focus on the boundary process itself if such models are to become more appropriate and more useful. The recognition that boundaries are human constructs, that they are part of the semiotic process of sense-making, that they are arbitrary and changeable, that they are purposeful and represent interests, and the role of power in sustaining them, transforms understanding of their significance. Given this awareness of the nature of boundary it becomes possible, not only to recognise boundaries themselves, but also to interrogate them in terms of how and why they are established, what purpose and which interests they are intended to promote. This is not to say that any particular boundary is inevitably inappropriate and/or inadequate, but to suggest that, given their importance and the consequences that flow from them, it should not be *simply assumed* that they are good boundaries just because members of the discourse say they are.

Once again, we are suggesting that, in order to advance our understanding of organisational behaviour, it is necessary to articulate and understand what purposes and interests are being served by the current state of the art. The point is not automatically to reject or to endorse them, but to promote effective understandings of organisational behaviour. After all, at the very least, it is well known that, if people know what they are doing and why they are doing it, they are likely to do it better than if they do not know. Awareness of the nature of the concept of boundary and of its applications in practice are fundamental to such an achievement.

A TALE FROM THE VILLAGE PUMP (*BOUNDARY*)

(See the Case Study in Appendix 2, pages 340-3)

Many instances of **boundary** location are crucial to the events described in this case. One example is the detailed map that was produced by Snow, as part of his investigation into the 1854 cholera outbreak, showing the geographical clustering of cases. This mapping clearly indicated a boundary beyond which there were no significant instances of the disease. The establishment of this boundary was a very important factor in adding weight to Snow's claim to be able to identify a specific cause of the cholera outbreak, and a very important factor in finding a solution to the problem. Another example is the **modelling** of the problem of identifying the causes of cholera. The miasma theory was a highly inclusive one, embracing a plethora of factors that could be seen as contributing to the existence of miasma, which then caused cholera, while Snow's hypothesis focused exclusively on contamination of water.

- In what ways did Farr's conceptualisation of the boundaries of the problem of cholera contribute to the delay in acknowledging that cholera was a water-borne disease?

Case

HOW TO FIND A MODEL EMPLOYEE?

Steady-Hobart is a medium-sized transport company, specialising in long-distance haulage for the engineering industry. At the moment it operates in the UK only, but it is looking to expand into European countries in the near future. The General Manager, Austin Carr, is a 30-year-old who trained as an accountant and who previously worked in the automotive industry, for a large international vehicle manufacturer. He had become rather disillusioned with working for a big multinational and wanted to try out his ideas about management in a smaller arena, where he could have greater impact on day-to-day affairs. One of his earliest actions at Steady-Hobart had been to appoint a Human Resource Manager. Prior to this appointment personnel matters – such as were perceived to exist – had been handled by the Transport Manager, with help from an administrative assistant. The Human Resource Manager, Helen Hurth, is just 25 years old and is Steady-Hobart's only female employee at managerial level, so far. She has an MA in Human Resource Management and also spent a year in Central Africa doing voluntary work with a major charity, organising relief convoys to a region hit by famine. One of her first tasks had been to draw up and implement an anti-discrimination policy for the company. The Transport Manager, Tom Wheeler, is 58 years old, an ex-army man who still insists on his military rank of Major being used – and indeed he is generally known within the company as 'the Major'. The Major has worked for Steady-Hobart since leaving the army after 21 years of service.

Last year a vacancy for a Shift Programmer arose. The job of Shift Programmer involves scheduling the necessary journeys, making sure that the necessary drivers and vehicles are available, and drawing up contingency plans to deal with unexpected problems, such as a driver going off sick, or vehicles being delayed. The company employs four Shift Programmers who are responsible for providing cover 24/7. The vacancy arose because one Shift Programmer left the company, unable to cope with the disruption to his domestic life caused by the shift patterns of the job.

Under the previous General Manager the recruitment of a Shift Programmer would have been left to the Major, who tended to recruit ex-army people through the informal contacts he maintained from his days in the army. (The Programmer who had resigned was not such a person and Tom Wheeler felt, privately, that this tended to prove his point.) But the new General Manager did not approve of this practice, which he felt was an amateurish approach to recruitment. He also had in mind developing some possibilities in relation to succession planning, especially replacement of the Transport Manager when he retired in a few years' time. He asked a recruitment agency to provide them with a short-list of four or five candidates. His brief to the agency had stressed that they wanted a person with potential, someone go-ahead, with a modern outlook. The qualifications for the post were a relevant technical certificate (a degree was not normally seen as necessary), at least 5 years' experience in a similar job (though not necessarily in transport), and computer literacy.

The Short-List:

Ted Male, 50 years old; Ted has no formal qualifications, but does have 25 years of experience scheduling with a transport company; he is described as steady and reliable, with a good sickness record; he has a Heavy Goods Vehicle (HGV) licence and is happy to stand in as a driver in an emergency; Ted wants the job because it would be more convenient geographically for him; his current salary is about £25,000 per annum.

James Male, 38 years old; James has recently gained an Open University degree in Business Studies; he is currently employed as a scheduler for a local parcels firm; he is married, with two children at secondary school; James wants the job because he is looking for a better wage, as well as the opportunity to use his newly acquired business studies skills; his current salary is about £18,000 per annum.

Tracy Female, 40 years old; Tracy is an ex-army driver with overseas service who is returning to work after a 5-year break, staying at home to look after her child; during that time, however, she has been scheduling delivery of meals to elderly people, as voluntary work, and has done odd driving jobs on a casual basis.

Ali Male, 30 years old; Ali is a refugee from the Middle East, where he had been Transport Manager for a large company, but had had to leave his home because of civil unrest; his English is good; Ali is over-qualified for this post, but has the potential to take on more responsibility in time; presently, he is driving for another company and wants to get back into management, as a step towards regaining his former status; his current salary is about £30,000 per annum, due to bonus earnings and working the maximum possible number of hours.

How the selection team ranked the candidates:

	General Manager:	Transport Manager:	Human Resources Manager:
(1)	Ali	Ted	James
(2)	Tracy	Tracy	Tracy
(3)	James	James	Ali
(4)	Ted	Ali	Ted

Rationales for the rankings:

General Manager, Austin Carr

Ali Past experience useful; good potential; international perspective; will come for less than his current pay in order to get a 'better' job; possible potential for succession plans.

Tracy Female; shows initiative; experience abroad; strong local ties, so less likely to move on; might have problems with shift patterns, but probably keen enough to resolve them.

James Open University degree shows commitment; local ties, but keen to progress so might move on elsewhere; again, potential for succession plans, but not as attractive as Ali.

Ted Unqualified, therefore expensive; good experience, but rather old.

Transport Manager, Tom Wheeler

Ted Excellent candidate, exactly what the company needs; great experience; willingness to drive a very positive asset; reliable; will fit in well; worth £25,000.

Tracy Background an asset; cheap to employ; though female will fit into the culture because of her military background.

James Unlikely to stay because expecting better things from his degree; previous experience not particularly relevant.

Ali Over-qualified; unlikely to stay; may be difficult and won't fit in.

Human Resource Manager, Helen Hurth

James Exactly the sort of person the company needs; go-ahead, educated, ambitious, and lots of potential.

Tracy Good to have more women in the company; voluntary work shows character; international experience would be useful.

Ali Possibly over-qualified, but very good CV; has potential, but expensive to employ.

Ted Unqualified; no potential.

- Why might the models of each member of the selection panel, of what is needed for this post, be different?

- What kind of bounding and modelling processes might explain the consideration given by the selection panel to factors such as gender, age and ethnicity, given the company's policy?

- In the event, they offer the job to Tracy. How might this choice be explained in terms of bounding processes? For example, which type of boundary is being prioritised?

- Clearly, Austin Carr wants to change the company. How might an understanding of bounding and modelling processes help him to do this?

(Other chapters that would be useful and relevant in analysing the case *include* Structure (3), Knowledge (4), Rationality (6), Self (8) and Decision-making (11).)

Bibliography

The issue of where an organisation's boundary is is rife in Organisation Studies. There is a lot of debate therein about various boundary locations and their advantages and disadvantages. This debate is particularly prominent in the contemporary conventional discourse of Organisational Behaviour, as represented in, for example, the Human Resource Management literature, where the issue is often one of how far an organisation can trespass into the non-work lives of its members in order to 'enhance', say, productivity or commitment, in work time – for example, requirements not to indulge in designated unhealthy activities such as over-eating, not taking exercise, smoking, and so on. However, while this debate is rife, there is really very little about what may constitute any such boundary, how 'real' it is.

There are a lot of books in the field that actually contain the words 'organisation' and 'environment' in their title, of which the best known are, probably, Lawrence and Lorsch (1967) and Karpik (1978). SWOT [Strengths, Weaknesses, Opportunities, Threats] analysis of environments, which, by implication, prioritises the organisation and its 'needs', is a common analysis of conventional organisational strategy texts – see, for example, Mintzberg (1994), Thompson (1997). Morgan (1990), however, represents a different approach, which focuses on the mutuality of organisation/society relationships. These issues are particularly pertinent in the context of multinational organisations – though venerable, Tugendhat (1971) contains some thought-provoking examples of the perception of boundary on the part of some senior managers of multinationals.

The nature of boundary is also very relevant in the realm of theory and conceptualisation. Reed's (1985) distinction between types of organisation theory that use a tight, inwardly-oriented boundary – the 'organisation as a discrete entity' view – and those that, to varying degrees, see organisations as embedded in their social context, is relevant. Burrell and Morgan's (1979) paradigms also model conceptual boundaries of thinking about organisations. An example of the significance of such differentiating devices in social theory generally is Jenks (1998).

It is actually easier to find critiques of the 'boundary as limit' approach than it is to find it openly articulated and defended, rather than treated as natural, given and obvious. For a poststructuralist analysis, see, for example, Cooper (1986, 1992a) – the former also includes the specific argument about separation and joining. Another relevant analysis is Cooper and Law (1995). The point that control of boundaries represents a source of power appears in, for example, Morgan (1997).

The notion of differentiation is central to semiotics, and to everything that derives from it – the point is not that differentiation itself is problematic, but that the idea, or belief, that it is fixed, obvious, impermeable, given, is. Perhaps the most salient use of this view is made in the approach known as Deconstruction, particularly associated with Derrida (for example, 1978), originally a technique applied to literary texts but later widely extended to social 'texts', including organisational 'texts'. Norris (1982) provides a good introduction to the approach. Derrida argued that all difference is ultimately 'undecidable' – see also his neologism 'differance', which emphasises the spatial and temporal aspects of differentiation. The premise is that the purposes of particular (conceptual) boundary locations, or differentiations, can be uncovered by examination of what is included and, thereby, what is excluded – and, since such inclusion and exclusion is not prescribable but a purposeful choice, it therefore represents the exercise of power. On the relevance of Derrida's work to analysis of organisation(s), see Cooper (1989). Foucault's concept of discourse (for example, 1970, 1971) is profoundly linked to issues of boundary location and differentiation, and, particularly, to the control and power associated with boundary. Lyotard (1988) focuses on very similar issues to both Derrida and Foucault.

From a somewhat different perspective, the New Physics writers, such as Bohm (1983), Capra (1983) and Zukav (1984), have challenged conventional views of boundary location precisely on the grounds that boundaries are not only not natural but also they do have major consequences. The issue of the responsibilities of organisations to society is one also taken up by the organisational/managerial ethics literature – see, for example, Maclagan (1998). See also Luthans, Hodgetts and Thompson (1987). On the issue of fragmentation central to Bohm's (1983) concerns but considered in the context of organisational behaviour see, particularly, Sievers (1994).

A very basic introduction to Systems Theory is contained in Cole (2004). The Open Systems Group (1981), Scott (1981) and Wilson (1990) also provide a good introduction to the main concepts and issues. Elliott (1980) provides a briefer summary of the issues surrounding the idea of organisations as systems. Several of the major relevant writers are represented in Lockett and Spear (1980). There are a number of different emphases within Systems Theory – for example, Katz and Kahn (1966) is regarded by many as a seminal text on open systems theory; the Tavistock Group is particularly associated with socio-technical systems theory – see, for example, Emery (1969); Checkland (1981) is associated with the concept of soft systems – see also Checkland and Scholes (1990); Beer (for example, 1994) is associated with the concept of viable systems; Flood and Jackson (1991) can be seen as an example of what is known as critical systems thinking. See also Sherman and Schultz (1998). One view of the interconnections between Systems Theory and Organisation Theory (particularly their critical varieties) can be found in Galliers, Mingers and Jackson (1997). Another, and very relevant, approach is to be found in Cooper (1992b). An approach that looks at systems thinking in terms of semiotics and communications is Wilden (1980).

Proponents of nuclear power have always stressed its safety and controllability, but a more independent literature has not shared this optimism. See, for example, Breach (1978) and Wynne (1982), both on the Windscale Inquiry, and Gosling and Montefiore (1977), which contains many interesting depositions from both proponents and opponents to an inquiry into the feasibility of fast breeder reactors. This is, undoubtedly, going to become a 'hot' issue again.

Stakeholder models of organisation have been around for some considerable time but have recently undergone a renaissance, especially in politics – see, for example, Hutton (1995, 1997) and also the communitarian literature cited in the bibliography to Chapter 8. See also Stead and Stead (1992). On the family as, potentially, having a stake in organisations see, for example, Goldsmith (1989) and Lewis and Lewis (1996). There is quite a large literature on the experience of women in work organisations – for a range of approaches see, for example, Marshall (1984), Walby (1986), Cockburn (1991). On the specific issue of sexual harassment see Collier (1995), Stockdale (1996) and Benokraitis (1997). On the same issue in the somewhat more general context of organisational analysis see, for example, Hearn, Sheppard, Tancred-Sheriff and Burrell (1989), Collinson, Knights and Collinson (1990), Mills and Tancred (1992), Reskin and Padavic (1994), Mills and Simmons (1995). (For an interesting exploration of connections between Feminism and Poststructuralism see Weedon (1987).)

Ecosystemic ideas are, explicitly or implicitly, widespread, and are increasingly penetrating into the literature on management and organisation, with a strong emphasis on behaviour in organisations, especially in the context of decision-making. The foundational ideas can be found in, for example, Boulding (1978) and Bateson (1973), as well as in the New Physics literature and, sometimes, the Systems Theory literature previously cited. The Gaia Hypothesis is particularly associated with Lovelock (1987) – see also Lovelock (2006) – and, for an introduction, see also Joseph (1990). Stead and Stead (1992) is an accessible source on implications for management. Books on management of the environment, in its ecological sense, are increasingly becoming available – see, for example, Wever (1996), McDonagh and Prothero (1997), Jones and Hollier (1997), Hutchinson and Hutchinson (1997).

Ecological issues have become an important element of poststructuralist thinking. This is a sophisticated, more 'eco-philosophical', approach, with strong links to Chaos Theory (see later in this bibliography), and to globalisation (see below).

Guattari has been particularly associated with this development – see, for example, Guattari (1995a, 1995b, 2000). For an overview of 'the environment in poststructuralist thought', see Conley (1997).

There is a very large, and growing, literature on globalisation. Steger (2003) offers 'a very short introduction'. For a collection of the debates, see Held *et al.* (2005), and also Held and McGrew (2002). Beck (2005) argues in favour of strengthening national boundaries in a context of transnational networks and interdependencies (see also Wallerstein (1984)). Bhagwati (2004) is an example of a very positive view of the potential impacts and implications of globalisation. See also Stiglitz (2002).

A must for anyone interested in modelling processes is Ashby (1970), in the generally relevant Stogdill (1970) – see also, for example, in the same book, the Appendix by March. Another useful book, more oriented towards organisational and management issues, is Harrison (1999). See also Pidd (1996). Pidd's book illustrates by example the prevalence of quantitative and/or quasi-quantitative models in texts on management, and texts on organisational behaviour are not exempt from this tendency. See, for example, Simon (1957), the mathematical symbolism of the concept of the motivational calculus (Handy 1976), or the testing of Expectancy Theory in, for example, Gibson, Ivancevich, Donnelly and Konopaske (2002). A much more advanced usage, but one that connects to a number of the issues raised here, is Wilden (1980). Beer's viable systems model – see, for example, Beer (1994) – and Morgan's metaphors of organisation – see, for example, Morgan (1997) – are well-known examples of models in use, and can stand as representative of some of the range of possibilities.

Issues of information are closely linked to poststructuralist approaches – central, for example, to Foucault's power/knowledge model (see Gordon (1980)), or to Derrida's (1994) model of techno-mediatic power – and not just questions of what constitutes information, but also how, where and why it is 'used'. Bateson (1973) has been influential in the original development of such themes – see his emblematic claim that 'information is the difference that makes a difference' (1973: 268). See, for example, Cooper (1987), and, again, Wilden (1980) – also, especially relevant to theorising about organisation, Cooper and Fox (1989). Townley (1994) is one example of a focus on the role of information in control in the context of 'human resources'. Indeed, any organisational text that relates to Poststructuralism is likely to contain information on information. Poster (1990) usefully brings together a number of poststructuralist writers in the general context of the role of information in contemporary society. For particular use of the analysis of processes of model-building and boundary location in the context of risk, see Carter and Jackson (1992, 1997).

That problem-solving is intimately connected with issues of model-building, boundary location and information ought to be quite obvious. It is worth noting, however, that Foucault (for example, 1974) describes all knowledge production as a problem-oriented activity – that is, that all knowledge production is related to some problem that the knowledge producer desires to solve, rather than to any pursuit of knowledge for its own sake. That problem-solving is fundamental to management practice is not contentious and can be seen as a theme in virtually any book on management and, particularly, on the management of organisational behaviour. There are, however, many different approaches to what this problem-solving activity might consist of – Margerison (1974) and Alvesson and Willmott (1996) represent just two examples of the range.

Bounded rationality is associated with Simon (1976) and bounded discretion with Shull, Delbecq and Cummings (1970). See also Bazerman (2006) for a discussion of 'bounded ethicality' and 'bounded awareness' in the context of (managerial) decision-making. On models of man (sic) see, as previously noted, Simon (1957), Leach (1972), Simons (1986), Schein (1988). For the use of models in Organisation Development see any OD text, such as French and Bell (1973). Tannenbaum and Schmidt's (1973) model of leadership styles and Blake and Mouton's (1964) managerial grid can stand as examples of the widespread use of models in that field. However, a somewhat more sophisticated understanding of role can be found in Goffman (1959). Role is often linked to the dramaturgical metaphor – see, for example, Mangham and Overington (1983).

A well-known introduction to Chaos Theory is Gleick (1988), though see also Prigogine and Stengers (1984) and Waldrop (1992). Lewin (1992) usefully links Chaos Theory to Gaia. Sources of relevance to issues of information and communication include, among many others, Serres (1982), Baudrillard (1985), Cooper (1987), Eco (1989), Poster (1990), Parker and Cooper (1998). For a different range of approaches to organisational communication, see, for example, Jablin (1987). Other areas mentioned in the 'Existing Applications' section of this chapter have been addressed elsewhere in this bibliography.

CHAPTER 10

Efficiency

This chapter addresses conceptualisations of efficiency, the fundamental, but largely unarticulated, premise of techniques for managing organisational behaviour. The nature of efficiency is reviewed in light of the issues raised in the preceding chapters: boundary, power, structure, discourse, ideology, self and semiotics. A view of efficiency emphasising its characteristics as a model is developed. Issues of the operationalisation of the concept of efficiency are then considered, focusing on aspects of measurement – in particular, how factors are selected for inclusion or exclusion; the emphasis on quantification and monetary values; the assessment of opportunity costs; assumptions relating to aggregations of efficiency – all in the context of the relevance and appropriateness of such techniques to the factors that would need to be considered in a meaningful conceptualisation of efficiency. The justifications for the dominant view of efficiency are examined in light of what it might mean to claim that an organisation is efficient and of issues surrounding the management of claimed scarcity. The need to understand efficiency in terms of its claimed and actual organisation is stressed, as is the impossibility of knowing whether this is achieved without a rigorous conceptualisation of what efficiency might mean. The significance of organisational behaviour, both in formulating and in acting out models of organisational efficiency, is emphasised.

We have stated unequivocally our own belief that the proper purpose of the project of the discourse of Organisational Behaviour should be the understanding of behaviour in organisations. However, the proper purpose that the discourse has, traditionally, defined for itself has been the discovery of ways of increasing labour efficiency. The discourse has always set out its stall of theories and techniques on the basis that they will increase efficiency – a moment's thought confirms the intuition that if, for example, a theory or technique offered a sure-fire way of increasing the 'self-actualisation' of employees without increasing their productivity, such a theory or technique would be extremely unlikely to be accepted. The productions of the discourse have consisted, predominantly, of the development of theories and techniques for managing people which claim to offer means of understanding and managing behaviour which would develop such behaviour to its point of maximum contribution of benefit to 'the organisation'. It is worth emphasising that such theories and techniques tend to presuppose an essential distinction between managers and managed, and that their object is usually the latter, rather than the former. It must also be pointed out that, since this is the basis on which claims to effectiveness are made, it must be the case that, if increased efficiency is *not* delivered by these theories and techniques, then the purpose of the discourse must be seen as unachieved – in effect, the discourse must be seen as having failed. Given such serious consequences, it is obviously important that there is a proper assessment of the extent to which the purpose *is* achieved. But one of the major difficulties with such assessment is that the concept of efficiency itself is not defined or interrogated but, at best, assumed to be obvious.

There is a very common ordinary language understanding of the concept of efficiency which construes its signification in terms of monetary values, and, indeed, that it encompasses only those things that can be given a monetary value. This assumption also permeates discursive assumptions about the concept. However, such a conceptualisation is simplistic, and deeply inadequate. Even if it were reasonable to assume that the defining characteristic of the concept of efficiency is monetary value, the then necessary exclusion of aspects that cannot easily be given a monetary value but that may have an important impact on efficiency would render it highly problematic. If we are to judge whether a practice or a process, a theory or a technique, is efficient, it is necessary to have a thorough understanding of the concept of efficiency itself. It is so important a concept that it warrants serious attention – and it is important, not just because it is the claimed purpose of understanding organisational behaviour, but also because, in the contemporary world, it obviously *is* imperative that organisations should be efficient, not wasteful of resources of whatever kind.

Organisations are, necessarily, concerned with efficiency and, thus, any understanding of what goes on in organisations needs to attend to the issues surrounding both the concept of efficiency and its operationalisation in practice. Understanding of organisational behaviour must have much to contribute to this project, as well as needing to be, itself, informed by a well-grounded understanding of what efficiency means. These are the issues that this chapter seeks to address.

The meaning of efficiency

Efficiency is deeply implicated in organisational behaviour and, thus, the ideas that have been developed in the previous chapters also have relevance for how efficiency may be understood. It is useful briefly to examine how these ideas call the conventional understandings of efficiency into question.

Efficiency is central to organisation. It is the function of organisation(s) to be efficient. Indeed, if organisations are not more efficient at what they do, compared to doing it without an organisation, then there is no point in having the organisation. **Efficiency is also, at its most basic, an extremely simple concept: it is merely the ratio of output to input of a particular process**. However, **what constitutes the inputs and outputs of a given process is not at all clear**, especially where the process involves people.

Boundary and efficiency

It was noted in Chapter 6 that the purpose of capitalist organisations is to create the maximum output of profit for a given input of investment. An organisation that gives a 10 per cent return on investment is more efficient than one that gives 5 per cent. However, it was also noted, in Chapter 9, that what constitutes an organisation is an issue of the human process of **boundary** formation, and that different people locate organisational boundaries in different places – and *that* leads to different calculations of what is efficient. Some years ago, a well-known car manufacturer sold a type of car that was known to have a particular fault which, under certain circumstances, led to the incineration of the car's occupants. The company decided that it was cheaper to pay out resulting insurance claims than it would be to redesign the car – in other words, it decided that this was more profitable, thus more efficient. However, it is unlikely that the victims of the car, or their heirs, would share this view of organisational efficiency. **What constitutes organisational efficiency, therefore, depends on what is seen as the organisation, what is seen to constitute its inputs and outputs – that is, depends on where the boundary is located.** We have already suggested that there are legal boundaries to organisations, and possibly even physical boundaries, but that **all boundaries are arbitrary and related to purpose or interest.**

Power and efficiency

It is this purpose or interest that informs the identification of what is to count as inputs and outputs. Other purposes and interests will identify other inputs and outputs, which may change dramatically the meaning and measurement of efficiency. This signifies that the answer to the question of what should be counted as inputs and outputs, and, thus, what constitutes efficiency, is not objective, neutral, scientific. It is an issue of **power** (see also Chapter 5). Those who can specify inputs and outputs and their related efficiency are those with the most power.

Structure and efficiency

Efficiency is also intimately connected to **structure**. The concept of efficiency itself implies a process – the conversion process in which something is done to inputs to convert them into outputs. It is obviously important to be able to distinguish what the process is from what it is not. For example, if we want to convert water into steam we need heat, and so heat is a part of the conversion process. However, what is *not* part of that process is the cost of the heat – the heat will do the same job regardless of its cost. The cost of the heat is, of course, a factor in the *cost efficiency* of the process, but its cost is not intrinsic to the process *per se*, and so relating the cost of the heat to the process of converting water into steam is inappropriate as a measure of *process efficiency*. Thus, heat is structurally related to the process of turning water into steam, but the cost of the heat is not.

Efficiency/effectiveness I

What is meant by efficiency generally receives little attention in the literature of the conventional discourse of Organisational Behaviour. Instead, there is a preference for linking efficiency and effectiveness, and then understating efficiency and emphasising effectiveness. The usual distinction made between the two is:

> Efficiency is doing things right.
> Effectiveness is doing the right things.

The strong implication of the emphasis on effectiveness is that it subsumes efficiency – if an organisation is being effective, it will necessarily be being efficient.

However, it could be argued that this assumption is over-confident, and blurs the issues. Certainly, organisations, or, rather, their managers, need to ensure that what they do is correct, in all the possible dimensions of that term, and necessary – but, having done that, then what they do should be done efficiently. Efficiency and effectiveness are two different concepts, two different activities, and one cannot subsume the other. In any case, doing 'the right thing' is also a matter of efficiency. For effort to be expended on doing something useless would be inefficient.

Taking an ecosystemic perspective might indicate that activities that are **effective** from a non-systemic point of view can be seen as singularly **ineffective** when the boundaries of the model are changed.

- Can you think of examples where this might be the case?

Efficiency and effectiveness are, of course, signifiers. Efficiency may be specified mathematically, but effectiveness cannot.

- What implications for their use follow from this?

The ability to distinguish what is **structurally** relevant to efficiency and what is not is of crucial importance. However, as was pointed out in Chapter 3, **when it involves human processes, structure is a wholly subjective phenomenon**. For example, in the 1960s and 1970s it was widely believed that labour efficiency, or productivity – which, in the context of organisational behaviour, can be taken to be the same – was not structurally related to earnings once a certain threshold of earnings had been reached. This led to the use of psychological incentives, which *were* held to be structurally related to productivity. The effort to increase productivity was attempted through widespread use of techniques such as job enrichment, and the prescriptions of approaches such as Organisation Development and those that focused on what was known as the Quality of Working Life. But under the preceding dominance of Taylorism the exact opposite was held to be the case: productivity *was* structurally linked to earnings. The contemporary organisational approach to productivity maintains this same Tayloristic understanding – indeed, has extended it, since the use of payment-by-results systems has penetrated areas where it was once thought that they could not be applied, such as the professions, education and health care. Thus, **what** processes are thought to be relevant, and so structurally related, to efficiency is very much a question of who is making the judgement.

Discourse and efficiency

The above examples also highlight the point that **knowledge paradigms** (see also Chapter 4) are also relevant to understanding efficiency: there is a **discourse** of efficiency. Decisions are made, rules established, about what is relevant to efficiency, who can contribute to knowledge about it and what form such knowledge should take, in order to be acceptable discursively. Thus, for example, before there was legislation on equal pay it was widely held that women should receive less pay for their work compared to men, because they were less efficient due to their physical and/or their psychological make-up. Needless to say, this was promulgated by a discourse composed almost entirely of men! We have already referred (in Chapter 8) to the current belief underlying the discursive understanding of the economy that it is necessary to keep wage rates as low as possible, at the same time as it is necessary to keep the remunerations of senior managers and directors as high as possible, if optimum efficiency is to be achieved. Again, it is hardly necessary to say that the discourse is dominated by those with high incomes.

Efficiency/effectiveness II

All organisations have rules to make them effective – that is, rules about 'doing the right thing'. These rules can also be assumed to contribute to the organisation's efficiency, in that their purpose is to 'prevent' dysfunctional behaviour. However, it is well known that **'working to rule'** is an excellent way of causing severe disruption to organisational activity. It seems that, if everyone in an organisation does exactly what they are supposed to do – follows the rules, then the organisation will grind to a halt. This implies that the procedures intended to make an organisation more effective actually have precisely the opposite effect.

■ How can this be explained?

Ideology and efficiency

It is but a short step from this to recognise that **ideology** is an important factor in efficiency. Much of the encouragement for organisations to be efficient derives from macro-economic pressure – from politicians briefed by economists. Government policies on industry and commerce, not to mention education, health, and so on, centre routinely on the need to make what has been called 'Great Britain plc' efficient, particularly with regard to its perceived competitors. Focusing particularly on the labour process, practices are encouraged, and supported, that seek to maintain wages at their lowest possible level and to weaken the power of labour by removing the safeguards – or 'restrictive practices', depending on your ideological point of view – 'enjoyed' by employees. Economic success is, it is often claimed, dependent on what is usually referred to as 'freeing up the labour market' – by which is signified driving down labour costs to the very minimum, whatever the consequences. Of course, it may be thought that if, for reasons of economics, that is what is necessary, then that is what needs to be done.

Economics, however, is not a neutral science, but deeply rooted in ideology – as, indeed, is only to be expected from a discourse so closely concerned with understanding and predicting human behaviour, individually and organisationally, as in, for example, the question of whether people will buy at a certain price, or whether they will choose work rather than leisure. There are various kinds of economics but all are founded on **axioms**: *statements which are claimed to represent self-evident truth but which cannot be demonstrated or proved to be true* – if they could, they would no longer be axioms but would be scientific facts. What the axioms are depends on which variety of economics is under consideration – in classical economics, for example, there is the notion of Rational Economic Man, which assumes that people (men) always act on the basis of a (the) rational calculation of their economic self-interest, and which underlies economic theory of this persuasion. However, this portrayal of human behaviour is believed only by some economists, some politicians and some managers. An axiom, in other words, is an unsubstantiated belief and, therefore, part of an ideology. The ideological nature of economics also explains why different political parties always claim that their own particular version of economics is the correct one. This ideological character used to be recognised through the title 'political economy'. The dropping of the word 'political', motivated by the desire to present economics as a value-neutral science, did not expunge its ideological nature, but only masked it.

In the discussion of ideology in Chapter 7 it was noted that certain ideas have a marked affinity with other ideas – and that is relevant here. While the economistic view of organisations is pertinent at a level of analysis beyond that of individual organisations, a similar view of efficiency permeates management thinking and practice. This is hardly surprising, since the dominant discourses of economics are, inevitably, congruent, in a capitalist society, with the beliefs of those who own capital and, consequently, of their agents, those who manage their capital-accumulating ventures. Thus, for example, economic theories that stress the benefits of public investment in alleviating unemployment, such as Keynesian and New Deal Economics, find little support from the owners of private capital and their agents, a response not unrelated to the interest of the latter in being able to control the supply of jobs, and that not unrelated to their interest in driving down labour costs as an instrument for maximising organisational efficiency. Thus it can be said that **concepts of organisational efficiency are human constructs rooted in ideology**.

Self and efficiency

Of course, people are central to issues of efficiency, conceptually and in practice, and, therefore, the **self** is also highly relevant, and in two particular ways: *the impact of self on efficiency*, and *the impact of efficiency on our sense of self*. It is often assumed that managers are rational pursuers of efficiency, but, in Chapter 8, it was pointed out that such a concept of a centralised, integrated, coherent self as is implied by this definition is not tenable. People – even managers – pursue their own interests defined in subjectively rational terms, and in ways that are often fragmentary and often contradictory. Even within the dominant view of what efficiency means this will be understood and interpreted in different ways by different individuals, and it is quite possible that any particular manager may feel that the undiluted pursuit of efficiency is not in their own interests. A personnel manager we know was given the task of making redundant all the employees in a particular factory by whatever means possible, and his final act was to be to make himself redundant. It could well be suggested that it was in his own interest to slow down the process as much as possible, if for no other reason than to remain in employment himself as long as he could, though one can easily assume that this approach would not meet the criteria of efficiency established within the organisation.

It is well known that managers indulge in, for example, nepotism, discrimination, favouritism and other such practices which are neither objectively rational nor, necessarily, contributions to efficiency, but which, presumably, they perceive to accord with self-interest and with their sense of self. Managers are people first, and managers second. It is easy to see, therefore, that the 'rational pursuit of efficiency' might induce conflict between different aspects of the sense of self. In the case of nepotism, for example, the sense of self as a family member may be more significant than that as a manager. Equally, if, as is likely, the 'rational pursuit of efficiency' led to conflict with the managed, it is possible that this might threaten other aspects of the sense of self, such as the belief that one is a nice person, fair and popular.

Performing efficiency?

According to conventional Organisation Theory, the function of organisation is 'the efficient production of goods and services', and anything which does not contribute to this goal is pathological and should be 'corrected'. This implies that everything that people are required to do in an organisation is, by definition, productive, even though it may not seem so. However, the French social theorist, Michel Foucault, suggested that labour power, as well as being used for the purposes of production, is also used for what he labelled **dressage.*** Dressage connotes discipline, training and performance. The term's most common usage is in the field of equestrianism, where it refers to the training of a horse to respond to controls, and in deportment. Success in the discipline of dressage involves getting the horse to perform unnatural movements and to obey control that is, thereby, for control's sake, for the gratification of the controller. (See also Chapter 12.)

Dressage is non-productive work. Whatever one is required to do in an organisation that does not contribute to (the received wisdom about, or the perception of, what constitutes) 'the efficient production of goods and services' is dressage. Dressage is an element of the labour process that is based on the demonstration of compliance, for the gratification of the desires of those with power – it has nothing to do with organisational efficiency, even though that is how it is usually rationalised.

▶

The practice of dressage in contemporary organisations is rife. Part of the dilemma for the organisational participant is that it is often difficult to know – certainly, to demonstrate as 'fact' – whether what we are required to do does actually contribute to the productive function or not. We have to assume that it does because we are told that it is required. But it is clear that some of what we are required to do has no other outcome than its own performance – nothing follows from it but a demonstration of compliance. For example, a well-known phenomenon in organisational life is a proliferation of meetings that people are required to attend but that have no recognisable utility. The demand that check-out operators should require their customers to 'have a good day', whether or not this is meaningful, or sincerely communicated, is another example where the *form* of labour is emphasised over its *content*.

The possibility of identifying part of the labour process as dressage is another obstacle to realising the idea, the ideal or the goal of organisational efficiency.

*Foucault also identified a symbolic function in the use of labour power, which, it might be argued, could be productive and could be dressage.

Sources: See Michel Foucault (1977) 'The Eye of Power', in C. Gordon (ed), *Michel Foucault: Power/Knowledge*. London: Harvester. See also Jackson and Carter (1998a).

Semiotics and efficiency

What is implied here is that people – whoever they are and whatever their relation to efficiency, whether proponents, practitioners or objects of it – have their own **models** of what efficiency signifies, and these models, as all models, are subjective and purposeful. This also means that efficiency is a **signifier** and, therefore, susceptible to analysis **semiotically**, rather than, for example, scientifically (see also Chapter 2). Such a semiotic analysis would necessarily emphasise that, as a signifier, its signifieds are arbitrary, subjectively defined and interpreted, local and contested. No particular signification can be treated as transcendent and, if we have the feeling that one *is* transcendent, **that is only because this particular meaning is prioritised and maintained by power**. That, in itself, signifies that other definitions, other significations, of efficiency are entirely possible and, potentially, just as valid, but are marginalised to de-value them.

Efficiency . . .

If efficiency were an objective phenomenon, then concepts like ideology, subjectivity, judgement, boundary, power and self would not be implicated in its operation. Efficiency would simply be the ideal, though its achievement might be seen to be impaired by the activities of people. However, given that organisations are social constructions, such a view must be a nonsense. Organisational efficiency is a meaningless concept independent of people. **Organisational efficiency does not have the status of a natural law, but is itself a model, constructed by people**. It does not make sense to talk about a debased ideal, always to be sought after, even if never to be actually achieved. What is needed is, simply, the inclusion of all these other factors in our understanding of efficiency.

However, if efficiency, in theory and in practice, is influenced by all these things, it cannot be objectively rational. Yet, given that, as previously noted, there is a profound reluctance to admit and accept the influence of subjectivity, let alone to assess its implications, it is not surprising that proponents of a particular view of efficiency do claim to be rational themselves, and claim that efficiency itself is an objectively rational phenomenon. Substantiation of this claim is, invariably, based on recourse to quantification, itself based on the claim that numbers cannot lie and an important rhetorical device in claims to be objectively rational. But quantification in the context of efficiency is extremely problematic. On one hand are issues of how to ascribe quantities to phenomena that have no known standard measure, such as motivation, satisfaction, culture, leadership, and so on. On the other hand, there remains the problem of what quantities, of what, should be included as inputs and outputs to the process whose efficiency is to be measured. If the meaning of efficiency is problematic so, too, is how it should be calculated and this also warrants some closer examination.

Measuring efficiency

When trying to measure efficiency it is important to include all significant factors if the outcome is to be a meaningful model of the process under consideration. However, as already suggested, the issue of what should be included is a matter of human judgement and influenced by, for example, ideology, power, concepts of the self, and so on, and, of course, by the capacity to process information. A particularly important aspect of the decision about what constitutes efficiency is *the judgement of where the boundary of the model is to be located* – in other words, the extent of the factors which are to be measured to decide whether a process is efficient or not. An ecosystemic approach, for example, might imply that absolutely everything should be included, but this may not be feasible, nor, probably, especially useful at the level of particular organisations. The skill in constructing a *useful* model of efficiency is, as with all models, a matter of purpose and significance.

The purpose for which a model is constructed is also a matter of human judgement and the inclusion or exclusion of factors (information) must be decided in relation to this idea of purpose. However, which real effects are to be included or excluded cannot be decided entirely on the basis of the desire of the modeller, since **any factor that has consequences for the efficiency of the process is, in practice, a given of the model**. For example, the managers of industrial processes, such as chemicals, coal mining, nuclear power, and others, have, historically, been reluctant to include in their calculations of the efficiency of a process the costs of cleaning up their waste products. Yet chemical discharges into rivers have threatened both the natural environment and the supply of water for human consumption. The coal industry dumped millions of tons of waste material in spoil heaps which, again, have destroyed natural environments and proved to be, in some cases, a real threat to human life through instability – one such spoil heap killed 144 children and adults when it slid onto a school in Aberfan. The nuclear industry knowingly produced waste for which there was no technology available for its permanent disposal, the cost of which was, therefore, unknowable, but also

From efficiency to inefficiency

The consequences of most human-made disasters have been, and are, know-able in advance. It was not impossible to predict that, if the *Herald of Free Enterprise* sailed with its bow doors open, it would sink. It was not impossible to predict that the lifeboats on the *Titanic* could not save everyone on board, if the ship were to sink. It was not impossible to predict that, if the O ring seals on the *Challenger* space shuttle failed, it would explode.

What characterises these, and other, disasters is that the managers involved thought that they were adopting the most efficient methods, until the failure proved them to be wrong – their efficient decisions turned out to be highly inefficient. This happened because they failed to include relevant variables in their model of efficiency.

In the case of the *Titanic* it took something less than 47 seconds to turn an 'efficient' closed system into a hopelessly inefficient open system. It was esti-mated that the iceberg was struck 37 seconds after first being sighted. Had the ship been lucky and turned fast enough, it might have missed the iceberg and retained its status as efficient. Having struck the iceberg, it took the iceberg 10 seconds to open up the hull. Sometime in this 10 seconds the fatal quantity of hull damage was exceeded – sealing the fate of the ship, and its passengers and crew.

11:40 pm
'Efficient' closed system

11:40:47 pm
Inefficient open system

produced *unintended* waste products which were not envisaged in any assessment of the process. In the case of the recent decision to decommission a nuclear power installation in the UK, it has been calculated that it will take one hundred years to complete, in the present state of knowledge of this process. Had that calcula-tion been included in the original estimates of the efficiency of nuclear power, a very different picture would have been presented, compared to the sunny view of cheap electricity to be had. In all these cases, managers were making routine assessments of efficiency, yet vast amounts of money have been, or will have to be, spent to eliminate problems caused which were not included in the original calculation of efficiency but which can now be seen to have major implications for the overall efficiency of the processes in question.

The contemporary debate, and concern, about global warming is another exam-ple, and one that particularly highlights the extensiveness of the boundaries that managers *ought* to be acknowledging, and for which they may be responsible. A prominent view is that global warming is caused by, or at least exacerbated by, organisational activity. One of the myriad consequences of global warming appears to be the melting of the polar ice fields, with the prospect of rising sea levels and inundation of large areas of the land mass. Surely, one way or another, this ought to be a factor in determining efficiency. The stark question that is raised by this debate is about what price it is reasonable to pay for organisational activity, when, ultimately, the price might be the extinction of human life. Yet there is very little evidence that global warming is being factored in to calculations of efficiency.

Inclusion or exclusion of factors

In considering how to construct an efficient understanding of efficiency and its measurement there are *five* salient issues to be examined. *Firstly*, there is the issue of **the evaluation of what factors are to be included in the calculation.** As noted, this is primarily an issue of perception and judgement of where the boundaries of the process are located. Some aspects may be relatively straightforward to identify, but others are much less clear and more open to interpretation. For example, if managers decide that they can maximise efficiency by making demands on employees which turn out to be excessive, resulting in employees becoming ill through overwork or injury – common cases being stress, exhaustion, back injury, repetitive strain injury, respiratory problems – the cost of repairing such damage is not borne by the organisation, but by the economy more generally, via the health service. If the cost is not borne directly by the organisation it could be, and often is, argued that it is not a factor influencing its efficiency calculations. This argument, however, is only tenable within a very narrowly bounded, and, indeed, naive, model. The counterargument is that the demands made on the national economy as an effect of an organisation's process should be included in calculations of that organisation's efficiency, since they are consequences emanating, solely, from its activities. Even the apparently clearer issues, such as the price of raw materials, are not as obvious as they may seem, when it is considered that, for example, these are supplied by organisations which have made efficiency calculations on the same uncertain basis of evaluation of what is to be included or excluded.

Theory is no less culpable than practice. For example, incentive theories, including popular theories of motivation to work as well as those based on financial incentives, themselves provide an illustration of this type of problem. Approaches to managing people that utilise techniques for encouraging greater levels of effort have been criticised for assuming, implicitly or explicitly, that people can increase their rate of working open-endedly, without any regard to the consequences of overwork – notwithstanding that death from overwork is now recognised as an industrial disease in at least one industrialised country, Japan. Excluding such factors from calculations of efficiency may seem attractive but might be seen as, at best, disingenuous and, at worst, actively misleading.

Generally, very few questions about what should be included or excluded in calculations of efficiency have obvious answers. But judgements about this are, inevitably, driven by desires to present a particular process as efficient, or not – which is to say that what is included or excluded is not driven by an objective assessment of facts but by subjective processes, and is purposeful, not in the service of absolute measures of efficiency, but of some other superordinate objective. **Efficiency is a means to an end, not an end in itself, but what that end is is, itself, a human construction and a reflection of human desires.**

Measurement

Secondly, there is the issue of **how what is to be included is to be measured**. Some things may seem to be fairly easy to measure, where there are standard units of measurement, such as gallons of water consumed or tons of fuel burned, and so on. The difficulty arises when things to be included are not readily susceptible to standard units of measurement. Good will, satisfaction and commitment are obvious examples of factors which are relevant to organisational efficiency but which have no known units of measurement. Where there are no meaningful scientific measures, however, the usual recourse is to fall back on **quasi-measures: giving quantities (from the Latin for how many?) to qualities (from the Latin for what kind?)**. There are, basically, two kinds of such measurement: ordinal and cardinal.

Ordinal measures typically rank the desirability of particular characteristics in relation to each other. The approach is often used (or ab-used) in questionnaires. Consider the following:

	(strongly disagree)				(strongly agree)
I am satisfied with my job	1	2	3	4	5
I work too many hours	1	2	3	4	5
I like my immediate boss	1	2	3	4	5

It is common practice to perform arithmetic routines, such as averaging responses, to produce a number which purports to represent an overall level of performance, but the logical basis for such practice is highly questionable. It often involves conflating very different phenomena – such as, above, satisfaction, evaluation of time, liking – which may also have very different significances. There is also the problem that absolute disagreement with a statement still results in a positive number: the worst case is not zero but one. There is an assumption of linearity and regularity: the difference between 'strongly disagree' and 'strongly agree' is represented by equal subdivisions. Some of these, and other, problems can be made more or less significant by the design of a questionnaire, but they remain inherent problems of ordinal measurement of non-quantitative factors.

Cardinal measures are those that ascribe a direct number value to such factors, usually independently of the views of the person concerned. An example of this process is the quantification of a person's situation which then represents a points total which symbolises their need. Such calculations often involve the mixing together of widely disparate factors as if they are mathematically related. A particularly notorious case is the QALY – Quality Adjusted Life Years – used in health care to assess the efficiency of an investment in medical treatment in terms of the quality of life of the patient. Of the two of us, one is a smoker and the other is not and, in the event of needing major surgery, for example, this would be taken into account in the question of whether the individual was worth the effort – whether it would be efficient to save that person's life, rather than someone else's life. Other factors would also be taken into account, however heterogeneous they might be, such as age, children, even income. Experience of work has received very similar attentions, notably from approaches associated with Quality of

Working Life, Organisational Culture and, latterly, Human Resource Management. The same fallacies have underwritten their use, most importantly the ignoring of what individuals feel about the quality of their working conditions in favour of the specifications of so-called experts.

It is quite routine in calculations of efficiency to ascribe quantitative values to factors that cannot, and ought not to, be measured in such a way. Quality of life is, simply, not to be encompassed by the sum of arbitrarily identified factors given numerical values, nor can it be judged independently of the person concerned. Furthermore, such measures cannot be standardised – the same element will be measured in different ways in different cases. **The reason for even attempting to do this is to provide numerical measures of efficiency – to give a spurious objectivity to what is a fundamentally subjective judgement.**

Money as the basis of measurement

The *third* aspect of the measurement of efficiency that needs to be considered is an extension of the second: **the attribution of money values to the measurements produced.** Where different types of factor are involved, there is a perceived need to reduce them to a common base and this, usually, is money. This involves allocating a notional money value, on the basis of a numerical measure, to factors that influence the efficiency of a process but that defy measurement. For example, it is common practice when selling a business to include a monetary evaluation of good will. Even if good will were not such an elusive quality for a business, there are no obvious units by which to measure good will and give it a monetary value – it can hardly be treated as a tangible commodity and so can hardly be bought and sold. Apart from the commodification of abstractions, however, there is a more important difficulty with this tendency: **money is only a symbolic language.** Currency is a signifier that has no intrinsic value in itself, but that merely signifies an amount of something else. As a signifier, money is characterised by *absence* – for example, what any particular piece of coinage represents is, notionally, an amount of gold held by a central bank, though it may not be there, either; *arbitrariness* – for example, it has no necessary form; *difference* – for example, it can be differentiated from anything else, including other money, and is defined by this difference. Additionally, as a signifier, it is open to interpretation and its meaning can change. **To talk about efficiency in terms of money, therefore, is to describe what is an arbitrary, uncertain and subjective model in a language which is also arbitrary, uncertain and subjective.**

A further difficulty in this conundrum is that **money is not the same as wealth: money only has exchange value, but wealth has both exchange value and use value.** A simple example will illustrate this. Suppose that you have a certain amount of money and you need to eat. You cannot eat the money, but you can exchange it for food. So you spend £1 of your money and buy a cheese sandwich, thereby satisfying your hunger. The following day you decide to repeat the purchase, but, overnight, the price of the cheese sandwich has risen to £1.10 pence. You buy your sandwich, but get no more use value out of it than when it cost £1. Thus, money is only a signifier with no direct relevance to use value. On the third day, there is a special offer of two cheese sandwiches for the price of one.

You eat one and are then left with one which you can sell or exchange for some other good. In this example, the cheese sandwich represents wealth because it has a particular value to you, independent of its price. Money is not wealth because it can only be exchanged for something useful. Money can stand as a surrogate for wealth, but only as long as its exchange value remains fairly constant, and only as long as someone is prepared to sell you what you need in exchange for your money. If the value of money changes rapidly, then it is a poor surrogate for wealth because wealth, as it has a use value, tends not to alter rapidly. This is precisely what happens in hyperinflation: money starts to lose its exchange value, so wealth held as money shrinks.

If no one will take your money in exchange for what you need, then, again, it is of no use: money is only worth what someone is prepared to exchange for it. A common illustration of this is the refusal of some English shopkeepers to accept Scottish bank notes, even though they are legal tender. Similarly, if your wealth is in Russian roubles, this currency will not be any use to you in England. In relatively stable economies money can be an efficient substitute (model) for wealth, but it is always vulnerable to changes of opinion as to its value, as in exchange rates for foreign currencies.

The point is that **money values are not reliable indicators of prosperity or of efficiency**. What citizens of a nation state should be concerned with is the increase in the wealth of that nation, because it is wealth that increases the standard of living, enhances freedom from want, ignorance, and illness, and so on. It is through organisations that wealth is increased, or not – in other words, the socio-economic purpose of organisations is to increase wealth. Conventional approaches to efficiency using money as a measure do not provide a reliable guide to this.

Efficiency = profitability?

In the years before the privatisation of the railways in the UK, it was reported that British Rail made a profit on its portfolio of property, but made a loss on running trains. Assuming that running trains could not be made to be profitable, it might then be argued that British Rail could maximise its efficiency by ceasing to run trains and concentrating on being a property owner.

- Would this have been a good idea?
- If it could be seen as a good idea, what are the implications for customers, who use rail transport because it is most efficient for them?
- If these customers then switched to, say, road transport, what would be the efficiency implications for the existing road network, road users and the environment?
- If it would not have been a good idea, what are the implications for the ways in which efficiency is measured?

Opportunity costs

The *fourth* issue relating to models of efficiency and its measurement concerns **the tendency to claim that a process is, or is not, efficient without reference to the opportunity costs of that process.** Opportunity cost is an accounting device which uses projections of estimates to identify the cost of choices forgone. The true opportunity costs of a decision would have to be based on the actual costs of the choice that is forgone when a decision is made. This cost can never be known because the events which would allow it to be known do not occur, but it is the only 'absolute' measure of comparative efficiencies. The decision between two options is a matter of human judgement; to claim that one's chosen option is optimally efficient is a statement of faith. For example, when the UK coal industry was, effectively, run down, it was claimed that it was more efficient to import coal. The opportunity cost of that decision is what it would have cost to produce the coal domestically rather than to import it, but this cannot be known since it did not happen. The estimate that it would have been higher depends crucially on being able accurately to predict those costs that did not occur: the forecast is susceptible to all the uncertainties that have been identified about modelling and about efficiency, and has the additional vulnerability that it is not a model of something in existence against which it could be checked but a model of something in the future that does not happen! To treat such forecasts as a basis for calculating the all-important matter of efficiency is tantamount to the negation of all claims to objective measurement in favour of the crystal ball.

Food for thought!

A current example of the problem of calculating **opportunity costs** in relation to questions of **efficiency** is the debate about 'food air-miles'. One particular case is that of asparagus. It is said, even by the French, that English asparagus is the best in the world, but it has a very short season of only a few weeks. Nonetheless, asparagus is available in UK supermarkets all the year round because it is imported from countries such as Peru, and this is even the case when English asparagus is in season, although, if the English variety is the best in the world, these imports must be less good. Being able to eat asparagus all the year round is not a nutritional requirement, but reflects a coalition of the desires of the consumer and those of the suppliers (growers, wholesalers, retailers, etc.). But to air-freight asparagus from South America to the UK has a number of costs which need to be balanced against these desires, such as the pollution caused by air traffic, which contributes, *inter alia*, to the world's rapidly escalating environmental problems. These costs are not included in the shipping rates, however – they would probably make it uneconomic, if they were. (There are also other environmental issues connected to the production of foods in South America for consumption in, for example, Western Europe, such as whether this is the most appropriate use of arable land, the clearing of rainforest to increase land available for such crops, as well as the economic issues surrounding cash-cropping, amongst other things.)

▶

> While for members of the supply chain shipping asparagus thousands of miles is an efficient (that is, acceptably profitable) process, in so far as there is a market for it, in ecosystemic terms it is extremely *in*efficient. The environmental costs of this trade simply cannot be justified by the desire of UK consumers to eat asparagus out of season. The opportunity 'costs' of the trade may not be precisely calculable, but would *appear* to far outweigh the benefits of this indulgence. Unfortunately, if we wish to try to halt, and even reverse, threats such as global warming, we may have to forgo such luxuries. *Quelle horreur!*

Aggregations of efficiencies

The *fifth* issue concerns **the tendency to assume that efficiencies are aggregated**. It is assumed, for example, that, if every sub-unit of an economic system is efficient, then the economy itself is efficient. That this is not the case is easily demonstrable. Take the case of the previously cited example of the wastage of so-called human resources: if a commercial organisation is highly efficient, as measured by, for example, earnings per share, or unit costs of production, but, in achieving this, overworks its employees who then go off sick and need to be treated by a highly efficient health service, as measured by, for example, costs per patient cured, these efficiencies cannot sensibly be added together. It is not unreasonable to argue that it would be more efficient not to work people into ill-health and then not to have to cure them of their illnesses. Unless the incremental benefits of overworking people are greater than the costs of curing them of the effects of overwork, such practices cannot be seen as examples of optimised efficiency.

If, as we have suggested, the theory and practice of organisational behaviour is governed by the guiding principle of increasing efficiency at the level of individual organisations, as measured by, say, benefit to shareholders, then it is especially remarkable how this approach can effectively mask the extent to which it can aggregate into serious *dys*functions if the boundaries are located at all differently. It might make sense if the limit of organisational activity represented the limits of the socio-economic world for any organisational participant, but this is not the case; people have to live in a world 'outside' the organisation. The consequences of such aggregations are, obviously, of great significance. This is equally the case 'within' the organisation. If each sub-unit of an organisation pursued maximisation of efficiency in its own terms, without reference to the rest of the organisation, it would be a recipe for disaster. Thus, for example, production departments might be producing units that could not be sold by marketing departments, or marketing departments might be selling units that could not be produced. The relentless pursuit of this particular version of efficiency, therefore, not only has dysfunctional effects (*inefficiencies*) for the people who are subjected to it, at whatever level, but also may be detrimental to the organisation as a whole, and to society in general. Given that the model of efficiency is also susceptible to so many problems, the risk of these accumulated dysfunctions would be hard to justify were the model not discursively and ideologically approved. This, however, is only to say that the claim that this model represents the ultimate possible model of efficiency is a claim based, not on science, but on desire and interest.

The fantasy of the perfect system

It could be argued that theorising in the conventional discourse of Organisational Behaviour, and that of Organisation Studies more generally, is predicated, at many levels, on a fantasy of perfection. A **fantasy** is defined as 'a preoccupation with thoughts associated with unobtainable desires'. Thus these discourses can be seen as preoccupied with a vision of organisation as it is wished that it is, rather than organisation as it 'is'. So, for example, as previously noted, conventional Organisational Behaviour seems to have a model of an 'ideal worker', towards whom techniques of organisational behaviour management and/or manipulation will tend. Much of the literature on Organisational Culture presupposes that there is a 'perfect culture' and that it can be achieved. The problem with this is that what this ideal worker or perfect culture looks like varies from theorist to theorist, and from practitioner to practitioner, and this is because perfection is very much in the eye of the beholder.

There is, nonetheless, a perhaps unconscious assumption, and an implicit promise, that everything about an organisation can be perfected. Once all these perfections have been achieved, they will aggregate into 'the perfect organisation'. The defining characteristic of this 'perfect organisation' is that it will be The Efficient Organisation. And the implicit message of conventional theory is that this is not tilting at windmills or chasing a dream, but very close – a few adjustments here or there are really all that is needed. It may be that progress towards the ideal type is asymptotic, with a need for continuous, but small, adjustments, but if we apply the theories correctly, do 'the right thing', then we will approach ever closer to the pinnacle of perfection.

The problem with this fantasy is that there could never be any such thing as '**The** Efficient Organisation', because efficiency is contingent on purpose and on a range of variables, and it is hardly conceivable that, even within one organisation, there could be unanimous agreement, even about what the significant variables are, or how to define them. One person's efficiency is another person's inefficiency. This is because what constitutes anyone's understanding of efficiency is based on human choices, human preferences, ideology, power. The characteristics of perfection, whatever they may be, are, almost by definition, unachievable.

Unfortunately, the fantasy that perfection is achievable, and the promise that what we have got now is almost there, blind us to other possibilities, other alternatives, for theory and for practice. There is no evidence that endless minor adjustments move us closer to any kind of perfection, or why would organisation, as a practice and as a process, still be the site of such unregenerate problems? Some would argue that it is exactly these other possibilities and other alternatives that must be examined if these problems of organisation(s) are to be addressed.

What's wrong with efficiency?

It may be necessary to restate at this point that we are *not* arguing against efficiency. What is being questioned is whether the dominant model of efficiency is meaningful and useful. Indeed, if it can be shown that claims for efficiency actually lead, in practice, to inefficiencies – that is, to dysfunctions and wastage of resources of whatever kind – can such an approach to efficiency be seen as itself efficient? Efficiency, however, is not merely useful, but wholly necessary – but this does not mean that there is only one version of what constitutes efficiency. The difficulty with current dominant notions of efficiency is that they are not even based on a proper recognition of what the term efficiency means, let alone a reasoned appreciation of other possible significations. The point of increasing efficiency is to gain more outputs for a given level of inputs. It is outputs that are used to provide quality of life, and, thus, quality of life is linked, inextricably, to organisational process and its effectiveness. **It is, therefore, important that organisations are efficient. What is at issue is what that efficiency consists of.** Models of efficiency have enormous impacts and consequences when they are operationalised in practice. Measures of efficiency are used to justify decision-making. The claimed rationality of such measures offers a supposed objectivity to such choices as are made. However, **understandings of efficiency are not rational and scientific, but value-laden, rooted in ideology, prioritise some interests over others and are enforced through power**.

It is important to stress that **efficiency is a comparative tool**. There is, therefore, no such thing as *the* efficient organisation, since calculations of the efficiency of a particular process, or of an organisation, only have meaning in relation to some other way of doing things which is less, or more, efficient than the one under consideration, in the context of particular purposes and interests. Decision-makers may be interested in, for example, whether it is more efficient to improve a manufacturing facility *or* to ship the whole thing to a Third World country, whether it is more efficient to try to change the culture in an organisation *or* to introduce a new payment system, whether it is more efficient to delayer an organisation *or* to maintain a steep hierarchy. Allocating supposedly objective and rationally calculated measures to such questions seems to allow the almost automatic generation of indicators that will tell decision-makers which is the 'better' course of action. But if these calculations are not rational and objective, then it is quite possible that the indicators point to inappropriate decisions – in other words, lead to inefficiency, even in their own terms.

The development of techniques for managing organisational behaviour illustrates the vulnerability of the process. The history of application of organisational behaviour techniques, while remarkably consistent in terms of their rationale, that they will increase efficiency, shows that most techniques have a relatively short life before being replaced by another technique making similar claims. This is rarely, however, supersession by new, more advanced, more efficient, techniques, but usually reversion to some previous technique – for example, as noted previously, Taylorism enjoys much popularity at the present time, even though it was supposedly abandoned many years ago in favour of more psychologically based approaches to increasing efficiency. Indeed, it can be said that very little that is genuinely new enters into the discourse of Organisational Behaviour – which, given the significance of discursive rules of appropriateness, is not very surprising. Typically, what happens is that the same approaches are endlessly recycled, under different names. Human Resource Management, for example, comprises many similarities with ideas that were associated with Organisation Development in the 1970s. The implication of this cycle of adoption and abandonment is that, whatever the indicators, such approaches do not actually, in practice, contribute to increases in the performance of individual employees.

The very limited definition of what might be taken to indicate that efficiency has been achieved is also problematic. In contemporary socio-economic conditions, money is the almost exclusive measure of increased efficiency. This means, inevitably, that intangible goods, such as education, health and the environment, either get price tags or get excluded from efficiency calculations. Attitudes to preservation of the natural environment provide an example. Organisations are facing increasing public pressure about their approach to depletion of, or damage to, the natural environment. The favoured proposed solution to this has been the idea of 'pollutor pays'. What this means in practice is that, on one hand, the health of the natural environment is given a money value, even though this could never reflect the actual significance or the complexity of the natural environment, and, on the other, that organisations can, if they wish, buy the right to pollute – they can pollute if they can afford the price. The one thing such an approach does not do is ensure that pollution of the environment is reduced, though this is its supposed objective.

Are organisations being efficient?

Notwithstanding the widespread commitment to increasing efficiency and the efforts made to that end, we rarely know what the effects of particular initiatives to improve efficiency are. Calculations of efficiency, whether actual or projected, are really just snapshots of a dynamic process. It is not possible, for example, to ascribe an increase in profits to particular events, such as trying to engineer a change in culture, because, clearly, profits are affected by influences too numerable even to identify, some of which are not even the results of managerial actions, but are attributable to externalities. The focus at, say, departmental level is no clearer. It has already been pointed out that departmental efficiencies can act against each other in terms of the overall efficiency of an organisation but, more than this, events, even in a relatively small department, are rarely so regular and consistent over time as to enable us to know, in some future time period, whether earlier projections of efficiency have actually been achieved, or what has, or has not, contributed to them. Organisational life is characterised by frequent changes in procedures, and so on, all designed to improve efficiency, yet the effects are barely demonstrable. **Most attempts to increase efficiency are really no more than acts of faith**.

Scarcity

It is worth pointing out that the justification for all measures – and, indeed, exhortations – to increase efficiency is almost always **the need to maximise utilisation of scarce resources**. However, it might be suggested that the nature of such scarcity is a fiction. There is certainly no shortage of labour power – for example, in the UK alone there are, depending on how the figures are calculated, at least 1–2 million people unemployed, and this has been the case continuously for the past three decades. There may be local shortages of skills, but nothing that could not be rectified, in a fairly short time, by proper investment in education and training. As regards scarcity of material resources, such as oil, steel or equipment, these only become wealth by the application of labour power. So, for example, if you own an oil well or a gold mine, they can only become of any use after labour power has been employed to extract, refine, transport, market, or whatever. The raw materials that form equipment can only do so after they have been furnished by labour power, and converted by more labour power into such equipment. Thus, for example, an ambulance is only an ambulance once labour power has made the steel, plastics, and so on, to be shaped, formed, fitted together, by more labour power to make a working ambulance. Since supplies of raw materials, even those that are finite, are available for conversion, and such supplies are relatively constant, any supposed scarcity must be scarcity of labour power to produce and shape materials into equipment. But labour power is not scarce.

That we may believe that resources are scarce is not because they actually are scarce, but an effect of the way that production of goods and services, and the distribution of benefits, is organised. In other words, **scarcity is used to justify the way we organise, but it is the way we organise that produces apparent scarcity**. For example, it is claimed that it is not possible to produce enough food to feed everyone in the world, yet the developed countries consume more food than is good for them and waste food extravagantly. It is common for overproduction in any good to be destroyed rather than to allow prices to come down because of increased supply, so that such goods might be available to those for whom they are otherwise scarce. On the other hand, **the claim that resources are scarce is very selectively applied**. That some resources *are* finite, most especially natural resources, does not prevent their profligate waste. Thus, for example, while water is a precious and increasingly scarce resource, this does not mean that it cannot be wasted, or that its distribution needs more careful management – in the UK it has been estimated that as much as one-third of water is simply lost due to leakage from water main pipes which are not properly maintained.

Similar levels of wastage can be found in the use of manufactured items. For example, only a generation ago most glass bottles were expected to be re-used several times in their lifetime, and this applied to any kind of bottle, whether for milk, medicine, beer, mineral water or anything else. Nowadays only milk bottles are routinely re-used. So, rather than being a handy, re-usable container, glass bottles, though in undiminished use, become an item of waste to be disposed of, exacerbating the already serious problem of waste disposal. Even bottles that are recycled through bottle banks are not re-used, but broken up and made into new bottles. This is, no doubt, claimed to be more efficient than re-using the existing bottle, but, if that is the case, why do we still re-use milk bottles?

Even though we know that resources such as natural gas and oil will run out in the relatively near future, we are still encouraged to increase our consumption of them. Indeed, an exemplar of the problems of efficiency and their relation to scarce resources can be found in consideration of the much-lauded privatisation of public utilities. Privatisation is claimed to have led to lower prices for, for example, fuel, through increased efficiency. This claimed increase in efficiency has been gained, to a large extent, by shedding labour – that is, by increasing unemployment. According to economic theory, lower prices should lead to increased consumption and, therefore, to the more rapid exhaustion of a finite and irreplaceable resource. It could be argued that keeping more people employed and prices higher, thus extending the period of availability of the resource while also providing people with the income to be able to buy it, might be a much more efficient course to take. The problem is that the husbanding of scarce resources is not really the issue at all.

Efficiency

What constitutes efficiency is highly debatable and depends, crucially, on the subjectively defined perceptions, meanings, judgements, interests and objectives which inform the bounding process in constructing the model. And, of course, the issues are compounded extensively because this bounding process is relevant, not only to models of efficiency themselves, but also to the processes to which the models are applied. This is why it is not unreasonable to say that efficiency *per se* is desirable, whilst being critical of the myriad shortcomings of the dominant model of efficiency: although it may be dominant, it is only a model. It needs to be recognised that all models of efficiency suffer from problems of measurement, but this only emphasises that **it is the objectives of such models that need to be articulated and assessed.** There could be many other versions of what it means to be efficient, with different objectives and different conditions, equally viable. What is needed is a comparison between the dominant and other models, in order to consider which objectives might be the more desirable and, then, which models of efficiency might be the more appropriate to achieve such objectives.

It was stated earlier that organisational behaviour is profoundly implicated in issues of efficiency at all levels. It is not unreasonable to suppose, therefore, that the discourse of Organisational Behaviour should be able to contribute to the consideration, even the resolution, of such issues. A department store magnate, John Wanamaker, is reported to have said that half the money spent on advertising was wasted, but the trouble was, he did not know which half it was. The same could be said of efficiency, in its current configuration. The problem is that finding out is a much more pressing issue.

Existing applications in Organisational Behaviour

There has been a general and widespread concern with efficiency, probably for centuries, probably coextensive with organisation itself – it could be said that the process of organisation is, and always has been, driven by the belief that people can increase their efficiency through organising. Everything in the canon of Organisational Behaviour, and in that of Organisation Studies more generally, is based on claims to increase efficiency. All technological change, for example, is predicated on this principle – the gun was a more efficient killing machine than the bow and arrow, railway transportation of goods was more efficient than that by canal, power looms produced cloth more efficiently than hand looms, electronic calculators were more efficient than slide rules, and so on, and on. For all the reasons already examined, however, this has not meant that the *application* of new technology has actually resulted in greater efficiency, though this has not dimmed the enthusiasm of proponents of organisational change in claiming efficiency as its justification.

Although there is a universal interest in increasing efficiency, the understanding of efficiency that predominates is subscribed to by a relatively small – though very powerful – group of people, principally capitalists, economists, politicians and managers. This understanding is deemed by others to be so self-evidently inadequate that most opponents to it often just dismiss it out of hand, rarely even spending time on dissecting it. Opponents from fields as various as Conflict Theory, Labour Process Theory, Moral Philosophy and History, among others, have all discounted the claims of this dominant model to increase efficiency, as well as questioning the desirability of the model's objectives, and its objectivity. Much of this disenchantment stems from dissension to the supposed over-arching power of 'The Market' and its claimed ability to dictate what is efficient. According to belief in The Market, inefficiency will be punished by annihilation by the efficient. Nonetheless, whether it is believed that The Market has supernatural powers which humans cannot effect or believed that The Market should serve human interests, all but the most utterly committed tend to intervene when The Market seems to be going against their interests. So, for example, in the UK politicians have shown no reluctance to intervene to support inefficiencies in agriculture, such as by paying farmers to keep land idle, but did not take the same approach to the coal industry. The long history of laws to regulate workplace behaviour similarly represents such intervention. The idea that The Market determines efficiency is not sustainable as long as the powerful are able, and willing, to intervene in its functioning. Even this suggests that The Market does operate according to some natural law, but this is widely disputed, and its ontological status highly contested.

However, as regards the conventional discourse of Organisational Behaviour there is no such uncertainty. The discourse has long subscribed to a naive model of organisational efficiency and it is this model which has consistently underwritten the development of theories and techniques for managing organisational behaviour, to the extent that no such theory or technique that does not claim to increase efficiency has achieved substantial recognition within the discourse. It could be said that the project of the discourse of Organisational Behaviour is, not the understanding of organisational behaviour itself, but to understand how organisational behaviour can be managed so as to increase efficiency, itself understood in terms of indicators such as shareholder benefit.

Much of the dissent from this dominant model of efficiency is based, not only on rejection of its principles, but also on the recognition that efficiency is both relational and comparative, that it is a relative condition and can, therefore, have different objectives and principles. There are theorists, for example, who argue that the prevailing model itself results in inefficiencies such as the wastage of people, either in general or in terms of particular groups who are discriminated against, and who suggest that such wastage is an inappropriate price to pay for the narrow sectional interest that is shareholder benefit. Other groups of theorists argue that the inappropriate price that is paid for this interest is degradation of the natural environment. Yet others argue that the inappropriate price is the social consequences, such as ghetto-isation and social deprivation for the non-privileged. From this it can be seen that other conceptualisations of the purposes and processes of organisational efficiency do exist, although they are not well represented in the official discourse.

Poststructuralist approaches, starting from a semiotic analysis, similarly do not give any credence to this official model. From such a perspective any claims to transcendence must, necessarily, be rejected, to be assessed from the perspective of the interests and assumptions that inform them. Again, specific focus on such analysis of organisational efficiency in the context of organisational behaviour is under-developed but, nonetheless, underwrites poststructuralist work in the area.

Further potential

It has already been suggested that there is a pressing need for the conventional discourse of Organisational Behaviour to acknowledge, articulate and examine the assumptions on which its theories and techniques are based, and the objectives which are, thereby, pursued. This is especially the case with the concepts and models of organisational efficiency which are dominant in the discourse. If the issues of organisational efficiency were to be addressed rigorously, it would have a marked impact on the discourse. The outcome might well be sustained adherence to present formulations, but, at least, their basis would be made clearer, and justified. If some reassessment and realignment were to follow from such an examination, however, the discourse would be changed substantially.

But the conventional discourse of Organisational Behaviour is not alone in being guilty of failing to articulate the assumptions and objectives of its model of organisational efficiency. Those who reject this model also tend to do so without rigorous exploration of the assumptions and objectives that are preferred. Additionally, the development of principles on which alternative models of organisational efficiency might be operationalised is patchy – in effect, although many dissent from the dominant model, alternatives are under-theorised, particularly in terms of what consequences might follow from their adoption. Given the enormous significance of, and need for, efficiency in organisational practice, it seems imperative that the concept be thoroughly explored, alternatives proposed, debates conducted, consequences considered. Such significance and necessity demand that **organisational efficiency should not be dismissed as obvious, or taken-for-granted**, whatever model is favoured. Many people have identified particular issues implicated in concerns for organisational efficiency, such as employee stress, or environmental pollution, but the general ramifications of changing our approach to organisational efficiency remain to be fully explored. Single issue concerns need to be integrated into coherent and comprehensive models. There are major and widespread implications for organisational behaviour in all this which should not be simply set aside – and if change, or even reinforcement, is to occur, it is in the context of organisational behaviour that it will begin. But, in the present parlous state of under-development, it all remains to be done.

Organisational behaviour and efficiency

Organisational behaviour and efficiency are inextricably interlinked. All the things that the discourse of Organisational Behaviour concerns itself with are informed by the objective of increasing efficiency and, in so doing, this has an enormous impact on the way we understand organisations. The discourse of Organisational Behaviour has helped to shape understanding of the management role, for managers themselves and for others, and has contributed substantially to prevailing views of what people are like, how they should be handled, what is good, or not good, for people, and so on. It has had equal significance for what are understood as appropriate working practices, to the extent that the very way we organise is influenced by this discourse of Organisational Behaviour. It is the repository of wisdom, for example, on whether material or psychological incentives should be used, on whether high levels of supervision or autonomous work groups are more effective, on whether leadership should be autocratic or democratic in style, on whether hierarchies should be flat or steep, on whether people can be successfully treated as workers or whether the 'whole' person should be taken into account, even on whether we can develop our own beliefs, attitudes and behaviours, or whether we need to be directed in this – for the benefit of 'the organisation'. At different times all of these approaches have represented current wisdom in the discourse, but the underlying principle has remained the same: pursuit of the supposedly objective, supposedly obvious and given, goal of increasing efficiency. But if these suppositions are incorrect, and if question marks can be placed over even the meaning of the concept of efficiency, let alone how it is operationalised in practice, how it is calculated and how its achievement is measured, then it is quite possible, even likely, that the discourse of Organisational Behaviour is having such huge impact on people's lives and on the way we organise for no good reason. This, surely, would be a risk too great to take.

However, if efficiency and its relationship to organisational behaviour is addressed on the basis of the considerations raised here, what is indicated is a completely new understanding of the meaning and purposes of work. Many of the practices imposed on people in organisations would, necessarily, change, not least as an effect of the articulation and justification of objectives which are inevitably required in order to legitimate organisational practice in the employment and management of people. The understanding of work as, primarily, the prerogative of managers to define, direct and organise would be dramatically supplemented by a much wider constituency of concerns. The physiological, psychological, social, environmental and political impacts of the ways in which work is organised would have to be treated much more seriously, to be taken into account much more thoroughly. Not least, they would have to be integrated into any calculation of what is, or is not, efficient.

A TALE FROM THE VILLAGE PUMP (*EFFICIENCY*)

(See the Case Study in Appendix 2, pages 340–3)

Issues of **efficiency** are obviously deeply implicated in any attempt to control an epidemic. In this case, Snow's success in getting the handle of the Broad Street drinking water pump removed – premised on his growing conviction that contaminated water was the problem in general, and that that pump was the problem in this particular epidemic – could be seen as a model of efficient action: cheap, fast and effective. The proponents of the miasma theory also had a wide range of proposals, for improving air quality, although these would have been very costly to implement and would have taken a long time to achieve (where their achievement was even possible – one of the proposals seems to have been that 'blocks' of clean air should be moved from high ground to lower ground). Additionally, in the end, these proposals addressed the wrong cause of the problem. In other words, whatever might have been done would have been, in any case, inefficient in controlling cholera, no matter how efficiently it was actually done. (It is, however, rather ironic that, from the perspective of today, one might wish that something had been done about improving the air quality anyway!)

■ Snow's objective can be seen as to bring under control the immediate epidemic. Farr's objective can be seen as the production of a mathematical model of the general case of the causes of cholera. What were the **opportunity costs** of each approach?

Case

HEALTH AND EFFICIENCY

The Pigg family lived in an old stone house on top of the hill, safely out of the reach of the Big Bad Wolf. The household comprised the widowed Ma Pigg and her three children, Chipolata, Ham and Bacon. One day Ma Pigg gathered her children together and told them that she was getting too old to look after them, and anyway they were now big enough to leave home and make their own way in the world. She proposed to give them their inheritance so that they could establish themselves in their own homes. The money was to be

▶

divided equally between them. It wasn't a large amount, so they would have to use all their resources efficiently to 'keep the wolf from the door', both literally and figuratively. However, local property prices had been rising and, each on their own, they would not be able to afford the type of house that they had been raised in. If they chose to buy independently, they would have to move down to the bottom of the hill, into wolf territory, but where cheaper houses were being built. If they pooled their resources, they could get a house at the top of the hill to share, but each of them relished the prospect of independence – there was a significant element of sibling rivalry between them.

Chipolata was easy-going, not really interested in work and wanted to live the 'good life'. Looking at the property around, she discovered that there were some cheap Straw houses available, well within her budget, but not wolf-proof. However, the Estate Agent pointed out that there were some very good wolf intruder alarms these days, and she could have one of these fitted at a bit of extra expense, to improve security. Should the Big Bad Wolf approach her house, the alarm would sound and would summon help. Chipolata realised that this solution would leave her with enough money to enjoy her desired lifestyle. She bought.

Ham was rather less worldly than his sister and was interested in living in an environmentally responsible way, as far as possible. He did not like the Straw houses because the straw had to be imported from less developed countries where there were sweatshop conditions for the straw gatherers. They also required fire-proofing with some very polluting chemicals that were rumoured to cause cancers. He could buy a brick house, but these cost more money than he had available, so he would have to borrow money, which he did not like doing. He finally settled on a new technology Wood house, though it would take all of his inheritance to buy it. He was a bit concerned about how wolf-proof the house might be, but they were made from a plentiful supply of local sustainable forest, and there were no dodgy chemicals involved. However, he was finally persuaded by the fact that, although untried in practice, tests had shown the houses to be highly wolf-resistant and, moreover, the builder was offering a no-quibble guarantee of 'wolf-proofness'. He bought.

Bacon was highly risk-averse where wolves were concerned. The only type of house that he would even consider was a brick one, since these were definitely totally wolf-proof. However, they cost more money than he had, so he would need a mortgage. But he had a good job, so he was not worried about that. He bought his Brick house.

All went along pretty well for a while, though some unforeseen problems did arise. One was that Chipolata's alarm tended to malfunction and to go off at random, with the effect that everyone began to ignore it – a very clear case of 'crying wolf'! There had still been no reliable empirical examples of Ham's style of house successfully resisting a wolf attack. As for Bacon, mortgage interest rates had been rising steadily, and he had a variable rate mortgage. However, each managed to reassure themselves that they had made the right decision, on the evidence so far.

One day the Big Bad Wolf turned up. He headed for Chipolata's house. The alarm went off but the Wolf ignored it – as did everyone else. He quickly blew the house down and ate Chipolata, with the alarm still sounding.

Ham and Bacon, while obviously grief-stricken at the loss of their sister, were nonetheless very glad that they had not gone for Straw, but had chosen better. They were both a bit smug that their modelling of the situation had resulted in more wolf-resistant homes than were offered by Straw. Things became quiet for a while but, inevitably, one day the Big Bad Wolf returned, this time to Ham's guaranteed wolf-proof house. It was certainly much harder to blow down but, with a bit of extra effort, he managed it, and ate Ham. Undoubtedly, had Ham survived, he could have claimed on his no-quibble guarantee, but, unfortunately, he did not.

Another period of quiet followed but, eventually, the Big Bad Wolf came back, to Bacon's house. This time he found that he could not blow the house down, no matter how hard he tried, though he was very persistent in his efforts, being hungry. So Bacon was safe in his house. The problem was that, with the Big Bad Wolf keeping the house under virtual siege, he could not leave the house to go to work to earn the money he needed to pay the mortgage. What with interest rates rising as they were, he rather quickly accumulated an enormous debt, and was defaulting on his mortgage payments. One day a letter arrived from Piggy Bank plc, telling him that the bank was seeking to repossess his house. Outside the Big Bad Wolf waited.

- Each sibling worked out a rational and efficient solution to the problem as they saw it. How might it be explained that, having gone through the same analytic process, they came to different conclusions?

- How did time influence the perception of the criteria of efficiency? Can efficiency be understood and evaluated other than with hindsight?

- The siblings opted to act independently rather than cooperatively because of their sibling rivalries, trading off increased security against some other sets of objectives. How did each compute the opportunity costs of their chosen course of action?

- Is it generally the case that personal and psychological preferences are likely to be more important than other kinds of information in justifying claims to efficient action? If that were to be the case, what would be the implications for evaluating such claims?

(Other chapters that would be useful and relevant in analysing the case *include* Structure (3), Knowledge (4), Rationality (6), Boundary (9) and Decision-making (11).)

Bibliography

Given its centrality to our notions of management and organisation, it is surprising how infrequently the issue of efficiency is directly addressed in books on these topics. Specifically in conventional Organisational Behaviour texts, it has been common to take an implicitly narrowly bounded and inwardly oriented view, by linking efficiency and effectiveness in terms of an individual organisation's goals – implying that efficiency is either obvious, or subsumed by effectiveness. For examples, see Boddy and Paton (1998), or Mullins (2005). For the same approach in a different field – management services – see, for example, Thorpe and Horsburgh (1991). This lack of direct attention to the meaning of efficiency creates certain problems. Thompson and McHugh (2001) talk about the taken-for-grantedness of what efficiency means. See also Jacques (1996). In a landmark study Baldamus (1961) makes the same point, emphasising the importance of asking the question 'what *is* efficiency?' – and, although the influential Simon (1976) devotes a whole chapter to efficiency, Baldamus notes (referring to the first edition of Simon's work in 1946) that, while efficiency is central to Simon's arguments, the concept is not defined by him either adequately or rigorously. To find that kind of discussion it is necessary to turn to more critical texts in the field of management and organisational behaviour, or to sources outside the field.

For example, in Labour Process Theory, Braverman (1974), Thompson and McHugh (2001) and Alvesson and Willmott (1996) represent a significant focus in the approach, over time, on the meaning and consequences of efficiency in organisational practice, especially through the critique of Taylorism, seen as the very epitome of the prioritisation of corporate efficiency. Efficiency is also a more common theme in approaches that focus generally on the labour process and employment relations – Baldamus (1961) is a prominent example here. Weber's work is widely seen as providing the underlying rationale for contemporary common-sense notions of organisational efficiency, but this interpretation of Weber, depending on an isomorphism between rationality and efficiency, has been contested – see, for example, Clegg and Dunkerley (1980), Clegg (1994). Ritzer (1993) sees such versions of efficiency, typified in the form of 'the one best way', as deeply implicated in what he calls 'the McDonaldization' of society, the characterisitics of which are prioritisation of efficiency, calculability, predictability and non-human technologies, resulting in the 'irrationality of rationality'. See also Bryman (2004) on Disneyization. Ritzer (1998) extends his analysis more generally, and includes the argument that theory too is susceptible to McDonaldization. See also Ritzer (2006). Marsden and Townley (1996) see efficiency and dehumanisation as the mutually defining characteristics of modernity. An interesting reflection on the systemic effects of the pursuit of organisational efficiency is in Bauman (2005, especially Chapter 4).

These references signify a connection between the negative effects of prioritising conventional notions of efficiency and the dominance of the metaphor of the machine in models of organisation. Marcuse (1986) is relevant here. Also relevant is his concept of the performance principle (Marcuse 1987), and the concept of performativity in Lyotard (1984). Rabinbach's (1990) study of the history of development of 'efficiency of effort' in work processes points to a conflation of 'economic efficiency' and 'technological efficiency' which has severe consequences for members of organisations. Gorz (1989) reflects a broader appreciation of these consequences. MacIntyre (1985) is also pertinent, with his focus on the absence of a knowledge base from which to claim efficiency.

However, it is very rare, in anything that actually focuses on efficiency, whether positively or negatively, to find claims that suggest that efficiency is easily calculated, or easily defined. It is, therefore, all the more remarkable that efficiency has such a taken-for-granted status in much of the literature which uses it as an underlying rationale for organisational practice. One of the major criticisms of these approaches is that they leave unexamined what factors ought to be included in the operant model of efficiency. A big factor here is where the boundary is located. Approaches that include, for example, ecological factors, or social factors, or even system viability factors, obviously imply extensive boundaries. There are various approaches that base their considerations on such extensive boundaries. Wallerstein's (for example, 1984) World Systems Theory provides a macro-level model of organisation which has huge implications for understanding efficiency. The previously cited increase in books on organisational strategy that focus on environmental management symbolise nascent redefinitions of what should be included in models of efficiency – see, for example, Wever (1996), Jones and Hollier (1997), Hutchinson and Hutchinson (1997). The issue of the efficient use of all resources, especially natural resources, is a strongly implied focus of all ecosystemic approaches. Capra (1983), for example, is explicit about this. Von Weizsäcker, Lovins and Lovins (1997) is also very specifically about ecological efficiency. See also Love and Love (1970). Fineman (1998) offers some interesting reflections on contemporary practice in the development of 'green capitalism'.

The ability to put numbers on things is very seductive, but numbers are not as unequivocal as they may seem, themselves part of a symbolic language – see, for example, Hofstadter (1980), Jones (1983), Rotman (1987). The measurement of attitudes is a highly developed art but, again, fraught with difficulties. Most books on research methods will contain techniques for doing this – for example, Frankfort-Nachmias and Nachmias (1992) – but the problems with such approaches are not unacknowledged – see, for example, Bryman (1989).

The issue of value is central to economic theory. For a discussion of the ontological status of money, see Baggott (2005). The problem of equating money and value and/or money and wealth is addressed by various approaches. One, though not the only, classic source on the nature of value is Marx – see, for example, Marx (1976), Bottomore (1991). Cole, Cameron and Edwards (1991) present a model of economic theories somewhat reminiscent of the paradigm approach outlined in Chapter 4, focusing on three different approaches to understanding value. Polanyi (1971) is useful on the symbolic nature of money. Guillet de Monthoux (1993) gives a historical and conceptual overview of the economic theories which underlie, and have informed, management theory and practice. Also relevant, and making the point that efficiencies do not necessarily aggregate from individual businesses to society as a whole, is Amey (1969).

The recycling of theories and techniques for managing organisational behaviour in the conventional discourse has been noted by various authors. Legge (1989) and Noon (1992), for example, note the conceptual relationship of Human Resource Management to Organisation Development.

The argument that the potential for freedom from scarcity exists is represented in a number of different traditions, often recognised as a problem of distribution rather than one of production – in other words, an issue of organisation. Drucker (1977), for example, implies that we can manage our way out of scarcity. Others, such as Marcuse (1986, 1987), take a more critical view of management's role in sustaining scarcity. For a brief discussion, see Carter and Jackson (1987).

Some of the sources of opposition to conventional common-sense notions of efficiency have already been cited in this bibliography. Dissent from the inevitability of the over-arching role of 'The Market' is equally widespread in terms of approach and discipline. For a range of views see Polanyi (1971), Harvey (1989), Jameson (1991), Heelas and Morris (1992), Beck (1992), Hutton (1995, 1997).

The general approach of the chapter, in terms of its underlying theory, builds very much on previous chapters – all previous bibliographies are, therefore, relevant. Given the general absence of specific reference to the concept of efficiency in texts on organisational behaviour, it is necessary to scrutinise them, analytically and critically, to discern their attitude and approach to it.

CHAPTER 11

Decision-making

This chapter focuses on decision-making as a ubiquitous activity in organisations, taking the view that organisational behaviour cannot be understood independently of the myriad decisions that inform it. Consideration is given to the possibility that decisions may tend towards objectivity and rationality – that is, be 'virtually rational' or 'as if rational' – and to the conventional distinction between what is taken to be rational for managers and what is taken to be rational for the managed. The process of decision-making is characterised in terms of the semiotics of self and emphasis is placed on the role of unconscious desires, psychological characteristics and perceptions of self. Decision-making is then examined in the context of each of the concepts developed in the preceding chapters. The elements of risk and moral judgement in decision-making are then highlighted. Given that objectively rational decision-making is not possible, the alternative is not necessarily unregenerate and random subjectivity, however, and it is suggested that, instead, decision-making can, and should, be construed as a process informed by meta-level objectives, themselves informed by understandings of the social, political and economic role of organisations. This issue is addressed through the concept of praxis. Such an approach implies the need to re-examine what the goals of organisations might be, in light of the impacts of organisational activity. Organisational activity is, of course, the product of organisational behaviour, hence the imperative need to understand organisational behaviour before such a process can even begin.

Organisation is the ongoing process of decision-making. Organisation requires a process of management and the process of management implies decision-making. Decision-making is what makes the process of organisation dynamic; it is the generic cause of all organisational activity, of whether an organisation is a good or a bad one, successful or unsuccessful, efficient or inefficient. The very task of management is to make decisions. However, *much more than this*, it must be said that everyone in an organisation, all the time, makes decisions. Any decision that involves people must be of interest to the field of organisational behaviour – and all decisions affect people, and are made by people. In other words, decision-making is utterly central to the study of organisational behaviour.

Given this significance of decision-making to all aspects of, and all perspectives on, organisational behaviour, it is obviously important that there is an appropriate understanding of what the decision-making process is and how it works. Everything that we have looked at so far contributes to a way of understanding decision-making and its process. However, this understanding is considerably different from more conventional approaches to decision-making, and has very different implications. Indeed, this difference even extends to the contention that decision-making is relevant to the whole of organisational behaviour and to the whole of organisation, since it is more common to see decision-making as having a role in, as being part of, organisational behaviour and organisation, but not the whole.

Decision-making is, ultimately, about choice. Everybody knows that decisions have consequences – that is, indeed, precisely their purpose – but the interesting questions about decision-making are, for example: Why does someone choose one option rather than another? What factors influence that choice? What factors influence the process of choosing? What consequences are hoped for, and why? It is these issues that this chapter seeks to address.

Decision-making as a rational, objective function

It is generally assumed that what constitutes a good decision is, not its consequence, but its basis in rational thought and objective information. Within the discourse of Organisational Behaviour there is a huge range of approaches to the achievement of this ideal. At one end of the range are approaches based on the firm belief in objectivity, while, at the other end, they are based on recognition that it may not be possible to make rational, objective decisions at all, for a variety of reasons. These reasons focus, in particular, on the recognition that information itself can be problematic, either in terms of limits to the ability to process information, or in terms of access to relevant information, or in terms of generalised uncertainty and the unknown, or in terms of acknowledgement that some factors do not lend themselves to measurement – though, as noted in Chapter 10, it is often attempted to resolve this latter difficulty by resort to quasi-quantification.

However, even where it is recognised that it may not be possible to make fully rational decisions, it remains a precept – a requirement – that decision-makers should get as close as they are able to rationality, by whatever means. One such means might be a generalised quantification process, another might be to eliminate, as far as possible, human intervention by, for example, applying statistical techniques or focusing on computation through technology. In other words, even where it is recognised that there are factors, especially human factors, that militate against the achievement of rationality and objectivity in decision-making, it is assumed that, on one hand, such factors can be minimised, or guarded against, or overcome, to the extent that decisions can be treated as **virtually rational**, or on the other hand, that such factors, perhaps because they are ubiquitous in all decision-making processes, can be effectively ignored, and the decisions treated **as if rational**.

Objectively rational decision-making for managers

For managers there are myriad techniques available to help them make 'virtually' or 'as if' rational decisions, such as Scientific Management, Discounted Cash Flow calculations, Business Process Re-Engineering, and so on. Much discursive activity is directed, specifically, towards furnishing such techniques to enhance the rational objectivity of decision-making. From this point of view, for all practical purposes, when managers make full and competent use of such techniques as are available, they are behaving as rationally as possible. On the other hand, workers are deemed to be acting as rationally as possible when they act in accordance with managers' wishes. This is not because they are to be subjugated, but because it is assumed that such obedience is in their best interests, since managers make decisions which are as rational and objective as possible. The significance of claims that everyone in an organisation pursues the same objective and that they co-exist in harmonious consensus is precisely that, if this is the case, it follows that there can be only one rational decision, that everyone will recognise this and that everyone will be pleased to obey its requirements.

One of the principal difficulties with this general approach to decision-making can be illustrated by looking at known failures of putatively rational decisions. Famous examples of such failures include the decision to sail the RMS *Titanic* at speed and in darkness into a known ice field; the decision to launch the *Challenger* Shuttle in temperatures low enough to affect the integrity of the rocket motors; the decision to set sail in the roll-on–roll-off ferry, *The Herald of Free Enterprise*, without the crew knowing that the bow doors had not been shut. It must be assumed that none of the managers involved in these decisions intended the subsequent failure, and that they made their decisions rationally, on the best information available. But in all these cases alternative decisions, based on the same information, were available but not taken. Thus, for example, in the case of the *Titanic*, other ships in the vicinity had stopped for the night so as to minimise the risk of hitting an iceberg; in the case of the *Challenger*, the leading expert on the component that failed, the O ring seals, had offered scientific data which predicted the failure; in the case of *The Herald of Free Enterprise*, requests for a signalling system to show the state of the bow doors, in recognition of the risk of sailing with them open, had been rejected. Common to all these cases is a known alternative decision forgone in favour of the decision actually made, presumably seen as the 'better' decision, and supposedly rational and objective. It has been suggested that the managers who made the decisions in these cases were simply mistaken, or made misjudgements, or misinterpreted the information available. But, if that is the case, then, on one hand, the decisions were not rational or objective and, on the other hand, this is equally likely in any decision situation.

Not all decisions have such dramatic and traumatic consequences but this does not mean that other decisions are less significant in their context, or that they will be more, or less, rational. Of course, it may be that the decisions cited above were potentially rational in the service of some particular interest, but that would be to say that they were not *objectively rational*, but *subjectively rational*. In any case, it could be suggested that the decisions were not in any sense rational, whether objectively or subjectively, but just wrong, because they resulted in failure. It is interesting to note that, in practice, decisions are judged to be rational or not with hindsight, but, as was pointed out in Chapter 6, rationality is future-oriented. Attribution of rationality with hindsight is not *rationality* but *rationalisation*.

Objectively rational decision-making for the managed

The matter of perceived interest is particularly relevant to the case of the managed, where workers are expected, routinely, to make decisions against their own (subjectively defined) interest, in favour of 'organisational interest', as (apparently, objectively) defined by managers. In other circumstances, people are generally thought to be acting rationally if they make decisions in line with their own interest, but in the context of work organisations this is not the case. Thus, for example, workers who resist attempts to increase efficiency which lead to fewer jobs are held to be acting irrationally. Consider the case of an operator of a widget-making machine, working in a department with poor industrial relations, under a supervisor who is particularly disliked because of autocratic behaviour: a new order for widgets requires recalibration of the machinery, a job performed by the supervisor; the operator notices that the supervisor has made an error in calculating the calibration, so that the widgets being produced are the wrong size, but keeps on churning them out all day knowing that they will be nothing but scrap. Is this rational or irrational? From a management point of view, the operator's decision to say nothing about the observed error and to keep on producing useless widgets would be seen as irrational because of its detrimental effect on the organisation – delays in filling the order, wastage of material, wages paid for no useful output, and so on. From the operator's point of view, keeping quiet may be a very rational decision – there may be a pleasure at seeing a disliked supervisor discomfited or, as is not unusual in work organisations, it may be seen as unwise to tell a person in authority that they have made a mistake. Neither of these possibilities would occur in an objectively rational organisation, but they do occur, as a matter of routine, in actual organisations.

Predictability, significance and preference

We have been using examples of major, or at least significant, decisions, even if such significance is retrospectively attributed in terms of the outcome – it is what happened next that makes it important rather than its significance being known at the time the decision was made. **But each significant decision is itself the product of infinite numbers of prior, and often seemingly minor, decisions.** Some might be clearly related to the problem under consideration, but, equally, many will not have clear relevance. Indeed, it is impossible to know at the time what the consequences or outcomes of such minor decisions as what you wear on a particular day, which street you walk down, what time you go to bed on a particular night, and so on, may be, or how they may relate to present problems. If you try to trace back as far as you can the decisions that led to you being in some present situation, you very quickly come to decisions you made which are, and which seemed at the time to be, utterly trivial, yet have made some very significant contribution to where you are now. Yet it could be argued that, for the major decision to be rational, it is also necessary for all these minor decisions to be rational. On reflection, this seems, simply, inconceivable.

It is often the case that it is not possible to know in advance whether a decision is significant or not, let alone what its outcome will be. For example, if you want to go to university to do an undergraduate degree, you will need to decide what you want to study and where you want to study it, though not necessarily in that order. You also need to decide which places are likely to accept you and which are unlikely to do so. There will be available a seeming mass of information, although, in practice, it will be highly attenuated. You need some decision criteria – and these are bound to be subjective, because they are concerned with your preferences. If you decide to study management or its related subjects, for example, there will be several hundred courses at over a hundred institutions in about sixty geographical locations, in the UK alone, which you, by making decisions, need to reduce, ultimately, to one or two. **However objective you try to be, that objectivity will be underwritten by your preferences**, which may derive from decisions you made, as a result of your experiences, at a very young age, when you could not possibly know what their significance might be in the future. You may have to decide between a reputedly good course at a first-rate institution in a dull or relatively isolated location and a lesser course at a lesser institution in a town famous for its night-life – you need to make this decision, although the factors that you are deciding between are not commensurable. There is no guarantee that taking the worthy (rational?) decision will bring about the best outcome in terms of your objectives. You cannot possibly know in advance whether you are making the 'best' decision, especially since you will never know what would have happened if you had made a different decision. The final irony is that whether you make a good decision or not may well be dependent on the aggregation of decisions made by other people – for example, your university experience will be profoundly affected by your peer group, who went through the same chancy process that you did.

Yet this is precisely what all decision-making, in any situation, is like. Some things may be more predictable, some decision criteria may be more easily specifiable, in some situations. Nonetheless, in principle and in practice, this is how we make decisions.

As these examples show, the factors that militate against rationality and objectivity in decision-making are so ubiquitous and so potent that they cannot be overcome, guarded against, ignored, swept aside. So to suggest that decisions can be '*virtually rational*' or '*as if rational*' is just inadequate and inappropriate when considering the way decisions are made in practice. It tells us nothing significant and, in the process, denies and masks those factors that have the greatest influence on decisions, that are most important to decision-makers and so require the fullest attention, by treating them as irrelevant because they do not fall into the category of rational and objective. Even if rationality and objectivity are to be judged (decided to be) ideal qualities, they are unachievable. It could be suggested, therefore, that the whole issue of objectivity and rationality in decision-making, or as a quality of decisions, is a red herring, irrelevant in the face of trying to understand how decisions are made, or even how to make decisions. For these purposes, what is needed is a thorough appreciation, not of *ideal*, but of *actual* conditions, not of what *ought to be* significant, but of what *is* significant in this process.

What if . . .?

Central to Modernism is the quest for, and the perceived necessity of, objective decision-making, whether in Science or in Management. It is the claimed objective quality of such decision-making that gives it legitimacy.

One often used excuse for relegating women to subordinate roles has been based on the argument that they exhibit a regrettable, though perfectly understandable, inability to make good – that is, objective – decisions *all* the time, because of their hormonal cycle. Therefore, it's obviously much better to leave the big decisions to men, who are untroubled by such natural weaknesses and imperfections.

However, some recently reported research, which will no doubt come as a great shock to all, shows that men's decision-making ability is affected by what are called 'sexual cues' – the opposite sex! It is, apparently, all to do with testosterone levels. Male decision-makers exposed to sexual cues are, apparently, more likely to accept 'unfair play', more likely to make risky decisions.

Perhaps, after all, we are all ruled by our hormones! What, then, will be the fate of objective decision-making?

Decision-making as the semiotics of self

In setting out to develop a different approach to thinking about decision-making and its processes, it is worth emphasising, first and foremost, that **decision-making is a universal activity.** For the sake of convenience we have often distinguished between 'managers' and 'workers', but this is a rather arbitrary distinction, especially in the context of decision-making. Workers are undoubtedly involved in the process of management and, to a large extent, managers are workers, in so far as they are, generally, employees. Certainly, managers usually have higher status and more formal authority than those denoted as workers, yet management is only a particular type of skilled work. Such distinctions are not very relevant in the context of decision-making, even though the decisions in question may be of a substantively different kind.

Decision-making is the process of choosing one option rather than others and, as such, is a ubiquitous process. Everybody makes decisions all the time, and **the nuts and bolts of that process are precisely the same in all cases** – though this is *not* to say that everyone will make the same decision under the same circumstances. However, it *is* to say that the decision-making process involved in, say, choosing to implement an appraisal scheme is just the same as the decision-making process involved in, say, choosing to have a cup of coffee or a cup of tea in the morning break, or choosing to write in pencil or in ballpoint. There is a general tendency in the literature on organisation and management, and that on organisational behaviour, to portray managers as people who make special kinds of decision in special ways, from the moment they arrive at work to the moment they leave it, and even, perhaps, beyond. Yet managers make decisions in the same way that everyone else does, and, often, the same *kind* of decision as everyone else does. To be sure, managers make decisions in a particular context – that of delivering an adequate performance from that which they manage – but, given the degree of uncertainty in any decision-making situation, they are as influenced by subjective factors and by personal predispositions as anyone else is. Managers do not shed their human-ness on entering an organisation, any more than any other employee does. They are likely to take as much care over where they have lunch as over appointing someone to a job. This is, simply, to be human.

The ways in which people approach decision-making can be seen as a product of **the semiotics of self**. Motivation to act, to decide to do a particular thing, is usually understood in the discourse of Organisational Behaviour by reference to the ensuing behaviour, but we have already suggested, especially in Chapter 8, that this is not a reliable way of understanding the process. **Decisions are better understood as manifestations of unconscious desires which function semiotically**. Because of what we know about semiotics, this cannot be taken to mean that such desires are constant, replicable or applicable to anyone else – and this variability is why, in the *same* situation, *different* people make *different* decisions.

Whatever such desires may be desires for, they will be superordinately significant in the way people approach decisions. **The unconscious desires that people have may not be obviously related to any aspect of the organisational or the management process, but they not only affect it, they constitute it**. For example, sexual desire is not considered, conventionally, to be directly relevant to the pursuit of management or organisational objectives – it is not an authorised aspect of them. But it is common knowledge that sexuality and sexual desire have important impacts on what takes place in organisations, such as, at the obvious level, people using their sexuality to gain advancement, or people with decision-making power using their influence to gain sexual favours.

People may be relatively more aware of **psychological characteristics** they have which are expressed in preferences which inform their approach to decision-making. For example, someone may have a desire for order and an abhorrence of disorder, and thus a desire for neatness, say, might influence attitudes to people who are less neat. Someone may find highly risky situations exciting, while someone else may be highly risk averse, which might lead them to find making decisions a stressful and difficult activity – though, of course, even a decision not to act is still a decision. These psychological attributes derive from personality, experience, culture, education, and so on, and may be developed at an early age, long before their relevance to a particular decision-making capacity could be known, and they are inaccessible to being changed once it *is* known. **Such attributes are not at all possible to set aside, or to parenthesise, while involved in a management process – they wholly inform it, and are an integral part of the decision-maker, whether they will it or not**. This is why not all those who manage are good at management.

More consciously involved in the decision-making process will be the **perceptions of self** held by any decision-maker. How a person desires to be seen by others, together with what they believe themselves to be like, can have a major impact, not only on how they approach the process of decision-making, but also on what decisions they are capable of making. Most decision-makers, for example, wish to be perceived by others as being competent at whatever they do, even if only for reasons of security, whether they are, in practice, competent or not, or seen to be competent or not. The desire to be so seen and the perception of what constitutes competence will influence how and what decisions are made. A person may desire to be liked by others and believe themselves to be likeable, whether or not this is the view of others, and this, too, will influence decision-making. A person may wish their superior to see them as, say, a democratically inclined, 'people-oriented' person, but their subordinates to see them as authoritative and not to be questioned. A person may wish to be seen as competent and as likeable, and these two desires may easily conflict in decision-making situations.

Indeed, any desires a person may have may be in conflict with other desires they have. The process of making decisions will be influenced profoundly by the need and the ability to juggle such conflicts so that they do not threaten the psychological stability of the sense of self – and such juggling may well be wholly absorbing of effort. In any case, **unconscious desires, psychological predispositions and the sense of self will be far more important and influential than any particular situation or conditions which accompany any particular decision**. Not rationality, not objectivity, but *these* are the elements that provide a basis for understanding the process of decision-making.

Semiotics and decision-making

Decisions are always made as a result of a semiotic interpretation of the decision situation. **All that is available to the decision-maker, all knowledge of perceived relevant factors, is present as signifiers**. As we know, signifiers have no particular signifieds attached to them; signifieds are specified (decided upon) by the individual interpreter. It is also the case that different people attach different signifieds to any particular signifier – this, of course, is another reason why different people make different decisions in the same situation. There is an enormous range of factors that predispose a person to a particular interpretation of a signifier and each interpretation of those factors is unique to each decision-maker. This, obviously, precludes any possibility of any decision being objectively rational, or even quasi-objectively rational, and, thus, highlights the irrelevance of emphasising this as a desirable quality of decisions. It does not, however, preclude contextually derived, intersubjective agreements about signifiers. Thus, for example, two accountants might agree that a particular balance sheet indicates a particular condition of a company, and even might agree what course of action should be followed. This intersubjective agreement, however, can only be partial, both in derivation and in prescription. What is more significant, and, possibly, more likely, is that two accountants might view the same balance sheet data and conclude completely different interpretations and prescriptions.

All decision-making is based on an interpretation of signifiers, on what they mean and which ones are relevant. There is no unmediated access to information. Decisions, therefore, are based on wholly subjective interpretations, influenced by all the factors that predispose people to particular significations and which may or may not be relevant to the decision itself, and to the decision-making process. The success of a decision depends on the ability of the decision-maker to enforce their interpretation of the signifiers.

Structure and decision-making

Decisions are rarely made about, or informed by, or contextualised within, single factors. Even a relatively simple decision will embody multiple factors and it is the configuration of these factors that indicates what sort of decision should be made. However, **this configuration – this structure – is not inherent in the factors, but is imposed on them by the deciding subject**. Take, for example, the apparently very simple decision about whether to choose tea or coffee to drink on a particular occasion. You will be influenced by a relative preference for one or the other, by a relative preference for the kind of one or the other that is on offer (for instance, decaffeinated or caffeinated coffee, leaf tea or tea bags), by availability of milk and sugar, and what sort, by the time of day, by medical opinion on the advisability of drinking tea or coffee, by location – the list is endless, and may also include the weather, the time of year, who your company is, and so on. Anything can affect this decision. How the factors are ordered, ranked, configured, structured is an entirely personal matter but, clearly, profoundly influences the decision. If such a simple event is so complex, how much more complex must be day-to-day organisational decisions. Again, the inherent variety in structuring information is yet another reason why different decisions are made by different people in the same situation, with the same information.

Knowledge and decision-making

When making decisions some appreciation of appropriate information is usual. However, this is not an impartial review of absolute facts, but a very partial review of subjectively interpreted signifiers. Not only are the signifiers subjectively interpreted, but they are also, inevitably, signifiers which are discursively approved as appropriate. **A decision-maker will take cognisance of what is approved by the relevant discourse not only in the decision situation, but also about how decisions should be made**. However, information which is not discursively approved may also be a factor. On one hand, there will be non-discursively approved information which may be relevant and available but which will not be considered, or which is relevant but simply not available, precisely because it is not approved as relevant by the discourse. On the other hand, there will be non-discursively approved factors or information which the decision-maker is aware of, knows are not approved by the discourse but which, nevertheless, influence the decision. Suppose, for example, that a decision-maker needs to make someone redundant and has two possible candidates, one not very able but popular, the other competent but unpopular. Popularity is not a discursively approved factor for this decision, while competence is. Nonetheless, it is quite possible that popularity may be a decisive factor.

Of course, given awareness of what is considered to be appropriate by the relevant discourse, decision-makers will seek to present the decision as commensurate with such appropriateness. This usually involves glossing the decision as rational – in effect, it is rational-ised. The desire to portray 'proper' decision-making processes as rational and objective is, effectively, a mask of respectability for what is, inevitably, a partial, subjective, value-laden activity.

Fares' fair

In August 1999 there was a total eclipse of the sun. In the UK the total eclipse was only visible in Cornwall. A press report in April 1999 publicised the decision of the railway company serving Cornwall to double its normal fare from London in the days prior to the eclipse, because of expected demand on its services ('Double rail fare to see eclipse', Keith Harper, *Guardian* 3.4.99). The railway company said that its decision was intended to 'dampen demand' so that passengers would not have to suffer over-crowding.

People travelling to see the eclipse are doing so for pleasure, and it might be argued that they should pay a market price for it. However, the railways are a public service and also carry passengers who travel for reasons other than pleasure, even when there is a solar eclipse – people might need to travel to Cornwall for any number of reasons, such as for business purposes, for an interview, because of a bereavement. Is it reasonable to require these people to pay double the usual fare in order to go about their normal business, because other people wish to view the solar eclipse?

■ What would be a reasonable decision in these circumstances, for any of the parties involved in the situation?

Power and decision-making

The power to make a decision is the power to determine what the signifiers are and what they mean, to determine what factors are relevant and how they are structurally related, to determine what constitutes knowledge, and so on. **Power is the ability to select (decide on) courses of action that reflect one's own desires and preferences.** It is the ability to declare that one's preferences and one's decisions are objective and rational, the one best way. But power is nothing to do with the *quality* of decision-making – being powerful does not mean that you make better decisions than those who are, comparatively, powerless. Power arises from the ability to ensure compliance, whatever the means of doing so. If you can get people to accept your interpretation of the situation and that your decision is the correct one, then you have power – it does not mean that others genuinely share your point of view, only that you possess the sanctions to make them comply with your point of view. **The ability to make decisions and to enforce them is the very signifier of power**, at whatever level it is considered, from micro-power to formal power. Equally, power does not have to justify or rationalise its decisions, unless challenged by a greater power: power is always its own justification for making decisions. The more power, the less need to present one's decisions as reasonable. All decisions, ultimately, are defined, positively or negatively, by power.

Rationality and decision-making

Extensive reference has already been made to the issue of rationality in decision-making, and there is no need to recapitulate this. Suffice it to say that, **in the context of people managing people, of organisational behaviour, there can be no**

such thing as objectively rational decision-making. All decisions reflect subjective preferences within the constraints of power, context and interest.

Ideology and decision-making

Even though each decision-maker's approach to the process of decision-making is based on unique perceptions and interpretations of the signifiers, this does not mean that each decision event is likely to be completely random. **A person's ideology will predispose them towards one type of decision outcome rather than another.** Furthermore, because certain formal ideologies are more or less congruent with certain interests and because there is a tendency for certain ideologies to coalesce, a degree of coherence may well inform decisions of a particular type. Ideology acts as a primary coarse filter on possibilities, to the extent that, in a given decision-making situation, some possibilities will never be considered because they are seen as being 'ideologically unsound'. Although over-simplifying the case, it could be suggested, for example, that managers, employed by owners to further the latters' interests through the management of labour, have sought, traditionally, to weaken the power, or perceived power, of trades unions, especially where trades unions are seen to reflect an ideology antithetical to that of the primacy of owners' interests. Therefore, decisions that appear to strengthen the position, or the power, of trades unions will tend not to be considered (although it must be said that decision-makers in management are not always very good at predicting what effect their decisions will have). The similarities in decisions which are observable across all kinds of capitalist organisation can be said to have much more to do with ideologically informed preferences than with agreement among managers on what constitutes an objective and rational decision, even though this apparent congruence gives them the appearance of, and is claimed to represent, a universal rationality to which this group has some special access.

Even so, while ideology may provide an early coarse selection of what is acceptable, there is still ample scope for the subjective evaluation of those options that *are* seen as ideologically appropriate, or 'sound'. Of course, what is ideologically unsound is not only defined by adherence to formal ideologies, but is also just as relevant in the context of what we called, in Chapter 7, personal ideologies, the general aggregation of ideas, beliefs, values, attitudes, and so on, which constitute one's 'world view'.

Self and decision-making

The involvement of the self in the decision-making process has already been addressed to some extent, earlier in this chapter, and those points do not need restating here. However, it is worth emphasising again that the perspective that sees people as units who work, as people whose life at work is somehow separable from the rest of their lives, whether they are, notionally, managers or workers, and who, therefore, make decisions at work in organisations which are uncontaminated by that life 'outside' work and are only interested in organisational benefit, is not a tenable one. In light of the approach being developed here, **it is clear that** this life 'outside' the organisation may very well predominate over all other considerations in the decision-maker's approach to making decisions. It is important to go further than simply positing a complex self who works, to point out that it follows from this that these selves have interests which they will seek, at least, to protect and, hopefully, to advance. Self interest clearly affects choices when it comes to making decisions.

That's interesting!

Morgan (1997: 162) suggests that there are three domains of interest which inform our actions – in other words, we make decisions based on these interests. The interests are the job we are paid to do, our career aspirations and our out-of-work interests. Morgan represents these as three inter-locking sets.

Source: From Morgan (1997) *Images of Organization*, Second Edition, London: Sage Publications Ltd.

The area where these interests coincide may be quite small. This means that decisions we make at work may, in practice, have little to do with work – we may decide a question on the basis of how it may best serve our career, or how it may best facilitate pursuit of our out-of-work interests.

Suppose, for example, that you have to arrange a meeting with colleagues and/or subordinates, but at the most suitable time for this meeting – that is, the most efficient time for it – you need to take your child to the dentist. The most likely decision is that you will arrange the meeting for a less suitable time, so that you can further your family interest.

Or, suppose, for example, that you spot an opportunity for promotion which requires an immediate written application. However, the only time available is time you have allocated to signing off your subordinates' expenses claims so that they can meet the deadline for the payroll run. Do you write your application and leave the expenses forms until after the payroll deadline so that your subordinates get paid their expenses a week, or a month, late? Or do you deal with the expenses forms and forgo the opportunity to apply for promotion?

Boundary and decision-making

Boundary location and the construction of models of the world which is being decided on are highly significant and primary mechanisms of dividing information which establish for the decision-maker what shall be included as relevant, excluded as irrelevant – and, once such boundaries and models are constructed in the mind, they are *treated as real*. The process of bounding is not necessarily a conscious one; people do not necessarily deliberately exclude factors that may be relevant. It is, often, a process which is informed and preformed by ideology, culture, values, attitudes, experience, and which simply 'slots into place' in what are seen as appropriate circumstances. However, **bounding is a process that prefigures all decision-making**.

Decisions about where the boundary lies, about what is relevant and what can be discounted, have as their purpose the specification of limits on the consequences of the decisions to be made, not in terms of their effect, but in terms of what is to be seen as the area of responsibility or influence of the decision-maker. Thus, for example, managers may be well aware that their activities are, for instance, polluting the environment but, because these effects are considered to be outside the relevant organisational boundary as defined by the operant model of the organisation, they can be ignored. This is not because there is no effect, or because the effect is wilfully denied, but because it has been declared to be external to the organisational boundary. Such pollution can be declared to be 'not their problem', even though it is known and recognised that it is being caused by their activities. It has already been pointed out, in Chapter 9, how potentially dangerous this approach to decision-making is, because it does not deal with actual consequences of decisions but with arbitrarily declared limits on responsibility. If such problems of actual consequences are to be avoided, it is necessary that issues of boundary location, and its process, are addressed, so that properly informed decision-making can become a possibility.

Efficiency and decision-making

Conventionally, the ultimate justification for all managerial decisions is their potential contribution to increased efficiency, a generally undemonstrable but extremely culturally powerful justification. But, precisely because claims for the efficient consequences of decision-making can rarely be demonstrated unequivocally, it should also be accepted that it is possible that supposedly efficient decisions in practice may well make things less efficient. For the efficient consequences of decisions to be demonstrable unequivocally would require, minimally, something analogous to a controlled experiment through which the consequences of the decision could be compared with a case where the decision had not been implemented – such a situation does not obtain in organisational decision-making in the usual course of events. **If the linking of decision-making and efficiency is disengaged, it becomes clear that the commitment to the efficient outcome of decisions requires an act of faith on the part of those involved in these decisions.** Given other, often negative, consequences of such decisions, this act of faith on the part of those affected by them seems a lot to expect. Indeed, the requirement for such a commitment might be seen, instead, as little more than a technique for exacting compliance under all circumstances and irrespective of impact, because of the claimed, and apparently unassailable, justification in terms of efficiency. That it amounts to no more than an act of faith makes management more akin to a religion than to a science.

The parenthesising, or even removal, of the fundamentally arbitrarily defined and insubstantial justification of increasing efficiency would have enormous implications for all organisational decision-making, and also for organisational legitimacy in general. It would necessarily imply that decision criteria should be more widely, and more openly, publicised, and that the rationale of possible alternative decisions should be more fully explored, independently of narrowly defined discursive and/or ideological appropriateness. It would also imply more rigorous consideration of the potential consequences of all decisions, in the context of their fullest possible range. Still, it is probably fair to say that, if managers were denied the justification of increasing efficiency for their decisions, there would be, at present, a considerable void, since other potential justifications are neither discursively approved, nor, thereby, even available. Imagine, for example, a manager who wanted to introduce an appraisal scheme but who admitted that they did not know whether it would improve or make worse the efficient operation of the organisation. Under contemporary conditions of knowledge about, and practice in, organisational behaviour, this would, indeed, be very difficult to justify!

Glad to be a woman

Gladys was a professional who worked in an industry where there were relatively few opportunities for promotion. Promotions occurred each February but, most years, most candidates were unsuccessful. There were two important features of the promotion process. The first concerned the track record of the individual. In Gladys' case, this was good. She was a long-serving member of the department and had established a good reputation for her work in terms of both quality and quantity. Promotion in this industry was a reward for past performance, rather than future potential, though it was recognised that Gladys scored highly in this respect also. The second important feature of the promotion process was that, although any eligible person could apply, success depended on having the support of their immediate boss, who could only support one candidate.

As February approached, Gladys applied for promotion. She was rather surprised, however, when her boss, Albert – who liked to be called Al – visited her office to tell her that he had decided not to support her in her application. Instead, he had decided to back an application from Tarquin. Tarquin had only joined the department in the past year, had a weaker track record than Gladys and was something of an unknown quantity in terms of ability and performance. Albert told Gladys that he was sure she would understand his decision – while she was, undoubtedly, an excellent candidate, Tarquin needed the promotion more than she did, because he was married and had young children, so needed the extra income the promotion would bring.

(You may think we have made this up, but it is a true story! Only the names have been changed . . .)

- How would you explain Albert's (call me Al) decision?
- How would you expect this episode to impact on Gladys' sense of self?
- How would you expect it to impact on Tarquin's sense of self?

Decision-making, risk, morality

All decisions always imply risk, in the sense that they involve making choices in conditions of uncertainty, particularly about the consequences of a decision, but also about information, decision criteria and the decision-making process itself. In the same way, **all decisions always imply moral judgement**, not least in the context of judging which risks it is appropriate to take and which it is not. More than this, however, decisions always involve achieving desired conditions, the way things should be, and, therefore, are always **normative**.

A risk common to all decisions is that things may end up worse than they were before, or worse than they would have been had some other choice been made. Of course, not all decisions are equally significant. It may not be of enduring consequence if you do not enjoy your coffee or tea, whichever you choose. At the other end of the spectrum there are decisions that are obviously highly significant, such as decisions that lead to injury or death for employees or members of the public. In between, there are many decisions that may seem to be relatively unimportant but which turn out to be very important as a result of their consequences – especially if they are bad decisions. For example, if the adoption of a particular working practice, no matter how well justified, results in a loss of trust, this loss is something that can never be fully regained and which may have serious medium- and long-term consequences for the future of employee relations and, particularly, for the likelihood of success of future initiatives. Bad decisions – that is, *decisions where risks have been incorrectly or inappropriately assessed* – have been known to lead to the entire collapse of an organisation – thus, for example, the supposedly inadequate supervision of a single employee apparently led to the collapse of a long-established and much-respected merchant bank. History, and especially business history, shows many examples of the inadequate assessment of risk in the consequences of a particular decision and many companies have paid dearly for failures in this respect – though, presumably, compensation is never as desirable to those who bear the consequences as would be not taking the risk in the first place.

If inadequate or inappropriate data on risk form part of the decision criteria, it is not surprising that such consequences follow, since they are combined with all the psychological and personal attributes that decision-makers bring to the decision-making process. If the reasons for making decisions are nothing to do with objective and rational criteria, but are to do with subjective interpretation of signifiers and subjective preferences for particular outcomes, and if relevant criteria are excluded merely because they do not conform to discursive requirements or to the ideological constraints and interests of those with the power to make decisions, then it is unlikely that the levels of risk attaching to the decision-making process can be minimised. In particular, it is the presentation of these interpretations and preferences as rational, objective and obvious – and, therefore, unchallengable – that increases the likelihood that risks will continue to be taken on behalf of those who bear their consequences without them being able to contribute to the decision-making process.

The power of decision-making

In 1984 a major gas leak occurred at a chemical plant in Bhopal, India. About 3,000 people died almost immediately, and some 300,000 others were affected by the gas. People were dying as a direct consequence of the gas many years later, and consequences are still being suffered today. The total number of people affected will probably never be known. The story of Bhopal makes fascinating study for those interested in decision-making in organisations, its characteristic feature being the manoeuvring for advantage of the main protagonists, while the victims received little or no recompense for their suffering.

The Bhopal Plant was operated by Union Carbide India Limited (UCIL), whose majority shareholder was the Union Carbide Corporation (UC) of the USA. Responsibility for the accident seemed to lie with UC, a view they seemed to share, initially. However, UC soon started to deny that they were responsible for the operation of the plant, claiming that UCIL was, effectively, an independent company. Acceptance of this argument would limit the liability of, and thus financial damage to, UC. They even suggested, though not convincingly, that the leak was the result of sabotage. However, UC's claims not to be responsible had little credibility – but they did influence the way the tragedy unfolded, channelling energies, not into alleviating its consequences, but into protracted litigation supporting their denial. They also, successfully, argued that any claims for damages should be resolved through the Indian courts, rather than the American courts, as limitations to claims were substantially lower in the former than in the latter. The saga does not end here, but even this prompts some interesting questions.

UC's responsibility seems fairly clear, morally at least, whatever the legal case – though the fact that they eventually made a multi-million dollar settlement might suggest acknowledgement of a wider responsibility. However, the success that UC had in limiting their liability certainly protected the interests of their shareholders. It could be argued that this is the primary responsibility of management and that, therefore, UC's strategy was a good decision. What do you think?

The attraction of settling through the Indian courts was that the valuation on, for example, a human life was less than it would be in the US – about $8,500, as opposed to $500,000, at 1985 prices. Thus, the total money that could be received in compensation by a victim, or a victim's family, would be much less. This was, obviously, a sound decision in economic terms.

- Are economic criteria the most important ones for business decisions?
- In cases such as Bhopal, is it appropriate to prioritise economic criteria?
- Do you think any other factors were involved in the decisions? Might, for example, racism, or First-World imperialism, have been influences?

Whatever the rationale for UC's approach to managing the crisis, the following seems to have been the case:

> WINNERS: UC shareholders, lawyers, UC insurers
> LOSERS: victims of the accident.

- Is this a justifiable outcome for any disaster caused by organisational decision-making?

Sources: The data and information on the Bhopal tragedy are to be found in Jones (1988), Shrivastava (1992).

Such aspects of the inherent risk in decision-making have obvious moral implications too. The moral dimension of decision-making has been the periodic focus of approaches based on concerns with the possibility of ethical behaviour on the part of organisations as collectivities. Although there is widespread support for the notion of ethical organisations, and equally widespread claims to be an ethical organisation, the issue is somewhat bogged down, if not moribund. It was previously noted that it is quite possible for an organisation to be (seen as), simultaneously, ethical and unethical, depending on the judgement (decision) criteria. This is because, while ethics relates to the way organisations ought to behave, without clear specification of what constitutes an ethical act, the desire to be ethical is fairly meaningless. **Because decision-making embodies, inevitably, normative values, it is obvious that all decisions are questions of ethics.** There is a tendency to dichotomise the ethical and the unethical organisation but this is an unsustainable distinction in consideration that *all* organisational decisions are made in line with what is wished to be the case – in other words, every single decision embodies moral judgements and is, therefore, implicated in the possibility of being ethical or otherwise. Of course, it is quite possible to change the understanding of what organisations *ought* to do but, unless this could accord with some generally accepted ethical code, it would be, again, not particularly meaningful.

It is also significantly relevant that capitalist organisations have, as their guiding principle, the objective of making profits for their owners. In such a context it is very difficult for such organisations to adopt some kind of moral code, especially if this were to be at odds with providing a 'respectable' return on investment, as is likely to be, or to be *perceived* to be, the case. This difficulty has been exemplified by the recurrent problem of establishing chartered status for managers, in order to establish management, in general, as a profession equivalent to, say, accountancy or engineering. Proposals to establish a chartered institute were around for many years. One of the difficulties has been that it is common for such charters to include a code of ethics which governs the professional behaviour of members and which is superordinate to the prevailing ethics of any employing organisation – in other words, members are required to conform to their professional code of ethics, even if there is a conflict between the professional code and the organisational code, or ethos.

Professionalising ethics?

In 2002 the Institute of Management was granted a Royal Charter and became the Chartered Management Institute. It published, in July 2002, a 'Code of professional management practice' (see **www.managers.org.uk**). This is a worthy, yet curious, document. Ethical values are referred to only twice, the first time in the Introduction to the Code, where it is stated that '[t]he discharge of your duties as a professional manager in all sectors of society involves the acceptance and habitual exercise of ethical values' – it could be suggested that this statement, although obviously well-intentioned, lacks any recognisably specific meaning. The Introduction further notes that it is possible for 'values, principles, rules and interests' to 'appear to conflict' and to be 'difficult to harmonise in practice', and advocates, in such cases, 'the personal

▶

and professional characteristics and qualities referred to and described in this Code'. However, while acknowledging that such conflict may, or may appear to, occur, the Code draws back from offering guidelines, for example, on how to apply such characteristics in order to resolve any conflict. Equally, it does not suggest what principles might be applied to prioritise, for example, significant aspects of any such conflict.

The Code has six sections regulating the conduct of professional managers in terms of 'the individual manager', 'others within the organisation', the organisation itself, those who might be called stakeholders, 'the wider community' and the Chartered Institute itself. The first section includes:

- Pursue managerial activities with integrity, accountability and competence.
- Disclose any personal interest which might be seen to influence managerial decisions.
- Practise an open style of management so far as is consistent with business needs.
- Keep up-to-date with developments in best management practice and continue to develop personal competence.
- Adopt an approach to the identification and resolution of conflicts of values, including ethical values, which is reasonable and justifiable.
- Safeguard confidential information and not seek personal advantage from it.
- Exhaust all available internal remedies for dealing with matters perceived to be improper, before resorting to public disclosure.
- Encourage the development and maintenance of quality and continuous improvement in management activities.

Source: From Chartered Management Institute, *Code of Professional Management Practice*. Reproduced with permission.

This seems to illustrate the problems outlined above. 'Ethical values' are referred to for the second, and last, time in the document, but only in a sub-clause, and without attempt to suggest what these might be. This vagueness is extended to the use of terms such as 'reasonable and justifiable', which could well be interpreted in a wide range of ways, and begs the question of 'reasonable and justifiable to whom?' – not to mention other terms, such as 'integrity', 'competence', 'quality', and so on. The ways in which these terms are used seems to imply an objective, or at least a universal, measure of good management practice against which any individual's practice can be judged. Clearly, this cannot be the case, but, unfortunately, the Code elides such issues of ambiguity and complexity. It also seems that the Code sidesteps the important issue of providing practical guidelines for resolving any potential conflict between the professional manager's responsibility to the owners of an organisation and the responsibility to society in general – though the third point does imply that the overriding responsibility is to (reified) 'business needs'.

The Royal Charter of the Chartered Management Institute states that its objectives are 'to promote for the public benefit the art and science of management' and 'to advance public education therein'. This phrasing seems to ignore that most of the organisations in which professional managers are employed are privately owned and dedicated to profitability, which – some would argue, legally – must be the first consideration of any manager. The silence on this important aspect of professional management may go some way to explain why the statements of the Code lack specificity to such an extent that they seem almost to be platitudes – they may do little more than describe the way that most managers would see themselves anyway. Perhaps more significantly, such vagueness leaves everything open to interpretation, with all the vulnerabilities to which interpretation is subject.

It has proved particularly difficult to provide a universally acceptable code of ethics for managers (that is, acceptable to *all* stakeholders, as well as to those who are professional managers) – not least in light of their role as agents of ownership who owe allegiance to owners, as well as to their professional institution. The establishment of, or the failure to establish, such a universally acceptable code of ethics has major implications for the formalisation of the moral content of decisions and of the process of decision-making. Whether the 2002 Code has the degree of definition necessary for the fulfilment of this role remains to be seen.

Decision-making and praxis

The aspects of decision-making that have been developed in this chapter are inherent to it. It is not possible to devise a process of decision-making which avoids them, or even which minimises their impact. It is, therefore, particularly important that such factors should *not* be ignored or swept aside, treated as unfortunate or, indeed, as if they do not exist, but that they should be recognised and incorporated into the understanding, and the practice, of the decision-making process. By recognising the arbitrary preferences, subjective judgements, uniqueness of perceptions and interpretations, the presence of the power/knowledge discourse, biases can be illuminated and even compensated. One particular approach to this is embodied in the concept of praxis.

A **praxis approach refers to a system of understanding theory and practice as integrated wholes.** In other words, theory and practice are seen to comprise a unity which cannot be divided: **theory is the ground of practice, and practice is the ground of theory.** The particular focus of a praxis approach is on the **achievement of outcomes and the knowledge that is necessary for their achievement.** It operates within a particular social, political and economic framework which emphasises particular preferences for the nature of social relationships, especially those based on *mutuality* and *mutual responsibility*.

For example, suppose that it is decided that it would be desirable to eliminate unemployment. It is not contentious to recognise that such an outcome would bring about huge gains, socially, politically, economically, psychologically, but we are, apparently, unable to achieve it. It is possible to send people to the moon, to harness nuclear power, to dam great rivers, to cure once-fatal diseases, but, in a wage labour economy, it is apparently impossible to find everyone a job. A decision that it would be desirable to eliminate unemployment would have major implications for organisations and, especially, for the management of organisational behaviour – to give just one small instance, it has been suggested that, in periods of full employment, styles of managing organisational behaviour need to be participative and democratic, while, in periods of high unemployment, styles of managing organisational behaviour usually tend to the autocratic, directive and repressive.

There are many possible ways to eliminate unemployment. It is possible, for example, to change the name – that is, to remove the *signifier* 'unemployment'; to redefine what it means to be unemployed by changing the criteria for being unemployed so that no one fits the category – that is, to change the *signified(s)* of 'unemployment'; to invest in a programme of publicly financed work so that people could be meaningfully employed; to invent non-jobs which give the impression that people are employed though there is no meaningful work for them to do; to force people into work, meaningful or otherwise, by reducing welfare support; to subsidise private organisations to employ more people. All these strategies have been tried in recent years, all developed on a theoretical basis of what was required, sound or otherwise. However, each possibility has greater or lesser attractions to various socio-economic perspectives, with the result that success or otherwise in achieving the objective has been secondary to ideological acceptability in the prevailing political culture – what was, arguably, the most successful of these strategies in genuinely reducing unemployment, investment in programmes of publicly financed works, was abandoned as ideologically unsound.

For the achievement of the objective it is obvious that the decision criteria are of major significance. **It is necessary for there to be congruence between the objective, the means of achieving it, and the prevailing socio-political culture.** In the context of an objective such as the elimination of unemployment, issues such as what motivates people, what constitutes a fair day's work, what constitutes a fair day's pay, what characterises reasonable working conditions, what impact organisations are allowed to have on the socio-economic 'environment' and on the physical 'environment', and so on, become integral parts of the *general* socio-political culture which seeks to solve the problem. It is not unreasonable to say that, ultimately, the problem of solving unemployment depends utterly on what people want organisations to be like and, in the balance, what organisations are prepared to offer.

What all this means is that unemployment is as much an organisational issue as is the introduction of an appraisal scheme, or the design of a production system, or the adoption of a programme of incentives. Although solving unemployment may be a generally larger issue than these other examples, the process of deciding is precisely the same – and even includes many of the same considerations. **A praxis approach focuses on what outcome is desired (decision consequences), and what means of achieving it are appropriate and acceptable (decision criteria), focuses on the relationship between means and ends in the context of the values embodied in them.** In this process it necessarily challenges all procedures of inclusion and exclusion, of boundary location and model-building, all procedures which are based in power and subjective preference. Specifically, it necessarily challenges the basis of decisions as to what is relevant to problem-solving. This process occurs because, **within such an approach, it is more important to solve the problem, to achieve the desired outcome, than it is to bow to discursive acceptability and what can claim to be ideologically appropriate.**

Existing applications in Organisational Behaviour

There is a vast literature in Organisation Studies in general and in Organisational Behaviour in particular on decision-making – indeed, it is not unreasonable to suggest that all such literature is, inevitably, about decision-making. However, it is possible to make a broad distinction within this literature. **The specific use of the term 'decision-making' is generally reserved to managerial activity**. Within this there is a lot of material on the process of decision-making itself and, in effect, all texts on management by function – such as Strategic Management, Marketing Management, and so on – will include something on decision-making. There are caveats to the rational objective model which are generally incorporated in this literature. On one hand, there is, notably, Herbert Simon's concept of **bounded rationality** (see Chapter 6), which concerns the limits to perfectly rational decision-making. On the other hand, there are, in particular, **studies of the management process** which describe constraints on managerial activity which limit the possibility of managers making decisions in the ideal, prescribed ways – that is, deliberate, planned decisions, based on rational and objective consideration of the balance of alternatives, detailed consideration of data, and so on. Such studies often emphasise the relatively chaotic nature of managerial activity in practice, which seems to lead managers generally to reactive rather than proactive decision-making. Another general caveat stresses that management takes place in conditions of uncertainty. However, notwithstanding recognition of these constraints, managerial decision-making is still generally treated as if it can attain a 'virtually objective' or an 'as if objective' status, and special emphasis is laid on the development of techniques which are designed to assist this achievement.

On the other side of the distinction is an equally large literature, especially in Organisational Behaviour, and especially concerning psychological characteristics, which extends the practice of decision-making to all organisational members – **but which rarely calls the processes described decision-making, preferring language such as subjective preference, choice, option**. Notable examples include types of motivation theory such as Expectancy Theory and the Motivation Calculus, theories of perception, Organisation Development, role theory, all of which emphasise that people actively make decisions about anything and everything. Yet, somehow, it is rarely deemed appropriate to grace this activity with the name of decision-making.

It is also important to note that, in both the above cases, much of the concern is directed towards purging 'irrationalities' in decision-making, such as the halo effect and stereotyping, rather than accepting that these are inevitable characteristics of all decision-makers which, therefore, should be included in the models and understood. Classing them as irrationalities to be purged merely drives them underground, masks their operation and increases rationalisation after the event.

The **poststructuralist** literature, in general, can also be seen as widely interested in decision-making and its process, though, again, not specifically by these names. In the work of Michel Foucault, for example, notably that concerning **power/knowledge** and the **development of discourses**, there is a very specific and consistent focus on the nodal points at which decisions are made and alternatives rejected, characterised in light of an analysis which emphasises the role of ideology, self-interest and power. Decision-making is also immanent in his concept of **micro-power**, which further stresses the extension of decision-making as an activity to every single person, all of the time. Foucault is not alone in this sharp attention to the making of decisions, whenever, wherever and by whomsoever. Typically, poststructuralist approaches shun the notion of deliberate and planned decision-making, in favour of a view of it as ubiquitous and all-pervasive, but, nonetheless, always with significant consequences. Thus, for example, in Foucault's discussion of what he calls **governmentality**, he specifically argues against the idea that this administrative tyranny is produced by a conspiracy of the powerful, in favour of the idea that it is a product of the tendency of those who have power and those who desire power to make like decisions based on what we have called coalitions of interest. Jacques Derrida's concept of **techno-mediatic power** conveys a very similar understanding of the process of decision-making. On a rather different tack, Gilles Deleuze and Félix Guattari have been interested in how desire can be colonised, so that people make decisions congruent with the interests of capitalism but fundamentally against their own interests.

There are poststructuralist studies of organisational life and organisational behaviour which carry forward these ideas about how people make decisions and the impacts and consequences they have on behaviour, attitudes, and so on. Again, such studies, notably in the fields of Human Resource Management and Personnel, treat decision-making as a ubiquitous activity motivated by self-interest and power relationships, but rarely call the process one of decision-making, perhaps because of the reservation of the term in the Functionalist literature to activity that is specifically managerial.

Further potential

It could be argued that it is important to challenge and resist this corralling of the term 'decision-making' to refer to managerial activity. Two immediate benefits would derive from such challenge: *firstly*, **the explicit recognition that everyone, all members of organisations, make decisions all the time, and all such decisions are germane to, and significant for, organisational process and organisational behaviour;** *secondly*, **the explicit recognition that managers make decisions in precisely the same way as everyone else, that they do *not* have some special access to rationality or objectivity, but only to greater autonomy and power.** It is particularly important that recognition should be given to the point that, just because someone is powerful and can, therefore, evade questioning of their decisions, it does not mean that those decisions are somehow inherently more objective or more rational.

Much of the impetus to ignore certain kinds of decision-making comes from the tendency to explain it in deterministic terms, determinism still being quite pervasive as an underlying motif in the discourse of Organisational Behaviour. This determinism sees the decisions made by individuals, not in terms of the exercise of free will, but, minimally, as conditioned responses to particular situations. The reluctance to accept voluntarism in trying to understand organisational behaviour leads to the tendency to dismiss much individual decision-making as irrelevant and the tendency to see much of the variety in decision-making as no more than inappropriate responses to a situation which should, therefore, be cured. For example, if your job is enriched but you decide not to work more productively, the problem will be defined in terms of your decision not to respond as you should do, rather than recognition that you are deciding to exercise your free will.

The prospects for an adequate and informed understanding of organisational behaviour will remain dim as long as this implicit or explicit determinism holds sway. **Observable organisational behaviour is not an issue of determinism but one of manipulation, the ability of people to be influenced to behave in certain ways.** It has often been noted that the process of management is one of manipulation, but how subtle and how all-pervasive such manipulation is and how it affects people's decision-making remains largely unexplored. This is an issue that cannot be detached from that of the way that organisations impact on the social and on the environment. How is it, for example, that people can work voluntarily in situations and conditions which are literally dangerous to themselves and to the wider environment, yet allow themselves to be convinced that this is not the case? Such questions, together with myriad others about the nature of organisational behaviour, will never be answered until we develop appropriate models of what people are like, and appropriate understandings of how and why they make the decisions that they do.

Organisational behaviour and decision-making

Before people behave they will have made a decision to behave, whether consciously or unconsciously, and it is only possible to make sense of behaviour by understanding the decision-making process. Traditional approaches in the discourse of Organisational Behaviour have ignored this, in favour of concentrating on observable behaviour – but, as we know, this observable behaviour is only a signifier whose signified is not available to be *determined* by theories of organisational behaviour. Attachment to the traditional approach in the discourse of Organisational Behaviour has led to a relatively poor and limited understanding of people in organisations, unable to go much beyond the notion that people are units who work, determined, reactive and manipulable. However, the development of theories associated, in particular, with Poststructuralism has opened up a new range of possibilities for expanding our understanding of behaviour in organisations, introducing new issues of relevance which have been widely ignored in the past but which are central to understanding people and their behaviour. This theorising provides a potential for the discourse to extend its horizons, and to answer questions that it has so far failed to answer.

Whichever way work in contemporary society is considered, it seems to be unrelievedly problematic. Although work is still the mainstay of society and the economy, the way wealth is produced for society and the way people provide for their own survival, and although we have thousands of years of experience of work and its organisation, it seems that we have not yet been able to find a way of organising work that minimises its attendant dysfunctions. On one hand, there is not enough work available to provide everyone with the means to ensure their own survival and, on the other hand, some people are killing themselves with overwork and workaholism is a widespread, serious and recognised disease. Some people do not receive sufficient wages to live on, others are burdened with telephone number salaries. Some face injury, physical and psychological, because of working conditions, or because they are stressed, others are simply bored to death. And so on. And all these phenomena are traceable to decisions that people have made.

Given the centrality of work in contemporary society, and, predominantly, of work in organisations, organisational behaviour could not be more significant or have a more important role to fulfil. Its lack of success, so far, in realising this significance is, largely, a result of the decision to adopt and sustain models of what people are like, and why they behave in the ways that they do, that lack sophistication, lack the ability to reflect the variety and complexity of real people, and, therefore, lack the penetration to provide an appropriate basis for understanding organisational behaviour. All organisational behaviour rests on decisions people make. Behaviour in organisations, in its broadest sense as well as in more specific instances, cannot be understood unless and until the ideal types of traditional Organisational Behaviour are discarded in favour of a more practical understanding of how and why decisions are made.

A TALE FROM THE VILLAGE PUMP (*DECISION-MAKING*)

(See the Case Study in Appendix 2, pages 340–3)

Everything in this case could be interpreted as being about **decision-making**. One of the reasons that this story is so famous is because of Snow's decision to take immediate action to get the pump disabled, rather than to pursue the more traditional means of getting his hypothesis tested and accepted before acting. This decision, today, has iconic status, symbolised, for example, in a plaque on the site of the Broad Street drinking water pump, and a pub close by called 'The John Snow' (somewhat disregarding Snow's views on the consumption of alcohol!) – there is also a John Snow Society, membership of which is accorded to those who have a drink in the pub. The miasma theorists, perhaps immobilised by information overload resulting from the inclusion of so many factors in their theory, decided, at the time, to observe, rather than to act.

- What factors seem to be significant in Farr's **decision** not to accept the hypothesis that cholera was water-borne?

Case

DISMAL PROSPECTS

The renowned economist and political commentator John Kenneth Galbraith suggested that economic forecasting only exists to make astrology look respectable! Alan Greenspan, another noted economist, expressed somewhat similar sentiments, rather differently, when he said of the Federal Reserve: 'The fact that our econometric models at the Fed, **the best in the world**, have been wrong for fourteen straight quarters, does not mean that they will not be right in the fifteenth quarter' (cited in Mayer 2001: 180, our emphasis).

However, whilst both might be sceptical regarding '*seeing*' the economic future, this was possibly the limit of their agreement. Galbraith's approach to economics tended towards the Keynesian. In his early life he was heavily involved in Roosevelt's 'New Deal' and subsequently served several Democratic presidents. He was critical of unfettered market capitalism and is regarded by some as a major inspiration of the contemporary anti-capitalist/anti-globalisation movement.

Greenspan's earlier life was associated with the, some would argue, cult-like Objectivists who espoused, *inter alia*, an extreme objectivism, libertarian individualism and unfettered capitalism. Latterly, he acted as advisor to Republican presidents and was the long-serving chairman of the Federal Reserve, until 2006. As regards capitalism, he is rather enthusiastic, claiming: 'Capitalism is based on self-interest and self-esteem; it holds integrity and trustworthiness as cardinal virtues . . . demanding that men survive by means of virtue, not vices. It is [a] superlatively moral system . . .' (Greenspan 1967: 121). Greenspan was also reported in the *New York Times* (28 October 2005) as having said on a later occasion: 'I guess I should warn you, if I turn out to be particularly clear, you probably misunderstood what I said'!

That two such ideologically opposed economists should disagree is not surprising (though if economics is as objective as its proponents like to claim, it should be). However, the following may surprise.

This report appeared in *The Guardian* newspaper, on 25 July 2001 (the reporters were Larry Elliott and Charlotte Denny; the emphasis is ours):

O'Neill insists recovery is near

The two men in charge of the American economy were at odds yesterday as the US Treasury Secretary, Paul O'Neill, shrugged off fears expressed by Alan Greenspan, chairman of the Federal Reserve, that conditions may get worse before they get better.

Mr O'Neill said he could see 'no barriers' to a recovery in growth by the final quarter of this year, and that higher productivity meant the US had the potential to grow by 3.5% a year 'and maybe more than that'.

The treasury secretary's comments, made during a visit to London, contrasted with Mr Greenspan's caution during his testimony to the Senate banking committee, in which he repeated a warning that there was a risk economic weakness 'will be greater than currently anticipated'.

With new evidence of strain on the US corporate sector yesterday, shares on Wall Street were again under pressure; the Dow Jones Industrial Average and the Nasdaq hi-tech index were down in early trading.

Mr O'Neill said that the six cuts in interest rates coupled with George Bush's tax cuts would work, and urged commentators to be patient rather than analyse the economy on a daily basis.

'. . . When you run the results [of the measures taken this year] through the models they show a real rate of growth of over 3% next year, which is not too bad.' Despite the complaints from US firms about the damage being caused by a high exchange rate, Mr O'Neill stressed that he believed in a strong dollar.

'One of the things that is pro-growth about the US is its flexibility and quickness to act. There is a lot of mobility and there is a quick reaction to demand and supply considerations. In other economies there is a slower ability to take on board the day-to-day signals coming from the economy and growth potential tends to be limited.'

There was, however, 'much to be admired about the operation of the UK economy'.

His visit marked the signing of a landmark double taxation treaty between Britain and the US which will shave tens of millions of pounds off the tax bills of British companies with American subsidiaries.

Source: Larry Elliot and Charlotte Denny, 'O'Neill insists recovery is near', *The Guardian*, 2 July 2001. Copyright © Guardian Newspapers Limited 2001. Reprinted with permission.

Googling 'Greenspan sneezes' throws up over 9000 hits. The problem with Greenspan sneezing was that it was followed by significant portions of the world, if not the entire world, catching a cold! In other words, Alan Greenspan was a very powerful man, the third most powerful in the world, according to some, after George W. Bush and Vladimir Putin, who were both elected – Greenspan, of course, was not. So, when he made a decision, it affected *you*, particularly as regards your wealth. Although he retired from the chair of the Federal Reserve in 2006, he held the post for eighteen years.

Paul O'Neill, as George W. Bush's first Secretary of the Treasury, was not quite so important in terms of global power, but, in terms of the US economy, he was certainly in the same league as Greenspan, with whom he had a long-standing and close association. Prior to his appointment by Bush he had been Chairman and CEO of Alcoa and had served under a number of Republican presidents and as a director of Kodak, the Rand Corporation, etc. He is on Harvard Business School's list of Great American Business Leaders.

Now, imagine that you are on a platform at Birmingham New Street railway station, and there is a train standing there. The monitor for the platform, which should give you information about where the train is going, is blank. You ask the driver and he tells you that the train is going to London. You double check by also asking the guard, and she tells you that the train is going to Manchester. So, here are the two people in charge of the train, one of whom thinks that the train is going south, the other of whom thinks that it is going north. Of course, such things do happen in dynamic systems, where there is inherent uncertainty. We might suppose that one of them (or possibly both) lacks up-to-date information resulting from a change in system conditions, but that, eventually, something will be resolved. Until then, however, this division of opinion about the immediate future will make decision-making for the intending passenger quite difficult.

The case of the US economy, however, is of a different order of magnitude. This report shows **two acknowledged, and very powerful, experts coming to opposite conclusions** about the immediate prospects for the US economy, about where it is heading. Unlike the train crew, we can assume that they have the same information available to them, on which to base their forecasts – if they have not, we should be very worried because their predictions are of enormous significance. We can also assume that, at the macro level, there will be a high degree of intersubjective agreement between them, about ideology, about the economic role of money, interest rates, inflation, the importance of the US economy, and so on. And no one can be in any doubt about the global importance attached to what they might say, and the impact of that on decision-making at every level, from the transnational to the national to the organisational, throughout the world. But they do not agree. What, then, are the implications for the process of decision-making?

■ How might an understanding of **semiotics** and **structure** help to explain the differences between Alan Greenspan and Paul O'Neill?

■ Any two people, however limited their **knowledge**, could make the same kind of rather basic but conflicting claims about the future of the US economy, but, given the absence of discursive authority, no one would take them very seriously. What impact does **discursive authority** give to the significance of the claims of Greenspan and O'Neill?

■ That there are two completely opposed authoritative claims emanating from the discourse does not apparently weaken the **power** of the discourse. Why might this be so?

■ Both Greenspan and O'Neill are known for their attachment to objectivity and 'the facts'. Can they both be objectively **rational**, if they hold diametrically opposed views on the future of the US economy?

■ It is likely that both Greenspan and O'Neill, given their attachment to objectivism, would see economists such as J.K. Galbraith as **ideological** and themselves as not ideological. How might this be explained?

■ O'Neill cannot have been unaware that what he was saying contradicted the views and public statement of Greenspan. What can be deduced from the report about the sense of **self** that motivated O'Neill to make these statements on this occasion?

■ O'Neill claims to 'see no barriers to recovery'. Given subsequent events, does this suggest an inappropriate **bounding** in his **model** of the world economy?

■ Given the immense influence on the global economy of these two men, how might others approach the issue of **efficiency**, based on these two conflicting views?

■ Could it be argued that management of US economic **decision-making** is a matter of faith rather than one of science?

And

■ Why might the passage of 49 days from this speech change everything?

O'Neill had been reluctant to take the job of Treasury Secretary and had given Bush a list of reasons why he was not suitable for the post. Bush waived aside O'Neill's doubts and insisted that he wanted him. In December 2002 O'Neill was required to resign (that is, he was fired by Bush), against a background and history of problems he had experienced while working for the Bush administration. In 2004 a book was published giving O'Neill's account of his time as Treasury Secretary (Suskind 2004). O'Neill was highly critical of both

▶

Bush and his administration – he described Bush in meetings 'like a blind man in a roomful of deaf people' (Suskind 2004: 149). One of the most sensational revelations of this book was that Bush had been planning the invasion of Iraq from the start of his presidency in 2000, although the official justification for the war had been as a response to 9/11 and Saddam Hussein's assistance for al-Qaeda, for which strong factual evidence did not exist (even at the time), and which has since been shown, along with the claim that Iraq possessed weapons of mass destruction, not to have been the case.

■ Does this tell us anything about Bush's **decision-making** skills? Is there any reason to assume that the way the White House makes decisions is any different to organisational decision-making generally?

(As the questions on this case demonstrate, all chapters are relevant to its analysis.)

Bibliography

There is a vast conventional literature on decision-making, which can be divided into two broad types: strict quantificational, statistical and computational approaches in which everything must be measured, and which are outside the scope here, and a literature which recognises issues of subjectivity, and so on, in varying degrees of complexity, but which tends to view such things as ultimately remediable – for example, from amongst many, Janis and Mann (1977), Harrison (1999), Gore, Murray and Richardson (1992), Jennings and Whattam (1998). Books on decision-making are variably oriented to its relevance to the context of organisational behaviour – see, for example, Matteson and Ivancevich (1989), Pugh (1990). A lot of the books on decision-making within an organisational behaviour framework reflect a behaviourist approach with all the attendant limitations of that – for example, Beach (1997), Bazerman (2006). There are, however, more sophisticated understandings of decision-making and its process in organisational contexts. A useful Interpretivist definition is given in Fineman, Gabriel and Sims (2005). An interesting analysis from a determinist perspective can be found in Simons (1986). An approach that views decision-making as an uncertain process and rescues the element of intuition is in Morton (1991). The inherent variety in approaches is represented in the still valuable Castles, Murray and Potter (1975). A poststructuralist and deconstructive approach is to be found in Chia (1994, 1996).

Information technology (IT) is increasingly recommended, and used, in decision-making, where its 'science-ness' is seen as enhancing rationality and objectivity. However, the idea that IT is not immune to human, subjective, purposes is also increasingly represented in various literatures. Solomonides and Levidov (1985), for example, discuss computerisation as a culture; McKenzie and Wajcman (1985), for example, examine the impact of social factors, values, and so on, on the development of technology in general; Attewell (1991), for example, discusses the misapplication of IT for purposes of control; Alvesson and Willmott (1996), for example, review the tendency to abdicate responsibility for decisions to IT, on the basis of its claimed – but impossible to substantiate – neutrality.

It has previously been noted (in Chapter 7, for example) that the unitary model of organisation is enjoying renewed popularity these days – see any standard Human Resource Management text – but its relevance and explanatory power remain contested by any approach that views organisations as composed of interest groups whose interests conflict.

Within the literature on decision-making there is a strong, and enduring, tendency to define decision-making as a managerial activity – see, for example, Coyle (1972), Harrison (1999), Bazerman (2006). That the managed are not seen as decision-makers, or expected to make decisions, is a widespread implication in conventional Organisational Behaviour texts, which tend to talk about subjective influences on worker behaviour, for example. Two classic illustrations are Taylor's (1911) idea that managers think and workers obey and the distinction between logics of efficiency (managers) and logics of sentiment (workers) in Roethlisberger and Dickson (1939). Carey (1977) finds a similar implication in Herzberg's work.

There are various studies of disasters which spring from managerial decision-making, from the particular perspective of the decision-making processes involved. See, for example, for a number of such cases, Hills (1987), Punch (1996). For extended illustrations of how decisions shaped events at Bhopal see Jones (1988), Shrivastava (1992). An approach that considers the role of decision-making in organisational failures is Anheier (1999). See also Drummond (2001).

Approaches that utilise psychoanalysis as a basis for understanding organisation and organisational behaviour are good sources on the role of unconscious desires in forming behaviour – see, for example, Schwartz (1990) and Sievers (1994), and others cited in the bibliography to Chapter 8. The role of sexuality in organisation(s) and organisational behaviour has received scant attention until relatively recently, but see Marcuse (1987) on the sublimation of sexuality into work – libidinal displacement – and also Freud (1963). More recently see, for example, Hearn and Parkin (1987), Hearn, Sheppard, Tancred-Sheriff and Burrell (1989), Burrell (1991, 1992, 1997). The concept of desire – not to be conflated with sexuality – is central to all post-Freudian analysis and, especially, to Poststructuralism – again, see the bibliography to Chapter 8. A particularly useful concept in terms of the present approach to decision-making is Deleuze and Guattari's (1988 or, more briefly, 1983) idea of the rhizome – see also Carter and Jackson (2004b), Goodchild (1996). See also Chapter 12.

The impact of psychological characteristics on decision-makers is most commonly, but rather limitedly, represented in conventional Organisational Behaviour in the literature on trait theories of leadership and in that on personality types – see, amongst many others, Gibson, Ivancevich, Donnelly and Konopaske (2002). The issue of perceptions of self is less well represented in this kind of literature, but its huge significance in forming the self is indicated in

Lacan's (for example, 1980) conceptualisation of I/Other relationships – yet again, the bibliography to Chapter 8 is relevant. The desire of managers, and others, to be seen as competent is reflected in the growing competency literature, though this, again, is not without its problems, both in what competency entails – see, for example, Brewis (1996), Lefebvre (1997) – and in the desire of managers to learn about it, or not – see, for example, Salaman and Butler (1990), Chia and Morgan (1996) and, especially, Thomas (1989).

In reference to the sections of this chapter that seek to apply the concepts developed in previous chapters to the process of decision-making, the bibliographic material of those previous chapters is all relevant. Some specific sources can be noted, however. For example, Nowakowska (1987) focuses on semiotic systems and decision-making, though somewhat briefly and somewhat algebraically. That accounting conventions can be used to signify different outcomes depending on the desire of the user is the message of Griffiths (1992). The unparalleled significance of structuring in handling information is an immanent concern of Foucault (for example, 1970, 1974) – see also Poster (1984) – and succinctly described in relation to Human Resource Management by Townley (1994). The impact of discursively disapproved factors, such as nepotism, bribery, discrimination, sexual favours, and so on, is the subject of much of the organisational and managerial ethics literature, and there are many case studies of such events – for example, Hills (1987), Punch (1996), Maclagan (1998), and see also Corbett (1994) and Hoffman and Moore (1990). In general, examples of such cases tend to be oriented towards ethical issues in terms of their analysis, and in the public domain, but that such factors influence decision-making is often a taken-for-granted assumption of organisational participants, though not of the conventional decision-making literature.

The idea that ideology can influence organisational decision-making has been around for a long time – see, for example, Child (1972), where it is raised but not really developed. Perhaps that has been the general fate of this observation – although, of course, Labour Process Theory and other Marxist and neo-Marxist approaches do focus on the role of ideology in forming organisational relations, from the starting point of two principal opposing ideologies brought together in organisations: Capital and Labour. An interesting macro-level analysis can be found in Zey (1998), who equates Rational Choice Theory with ideology. Several of Morgan's (1997) metaphors – notably, organisations as cultures, political systems and psychic prisons – represent approaches to understanding organisations and organisational behaviour which particularly focus on the impact of the self.

It was explicit in Chapter 9, on boundary, that boundary location and model-building are profoundly implicated in all decision-making. The problems of boundary are becoming increasingly widely recognised, and have even made their appearance in the 'pop' management literature – see, for example, Ashkenas, Ulrich, Jick and Kerr (1995). Mitroff and Linstone (1993) specifically exhort decision-makers to abandon constrictive boundary conceptions. They take a systemic approach. Indeed, approaches based in Systems Theory generally have a broad focus on decision-making in the context of bounding processes. The work of Stafford Beer is notable in this respect (for example, 1966, 1978 [which, unlike its 1994 reprint, has usefully coloured paper], 1994) – see also Van Gigch (1987). The idea that many management techniques involve acts of faith, and that management itself exhibits characteristics of a religion, is not uncommon – see, for example, Thomas (2003). Perhaps another facet of this is in terms of the ideal types represented by many accounts, and conceptualisations, of management – see, for example, Willmott (1984). See also Wynne (1982), who characterises much decision-making activity in terms of ritual.

Beck (1992) characterises late modernism as, quintessentially, a risk society. See also Beck (1999). Douglas (1986) develops the interesting concept of 'subjective immunity', which encapulates the common assumption of decision-makers (that is, people) that 'accidents' never happen to us, but always to other people. For a Foucauldian approach to risk analysis, see Carter and Jackson (1997). Hills (1987) contains several cases on industrial disease as an outcome of organisational decision-making. Parker (1998a) contains a range of contributions on issues of moral and ethical interest which are outcomes of organisational decision-making – see, especially, Parker's own contribution, entitled 'Against Ethics'. Previously cited organisational and managerial ethics literature is also relevant. For a volume of case studies on such issues, see Hoffman and Moore (1990).

Praxis is a concept used in various ways and which seems to defy universal definition. See, for example, Bernstein (1983), Kilminster (1979). On its potential relevance to studying organisation, see Heydebrand (1983). Foster's (1985) concept of resistance is closer to the use of the term praxis made here – see also Jackson and Willmott (1987), Carter and Jackson (1990), Jackson and Carter (1992, 1995a). The argument about the connection between boom and slump and management style is in Ramsie (1977). For a nice illustration of the argument on the ideological unacceptability of curing poverty through relieving unemployment, even though it works, see Elliott (1999).

The tendency to reserve decision-making to a managerial context was noted earlier in this bibliography. For a commentary on bounded rationality, including some more recent comment by Simon, see Rubinstein (1998). Harrison (1999) specifically locates decision-making as part of the management process. Well-known studies of the management process are Mintzberg (1980), Stewart (1988). Watson (1994) provides an interesting slant on these issues. All the examples noted of the influence of subjective preference, and so on, on organisational behaviour have been previously cited. It is worth noting, however, that characteristically, such approaches assume that either these influences can be parenthesised or they are remediable. This tendency is epitomised in the literature on perception in the context of organisational behaviour – see, amongst many others, Buchanan and Huczynski (2004).

Foucault's concept of power/knowledge is immanent in his work – see, for example, Gordon (1980). The key references on discourse – though, again, an immanent concept in his work – are Foucault (1970, 1971, 1974), but see also his studies of particular discourses, such as Foucault (1967, 1979a). The concept of governmentality is introduced in Foucault (1979b) – see also Burchell, Gordon and Miller (1981). Various commentaries on, and introductions to, Foucault's work were noted in the bibliography to Chapter 3. Derrida's concept of techno-mediatic power is explored in Derrida (1994). It seems almost too obvious to point out that Derrida's influential concept of 'undecidability' is also relevant – see, for example, Derrida (1981), also Norris (1987), Wood (1992), Cooper (1986, 1989). Deleuze and Guattari's ideas are represented in Deleuze and Guattari (1984, 1988), but see also, for example, Descombes (1980) or, for an organisational perspective, Carter and Jackson (2004b).

CHAPTER 12

Conclusions

This final chapter, rather than seeking to provide a summary, focuses on the rationale of our central thesis, that we need to *rethink organisational behaviour*. Following a brief recapitulation of 'the story so far', there is a consideration of why understanding organisational behaviour matters, particularly in the context of how we think about organisation. From this is developed the metaphor of the organisation as rhizome (based on an insight in the work of Deleuze and Guattari). We then go on to look at what might be signified by Postmodernism, especially the question of what possibilities Postmodernism might offer in terms of rethinking the discourse of organisational behaviour.

The plot so far, in 333 words

Understanding behaviour is accomplished through symbolic interpretation, the subject matter of **SEMIOTICS**. Semiotics provides a way to understand how meaning is constructed. However, meanings are not intrinsic to symbols but are a function of the understanding subject. Subjects create what might be seen as personal meanings through their attempts to **STRUCTURE** and make sense of the world. These structures are tools for thought, rather than corresponding to some objective, given, reality. But **KNOWLEDGE** is constructed from more than these infinitely variable and personal meanings, and requires some intersubjective agreement among 'experts', at whatever level. Expertise is not a function of superior understanding, but is constituted by membership of groups who have the **POWER** to prioritise meaning, which, as noted, is nevertheless rooted in a particular subjective rationality. **RATIONALITY** is always informed by specific **IDEO-LOGICAL** preferences which form the basis for judgements about what is, or is not, real. Ideologies in their turn reflect and inform some concept of the **SELF**: that is, how we understand ourselves and others as individuals. All of this is made possible by some cognitive **BOUNDING** process which attempts to separate the significant from the unimportant. Bounding is a necessary but fallible process which operates to limit variety/information at whatever level understanding is sought: for example, self/other, manager/worker, organisation/environment. The success of bounding processes can be seen, generically, in terms of **EFFICIENCY**, which can be psychological, economic, organisational and many other possibilities. Inefficient perceptions of boundaries lead inevitably to systemic sub-optimisation, because what are significant factors remain unrecognised and therefore excluded. In other words, **DECISION-MAKING**, which can be seen as the essence of organisational behaviour, at all levels of action, is the outcome of all the above elements, and it is the quality of their operation which fundamentally impacts on whether the decision is an appropriate one. Decision-making is a response to **SEMIOTIC** readings and generates yet more semiotic readings, continuously engaging the whole process, which is both dynamic and constantly changing.

Why organisational behaviour matters

At the outset of this book we stated that it was not intended to be a conventional Organisational Behaviour text, and that the reader would probably find nothing in it about how to manage organisational behaviour. Rather, our intention was to try to rescue an aspect of understanding organisation which has become somewhat moribund, but whose significance could hardly be overestimated, and **to build a framework for *rethinking organisational behaviour*** which could reflect more effectively the complexity of people's behaviour in organisations and which could reflect the potential contribution to our understanding of it offered by contemporary social theorising. In this respect, our intention was **to recontextualise attempts to understand organisational behaviour**. Traditionally, the discourse of Organisational Behaviour has tried to reconstruct meaning from observed behaviour. We have sought to focus on the construction of meaning itself, in order to demonstrate the complexity and, indeed, ungeneralisability of the behaviour that springs from it.

We have stated on a number of occasions in this book our own conviction that the proper purpose of the study of organisational behaviour is to understand organisational behaviour in itself, rather than to provide strategies and techniques with which behaviour may be moulded and manipulated in accordance with the demands of particular interests. Such a purpose, in itself, suggests the importance of developing as comprehensive a model of what informs behaviour in organisations as possible. But that is not all. It could be said that we now live in a world which is more organised than ever before.

It is extremely difficult to escape or evade formal organisation in any aspect of our lives. For most people, most of the time – waking, sleeping, working, playing – we are organised. Surely, something that probably affects every moment of our lives ought to be clearly understood, by us all? And, in all these instances, we are, literally, *behaving in organisations*. More than that, all this behaving, this activity, produces **outcomes**. These outcomes reproduce society – that is, enable society to continue, give it its particular direction and trajectory. This, then, is another reason why it matters whether we have appropriate models of behaviour in organisations: whatever outcomes we may desire from organisations, it would be optimistic indeed to assume that these outcomes will somehow just occur. We need to understand what outcomes are desirable *and* what organisational processes will produce these outcomes.

Escaping organisation?

Consider the relatively simple activity of going for a walk in the countryside.

For centuries, landowners have organised the countryside into areas where walking is permitted and other areas where it is not. Even where walking is generally permitted, it is usually organised, for example, on to footpaths, or in ways that seek to limit environmental impact. If, like us, you live in a city, you need to get to the countryside in which you want to walk and, to do that, you need to utilise some form of organised transport. For example, if you go by road, you will need a vehicle, which must be taxed, licensed and road-worthy, a road system, organisations that will provide you with fuel, and, probably, parking facilities. Perhaps it is appropriate to be a member of a motoring organisation which will assist you if you need help of any kind. You may need maps – produced by an organisation. You will need clothes – produced by, and acquired through, organisations. To pay for those clothes, you will probably have to belong to a bank, or a credit card company, and, of course, you may have had to work in an organisation to earn the money to pay for these pleasures – in which case, the time available for you to go walking is also being organised.

You may prefer to walk in company, in which case you can join an organisation dedicated to that, or some other special-interest group organisation associated with walking, such as the Ramblers' Association. Or you may prefer to walk on your own. But, when you stand on top of a hill with the free wind in your hair, just reflect on how much organisation you have had to submit to, to get you there! And, if you want to go somewhere 'remote', don't forget to notify some appropriate organisation of your itinerary, so that, if anything should befall you, a rescue-organisation can find you.

Walking is often a rather escapist activity – and, perhaps, organisation is the very thing from which escape is desired. It is not a very complicated activity. But even the simplest activities are virtually impossible without the involvement of organisation(s).

Well, where do we go from here?

Even though we have not set out to be prescriptive, it must be acknowledged that the reader is likely to get to this point wondering where it leads. So, we will try to sketch out one possible scenario.

In order to understand organisational behaviour it is necessary to have an understanding of what an organisation is. However, there is no agreed definition of what constitutes an organisation. There are just different models, and, as was pointed out in Chapter 9, models are always interested and purposeful. Furthermore, from a subjectivist point of view, any organisation must be understood semiotically. The most popular semiotic model currently available in the study of behaviour in organisations is that of metaphors of organisation, as developed by, for example, Gareth Morgan. Long experience of studying organisations has led *us* to the view that ***organisations are rhizomic*** in character, as will be developed in a moment.

The ins and outs of organisation

It has been popular in the discourse of Organisation Studies in general to see what an organisation produces as being produced *because* of the way it is organised. This, essentially Functionalist, view sees the overt purpose of an organisation as being achieved through the conscious analysis of that purpose in terms of the implied necessary operations and structures. In other words, if you want to produce widgets, you work out what productive and service facilities are necessary and how these should be structured internally and relative to each other. So the argument goes, if you then operate this organisation efficiently, you will be a successful purveyor of widgets. Even more radical models of organisation tend to follow this basic logic, although reasons for organising would be likely to include elements such as class interest and social control and the productions of organisation to include consequences such as social domination, as well as widgets. Organisations are often defined in terms of their outcomes – but this is a reverse process of reasoning. By a further logical twist, it is also often claimed that a successful organisation is successful because of the way it is organised.

It is necessary for the model of organisation implied in this book, however, to separate outcomes and judgements of success or otherwise from the formal structures and operations. There are two reasons for this. ***Firstly***, while it cannot be denied that organisations produce goods and services – their intended and formal function – and that from this, benefit or disbenefit, depending on one's view of what is produced, flows for society generally, it must also be acknowledged that **goods and services are not the only things that organisations produce**. There are many other products which are not part of the formal function but which also have consequences for, for example, individuals, society in general, and/or the natural environment. These other products have an enormous range of types and forms. They may include, for example, pollution and waste products, but also the production of artificial scarcity through monopolisation of resources; crime, such as the misappropriation of employee pension funds, or price fixing; subversion of the political process, from economic threats to more extreme cases like the involvement of ITT in Chile; or the manufacturing of poverty through control of economic resources, as well as more personal events such as the production of accidents and injury. Such products cannot be seen simply as by-products of the formal function – the goods and services intended to be produced – *because they are not inherently necessary to their production*. It may be the case that if, for example, pollution is not to be produced, this would have negative consequences for the viability of producing a particular product. But, then, it should be considered whether pollution is a reasonable price to pay for that organisation's activities – in other words, whether private profit is more important than the public disadvantage of pollution. Since organisations are judged in terms of what they do, there needs to be a holistic appreciation of that, one that does not focus only on ***intended*** products and consequences but also includes ***unintended*** products and consequences, because, although unintended, they are, nonetheless, products and consequences.

Secondly, many of the things that happen in an organisation do not contribute to either the intended or the unintended products of that organisation. It is conventional in the analysis of organisations to distinguish between *productive work* and *non-productive work* and, in the case of the latter, to distinguish between *necessary* non-productive work and *unnecessary* non-productive work. In work design the conventional objective is to minimise the amount of necessary non-productive work and to eliminate altogether the unnecessary non-productive work. But, although this may be a highly laudable objective, there is no way of identifying, unequivocally, what might be both unnecessary and non-productive.

Much of what happens in organisations can be seen as the outcome of managerial fiat – that is, it is the outcome of decisions made by those with the power to make decisions. Understanding power in the sense that it has been used here, however – with the emphasis on micro-power – implies that everyone in an organisation is making decisions, all the time, and always by fiat. Suppose, for example, that a manager decides to go to a conference in New York: there is no way of knowing whether this is likely to be of practical benefit for the organisation or is just a 'jolly' for the manager. At the other end of the spectrum, if a word processor operator decides to spend time cleaning a mouse mat, there is no way of knowing whether this is of practical benefit to the organisation, or a welcome break from pressing keys, or just an obsession with cleanliness on the part of the operator. Even the most ardent application of management services techniques to the organisation of work cannot resolve these questions. In any case, while there may not be direct practical benefit, there may well be indirect benefit, if the activity makes the actor 'feel better'.

Micro-power in action

A prominent US politician and ex-basketball superstar, Bill Bradley, was invited to make a speech at a large political banquet. During the meal the waiter came round and served Bradley with a pat of butter. Bradley reacted to this by asking if he could have two pats of butter.

'Sorry,' the waiter replied. 'Just one pat of butter each.'

'I don't think you can know who I am,' Bradley responded. 'I'm Bill Bradley, Rhodes Scholar, professional basketball player, world champion, United States senator.'

'Well,' the waiter said. 'Maybe you don't know who I am.'

'As a matter of fact I don't,' Bradley replied. 'Who are you?'

'I'm the guy,' said the waiter, 'who's in charge of the butter.'

Source: Reported in M. Kettle, 'Ten Steps to the White House', *The Guardian*, 1 March 1999, from which the speech here is directly quoted.

Clearly, some decisions may be key decisions in terms of achieving the outputs, intended or unintended, of the organisation. But far more decisions made in the organisation have nothing to do with that – particularly in consideration that alternative decisions could have been made with precisely the same effect. The manager could have chosen to go and play golf, for example, or the word processor operator could have chosen to go and have a cigarette in the toilets. *Most* decisions are probably not important in terms of what 'the organisation' does. Equally, the decisions which *are* important are not hierarchically distributed, so that the more senior you are, the more key your decisions are. The ability to make key decisions, or the possibility of making key decisions, may even be randomly distributed throughout an organisation. **There are many things that go on in organisations that need to be understood as part of them, but which have no relevance to the intended outcomes – yet there is no way of knowing what their contribution may be.** These things, too, should not be excluded from the model of organisation.

Parking? Fine!

Each of us works in a different university. Each organisation has the same intended 'product', and each is relatively successful in achieving this formal intention. The formal structures and processes of the two institutions are similar, but by no means identical – though, if success is a product of structure and process, as conventional wisdom implies, one would expect them to be identical. Some of the differences might, at first sight, appear to be trivial but, on closer examination, it can be seen that their ramifications may be very far from trivial.

In recognition that it is functional for people to be able to park their car on campus, each university provides car parking space. To be able to park legitimately it is necessary to have an official sticker on your car. It is acknowledged that members of the organisation, being, generally, middle-class professional people, may have access to more than one car and it is quite legitimate to use a different car with the same permit – but not to use more than one car at a time. But in one university it is possible to have a sticker per car to be used and in the other university only one sticker is provided, which has to be transferred from car to car. The objective is the same – to control the use of parking space – but the means is different.

A possible explanation for this difference is that, in the former case, members of the organisation are trusted not to use two cars at once, while, in the latter case, trust is withheld by making it impossible to use two cars at once.

The whole issue of car parking has no direct relevance to the intended products of the organisation – but there may be very significant consequences of the recognition that, even in such minor matters, your organisation regards you as trustworthy . . . or not.

These circumstances are the consequence of someone making a simple decision on whether one or two permits should be issued. Obviously the intention behind the decision is not to make a statement about trust, yet that is the outcome. The decision made is, clearly, a function of *who* makes it, not a matter of functional necessity, because, if it were an issue of functional necessity, the decision would be the same in both cases.

The decision produces behaviour. But the behaviour is not simply parking a car, and the behaviour effects may permeate myriad other activities at work.

Michel Foucault identified three types of labour in organisations: productive labour, symbolic labour and dressage (see also Chapter 10). Productive labour is that which is necessary to the production of outputs. Symbolic labour is labour associated with prevailing cultural conditions and may include ritualistic aspects. An example is a graduation ceremony. Students do not actually graduate until they have been processed through a graduation ceremony which usually involves dressing up in an otherwise rare form of academic uniform, parading, the use of archaic language, shaking someone's hand and, perhaps, being handed a blank roll of paper. However, this is not necessarily directly non-productive labour. Although it may seem a somewhat ridiculous exercise in the context of the educative aims of both student and organisation, it can, even so, constitute, for example, a useful marketing exercise, or satisfy a felt need for a rite of passage. Labour as dressage, however, has no such useful function. It is labour whose sole purpose is to discipline, to produce a performance, in its theatrical sense, not because such discipline and performance is necessary, but to demonstrate submission to control. It is not enough simply to do, but required to do in particular prescribed ways, whether or not what is prescribed is appropriate or relevant to the actual task.

Thus, there are two things that need to be recognised and acknowledged about organisations. *Firstly*, **they produce consequences from their activities beyond those that they formally intend to produce.** *Secondly*, **a lot of the activities within organisations are unconnected with the formal purposes and could be done differently to the same effect.** If we seek to understand organisation and organisational behaviour it is imperative that these activities, too, be included in our models of what an organisation is.

The rhizome: a root metaphor?

In this book, we started out with the simple but basic concept of the **signifier/ signified relationship** as the key building block to all that followed. Another key concept in the book is that of **micro-power**, which constitutes a matrix of decision-making events in organisations. Micro-power is not just dyadic, interpersonal and episodic, but a totalising presence. We suggested that any explanation of organisation and organisational behaviour needs to acknowledge its process as a defining characteristic of behaviour. Gilles Deleuze and Félix Guattari use, in their work, a somewhat similar concept, **micropolitics**, in preference to micro-power. They describe micropolitics as flows of belief and desire, which operate at all levels of interaction, and which are ubiquitous and universal. For Deleuze and Guattari, micropolitics are the essence of what they call 'rhizomatics'. It is this concept of the **organisation as rhizome** that we want, briefly, to develop.

The rhizome is not an easy concept to define and it is worth exploring what is meant by it. Literally, rhizome is a botanical term and refers to a particular type of plant root – 'an underground stem producing roots and leafy shoots', as *Chambers Dictionary* describes it. A rhizome is quite distinct from any other plant root types, such as the tap root or the tree-like branching kind – the etymology of rhizome is 'root mass'. Think of a rhizome as a network of interconnections or of interconnectedness, but not one that follows any pattern or regularity. Deleuze and Guattari define it like this:

'. . . the rhizome connects any point to any other point . . . It is composed not of units but of dimensions, or rather directions in motion. It has neither beginning nor end, but always a middle from which it grows and which it overspills . . . The rhizome operates by variation, expansion, conquest, capture, offshoots.' (1988: 21)

and

'. . . any point of a rhizome can be connected to anything other, and must be'. (1988: 7)

and

'A rhizome may be broken, shattered at a given spot, but it will start up again on one of its old lines, or on new lines.' (1988: 9)

In other words, a rhizome is a tangled mass of randomly developing connections following no logical pattern. It is always connecting points to other points. If disrupted, it can start up again in multitudinous ways. The rhizome produces a plant superstructure, but not in a way that is directly related to the organisation of its root network. Plants are not the only things that are rhizomic. Deleuze and Guattari themselves illustrate the idea with examples of animal communities, such as that of rats, and burrows such as rabbit warrens can be seen as rhizomic. The rhizome which is of most interest here is the human. Furthermore, **not only are humans organised rhizomically, but, also, they organise rhizomically**.

To talk about organisations as rhizomes is to say that they are, in effect, constituted by flows of desire, belief, micropolitics, micro-power, which are unspecifiable, unpredictable and uncapturable and which may, or may not, lead to specific, predictable

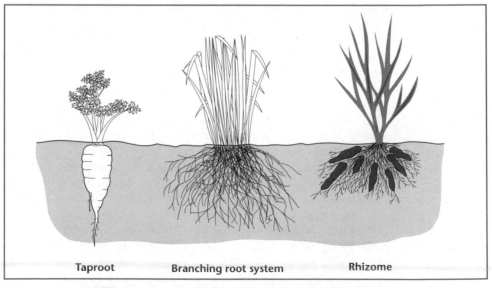

Taproot   Branching root system   Rhizome

Different ways in which plants can be rooted to the spot

and identifiable outcomes. **Organisational activity, organisational behaviour, is, in such terms, a tangled mass of randomly developing connections which, as a totality, follow no logical pattern, can occur in multitudinous ways and connect everything to everything else.** The decision-making which goes on in organisations, ubiquitous and universal, is itself rhizomic and produces activity and behaviour which is rhizomic – unspecifiable, unpredictable, uncapturable. As a model of organisation, the rhizome also has the virtue that it represents the profoundly dynamic quality of organisation and organisational behaviour, ongoing, constantly moving, developing, but in unspecifiable directions.

The rhizome as metaphor

To recapitulate, briefly: a metaphor is a device that aids our understanding through perception of similarities between concepts, or objects, which are dissimilar. In other words, entities which, for all practical purposes, are unlike each other can be seen to share certain characteristics, or isomorphisms (from the Greek iso- meaning equal, and -morph, meaning form). It is, indeed, their very dissimilarity which makes a metaphor effective, by encouraging us to think about something in a different way.

Take, for example, the metaphor of organisation as machine. Both organisations and machines have components which interact with other components within a structure, which produces an output. In this respect they can be seen as isomorphic. But an organisation is *not* a machine.

Metaphors are models. They contain less information than that which they represent. As with all models, there are no absolutely good or absolutely bad metaphors – they are good or bad only in so far as they serve the purpose of the user. The purpose is to enhance our understanding of, in this case, what an organisation is.

The metaphor of the **organisation as rhizome** suggests two obvious isomorphisms. *Firstly*, the processes of organisation can be likened to the root growth of a rhizome – tangled, interconnected, developing randomly, able to overcome fracture, and so on. *Secondly*, out of this confusion an outcome is produced. In the case of a literal rhizome, this is the above-ground plant growth, which, although deriving from the confused root mass, is not a product of a particular configuration, since many variations of the root mass will produce similar plants. Similarly, the confusion of organisation produces intended outcomes, its goods and services. Similar goods and services can be produced from widely varying organisational configurations and processes.

There is also, however, a *third* isomorphism which adds to the utility of the rhizome metaphor. This is best illustrated through an example. A potato is a rhizome. A tangled root mass produces a plant, but that is not 'the potato'. The root mass produces, within itself, random growths – actually food reserves for the plant – which we harvest. Thus, although, as far as the organism is concerned, the top-growth is its 'intended' outcome, from our point of view, it is the growths on the root that are the most important. In other words, organisations, as well as producing intended, or formal, outputs, produce other random outputs which may be of greater significance than the intended outputs.

▶

Think, for example, of Chernobyl. Although the complex organisation that was a nuclear power station formally produced electricity, certain behaviour by some of its members produced the explosion – of far greater, perhaps even inestimable, significance. Or, more positively, remember that it was only Fleming's poor housekeeping (behaviour) that led to the discovery of penicillin. Products such as the non-stick pan and the 'post-it' note were also accidental by-products. More mundanely, think of the person who has to retire early through illness caused by years spent working at a badly designed task, or the couple who meet for the first time over the photocopier at work and live happily ever after. All these are potatoes in the rhizome of their respective organisation.

It is not meant to be implied that this rhizomic organisation exists alongside the formal organisation, somehow in parallel to it. The formal organisation, its structures and processes, its formal function, its necessary productive work, are all part of the rhizome, not as a package but distributed within it, perhaps identifiable as, or at, nodal points, but escaping pattern, prediction and definition. Most of all, it is impossible to isolate from everything else that makes up the rhizome.

The rhizome is a purely descriptive model of organisation. It is not intended that organisations should be like a rhizome – indeed, that is precisely the point: that is how they are, whether one intends it or not. The rhizome is not controllable. That does not stop people trying to control it, but, as noted earlier, the nature of the rhizome is such that, if it is 'broken', it simply restarts itself in the same or different ways. This is why, for example, attempts to control organisational behaviour through cultural engineering never work, because culture, as organisation, is rhizomic and thus is not amenable to being engineered.

It is also interesting to note that, for a very long time, it has been acknowledged, in the conventional discourse of Organisational Behaviour, that there is a 'part' of organisation that is not controllable – traditionally called the informal organisation. It is in the nature of this informal organisation that it is not available to be managed – if it were, it would become part of the formal organisation – and so it has been treated as a sort of vaguely defined subset of the formal, running perhaps parallel, perhaps counter, to it. Seen rhizomically, the distinction between the two is irrelevant. In terms of the dynamics of micropolitics, micropower, decisions are just decisions and their province or status is not only meaningless, it is even unspecifiable. It is not possible to say definitively – or, perhaps, even at all – which behaviours are affecting, or effecting, which outcomes.

However, there is a cautionary note to be sounded. Rhizomic organisation still functions within the macro-ideology of capitalism. Desire and belief are not wholly unfocused, wholly unfettered. Capitalism needs capitalist organisations in order to survive, although it may not be particularly significant how those organisations operate in detail – as long as the desire is desire for those things that capitalism can produce and the belief is belief in the efficacy and inevitability of capitalism. This is why we have suggested that **capitalism as a regime of truth must be included in any attempt to understand organisation and organisational behaviour**, and must be questioned in terms of its efficacy (its inevitability is demonstrably a false claim) in providing a sustainable, equitable socio-economic system.

Thus, it is our view that organisational behaviour is the product, or outcome, of decision-making, and decision-making, (influenced by, for example, semiotics, perceptions of structure, discourses of knowledge and power, subjective rationalities, ideologies, issues of self, bounding processes and implicit concepts of efficiency which inform the process of organisation) is structured rhizomically – that is, by flows of belief and desire. This is *not* to say that organisational behaviour is a dead duck because nothing can influence or affect it, but it *is* to say that understanding what constitutes 'effective' organisational behaviour is a hugely complicated and difficult process – which, nonetheless, must be addressed. The point of understanding organisational behaviour, however, cannot be to manipulate behaviour, because, although, clearly, that can be done, such manipulation can never be total or even known to be decisively or effectively focused. What is more, there will always be areas of the decision-making to be manipulated, potentially the major part of it, which will escape manipulation.

The picture that emerges is:

'INFLUENCES'
  LEAD TO
    RHIZOMIC DECISION-MAKING
      LEADS TO
        BEHAVIOUR
          LEADS TO
            OUTCOMES

(though it needs to be remembered that the apparent linearity of this is simply a consequence of the written medium, a model, not a literal representation of the actual process). The task for the study of organisational behaviour is twofold – *analytically*, to explain how things are and, *synthetically*, to suggest ways of doing things differently. To do either of these things the focus must be on the 'influences' that go into decision-making. **The big question is, always, why does someone decide to do one thing rather than another?** What is implied here is that the answer to this question is far greater than any individual psychology or process of perception, but a complex texture of macro(politics) and micro(politics). The challenge is to achieve desired outcomes.

For example . . .

Let us try to illustrate this with an example referred to on a number of occasions elsewhere in this book: organisational stress. High levels of experienced stress are an apparent and widespread feature of contemporary organisations. Current wisdom is that this is inevitable and that the solution is to minimise the dysfunctions by training people to cope with stress. However, such an explanation, rooted in determinism, is not tenable in light of the models developed here. Stress, as an organisational outcome, results from particular behaviours emanating from particular decisions. If we want to reduce, or eliminate, organisationally related stress, then we need to make different decisions. To do that we need to understand how or why we made the current decisions, and, to do that, we need to look at the influences on those decisions.

It is feasible to suggest a few possibilities. In terms of *ideological* influences, for example, it may be held that, if employees experience stress, then that is an unfortunate, but inevitable, consequence of them having to earn their living – it is the worker's job to work and if work is stressful, so be it. There may even be an element of Social Darwinism, such as, stress is for wimps and the sooner these people are stressed out of the organisation and replaced by people who can cope, the better. In terms of *modelling*, perhaps those with power in the organisation do not believe that stress really exists – they may have attenuated it out of their model of organisation. In terms of the influences of the *discourse of power/knowledge*, perhaps it is felt that it is a good thing to keep people stressed, because it keeps them in their place and helps maintain power differentials. In terms of the influence of concepts of *efficiency*, it may be felt that organisational efficiency is served by maintaining high levels of experienced stress, and that it is cheaper to get people cured of the dysfunctions outside the organisation than it would be to reduce the stressors. In terms of the *semiotics*, it may be believed that indications of experienced stress do not really signify stress, but signify recalcitrant behaviour. And so on.

If the desired outcome is to reduce experienced stress in organisations, then all such models have to be uncovered, and changed. Obviously, not all decisions made in organisations actively contribute to increasing levels of stress and one of the 'forensic' aspects of the study of organisational behaviour should be to discover which are the ones that do. Of course, there are also those who would argue that we should simply forget about what causes stress now, and just re-engineer our organisations as stress-free zones. Either way, at first glance it may seem that what we are suggesting is an overly rationalistic and analytical approach – but it is not. What we are saying is that **human actions can change things**. Whether desired outcomes are achieved is an empirical issue, a matter of testing actual outcomes, not one of prescription or of predetermination. It is an issue of **praxis**. It must also be remembered that, even if the stress-free organisation were ever to be achieved, it would still be rhizomic, full of (arbitrary) decision-making.

So, what are the chances of such an approach gaining discursive approval? Within the conventional discourse of Organisational Behaviour, very small. However, the claimed advent of postmodernity is producing the opportunities for new discourses to appear – and the study of organisational behaviour is no exception in this.

Postmodernism

Postmodernism is yet another complex concept, defying easy description or explanation. While the relevance of Poststructuralism to understanding organisational behaviour is well established, it is still quite unclear what will be the impact of Postmodernism. That it has relevance to the understanding of organisational behaviour is not in doubt, if only because of its ontological, epistemological, cultural role in the contemporary social world. But one of the problems is that any meaning of the term has become obscured by its popular application to just about anything, regardless of whether or not it is appropriate. Even in its most rigorous usage, Postmodernism, as a signifier, has the confusing quality of being able to signify complete opposites – such as, increasing ambiguity or flexibility *and* increasing subjugation to the demands of capitalism. Fortunately, however, all variations of the (rigorous) use of the term 'Postmodernism' do embody a core concept, irrespective of whether it is specifically articulated or not. This core characteristic is **the loss of faith in *the* rational**. But, before exploring this loss of faith, it is useful to situate Postmodernism in relation to that which it comes 'after', Modernism.

Modernism

Modernism is, perhaps, best understood as an epoch, a period in which the 'set' of ideas which we associate with Modernism predominated, and which is often seen as opposing other 'sets' of ideas, especially Romanticism, Mysticism, Classicism, and so on. Modernism permeated all aspects of human endeavour – the arts, architecture, medicine, education, management, to name a few – and reflected a belief in the rational solution of all human problems through the application of Science. Science, the epitome of 'the rational', could, it was held, solve the problems, not just of the natural world, but also of the social world. It would solve, for example, problems of health through the development and use of antibiotics, and public sanitation, problems of ignorance through mass education in large schools, problems of hunger through the use of pesticides to maximise agricultural output, problems of housing through the development of techniques to build high-rise flats, and so on. Most important for our purposes, the problems of organisational behaviour could be solved through Scientific Management, or, more generally, management as science. The application of Science to social problems promised a utopia of well-fed, healthy, educated and happy people. The gloss would be provided by the arts, through realism – kitchen-sink drama rather than Jane Austen – and by freeing people's ability to see the underlying signifieds, rather than merely observing the pretty signifiers – Picasso rather than Gainsborough.

However, it eventually started to become apparent that Science was not solving social problems – and was even creating new ones. This realisation did not occur with a bang and did not occur simultaneously in all aspects of human activity. If it has occurred at all, it has been a gradual, uneven, episodic process, taking place over many years. We say 'if it has occurred' because some commentators do not accept that there is such a 'thing' as Postmodernism and, even among those who do accept it, there is so little agreement about what, exactly, it is. Some argue that Postmodernism represents a distinct break with Modernism, others that it is merely the latest phase of Modernism. For our purposes here, Postmodernism can best be seen as an irregular emergent process, becoming recognisable some time after the Second World War – though, as an illustration of the diversity of opinion regarding Postmodernism, one commentator, Charles Jencks, emblematically dates the start of Postmodernism in architecture as 3.32 p.m. on 15 July 1972, the moment when the Pruitt-Igoe housing development in St Louis, Missouri, a symbol of the modernist development of 'machines for living', was dynamited; others suggest that it pre-dates the twentieth century.

With regard to the conventional discourse of Organisational Behaviour, however, it could be argued that this is still firmly rooted in Modernism,

though with emergent signs that, in this aspect of the social world as in others, Science has failed to solve organisational problems, as noted in this book. Whether Postmodernism will provide the answers remains to be seen.

We said earlier that the one irreducible premise of Postmodernism was the loss of faith in *the* rational. This has led one commentator, Hal Foster, to suggest that Postmodernism can be seen in terms of two distinct and opposite approaches, which can be used to highlight the many contradictions and the lack of coherence which characterises the so-called postmodern epoch.

The Postmodernism of Reaction

The first of these approaches responds to the realisation that rational thinking and Science have not solved social problems by resorting to a reliance on instinct, gut feelings, simplification and faith. At the macro level, this might be seen as an explanation for the contemporary upsurge in, for example, nationalism, or football violence. If there is no absolute or transcendent rationality, then there can be no absolute or transcendent right and wrong – there can be moral rights and wrongs, but these are just matters of opinion. Thus, for example, if you support football Team A and feel an instinctive dislike for supporters of football Team B, from a modernist point of view this is irrational. It might be argued, amongst other reasons, that they are just people like you, who enjoy football for the same reasons as you do, that their preference for a different team makes perfectly good sense – for example, they live in Town B and it is both sensible and easier to support your local team, that if no one supported Team B there would be no Team B and, therefore, no one for Team A to play against, and, therefore, no football, and so on. Yet, clearly, there is violence associated with supporters of football teams and so, equally clearly, the reasoned case as to why there should not be, fails.

What can be seen emergent here is what some theorists of Postmodernism have labelled 'neo-tribalism'. As the rational basis for living in social proximity to others fails, we fall back on a form of tribalism where hostility to, and conflict with, other tribes creates identity and sanctions such rules as a basis for social existence. On a larger scale, the conflict in the former Yugoslavia can be seen in this same light. The loss of faith in *the* rational results in a general regression to premodern behaviour patterns, fuelled by belief in some Golden Age which was lost but can be regained.

The most obvious example of this, and which has the strongest implications for behaviour in organisations, is the rise of Authoritarianism. In the liberal 1960s, managers used to claim that they managed through the consent of those who were managed. Today, the justification for managerial action is the claim to the manager's *right* to manage. The ideas of democratic, participative, management, of satisfying, enriching, labour, have, despite the rhetoric of Human Resource Management theory and practice, given way to a more brutal approach to managing people – increased working hours, more stress, less security, zero hours contracts, child labour, sweat shops, increased surveillance, panopticism, and so on. The Postmodernism of Reaction implies a return to styles of management popularly associated with nineteenth-century factory culture, and, indeed, there are many indications that this is the direction in which we are going.

The Postmodernism of Resistance

Starting from the same point as the Postmodernism of Reaction, this approach moves off in a totally different direction. **For the Postmodernism of Resistance, the loss of faith in *the* rational provides, not a threat, but an opportunity.** Escaping the shackles of a supposed dominant rationality, embodied in those with power, allows the emergence of different ways of thinking, of different perspectives, of legitimate challenge to the orthodoxy. One arena where this response has been particularly prominent is the arts, represented in, for example, the challenge to what is often referred to as 'high culture'. This 'high culture' reflects the view that there is, or ought to be, objectively defined merit in art, that experts can tell good art from bad art, that aesthetics is a science and should be understood scientifically. Thus, Shakespeare, Beethoven and Rembrandt are good, while Agatha Christie, Andrew Lloyd-Webber and Tretchikoff are not; white art is good, black art is not; and so on. But the Postmodernism of Resistance reflects the view that experts are not the arbiters of taste, of quality, of absolute definitions of merit – all that experts do is exercise power, maintain particular and partial interests, sustain the discourse of High Culture.

The liberating tendency of this approach has had little impact in the conventional discourse of Organisational Behaviour, challenging as it does the expert status of both Organisational Behaviour theorists and managers. On the other hand, it could be suggested that their shortcomings are well recognised by, for example, the managed, and, probably, by many others not associated with the profession. The managed have rarely subscribed to the dominant logic of management, to the received interpretation of rationality represented by managers' claims. For the most part, they merely tolerate it because of their relative inability to challenge the dominant discourse. The managed have always had less faith in the techniques of the managers, and have their own logics, rationalities and reasons to describe the process of being managed. A simple test of this is to read accounts of being managed by those who have experienced it. They bear no relation whatever to the accounts of management produced by the 'experts'.

The force of the Postmodernism of Resistance is not just to challenge the claim that there is an over-arching or transcendent rationality, objective, scientific, impartial, but also, in that process, to legitimate alternative approaches, legitimate critique of the existing dominant discourse without having to embrace its logic, and to 'resist' any tendency of any approach to become dominant. **What that legitimation achieves is the opening up of possibilities and opportunities for genuine choice about desired outcomes for organisation.** The rationality of Science focuses on means, claiming that if you get the means right – that is, use means appropriate to Science – the ends simply follow from that. In that sense, the ends are predetermined by the means. Within the Postmodernism of Resistance, on the other hand, nothing can be seen as predetermined, because everything is the result, or effect, of human construction. Thus, means and ends are both opened up, through praxis, to development and articulation within the context of rationalities other than that of a science and an objectivity in the service of capitalism. *This does not mean that the abandonment of objectivism, characteristic of all versions of Postmodernism, necessarily implies an irremediable relativism, where nothing definitive can be said about anything, no judge-*

ments can be made and morality is reduced to personal opinion. On the contrary, it provides possibly the first opportunity since the onset of Modernism for a genuine and meaningful debate about the plurality of possibilities for human development, based on rigorously conceptualised alternatives rooted in intersubjective agreement and interests.

All this is represented in the field of knowledge about organisation(s) by the gradual emergence of a new discourse, reflected in many of the references cited in this book. This new discourse does not take its inspiration from the existing discourse but is driven by the desire to escape its inherent limitations and to provide models of organisational behaviour which have better explanatory power, in particular by rooting its considerations in more comprehensive models of what people are like and of the social context in which they behave. This nascent discourse is characterised by an extraordinary variety of approaches to understanding organisation and organisational behaviour, reflecting an extraordinary variety of concerns, notably about the impacts of conventional organisational theory and practice. That this discourse fits into the framework of the Postmodernism of Resistance is signified by the apparent lack of coherence about the means and ends that organisations should adopt. However, it is precisely the point that a discourse within the Postmodernism of Resistance should not adopt an artificial coherence, but be a process of providing as wide a range as possible of information and conceptual development, from which those who participate in organisations can make an informed choice about the means and ends that are desirable.

It is worth noting that, so far, the 'reaction' of the conventional discourse of Organisational Behaviour to this nascent alternative has been to ignore it. If the alternative discourse continues to gain ground in the legitimation of its concerns, it cannot be expected that such negligence will also continue. It will, undoubtedly, try to stifle it and, almost certainly, to do this through incorporation and maintaining its grip on the rewards and sanctions associated with discursive acceptability. Under conditions of postmodernity, this will occur through the Postmodernism of Reaction. However, **we cannot un-know what we know about organisations**.

One of the defining features of Postmodernism is the abandonment of the idea that progress, and thought, develop in a linear fashion. In this sense, Postmodernism could be seen as embodying the articulation of the rhizomic condition. Whatever ensues from this recognition by Postmodernism will develop rhizomically – as ever. If thought, behaviour and action are rhizomic it is hardly to be wondered at that they result in rhizomic organisation(s). The recognition of this can only be beneficial in terms of organising society, and organising organisations, for desired outcomes.

In the end

The point of understanding organisational behaviour is not to control it in the service of particular and partial interests. Of course, such control can be achieved, though it is not necessary to understand organisational behaviour in order to be able to control it, because the only way to control it is through the exercise of power and coercion. Such means can never be effective indefinitely and so it is not surprising that attempts to achieve such control end, not only in dysfunctions, but also in failure. This does not mean that there is nothing to be done. On the contrary, given the unparalleled significance of behaviour in organisations in constructing the world we live in, it means that it is imperative that we try to achieve an adequate and appropriate understanding of what influences organisational behaviour if we are ever to achieve desired outcomes in the context of responsible organisations – whatever we might take these terms to signify.

We started out studying organisational behaviour a long time ago, motivated by awareness of the utterly unsatisfactory explanations of organisational behaviour offered by the conventional discourse, as witnessed by our own extensive experience of being members of organisations. This conventional discourse has focused its efforts on the micro-manipulation of behaviour in organisations in service of increasing the efficiency of individual organisations. As such, it is not only very narrowly focused, but also ignores the wider context of organisational behaviour, its shaping of our natural and social world. Most importantly, it fails to acknowledge that most of what happens in the world, for good or for ill, is the outcome of organisational behaviour.

What we have proposed here is *a rethinking of organisational behaviour*. This rethinking is aimed at providing a new, or, at any rate, different, basis for thinking about organisational behaviour which will enhance our understanding of it. It is also about *rethinking the role of understanding organisational behaviour*. It is our view that, because everything is affected, and effected, by organisational behaviour, and organisational behaviour affects, and effects, everything, it is necessary to understand organisational behaviour in all its complexity and variety and to put it in a holistic context.

We may progress towards universal health and happiness through the unalloyed development of democratic capitalism, or we may utterly destroy the social and natural world by their exploitation. We may do something completely different, such as finding ways to enjoy the benefits of what we do now while eliminating the disbenefits. We may even construct a radical change which is as yet inconceivable. But, whatever happens, it will be done by people behaving in organisations.

Afterword

Revisiting the arguments of this book for the second edition, in light of the events and developments of the intervening period since the first edition, has reinforced our view that, because organisation(s), and thus organisational behaviour, are so significant in producing the world that we live in, both the good and the bad, it is profoundly important to understand why people do the things that they do, and especially what constraints and opportunities characterise that behaviour. The 'official science' for doing this is formalised in the discourse of Organisational Behaviour, but that discourse manifests little interest in this broad task, preferring, instead, to focus on the manipulation of behaviour in organisations in accordance with the interests of management. If we seek to understand organisational behaviour, we need different concepts, with better explanatory power, compared to those currently to be found in the orthodox discourse. This is what this book tries to provide.

And what of the organisational world since the first edition? As far as the kind of problems that we identified as characterising organisational behaviour are concerned, they are, not surprisingly, still with us. As we noted in Chapter 1, when we look for examples of these problems we are really spoilt for choice. A random selection includes: a gerrymandered presidential election in the USA, a country that sees its current mission as to export 'democracy' to other, sometimes unwilling, 'less enlightened' countries; a disastrous outbreak, in the UK, of foot and mouth disease, caused by the mismanagement of one farm in the north of England; the implosion of Enron, taking with it the consultancy Arthur Andersen, and resulting, in 2006, in the conviction of Enron's 'chief culprits', who have been given prison sentences that may well see them spending the rest of their lives behind bars; other major corporate collapses based on one kind of mismanagement or another, such as WorldCom, and the Martha Stewart affair; a series of rail accidents in the UK, caused by poor track maintenance, and leading to the collapse of Railtrack; the continuing spread of the MRSA virus in hospitals, facilitated by poor organisational practice; the growing pensions scandal; the acknowledgement by the UK government that the Home Office has become, in effect, unmanageable, and so 'unfit' for its crucial role in national governance; the organisational devastation of both health and education provision; and so it goes on! This, of course, is without even mentioning terror attacks in New York, Bali, Madrid, London, or global warming and other environmental problems, such as Hurricane Katrina, destruction of the Amazon's rain-forest, desertification, rising sea levels . . . At the more localised level, the degradation of work continues; work-related dysfunctions proliferate; unemployment remains a problem; wage rates at the bottom of the hierarchy continue to be squeezed, while executive salaries rocket; industrial disputes are on the increase . . .

One can say with some confidence that organisational problems have not been resolved, and nor has the ability of Organisational Behaviour to illuminate them. So, is there any cause for optimism? On one hand, perhaps not. As we have suggested, challenges to the orthodoxy in the social sciences do not rest on their explanatory power, and do tend to stimulate responses designed to protect the established 'truth'. The apparently undiminished attack on the concept of incommensurable knowledge paradigms still chases, implicitly or explicitly, the dream of an ultimately unified knowledge – which will, of course, be the knowledge approved by, acceptable to, the powerful. This trend may also be symbolised in the resurgence detected by some writers, of the comfort blanket of Realism in theorising about organisation(s), which, again, implies, as a logical consequence, the potential to achieve objective truth.

On the other hand, perhaps there is cause for optimism. The critique of the orthodoxy of Organisation Theory in general, and of Organisational Behaviour in particular, grows unabated, and represents new developments and new directions for the field. There is a re-emergence of interest in Political Economy and its relevance for organisation. The work of thinkers such as Hardt and Negri is proving to be influential, developing links between Poststructuralism and a 'new' Marxian activism. Among journals that represent critical approaches to the field, a relatively recent addition, the on-line journal *Ephemera*, proclaims a concern with the theory *and politics* of organisation. There are increases in demands for the study of organisation to 'reposition' and to 'repoliticise' itself. One publication gathered more than thirty writers to offer a vision of the future non-Functionalist Business School. What is significant about such work is that it proceeds untroubled by the attempts of the conventional discourse to impose a dominant unitary approach, and is often characterised by a sense of the urgency of developing adequate ways to think about and understand the contemporary organisational world. And, despite the uncertain status of Postmodernism, there continues to be a proliferation of 'voices' considering aspects of organisation(s) from a wide range of perspectives outwith the official discourse, perspectives as varied as queer theory, science fiction, monstrosity, postcolonialism, for example. However tempted the orthodoxy may be to seek to repress such voices, it is unlikely to be able to do it – to replace the lid on this particular Pandora's box!

Perhaps the final word could go to the cybernetician Ashby, and his Law of Requisite Variety, which has been neatly summarised as stating that 'only variety can absorb variety'. In other words, if you want to control a system – a car, a person, an organisation, an economy, an eco-system, for example – you have to be as smart as the system is complex. If you are not, the system will be beyond your ability to control – the car will crash, the prisoner will escape, the company will go bankrupt, the planet will become unfit for human life, or, indeed, any other kind of life. These are exactly the sort of problems that we now face. Some are of *relatively* minor importance, but many are not. To solve these problems we need to be smart, but it seems that we are not, or, anyway, not smart enough. It is action informed by *adequate* thinking – in other words, by praxis – that is needed. Simple, and simplistic, solutions will not help us to understand the complex problems of organisational behaviour.

Bibliography

During the preparation of this book we have been aware of an undiminished stream of books on the subject of organisational behaviour appearing, which are, in essence, restatements of the orthodox understanding of the subject. Yet it has been our proposal that organisational behaviour needs to be 'rethought' and that this particular straitjacket needs to be escaped. It is not possible to rethink organisational behaviour from within the dominant discourse of the subject – this would be, simply, a contradiction in terms. In this book we have sought to demonstrate how a different way of thinking, especially that offered by Poststructuralism, can expand our understanding and contribute to a different way of thinking about organisational behaviour. Much of the source literature we have used does not directly focus on organisations as they are conventionally understood, though it has provided a lot of inspiration for writers on organisations outside the dominant discourse. For example, the work of Michel Foucault, whilst addressing issues of organisation and organisations, was not conceived specifically as a contribution to the discourse of Organisation Studies, though his work is increasingly being applied to that purpose – see, for example, among others, Burrell (1988), Townley (1994), McKinlay and Starkey (1998). However, a generalised concept of organisation as a process is central to the poststructuralist literature. Any particular organisation is merely an example of this generalised process of organisation, and a historically specific one, at that.

One of the omissions of the conventional discourse that we have noted is its failure to consider Capitalism in its role as the informing context, the regime of truth, of organisation, a context, however, of considerable significance to post-structuralist writers. Gilles Deleuze and Félix Guattari have, perhaps, been two of the most explicit of those writers in this tradition who have linked Capitalism and organisation. Their work has long been regarded as seminal by poststruc-turalists, and in the development of Poststructuralism, and is, increasingly, being seen as relevant to those interested in the 'Postmodernism of Resistance'. In our view, the key texts are Deleuze and Guattari (1984, 1988) – *Anti-Oedipus* and *A Thousand Plateaus*, both sub-titled *Capitalism and Schizophrenia*. Deleuze and Guattari (1983) is a brief abstraction, focusing on the rhizome, from *A Thousand Plateaus*. They have written other books, both separately and together, which are also relevant – see, for example, Guattari (1984), Deleuze and Guattari (1994), or Deleuze and Parnet (included in Deleuze and Guattari (1983)).

It needs to be acknowledged that their work is regarded as difficult, though very rewarding of effort. It can even be said that a lot of the commentaries on their work, though somewhat more accessible, are, perhaps, still less than an easy read – for example, Massumi (1992), Goodchild (1996) – though we ourselves have written on Deleuze and Guattari's relevance to organisation, in what we *hope* is a rather more accessible way – Jackson and Carter (1986), Carter and Jackson (2004b). There is a considerable amount of interest in their work these days, and it would be reasonable to expect more, and possibly more accessible, material to appear. Of course, being difficult to read does not mean that it is not worth reading what already exists! The concept of the rhizome is developed par-ticularly in Deleuze and Guattari (1988) – but it rewards reading in the context of Deleuze and Guattari (1984).

There are an amazing number of books that have 'Postmodernism', in some linguistic version, in their title, let alone those that do not use the word in the title but which do consider it in some way. It would not be useful to attempt to list all these books. It is worth noting, however, that it is important to remember that writers have a wide range of orientations towards Postmodernism, and this needs to be taken into account when reading about it. In our view, reading Hal Foster's 'Postmodernism: A Preface', the introduction to his collection *Postmodern Culture* (1985), which sets out the distinction we have used, is an excellent place to start with Postmodernism, even if you know nothing else about it. There are a number of introductory texts – an *Introducing Postmodernism* (Appignanesi and Garratt 2004) – also available as a double audio cassette, a Key Ideas book (Smart 1993), a Teach Yourself book (Ward 1997), and various readers. See also, for example, Waugh (1992), Lyon (1994), Anderson (1995), Natoli (1997).

There are some texts which are regarded as seminal, notably Lyotard (1984) – *The Postmodern Condition: A Report on Knowledge*. A counterposition is to be found in Habermas (1981) – 'Modernity Versus Postmodernity', which also appears in Foster (1985), but as 'Modernity – An Incomplete Project'. And then, of course, there is anything by Baudrillard. A number of other texts are also important – for example, Featherstone (1988), Harvey (1989), Jameson (1991), Bauman (1992, 1993) – though, again, their attitude to Postmodernism is not uniform. Generally, attitudes can be seen as ranging through seeing it as the 'new reality', seeing it as an aberration to be corrected, seeing it as non-existent, as well as those who see it as both positive and a cause for celebration.

There are a number of texts that discuss Postmodernism in relation to Modernism – see, for example, B.S. Turner (1990), Best and Kellner (1991), Norris (1992), Smart (1992), Brooker (1992). See also Bauman (1991). Postmodernism even has a history now – Bertens (1994) – while Latour (1993) argues that 'we have never been modern' yet, also implied by Giddens (1990) and, of course, Habermas (1981). A different group of writers suggest that the experienced change of contemporary society is explicable through Postmodernism – for example, Crook, Pakulski and Waters (1992), Kumar (1995). Two books which specifically relate Postmodernism to the Social Sciences are Rosenau (1992) and Hollinger (1994).

There are also an increasing number of books and articles that purport to relate Postmodernism to various aspects of the study, and practice, of organisations. These vary enormously in rigour, relevance and perspective. Cooper and Burrell (1988) is widely regarded as a significant introduction. Other examples include Clegg (1990), Carter and Jackson (1990, 1993), Jackson and Carter (1992, 1995a), Hassard and Parker (1993), Boje, Gephart and Thatchenkery (1996), Chan (2000), Hancock and Tyler (2001) and Linstead (2004). There are even books that seek to relate Postmodernism to specific organisational functions, such as Brown (1995, 1998).

Since the first edition of this book there have been some notable developments in the field, although these are less apparent in the conventional discourse of Organisational Behaviour in particular, or that of Organisation Studies more generally – of note here are, for example, an impressive number of new editions of established texts. Amongst those who engage in the development of critique, however, there has been a broadening out, both in terms of theoretical diversity and in terms of diversity in focuses. There has also been some reflection on this diversity, and its potential to contribute to the adequacy of the discourse to generate understanding, and amelioration of the problems of organisation that we now face. *Organization* (2003b) may stand as an example of this reflective tendency, but one that is couched in terms of a 'manifesto' for the (re)direction of research efforts. The broadening out of theoretical diversity can be symbolised by the increasing range of philosophies, theories and ideas that are being examined in terms of their potential to contribute to understanding organisation(s), and, thereby, organisational behaviour. One example of this literature is Jones and Munro (2005). Their introduction offers an interesting view of the issues that have characterised work in the field in the two decades to 2005, and the range of theorists covered in the book includes what they call 'organization theorists', 'theorists of organization' and 'theorists with concepts for understanding organization' (2005: 8). It is perhaps too soon to say what may have lasting impact, but it can certainly be said that these are interesting times for the study of organisation.

The 'Afterword' refers specifically to a range of texts. The re-emergence of Realism in organisation theory is considered by Reed (2005) – for a different approach to this, see also Miles (2001). The best known works by Hardt and Negri are *Empire* (2000) and *Multitude* (2005). An example of the argument that there is a need for the study of organisation to 'reposition' itself is in Böhm (2005). The vision of a future non-Functionalist Business School is in Jones and O'Doherty (2005). An accessible introduction to Ashby's Law of Requisite Variety is in Beer (1981) – the summary phrase is from Beer (1981: 308).

Lecourt (2001) warns of the existence of, and dangers of, a developing 'mediocracy' amongst thinkers. Baudrillard (2005) is a very readable exposition of, amongst other things, the immanent denial that meets any questioning of the concept of objective reality, and the dangerous retreat ever further into the hyper-real that this entails. For Baudrillard, **'we are certainly further and further removed from the solution, but nearer and nearer to the problem'** **(2005: 34). There is certainly much to do!**

Glossary

Below are elaborations of some of the terms used in this book, but none of them is, or could be, definitive. The slant we have put on these terms emphasises the particular use that we have made of them. Many people would disagree and/or emphasise other aspects.

Analytic/Synthetic: These terms have complex and technical uses in Philosophy but have been used to signify something rather simpler here. Analysis is the attempt to understand the formative influences on the subject of study, such as semiotics, power, modelling, and so on, and how these influences affect outcomes. Synthesis is the attempt to construct a new holistic understanding, which may be more than an amalgam of what we already know, such as the ecosystemic organisation.

Behaviourism: A school of Psychology that aims to understand, and thereby to manipulate, human action through the observation of behaviour (behaviour modification). Behaviourism underpins much of the conventional discourse of Organisational Behaviour and is popular in all areas of Management and Organisation Studies, though its popularity has declined in other areas of applied psychology. According to Behaviourism, the primary influence on behaviour is environmental conditions – for example, if it is hot, you will feel thirsty and seek out a drink; if you are given an enriched job, you will work harder. Cultural Engineering is a classic example of trying to modify behaviour by changing ('improving') the cultural environment, with culture understood as independent of the people who 'inhabit' it. A difficulty for Behaviourism is identifying which stimuli affect action, in which way. For example, action may be stimulated, not by the enrichment of a task, but by fear that someone in authority is taking a close interest in your job! Behaviourism is a deterministic (q.v.) approach, and is not given much credence by more critical approaches to understanding organisational behaviour.

Bricolage: Literally, the French for do-it-yourself, this term is particularly associated with the work of the structuralist anthropologist, Claude Lévi-Strauss, who distinguished between two kinds of 'mind' – the 'Western' mind, trained in abstract and analytical ways of thinking, and the less formalised thinking of the 'savage' or 'primitive' mind. While the former will attempt to understand novel phenomena, concepts, problems, by constructing appropriate thinking tools, the latter re-uses whatever tools are already available. This is the analogy with DIY. The handyman lacks the specialist tools that a skilled artisan would have, but improvises with whatever is available. Thus, the trained mind understands aeroplanes in terms of aerodynamics, while the primitive mind might see them in terms of metal 'birds', birds being the best already available explanation of the phenomenon. In organisational terms, the management theorist may see the Chief Executive Officer as the product of a meritocracy, while the primitive mind might see this person as a tribal chief. The term is used, not to distinguish between, for example, developed and undeveloped societies, but to distinguish between different ways of thinking which are more or less present in all societies. The analogy with different societies simply serves the purpose of a metaphor. Both types of thinking have their advantages. The introduction of a new technology may be best realised through the application of the trained mind; launching a new product might benefit from more DIY thinking.

Chaos Theory: It seems increasingly common to see mention of Chaos Theory in the context of analysis of organisations, but, in that context, it is often best understood as a metaphor. Strangely, Chaos Theory is less about chaos, and more to do with identifying changing patterns of order that underlie apparently chaotic systems (which is why it is seen to have relevance to organisations). It seeks to explain complex, dynamic, non-linear systems, of which an organisation, a market, or an economy, are appropriate examples. Such systems may appear to exhibit low levels of predictability, but they may exhibit recognisable patterns of behaviour over time. They operate at the 'edge of chaos', never descending into total randomness, never coalescing into a fixed and stable order. They have the ability to switch, unpredictably and suddenly, from one sort of 'order' to another. The labour relations of an organisation can be used as an example: such relations are, clearly, complex, dynamic and non-linear, and, according to Conflict Theory (q.v.), a constant struggle between the will of managers and the desires of workers, individually and collectively. Such a system can remain *relatively* stable for long periods, but a small alteration to a variable – a supervisor swears at a worker, a bonus payment appears too small, the coffee machine breaks down – can tip the balance from stability into a strike. Various versions of Chaos Theory are used to study organisations, and it is sometimes linked to Complexity Theory. There are also links with Poststructuralism, notably with Deleuze and Guattari's rhizomatics. Chaos Theory offers a different type of explanation for organisational behaviour than does the simple determinism (q.v.) of the conventional discourse of Organisational Behaviour.

Conflict Theory: see **Unitarism**.

Critical Modernism: Critical Modernists, though sharing much of the disillusion felt regarding the failures of Modernism (q.v.), do not subscribe to the solutions offered by Postmodernism (q.v.). They retain faith in reason and objective rationality, arguing that the failures of Modernism are remediable and that the future utopia is to be gained by the increased, and improved, application of rational thought, but in a context of expressed social values. Work in this area is particularly closely associated with Critical Theory (q.v.).

Critical Theory: The more general term for a movement emerging around 1930, particularly associated with The Frankfurt School, which continues to be popular and which furnishes one of the major critiques of organisational life. Initially seen as a radical revision of Marxist thought, it has also incorporated a strong Freudian tradition and is closely associated with the attempt to synthesise the thinking of Marx and Freud. Critical Theory has an attachment to the idea of transcendent rationality, but sees this as a product of individuals, rather than a quality of an external world. Various forces intervene to prevent the achievement of this potentially transcendent rationality, the principal one being power.

Deconstruction: This is often referred to, but erroneously, as a method of discovering the concealed meaning in a text. Rather, Deconstruction is the theory that texts do contain multiple meanings, and that these can be accessed, potentially, by a variety of methods. Meanings may be 'contained' in a text by the very evidence that they have been deliberately unarticulated – for example, one word, concept, signifier, is chosen rather than another, which is, thereby, excluded. Meanings, as texts, are composed of signifiers, and can be as varied as the readers. Though we should not ignore the authorial intention, as far as it can be known, since this itself contains meaning, it cannot be given priority over any other reading. Some meanings might only materialise in some future period of reading – for example, reading Charles Dickens in the present day might produce a meaning which would have been impossible to conceive in Dickens' time, because of, say, intervening events which colour our understanding. Deconstruction allows the possibility of thinking to the limit of what can be thought, triggered by a literal or metaphorical text. (See also **Undecidability**.)

Description/Prescription: Analyses or theories that claim to be Descriptive claim, as the term suggests, to portray the world 'as it is'. Those that are Prescriptive are informed, implicitly or explicitly, by the claim that things are not the way that they *should be*, and that, by following their precepts, it will be possible to move from where we are now to the desired, and recommended, state. The claim to be Descriptive is typical of objectivist (q.v.), 'scientific' approaches. It is, however, important to note that many theories in Organisational Behaviour that claim to be Descriptive are, implicitly, Prescriptive – 'prescriptive' because they are imbued with value-laden assumptions that someone is not doing what they should be doing and that this can, and should, be put right, and 'implicitly' because such assumptions are neither articulated nor interrogated. (See also **Positive/Normative**.)

Determinism/Voluntarism: These concepts are often linked to objectivism (q.v.) and subjectivism (q.v.). Determinism is the belief that action in a given situation follows precisely from antecedent conditions. Thus, in ordinary language, water freezes at $0°$ Centigrade, an object released in free space 'falls' to the ground, and so on. Determinism underpins all (popularly understood) science. In other words, water cannot choose not to freeze, the released object cannot choose to head skywards. Some Determinists believe that every subsequent event was determined at the creation of the universe, whether by God or by the Big Bang, including you reading this at this point in time, in this place, and your reaction to it. The conventional discourse of Organisational Behaviour is, explicitly or implicitly, imbued with Determinism.

Voluntarism is the belief in free will. While the question of free will is not really a problem in the Natural Sciences, it certainly is in the Social Sciences. The desire of some to see Social Science as part of, or as emulating, the Natural Sciences implies that people do not have free will – you do not choose, at this moment, whether or not to scratch your left ear, whether you do, or do not, do so is determined by the immediately preceding conditions. Although we may have a sense that we are able to choose our actions, to the Determinist this is simply an illusion. If free will is only an illusion, this causes problems, in particular, for the possibility of ethics. If we have no choice, how can we be ethical, how can we be right or wrong, good or bad? If, for example, everything that Hitler did was predetermined at the creation of the universe, how can he be blamed for it? In this view, we all just act out scripts given to us and cannot do differently. Some theorists prefer to believe in a compromise position: some things are determined, others are not, though it is difficult to say which is which. Voluntarism is a subjectivist position.

Discourse: In the sense used in this book, a concept associated with the work of Michel Foucault which describes the functioning of power/knowledge relationships. Power and knowledge are inextricably linked and serve some particular, and partial, interest – in utter contrast to the Enlightenment (q.v.) view of knowledge as a good in itself and tending towards the identification of absolute truths. Discourses can be seen as configurations of practices and people, and members of a discourse control what constitutes a field of knowledge, what can be said about it, by whom, where and how. Discourses are associated with regimes of truth, the conditions which must be satisfied for anything to be declared to be true in any particular epoch – for example, religion, or science, or Capitalism, at various times. Discourses can change, but do not do so very often.

Emancipation: A goal and ideal associated with Marxist theorising generally and, in its most conceptually developed form, with Critical Theory (q.v.). Emancipation refers to an achievable future state where there is not merely freedom from oppression, but also the opportunity for people to realise their full human potential. Thinking based on Marx's later work tends to see Emancipation as, primarily, a socio-economic problem, where the forces preventing Emancipation are part of an external world, while thinking which draws on the earlier work of Marx, notably Critical Theory, would add a necessary psychological component, where the forces preventing Emancipation – although undoubtedly having an important external component – are also influenced by an 'internal' inability to think our way out of our oppression. In Poststructuralism, the latter is often seen in terms of self-policing: setting our own boundaries and limitations and then treating them as external givens. Another term popularly associated with this condition is 'the psychic prison'. (See also **Panopticism**.)

The Enlightenment: An imprecise period, but about 1600 is as good a starting date as any other, and lasting until well after the French Revolution, (some argue it started with the French Revolution – you see the problem?). It saw the emergence of a science unconstrained by the dogma of the Christian Church and the triumph of Reason over superstition. It is supposed to have witnessed, or encouraged, a flowering of the growth of knowledge, the secularisation of society, the rise of democratic freedoms and the release of the arts from their role of religious/moral illustration. The word itself, Enlightenment, symbolises the significance accorded to this period. (See also **Modernism**.)

Epistemology: see **Ontology**.

False Consciousness: A much neglected concept in the study of organisational behaviour, False Consciousness provides an explanation of why some people seem eager to identify themselves with the interests of their oppressors. This phenomenon is widespread in contemporary organisations – for example, the enthusiasm for being appraised. It would appear that the desire of some people to be like, or to join, those who rule them is so strong that they are willing to adopt the rationality of those rulers, even though their own immediate interests are not served by this and even though their chances of joining the rulers are zero. Some versions of this concept imply an objective definition of interests, of a state of consciousness that would not be false. The version used in this book seeks to avoid that implication by emphasising that people can pursue, or adopt, interests inimical to their own, even by their own definition of their interests. (See also **Emancipation**.)

Homeostasis: The tendency of a system when disturbed to self-correct. Systems have limits – stability criteria – within which they can tolerate disturbance, or perturbation, and still correct towards equilibrium. If these limits are exceeded, the system will become unstable and fail. The 'device' that maintains homeostasis is the homeostat. Homeostats can be biological, mechanical, electrical, and so on. A common example is a thermostat, but the term is widely used in a conceptual sense in the context of social system equilibrium and the attempt to identify what may cause instability. It is difficult to say what a homeostat in, say, an organisation might look like, but it is not difficult to identify the processes involved.

Labour Process Theory: A Marx-inspired mode of enquiry, focusing on the role of management in mediating the relationship between the owners of the means of production (Capital) and those who do the producing (Labour). This mediation is seen to favour the former at the expense of the latter. Labour Process Theory represents both the later scientific work of Marx, with its emphasis on class struggle, and the earlier Hegelian Marxism, as represented in Critical Theory (q.v.). More recently, some Labour Process Theorists have been exploring possible connections with Poststructuralism. Labour Process Theory is a very well-established approach within organisation studies and has offered an important alternative to the managerialist (q.v.) orientation of the conventional discourse.

Managerialism: A term used in various ways, but generally relating to the interests and/or philosophy of those who manage. It tends to reflect a particular rationale for action, serving an end which is seen as a good in itself. It indicates an inability to recognise or accept that there are other legitimate interests in an organisation which have an equal right to be served. Managerialism is especially associated with a body of knowledge about organisation which emphasises definitions and solutions to problems which only consider what is acceptable to managers.

Modernism: For our purposes here, the logical outcome of the Enlightenment (q.v.), and so to be seen as blossoming after, say, 1830, though some people see it as coextensive with the Enlightenment. Modernism has continued since its onset until the (possible) advent of Postmodernism (q.v.), about now, though some people do not agree that it is no longer dominant, and others argue that it ceased to be dominant much earlier in the twentieth century. It can be understood in terms of belief in the efficacy of applying Reason/Science to the solution of human problems. It developed unevenly in different aspects of social life. Thus, Engineering was quick off the mark with improved transport systems – canals, railways, steamships, etc. – and innovations in machinery. Public Health was not far behind with the great water and drainage schemes for the major towns. Agricultural Science furnished improved farming methods, leading to greater yields. Education for the masses really got going in the late nineteenth century, Architecture and the Arts in the early twentieth century. In many ways, management is a classically modernist practice. (See also **Postmodernism**, **Critical Modernism**.)

The New Physics: A development in Physics rooted in the realisation of the implications of post-Einsteinian relativism. Its implications for the social world were readily seized upon by writers, especially in the 1980s, usually natural scientists alarmed at the disastrous social and environmental consequences following from the old Newtonian model of science, which still predominates. The New Physics made a major contribution to the legitimation of relativism in the social sciences and, indeed, for some has suggested a narrowing of the traditional gap between the natural and the social sciences, by reversing the previous wisdom, that the social sciences should become more like the (Newtonian) natural sciences. The New Physics has been influential in the development of holistic, ecological and ecosystemic approaches to understanding organisation.

Normative: see **Positive**.

Objectivism/Subjectivism: These concepts relate to issues of ontology (q.v.) and epistemology (q.v.). In the hard, concrete, available to all, person-independent world of the Realist, there is knowledge which is characterised as objective, comprising hard facts, discovered by the application of rational thought, and which have the status of being true in all time and all space, equivalent to the facts of the natural world. In the ephemeral, person-specific world of the Relativist, there are no facts, only understandings gained empathetically, and which are unique to their own situation, since all situations are different. From whatever you believe the world to be like will, necessarily, follow these different understandings of what can be known about it, and what methods are appropriate to discovering, or creating, that knowledge.

Oligarchy: A system of rule (or control) by the few, as opposed to, for example, monarchy – rule by the one, or democracy – in theory, rule by all the people. In other words, a state, or an organisation, run by a small, generally self-perpetuating, elite who eschew democratic principles and practice, seen as inefficient and ineffective, in favour of the pursuit of their own interests, usually portrayed as being to the advantage of all.

Ontology/Epistemology: Ontology is the theory of what is real, or exists. There are lots of different ontologies – none can be *proved* and, therefore, they are just acts of faith, notwithstanding their inestimable importance for everything we do, and for our ability to survive in the world. They range from the belief that nothing is real but our awareness of existing (Solipsism – think about it: if all our knowledge of the external world is achieved through sense data and we know that our senses can be fooled – mirages, optical illusions, feelings of limbs which have been amputated, etc. – how do we know that our senses are not fooling us all the time and that, really, there is nothing out there?) – to the belief that there is a hard, tangible, external world out there and common to us all, and independent of our awareness of it. (Ask yourself: do you and, say, your parents really live in the same world?)

Having established what is real, what will you take to be knowledge of it? This is the realm of **Epistemology**, and it follows from your Ontology, because it is only possible to have knowledge of what you believe to be 'real'. Think of a person whom you accept as existing. Suppose you wish to know how long they have existed – that is, how old they are. There are various methods you can use, but which will you accept as giving you knowledge? You could ask them, but people can tell lies and, anyway, how do they know? You could look at their birth certificate, but how do you know it is theirs? It could belong to someone else, it could be a forgery, it might contain an error. You could ask their parents, but memories can be faulty. You can see the problem.

Clearly, what you will accept as knowledge will be influenced, to some extent, by your purpose in wanting to know. If you are checking their eligibility for an 18–30 holiday, you may accept a 31-year-old claiming that they are only 29. But if you are anxious to avoid employing someone under-age, you might be much more rigorous in ensuring that the apparent 16-year-old is not really 14. Suppose you are a manager, and a consultant wants to sell you a sure-fire scheme for improving labour productivity – how about a job enrichment programme? – what will you take to be knowledge of its claimed potential? Perhaps you will accept the consultant's sales pitch (if so, be careful when you buy a used car or you may be disappointed!). Perhaps you will want to see an example of it in use, or to talk to another manager who has used it. Say you implement the proposal, what will you take to be knowledge of its success?

All your decisions about what might constitute knowledge of something depend on what you believe the world to be like – and why you want to know.

Organisation Development: A movement popular in the 1960s and 1970s which used applied behavioural science (see, for example, **Behaviourism**) techniques to try to improve organisational performance and ability to cope with change. It was a diagnostic, interventionist, approach which used a facilitator, or change agent. It avoided being directive, instead encouraging diagnoses and solutions to be generated organically, via the use of appropriate behavioural techniques. Organisation Development focused on intra-group and inter-group relationships, rather than on individuals. It was an approach very much in tune with the liberal socio-political climate of the time and its popularity declined with the return of a more authoritarian climate. It was difficult to quantify the benefits of Organisation Development interventions and so it fell foul of the new dogma of economic fundamentalism. There is some evidence of a resurgence of use of some of the more dubious techniques associated with Organisation Development – T Group-type management training, for example – though in a less rigorously controlled environment than that considered important in the Organisation Development years.

Panopticism: A concept associated with Poststructuralism and relevant to the issue of Emancipation (q.v.). It refers to the increasing levels of surveillance experienced in ordinary life, and, particularly, in organisational life. Increased levels of surveillance provide the means for increased levels of control, and reduce the possibilities for emancipation. Eagerness on the part of some people to participate in, and accept, this being observed is often seen as a case of False Consciousness (q.v.). The word 'panoptic' literally means 'all-seeing'. The concept is related to the 'panopticon', a design for a prison developed in the early nineteenth century by Jeremy Bentham.

Pluralism: see **Unitarism**.

Positive/Normative: Positive statements are about what 'is', as opposed to Normative statements, which are about what 'ought to be'. Positive statements are associated with Science: 'oxygen is an element', 'heroin is addictive', for example. It is the ability to say what 'is' and, thus, what is true and real, that gives Science its legitimacy. Traditionally, Science avoids statements about what 'ought to be' the case. Positive statements relate to Nature and can be proved – or, more correctly, **dis**proved. Normative statements, because they refer to what 'ought to be', are the province of Philosophy: 'criminals ought to be punished',' food ought to taste good', for example. Normative statements refer to opinion and cannot be proved or disproved. However, (and commonly in the world of management), normative statements often masquerade as positive ones: 'the employee is our most important asset', 'money is not a motivator', for example. To claim opinion as fact is a rhetorical device (see also **Rhetoric**) that gives weight to statements. Semiotically, to be able to claim opinion as fact is a function of power. (See also **Description/Prescription**.)

Postmodernism: Postmodernism can be seen as emerging some time after the Second World War and as continuing still, if it can be seen to exist at all. Some people have argued that Postmodernism is less a matter of real effects, more a change in the ways we understand the world – an **Epistemology** (q.v.). It is a response to a lack of faith in the ability of Modernism (q.v.) to solve social problems. Thus, for example, pesticides and antibiotics have led to resistant and far worse strains of the very things they were supposed to control; fertilizers have led to pollution problems; factory-style schools fail to educate; high-rise housing has led to vandalism, isolation and related social problems; Scientific Management (see **Taylorism**) has led to unemployment, overwork, work-related illness; and so on. The postmodern response to all this takes two principal and opposing forms. One is a nostalgia for a supposed Golden Age when things were 'better', when society was ordered and well regulated and when everyone knew their (God-given) place. This form implies a necessary return to authoritarianism. The other form denies authority and celebrates the proliferation of alternative voices, seeing order, or the belief in order, or the search for order, as themselves a problem. In this form, the solution must be to learn to live with uncertainty and ambiguity. The former version of Postmodernism has been the more prominent in the management of organisations.

Praxis: This is an imprecise term with a wide range of uses. As used in this book, it relates to approaches to understanding organisation(s) which focus on decisions, actions and behaviour in the context of what the emancipated (q.v.) person would do, under conditions in which organisations served appropriate and consensually established social purposes, rather than mere individual interests sustained through power. Praxis always refers to the unity of theory and practice.

Prescription: see **Description**.

Quality of Working Life: This phrase describes both a philosophy and a movement, rooted in the belief that work should be humane, interesting and satisfying. It developed out of preceding interests in job satisfaction, job enrichment, job redesign, Organisation Development (q.v.), etc. It was popular in the 1970s but lost much of its early optimism in the face of the emergence of a more brutalist management style in the 1980s, as it became clear that its outrageous objectives were incompatible with the new economic realism.

Rhetoric: In Aristotelian terms, a form of logic, sometimes called the science, sometimes called the art, of argumentation. Certainly as regards knowledge of the social world, rhetoric is the way knowledge is communicated. There are many rules of rhetoric and there are rhetorical devices for portraying the knowledge communicated in ways that cloak it in apparent legitimacy – for example, in contemporary circumstances, appeals to science and quantification which seek to portray knowledge as fact, objectively true. An example of a rule of rhetoric is that one should only speak to sympathetic audiences, which ensures the success of the argument presented. Rhetoric is closely related to Semiotics (q.v.), Discourse (q.v.) and power.

Semiotics/Semiology: The field, or discipline, of Semiotics is far more extensive and comprehensive than we have suggested in this book. Its main development has been in the fields of Linguistics, and Literary and Cultural Studies. Its use in the study of organisations is relatively under-developed. Indeed, it is likely that 'organisational semiotics', as a discrete subject, would involve the development of a new lexicon, not of foundational concepts, but of concepts through which it could be applied and operationalised.

Subjectivism: see **Objectivism**.

Synthetic: see **Analytic**.

Taylorism: This is, effectively, a synonym for Scientific Management, and derives from F. W. Taylor, the so-called 'Father of Scientific Management'. Taylorism comprises both the belief that management can be practised scientifically and the techniques which, it is claimed, will allow this to be done, such as, work measurement, method study, etc. Taylorism is still popular with managers (though often in other guises and under other names), some politicians and some management academics, though virtually no one else. It was widely criticised at the time Taylor was developing it, and has continued to be criticised ever since. A particularly well-articulated and influential critique of Taylorism is closely associated with Labour Process Theory (q.v.).

Undecidability: Take, for example, the conventional oppositions, good/bad, inside/outside. If words are understood as signifiers, then they have no objective, received, meanings, and the distinction, or division between them, has no intrinsic, obvious, uncontentious meaning – it is undecidable. For example, is it good that an organisation gives its employees the best possible quality of working life (q.v.) at the expense of profit, or is it good that it does not and makes more profit for the owners? Clearly, what is good is undecidable – it depends on your point of view, or on how you read the organisational text. Similarly, is the river into which an organisation discharges its waste, and which then provides drinking water for its employees in their homes, inside the organisation or outside it? Legally, it may be outside but, systemically, it is inside. A nice illustration of the idea of undecidability is furnished by *the strand* – the space on the shore between low water and high water. At low water the strand is land, but at high water it is sea. Thus, it is neither land nor sea, yet, at the same 'time', both.

Because things are undecidable, however, does not mean we do not decide. It means that decisions are a function of the one who decides, not given in the thing which has to be decided. We cannot shelter behind supposed truths, such as efficiency is good, low motivation is bad. Undecidability points out, inexorably, that human beings are responsible for human decisions.

Unitarism, Pluralism, Conflict Theory: Three competing theories of society which are equally applicable to organisations and which, in organisation theory, have often been used in the contexts of industrial relations and the management of conflict.

Unitarism sees all members of a particular group as sharing a common interest, so that decisions about what to do should, and are likely to, reflect that interest. Unitarism is widely regarded as a very naive approach which is usually promulgated by those in power, who declare their own interests to be those of everyone, especially the powerless. It has lately exhibited a resurgence of popularity, particularly since the advent of Thatcherism. Unitarism is particularly favoured, explicitly or implicitly, in organisational management.

Pluralism is held to be an essential quality of a democratic society and, as such, not obviously applicable to organisations, which show little evidence generally of being democratic. However, it has been the most enduring model of organisational relations, especially favoured by those who control them, but often seen by its critics as no more than a sophisticated version of Unitarism. For our purposes here, Pluralism can be seen as the recognition that organisational members have a variety of interests, not all of which can be satisfied. In acceptance of this, organisational members use a variety of mechanisms rationally to trade interests until a decision can be made which reflects a consensus by members as to what should be done. This requires some – or, possibly, all – members to forgo their interest for the benefit of the whole. In practice, outcomes always favour those with the most power to protect their interests.

Conflict Theory starts from the same position of seeing organisations as comprised of competing interests, but sees these conflicts of interest as inevitable, ubiquitous and insoluble. Outcomes are achieved solely as the effect of struggles for power. Those with most power win through, those with less power can make things difficult for them in the short term, and may even have some fun in the process. Conflict Theory has the virtue of representing organisational relations as highly dynamic.

Voluntarism: see **Determinism**.

APPENDIX 1

History and ideas

To provide a comprehensive, and comprehensible, model of the development of the ideas that inform this book is an impossible task. Ideas do not appear on the scene fully formed but evolve. Their development rarely fits into a recognisably regular pattern, but is typically rhizomic (see Chapter 12). It is often not immediately clear what their impact might be. However, all ideas are intimately connected with the social, economic, political, cultural conditions that contextualise them and new ideas tend to emerge in response to perceived shortcomings in the prevailing ways of understanding the world, especially as the contextual conditions change – so, for example, once slavery was seen as reasonable, right and good but ideas changed (and this is reflected in the development of, for example, Postcolonial Studies); once discrimination against women was seen as reasonable, right and good but now it is not (intimately related to the development of Feminism and, for example, Gender Studies). It is, therefore, both possible and useful to have some sense of how thinking changes, of how new and powerful ideas emerge, and of how the conditions that mark their emergence connect to them.

The small print

First, however, it is appropriate to make some framing comments. The ideas and events that we (very selectively, subjectively and from an inevitably somewhat Anglocentric viewpoint) choose to highlight here are all matters of public record – who knows how many times, and by whom, ideas have been developed, but not published or publicised, and of which there is, therefore, no trace? Nonetheless, it is also extremely uncommon to find, or even to think, an idea that is totally new, though the significations of any idea are likely to be different in different epochs – for example, the democracy of the ancient Greek city states was very different to modern democracy. The ideas and events mentioned below are very complex and it is simply not possible to re-present that complexity (nor would that be particularly useful). We are offering a model, but it should not be forgotten that, although unrepresented, that complexity is entirely relevant to understanding. Developments occur at different times (and) in different fields;

they are not necessarily connected, but they may be. The course of ideas rarely runs smoothly, and, certainly in the case of ideas that generate important changes in the way we understand the world, they usually experience resistance – sometimes for very long periods of time, until a critical mass of people believe in and adopt the idea. Sometimes ideas are resisted to the extent that they suffer total eclipse for long periods, to be rediscovered by later generations. Even once accepted, or at least adopted, it can be decades, or even centuries, before the full impact of an idea is understood. But what has been thought once cannot be un-thought. Ideas, once expressed, have life.

We have suggested above that what we are offering here is a model, and it will be recalled (from Chapter 9) that the crucial characteristic of models is that they are purposeful – and, of course, this model is no different. The ideas and events that we select as part of our model are those that seem to us to chart the development of, or to have a significant impact on, what has been called an emancipatory interest. An emancipatory interest has two principle elements: the realisation of autonomy and responsibility for all and critical reflection on those factors – political, social, psychological, etc. – that inhibit the development of human potential and act as a barrier to, or actively repress, the achievement of autonomy and responsibility for all. The term 'originates' in the work of Jürgen Habermas, who argued, in *Knowledge and Human Interests* (1976), that all knowledge production reflects the purposes and interests of those who produce it – he called these 'knowledge constitutive interests'. There were, he thought, three kinds of such interest, the interest in control, the interest in understanding and the interest in emancipation. (Others have suggested further knowledge constitutive interests, such as Ulrich Beck (1992), who proposed a 'productivity interest'.) It is also to be noted that some of the most significant ideas and events cited here could not be seen as motivated, in themselves, by an emancipatory interest, such as the development of the steam engine, or, at another extreme, the death camps of the Second World War. But it can be argued that their impact has included the stimulation in others of an emancipatory interest – in the latter case, for example, to demand the development of ideas that might help to make the possibility of such a thing ever happening again 'unthinkable'. This is not to say that such optimism has been realised, but this does remain a significant emancipatory goal.

We have chosen here to identify a few key dates, in relation to the emergence of new thinking. By noting the events that surround these dates, it is possible to see how ideas are embedded in, and emerge from, prevailing socio-historic conditions. This is to emphasise that ideas are not free-floating entities but dependent on, and relevant to, perceptions about the world – in that sense, one might almost call them functional. The dates are intended to symbolise turning points in the history of the human condition, to symbolise nodal points of change in the intellectual climate and the emergence of ideas that both reflect those changes and offer new directions in response to them. To mark, for example, the date of the publication of Freud's book, *The Interpretation of Dreams*, in 1900, is not to make any special claim for this particular work (though many see it as his greatest work), but it is to highlight that, at this particular time, influential ideas about human psychology were emerging, ideas that articulated new and different views about how the world in general, and human society in particular, might be understood and that were to have a profound impact on the understandings of those who followed after.

The big picture

The year **1600** can be taken as emblematic of the Enlightenment. The Enlightenment, in so far as it can be taken to be a meaningful concept – and not everyone agrees that it is – did *not* start in 1600; again, even those who believe in the idea of the Enlightenment do not agree about its dates. What can be said, however, is that around 1600 changes were occurring that led, directly or indirectly, to the understandings of knowledge and the socio-political order that we 'enjoy' today. Fifty years previously Copernicus had theorised heliocentrism. Galileo would soon refine the telescope, which would give empirical confirmation of this theory. Another fifty years would see the birth of Isaac Newton, a very significant figure in the founding of modern physics, and the publication of Hobbes' *Leviathan*, often seen as the first work of modern political philosophy, and as having set the agenda for political life that we still use today. The Reformation was breaking the Catholic hegemony in Europe, and, in England, the subordination of the Church to the State can be seen as an early move in the direction of secularisation of government. By 1642 England was embroiled in civil war, which, eventually, effectively ended the doctrine of the divine right of kings, and established the supremacy of Parliament – though it took almost 300 years longer to establish mass franchise.

Another particularly significant year was **1848**. This is not to suggest that nothing significant happened in the years in between, which were characterised by the sometimes dramatic spread of Enlightenment ideals such as Science, Reason and Freedom (see also Glossary). These years saw, for example, publication of the enormously influential works of Hume and of Rousseau, who can be seen as representative of opposite poles in the classic Enlightenment debate about reason and nature, and whose work still resonates in the intellectual climate of today. And there was, for example, the French Revolution and the American War of Independence – Republicanism flourished and, in 1791, Thomas Paine published *The Rights of Man*. In Britain there was the Industrial Revolution. By 1848 slavery, in the context of Britain, had, more or less, been outlawed. Science had ushered in the Steam Age and the development of the railway locomotive had ushered in the age of mass transportation. The first international travel agency, Thomas Cook, had been established in 1841. The roots of Modernism were clearly discernible.

The year 1848 symbolises, however, a significant turning point. This year, sometimes known as 'the year of revolution', saw upheavals in France, Germany, Italy and Poland in Europe, and others much further afield. Although repressed, these events represented the active pursuit of civil liberties on an unprecedented scale. In Britain there was nothing comparable to the revolutions elsewhere – often attributed to the passing of the Reform Act in 1832, which, amongst other things, extended the franchise, in the middle classes at least – but 1848 was the year that the Chartist movement presented its massive petition to Parliament, demanding universal suffrage, secret ballots, pay for Members of Parliament and annual elections to Parliament. All of this can perhaps be symbolised in the publication in that year, by Marx and Engels, of the inestimably influential *Communist Manifesto*. This relatively brief manuscript was the precursor of thinking and ideas offering, specifically, an antithesis to the burgeoning philosophy of

Capitalism, represented by thinkers such as Adam Smith. Marx's thinking continues to be extremely influential philosophically. He is often regarded as one the most significant original thinkers to influence the development of ideas in the years since then. Another such thinker is Freud.

Another year that can be seen as a turning point is **1900**. As noted above, this was the year that Freud published what many believe is his most important work, *The Interpretation of Dreams*. The intervening fifty-odd years since 1848, saw, in Britain, the development of the ideals of Modernism at an impressive rate – for example, the extension of the franchise to some working-class males, education acts, acts to control the exploitation of labour, general extensions of public works in terms of public health and welfare. The founding of the Football Association in 1863, and the first FA Cup competition in 1871, can be taken to symbolise the establishment of the principle of formalised leisure activities, and it was during this period that the phenomenon of the seaside holiday appeared. The year 1900 also saw the death of Nietzsche.

The particular relevance here of Freud and Nietzsche can be summarised in terms of subjectivism. One of the ideas on which Nietzsche placed special emphasis is what he called 'the death of God', the recognition that we do not live in a divinely ordered world, acting out our roles in accordance with divine purpose. Life, therefore, has no externally determined logic – the world we know results from human action and reflects the effects of power, rather than of transcendent truth. According to Nietzsche, our experienced reality is shaped by what he defined as 'man's will to power'. What we should understand by this concept is a matter of considerable dispute, but the idea that it is power that shapes experienced reality has very wide currency – for example, looking back to the materialist ideas of Marx and Engels, who had pointed out in the *Communist Manifesto* that the dominant ideas in any epoch are those of its ruling class, and looking forward to more non-materialist contemporary thinking. Freud's contribution lies in the development of psychoanalytic understandings of behaviour, especially in relation to the role of the unconscious in motivation. Rather than action following from objective reasoning processes, according to Freud, it is unconscious desire that motivates – though, again, there is considerable debate about how this functions. Together, Nietzsche and Freud present us with a model of human action that is focused on the pursuit of unconscious desire in a world devoid of predetermined purpose, where outcomes reflect people's ability to impose their will. This model, of course, poses some difficulty for the Enlightenment ideal of reason, and for Modernism's ideal of the rational solution to human problems.

The years between 1900 and our next date – **1914** – saw peak rates of emigration to the United States of America, principally of the European poor escaping harsh regimes and persecution. In the Arts, we have the appearance of Cubism, to be followed shortly by Surrealism and Dadaism, each 'representing' the denial of a rational objective world and celebrating the life of the mind beyond immediate perception. James Joyce wrote his first major work, *Dubliners*. Marconi made possible the first transatlantic radio transmission in 1901 and the Wright brothers flew the first powered aircraft in 1903. Einstein published his *Special Theory of Relativity*. 1914 is also symbolically significant for the work being done to prepare for publication the notes produced from the lectures of Saussure, who had died in 1913 and who can be seen as the precursor of modern Structuralism, which itself was the precursor of Poststructuralism. His understanding of the role of language, particularly in creating 'reality', has been central to many, and diverse, aspects of contemporary thought.

1914 is, of course, most significant as the year of the outbreak of the First World War, the first industrialised war, allowing killing on an unprecedented scale. The First World War also gave rise to immense social and political change. For example, women were allowed, albeit only for the duration of the war, to do work that had previously been the sole preserve of men, which led, directly, to their getting the right to vote for the first time, in 1918 (for women aged over thirty), and to the first woman Member of Parliament. The first attempt at international governance was established in the League of Nations, the precursor of the United Nations. The First World War also engendered profound changes in social attitudes, notably the decline of deference.

The year **1930** saw the emergence of the Critical Theory of the Frankfurt School, the influence of which on thinking in the twentieth century and beyond cannot be over-estimated. The period following the First World War was characterised by the polarisation of political ideologies. In the Soviet Union Stalin was in control. In Italy Mussolini had established a Fascist regime and in Germany Hitler had begun his rise to power. In many European countries, and beyond, there was a growing confrontation between the politics of the Right and the politics of the Left, and much civil unrest. This period also saw the establishment of radio broadcasting, with its huge impact on the availability of information, and the invention of television, the discovery of penicillin, Prohibition, the Wall Street Crash and the first 'talkies'.

All of this was pertinent to Critical Theory, as one of its ambitions has been to understand the experienced life in its totality, and to understand how the institutions, practices, values, and so on, of contemporary society contribute to social domination – for Critical Theory nothing is irrelevant. The distinctive approach that Critical Theory brought to this quest involved the rejection of the determinism of the late Marx, to find inspiration in his earlier Hegelian Idealism. This informed a more subjectivist approach to Marxian analysis and facilitated a later attempt by Critical Theorists to synthesise the work of Marx with that of Freud. The inclusiveness of the approach also drew attention to the role of power in language. Such power was also very much part of the experienced reality of the members of the Frankfurt School, who, along with many others, were forced by the rise of Hitler to flee Germany in 1933. The Frankfurt School was first re-established in Switzerland and then moved to the USA. Not all associates of the School escaped – Walter Benjamin, for example, committed suicide in 1940, at the Franco-Spanish border, believing that he would be refused entry to Spain in order to escape the Nazis.

1945 was another year of turning points, and obviously significant as the year that saw the end of the Second World War. One of the 'by-products' of war is the stimulus to technological innovation and development – this period saw the dawn of the 'Computer Age', for example. Another such 'by-product' is the desire for change. By the end of the Second World War we had the jet aeroplane, the 'Atomic Age', the precursor of the intercontinental ballistic missile, nylon, antibiotics and the jeep. On the social front, in Britain, the 1944 Education Act had provided for free secondary level education for all, and the Beveridge Report of 1942 had laid down the foundations for the Welfare State, especially for the National Health Service which gave free health care to all for the first time in Britain.

Another important outcome of the war was the questioning of the precepts of Modernism. This was particularly associated with the uncovering of the industrial-scale genocide practised by the Germans during the war. Clearly, science, technology and rational thought could no longer be seen as inevitably benign products of the Enlightenment, not inevitable 'forces for good'. They worked equally well for those whose goals did not include universal freedom and the opportunity for everyone to develop their 'human potential'. This crisis of belief in Modernism can be seen as giving rise to what later became known as Postmodernism. In terms of ideas, a number of important thinkers were working at this time, whose ideas would have influence on the generations of thinkers to come. For example, Wittgenstein argued that the meaning of a word is its use in language, an understanding sympathetic with what would become known as Poststructuralism. The anthropologist Lévi-Strauss was developing Structuralism, which would also be an important influence on the development of Poststructuralism (see also Chapter 3). Sartre was extending the concept of Existentialism, of which Nietzsche's work was seen as a foundational influence. Another idea that was to make a big impact was that of 'Big Brother', in Orwell's book, *Nineteen Eighty-Four*. This book also gave us the concept of Newspeak, of which Management-speak is a relevant descendant. Television broadcasting, which had been suspended for the duration of the Second World War, was resumed in 1946.

1963 was the year that, according to the poet Philip Larkin, sex was discovered, but, fortunately, the contraceptive pill had already been introduced in 1961. The following year James Bond was getting Pussy Galore in the film *Goldfinger*. Beatlemania was in full swing, the Rolling Stones released their first single and the 'recreational drugs culture' was emerging. 1963 was also the year that the American President, J.F. Kennedy, was assassinated, and the Vietnam War was poised for escalation. The first woman, a Russian, was sent into space. There was the Civil Rights march on Washington at which Martin Luther King gave his 'I have a dream' speech and the USA enacted Equal Pay legislation.

It was in the mid-1960s that Critical Theory began to move into the mainstream, especially with the publication, in 1964, of Marcuse's book, *One Dimensional Man* – these ideas would become very influential in the widespread student unrest of 1968. It was also at around this time that Poststructuralism began to emerge as a distinctive analytical approach. Early Poststructuralist theorists, such as Michel Foucault, Jacques Derrida and Gilles Deleuze, were already publishing their work, but it would be the 1970s before they started to become available in English translations.

The small picture

Up to this point Organisation Theory, and Organisational Behaviour in particular, had been dominated by ideas from the USA, although it was already a matter of some debate whether the cultural specificity of the American context was particularly appropriate to a European context. The advent of accessible social theory from a European context was to have a major impact on Organisation Studies, especially in the arena of critique of mainstream organisation, in theory and in practice. Critical Theory had been part of these approaches for some time, but the arrival of Poststructuralism was to provide a second pillar of critical thought, most significantly, perhaps, in the realm of inquiry into the ontology and epistemology of organisation.

One of the most important contributions to the legitimisation of critique in the field of Organisation Studies was the publication, in 1979, of Burrell and Morgan's influential book, *Sociological Paradigms and Organisational Analysis*. This book introduced the idea of incommensurable synchronic knowledge paradigms. (It is interesting to note that the prevailing political ideology of the time, proclaimed by Margaret Thatcher, who had become the first female Prime Minister in Britain in that same year, was 'There Is No Alternative', usually abbreviated to TINA.) Burrell and Morgan's book makes no mention of poststructuralist ideas, but within a short space of time these ideas would start to appear in the discourse, particularly as a result of the work of Robert Cooper. An influential series of articles by Cooper and Burrell, published in the late 1980s in the journal *Organization Studies*, discussed the relevance of, amongst others, Foucault and Derrida to the study of organisation – by now their ideas were being specifically linked to Postmodernism, although not everyone agrees with this linkage. The years since then have seen a proliferation of non-Functionalist, especially subjectivist, approaches to the study of organisation(s). A substantial body of work in the field has been built up using the ideas of Poststructuralism. Critical Theory has also continued to flourish, and there have been some attempts, not always successful, to develop a *rapprochement* between Critical Theory and Poststructuralism. Another substantial body of work deals, in various ways, with the ideas that inform Postmodernism (though some cultural commentators claim that Postmodernism has already passed). An important exemplar of the range and implications of such thinking was represented in the publication, in 1997, of Burrell's book, *Pandemonium*. However, for an even more recent example of the direction in which thinking about organisation is moving, see the (freely available) *Manifestos for the Business School of Tomorrow*, edited by Jones and O'Doherty in 2005.

The fuzzy picture

Given the slow pace at which ideas develop, it is really only with hindsight that it becomes meaningful to attach symbolic significance to particular points in time. It is impossible to say whether we are now in a period of historically important change, and, if so, what is changing, and where it is leading. Is the change we are experiencing incremental or dramatically different to what has gone before? Which are the events of the last twenty-five or so years that will, later, be seen as genuinely significant moments of change? Many people would cite 1989 as a year of significant importance. Most of the twentieth century was characterised by high levels of antagonism between the capitalist 'West' and the communist 'East'. The end of the Second World War saw the onset of the Cold War, the end of which was symbolised by the collapse of the Berlin Wall in 1989, though the vestiges of antagonism drifted on until 1991. Some people proclaimed 1989 as the year that Communism 'died', and Capitalism 'won'.

One effect of the Cold War was to mute critique of Capitalism. Whatever its faults, it was argued, Capitalism had popular appeal, compared to its supposed alternative, Communism. The Cold War had bound those of each side together, in the face of what was, often quite literally, an external threat. But with the 'death' of Soviet Communism that sense of external threat was lost, and there has been a marked increase of attention paid to the inherent problems of Capitalism. Whereas Capitalism represented, historically, a bastion against its 'opponent', Communism, it is now, increasingly, being seen as part of the 'new' problem: the despoliation of the planet, politically, economically and, especially, environmentally. It is interesting to speculate whether the identification of a new 'external threat' – global terrorism – will reassert the bonding process characteristic of the Cold War period, though, at the present time, this seems unlikely to have the power to paper over the cracks found in the capitalist façade, not least because, to many, Capitalism is, itself, implicated in this new development. While it could be suggested that Capitalism and Communism were opposing socio-economic ideologies – perhaps, mirror images of each other – Capitalism and global terrorism are, fundamentally, of different orders.

Perhaps the most prominent resistance to Capitalism is to be found in the Anti-Globalisation Movement. These ideas undoubtedly have immense significance for organisational behaviour, in theory and in practice. If the problems claimed to emanate from the attempt of Capitalism to colonise the planet – for example, oil wars, deforestation, exhaustion of scarce resources, remorseless exploitation of less developed economies, and so on – are real, then organisations, and those behaving in them, are heavily implicated. In this sense, it is possible to detect, since the first edition of this book, a new, emergent, focus. This focus can, perhaps, be symbolised by the work of two writers, Hardt and Negri (2000, 2005), who reflect a view, associated with Postmodernism, that the nation state has declined in importance in the face of overwhelmingly global forces. Clearly, some states are more powerful than others, but none *controls*. Even the United States of America, the sole superpower – pending the arrival to that status of China – is subject to these new forces. Both capital and jobs are traded in the global marketplace, relatively unimpeded. Terrorism is transnational, as is disease, communication, culture, eco-catastrophe.

In the more specific context of studies of organisation, the re-emergence of the concept of Political Economy – eclipsed for many decades (see also Chapter 10) – is one area providing a focus for a new generation of critique. Critiques of Capitalism are now much more evident, and more widespread, in the intellectual context, as well as amongst political activists, and also in popular culture, where they have become part of the entertainment industry, and so reach an ever wider audience.

In recognition of these global issues associated with Capitalism, the questions for the study of organisational behaviour become ever more pressing. What is it, exactly, that we are motivating people to do? Where are people being led? What sort of cultures are we trying to engineer? Whose ethical views should we accept?

Fragments?

It is inevitable that an overview like this one will miss out many important ideas and events, and, in some cases, it is hardly possible to do justice to some of the most significant themes of an epoch. The twentieth century, for example, was characterised by almost continuous international conflict, and it is indisputable that this has had a profound impact on ideas, and vice versa. The globalisation of communication is another significant thread through that century that has undoubtedly had a major impact. We have not made much reference to the Arts, but they too have a profoundly symbiotic relationship with ideas and events. Our purpose, however, has been to illustrate the interconnectedness of ideas and events in a particular context and over a period of time. Some ideas have impressive durability, others turn out to be ephemeral. Which is which in the contemporary world will only become clear in time.

APPENDIX 2

Continuous case study

This case study describes the significant elements of a real event. It offers material that can be analysed in terms of each of the concepts developed in the foregoing chapters. Questions, together with some additional material, are included towards the end of each chapter.

A tale from the village pump

The situation

During the nineteenth century, Britain was 'plagued' by recurrent outbreaks of what was known as Asiatic cholera – between 1831 (apparently, the first year of its appearance in Britain) and 1866 there were nearly 40,000 deaths from Asiatic cholera in London alone. The view then prevailing was that cholera was transmitted by bad air: miasma. One of the leading proponents of this theory was William Farr, who was interested in statistical approaches to understanding epidemics. From his data on the occurrence of cholera, he demonstrated that, in relation to London, the incidence of cholera declined with increased distance from the River Thames. At this time the River Thames was, in effect, a notorious open sewer. The stench arising from the river was believed to carry cholera and so the further from the river, the better the quality of the air and the less cholera was found. The crucial factor, according to Farr's theory, was the land gaining height as it moved away from the River Thames. The further back from the river people were, the cleaner the air, because the higher the land. Farr had produced a mathematical model to demonstrate that this was the case. The model was also applied in Liverpool, where it showed the same result. Farr was a representative of the orthodox view of the day on the causes of cholera. Another such supporter of the miasma theory was the influential Edwin Chadwick, whose particular interest in this context was improvement of sanitation. This belief in the miasma theory was, however, challenged in 1849 by John Snow.

The people

William Farr (1807–83) came from a relatively poor Shropshire family but, from the age of two, was 'adopted' by a local squire who eventually bequeathed £500 to him, which he used to finance studies in Paris and Switzerland. On his return to England he became an apothecary in the Bloomsbury district of London (1833), even then a very well-to-do area. He started writing for *The Lancet*, still a major medical publication in the UK, in 1835. In 1838 he was appointed Compiler of Abstracts (Chief Statistician) to the Office of the Registrar-General, at £350 per annum. He held this position for most of his professional life. In other words, Farr quickly became part of the medical establishment of the day. He eventually became known as 'the father' of the use of statistics in medicine, with especial reference to epidemics.

John Snow (1813–58) was the son of a Yorkshire farmer who worked his way up the medical hierarchy, practising medicine in Newcastle upon Tyne and Pateley Bridge – a small town in the Yorkshire Dales – before eventually moving to London, where he became a member of the Royal College of Surgeons in 1838, qualified as an MD in 1844 and was appointed a Licentiate of the Royal College of Physicians in 1850. He had very effectively pioneered the use of ether and chloroform as anaesthetics before turning his attention to cholera. He first published his theory that cholera was a water-borne disease in 1849, following a particularly virulent outbreak starting late in 1848. In developing this theory, Snow had used some of Farr's own data, but Snow had reached very different conclusions in interpreting the data than those reached by Farr. Snow's publication was awarded a (monetary) prize by the Institut de France, but was, however, derided in Britain. This did not prevent him later becoming known as the 'Father of Epidemiology'.

The Soho outbreak

Another serious outbreak of cholera occurred in 1854, in the Broad Street area of London. John Snow, already interested in the causes of cholera and, fortuitously, living nearby, took the opportunity to try to discover the source of this outbreak. He established the technique of mapping the occurrences of the disease, using a sort of cluster analysis. At this time, drinking water was obtained from public pumps and Snow suspected that one particular pump was instrumental in this outbreak. There were more than 500 deaths from cholera within ten days, in a very small area of Broad Street, and Snow became increasingly convinced that the local pump was the crucial factor. Not without considerable opposition, on 7 September he persuaded the local parish dignitaries, the Board of Guardians, to disable this pump by removing its handle, thus forcing people to get their drinking water from other pumps. The Board of Guardians did this the next day and there seemed to be an immediate effect. As it happened, the outbreak was already in decline, going from 142 deaths on 1 September to only 14 on 8 September. Still, it seemed that the water from the Broad Street pump was indeed contaminated, and Snow was convinced that he had demonstrated a connection between contaminated drinking water and incidence of cholera.

There were several deaths from cholera in this outbreak that did not seem to be connected to the Broad Street pump. Ten were associated with people who might have been expected to use a neighbouring pump but, on investigation, it turned out that some of them did use the Broad Street pump, because they liked the water from there, and three others were schoolchildren who had stopped at the pump for a drink on their way to school. There were some other relatively isolated cases during the outbreak, but it transpired in one case, for example, that the elderly lady concerned had previously lived in the Broad Street area and particularly liked the water from that pump, so sent her servant especially to get water there for her. Gradually, it became possible to trace all the cases to usage of the Broad Street water pump. A report published after the outbreak identified the existence of a previously uncharted cess pool beneath the ground only 3 feet from the pump, which had leaked into the water supply for the pump and which was acknowledged as a likely cause of the outbreak of cholera.

The aftermath

Convinced of his own theory (as it eventually turned out, correctly), Snow advocated the use of filters by water companies and boiling water during cholera outbreaks, but this was not generally accepted, and the miasma theory continued to hold sway. In 1855 Snow was criticised, in print, by *The Lancet*, for being 'unscientific' – *The Lancet* supported the miasma theory. However, also in 1855, a Parliamentary Committee was set up to devise amendments to the Nuisances Removal and Diseases Prevention Act of 1846, known generally as 'The Cholera Bill'. Snow gave evidence to this committee. Its intention had been to require organisations to do something about cleaning up their emissions, in accordance with the miasma theory. But Snow succeeded in persuading them to focus on cleaning up drinking water, and protecting it from contact with sewers, cess pools, and so on – much to the irritation of *The Lancet*.

William Farr, who sat on the Committee for Scientific Enquiry, presented his data on the 1854 cholera epidemic to the committee that same year of 1855. These data showed that proximity to the Thames was a problem, with the exception of the area around the Broad Street pump. Farr's own data showed that there was a strong possibility that cholera was water-borne, yet he still clung to the orthodox miasma theory. By 1856 he was starting to hedge his bets a bit, though he did this, in effect, by including water pollution as one of the many elements of the miasma theory. In 1866, however, after Snow's death, Farr himself was instrumental in tracing an outbreak of cholera in East London to drinking water contaminated by sewage (as in the case of the Broad Street outbreak), exposing misconduct on the part of the relevant water company in the process.

(There is a very large amount of information about these events available on the Internet, as well as in books, such as Stephen Halliday's *The Great Stink of London* (1999), and articles. A particularly comprehensive and accessible site can be found at **www.ph.ucla/epi/snow.html**)

APPENDIX 3

Extended case studies

These case studies (which are not referred to elsewhere in this book) are presented for analysis using the full range of the concepts developed in the main body of the book.

CASE STUDY 2

RatGames

The company

RatGames was a very successful company that produced advanced specialist computer games, located in a small town in Germany. It was a cash-rich company, with a history and organisation typical of the sector. It was started about 20 years ago, by Friedrich Reisz, a computer graduate, and had experienced rapid growth right from the start. At the present time it had a small managing Board running the company along very informal lines. The only traditional professional on the Board was the accountant, Max Schilling, whose role was to ensure that the financial management of the company was in line with current legislation and that all proper procedures were followed. The other Board members were all technologists, friends of the owner. While there were some notional responsibilities allocated to these people – especially, responsibility for Marketing, and for Human Resource Management – there was, in practice, very little attention paid to these areas, as, because of the culture of the company, it was not really seen as necessary.

The company's strength lay in its creative skills, which ensured a steady stream of new products that almost sold themselves, so Marketing was not really an issue. As for Human Resource Management, the main asset of the company was undoubtedly the people who thought up the games and developed them into a saleable product. They tended to be men who were obsessed with computers. They were recruited for their technological and creative skills rather than for their education – they ranged from people with doctorates to high school drop-outs – and certainly not for their social skills. They were paid well and, more or less, left on their own to do the work as they pleased, being judged solely on their ability to supply a range of marketable games, and on their loyalty to the company – there was an understanding that they would work only for RatGames, rather than offer their services anywhere else as well. These technophiles, known in the company as 'the gamers', were generally employed on a casual basis but tended to be highly committed to a job that paid them well for doing what they wanted to do, and would be doing anyway. They were not really amenable to conventional management practices, which was just as well, since the members of the Board did not possess such skills or the inclination to try to apply them. Some of the people produced games as and when they felt like it, or when they needed some money. Others spent all their waking hours working. The rewards system was based on payment-by-results. All in all, there seemed to be very few Human Resource problems to worry about.

Decisions at Board level were often made in the atmosphere (sometimes literally) of a hippy commune, though with the exception of the accountant, who tried to take, and to encourage the others to take, a more formal approach. Friedrich Reisz often made important decisions without reference to the Board, but no one objected to this – it seemed to work. However, at other times there was some attempt at a more 'collective' approach to management. But the 'workers' had no real interest in how the company was run or how healthy it was. Typically, they were young – 25 was considered to be old – and unattached. They spent their money on things like fast cars and electronic gadgetry. They tended to be loners, with only sporadic interest in a social life, and with zero interest in careers or pensions. Burn-out was a common problem, and new talent was not easy to find, but the company needed a fairly steady stream of new talent to maintain its success rate – without good people the company would be in trouble very quickly. In spite of this, and although cash-rich, no provision had been made for hard times. Income was spent freely on equipment and on 'expenses'.

The problem

Some time ago, a large amount of money was spent on acquiring some very new technology that would allow games of greater complexity and realism to be developed. Although they were not very interested in Marketing, the Board was very aware of their market, and they knew that, once this technology was fully functioning, it would generate big rewards. But it did not work. The problem was that the sort of skills that abounded within the company were creative ones, and the people were not suited to, nor did they possess, the sort of skills needed to make the new equipment function. There did not seem to be any actual faults with the equipment, so the various manufacturers were unable to help, and there was no competent 'Production Manager' in the company who could have made the most of any manufacturing expertise on offer. Because of the risk of 'espionage', they refused to use consultants or contractors. To do work for the company, people had to be on the payroll, and loyal. They had tried to recruit someone but had not had any success so far – potential recruits were thin on the ground and seemed to feel that the company was unattractively located, amongst other things, and perhaps the job specification was too vague. The problem was one of making the 'bits' fit together as a whole. Due to a lack of expertise and 'can't be asked', the equipment was sitting there gathering dust, much to the distress of Max Schilling.

As it was a fairly small sector, the problems that RatGames was experiencing in this respect were well known to their competitors within the sector. Generally speaking, the competitors were quite happy about it. If RatGames got the new technology to work it would leap ahead, and force them to follow suit, to catch up. Because of the expense and uncertainty involved, no one else wanted to try to be the first to use it. The status quo was pretty acceptable to everyone, except RatGames.

The solution?

One day a strange young woman turned up at the offices of RatGames and asked to see the boss. Not only was she strange in so far as they did not know her, but she was also a bit strange because she was dressed in a business suit and looked as if she would be more at home in a conventional organisational setting. Leni Peiper explained to Friedrich Reisz that she was aware of their problem with the new technology and that she could fix it for them, fairly quickly. Her services would cost them 100,000 euros, in cash. Normally he would not have countenanced such an approach, for all the reasons already noted, but this young woman was no threat, and 100K euros was, relatively, peanuts to them. Friedrich Reisz was in a particularly benign mood, feeling very laid back, so he thought, well, why not? 'Fix it and I would gladly pay you 500K,' he said. 'When can you start?' Leni said that she could start the next day. So it was agreed. Being the sort of company they were, contracts were not the usual way of doing things, arrangements were often made, jobs agreed, on an *ad hoc* basis, and mutual trust was considered more important than formality, so Friedrich and Leni just shook hands on it. He told the Board the news and they agreed that it would be a bargain, if she could do it. A couple of days later the job was done, the problem fixed, the equipment usable.

The disagreement

The Board was informed of the good news. The uniform response was 'So soon? Well, in that case, it could not have been much of a problem!' 'Hardly worth 500K,' said Max Schilling, and with this comment there was general agreement. They felt that they were being ripped off. No one should be able to earn that sort of money. The next day Leni turned up and asked for her cash.

'It can't have been much of a problem,' said Friedrich. 'Not 500,000 euros' worth of a problem, anyway, for sure.'

'I didn't ask for 500K,' replied Leni. '100K is what I asked for, and what I want.' Something in Leni's manner suddenly irritated Friedrich.

'It's not even worth 100K,' he said. 'Two days work? I'll pay you 10,000 euros, no more. There's no contract, so you can take it or leave it.'

Leni was clearly annoyed at this response, though she remained very calm.

'Is this how you usually conduct your business?' she asked. 'We agreed the price and now you should pay it.'

Friedrich repeated that his top offer was 10,000 euros.

An argument ensued, but he felt that he was in a strong position. She was very young. She could hardly undo the work that she had done. He thought that her only option was to accept his offer and to put it down to experience. He decided to give her some free advice, that, next time she took on such a job, she should take a bit longer over it and make it seem more difficult – though, in all honesty, he knew that it had been a difficult problem, since they had been unable to solve it themselves. As it was Friday afternoon, he gave her the weekend to consider his offer (which was really a non-negotiable ultimatum). Still very calm, she repeated that he should pay her what they had agreed. 'If you do not, you will regret it, I assure you,' she warned. But Friedrich could not think of any way that she could force him to pay 100K euros for her work. She couldn't even damage his reputation among his competitors, in his view, because it would be more damaging for them to know, as they assuredly would, that he had paid someone none of them knew 100K euros for two days' work. He went off for the weekend feeling justified in his firmness, and elated that the new technology was now available for use.

The pay-off

At about lunch-time on Monday, Friedrich received a telephone call from Max Schilling, to say that none of the gamers had arrived for work. Friedrich was slightly surprised but this did occasionally happen when, for example, there had been some event over the weekend that they had all attended, though he had not known of any such event pending. But then, he had been tied up for a while in the 'pay negotiations' with the young woman. He reassured Max that there was probably a perfectly good explanation for it, even if it was a bit irritating. However, on Tuesday Max phoned again, to report that there was still no one at work. This time Friedrich was worried. He asked Max to phone around a bit, to see if he could find anything out. Later that afternoon Max phoned back, with some shocking news. Every single one of his gamers had been poached by Leni – they had all agreed to work for her. What Friedrich had failed to appreciate was that she was way ahead of RatGames technologically, and she had offered all the gamers the prospect of bigger and better 'toys' to play with. Since they were not under contract to RatGames, they had taken all their works-in-progress with them so that they could finish them, and that work could form the basis of their contribution to the assets of the new company. The availability of the bigger and better technology would make these games themselves bigger and better. For a gamer, it was an opportunity that was irresistible. On top of that, Friedrich's new technology was no use, at the moment, since there was no one around to try it out and to use it.

Max also told him that he had not had to phone around at all, as it happened, because Leni had phoned him to tell him what had occurred, and to offer him a job as well. Under the circumstances, there did not seem much point in him staying at RatGames, so this was, he told Friedrich, goodbye.

In light of the issues discussed in this book:

- What are the various power relations that are being played out in this case?
- What kind of elements in Friedrich Reisz's sense of self might have influenced him to behave in the way that he did?
- In what ways are issues of structure relevant to the various problems that RatGames experienced?
- What competing rationalities are evident in the case?

CASE STUDY 3

WaReady

The company

WaReady was a fairly small company engaged in the defence industry. It was located in a relatively remote part of northern England. It occupied a small stately home that, because of its remote location, had been requisitioned during the Second World War for top-secret military work and had since somehow remained a site for related kinds of work, though no longer under government control. The site had acquired a number of extra buildings over the years, the sort of buildings that seem intended to be temporary but seldom are. WaReady was, basically, a family-owned firm which had, in the past, been quite successful but which was beginning to experience heightened competitive pressures. The management of WaReady was, typically, autocratic and paternalistic in style. The company was non-unionised, a situation encouraged by the managers, although the 'industrial relations' in the company had not always run smoothly, and it sometimes seemed that tensions were not very far from the surface. Problems and disputes were put before a relatively compliant Works Committee.

Will Flower

One of the key workers at WaReady was William Flower. He was a highly skilled craftsman, a 'scarce resource'. Will had been poached from another company, Thomas Paines, which was not directly part of the defence industry but which used technologies similar to those used by WaReady. WaReady had made William Flower an offer that he could not refuse, and one that could not be matched by Thomas Paines, although they were very sorry to lose him. The reason for this was not just the particular and scarce skills that Will had, but also connected to the informal role that he had come to fill in the company. Thomas Paines had been plagued with fractious interpersonal relations until Will had joined them. His generally conciliatory character and his ability to deploy reasonable arguments had had a very calming influence on all at Thomas Paines. He was popular, and valued as much for himself as for his work. Will was a happy-go-lucky sort of person, open and unselfconscious, straightforward and unsophisticated. He always thought well of people, did not suspect or understand malice. He did have one weak spot, though, which was that, if he came under a lot of emotional pressure, he would become aggressive – he was well aware of this problem with his temper and was always anxious to avoid trouble of any kind, especially personal confrontation.

WaReady was a somewhat larger company than Will had been used to at Thomas Paines, but he readily accepted its offer, and settled in quickly there. He was considered to be very good at his job, and was popular with his workmates. His superiors also appeared to like him, generally. After a settling-in period, it was decided to attach Will to a special project group that was working on new product development. The project was an important part of WaReady's strategic plans but was also highly speculative. Will's special skills were potentially valuable to this project. However, after a while Will found that he was incurring adverse comments from the Assistant Foreman, usually over really trivial things, such as criticism because his workbench was untidy, because his writing was a scrawl, because, allegedly, he took longer than was necessary to go to the factory stores. Will was puzzled by these criticisms and they irritated him somewhat, but, as ever, he let them pass, to avoid trouble. Nonetheless, he felt that he was being harassed. One day, when feeling especially down about this, he mentioned it to Dan Skerry, an older and more experienced worker who was not part of the project group but who had been with WaReady many years, and to whom he sometimes chatted in their breaks. Since Will had raised the issue, Dan was moved to warn him that the General Foreman, Bob Clay, had taken a dislike to him and that Will should, therefore, watch his step. Will generally trusted Dan's opinion, but was amazed by this view and could not credit it. Bob Clay had a reputation for being very competent at his job. He certainly could be severe, even unpleasant, to those in his charge, but had never been so to Will – on the contrary, he had always seemed friendly and pleasant.

Bob Clay

Bob Clay was also relatively new to WaReady, though not quite as recent an addition as Will was. His reputation for competence was justified, but he could not be described as popular. Not that he minded that, since he felt that popularity was not a necessary qualification for a General Foreman. He was rather distant towards most people. Not much was known about Clay's life before he joined WaReady and, although rumours abounded, he discouraged any overt curiosity, either in himself or in his past. But, as Dan Skerry, and others, had noticed, he had indeed taken a dislike to Will, though it was not at all clear, even to him, why. Perhaps it was something more than dislike. Such popular and pleasant people do sometimes occasion hostility in others. It was also thought by some that Will, whose own history was uncertain – it was known to have been disadvantaged, but something in his mannerisms and language led some to think that he had originally come from a privileged background – unwittingly irritated Clay because he did not seem to belong on a shop floor. Clay had been moaning about Will and denigrating him to the Assistant Foreman and to other supervisors who, because of Clay's position, had come to be influenced by this dislike for Will on Clay's part. This was the cause of the petty harassments that Will had experienced. Clay had even tried, through others, to set Will up, in the hope that he would commit some indiscretion, but unsuccessfully. This lack of success was not at all surprising, given Will's character. He did realise that he had been targeted, but did not understand why, and did not mention it to anyone else – he did not want to be seen as a tell-tale. However, an opportunity for Clay to pursue his dislike of Will did soon arise, when the project on which Will was working failed to deliver the expected benefits. Clay resolved to put some blame on Will, and to complain to the Project Manager about this.

'Lucky' Starr

The Project Manager was Zachary Starr, universally known in the company (though never to his face) as 'Lucky' Starr – the reasons for this nickname must have been lost in the obscurities of the history of the company culture, because it did not seem to suit him particularly. Starr was another well-regarded member of the company. He was thought to be fair and honest, though somewhat unimaginative. He was also seen as a deeply moral man, unusual in an industry rife with corruption – and a man of deep religious faith. Starr was, like Clay, something of a disciplinarian, and, again like Clay, prided himself on being neutral and impartial, the professional, eschewing emotion. Lucky Starr was very conscious of his status, and enjoyed the outward signs of it. He expected others to acknowledge it – he was not the sort of person to encourage familiarity, he did expect to have a decent office, his own parking space, a good company car, and whatever else was his due. Yet he saw himself as taking a fatherly role towards those he managed, however distant a father that would seem to be. Part of the respect that was accorded to him by others was due to his alertness to all aspects of the workings of the company, his ability to resolve a wide range of issues. Starr was considered to be good at making quick decisions, and inclined to prompt action. Despite Will's minor role, Starr was aware of him and had formed the opinion that he was a good worker. He was considering promoting him to a more responsible position. He was rather less convinced of Clay's qualities, although he had had a bit more contact with Clay because of the latter's more senior position. Still, he did not know either Will or Clay well.

The accusation

Clay asked for an informal chat with Starr, at which he told Starr that he was sure that Flower had deliberately sabotaged the project. Starr was incredulous at this accusation, not least because of Will's relatively junior role in the project. Realising the significance of the accusation, he immediately cautioned Clay about the seriousness of lying about it. He demanded to know why Clay should say such a thing, but Clay stuck to his guns and insisted that he had proof. He was very indirect in his explanations but he seemed to imply that Flower had been bribed by a competitor to try to damage the project. Starr was not sure what to do. Instinctively, he did not believe Clay but, equally, he could not imagine why he should lie about it. He could not risk ignoring such a problem but did not want to act in haste. He decided to investigate informally, by summoning Will Flower and asking Clay to repeat his accusation in front of him – he assumed that the craftsman would be able to refute the allegations straight away. Clay agreed to proceeding in this way, and so it was done.

The impact

Will Flower was so astounded at Clay's accusations that he was totally lost for words. This turn of events was completely unexpected. He felt both outraged and threatened by the lies that were being told. He lost his temper. He was too angry to articulate a coherent response, but was very aware that some response was needed, immediately. Unable to do anything else, he simply physically attacked Clay. He lashed out at him. Clay did not retaliate and it was all over in a moment. By this time Starr was quite convinced that Clay had slandered Will, for whatever reason, but suddenly the situation had changed, and had escalated dramatically. This was not the sort of problem that Starr could welcome.

What to do now?

He did not know what to do next. Clay was obviously being malicious, but Flower should not have hit him, under any circumstances. It had become a very complicated situation. If the situation were to be taken seriously – as, minimally, discipline required that it should – he would lose a key, and hard to replace, worker, but he would also lose faith in Clay's usefulness as a supervisor. To take it seriously would mean that one, and possibly both, would have to go. He thought of turning a blind eye: if Clay made an official complaint, he could say that he had seen nothing and it would be Clay's word against Flower's word, and Flower, if he were sensible, would say nothing. He saw immediately that this would never work, as he, Starr, would have to lie about what had happened, and he was not sure that Flower would be able to lie either. He realised that he could not even rely on the events remaining a private matter, and there would, inevitably, be repercussions amongst the other workers who, if nothing was done, might no longer respect discipline, but who, if an example was made, might be aggrieved at the loss of someone who was, to them, a popular and hard-working colleague. Equally, although Clay certainly had a surveillance role, Starr did not want to seem too ready to accept whatever Clay said, as this would undoubtedly aggravate any tensions among the workers. At the same time, there was no point in denying this surveillance role altogether, as that, too, would be bad for discipline. There was also the problem that, if he did nothing, Clay would have a hold over him – if he was capable of lying about this, who knew what he might also be capable of doing? On top of all that, perhaps the company really was being targeted unethically by competitors.

The meeting

Starr wanted to try to keep the situation under wraps, to avoid premature provocation of any of the further escalations that seemed likely, once it was more widely known what had happened. For the time being, he decided to consult, informally, the Human Resources Manager, Louis Tenant, and so promptly phoned him. Starr briefly described the situation to Tenant and asked his advice about how to proceed. Tenant suggested that they should summon the Workers' Representative and then meet together with Starr and Flower – by this time, Clay had made it clear that he was not going to lodge an official complaint, so his presence was considered unnecessary to their deliberations. When contacted about a meeting, the Workers' Representative, who was called Ian Cumming, made himself available immediately, and so the meeting convened straight away.

The meeting took place in Starr's office, which, although well-appointed, was not very big. Though Tenant was, notionally, the chair of the meeting, Starr sat behind his rather large desk and the others, including Will Flower, perched wherever they could, facing Starr. No refreshments were provided. To start with, Starr described what had happened, including why the confrontation had taken place, and added that he did not believe Clay's accusation although he had no idea why Clay might lie. Flower then agreed that it was as Starr had said, and asserted that the accusation was indeed false, though he too did not know why it had been made. He was then asked to wait outside the room, while the matter was discussed.

The alternatives

Tenant suggested that they had two options. One was to regard the event as an open-and-shut case of assault, which would be an automatic sacking offence according to the company rules. The assault was not disputed, and so the matter could be resolved immediately. The alternative was to regard the assault as having been provoked maliciously, in which case there were grounds for an investigation. This would require a full inquiry into Clay's allegations, which would, itself, involve seeking out evidence and witnesses. If Clay were found to be correct, again this would result in Flower's dismissal. If it was found that he was not correct, then, presumably, Clay would have to be dismissed, not least because his position would become untenable in practice, as well as because he had lied. Tenant added that, as far as he could understand it, there did seem to be a case for some investigation, though, of course, this would take time and effort and would necessitate the whole situation becoming public knowledge. Cumming also said that he felt that there might be more to the situation than met the eye. Tenant was obviously looking for some sort of lead from Starr on which option he, Starr, preferred to pursue.

Starr pondered on this for a while. It was clear that the easiest solution was just to get rid of Flower – even if they did pursue an investigation, it could still end up with Flower's dismissal, and the disruption would then have been for nothing. However, he did not really want to lose Flower and, more importantly, there was the matter of doing justice. If Flower had been slandered and provoked, it would be unfair simply to dismiss him, and his skills would be lost needlessly. Just as significantly, if the matter were not investigated, Starr would never know whether Clay could be trusted in future. If he took the easy way out, he would certainly lose a key worker. If he took the longer route, he might still lose him, and create other problems in the process. Should he just follow the rules, or should he exercise moral judgement, with all the attendant risks of doing that? In the end, from a disciplinary point of view, were the motives relevant in light of the consequences? An assault was an assault, and, according to the rules, the penalty was dismissal. It was difficult to balance things out. He was also beginning to feel rather stressed by his own sense that some decision had to be reached quickly.

The decision

At last, Starr spoke. He told Tenant and Cumming that, in his view, the decision should be made by the three of them together. He added that, while not seeking to influence them, it seemed clear to him that the rules dictated that there was no excuse for assault and dismissal was the only appropriate action. Neither Tenant nor Cumming relished the implications of this course of action, and both thought that, when the news got out, as inevitably it would do, this would not be seen as a popular decision by Flower's colleagues, in particular. On the other hand, neither did they relish the implications of the other option. And so they agreed to follow Starr's lead. They recalled Will Flower to the room and he was, there and then, informed that he was to be dismissed for gross misconduct. And that was that.

In light of the issues discussed in this book:

- What can be seen as the factors that affected the decision-making process?
- The attempt to resolve the problem can be seen as informed by four competing demands: justice, ethics, rules and efficiency. Is it inevitable that these demands be in conflict with each other? Were they inevitably in conflict with each other in the case?
- In effect, the management team chose to remain in ignorance about the causes of the problem and about whether the accusation was justified, or not. How was the management of boundaries used by the various key actors to define and resolve the problem?
- How might (a) consequentialism and (b) deontology explain the decision arrived at?

APPENDIX 4

The art of the case study

In the use of case studies in a management education context, it is most common to present examples of 'actual' events. Indeed, it is held to be one of the strengths of the case study method that it supplements abstract learning with relevant situations from 'the real world'. The clock can be put back and, with the benefit of hindsight, we can 're-run' problems and, perhaps, this time, do things better – even if it is only pretend. However, this understanding is problematised by the ideas and concepts that inform Poststructuralism.

Firstly, there is an **ontological/epistemological** issue. How do we know what occurred? All that we have for evidence in a case is a text – even supplementary information that might be available is only a text. If we were not present when the events occurred, how can we know that the events described actually happened, or actually happened in the way that they are described? (Could we know even if we were there?) The ontology of a text is a difficult problem to resolve. Take *The Bible*, for instance. To some people it is a work of literal truth, to others it is a literary fiction. As no one is around now who witnessed the events portrayed, how can we judge its accuracy? And, in the instance of more recent events where we do have eye-witness accounts, the picture is no clearer. Take, for example, the very public assassination of the American President, John F. Kennedy, in 1963. Not only was this witnessed by hundreds of people, it was also recorded on film, and yet there is still dispute about whether Lee Harvey Oswald was the perpetrator; nor is it believed that witnesses or film are infallible records. Even official attempts to establish what happened have not clarified the situation. A further complication for case studies trying to access the truth about a real event is that they are, inevitably, models, and thus much of the information about the events portrayed will be filtered out. What is filtered out reflects the purpose of the 'model-builder' – that is, reflects the model-builder's particular biases, preferences and perceptions, and their view of the use to which the material is to be put.

The second problem arises from the 'nature' of **semiotics**. All texts, including case studies, are made up of signifiers that have no simple, fixed signifieds. The 'story' that a text tells, therefore, is contained, *not in the text, but in the reader*. Every reader 'reads' the text in their own particular way. Even if a case study (a text) could be claimed to be an utterly accurate representation of an actual set of events (which is, anyway, impossible), by the time it was read it would be a different story. And, if five people read it, there will be five more different stories. **All case material is, therefore, fiction**. The pedagogic value of a case study resides, not in the material itself, but in the individual readings that are produced by it. Does the particular juxtaposition of signifiers evoke an image, an understanding, a meaning that is useful to the reader? Does it contribute to 'seeing' the relevance of the various ideas that it is hoped it will illustrate?

There is another reason to see 'fiction' as a potentially useful tool where the study of organisational behaviour is concerned. The conventional discourse of Organisational Behaviour seeks to legitimate its claims by reference to reason, rationality, value-neutrality and rigour – in other words, by reference to Science. Science, it is argued, deals with objective truths and so furnishes us with a true account of reality. In contrast to this we have the Arts. The Arts, it is claimed by those who prefer Science, deal in imagination, give form to what is not 'real'; the Arts 'lie'. Unsurprisingly, this is not the view of Poststructuralism. While Science claims to give us answers, and requires us only to believe in its power, the Arts tell us nothing absolute and require us to think and to feel.

A 'scientific' understanding of organisational behaviour is necessarily sterile, the people who are its object of study purged of emotion and feeling (except where it is believed that (certain kinds of) emotion might be helpful to managers). People who lie, cheat, desire, love, hate, are kind or malicious, devious or deviant, do not exist in the fantasy world of the conventional discourse of Organisational Behaviour, but they do exist in organisations. They are also central to the Arts. Take, for example, the Irish airman, in the poem by Yeats that is included in Chapter 6. He has a very low level of identification with the organisation to which he belongs, he does not believe in its objectives, he thinks that the management of the organisation is ineffectual, he cares nothing for the extrinsic rewards the organisation offers to him, he sees no future for himself in the organisation and he is not motivated by the task. It is all just a means to satisfy his desire to zoom around the sky in an aeroplane. In contemporary terms, he must be seen as unmanageable, and he should be sacked immediately! Yet, we would argue, he is not such a rare beast, in contemporary terms, or in the terms of his own time. More importantly, the expressing of all this in the poem is done with economy and power – and is more memorable by far than the description of it above! Or take, for another example, the self-portrait by Picasso that is included in Chapter 8. Who has never felt like that? Who cannot empathise with this portrayal? And how much more striking is this picture than would be most attempts to define it in words – or in terms of bio-chemical processes? How does this self-portrait compare to the happy smiling faces of corporate publicity? If understanding of what people are like is our aim, perhaps the Arts will tell us more than Science ever can!

As noted in Chapter 1, the two extended case studies in Appendix 3 are both based on reworkings of literary 'texts' – one on Herman Melville's short story *Billy Budd, Sailor* (1967), and the other on the traditional story, *The Pied Piper of Hamelin*. This approach is not used just to show that it can be done. While transferring the action into a contemporary context, and, in the case of the former, stripping away much of the enfolding narrative, we have sought also to utilise the insights of the originals, and to illustrate the timelessness of human concerns and of behaviour in organisations. Of course, such texts can be illuminating to students of organisational behaviour even without such recontextualisations. It has often been remarked, for example, that Kafka's novel, *The Trial* (1963 [1925]), and his last, unfinished, work, *The Castle* (1983 [1926]), offer the most powerful descriptions of the workings of bureaucracy that can be found anywhere – certainly more powerful than anything that might be found in a text-book. Charles Bukowski's book, *Post Office* (1971), is another example of the power of a 'novel' to re-present what it can be like to work in an organisation, how people behave in organisations, and why. Robbe-Grillet's detective story *The Erasers* (1964 [1953]) is a novel that powerfully illustrates poststructuralist ideas, as well as the non-linearity of organisational life, and of organised life. These few examples are merely the tip of a massive iceberg. (There is a literature on art, aesthetics and organisation; see, for example, Carr and Hancock (2003), Linstead and Hopfl (2000), Strati (1999) and Hassard and Holliday (1998).) Being part of the Arts, rather than a quasi-scientific text-book, certainly does not mean that a work has nothing to say about the interests and concerns of someone who is trying to understand organisation in general, and organisational behaviour in particular – such a claim could hardly be further from the case. And it is worth remembering that most people have much better recall of any novel that they have read than they do of most text-books that they have read!

There is, indeed, a world of interesting and thought-provoking material around that illuminates the practice of behaving in organisations.

References

Abercrombie, N., Hill, S. and Turner, B. (1980) *The Dominant Ideology Thesis*. London: Allen and Unwin.

Adams, G. and Balfour, D. (2004) Human rights, the moral vacuum of modern organisations and administrative evil. In Campbell, T. and Miller, S. (eds) *Human Rights and the Moral Responsibilities of Corporate and Public Sector Organisations*. Dordrecht: Kluwer.

Aktouf, O. (1996) Competence, symbolic action and promotability. In Linstead, S., Grafton-Small, R. and Jeffcutt, P. (eds) *Understanding Management*. London: Sage.

Allaire, Y. and Firsirotu, M. (1984) Theories of organizational culture. *Organization Studies*, 5, 3, 193–226.

Allport, F.H. (1924) *Social Psychology*. Boston: Houghton Mifflin.

Alvesson, M. (1987a) *Organization Theory and Technocratic Consciousness*. Berlin: De Gruyter.

Alvesson, M. (ed.) (1987b) Organizational culture and ideology. *International Studies of Management and Organization* (special issue), xvii, 3.

Alvesson, M. (2002) *Understanding Organizational Culture*. London: Sage.

Alvesson, M. and Berg, P.-O. (1992) *Corporate Culture and Organizational Symbolism: An Overview*. Berlin: De Gruyter.

Alvesson, M. and Deetz, S. (2000) *Doing Critical Management Research*. London: Sage.

Alvesson, M. and Willmott, H. (eds) (1992) *Critical Management Studies*. London: Sage.

Alvesson, M. and Willmott, H. (1996) *Making Sense of Management*. London: Sage.

Amey, L.R. (1969) *The Efficiency of Business Enterprises*. London: George Allen and Unwin.

Analoui, F. and Kakabadse, A.P. (1991) *Sabotage – How To Recognise and Manage Employee Defiance*. London: Mercury.

Anderson, W.T. (ed.) (1995) *The Fontana Post-modern Reader*. Glasgow: Fontana.

Anheier, H.K. (ed.) (1999) *When Things Go Wrong: Organizational Failures and Breakdowns*. Thousand Oaks, CA: Sage.

Anthony, P.D. (1977) *The Ideology of Work*. London: Tavistock.

Anthony, P.D. (1986) *The Foundation of Management*. London: Tavistock.

Appignanesi, R. and Garratt, C. (2004) *Introducing Postmodernism*. Cambridge: Icon.

Argyris, C. (1957) *Personality and Organization*. New York: Harper and Row.

Ashby, W.R. (1970) Analysis of the system to be modeled. In Stogdill, R.M. (ed.) *The Process of Model-Building in the Behavioral Sciences*. Columbus, Ohio: Ohio State University Press.

Ashkenas, R., Ulrich, D., Jick, T. and Kerr, S. (1995) *The Boundaryless Organization*. San Francisco, CA: Jossey Bass.

Attewell, P. (1996) Information technology and the productivity challenge. In Kling, R. (ed.) *Computerization and Controversy*, 2nd edn. London: Academic Press.

Avineri, S. and de-Shalit, A. (eds) (1992) *Communitarianism and Individualism*. Oxford: Oxford University Press.

Baggott, J. (2005) *A Beginner's Guide to Reality*. London: Penguin.

Bakan, J. (2005) *The Corporation: The Pathological Pursuit of Profit and Power*. London: Constable.

Baldamus, W. (1961) *Efficiency and Effort*. London: Tavistock.

Baran, P.A. and Sweezy, P.M. (1966) *Monopoly Capital*. New York: Monthly Review Press.

Baritz, L. (1975) The servants of power. In Esland, G., Salaman, G. and Speakman, M.-A. (eds) *People and Work*. Edinburgh: Holmes McDougall.

Barthes, R. (1967) *Elements of Semiology*. Trans. A. Lavers & C. Smith. London: Jonathan Cape.

Barthes, R. (1968) *Writing Degree Zero*. Trans. A. Lavers & C. Smith. New York: Hill & Wang.

Barthes, R. (1972) *Mythologies*. Trans. A. Lavers. London: Jonathan Cape.

Bateson, G. (1973) *Steps To An Ecology of Mind*. London: Paladin.

Baudrillard, J. (1985) The ecstasy of communication. In Foster, H. (ed.) *Postmodern Culture*. London: Pluto Press.

Baudrillard, J. (1988) Simulacra and simulations. In Poster, M. (ed.) *Jean Baudrillard, Selected Writings*. Oxford: Polity/Basil Blackwell.

Baudrillard, J. (2005) *The Intelligence of Evil or the Lucidity Pact*. Trans. C. Turner. Oxford: Berg.

Bauman, Z. (1991) *Modernity and Ambivalence*. Oxford: Blackwell.

Bauman, Z. (1992) *Intimations of Postmodernity*. London: Routledge.

Bauman, Z. (1993) *Postmodern Ethics*. Oxford: Blackwell.

Bauman, Z. (2005) *Work, Consumption and the New Poor*, 2nd edn. Maidenhead, Berks.: Open University Press.

Baxter, B. (1982) *Alienation and Authenticity – Some Consequences for Organised Work*. London: Tavistock.

Bazerman, M. (2006) *Judgement in Managerial Decision Making*, 6th edn. New York: John Wiley.

Beach, L.R. (1997) *The Psychology of Decision Making: People in Organizations*. Thousand Oaks, CA: Sage.

Beck, U. (1992) *Risk Society*. Trans. M. Ritter. London: Sage.

Beck, U. (1999) *World Risk Society*. Cambridge: Polity.

Beck, U. (2005) *Power in the Global Age*. Trans. K. Cross. Cambridge: Polity.

Beer, S. (1966) *Decision and Control*. Chichester: John Wiley.

Beer, S. (1978) *Platform For Change*. Chichester: John Wiley.

Beer, S. (1981) *Brain of the Firm*. Chichester: John Wiley.

Beer, S. (1994) *The Heart of Enterprise*. Chichester: Wiley.

Bell, D. (1960) *The End of Ideology*. New York: The Free Press.

Bendix, R. (1966) *Work and Authority in Industry*. New York: John Wiley.

Bendix, R. (1970) The impact of ideas on organizational structuring. In Grusky, O. and Miller, G.A. (eds) *The Sociology of Organizations: Basic Studies*. New York: The Free Press.

Bennett, W.L. and Feldman, M.S. (1981) *Reconstructing Reality in the Courtroom*. London: Tavistock.

Benokraitis, N.V. (1997) *Subtle Sexism: Current Practice and Prospects for Change*. Thousand Oaks, CA: Sage.

Benvenuto, B. and Kennedy, R. (1986) *The Works of Jacques Lacan: An Introduction*. London: Free Association Books.

Berg, M. (1994) *The Age of Manufactures: Industry, Innovation and Work in Britain 1700–1820*, 2nd edn. London: Routledge.

Berger, P. and Luckman, T. (1967) *The Social Construction of Reality*. Harmondsworth: Penguin.

Berle, A.A. and Means, G.C. (1932) *The Modern Corporation and Private Property*. New York: Macmillan.

Bernstein, R.J. (1979) *The Restructuring of Social and Political Theory*. London: Methuen.

Bernstein, R.J. (1983) *Beyond Objectivism and Relativism*. Oxford: Basil Blackwell.

Bertens, H. (1994) *The Idea of the Postmodern: A History*. London: Routledge.

Best, S. and Kellner, D. (1991) *Postmodern Theory: Critical Interrogations*. Basingstoke: Macmillan.

Beynon, H. (1973) *Working For Ford*. Wakefield: EP Publishing.

Beynon, H. and Glavanis, P. (1999) *Patterns of Social Inequality*. Harlow, Essex: Pearson.

Bhagwati, J. (2004) *In Defense of Globalization*. Oxford: Oxford University Press.

Blackburn, R. (ed.) (1972) *Ideology in Social Science: Readings in Critical Social Theory*. London: Fontana.

Blake, R. and Mouton, J.S. (1964) *The Managerial Grid*. Houston, Tex.: Gulf.

Blauner, R. (1964) *Alienation and Freedom – The Factory Worker and His Industry*. Chicago: University of Chicago Press.

Blytheway, R. (1995) *Ageism*. Buckingham: Open University Press.

Blyton, P. and Turnbull, P. (eds) (1992) *Reassessing Human Resource Management*. London: Sage.

Boddy, D. and Paton, R. (1998) *Management: An Introduction*. Hemel Hempstead: Prentice Hall.

Bogard, W. (1996) *The Simulation of Surveillance – Hypercontrol in Telematic Societies*. Cambridge: Cambridge University Press.

Bohm, D. (1983) *Wholeness and the Implicate Order*. London: Ark Paperbacks.

Böhm, S. (2005) *Repositioning Organization Theory*. Basingstoke: Palgrave Macmillan.

Boje, D.M., Gephart, R.P. and Thatchenkery, T.J. (eds) (1996) *Postmodern Management and Organization Theory*. London: Sage.

Borgmann, A. (1992) *Crossing the Postmodern Divide*. Chicago: University of Chicago Press.

Bottomore, T. (1991) *A Dictionary of Marxist Thought*. Oxford: Blackwell.

Boulding, K.E. (1978) *Ecodynamics*. London: Sage.

Bourgeois, V.W. and Pinder, C.C. (1983) Contrasting philosophical perspectives in administrative science: A reply to Morgan. *Administrative Science Quarterly*, 28, 608–13.

Bowie, M. (1991) *Lacan*. London: Fontana.

Bradley, H. (1989) *Men's Work, Women's Work*. Cambridge: Polity.

Brady, R.A. (1943) *Business as a System of Power*. New York: Columbia University Press.

Braverman, H. (1974) *Labor and Monopoly Capital: The Degradation of Work in the Twentieth Century*. New York: Monthly Review Press.

Breach, I. (1978) *Windscale Fallout*. Harmondsworth: Penguin.

Brewer, A. (1984) *A Guide to Marx's Capital*. Cambridge: Cambridge University Press.

Brewis, J. (1996) The 'making' of the 'competent' manager. *Management Learning*, 27, 1, 65–86.

Broms, H. and Gahmberg, H. (1987) *Semiotics of Management*. Helsinki: Helsinki School of Economics.

Brooker, P. (ed.) (1992) *Modernism/Postmodernism*. London: Longman.

Brown, G. (1977) *Sabotage*. Nottingham: Spokesman Books.

Brown, S. (1995) *Postmodern Marketing*. London: Routledge/International Thomson Press.

Brown, S. (1998) *Postmodern Marketing Two: Telling Tales*, 2nd edn. London: International Thomson Press.

Bryman, A. (1984) Organization studies and the concept of rationality. *Journal of Management Studies*, 21, 4, 391–408.

Bryman, A. (1989) *Research Methods and Organization Studies*. London: Unwin Hyman.

Bryman, A. (2004) *The Disneyization of Society*. London: Sage.

Buchanan, D. and Huczynski, A. (2004) *Organizational Behaviour: An Introductory Text*, 5th edn. Hemel Hempstead: Prentice Hall.

Bukowski, C. (1971) *Post Office*. London: W.H. Allen.

Burchell, G., Gordon, C. and Miller, P. (eds) (1991) *The Foucault Effect: Studies in Governmentality*. London: Harvester Wheatsheaf.

Burnham, J. (1942) *The Managerial Revolution*. London: Pitman.

Burns, T. and Stalker, G.M. (1961) *The Management of Innovation*. London: Tavistock.

Burns, T.R., Karlsson, E. and Rus, V. (eds) (1979) *Work and Power*. London: Sage.

Burrell, G. (1988) Modernism, Postmodernism and organizational analysis (2): The contribution of Michel Foucault. *Organization Studies*, 9, 2, 221–35.

Burrell, G. (1991) The organization of pleasure. In Alvesson, M. and Willmott, H. (eds) *Critical Management Studies*. London: Sage.

Burrell, G. (1992) Sex and organizational analysis. In Mills, A. and Tancred, P. (eds) *Gendering Organizational Analysis*. London: Sage.

Burrell, G. (1996) Normal science paradigms, metaphors, discourses and genealogies of analysis. In Clegg, S.R., Hardy, C. and Nord, W.R. (eds) *Handbook of Organization Studies*. London: Sage.

Burrell, G. (1997) *Pandemonium – Towards a Retro-Organization Theory*. London: Sage.

Burrell, G. and Dale, K. (2006) *Organisations, Space and Architecture*. Basingstoke: Palgrave Macmillan.

Burrell, G. and Morgan, G. (1979) *Sociological Paradigms and Organisational Analysis*. London: Heinemann.

Capra, F. (1983) *The Turning Point*. London: Fontana.

Carey, A. (1967) The Hawthorne studies: A radical criticism. *American Sociological Review*, 32, 403–16.

Carey, A. (1977) The Lysenko Syndrome in Western social science. *Australian Psychologist*, 12, 1, 27–38.

Carr, A. and Hancock, P. (eds) (2003) *Art and Aesthetics at Work*. Basingstoke: Palgrave Macmillan.

Carter, P. and Jackson, N. (1987) Management, myth, and metatheory – from scarcity to postscarcity. *International Studies of Management and Organization*, xvii, 3, 64–89.

Carter, P. and Jackson, N. (1990) The emergence of Postmodern management? *Management Education and Development*, 21, 3, 219–28.

Carter, P. and Jackson, N. (1992) The perception of risk. In Ansell, J. and Wharton, F. (eds) *Risk: Analysis, Assessment and Management*. Chichester: Wiley.

Carter, P. and Jackson, N. (1993) Modernism, Postmodernism and motivation, or why Expectancy Theory failed to come up to expectation. In Hassard, J. and Parker, M. (eds) *Postmodernism and Organizations*. London: Sage.

Carter, P. and Jackson, N. (1997) *Risk 'analysis' as discourse*. University of Hull: School of Management Working Paper HUSM/PC/32.

Carter, P. and Jackson, N. (2004a) For the sake of argument: Towards an understanding of rhetoric as process. *Journal of Management Studies*, 41, 3, 469–91.

Carter, P. and Jackson, N. (2004b) Deleuze and Guattari: A 'minor' contribution to organization theory. In Linstead, S. (ed.) *Organization Theory and Postmodern Thought*. London: Sage.

Cashmore, E.E. and Mullen, B. (1983) *Approaching Social Theory*. London: Heinemann.

Castles, F.G., Murray, D.J. and Potter, D.C. (eds) (1975) *Decisions, Organizations and Society*. Harmondsworth: Penguin/Open University.

Chan, A. (2000) *Critically Constituting Organization*. Amsterdam: John Benjamins.

Chandler, D. (2002) *Semiotics: The Basics*. London: Routledge.

Chatwin, B. (1987) *The Songlines*. London: Picador.

Checkland, P.B. (1981) *Systems Thinking, Systems Practice*. Chichester: Wiley.

Checkland, P.B. and Scholes, J. (1990) *Soft Systems Methodology in Action*. Chichester: Wiley.

Chia, R. (1994) The concept of decision: A deconstructive analysis. *Journal of Management Studies*, 31, 6, 781–806.

Chia, R. (1996) *Organizational Analysis as Deconstructive Practice*. Berlin: De Gruyter.

Chia, R. (ed.) (1998) *In the Realm of Organization: Essays for Robert Cooper*. London: Routledge.

Chia, R. and Morgan, S. (1996) Educating the philosopher-manager. *Management Learning*, 27, 1, 37–64.

Child, J. (1972) Organizational structure, environment and performance: The role of strategic choice. *Sociology*, 6, 1–22.

Clarke, J. and Newman, J. (1997) *The Managerial State*. London: Sage.

Clarke, T. and Salaman, G. (1996) The management guru as organizational witch doctor. *Organization*, 3, 1, 85–107.

Clayre, A. (ed.) (1977) *Nature and Industrialization*. Oxford: Oxford University Press.

Clegg, S.R. (1989) *Frameworks of Power*. London: Sage.

Clegg, S.R. (1990) *Modern Organizations: Organization Studies in the Postmodern World*. London: Sage.

Clegg, S.R. (1994) Max Weber and contemporary sociology of organization. In Ray, L.J. and Reed, M. (eds) *Organizing Modernity*. London: Routledge.

Clegg, S. and Dunkerley, D. (1980) *Organization, Class and Control*. London: RKP.

Clegg, S.R., Hardy, C. and Nord, W.R. (eds) (2006) *Handbook of Organization Studies*, 2nd edn. London: Sage.

Clegg, S.R. and Palmer, G. (eds) (1996) *The Politics of Management Knowledge*. London: Sage.

Cobley, P. and Jansz, L. (1997) *Semiotics For Beginners*. Cambridge: Icon.

Cobley, P. and Jansz, L. (2004) *Introducing Semiotics*. Cambridge: Icon.

Cockburn, C. (1983) *Brothers: Male Domination and Technological Change*. London: Pluto.

Cockburn, C. (1991) *In the Way of Women*. Basingstoke: Macmillan.

Cockburn, C. and Ormrod, S. (1993) *Gender and Technology in the Making*. London: Sage.

Cohen, M.D., March, J.C. and Olsen, J.P. (1982) A garbage can model of organizational choice. *Administrative Science Quarterly*, 17, 1–25.

Cohen, S. and Taylor, L. (1992) *Escape Attempts – The Theory and Practice of Resistance to Everyday Life*, 2nd edn. London: Routledge.

Cole, G.A. (2004) *Management: Theory and Practice*, 6th edn. Eastleigh: D.P. Publications.

Cole, K., Cameron, J. and Edwards, C. (1991) *Why Economists Disagree*, 2nd edn. London: Longman.

Collier, R. (1995) *Combatting Sexual Harassment in the Workplace*. Buckingham: Open University Press.

Collins, D. (2000) *Management Fads and Buzzwords*. London: Routledge.

Collins, J. and Mayblin, B. (2005) *Introducing Derrida*. Cambridge: Icon.

Collinson, D., Knights, D. and Collinson, M. (1990) *Managing to Discriminate*. London: Routledge.

Conley, V. (1997) *Eco-Politics – The Environment in Poststructuralist Thought*. London: Routledge.

Cooper, C.L., Cooper, R.D. and Eaker, L. (1988) *Living With Stress*. London: Penguin.

Cooper, R. (1983a) The Other: A model of human structuring. In Morgan, G. (ed.) *Beyond Method*. London: Sage.

Cooper, R. (1983b) Some remarks on theoretical individualism, alienation and work. *Human Relations*, 36, 8, 717–24.

Cooper, R. (1986) Organization/disorganization. *Social Science Information*, 25, 2, 299–335.

Cooper, R. (1987) Information, communication and organization: A post-structuralist revision. *Journal of Mind and Behaviour*, 8, 3, 395–416.

Cooper, R. (1989) Modernism, Postmodernism and organizational analysis: The contribution of Jacques Derrida. *Organization Studies*, 10, 4, 479–502.

Cooper, R. (1992a) Formal organization as representation: Remote control, displacement and abbreviation. In Reed, M. and Hughes, M. (eds) *Rethinking Organization*. London: Sage.

Cooper, R. (ed.) (1992b) Systems and organizations: New directions. *Systems Practice* (special issue), 5, 4.

Cooper, R. (1993) Technologies of representation. In Ahonen, P. (ed.) *Tracing the Semiotic Boundaries of Politics*. Berlin: De Gruyter.

Cooper, R. and Burrell, G. (1988) Modernism, Postmodernism and organizational analysis: An introduction. *Organization Studies*, 9, 1, 91–112.

Cooper, R. and Fox, S. (1989) Two modes of organization. In Mansfield, R. (ed.) *Frontiers of Management*. London: Routledge.

Cooper, R. and Law, J. (1995) Organization: Distal and proximal views. In Bacharach, S., Gagliardi, P. and Mundell, B. (eds) *Research in the Sociology of Organizations (Vol. 13): Studies of Organizations in the European Tradition*. Greenwich, CT: Jai Press.

Copley, F.B. (1923) *Frederick W. Taylor: Father of Scientific Management*. 2 Volumes. New York: Harper and Brothers.

Corbett, J.M. (1994) *Critical Cases in Organisational Behaviour*. Basingstoke: Macmillan.

Cousins, M. and Hussain, A. (1984) *Michel Foucault*. London: Macmillan.

Coyle, R.G. (1972) *Decision Analysis*. London: Nelson.

Crook, S., Pakulski, J. and Waters, M. (1992) *Postmodernization: Changes in Advanced Society*. London: Sage.

Cyert, R.M. and March, J.G. (1963) *A Behavioural Theory of the Firm*. Englewood Cliffs, NJ: Prentice-Hall.

Czarniawska-Joerges, B. (1992) *Exploring Complex Organizations*. London: Sage.

Czarniawska-Joerges, B. and Guillet de Monthoux, P. (eds) (1994) *Good Novels, Better Management*. Chur, Switz: Harwood Academic.

Dahrendorf, R. (1959) *Class and Class Conflicts in Industrial Society*. London: RKP.

Dale, K. and Burrell, G. (2003) An-Aesthetics and architecture. In Carr, A. and Hancock, P. (eds) *Art and Aesthetics at Work*. Basingstoke: Palgrave Macmillan.

Danaher, G., Schirato, T. and Webb, J. (2000) *Understanding Foucault*. London: Sage.

Daudi, P. (1986) *Power in the Organisation: The Discourse of Power in Managerial Praxis*. Oxford: Blackwell.

Davies, S. (1996) *Big Brother*. London: Pan.

Davis, P. and Donaldson, J. (1998) *Co-operative Management: A Philosophy for Business*. Cheltenham: New Harmony Press.

Deal, T. and Kennedy, A. (1988) *Corporate Cultures*. London: Penguin.

De Board, R. (1978) *The Psychoanalysis of Organizations*. London: Tavistock.

Deetz, S.A. (1992) *Democracy in an Age of Corporate Colonization*. New York: SUNY Press.

Deetz, S. (1994) The new politics of the workplace: Ideology and other unobtrusive controls. In Simons, H.W. and Billig, M. (eds) *After Postmodernism: Reconstructing Ideology Critique*. London: Sage.

Deleuze, G. and Guattari, F. (1983) *On the Line*. Trans. J. Johnstone. New York: Semiotext(e).

Deleuze, G. and Guattari, F. (1984) *Anti-Oedipus – Capitalism and Schizophrenia*. Trans. R. Hurley, M. Seem and H.B. Lane. London: Athlone.

Deleuze, G. and Guattari, F. (1988) *A Thousand Plateaus*. Trans. B. Massumi. London: Athlone.

Deleuze, G. and Guattari, F. (1994) *What is Philosophy?* Trans. H. Tomlinson and G. Burchill. London: Verso.

Deleuze, G. and Parnet, C. (1983) Politics. In Deleuze, G. and Guattari, F. *On the Line*. Trans. J. Johnston. New York: Semiotext(e).

Derrida, J. (1976) *Of Grammatology*. Trans. G.C. Spivak. Baltimore, MD: Johns Hopkins University Press.

Derrida, J. (1978) *Writing and Difference*. Trans. A. Bass. London: Routledge and Kegan Paul.

Derrida, J. (1981) *Dissemination*. Trans. B. Johnson. London: Athlone.

Derrida, J. (1994) *Specters of Marx*. Trans. P. Kamuf. London: Routledge.

Descombes, V. (1980) *Modern French Philosophy*. Trans. L. Scott-Fox and J.M. Harding. Cambridge: Cambridge University Press.

Dews, P. (1987) *Logics of Disintegration: Poststructuralist Thought and the Claims of Critical Theory*. London: Verso.

Diamond, M.A. (1993) *The Unconscious Life of Organizations: Interpreting Organizational Identity*. Westport, CT: Quorum.

Domhoff, G.W. (2005) *Who Rules America? Power, Politics and Social Change*. 5th edn. Boston: McGraw Hill.

Donaldson, L. (1985) *In Defence of Organization Theory*. Cambridge: Cambridge University Press.

Donaldson, L. (1996) *For Positivist Organization Theory*. London: Sage.

Donzelot, J. (1991) Pleasure in work. Trans. C. Gordon. In Burchell, G., Gordon, C. and Miller, P. (eds) *The Foucault Effect: Studies in Governmentality*. London: Harvester Wheatsheaf.

Doray, B. (1988) *From Taylorism to Fordism: A Rational Madness*. Trans. D. Macey. London: Free Association Books.

Douglas, M. (1986) *Risk Acceptability According to the Social Sciences*. London: Routledge and Kegan Paul.

Dreyfus, H.L. and Rabinow, P. (1982) *Michel Foucault: Beyond Structuralism and Hermeneutics*. Brighton: Harvester.

Drucker, P. (1968) *The Practice of Management*. London: Pan.

Drucker, P. (1977) *People and Performance: The Best of Peter Drucker on Management*. London: Heinemann.

Drucker, P. (1980) *Managing in Turbulent Times*. London: Heinemann.

Drucker, P. (1981) *Towards the Next Economics*. London: Heinemann.

Drucker, P. (1993) *Post-Capitalist Society*. London: Heinemann.

Drummond, H. (2001) *The Art of Decision Making*. Chichester: John Wiley.

Dubois, P. (1979) *Sabotage in Industry*. Trans. R. Sheed. Harmondsworth: Penguin.

Du Gay, P. (1996) *Consumption and Identity at Work*. London: Sage.

Dye, T. R. (2000) *Who's Running America?* 6th edn. Upper Saddle River, NJ: Prentice-Hall.

Eagleton, T. (ed.) (1994) *Ideology*. London: Longman.

Eco, U. (1976) *A Theory of Semiotics*. Bloomington, IN: Indiana University Press.

Eco, U. (1984) *The Name of the Rose*. Trans. W. Weaver. London: Pan.

Eco, U. (1987) *Travels in Hyper-Reality*. Trans. W. Weaver. London: Pan.

Eco, U. (1989) *The Open Work*. London: Hutchinson.

Edel, A. (1979) *Analyzing Concepts in Social Science – Science, Ideology and Value*. New Brunswick, NJ: Transaction Books.

Eldridge, J.E.T. and Crombie, A.D. (1974) *A Sociology of Organisations*. London: George Allen and Unwin.

Elliot, D. (1980) The organization as a system. In Salaman, G. and Thompson, K. (eds) *Control and Ideology in Organizations*. Milton Keynes: Open University Press.

Elliott, L. (1999) The real value of the Victorians. *The Guardian*, 29 March.

Ellis, R. and McClintock, A. (1994) *If You Take My Meaning*, 2nd edn. London: Edward Arnold.

Elster, J. (1983) *Sour Grapes: Studies in the Subversion of Rationality*. Cambridge: Cambridge University Press.

Emery, F.E. (ed.) (1969) *Systems Thinking*. 2 Volumes. Harmondsworth: Penguin.

Etzioni, A. (1988) *The Moral Dimension*. New York: Free Press.

Featherstone, M. (ed.) (1988) Postmodernism. *Theory, Culture and Society* (special issue), 5, 2–3.

Feyerabend, P. (1978) *Against Method*. London: Verso.

Fillingham, L.A. (1993) *Foucault For Beginners*. New York: Writers and Readers.

Fineman, S. (ed.) (1993) *Emotion in Organizations*. London: Sage.

Fineman, S. (1998) The natural environment, organization and ethics. In Parker, M. (ed.) *Ethics and Organizations*. London: Sage.

Fineman, S. and Hosking, D.-M. (eds) (1990) The texture of organising. *Journal of Management Studies* (special issue), 27, 6.

Fineman, S., Gabriel, Y. and Sims, D. (2005) *Organizing and Organizations*, 3rd edn. London: Sage.

Fiske, J. (1990) *Introduction to Communication Studies*, 2nd edn. London: Routledge.

Flanders, A. (1964) *The Fawley Productivity Agreements – A Case Study of Management and Collective Bargaining*. London: Faber & Faber.

Flood, R.L. and Jackson, M.C. (eds) (1991) *Critical Systems Thinking: Directed Readings*. Chichester: Wiley.

Foster, H. (ed.) (1985) *Postmodern Culture*. London: Pluto Press.

Foucault, M. (1967) *Madness and Civilization*. Trans. R. Howard. London: Tavistock.

Foucault, M. (1970) *The Order of Things*. London: Tavistock.

Foucault, M. (1971) Orders of discourse. Trans. R. Swyer. *Social Science Information*, 10, 2, 7–30.

Foucault, M. (1974) *The Archaeology of Knowledge*. Trans. A. Sheridan-Smith. London: Tavistock.

Foucault, M. (1977) The eye of power. Trans. C. Gordon. In Gordon, C. (ed) (1980) *Michel Foucault – Power/Knowledge*. Brighton: Harvester.

Foucault, M. (1979a) *Discipline and Punish*. Trans. A. Sheridan. Harmondsworth: Penguin.

Foucault, M. (1979b) Governmentality. Trans. R. Braidoth. *Ideology and Consciousness*, 6, 5–21.

Foucault, M. (2003) *Society Must Be Defended*. Trans. D. Macey. London: Allen Lane.

Fox, A. (1966) *Industrial Sociology and Industrial Relations: Royal Commission on Trades Unions and Employers' Associations*. London: HMSO.

Fox, A. (1973) Industrial relations: A social critique of pluralist ideology. In Child, J. (ed.) *Man and Organisation*. London: Allen and Unwin.

Fox, A. (1974) *Beyond Contract: Work, Power and Trust Relations*. London: Faber and Faber.

Fox, A. (1980) The meaning of work. In Esland, G. and Salaman, G. (eds) *The Politics of Work and Occupations*. Milton Keynes: Open University Press.

Frankfort-Nachmias, C. and Nachmias, D. (1992) *Research Methods in the Social Sciences*, 4th edn. London: Edward Arnold.

French, J.R.P. and Raven, B. (1968) The bases of social power. In Cartwright, D. and Zander, A.F. (eds) *Group Dynamics: Research and Theory*, 3rd edn. New York: Harper and Row.

French, W.L. and Bell, C.H. (1973) *Organization Development*. Englewood Cliffs, NJ: Prentice-Hall.

Freud, S. (1963) *Civilisation and Its Discontents*. Trans. J. Riviere. London: Hogarth Press.

Fromm, E. (1979) *To Have Or To Be?* London: Abacus.

Frost, P.J., Moore, L.F., Louis, M.R., Lundberg, C.C. and Martin, J. (eds) (1985) *Organizational Culture*. London: Sage.

Frost, P.J., Moore, L.F., Louis, M.R., Lundberg, C.C. and Martin, J. (eds) (1991) *Reframing Organizational Culture*. London: Sage.

Gabriel, Y. (1999) *Organizations in Depth*. London: Sage.

Gabriel, Y. (2000) *Storytelling in Organizations*. Oxford: Oxford University Press.

Galliers, R., Mingers, J. and Jackson, M. (1997) Organization theory and systems thinking: The benefits of partnership. *Organization*, 4, 2, 269–78.

Gergen, K. (1992) Organization theory in the postmodern era. In Reed, M. and Hughes, M. (eds) *Rethinking Organization*. London: Sage.

Gherardi, S. (1995) *Gender, Symbolism and Organizational Culture*. London: Sage.

Gibb, J. (2005) *Who's Watching You?* London: Collins and Brown.

Gibson, J.L., Ivancevich, J.M., Donnelly, J.H. and Konopaske, R. (2002) *Organizations: Behaviour, Structure, Processes*, 11th edn. Burr Ridge, IL: Irwin.

Giddens, A. (1979) *Central Problems in Social Theory*. London: Macmillan.

Giddens, A. (1990) *The Consequences of Modernity*. Cambridge: Polity.

Giddens, A. (1991) *Modernity and Self-Identity*. Cambridge: Polity.

Giddens, A. and Mackenzie, G. (eds) (1982) *Social Class and the Division of Labour*. Cambridge: Cambridge University Press.

Gleick, J. (1988) *Chaos*. London: Sphere.

Goffman, E. (1959) *The Presentation of Self in Everyday Life*. Harmondsworth: Penguin.

Goldsmith, E.B. (ed.) (1989) *Work and the Family*. London: Sage.

Goodchild, P. (1996) *Deleuze and Guattari: An Introduction to the Politics of Desire*. London: Sage.

Gordon, C. (ed.) (1980) *Michel Foucault – Power/Knowledge*. Trans. C. Gordon, L. Marshall, J. Mepham and K. Soper. Brighton: Harvester.

Gore, C., Murray, K. and Richardson, B. (1992) *Strategic Decision-Making*. London: Cassell.

Gorz, A. (1989) *Critique of Economic Reason*. Trans. G. Handyside and C. Turner. London: Verso.

Gosling, D. and Montefiore, H. (eds) (1977) *Nuclear Crisis*. Dorchester: Prism Press.

Gouldner, A.W. (1967) Reciprocity and autonomy in functional theory. In Demerath, N.J. and Peterson, R.A. (eds) *System Change and Conflict*. New York: Free Press.

Gouldner, A.W. (1969) The unemployed self. In Fraser, R. (ed.) *Work*, Vol. 2. Harmondsworth: Penguin.

Gouldner, A.W. (1970) *The Coming Crisis of Western Sociology*. London: Heinemann.

Gouldner, A.W. (1976) *The Dialectic of Ideology and Technology: The Origins, Future and Grammar of Ideology*. London: Macmillan.

Grahame, K. (1951) *Wind in the Willows*. London: Methuen.

Green, P. and Ward, T. (2004) *State Crime – Governments, Violence and Corruption*. London: Pluto.

Greenspan, A. (1967) The assault on integrity. In Rand, A., Bransen, N., Greenspan, A. and Hessen, R., *The Unknown Ideal*. Harmondsworth: Signet/Penguin.

Griffiths, I. (1992) *Creative Accounting: How To Make Your Profits What You Want Them To Be*. London: Routledge.

Guattari, F. (1984) *Molecular Revolution*. Trans. R. Sheed. Harmondsworth: Penguin.

Guattari, F. (1995a) *Chaosmosis – An Ethico-Aesthetic Paradigm*. Trans. P. Bains and J. Pefanis. Bloomington, IN: Indiana University Press.

Guattari, F. (1995b) *Chaosophy*. New York: Semiotext(e).

Guattari, F. (2000) *The Three Ecologies*. Trans. I. Pindar and P. Sutton. London: Athlone.

Guba, E.G. (ed.) (1990) *The Paradigm Dialog*. Newbury Park, CA: Sage.

Guillet de Monthoux, P. (1993) *The Moral Philosophy of Management – From Quesnay to Keynes*. New York: M.E. Sharpe.

Habermas, J. (1976) *Legitimation Crisis*. Trans. T. McCarthy. London: Heinemann.

Habermas, J. (1978) *Knowledge and Human Interests*, 2nd edn. Trans. J.J. Shapiro. London: Heinemann.

Habermas, J. (1981) Modernity versus Postmodernity. Trans. S. Ben-Habib. *New German Critique*, 22, 3–14.

Habermas, J. (1987) *Towards a Rational Society*. Trans. J.J. Shapiro. Boston: Beacon Press.

Habermas, J. (1994) Ideology. In Eagleton, T. (ed.) *Ideology*. London: Longman.

Hall, S. (1977) The hinterland of science: Ideology and the "Sociology of Knowledge". In Centre for Contemporary Cultural Studies: *On Ideology*. London: Hutchinson.

Halliday, S. (1999) *The Great Stink of London*. Stroud: Sutton Publishing.

Hancock, P. and Tyler, M. (2001) *Work, Postmodernism and Organization*. London: Sage.

Handy, C. (1976) *Understanding Organisations*. Harmondsworth: Penguin.

Handy, C. (1984) *The Future of Work*. Oxford: Basil Blackwell.

Handy, C. (1994) *The Empty Raincoat: Making Sense of the Future*. London: Hutchinson.

Hardt, M. and Negri, A. (2000) *Empire*. Cambridge, Mass.: Harvard University Press.

Hardt, M. and Negri, A. (2005) *Multitude*. London: Penguin.

Harland, R. (1987) *Superstructuralism: The Philosophy of Structuralism and Post-Structuralism*. London: Methuen.

Harris, N. (1968) *Beliefs in Society: The Problem of Ideology*. London: C.A. Watts.

Harris, R. (2003) *Political Corruption – In and Beyond the Nation State*. London: Routledge.

Harrison, E.F. (1999) *The Managerial Decision-Making Process*, 5th edn. Boston: Houghton Mifflin.

Harvey, D. (1989) *The Condition of Postmodernity*. Oxford: Basil Blackwell.

Hassard, J. (1988) Overcoming hermeticism in organization theory: An alternative to paradigm incommensurability. *Human Relations*, 41, 3, 247–59.

Hassard, J. and Holliday, R. (eds) (1998) *Organization-Representation: Work and Organization in Popular Culture*. London: Sage.

Hassard, J. and Keleman, M. (2002) Production and consumption in organizational knowledge: the case of the 'paradigms debate', *Organization*, 9, 2, 331–55.

Hassard, J. and Parker, M. (eds) (1993) *Postmodernism and Organizations*. London: Sage.

Hawkes, T. (1983) *Structuralism and Semiotics*. London: Methuen.

Hearn, J. and Parkin, W. (1987) *Sex At Work: The Power and Paradox of Organization*. Brighton: Wheatsheaf.

Hearn, J., Sheppard, D.L., Tancred-Sheriff, P. and Burrell, G. (eds) (1989) *The Sexuality of Organization*. London: Sage.

Heelas, P. and Morris, P. (eds) (1992) *The Values of the Enterprise Culture*. London: Routledge.

Held, D, and McGrew, A. (2002) *Globalization and Anti-Globalization*. Cambridge: Polity.

Held, D. *et al.* (2005) *Debating Globalization*. Cambridge: Polity.

Herzberg, F., Mausner, B. and Snyderman, B. (1959) *The Motivation to Work*. New York: John Wiley.

Heydebrand, W. (1983) Organization and praxis. In Morgan, G. (ed.) *Beyond Method*. London: Sage.

Hills, S.L. (1987) *Corporate Violence: Injury and Death for Profit*. Totowa, NJ: Rowman and Littlefield.

Hodge, R. and Kress, G. (1988) *Social Semiotics*. Oxford: Polity/Basil Blackwell.

Hoffman, W.M. and Moore, J.M. (eds) (1990) *Business Ethics*, 2nd edn. New York: McGraw-Hill.

Hofstadter, D. (1980) *Gödel, Escher, Bach: An Eternal Golden Braid*. London: Penguin.

Hofstede, G. (1991) *Cultures and Organizations*. Maidenhead, Berks.: McGraw-Hill.

Hollinger, R. (1994) *Postmodernism and the Social Sciences: A Thematic Approach*. London: Sage.

Hollis, M. (1975) *Rational Economic Man: A Philosophical Critique of Neo-Classical Economics*. Cambridge: Cambridge University Press.

Hollis, M. and Lukes, S. (eds) (1982) *Rationality and Relativism*. Oxford: Basil Blackwell.

Holub, R.C. (1991) *Jürgen Habermas: Critic in the Public Sphere*. London: Routledge.

Horrocks, C. and Jevtik, Z. (2004) *Introducing Foucault*. Cambridge: Icon.

Hosking, D.-M., Dachler, H.P. and Gergen, K. (eds) (1995) *Management and Organisation: Relational Alternatives to Individualism*. Aldershot: Avebury.

Huczynski, A.A. (1993) *Management Gurus*. London: Routledge.

Hughes, E.C. (1958) *Men and Their Work*. Glencoe: Free Press.

Hutchinson, A. and Hutchinson, F. (1997) *Environmental Business Management*. London: McGraw-Hill.

Hutton, W. (1995) *The State We're In*. London: Jonathan Cape.

Hutton, W. (1997) *The State To Come*. London: Vintage.

Hyman, R. (1977) *Strikes*, 2nd edn. London: Fontana.

Jablin, F.M., Putnam, L.L., Roberts, K.H. and Porter, L.W. (eds) (1987) *Handbook of Organizational Communication*. Newbury Park, CA: Sage.

Jackall, R. (1988) *Moral Mazes: The World of Corporate Managers*. Oxford: Oxford University Press.

Jackson, B. (2001) *Management Gurus and Management Fashions*. London: Routledge.

Jackson, N. and Carter, P. (1985) The ergonomics of desire. *Personnel Review* 14, 3, 20–8.

Jackson, N. and Carter, P. (1986) Desire versus interest. *Dragon*, 1, 8, 48–60.

Jackson, N. and Carter, P. (1991) In defence of paradigm incommensurability. *Organization Studies*, 12, 1, 109–27.

Jackson, N. and Carter, P. (1992) Postmodern management: Past-perfect or future-imperfect? *International Studies of Management and Organization*, 22, 3, 11–26.

Jackson, N. and Carter, P. (1993) 'Paradigm Wars': A response to Hugh Willmott. *Organization Studies*, 14, 5, 721–27.

Jackson, N. and Carter, P. (1994) Looking forward to the past of business ethics. *Industrial and Commercial Training*, 26, 10, 23–5.

Jackson, N. and Carter, P. (1995a) The 'fact' of management. *Scandinavian Journal of Management*, 11, 3, 197–208.

Jackson, N. and Carter, P. (1995b) Organisational chiaroscuro: Throwing light on the concept of corporate governance. *Human Relations*, 48, 8, 878–89.

Jackson, N. and Carter, P. (1998a) Labour as dressage. In McKinlay, A. and Starkey, K. (eds) *Foucault, Management and Organization Theory*. London: Sage.

Jackson, N. and Carter, P. (1998b) Management gurus: What are we to make of them? In Hassard, J. and Holliday, R. (eds) *Organization-Representation: Work and Organization in Popular Culture*. London: Sage.

Jackson, N. and Willmott, H. (1987) Beyond epistemology and reflective conversation: Toward human relations. *Human Relations*, 40, 6, 361–80.

Jacques, R. (1996) *Manufacturing the Employee*. London: Sage.

Jahoda, M. (1982) *Employment and Unemployment*. Cambridge: Cambridge University Press.

Jahoda, M., Lazarsfeld, P.F. and Zeisel, H. (1972) *Marienthal*. London: Tavistock.

Jameson, F. (1991) *Postmodernism, Or, The Cultural Logic of Late Capitalism*. London: Verso.

Jamieson, G.H. (1985) *Communication and Persuasion*. London: Croom Helm.

Janis, I.L. and Mann, L. (1977) *Decision Making: A Psychological Analysis of Conflict, Choice and Commitment*. New York: Free Press.

Jay, M. (1973) *The Dialectical Imagination*. Berkeley, CA: University of California Press.

Jencks, C. (1985) *Modern Movements In Architecture*, 2nd edn. London: Penguin.

Jenks, C. (ed.) (1998) *Core Sociological Dichotomies*. London: Sage.

Jennings, D. and Whattam, S. (1998) *Decision Making: An Integrated Approach*, 2nd edn. London: Financial Times Pitman.

Jermier, J.M., Knights, D. and Nord, W.R. (eds) (1994) *Resistance and Power in Organizations*. London: Routledge.

Jones, C. and Munro, R. (eds) (2005) *Contemporary Organization Theory*. Oxford: Blackwell.

Jones, C. and O'Doherty (eds) (2005) *Manifestos for the Business School of Tomorrow*. The Netherlands: Dvalin Publishing.

Jones, C., Parker, M. and ten Bos, R. (2005) *For Business Ethics*. Abingdon: Routledge.

Jones, G. and Hollier, G. (1997) *Resources, Society and Environmental Management*. London: Paul Chapman.

Jones, M.O. (1996) *Studying Organizational Symbolism: What, How, Why?* Thousand Oaks, CA: Sage.

Jones, R. (1983) *Physics As Metaphor*. London: Abacus.

Jones, T. (1988) *Corporate Killing: Bhopals Will Happen*. London: Free Association Books.

Joseph, L.E. (1990) *Gaia: The Growth of an Idea*. London: Penguin.

Kafka, F. (1963 [1925]) *The Trial*. London: Penguin.

Kafka, F. (1983 [1926]) *The Castle*. London: Penguin.

Kane, P. (2004) *The Play Ethic*. London: Pan.

Karpik, L. (ed.) (1978) *Organization and Environment*. London: Sage.

Katz, D. and Kahn, R.L. (1966) *The Social Psychology of Organizations*. New York: John Wiley.

Kilminster, R. (1979) *Praxis and Method*. London: Routledge and Kegan Paul.

Kingdom, J. (1992) *No Such Thing As Society? Individualism and Community*. Buckingham: Open University Press.

Kling, R. (ed.) (1991) *Computerization and Controversy*, 2nd edn. London: Academic Press.

Knights, D. and Willmott, H. (eds) (1990) *Labour Process Theory*. Basingstoke: Macmillan.

Kritzman, L.D. (ed.) (1988) *Michel Foucault – Politics, Philosophy, Culture*. Trans. A Sheridan and others. New York: Routledge.

Kuhn, T.S. (1970) *The Structure of Scientific Revolutions*, 2nd edn. Chicago: University of Chicago Press.

Kumar, K. (1995) *From Post-Industrial to Post-Modern Society*. Oxford: Blackwell.

Lacan, J. (1977) *The Four Fundamental Concepts of Psycho-Analysis*. Trans. A. Sheridan. Harmondsworth: Penguin.

Lacan, J. (1980) *Écrits – A Selection*. Trans. A. Sheridan. London: Tavistock.

Lakatos, I. and Musgrave, A. (eds) (1972) *Criticism and the Growth of Knowledge*. Cambridge: Cambridge University Press.

Larrain, J. (1979) *The Concept of Ideology*. London: Hutchinson.

Latour, B. (1987) *Science in Action*. Milton Keynes: Open University Press.

Latour, B. (1993) *We Have Never Been Modern*. Trans. C. Porter. Hemel Hempstead: Harvester Wheatsheaf.

Lawrence, P.R. and Lorsch, J.W. (1967) *Organization and Environment: Managing Differentiation and Integration*. Boston, MA: Harvard Business School Press.

Lawson, H. and Appignanesi, L. (eds) (1989) *Dismantling Truth: Reality in the Postmodern World*. New York: St. Martin's Press.

Leach, E. (1972) Models of Man. In Robson, W. (ed.) *Man and the Social Sciences*. London: George Allen and Unwin.

Leader, D. and Groves, J. (2005) *Introducing Lacan*. Cambridge: Icon.

Leather, P. (1983) Desire: A structural model of motivation. *Human Relations*, 36, 2, 109–22.

Lechte, J. (1994) *Fifty Key Contemporary Thinkers – From Structuralism to Postmodernity*. London: Routledge.

Lecourt, D. (2001) *The Mediocracy*. Trans. G. Elliott. London: Verso.

Lefebvre, E. (1997) *The Monk/Manager*. Leuven: Acco.

Legge, K. (1989) HRM: A critical analysis. In Storey, J. (ed.) *New Perspectives on Human Resource Management*. London: Routledge.

Legge, K. (1995) *Human Resource Management – Rhetorics and Realities*. Basingstoke: Macmillan.

Lemaire, A. (1977) *Jacques Lacan*. Trans. D. Macey. London: Routledge and Kegan Paul.

Lévi-Strauss, C. (1972) *The Savage Mind*. London: Weidenfeld & Nicolson.

Lewin, R. (1992) *Complexity: Life at the Edge of Chaos*. New York: Macmillan.

Lewis, S. and Lewis, J. (eds) (1996) *The Work–Family Challenge*. London: Sage.

Lichtheim, G. (1967) *The Concept of Ideology and Other Essays*. New York: Random House.

Lincoln, Y.S. (ed.) (1985) *Organization Theory and Inquiry: The Paradigm Revolution*. Beverley Hills, CA: Sage.

Linhart, R. (1981) *The Assembly Line*. Trans. M. Crosland. London: John Calder.

Linstead, S. (ed.) (2004) *Organization Theory and Postmodern Thought*. London: Sage.

Linstead, S. and Grafton-Small, R. (1992) On reading organizational culture. *Organization Studies*, 13, 3, 331–55.

Linstead, S. and Hopfl, H. (eds) (2000) *The Aesthetics of Organization*. London: Sage.

Linstead, S., Grafton-Small, R. and Jeffcutt, P. (eds) (1996) *Understanding Management*. London: Sage.

Lockett, M. and Spear, R. (eds) (1980) *Organizations as Systems*. Milton Keynes: Open University Press.

Lounsbury, M. and Ventresca, M. (2003) The new structuralism in organization theory, *Organization*, 10, 3, 457–80.

Love, G.A. and Love, R.M. (eds) (1970) *Ecological Crisis: Readings for Survival*. New York: Harcourt Brace Jovanovich.

Lovelock, J. (1987) *Gaia: A New Look at Life on Earth*. Oxford: Oxford University Press.

Lovelock, J. (2006) *The Revenge of Gaia*. London: Allen Lane.

Lukes, S. (1973) *Individualism*. Oxford: Basil Blackwell.

Lukes, S. (2005) *Power – A Radical View*, 2nd edn. Basingstoke: Macmillan.

Luthans, F., Hodgett, R.M. and Thompson, K.R. (1987) *Social Issues in Business*, 5th edn. New York: Macmillan.

Lyon, D. (1994) *Postmodernity*. Buckingham: Open University Press.

Lyotard, J.-F. (1984) *The Postmodern Condition – A Report on Knowledge*. Trans. G. Bennington and B. Massumi. Manchester: Manchester University Press.

Lyotard, J.-F. (1988) *The Differend – Phrases in Dispute*. Trans. G. Van Den Abbeele. Manchester: Manchester University Press.

MacCannell, J.F. (1986) *Figuring Lacan*. London: Croom Helm.

MacIntyre, A. (1985) *After Virtue*, 2nd edn. London: Duckworth.

Maclagan, P. (1998) *Management and Morality*. London: Sage.

Mangham, I. (1986) *Power and Performance in Organizations*. Oxford: Blackwell.

Mangham, I. (1995) MacIntyre and the manager. *Organization*, 2, 2, 181–204.

Mangham, I. and Overington, M.A. (1983) Dramatism and the theatrical metaphor. In Morgan, G. (ed.) *Beyond Method*. London: Sage.

March, J.G. (1970) Problems in model-building. In Stogdill, R.M. (ed.) *The Process of Model-Building in the Behavioral Sciences*. Columbus, OH: Ohio State University Press.

Marcuse, H. (1968) *Negations*. New York: Free Association Books.

Marcuse, H. (1986) *One Dimensional Man*. London: Ark Paperbacks.

Marcuse, H. (1987) *Eros and Civilization*. London: Ark Paperbacks.

Margerison, C.J. (1974) *Managerial Problem Solving*. London: McGraw-Hill.

Marglin, S. (1980) The origins and functions of hierarchy in capitalist production. In Nichols, T. (ed.) *Capital and Labour*. London: Fontana.

Marsden, R. and Townley, B. (1996) The owl of Minerva: Reflections on theory in practice. In Clegg, S.R., Hardy, C. and Nord, W.R. (eds) *Handbook of Organization Studies*. London: Sage.

Marshall, J. (1984) *Women Managers – Travellers in a Male World*. Chichester: John Wiley.

Martin, J. (1992) *Cultures in Organizations: Three Perspectives*. Oxford: Oxford University Press.

Martin, J. (2002) *Organizational Culture: Mapping the Terrain*. Thousand Oaks, CA: Sage.

Marx, K. (1975) *Early Writings*. Trans. R. Livingstone and G. Benton. Harmondsworth: Penguin.

Marx, K. (1976) *Capital,* Vol. 1. Trans. B. Fowkes. Harmondsworth: Penguin.

Massumi, B. (1992) *A User's Guide to Capitalism and Schizophrenia*. Cambridge, MA: Massachusetts Institute of Technology.

Matteson, M.T. and Ivancevich, J.M. (eds) (1989) *Management and Organizational Behavior Classics*, 4th edn. Holmewood, IL: Irwin.

Mayer, M. (2001) *The Fed – The Inside Story of How the World's Most Powerful Financial Institution Drives the Markets*. New York: Free Press.

Mayo, E. (1933) *The Human Problems of an Industrial Civilization*. London: RKP.

McDonagh, P. and Prothero, A. (eds) (1997) *Green Management: A Reader*. London: Dryden.

McEwen, E. (ed.) (1990) *Age: The Unrecognised Discrimination*. London: Age Concern.

McGregor, D. (1960) *The Human Side of Enterprise*. New York: McGraw-Hill.

McHoul, A. and Grace, W. (1993) *A Foucault Primer*. London: UCL Press.

McKenzie, D. and Wajcman, J. (eds) (1985) *The Social Shaping of Technology*. Milton Keynes: Open University Press.

McKinlay, A. and Starkey, K. (eds) (1998) *Foucault, Management and Organization Theory*. London: Sage.

McLellan, D. (ed.) (1980) *Marx's Grundrisse*, 2nd edn. Basingstoke: Macmillan.

Meakin, D. (1976) *Man and Work*. London: Methuen.

Meek, V.L. (1988) Organizational culture: Origins and weaknesses. *Organization Studies*, 9, 4, 453–73.

Melville, H. (1967) *Billy Budd, Sailor & Other Stories*. London: Penguin Books.

Merton, R.K. (1949) *Social Theory and Social Structure*. Glencoe, IL: Free Press.

Meszaros, I. (1986) *Philosophy, Ideology and Social Science*. London: Harvester Wheatsheaf.

Michels, R. (1968) *Political Parties*. Trans. E. and C. Paul. New York: The Free Press.

Miles, S. (2001) *Social Theory in the Real World*. London: Sage.

Mills, A. and Tancred, P. (1992) *Gendering Organizational Analysis*. London: Sage.

Mills, A. and Simmons, T. (1995) *Reading Organization Theory: A Critical Approach*. Toronto: Garamond.

Mintzberg, H. (1980) *The Nature of Managerial Work*. Englewood Cliffs, NJ: Prentice-Hall.

Mintzberg, H. (1994) *The Rise and Fall of Strategic Planning*. Hemel Hempstead: Prentice Hall.

Mitroff, I. and Linstone, H.A. (1993) *The Unbounded Mind: Breaking the Chains of Traditional Business Thinking*. Oxford: Oxford University Press.

Moore, B. (1965) Tolerance and the Scientific Outlook. In Wolff, R.P., Moore, B. and Marcuse, H., *Critique of Pure Tolerance*. Boston: Beacon Press.

Morgan, G. (1980) Paradigms, metaphors and puzzle solving in organization theory. *Administrative Science Quarterly*, 25, 605–22.

Morgan, G. (ed.) (1983a) *Beyond Method: Strategies for Social Research*. London: Sage.

Morgan, G. (1983b) More on metaphor: Why we cannot control tropes in administrative science. *Administrative Science Quarterly*, 28, 601–7.

Morgan, G. (1989) *Creative Organization Theory*. London: Sage.

Morgan, G. (1990) Paradigm diversity in organizational research. In Hassard, J. and Pym, D. (eds) *The Theory and Philosophy of Organizations*. London: Routledge.

Morgan, G. (1997) *Images of Organization*, 2nd edn. London: Sage.

Morgan, Glen (1990) *Organizations in Society*. London: Macmillan.

Morton, A. (1991) *Disasters and Dilemmas: Strategies for Real-Life Decision Making*. Oxford: Basil Blackwell.

Moss, J. (ed.) (1998) *The Later Foucault: Politics and Philosophy*. London: Sage.

Mouzelis, N. (1975) *Organisation and Bureaucracy*, 2nd edn. London: RKP.

Mullins, L.J. (2005) *Management and Organizational Behaviour*, 7th edn. London: Financial Times Prentice Hall.

Mumby, D.K. (1988) *Communication and Power in Organizations: Discourse, Ideology and Domination*. Norwood, NJ: Ablex.

Natoli, J. (1997) *A Primer to Postmodernity*. Malden, MA: Blackwell.

Newton, T., Handy, J. and Fineman, S. (1995) *'Managing' Stress: Emotion and Power at Work*. London: Sage.

Nichols, T. (1969) *Ownership, Control and Ideology*. London: Allen and Unwin.

Nichols, T. (ed.) (1980) *Capital and Labour: A Marxist Primer*. London: Fontana.

Nichols, T. and Armstrong, P. (1976) *Workers Divided*. Glasgow: Fontana.

Noon, M. (1992) HRM: A map, model or theory? In Blyton, P. and Turnbull, P. (eds) *Reassessing Human Resource Management*. London: Sage.

Norris, C. (1982) *Deconstruction: Theory and Practice*. London: Methuen.

Norris, C. (1987) *Derrida*. London: Fontana.

Norris, C. (1992) *Uncritical Theory*. London: Lawrence and Wishart.

Norris, C. (1996) *Reclaiming Truth*. London: Lawrence and Wishart.

Novarro, V. (1980) *Women's Work, Men's Work – The Ambivalence of Equality*. London: Marion Boyars.

Nowakowska, M. (1987) The dynamics of knowledge structure: Semiotic sytems. In Van Gigch, J.P. (ed.) *Decision Making About Decision Making*. Cambridge, MA: Abacus.

Nuckolls, C.W. (1998) *Culture: A Problem that Cannot be Solved*. Madison, WI: University of Wisconsin Press.

Offe, C. (1985) *Disorganised Capitalism*. Cambridge: Polity.

Open Systems Group (eds) (1981) *Systems Behaviour*, 3rd edn. London: Harper and Row.

Organization (2003a) Ethics, politics and organizing. (Special Issue) 10, 2.

Organization (2003b) Speaking out on organization studies/W(h)ither organization studies? (Special Issue) 10, 3.

Parker, M. (ed.) (1998a) *Ethics and Organization*. London: Sage.

Parker, M. (1998b) Business ethics and social theory: Postmodernizing the ethical. *British Journal of Management*, 9, 27–36.

Parker, M. (1998c) Judgement day: Cyborganization, humanism and postmodern ethics. *Organization*, 5, 4, 503–18.

Parker, M. (2000) *Organizational Culture and Identity*. London: Sage.

Parker, M. (2002a) *Against Management*. Cambridge: Polity.

Parker, M. (ed) (2002b) *Utopia and Organization*. Oxford: Blackwell.

Parker, M. and Cooper, R. (1998) Cyborganization: Cinema as nervous system. In Hassard, J. and Holliday, R. (eds) *Organization-Representation*. London: Sage.

Parsons, T. (1949) *The Structure of Social Action*. Glencoe, IL: Free Press.

Perelman, Ch. (1979) *The New Rhetoric and the Humanities*. Trans. W. Kluback. Dordrecht, Holland: D. Reidel.

Perelman, Ch. (1982) *The Realm of Rhetoric*. Trans. W. Kluback. Notre Dame, IN: University of Notre Dame Press.

Peters, T.J. and Waterman, R.A. (1982) *In Search of Excellence*. New York: Harper & Row.

Pidd, M. (1996) *Tools For Thinking: Modelling in Management Science*. Chichester: Wiley.

Pinder, C.C. and Bourgeois, V.W. (1982) Controlling tropes in administrative science. *Administrative Science Quarterly*, 27, 641–52.

Playford, J. (1971) The myth of pluralism. In Castles, F., Murray, D.J. and Potter, D.C. (eds) *Decisions, Organisations and Society*. Harmondsworth: Penguin.

Polanyi, K. (1971) *Primitive, Archaic and Modern Economies*. Boston, MA: Beacon Press.

Polanyi, M. (1962) *Personal Knowledge*. London: RKP.

Pondy, L.R., Frost, P., Morgan, G. and Dandridge, T. (eds) (1983) *Organizational Symbolism*. Greenwich, CT: Jai Press.

Porter, R. (2000) *Enlightenment*. London: Penguin

Poster, M. (1984) *Foucault, Marxism and History*. Cambridge: Polity.

Poster, M. (1990) *The Mode of Information*. Cambridge: Polity.

Power, M. (1990) Modernism, Postmodernism and organization. In Hassard, J. and Pym, D. (eds) *The Theory and Philosophy of Organizations*. London: Routledge.

Pratt, V. (1991) *The Philosophy of the Social Sciences*, 2nd edn. London: Routledge.

Prigogine, I. and Stengers, I. (1984) *Order Out of Chaos*. London: Fontana.

Pugh, D.S. (ed.) (1990) *Organization Theory: Selected Readings*, 3rd edn. London: Penguin.

Pugh, D.S. and Hickson, D.J. (eds) (1989) *Writers On Organizations*, 4th edn. London: Penguin.

Punch, M. (1996) *Dirty Business*. London: Sage.

Rabinbach, A. (1990) *The Human Motor: Energy, Fatigue and the Origins of Modernity*. New York: Basic Books.

Ramsie, H.A. (1977) Cycles of control: Worker participation in social and historical perspective. *Sociology*, 11, 3, 481–506.

Ravetz, J.R. (1971) *Scientific Knowledge and its Social Problems*. Oxford: Clarendon.

Ravetz, J.R. (1990) *The Merger of Knowledge with Power*. London: Mansell.

Ray, L. and Sayer, A. (eds) (1999) *Culture and Economy after the Cultural Turn*. London: Sage.

Reed, M. (1985) *Redirections in Organizational Analysis*. London: Tavistock.

Reed, M. (2005) Reflections on the 'realist turn' in organization and management studies. *Journal of Management Studies*, 42, 8, 1621–44.

Reed, M. and Hughes, M. (eds) (1992) *Rethinking Organization*. London: Sage.

Rejai, M. (ed.) (1971) *The Decline of Ideology?* Chicago: Aldine Atherton.

Reskin, B. and Padavic, I. (1994) *Women and Men at Work*. Thousand Oaks, CA: Pine Forge.

Rex, J. (1961) *Key Problems in Sociological Theory*. London: RKP.

Ritzer, G. (1993) *The McDonaldization of Society*. Thousand Oaks, CA: Pine Forge.

Ritzer, G. (1998) *The McDonaldization Thesis*. London: Sage.

Ritzer, G. (ed.) (2004) *Handbook of Social Problems*. Thousand Oaks, CA: Sage.

Ritzer, G. (ed.) (2006) *McDonaldization: The Reader*, 2nd edn. Thousand Oaks, CA: Pine Forge.

Robbe-Grillet, A. (1964 [1953]) *The Erasers*. Trans. R. Howard. London: Calder and Boyars.

Robbe-Grillet, A. (1977) Order and disorder in film and fiction. *Critical Inquiry*, 4, 1, 1–20.

Roethlisberger, F.J. and Dickson, W.J. (1939) *Management and the Worker*. Cambridge, MA: Harvard University Press.

Rogers, R. (1990) *Architecture – A Modern View*. London: Thames and Hudson.

Rorty, R. (1982) *Consequences of Pragmatism*. Brighton: Harvester.

Rose, M. (1978) *Industrial Behaviour*, 1st edn. Harmondsworth: Penguin.

Rose-Ackerman, S. (1999) *Corruption and Government*. Cambridge: Cambridge University Press.

Rosen, M. (1985) Breakfast at Spiro's: Dramaturgy and dominance. *Journal of Management*, 11, 31–48.

Rosen, M. (1986) Christmas time and control: An exploration in the social structure of formal organizations. *Dragon*, 1, 5, 51–73.

Rosenau, P.M. (1992) *Postmodernism and the Social Sciences*. Princeton, NJ: Princeton University Press.

Rothschild, J. and Whitt, J.A. (1986) *The Cooperative Workplace*. Cambridge: Cambridge University Press.

Rotman, B. (1987) *Signifying Nothing: The Semiotics of Zero*. Basingstoke: Macmillan.

Roy, D. (1960) Banana time: Job satisfaction and informal interactions. *Human Organization*, 18, 2, 156–68.

Rubinstein, A. (1998) *Modeling Bounded Rationality*. Cambridge, MA: MIT Press.

Russell, B. (1961) *History of Western Philosophy*. London: George Allen and Unwin.

Russell, B. (1976) *In Praise of Idleness*. London: George Allen and Unwin.

Ryan, A. (1970) *The Philosophy of the Social Sciences*. Basingstoke: Macmillan.

Salaman, G. (1979) *Work Organisations: Resistance and Control*. London: Longman.

Salaman, G. and Butler, J. (1990) Why managers won't learn. *Management Education and Development*, 21, 3, 183–91.

Salaman, G. and Thompson, K. (eds) (1980) *Control and Ideology in Organizations*. London: Open University Press.

Saussure, F. de (1983) *Course in General Linguistics*. Trans. R. Harris. London: Duckworth.

Sautet, M. and Boussignac, P. (1990) *Nietzsche for Beginners*. New York: Writers and Readers.

Savage, C.I. and Small, J.R. (1975) *Introduction to Managerial Economics*, 2nd edn. London: Hutchinson.

Scarborough, H. and Corbett, J.M. (eds) (1992) *Technology and Organization: Power, Meaning and Design*. London: Routledge.

Schein, E. (1988) *Organizational Psychology*, 3rd edn. Englewood Cliffs, NJ: Prentice-Hall.

Scherer, A.G. (ed.) (1998) Pluralism and incommensurability in strategic management and organization theory: Consequences for theory and practice. *Organization* (special issue), 5, 2.

Schirer, W.L. (1960) *The Rise and Fall of the Third Reich*. London: Pan/Secker and Warburg.

Schneider, S.C. and Powley, E. (1986) The role of images in changing corporate culture: The case of A. T. & T. *Dragon*, 1, 2, 5–44.

Schwartz, H. (1986a) Totalitarianism and cultural engineering – Part 1. *Dragon*, 1, 6, 78–100.

Schwartz, H. (1986b) Totalitarianism and cultural engineering – Part 2. *Dragon*, 1, 7, 24–48.

Schwartz. H. (1990) *Narcissistic Process and Corporate Decay: The Theory of the Organizational Ideal*. New York: New York University Press.

Scott, J. (1991) *Who Rules Britain?* Cambridge: Polity.

Scott, J. (1997) *Corporate Business and Capitalist Classes*, 3rd edn. Oxford: Oxford University Press.

Scott, W.R. (1981) *Organizations: Rational, Natural and Open Systems*. Englewood Cliffs, NJ: Prentice Hall.

Selznick, P. (1949) *TVA and the Grass Roots*. Berkeley, CA: University of California Press.

Sennett, R. (2006a) Workers will carry on striking until they get a life. *The Guardian*, 25.05.2006.

Sennett, R. (2006b) *The Culture of the New Capitalism*. New Haven: Yale University Press.

Serres, M. (1982) *The Parasite*. Trans. L.R. Schehr. Baltimore, MD: Johns Hopkins University Press.

Sewell, G. and Wilkinson, B. (1992) Empowerment or Emasculation? Shopfloor surveillance in a total quality organization. In Blyton, P. and Turnbull, P. (eds) *Reassessing Human Resource Management*. London: Sage.

Sheridan, A. (1980) *Michel Foucault: The Will to Truth*. London: Tavistock.

Sherman, H. and Schultz, R. (1998) *Open Boundaries – Creating Business Innovation through Complexity*. Reading, MA: Perseus.

Shrivastava, P. (1992) *Bhopal: Anatomy of a Crisis*, 2nd edn. London: Paul Chapman.

Shull, F.A., Delbecq, A.L. and Cummings, L.L. (1970) *Organizational Decision Making*. New York: McGraw-Hill.

Sievers, B. (1994) *Work, Death and Life Itself: Essays on Management and Organization*. Berlin: De Gruyter.

Silverman, D. (1970) *The Theory of Organisations*. London: Heinemann.

Simon, H.A. (1957) *Models of Man: Social and Rational*. New York: Wiley.

Simon, H.A. (1976) *Administrative Behaviour: A Study of Decision-Making Processes in Administrative Organizations*, 3rd edn. New York: Macmillan.

Simons, G. (1986) *Is Man A Robot?* Chichester: Wiley.

Simons, H.W. and Billig, M. (eds) (1994) *After Postmodernism: Reconstructing Ideology Critique*. London: Sage.

Simons, J. (1995) *Foucault and the Political*. London: Routledge.

Simpson, P. (1993) *Language, Ideology and Point of View*. London: Routledge.

Skoldberg, K. (2002) *The Poetic Logic of Administration*. London: Routledge.

Smart, B. (1985) *Michel Foucault*. London: Tavistock & Ellis Horwood.

Smart, B. (1992) *Modern Conditions, Postmodern Controversies*. London: Routledge.

Smart, B. (1993) *Postmodernity*. London: Routledge.

Smiles, S. (1897) *Self Help*. London: J. Murray.

Smircich, L. (1983) Concepts of culture and organizational analysis. *Administrative Science Quarterly*, 28, 339–59.

Smircich, L. and Calas, M.B. (1987) Organizational culture: A critical assessment. In Jablin, F.M., Putnam, L.L., Roberts, K.H. and Porter, L.W. (eds) *Handbook of Organizational Communication*. London: Sage.

Smith, D. and Evans, P. (1983) *Marx's Kapital for Beginners*. New York: Writers and Readers.

Solomonides, T. and Levidov, L. (eds) (1985) *Compulsive Technology: Computers as Culture*. London: Free Association Books.

Spender, D. (ed.) (1981) *Mens Studies Modified*. Oxford: Pergamon.

Stead, W.E. and Stead, J.G. (1992) *Management For a Small Planet*. Newbury Park, CA: Sage.

Steger, M.B. (2003) *Globalization: A Very Short Introduction*. Oxford: Oxford University Press.

Stewart, R. (1988) *Managers and Their Jobs*, 2nd edn. Basingstoke: Macmillan.

Stiglitz, J. (2002) *Globalization and its Discontents*. London: Penguin.

Stockdale, M.S. (1996) *Sexual Harassment in the Workplace*. Thousand Oaks, CA: Sage.

Stogdill, R.M. (ed.) (1970) *The Process of Model-Building in the Behavioral Sciences*. Columbus, OH: Ohio State University Press.

Strati, A. (1999) *Organization and Aesthetics*. London: Sage.

Sturdy, A., Knights, D. and Willmott, H. (eds) (1992) *Skill and Consent*. London: Routledge.

Sturrock, J. (ed.) (1979) *Structuralism and Since*. Oxford: Oxford University Press.

Sturrock, J. (1993) *Structuralism*, 2nd edn. London: Fontana.

Suskind, R. (2004) *The Price of Loyalty*. London: Free Press.

Swingle, P.G. (1976) *The Management of Power*. Hillsdale, NJ: Lawrence Erlbaum.

Tannenbaum, R. and Schmidt, W.H. (1973) How to choose a leadership pattern. *Harvard Business Review*, May/June, 162–80.

Taylor, F.W. (1911) *The Principles of Scientific Management*. New York: Harper.

Taylor, L. and Walton, P. (1971) Industrial sabotage: Motives and meanings. In Cohen, S. (ed.) *Images of Deviance*. Harmondsworth: Penguin.

ten Bos, R. (2000) *Fashion and Utopia in Management Thinking*. Amsterdam: John Benjamins.

Terkel, S. (1975) *Working*. [Revised edition]. Harmondsworth: Penguin.

Thomas, A.B. (1989) One minute management education: A sign of the times? *Management Education and Development*, 20, 1, 23–38.

Thomas, A.B. (2003) *Controversies in Management*, 2nd edn. London: Routledge.

Thompson, E.P. (1968) *The Making of the English Working Class*. Harmondsworth: Penguin.

Thompson, J.L. (1997) *Strategic Management: Awareness and Change*, 3rd edn. London: International Thompson Press.

Thompson, K. (1986) *Beliefs and Ideology*. London: Ellis Horwood/Tavistock.

Thompson, P. (1983) *The Nature of Work*. Basingstoke: Macmillan.

Thompson, P. and McHugh, D. (2001) *Work Organisations: A Critical Introduction*, 3rd edn. Basingstoke: Macmillan.

Thorpe, R. and Horsburgh, S. (1991) *Productivity*. In Bentley, T.J. (ed.) *The Management Services Handbook*, 2nd edn. London: Pitman.

Thrift, N. (1999) Capitalism's cultural turn. In Ray, L. and Sayer, A. (eds) *Culture and Economy after the Cultural Turn*. London: Sage.

Tönnies, F. (1974 [1887]) *Community and Association*. Trans. C.P. Loomis. London: Routledge and Kegan Paul.

Townley, B. (1994) *Reframing Human Resource Management*. London: Sage.

Tressel, R. (1965 [1914]) *The Ragged Trousered Philanthropists*. London: Granada.

Tsoukas, H. (1998) Forms of knowledge and forms of life in organized contexts. In Chia, R. (ed.) *In the Realm of Organization*. London: Routledge.

Tugendhat, C. (1971) *The Multinationals*. Harmondsworth: Penguin.

Tunstall, J. (1962) *The Fishermen*. London: McGibbon and Key.

Turner, B.A. (ed.) (1990) *Organizational Symbolism*. Berlin: De Gruyter.

Turner, B.S. (ed.) (1990) *Theories of Modernity and Postmodernity*. London: Sage.

Turner, S. (1983) Studying organizations through Lévi-Strauss's structuralism. In Morgan, G. (ed.) *Beyond Method*. London: Sage.

Ure, A. (1967 [1835]) *The Philosophy of Manufactures*. London: Cassell.

Urry, J. and Lash, S. (1987) *The End of Organized Capitalism*. Cambridge: Polity.

Urry, J. and Wakeford, J. (eds) (1973) *Power in Britain*. London: Heinemann.

Van Gigch, J.P. (ed.) (1987) *Decision Making About Decision Making*. Cambridge, MA: Abacus.

Vanek, J. (ed.) (1975) *Self Management: Economic Liberation of Man*. Harmondsworth: Penguin.

Veblen, T. (1924) *The Theory of the Leisure Class*. London: George Allen and Unwin.

Von Weizsäcker, E., Lovins, A.B. and Lovins, I.H. (1997) *Factor Four: Doubling Wealth – Halving Resource Use*. London: Earthscan.

Vroom, V.H. (1964) *Work and Motivation*. New York: Wiley.

Walby, S. (1986) *Patriarchy At Work*. Cambridge: Polity.

Waldo, D. (1968) *The Novelist on Organization and Administration: An Inquiry into the Relationship Between Two Worlds*. Institute of Governmental Studies, University of California.

Waldrop, M.M. (1992) *Complexity*. London: Penguin.

Wallerstein, I. (1984) *The Politics of the World-Economy*. Cambridge: Cambridge University Press.

Walton, C.C. (1988) *The Moral Manager*. New York: Harper and Row.

Ward, G. (1997) *Teach Yourself Postmodernism*. London: Hodder.

Watson, J. and Hill, A. (1997) *A Dictionary of Communication and Media Studies*, 4th edn. London: Arnold.

Watson, J.D. (1968) *The Double Helix: A Personal Account of the Discovery of the Structure of DNA*. London: Weidenfeld & Nicolson.

Watson, T.J. (1994) *In Search of Management*. London: Routledge.

Waugh, P. (ed.) (1992) *Postmodernism: A Reader*. London: Edward Arnold.

Weber, M. (1930) *The Protestant Ethic and the Spirit of Capitalism*. Trans. T. Parsons. London: George Allen and Unwin.

Weber, M. (1947) *The Theory of Social and Economic Organization*. Trans. A. Henderson and T. Parsons. Glencoe, IL: Free Press.

Weedon, C. (1987) *Feminist Practice and Poststructuralist Theory*. Oxford: Blackwell.

Wever, G. (1996) *Strategic Environmental Management: Using TQEM and ISO 14000 for Competitive Advantage*. New York: Wiley.

Whitley, R. (1984) The scientific status of management research as a practically-oriented social science. *Journal of Management Studies*, 21, 4, 369–90.

Wilden, A. (1980) *System and Structure*, 2nd edn. London: Tavistock.

Williams, R. (1976) *Keywords: A Vocabulary of Culture and Society*. Glasgow: Fontana/Croom Helm.

Willmott, H. (1984) Images and ideals of managerial work: A critical examination of conceptual and empirical accounts. *Journal of Management Studies*, 21, 3, 349–68.

Willmott, H. (1993) Breaking the paradigm mentality. *Organization Studies*, 14, 5, 681–720.

Willmott, H. (1997) Management and organization studies as science? *Organization*, 4, 3, 309–44.

Willmott, H. (1998) Re-cognizing the Other: Reflections on a 'New Sensibility' in social and organization studies. In Chia, R. (ed.) *In the Realm of Organization*. London: Routledge.

Wilson, B. (ed.) (1970) *Rationality*. Oxford: Basil Blackwell.

Wilson, B. (1990) *Systems: Concepts, Methodologies and Applications*, 2nd edn. Chichester: Wiley.

Wilson, F. (1995) *Organizational Behaviour and Gender*. London: McGraw-Hill.

Winch, P. (1958) *The Idea of a Social Science and Its Relation to Philosophy*. London: RKP.

Wood, D. (ed.) (1992) *Derrida: A Critical Reader*. Oxford: Blackwell.

Woodward, J. (1965) *Industrial Organisations – Theory and Practice*. London: OUP.

Woolgar, S. (1989) The ideology of representation and the role of the agent. In Lawson, H. and Appignanesi, L. (eds) *Dismantling Truth*. New York: St. Martin's Press.

Wynne, B. (1982) *Rationality and Ritual: The Windscale Inquiry and Nuclear Decisions in Britain*. Chalfont St. Giles: The British Society for the History of Science.

Yeats, W.B. (1994) *The Poems* (ed. D. Albright). London: J.M. Dent.

Zey, M. (1998) *Rational Choice Theory and Organizational Theory: A Critique*. Thousand Oaks, CA: Sage.

Zizek, S. (ed.) (1994) *Mapping Ideology*. London: Verso.

Zukav, G. (1984) *The Dancing Wu Li Masters*. London: Fontana.

Index